Windows® 95
Bible

Windows® 95 Bible

Alan Simpson

IDG Books Worldwide, Inc.
An International Data Group Company

Foster City, CA ✦ Chicago, IL ✦ Indianapolis, IN ✦ Southlake, TX

Windows® 95 Bible

Published by
IDG Books Worldwide, Inc.
An International Data Group Company
919 E. Hillsdale Blvd.
Suite 400
Foster City, CA 94404
www.idgbooks.com (IDG Books Worldwide Web site)

Library of Congress Catalog Card No.: 96–80448

ISBN: 0-7645-3069-0

Printed in the United States of America

10 9 8 7 6 5 4 3 2 1

IB/SU/QX/ZX/FC

Distributed in the United States by IDG Books Worldwide, Inc.

Distributed by Macmillan Canada for Canada; by Transworld Publishers Limited in the United Kingdom; by IDG Norge Books for Norway; by IDG Sweden Books for Sweden; by Woodslane Pty. Ltd. for Australia; by Woodslane Enterprises Ltd. for New Zealand; by Longman Singapore Publishers Ltd. for Singapore, Malaysia, Thailand, and Indonesia; by Simron Pty. Ltd. for South Africa; by Toppan Company Ltd. for Japan; by Distribuidora Cuspide for Argentina; by Livraria Cultura for Brazil; by Ediciencia S.A. for Ecuador; by Addison-Wesley Publishing Company for Korea; by Ediciones ZETA S.C.R. Ltda. for Peru; by WS Computer Publishing Corporation, Inc., for the Philippines; by Unalis Corporation for Taiwan; by Contemporanea de Ediciones for Venezuela; by Computer Book & Magazine Store for Puerto Rico; by Express Computer Distributors for the Caribbean and West Indies. Authorized Sales Agent: Anthony Rudkin Associates for the Middle East and North Africa.

For general information on IDG Books Worldwide's books in the U.S., please call our Consumer Customer Service department at 800-762-2974. For reseller information, including discounts and premium sales, please call our Reseller Customer Service department at 800-434-3422.

For information on where to purchase IDG Books Worldwide's books outside the U.S., please contact our International Sales department at 415-655-3200 or fax 415-655-3295.

For information on foreign language translations, please contact our Foreign & Subsidiary Rights department at 415-655-3021 or fax 415-655-3281.

For sales inquiries and special prices for bulk quantities, please contact our Sales department at 415-655-3200 or write to the address above.

For information on using IDG Books Worldwide's books in the classroom or for ordering examination copies, please contact our Educational Sales department at 800-434-2086 or fax 817-251-8174.

For press review copies, author interviews, or other publicity information, please contact our Public Relations department at 415-655-3000 or fax 415-655-3299.

For authorization to photocopy items for corporate, personal, or educational use, please contact Copyright Clearance Center, 222 Rosewood Drive, Danvers, MA 01923, or fax 508-750-4470.

is a trademark under exclusive license to IDG Books Worldwide, Inc., from International Data Group, Inc.

ABOUT IDG BOOKS WORLDWIDE

Welcome to the world of IDG Books Worldwide.

IDG Books Worldwide, Inc., is a subsidiary of International Data Group, the world's largest publisher of computer-related information and the leading global provider of information services on information technology. IDG was founded more than 25 years ago and now employs more than 8,500 people worldwide. IDG publishes more than 275 computer publications in over 75 countries (see listing below). More than 60 million people read one or more IDG publications each month.

Launched in 1990, IDG Books Worldwide is today the #1 publisher of best-selling computer books in the United States. We are proud to have received eight awards from the Computer Press Association in recognition of editorial excellence and three from *Computer Currents'* First Annual Readers' Choice Awards. Our best-selling ...*For Dummies*® series has more than 30 million copies in print with translations in 30 languages. IDG Books Worldwide, through a joint venture with IDG's Hi-Tech Beijing, became the first U.S. publisher to publish a computer book in the People's Republic of China. In record time, IDG Books Worldwide has become the first choice for millions of readers around the world who want to learn how to better manage their businesses.

Our mission is simple: Every one of our books is designed to bring extra value and skill-building instructions to the reader. Our books are written by experts who understand and care about our readers. The knowledge base of our editorial staff comes from years of experience in publishing, education, and journalism — experience we use to produce books for the '90s. In short, we care about books, so we attract the best people. We devote special attention to details such as audience, interior design, use of icons, and illustrations. And because we use an efficient process of authoring, editing, and desktop publishing our books electronically, we can spend more time ensuring superior content and spend less time on the technicalities of making books.

You can count on our commitment to deliver high-quality books at competitive prices on topics you want to read about. At IDG Books Worldwide, we continue in the IDG tradition of delivering quality for more than 25 years. You'll find no better book on a subject than one from IDG Books Worldwide.

John Kilcullen
CEO
IDG Books Worldwide, Inc.

Steven Berkowitz
President and Publisher
IDG Books Worldwide, Inc.

Eighth Annual Computer Press Awards ≥1992

Ninth Annual Computer Press Awards ≥1993

Tenth Annual Computer Press Awards ≥1994

Eleventh Annual Computer Press Awards ≥1995

To Susan, Ashley, and Alec, as always.

Credits

Acquisitions Editor
Greg Croy

Development Editor
Amy Thomas

Technical Editor
Yael Li-Ron

Copy Editor
Marcia Baker

Project Coordinators
Susan Parini
Ben Schroeter

Production Staff
Laura Carpenter
Tom Debolski
Renée Dunn
Stephanie Hollier
Stephen Noetzel
Andreas Schueller

Quality Control Specialist
Mick Arellano

Proofreader
Mary Oby

Indexer
James Minkin

About the Author

Alan Simpson is a freelance computer/Internet nerd and veteran author of *digilit* (digital literature). Alan's experience with Windows 95 began in 1993 when the product was still in its nonpublic infancy. Since then, Alan has spent many thousands of hours learning the ins and outs of Windows 95, the Internet, and Windows 95 applications. Although he's a bit of a guru, Alan is best known for his light, conversational writing style, which appeals to most people who are put off by the dense, unintelligible text that fills so many manuals and large computer books.

Alan lives with his wife, two children, three dogs (Clifford, Lana, Tracker), a cat, a rabbit, and some fish in San Diego, California. He works at home. A lot. Alan is probably the least suntanned person in southern California. He can be reached at:

Alan Simpson
P.O. Box 630
Rancho Santa Fe, CA 92067
Fax: (619) 756-0159
E-mail: alan@coolnerds.com
Web: http://www.coolnerds.com

Preface

Welcome to *Windows 95 Bible*!

A Little History

I started using Windows 95 way back in December of 1993. Like many first-time users, I was a bit perplexed by the new interface. Little things that were effortless in Windows 3.x suddenly were difficult again. I was forever jumping into Help just to figure out how to perform the simplest tasks. I was stymied by many of the new features in Windows 95. Some features, I couldn't get to work; some, I didn't understand; and, some I couldn't even find.

But I got hooked — big-time. I decided I must know everything about this beast; I must be able to use it fluently and effortlessly; I must learn about, and master, every feature. I was challenged, enthralled, and consumed. Don Quixote had his windmills; I had my Windows 95.

As the weeks and months rolled by, I did gain that mastery. I tackled each feature in Windows 95 one by one and didn't quit until everything worked. And when I say every feature, I mean *every* feature: Briefcase, the Microsoft Network (MSN), local area networking, Microsoft Exchange, Microsoft Fax, Sound Recorder, Media Player, CD Player, HyperTerminal, Phone Dialer, DriveSpace, dial-up networking, direct cable connection, WinPopup, PCMCIA . . . on and on. Yes, indeed, if Windows 95 can do it, it can do it right here in my office.

Months and years rolled by, and things didn't change much. Until, suddenly, the Internet was upon us all, offering new ways to use our computers and new ways to communicate. Then, in 1997, came Microsoft Internet Explorer 4.0 (well, in beta anyway), and this added a whole lot of new features to Windows 95. In fact, the very appearance of Internet Explorer 4 prompted me to write this book. Or, rather, I should say, prompted me to produce this new edition of an earlier book. Let me explain what I mean.

This book is actually the second edition of my Windows 95 work. The first edition was titled *Windows 95 Uncut,* but this edition is titled *Windows 95 Bible* to fit into IDG Books' *Bible* series.

Normally a second edition of such a big book wouldn't be done until a new product, such as Windows 98, existed. But, because so much of the world *around* Windows 95 has changed, the original *Windows 95 Uncut* didn't seem to do justice to all the Windows 95/Internet Explorer 4 combination has to offer. So in this new edition, you'll find all the important stuff about working privately on your desktop and setting up and using a local area network, just as before. In addition you'll find:

- ✦ Greatly expanded coverage of connecting to, and using, the Internet with Microsoft Internet Explorer 4, Outlook Express, Microsoft NetMeeting, and Microsoft Chat.
- ✦ Lots of information on the new Active Desktop and live desktop components.
- ✦ All new 32-bit Windows 95 programs on the CD-ROM.
- ✦ More coverage of advanced topics like corporate computing and using the Registry.

Many new topics covered here are based on questions and suggestions I've received from readers, just like you. Keep those e-mails coming. My mail info is in the About the Author section near the front of the book.

Whom This Book Is For

I wouldn't recommend this book to an absolute beginner. You should be familiar with basic PC terminology, and you should have some hands-on experience with the mouse and keyboard. But I don't expect you to have any formal training in computer science, and you certainly don't need to know anything about programming to use this book.

If words such as *keyboard* and *click* no longer shoot waves of anxiety through you, you're probably OK. If you actually like the PC and want the productive and creative power it can give you, so much the better. If you're flat-out "wired," ambitious, and only a little scared — perfect. We'll get along just fine.

Features of This Book

Have you ever noticed that computer books have become a little like computer programs? The books are heavy on "features": pictures you have to read around, characters shouting and waving at you from the margins, little boxes of text here and there, maybe the occasional famous quote from some ancient scholar. I didn't do any of that in this book.

This book is pretty much just me talking on paper (as I like to call it) and showing you pictures. Most of the book is based on personal experience: those umpteen months of bringing Windows 95 to its knees and making it my personal slave. (That's probably not a great sales pitch, I realize. But it's the truth, so what the heck.)

The book does have some margin icons. So I guess I'd better explain what those mean:

 This icon signifies your basic tip: a trick, technique, or other tidbit worth calling special attention to, just so you don't miss it.

 When I was struggling with the "unpleasant" portion of the Windows 95 learning curve, a lot of things confused and puzzled me. Eventually, though, I'd discover something that would make me say, "Oh, now I get it." The "Puzzled?" icon is an attempt to predict where you may get that Rubik's Cube feeling and an attempt to bring you the "Ah ha!" experience a little sooner.

 This icon refers to a source of additional information on a topic (just in case I didn't already tell you enough to bore you to tears).

 This icon points out a technique you really need to think about before you act. Tread carefully, because if you make a mistake, it'll be difficult — or impossible — to undo the mistake.

 If there *is* a way to undo a mistake, fix a problem, or get out of a jam, this icon points the way.

About the CD-ROM

The CD-ROM that comes with this book is largely optional. That is to say, if you don't have a CD-ROM drive, don't worry about it. But if you *do* have a CD-ROM drive, by all means take a look. The disc has some really great programs and all kinds of fun and useful stuff. When you feel like taking the CD-ROM for a spin, refer to Appendix C.

How to Use This Book

I recommend you start by browsing through the table of contents to get a feel for the way topics are organized. You'll see this book contains parts on topics such as portable computing and cyberspace, and that each part is divided into chapters dealing with a specific topic or feature, such as the Briefcase or the Internet. Feel free to read any chapter at your convenience; I don't expect you to plow through this book cover to cover.

You need to pay special attention to one part, though: Part I, which is titled "Know This or Suffer." All the stuff you *really* need to know to get along with Windows 95 is in this part. You may have to bite the bullet and actually read through those chapters to get some grounding and some skill. Otherwise, the later parts and chapters may be a bit overwhelming.

Getting Updates on Internet Explorer 4

This printing of *Windows 95 Bible* is based on the beta release of Internet Explorer 4.0. Because Microsoft reserves the right to change Internet Explorer, some differences may exist between the descriptions in this book and the final release of Internet Explorer 4.0. Please check the IDG Books Worldwide Web site at www.idgbooks.com for updates.

To help you retrieve and print Internet Explorer 4.0 updates from the Web easily, you can download an evaluation version of WebPrinter for Windows 3.x/95 v2.0 from the IDG Books Worldwide Web site. WebPrinter enables you to print Web pages as minibooklets. This application automatically intercepts standard-sized pages as they are sent to your laser/ink jet printer, and then reduces, rotates, and paginates the pages to print as double-sided booklets.

 You can print up to four documents before you have to purchase the full version of WebPrinter. For more information, visit the ForeFront Group's Web site at www.ffg.com, or call (800) 475-5831.

Acknowledgments

I always say that book writing is a prima donna sport. In football, the quarterback gets to be the prima donna; in baseball, it's the pitcher. In book writing, the author gets the glory (and all the heat as well). But, in truth, all these enterprises are team sports, and it's the team — not any individual — that makes it all work.

Nonetheless, it's up to the prima donna to give credit where credit is due. So here goes. First of all, many, many thanks to everyone at IDG Books who made this book happen. You were all very supportive, very professional, and very patient. In particular, I'd like to thank Amy Thomas, Development Editor; Greg Croy, Acquisitions Editor; Marcia Baker, Copy Editor; Yael Li-Ron, Technical Reviewer; Melisa Duffy, Marketing Manager; Susan Parini and Ben Schroeter, Project Coordinators; and Laura Carpenter, Tom Debolski, Renée Dunn, Stephanie Hollier, Stephen Noetzel, and Andreas Schueller, Graphics and Production Specialists.

Many thanks to everyone at Microsoft for helping me get an early start on this great product and for all the support and answers you provided along the way.

To Matt Wagner and everyone at Waterside: Thanks for getting this opportunity to me and making the deal happen.

And, of course, to my family: Thank you, thank you, thank you for your patience and understanding. I *really* had to concentrate on this one and I appreciate your support.

Contents at a Glance

Contents

PART II: HAVE IT YOUR WAY   101

Chapter 5: General Housekeeping (Copying, Deleting, and So On) 103

Chapter 6: Personalizing the Screen...119

PART III: GROWTH, MAINTENANCE, AND GENERAL TWEAKING   177

PART VI: HOPPING ON THE INFO SUPERHIGHWAY   393

Chapter 21: Cruising the Microsoft Network (MSN).....................395

Chapter 22: Connecting to a Bulletin Board System (BBS) or PC 413

Chapter 27: Using Microsoft NetMeeting 581

Chapter 28: Fun with Microsoft Chat 599

Know This or Suffer

How to Do Anything in Windows 95

Hullo. In the introduction (which you may have skipped), I promised this book will be an "empowering" book. That is, I don't want to get into the theory or design of Windows 95, don't wanna laud its merits or whine about its shortcomings. You've probably already gotten plenty of that from the trade press. I just want to give you the power to do whatever you want with Windows 95.

Also, I don't want you to feel you must read this entire book to use Windows 95 effectively. As I mentioned in the introduction, I'll put all the "need to know" stuff up here in Part I. Anything beyond Part I is optional; you can read those chapters at your leisure and ignore any chapters that aren't pertinent to your work. And like any good reference book, this one has a table of contents, glossary, and index, so you can just look up information as needed.

Now, first on the list of things you really need to know is . . .

How to Start Windows 95

Assuming you have installed Windows 95 on your machine, there's really nothing special you need to do to start it. Just turn on the computer, monitor, printer, and so forth, and wait. If you're on a local area network (LAN), you may be asked to supply a user name and password. Fill in the blanks with whatever information your network administrator gave you, or just press Esc to get right into Windows 95. (If you press Esc, however, you won't be able to use shared resources on the LAN.)

Installing Win 95

I'm going to start off assuming you have (or somebody else has) already installed Windows 95 on your PC. If you haven't installed Windows 95 yet and want some help with this, see Appendix A. If you're a corporate information systems manager and need to upgrade lots of PCs on a LAN, see Part IX first. Those chapters discuss using Windows 95 in a corporate setting, large-scale installation alternatives, and adding Windows 95 to an existing Novell or Windows NT LAN.

When Windows 95 is ready to roll, your screen will look something like Figure 1-1, which also points out the names of various desktop doodads.

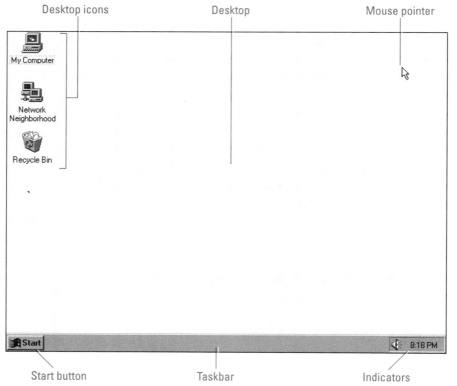

Figure 1-1: The Windows 95 desktop

When you first get to the desktop, you may see a big *Welcome to Windows 95* window. I'll talk about that window a little later in this chapter. For now, if you're looking at the Welcome window, you can click on its Close button to make your screen look more like Figure 1-1. The following sections provide a quick overview of what's on the screen to get you started using Windows 95.

Desktop

The desktop is the large blank area that acts sort of like your real (wooden or metal) desktop; it's always there, and it's where you put whatever you're working on at the moment.

 You can right-click on the desktop to display a shortcut menu of commands for rearranging and customizing the desktop.

Mouse pointer

The mouse pointer moves when you move the mouse. To *point to* something on the screen, you move the mouse until the mouse pointer is touching the thing to which you want to point. To *click* something, you point to that thing and then press and release the main (usually, left) mouse button. To *double-click* something, point to it and then press and release the main mouse button twice, as fast as you can (click-click!). To *right-click* something, point to it and then press and release the secondary mouse button (usually, the button on the right side of the mouse).

Desktop icons

You may see a few desktop icons displayed down the left side of the desktop. You can double-click any one of those icons to open it into a window or right-click any icon to see what other options are available. After you open an icon into a window, you can click the *X* in the upper-right corner of that window to close the window. The desktop icon for that window remains on the desktop.

Taming the mouse

In this book, I'm assuming you already know how to work a mouse. If you have any problems with the mouse, see Chapter 7, where you'll learn how to control the tracking speed of the mouse, the double-click speed, and so on. If you're a lefty, you can use techniques discussed in that chapter to reverse the mouse buttons so the main mouse button is below your index finger.

Start button

The Start button is the way you'll probably start 99 percent of the things you do in Windows 95. You can click the Start button to display the Start menu; then you can point to any option with a right-pointing triangle next to it to see a submenu. If an option does not have the right-pointing triangle next to it, then you have to click (once) the option to select it.

 You can customize the Start menu and taskbar in many ways, as you'll learn in Chapter 8.

Taskbar

Although it appears empty in Figure 1-1, the taskbar eventually will contain a button and icon for every open window on your desktop. If you want to get to a window currently not visible on the desktop (because it's minimized or covered by other windows), you can click the appropriate button in the taskbar. You can right-click the taskbar to customize it, and you can drag the taskbar to any edge of the screen.

Indicators

The right edge of the taskbar displays the current time and indicators that will change periodically, depending on what you're doing at the moment. You can double-click the current-time display to change the date and time. Typically, you also can click any other small icon that appears near the clock to do something with the hardware the icon represents. If I click the little speaker icon, for example, I get the volume control for my speakers, as shown in Figure 1-2.

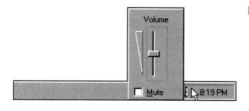

Figure 1-2: Volume control appears when you click the Speaker indicator.

Starting Programs

The first thing most people want to do when they get to an operating system is launch some other program. I'll discuss how you do that right off the bat. Follow these steps:

1. Click the Start button and then point to <u>P</u>rograms.

A menu of program groups and icons appears, as shown in Figure 1-3. Notice that if you installed Windows 95 over an earlier version of Windows, just about every option in this menu actually is a program group from your old Program Manager.

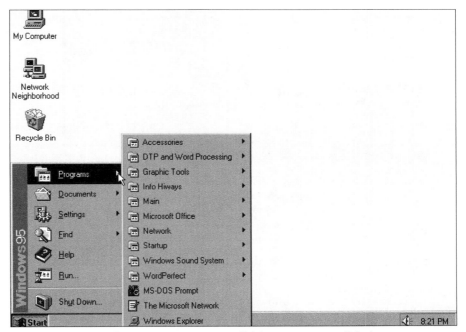

Figure 1-3: To see the program groups available on your PC, click the Start button and then point to <u>P</u>rograms.

2. To start a program, click its icon or point to its folder.

For example, suppose you have Microsoft Office (which includes Microsoft Word) on your PC. To start Microsoft Word you would point to (or click) the Microsoft Office folder and then click the Microsoft Word icon, as shown in Figure 1-4.

If a right-pointing triangle appears next to a menu item, you don't have to click that item to see what's next (although you can if you want to); all you must do is point to it. If an option *doesn't* have that little triangle next to it, pointing to the item does nothing, and you have to click the item to open it.

This method seems a little weird when you're getting started, especially if you're accustomed to double-clicking everything to get to a program, as in Windows 3.x. Also, you'll feel like a mouse klutz for a while, because you have to glide from one menu to another without taking the mouse off the menus for any length of time. Trust me, though, you'll get used to it.

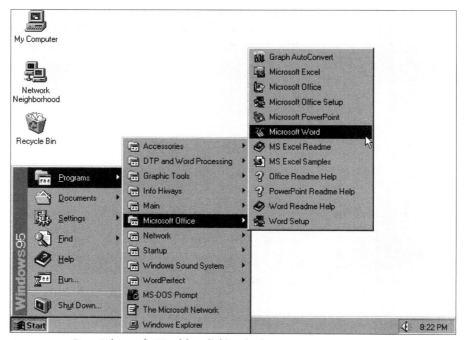

Figure 1-4: Start Microsoft Word by clicking its icon.

More Info You can start programs and open documents in Windows 95 in many ways, as I'll discuss in Chapter 3. Using the Start button is just one of many approaches.

Note, starting a program and then choosing File ➪ Open from its menu bar to open an existing document is somewhat dated now. In Windows 95, a much quicker way to open a recently saved document is to click the Start button, point to Documents, and then click the name of the document you want to open. Or just double-click the name of the document you want to open.

Closing Programs

When you want to close a program, use whichever of these three techniques is handiest:

✦ Click the Close button (X) in the upper-right corner of the window you want to close.

✦ Double-click the icon in the upper-left corner of the window you want to close.

✦ Click File in the program's menu bar and then click Exit.

Your options are illustrated in Figure 1-5, which uses Microsoft Word as the example program.

To close a program . . .

... double-click here   ... or click here

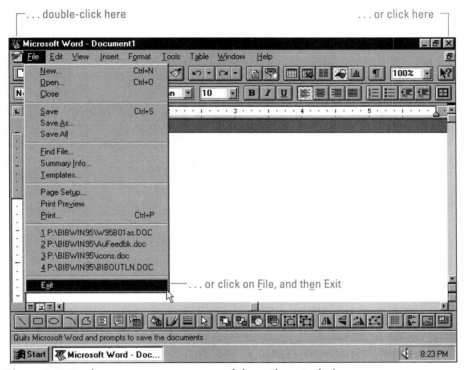

... or click on File, and then Exit

Figure 1-5: To close a program, use any of these three techniques.

Fleeing to DOS

If you're an ex-DOS user, you may feel some anxiety about being in this new environment. Not to fear though, because you can easily get to the Windows 95 command-line mode, which, for all intents and purposes, is identical to DOS. Follow these steps:

1. Click the Start button and then point to Programs to display the Programs menu.

2. Click the MS-DOS Prompt icon (near the bottom of the menu).

   You go to a DOS-like screen, as shown in Figure 1-6.

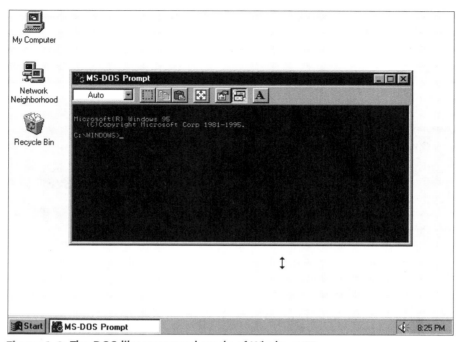

Figure 1-6: The DOS-like command mode of Windows 95

You can enter any DOS command with which you're familiar and then press Enter, just as you do in "real" DOS.

Hot Stuff If you enter the DOS VER command at the C:\> prompt, you'll see you're not really in DOS after all. (In case you're not near a PC, I'll just tell you what the screen says; it says *Windows 95* where it used to say *MS-DOS*.)

Fleeing from DOS

The little DOS window is pretty much like any other window. If you run a program within the DOS window, however, you typically have to exit that program before you can close the DOS window. Instructions on the screen will tell you if this is the case. Other than that, to close the DOS window, you can do any of the following things:

✦ Click the Close (X) button in the upper-right corner of the DOS window.

✦ Double-click the icon in the upper-left corner of the DOS window.

✦ Type **exit** and press Enter at the C:\> prompt.

If you're not already familiar with DOS, you needn't worry; you don't have to know *anything* about DOS to use Windows 95. I included this section only because I know experienced DOS users probably will want to switch to DOS occasionally to do things they haven't figured out how to do in Windows 95. For example, you might want to use the DOS COPY command to copy some files, or DIR to look for a file.

Starting in DOS mode

The techniques I just described are fine for entering the occasional DOS commands. In some situations, however, you might not find this technique suitable for running old DOS programs. Here's a quick trick that often works for getting a stubborn DOS program to run right away:

1. Close any open programs and save your work, if necessary.
2. Remove any floppy disks from floppy disk drives.
3. Click the Start button and then click Shut Down.
4. Choose Restart the computer in MS-DOS mode? And click Yes.
5. When you get to the C:\> prompt, run the DOS program just as you did on the old DOS machine.

For example, you might just be able to type the program's name (**wp**) and press Enter. Or, you may have to navigate to the program's directory first by typing something like this:

cd \wp

and pressing Enter, and then enter the program's startup command.

When you've finished with the DOS program for the time being, exit it as you normally would. You'll be returned to the C:\> prompt. To get to Windows 95, type **exit** and press Enter.

If the technique I just described still doesn't get your old DOS program running, don't fret. I'll talk about several techniques installing and running DOS programs in Chapters 3 and 9, and something along the way is bound to work.

Ye Olde Program Manager

If you're in a hurry to get some work done and you aren't yet accustomed to the Windows 95 techniques for launching a program, you can call up a reasonable facsimile of the Windows 3.1 Program Manager. To do so:

1. Click the Start button and then click Run.
2. Type **progman** and press Enter or click the OK button.

You can maximize the Program Manager window to fill the screen by double-clicking its title bar (or right on the title Program Manager). Or by clicking the large square near the upper-right corner of the Program Manager window.

I say this version of Program Manager is a reasonable facsimile of the original because there are a few differences:

✦ Closing Program Manager no longer shuts down Windows. Instead, you're taken back to the Windows 95 desktop.

✦ Pressing Ctrl+Esc takes you to the Start menu rather than the Task List.

✦ Pressing Ctrl+Alt+Del does not reboot your computer but, instead, takes you to a Close Program dialog box where you can close down individual programs, or reboot if you wish.

✦ Minimized group windows appear as buttons near the bottom of the Program Manager window, rather than as icons.

If you're accustomed to using the Windows 3 Program Manager, it might be tempting to stay in this Windows 95 version of this program. But, personally, I wouldn't recommend it. With a little experience outside of Program Manager you'll eventually see the Windows 95 way of doing things is much easier and quicker. You can close down Program Manger just like any other program:

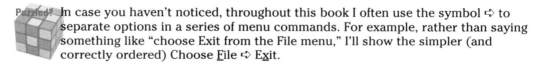

Puzzled? In case you haven't noticed, throughout this book I often use the symbol ➪ to separate options in a series of menu commands. For example, rather than saying something like "choose Exit from the File menu," I'll show the simpler (and correctly ordered) Choose File ➪ Exit.

✦ Choose File ➪ Exit from the Program Manager's menu bar

✦ Or, click the Close (X) button in the upper-right corner of Program Manager's window.

✦ Or, double-click the little icon at the left side of Program Manager's title bar.

You'll be returned to the "normal" Windows 95 desktop.

File Manager

Although not readily accessible from the desktop or menus, a copy of the old Windows 3.1 File Manager is in Windows 95. To start it:

1. Click the Start button and choose Run.

2. Type **c:\windows\winfile.exe** and then press Enter or click the OK button.

The file manager program that appears is the spitting image of the old File Manager. As an alternative to going through the Start ➪ Run business to use the Winfile program, you can make the Windows 95 Explorer look very similar to the old File Manager. To take a quick peek follow these steps:

1. Click the Start button and point to Programs.

2. Click Windows Explorer.

3. Choose View ➪ Details from the menu bar in the Exploring window that appears, to make Explorer look more like the old File Manager.

I'll talk more about Windows Explorer and general file management in Chapter 5. For now, you can exit File Manager like any other program: choose File ➪ Exit or click the Close (X) button.

Take the Guided Tour

A great starting point for getting the hang of Windows 95 is the built-in guided tour. It's only available if you installed Windows 95 from a CD. So, if you did, follow these steps to start the tour:

1. If you didn't close the Welcome window described at the start of this chapter, Skip to Step 3 now.

2. To reopen the Welcome window, click the Start button, click Run, type **welcome**, and then click OK.

3. In the Welcome window (see Figure 1-7), click the Windows Tour button, and then follow the instructions on the screen.

Hot Stuff   If you have Windows 95 on CD, but your Welcome window doesn't have a Windows Tour button, that component isn't installed on your hard disk. To install it, first close the Welcome window and then see the instructions in "Installing Missing Windows Components" in Chapter 10.

While you're in the Windows tour, be sure to take the Using Help tour. The help system in Windows 95 is *vastly* improved from Windows 3.1. So you'll want to learn how to use the online help as soon as possible. For more information, see "How to Do Anything" a little later in this chapter.

If you're an experienced Windows 3.1 user, you'll probably want to explore the online What's New documentation to ease the transition to Windows 95. To see what's new, follow these steps:

1. If the Welcome window isn't visible on your screen at the moment, click the Start button, click Run, type **welcome**, and then click OK.

2. Click What's New.

Figure 1-7: The guided tour

You see a window titled Windows Help (shown in Figure 1-8) that presents frequently asked questions for experienced Windows users.

3. Follow the instructions on the screen.

This online document is presented in question-and-answer format. Click any question to view the answer. When you're done, you can click the Close button (X) in the upper-right corner of the Windows Help window.

How to Do Anything

The Windows tour and What's New online document definitely will help you get your feet wet in Windows 95. But the tours can do only so much. Many new questions surely will arise in your daily use of Windows 95. Obviously, the main purpose of this book is to answer all those questions. But before you become totally reliant on this book (or any other book), you really should master the online help and documentation. These features are much better than anything I've seen before and usually are the quickest and easiest way to learn how to do something — even troubleshoot a problem.

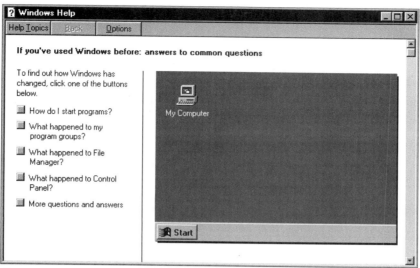

Figure 1-8: If you click What's New in the Welcome window, you see this window.

I'm not harping on the online help just because it's the hip thing to do these days. The fact of the matter is I became a Windows 95 "expert" *without any written documentation whatsoever*. From the time I received my first copy of the prerelease version of Windows 95 (in December 1993) until I wrote this chapter (15 months later), I was given barely one stitch of printed documentation. Yet I consider myself an expert for the simple reason that I can make Windows 95 do whatever I want it to do, whenever I feel like it. (I assume making something do whatever you want defines *expertise,* no?)

Now you may be wondering whether you wasted your money buying this book. After all, if I mastered the system without printed documentation, can't you? The answer to this question is "It depends." One of the advantages of going through the online documentation is I know Windows 95's strengths and weaknesses. I know where more depth would be helpful, what topics are not discussed in detail, and so on. So by writing this book, I can help fill in lots of gaps. Also, other people's experience is always a good thing when you're learning something new. Much of my goal in writing this book is to empower those of you who have less experience than I do by handing you my experience on a silver platter (that is, in a format I hope you can understand, even if you're not already a hard-core computer whiz).

Anyway, the point is, *don't skimp on learning to use the Windows 95 built-in help and documentation.* Take some time to read the rest of this chapter so you can learn how to get answers and solve problems quickly.

The following sections show you all the different ways to get help and information right on your screen. You'll start with a quick, simple method and work your way to techniques that require digging.

Instant help

You can use any of the following techniques to get brief, but immediate, help with just about anything you see on your screen at the moment:

✦ To get help with a command button, point to it. A tooltip usually appears (see Figure 1-9).

Figure 1-9: Tooltips pop up when you rest the mouse pointer on a button.

✦ To see what options a particular button or icon offers, try right-clicking that button or icon. You may see a menu of options, as shown in Figure 1-10.

✦ If you're already in a dialog box or window, you typically can press F1 for help. Or, if you see the little question-mark button in the upper-right corner of the current window, click that button, and then click whatever item you need explained.

When you use the last method, a brief help window pops up, as shown in Figure 1-11. After reading the window's contents, click anywhere in that window to remove it from your screen.

In case you're wondering, I double-clicked the time indicator near the lower-right corner of the screen to get to the dialog box shown in Figure 1-11.

Figure 1-10: Right-clicking a button or icon may display a pop-up menu.

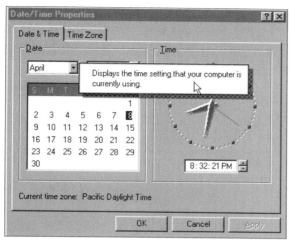

Figure 1-11: To get help, you can press F1 or click
the ? button, and then click an object.

Your electronic table of contents

For general information or background on a particular topic, try using the table of
contents for the help system (see Figure 1-12). Follow these steps:

1. Click the Start button, click Help, and then click the Contents tab.

2. Open any book by double-clicking the book, or by clicking the book once,
   and then clicking the Open button.

3. To explore a topic (indicated by a page with a question mark on it), double-
   click the topic, or click it, and then click the Display button.

When an unopened book is highlighted, the left button at the bottom of the Help
Topics menu is labeled Open. When a topic within a book is highlighted, that
leftmost button is labeled Display.

The table-of-contents technique is most useful when you want to explore a large
subject area, such as "How to Use a Network" or "Tips and Tricks for Running
Programs." If you want to search for a more specific topic, use the electronic
index, as described in the following section.

Your electronic index

The online help system's electronic index is basically the same as the index in the
back of a printed book. To use it, click the Start button, choose Help, and then
click the Index tab. Type the word or phrase you want to look up. Then, in the list
box, click the index entry you want (see Figure 1-13).

Figure 1-12: The Contents tab in Windows Help

You're taken to the help entry for that particular topic, as in the example shown in Figure 1-14.

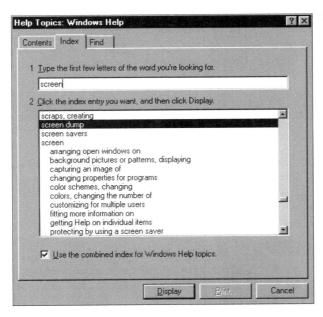

Figure 1-13: Use the help index as you would the index in the back of a printed book.

When you arrive at the help window for a particular topic, you can do any of the following things:

✦ If the help window has a Click Here button, you can click it to go straight to the appropriate dialog box or folder. (This feature of Windows 95 *alone* justifies making the change from Windows 3.x.)

✦ If the window has a Related Topics button, you can click that button for information on related topics.

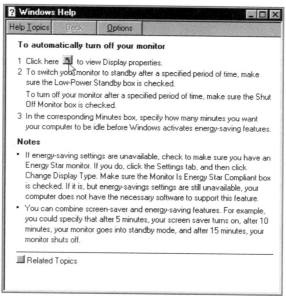

Figure 1-14: A help topic displayed on the screen

✦ You can click Help Topics to return to the electronic index (or wherever you came from)

• Or click Back to move back to the preceding help topic (if any).

• Or click Options to choose among a variety of options, including keeping the help window on top of other windows.

• When you want to close the help window, click its Close button (X).

Searching for a word or phrase

When you're in the help window, you may notice, in addition to the Contents and Index tabs, the window has a tab called Find. When you use it, the Find tab may seem to be almost identical to the Index tab, but there are some differences.

For one thing, the Index tab takes you to a professionally prepared index that contains topics (words) that the person who created the Index felt were appropriate for the index. (As I mentioned earlier, the index in Windows Help is virtually identical to the index in the back of a book.) The Find tab, however, takes you to a computer-prepared index, which lists every word appearing in the online document — even words such as *a* and *the*. In short, Find provides a much broader search of the material than Index does.

The word list Find uses generally is not shipped with a product. Instead, the first time you use a help file, the Find word list is created automatically. During that phase, a little book animation appears on the screen. (In some cases, you may first see a Wizard window. Don't worry about it; just follow the instructions on the screen.)

Another difference is the Find tab uses a three-step process, rather than a two-step process. In the Step 1 section of the tab, you type a word. In the Step 2 section, you click any word to narrow your search, if you like. You also can Ctrl+click (hold down the Ctrl key while clicking the mouse) several words or phrases to narrow your search. A list appears in the Step 3 section of the tab, displaying all related topics.

When you see the topic you want, you can double-click the topic to open it immediately. Or, you can click several topics, and then click the Display button to explore all the checked topics (see Figure 1-15).

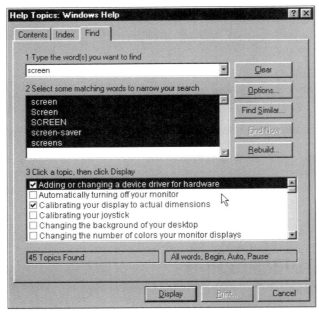

Figure 1-15: The Find tab searches every word in the online help system.

You can customize the way Find does its thing, if you're so inclined. For example, after you click the Find tab in a help window:

✦ You can click the Options button to specify how Find treats multiple search words and when it performs its search (see Figure 1-16).

✦ After you click a topic in the Step 3 section of the Find tab, you can click the Find Similar button to review topics related to the checked topic(s).

✦ You can click the Rebuild button to rebuild the word list Find uses.

The bottom line here is this: If Index doesn't seem to come up with the word or phrase you're looking for, try using Find instead.

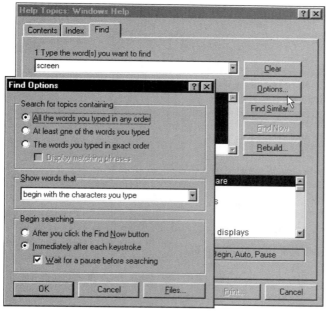

Figure 1-16: The Find Options dialog box

Instant Troubleshooting

One of the best new features of Windows 95 is its Troubleshooting help feature. I can't even count how many times this feature solved problems for me in the early days of beta testing Windows 95 without written documentation. I *can* tell you with confidence that any time something doesn't work as expected in Windows 95, the first place you should look for a solution is the help system's Troubleshooting feature. Follow these steps:

1. Click the Start button and then click Help.
2. Click the Contents tab and then double-click the Troubleshooting book.

   The book opens, as shown in Figure 1-17.
3. Double-click whichever document is appropriate to your problem.
4. Follow the instructions on the screen.

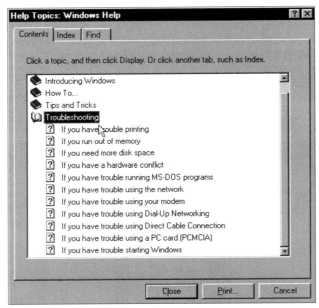

Figure 1-17: Topics in the Troubleshooting book

Shutting Down Your PC

If you are an ex-Windows 3.1 user, you're probably accustomed to exiting Windows and returning to the DOS command prompt to ensure all your work is saved before you turn off your PC. In Windows 95, you have no DOS to exit to — but this doesn't mean you can just turn off your PC whenever you feel like it.

To ensure all your work is saved and no files are corrupted, you should always shut down Windows 95 before you turn off your computer. Follow these steps:

1. Click the Start button and then click Shut Down.

   You see the little dialog box shown in Figure 1-18.
2. Click the first option (if it isn't already selected) and then click Yes.
3. Respond to any and all prompts that appear on the screen.

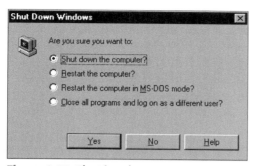

Figure 1-18: Shutting down

Don't turn off your computer until the screen tells you it's safe.

Summary

In this chapter you've learned about the following important basic skills:

✦ To start Windows 95, just start your computer.

✦ To get started doing anything in Windows 95, click the Start button.

✦ To run a program, click the Start button, point to Programs, then choose a program name or program group from the menu that appears.

✦ To exit a program, click the Close (X) button in the upper-right corner of its window.

✦ The quickest way to get help in Windows 95 is through the built-in help system. And there are several ways to use the help system:

For instant help with whatever you're doing at the moment, press the Help key (F1).

In some windows and dialog boxes, you can click the ? button near the upper-right corner of the window, then just click the item with which you need help.

From the desktop, you can click the Start button and then click Help. In the help window that appears you can choose the Contents (like a table of contents), Index (like a book index) or Find (an electronic "super-index") tab to look up the information you need.

✦ You should always exit Windows 95 before you shut down your PC. Just click the Start button, choose Shut Down, then click the Yes button.

✦   ✦   ✦

Getting Around

The guided tours described in the preceding chapter give you a little hands-on practice in the mechanics of managing objects on your screen. In this chapter, I'll review some of those mechanics. But I want to go into more depth, showing you the many tricks you can use in managing objects on the desktop. In addition, I want to show you how to actually find things on the computer.

I realize I've already told you I assume you have *some* experience with PCs, so you may feel much of the material covered here is stuff you already know. Many people, though, have little holes in their knowledge and understanding of these basic concepts; I want to review them all so I know we're on the same track and using similar terminology.

Understanding Icons

Imagine, for a moment, a desk with all the usual accouterments: telephone, calculator, calendar, pens and pencils, documents you're using. Now imagine you have the power to touch any of those objects and shrink it to the size of a pea, just to get it out of the way for the moment. That power would certainly help unclutter your desktop. When you needed to use one of those pea-size objects, you could just tap it with your finger, and bingo — the object would open in its natural size.

Of course, no real-world desktop works this way. The *virtual desktop* that is Windows 95, on the other hand, works exactly this way. You can make things appear and disappear just by touching them with your mouse pointer.

A pea-size object on your computer screen is called an *icon*. Initially, you'll see at least two icons on your Windows 95 desktop: one named *My Computer* and another named *Recycle Bin*. As you start opening icons into windows, you'll see many icons contain still other icons (see Figure 2-1).

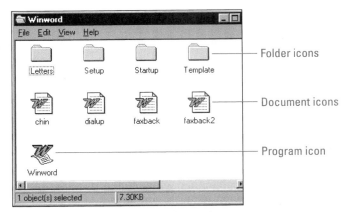

Figure 2-1: Some examples of icons in Windows 95

The appearance of an icon gives you some clue as to what kind of stuff is inside the icon and, hence, to what will likely appear when you double-click the icon. The following list summarizes the main types of icons you'll come across:

✦ *Folder icon:* contains its own set of icons. When you open a folder icon, you see more icons.

✦ *Program icon:* represents a program. When you open a program icon, you start the program it represents. Double-clicking the Winword icon in Figure 2-1, for example, would start the Microsoft Word for Windows program.

✦ *Document icon:* represents a document; typically this is something you can print. The icon usually has a little dog-ear fold in the upper-right corner to resemble a paper document. Opening a document icon typically launches whatever program is required to view/change/print that document, as well as the document itself.

You'll also come across icons that don't fall into any of these categories. Some icons represent disk drives, printers, help files, settings, and so on. But you can manipulate virtually all icons by using the set of basic skills in the following list:

✦ To open an icon, double-click it. The icon's contents appear in a *window* (discussed in the following section).

✦ To move an icon, drag it to any new location on the screen.

✦ To see all the options available for an icon, right-click the icon to see its shortcut menu.

✦ To organize all the icons on the desktop, right-click the desktop, and point to Arrange Icons on the shortcut menu that appears. Then click whichever option you prefer, by Name, by Type, and so forth.

✦ To have Windows 95 automatically arrange icons for you, right-click the desktop and choose Arrange Icons ➪ Auto Arrange.

Managing Windows

When you click an icon, it opens into a *window*. You really must know how to work with those windows to accomplish things. This section discusses what a window really is and what you can do with all windows.

In the olden days of computers, you would run a program, and that program would take over the entire screen. To use a different program, you had to exit the one you were in and then start the other program. That program, in turn, hogged the entire screen.

The days of running one program at a time ended when Windows was created. With Windows, you can run as many programs as you want (well, as many programs as you can fit into your PC's RAM). Rather than hogging the entire screen, each program occupies only a window onscreen. In Figure 2-2, for example, two programs are running and visible on the screen: Paint (a drawing program) and WordPad (a simple word processor that comes with Windows 95). Each program appears in its own window.

Window dressing

Notice, each window in Figure 2-2 has its own unique contents. If you look closely, however, you may notice the frames surrounding those windows are similar. The reason for this similarity is simple: all the tools you use to manage the window are in this frame. This arrangement means that no matter how perplexed you may be by the contents of a window, you can always use the tools on the window's border to manipulate the window. Figure 2-3 shows the tools that frame most windows.

Not every window has exactly the same set of tools. Some small windows can't be sized and, therefore, have no sizing pad; some windows don't have toolbars. But most windows have at least some of the tools shown in Figure 2-3.

The following sections describe how you work with each tool.

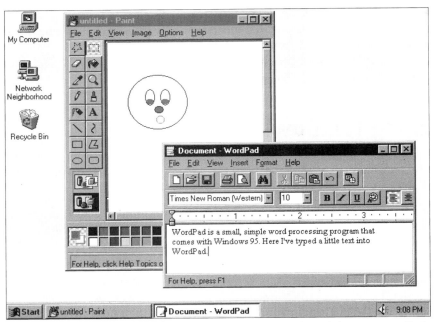

Figure 2-2: In Windows, each program occupies a portion of the screen called a *window*.

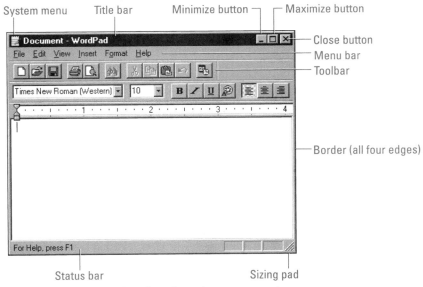

Figure 2-3: Every window has these important tools around its border.

Title bar

The *title bar* shows the icon and name of the stuff inside the window. You can then double-click the title bar to expand the window to full-screen size and to shrink the window to its previous size. More important, you can move a window anyplace on the screen by dragging its title bar.

Minimize button

When you click the *Minimize button*, the window shrinks to just a button in the taskbar. To reopen the window, just click that taskbar button.

Maximize button

Clicking the *Maximize button* expands the window to full-screen size (a quick way to hide other windows that may be distracting you). When the window is full-screen size, the Maximize button turns into the Restore button. To return the window to its previous size, just click that Restore button (between the Minimize and Close buttons.)

Close button

Clicking the *Close button* closes the window, taking it off the screen and out of the taskbar as well. You'll learn more about closing windows in Chapter 3.

When you open a series of windows, you can close the last window and all the windows that led up to it in one fell swoop. Just hold down the Shift key and then click the Close (X) button on the last window you opened.

Border and sizing pad

The frame, or *border*, that surrounds a window is an important tool. You size the window by dragging its border. Many windows have a large *sizing pad* in the lower-right corner; this pad is especially easy to drag.

To size and arrange all the open windows instantly so you can see their title bars, right-click the taskbar between any buttons and away from any indicators. Then click Cascade in the menu that appears. To bring any open window to the forefront instantly, click its taskbar button.

Menu bar

Many windows have a *menu bar* just below the title bar. This menu bar gives you access to commands that affect only those things inside the current window. The View menu is especially important, because it lets you arrange the contents of the window in whatever format is most convenient for you.

Toolbar

Some windows also have a *toolbar* just below the menu bar. The toolbar provides one-click access to the most frequently used menu commands. Sometimes, the menu bar is available but turned off. To display the toolbar, choose View ➪ Toolbar (see Figure 2-4).

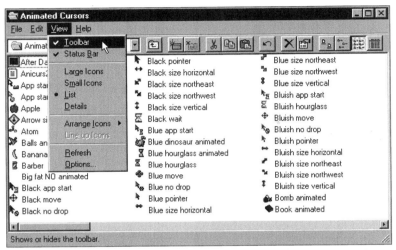

Figure 2-4: The View menu and toolbar are available in many windows.

Status bar

The *status bar* along the bottom of a window shows you the status of various things inside the window. You'll see some examples as you go along in this book. For now, be aware that in many windows, you can hide or display the status bar by choosing View ➪ Status Bar.

System menu

The *System menu* lets you move, size, and close the window by using the keyboard rather than the mouse. To open the System menu, click the icon in the upper-left corner of the window. Or press Alt+spacebar. You also can double-click the System menu icon to close the window.

Scrollbars

If there's more stuff inside a window than can fit into that window, *scrollbars* appear to allow you to move around inside the window. You can use the arrow keys and PgUp and PgDn to move around, or you can use the mouse techniques shown in Figure 2-5.

Top Ten tips for managing windows

If all the various gizmos on the window's border have your mind reeling, perhaps it would be easier to think from the standpoint of what you actually want to do with the windows open on your desktop. Following, in a nutshell, are the main things you need to know how to do:

✦ To open a window, double-click its icon.

✦ To hide an open window temporarily (to unclutter your desktop a bit), click the window's Minimize button.

✦ To view an open window currently covered by other windows or is minimized, click that window's taskbar button.

✦ To move a window, drag it by its title bar to some new location onscreen.

✦ To size a window, drag its lower-right corner or any border.

✦ To enlarge a window to full-screen size, so it completely covers any other windows, double-click its title bar or click on its Maximize button.

✦ To restore a maximized window to its previous size, double-click its title bar or click its Restore button.

✦ To arrange all open windows in a stack with their title bars showing, right-click any "neutral" area (the space between, above, or below buttons) on the taskbar. Then choose Cascade from the pop-up menu.

✦ To close a window, click the Close button (X) in the upper-right corner of the window.

✦ To reopen a closed window, you must repeat whatever steps you took to open it the first time; closing a window also removes its little button from the taskbar.

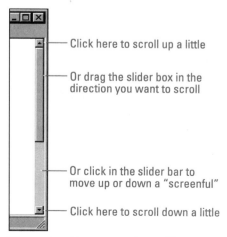

Click here to scroll up a little

Or drag the slider box in the direction you want to scroll

Or click in the slider bar to move up or down a "screenful"

Click here to scroll down a little

Figure 2-5: How to work scrollbars

Closing versus minimizing a window

Think of minimizing a window as taking some document on a real desktop and sliding it into a desk drawer. The document is not cluttering your desk anymore, but it is within easy reach. Closing a window, on the other hand, is more like putting a real folder back in the file cabinet. You can still get back to the document when you want it, but the process is a little more of a hassle than yanking it out of the desk drawer.

From a technical standpoint, closing a window has two advantages: It frees the memory (RAM) the program was using, and it gives you an opportunity to save your work. Minimizing a window does neither of those; it just shrinks the window to a taskbar button to get it out of the way for the moment.

Using the Taskbar

The taskbar at the bottom of the screen contains a button for each open window on the desktop. Figure 2-6 shows an example.

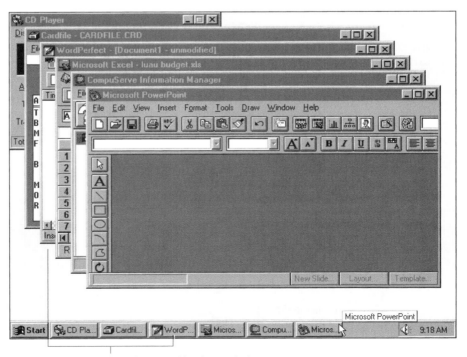

Each open window above has a taskbar button below.

Figure 2-6: The taskbar, showing a button for each open window

At first, it may seem stupid to show buttons for only *open* windows. If a window is already open, why do you also need to see a button for it? The answer is: A window being open is no guarantee that you can *see* that window. Windows can (and often do) overlap or completely cover one another. The beauty of the taskbar is you can bring any open window from hiding simply by clicking its taskbar button.

You can do many cool things with the taskbar, as summarized in the following list:

✦ To bring an open window to the forefront, click its taskbar button.

✦ To see the options for a particular window, right-click its taskbar button.

✦ To arrange all the open windows on the desktop, right-click the taskbar and then choose <u>C</u>ascade, Tile <u>H</u>orizontally, or Tile <u>V</u>ertically. Experiment with these options whenever you have two or more open windows on the desktop, to see for yourself how each option arranges the windows.

✦ To see what a taskbar button represents, point to the button and wait for the tooltip to appear. Pointing to the Micros button in Figure 2-6, for example, shows the button is actually for Microsoft PowerPoint.

Hot Stuff Notice the icon in each taskbar button (CD Pla..., Cardfil..., WordP..., and so on) matches the corresponding icon in the upper-left corner of each open window (CD Player, Cardfile, WordPerfect, and so on).

✦ To minimize (or unminimize) all open windows, right-click the taskbar and then choose <u>M</u>inimize All Windows or <u>U</u>ndo Minimize All.

More Info Chapter 8 presents tips and tricks for personalizing the taskbar.

✦ To move the taskbar to some other edge of the screen, drag it to that edge.

✦ To size the taskbar (to make it thinner or thicker), drag its inner edge (the edge nearest the center of the screen).

How Stuff Is Organized

Everything I've discussed so far is vitally important to using Windows 95, because you must be able to manipulate the various objects on your screen to get anything done. In the real world, managing windows and icons onscreen is as important as managing papers and other objects on your real desktop.

A big difference between your real desktop and your virtual Windows 95 desktop, however, is where you get the stuff you put on the desktop. In a real-world desktop, most of the documents you work with are probably stored in a file cabinet. On a computer, all the objects you can bring to the desktop are stored on a computer disk.

In a real-world file cabinet, you go through the following steps to fetch whatever it is you want:

1. Go to the appropriate file cabinet.
2. Open the appropriate drawer.
3. Pull out the appropriate file.

On a computer, you do this instead:

1. Go to the appropriate disk drive.
2. Open the appropriate folder(s).
3. Double-click the appropriate file icon.

You're probably somewhat familiar with these terms from earlier computer experience. To play it safe, though, the following sections define those terms.

Drive

Anything in the computer is actually stored on a disk. The disk spins around like a CD in a CD player so the computer can read and write stuff to the disk. The device that actually spins the disk around is called a *disk drive* (or *drive* for short).

A disk drive generally has a one-letter name. Your floppy-disk drive, for example, is named A; you may have a second floppy-disk drive named B. In general, you use the floppy-disk drives to copy files to and from the hard disk inside your computer, to make backups, or to copy stuff from one PC to another.

Most of the stuff in the computer is actually stored on your *hard disk drive,* which usually is named C. Unlike floppy disks, you never actually see the hard disk, because it's hermetically sealed in an airtight compartment within the PC. Typically, a hard disk can hold as much information as hundreds (or even thousands) of floppy disks.

You may have some other drives attached to your computer. If you have a CD-ROM drive, it may be named D.

To see what drives are available on your computer, double-click the My Computer icon on the desktop. When the My Computer window opens, you see an icon for each drive (and perhaps a few folders that represent other hardware on your computer). In Figure 2-7, for example, you can see that my computer has a 3 ½-inch floppy drive named A, a 5 ½-inch floppy drive named B, a hard disk named C, and a CD-ROM drive named D.

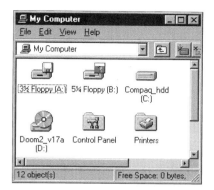

Figure 2-7: This computer has two floppy drives (A and B), a hard disk (C), and a CD-ROM drive (D).

You may notice my hard disk, C, also has another name: Compaq_hdd. This name is the disk's electronic *label*. You can create or change your own hard disk's label, if you like, to any name of 11 characters or fewer, with no spaces. Right-click the drive's icon in the My Computer window. Choose Properties, and fill in the option titled Label. Then choose OK.

Folder

A hard disk or CD-ROM can contain hundreds, even thousands, of files. If you put all those files on the disk without organizing them, finding things later could be difficult. The process would be similar to taking all the files from your file cabinet and dumping them into a large box.

Many folders are created automatically when you install new programs. If I were to double-click the icon for drive C shown in Figure 2-7, a new window would open, showing me the names of the folders (and files, if any) on that drive, as shown in Figure 2-8.

One thing that makes a folder different from a drive or a file is a folder can contain other folders. For example, I could have a folder named All My Stuff. Within this folder, I could have other folders: My Documents, which contains written documents; My Pictures, which contains photos and drawings; and My Clips, which contains sound clips, video clips, and so on.

In case you're wondering, a *folder* is what we used to call a *directory* or *subdirectory* in DOS and Windows 3.x.

I'll talk about how you create, manage, and delete folders in Chapter 8. For now, it's sufficient to know that a folder can contain many files and also other folders.

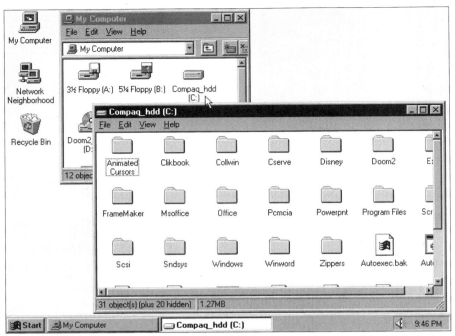

Figure 2-8: Opening a drive icon displays the names of folders and/or files on the disk in that drive.

Files

A *file* is most like the contents of a manila file folder in a desk drawer. Each item in the computer is in its own file. Suppose you use a word processing program to type a letter. When you save that letter, it's saved in a file.

Programs are also stored in files. When you installed Windows 95, it created a folder named Windows. Within this folder are all the files (and perhaps some folders) that make up the Windows 95 program.

As mentioned earlier, a file's icon gives you some clue about the type of information in the file. Program files have icons that represent those programs. Document icons look like dog-eared sheets of paper (refer to Figure 2-1).

Browsing with My Computer

You can find stuff in the computer in three main ways: you can use My Computer or Windows Explorer to browse around to see what's available, or (if you know the exact name of the file or folder you want) you can use the Find command on the

Start menu to go right to that folder or file. I'll discuss browsing with My Computer first, only because I've already touched on this method.

My Computer is a tool that lets you to browse all the disks physically attached to your computer. To start My Computer, double-click its icon, which opens into a window. In the example shown in Figure 2-7, this window contains icons for two floppy-disk drives (A and B), a hard disk (C), and a CD-ROM drive (D).

 Any network drives to which you have mapped a drive letter also appear in My Computer; you can treat them just like drives physically attached to your computer. I know, however, many of you are using stand-alone PCs, so I won't confuse matters by discussing network drives just now. Part VII of this book discusses local area networks in depth.

Working My Computer is easy. To start My Computer, double-click its icon. Then you can do any of the following things:

✦ To see what's on the disk in a particular drive, double-click this drive's icon.

✦ To see what's in a folder, double-click that folder.

✦ To see what's in a file, double-click this file's icon.

✦ To back up (close anything you've opened), click the Close button in the upper-right corner of the window you want to close.

Changing your view in My Computer

When you first open a window in My Computer, the contents usually are displayed in Large Icons view. You can decide for yourself how you want the contents to be displayed. Your choices — Large Icons, Small Icons, List, and Details — are depicted in Figure 2-9. Notice the mouse pointer in each example is pointing to the button I clicked to select that particular view.

Why your screen doesn't look like mine

If you followed along with this section by double-clicking My Computer and other icons on your own PC, your screen probably won't match mine exactly. That's because every PC starts out as sort of a big, empty electronic file cabinet. You fill this file cabinet by adding whatever folders and files are appropriate to your own work.

One way to create files is to create and save documents, as discussed in Chapter 3. You also can create folders and files by using menu commands, as discussed in Chapters 4 and 5. Also, when you install a new program, the installation procedure automatically creates folders and files for storing that particular program, as discussed in Chapter 9.

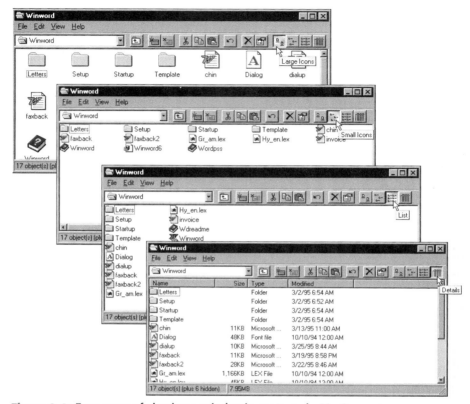

Figure 2-9: Four ways of viewing a window's contents in My Computer

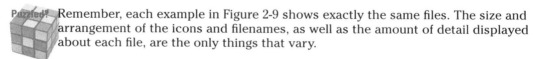 Remember, each example in Figure 2-9 shows exactly the same files. The size and arrangement of the icons and filenames, as well as the amount of detail displayed about each file, are the only things that vary.

To choose a view, click <u>V</u>iew in the window's menu bar and then choose Large Icons, S<u>m</u>all Icons, <u>L</u>ist, or <u>D</u>etails, as appropriate. Alternatively, click the appropriate button in the toolbar. If you can't see the toolbar, first choose <u>V</u>iew ➪ <u>T</u>oolbar.

Figure 2-10 shows the <u>V</u>iew menu open.

Arranging My Computer contents

In addition to deciding the size of the icons in a My Computer window, you can choose the order in which you want to see those items. The normal order is to list all the folders (if any) within the current folder in alphabetical order, followed by all the files (if any) within the current window, also in alphabetical order (see Figure 2-11).

Figure 2-10: The View menu in a My Computer window

Figure 2-11: By default, folders and files are listed in alphabetical order in a My Computer window.

To change the order, follow these steps:

1. Choose View ➪ Arrange Icons.

2. Click one of the following options:

   • by Name: presents folders and files in alphabetical order by name (the usual method).

   • by Type: organizes the folders by type.

   • by Size: organizes everything by size (smallest to largest).

- by <u>D</u>ate: organizes files by date last modified, with most recently modified files listed first. (This option is handy when you're looking for a file you created recently, whose name you can't quite remember.)

Details view (the one that shows all the file details) offers a shortcut for rearranging the icons within the window. Click the column heading to sort everything by that column; click the heading a second time to reverse the sort order in that column. If you click the Modified column heading, for example, the icons are instantly arranged in ascending date (newest to oldest). Clicking Modified a second time reverses the sort order (oldest to newest).

Hot Stuff Here's another little trick that pertains only to Details view: You can widen or narrow the columns. Point to the line that separates two column heads until the mouse pointer turns into a two-headed arrow; then drag the column line to the left or right.

Navigating in My Computer

If you think about it, you'll realize what My Computer really does is let you drill down to more specific areas of the disk. For example, you may open My Computer and double-click the C drive just to look on drive C. Then you may click a folder to drill down and see what's in that folder. Within that folder, you may click yet another folder to drill down and see what's in there.

You also can work your way back up through the drill-down procedure or even jump to an entirely different drive, folder, or whatever without drilling at all. Follow these steps:

1. Make sure the toolbar is visible in the current window.

   Choose <u>V</u>iew ➪ <u>T</u>oolbar if it isn't.

2. Use the first two buttons in the toolbar as follows:

   - To move up to the parent folder, click the Up One Level button. The current folder closes, and you return to the previous folder (assuming you have a "previous folder.").

   - The first tool in the toolbar is a drop-down list box named *Go to a different folder* (when you view its tooltip). To jump to another place altogether, you can click that drop-down button, then choose a destination from the list that appears. The contents of the current window are replaced by the contents of whatever folder you select.

Figure 2-12 shows an example in which the mouse pointer is pointing to the Up One Level button in the toolbar. The Go to a different folder drop-down list box is just to the left of that button.

Figure 2-12: The first two buttons in a My Computer window help you navigate.

Ye olde DOS directories and extensions

Three things about using My Computer are especially awkward for people who are familiar with DOS and/or Windows 3.x:

✦ An icon always shows the actual filename (not an alias), which has dire consequences for renaming and deleting things. (I'll discuss all this in detail in Chapters 4 and 8.)

✦ The extension of that filename may be hidden.

✦ The title bar usually displays the name of the current folder (for example, Letters) without showing the full path of how you got to that folder (for example, C:\WinWord\Letters).

For an example, refer to Figure 2-12, which displays the contents of a folder named Letters. That folder contains some files that have something to do with Microsoft Word for Windows (guessing from the large letter *W* within each icon).

Now suppose you want to see where this Letters folder is on the disk and what types of files these icons represent. Follow these steps:

1. In any open My Computer window, choose <u>V</u>iew ➪ <u>O</u>ptions.

   The Options dialog box appears.

2. Click on the View tab.

   You see the options shown in Figure 2-13.

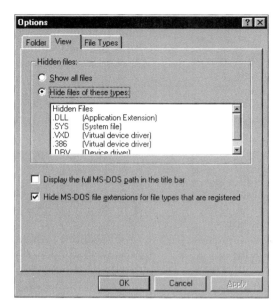

Figure 2-13: The View tab of the Options dialog box

3. To display the full DOS path name in the title bar of My Computer windows, choose Display the full MS-DOS path in the title bar.

4. To display the extension of every filename displayed in a My Computer window, clear (deselect) the Hide MS-DOS file extensions for registered file types.

5. Click OK to return to the desktop.

Now the title bar shows the complete path to the current folder, and each icon shows the name and the extension of the file it represents. Figure 2-14 shows the window from Figure 2-12 after I completed Steps 1-5. If you're accustomed to DOS path names and the role of .DOT (document templates) files in Word, this information probably is useful to you.

Other My Computer tricks

The following sections provide some tips and tricks for getting the most out of My Computer:

Refreshing the My Computer icons

If you're on a LAN or using lots of programs and My Computer doesn't show something it should be showing, choose View ➪ Refresh to reread the contents of the folder.

What the heck are registered files?

In Windows 95, certain types of files are automatically identified as belonging to certain programs. Files with the .DOC extension, for example, are registered to Microsoft Word. This means if you double-click an icon for a file with the .doc extension, Windows 95 automatically opens Microsoft Word and then displays the document you double-clicked.

This approach has two advantages. For one, you needn't go through the usual method of opening a program and then choosing File ➪ Open within that program to open a specific document. Instead, you just open the document. Also, a naive user needn't know with which program a particular document goes. Suppose that Kyle Klewless, who knows nothing about computers, wants to see what's in a file named Please review me Kyle. He doesn't need to know what program is required to open that document; he just has to double-click the document.

Because all the registration business generally is handled behind the scenes, automatically, in Windows 95, there isn't even a reason to display filename extensions. Showing Kyle Klewless the filename Please review me Kyle.doc does him no good; the name Please review me Kyle is sufficient. So that's the reason extensions on registered filenames are hidden by default in Windows 95.

Of course, the automatic registrations may not always be exactly what you want them to be. You can change them. In Chapter 4, I'll show you many shortcuts for opening documents, including techniques for associating different types of files with different programs.

Displaying system and hidden files

Normally, My Computer hides system files, such as dynamic link libraries (.DLL), system files (.SYS), and device drivers (.VXD, .386, and .DRV), the reason being there isn't any reason for the average user to be messing with them. If you need to see those files, choose View ➪ Options in any My Computer window. Click the View tab, and choose Show all files. Then click OK.

Danger Zone Before you delete an entire folder, remember there may be some hidden files on there. As a general rule, you should inspect the folder with Show all files turned on, before you delete it, so you know for sure which files you're about to delete.

Minimizing window pileups

If you don't want My Computer to stack up so many windows as you drill down through folders, choose View ➪ Options; click the Folder tab; and then choose the second option, Browse folders by using a single window....

Hot Stuff Piling up My Computer windows eats up system resources. If memory is tight, you'll probably need to use the Browse folders by using a single window option.

Figure 2-14: The window shown in Figure 2-12 with the full path in the title bar and file extensions.

Even if you minimize window pileups in My Computer, you still have to drill down through folders one window at a time. Although this procedure is good for many people, more experienced users may prefer to use Windows Explorer to browse their PCs.

Browsing with Windows Explorer

Like My Computer, *Windows Explorer* is a tool for browsing around on your hard disk (or on any disk, for that matter) to see what's available. Explorer doesn't use the one-window-at-a-time technique. Instead, Explorer presents your drives, folders, and files in a single window, and you navigate within that window.

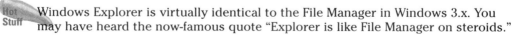 Windows Explorer is virtually identical to the File Manager in Windows 3.x. You may have heard the now-famous quote "Explorer is like File Manager on steroids."

To open Windows Explorer, do any of the following things:

   ✦ Click the Start button, point to <u>P</u>rograms, and then click Windows Explorer.

   ✦ Right-click the My Computer icon and then choose <u>E</u>xplore.

   ✦ Right-click the Start button and then choose <u>E</u>xplore.

Regardless of which method you use to start Explorer, you go to the Explore window, which will look something like Figure 2-15.

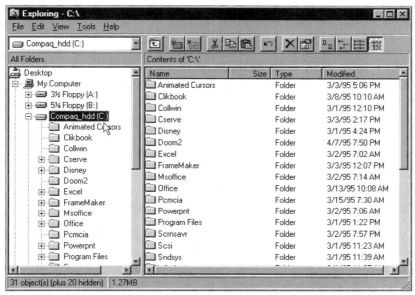

Figure 2-15: The Windows Explorer

To use the Explorer to go exploring, follow these steps:

1. If the toolbar isn't visible, choose View ➪ Toolbar.

2. Click the drop-down list button in Go to a different folder (the first tool in the toolbar), and then click the drive or folder you want to explore.

3. In the leftmost column, click the folder whose contents you want to view.

4. If additional folders are within the currently selected folder, you see a plus sign (+) next to the folder name; click that plus sign to view the names of folders within the folder.

   You can repeat this step until you've drilled down to the folder you want to view.

5. To see what's in the currently selected folder, look in the pane to the right of the folder list.

6. When you finish exploring, click the Close button in the upper-right corner of the Explorer window.

Many of the tricks discussed in the My Computer section work in Explorer as well, including the following:

✦ To view large icons, small icons, a list, or details in the rightmost pane of the Explorer window, click the appropriate button in Explorer's toolbar, or choose <u>V</u>iew ➪ Arrange <u>I</u>cons and then click the arrangement you want.

✦ To update the list of folder and filenames in the Explorer window, choose <u>V</u>iew ➪ <u>R</u>efresh.

✦ To display file extensions, DOS path names, and hidden files, choose <u>V</u>iew ➪ <u>O</u>ptions, click on the View tab, and then choose options to view or hide whatever you want.

As you'll learn in Chapters 3 and 4, you can use either My Computer or Explorer to open, copy, move, and delete files and folders.

When you finish with Explorer, you can close it as you would any other window: Click its Close button, or choose <u>F</u>ile ➪ E<u>x</u>it.

Finding a Specific File or Folder

My Computer and Explorer are fine for browsing around to see what's on a disk and even OK for drilling down to a particular file when you already know what folder that file is in. But in some situations, you may not know where a file is located. You may know the file's name, the date it was last modified, or something about the folder's contents, but you don't know, or can't remember, *where* that file is.

No problem — you can use the Find feature to search an entire disk (all its folders and subfolders) for a specific file. Follow these steps:

1. Click the Start button and then point to <u>F</u>ind.

2. Click Files or <u>F</u>olders.

   You're taken to the Find dialog box, shown in Figure 2-16.

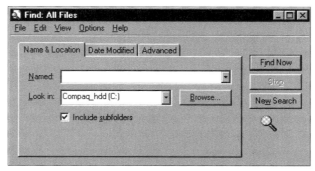

Figure 2-16: The Find dialog box

3. If you want to search the entire hard disk, leave the <u>L</u>ook in setting set to C:, and make sure the Include <u>s</u>ubfolders check box is checked. If you want to search some other disk, select the icon or folder, use the <u>B</u>rowse button to

navigate to that drive or folder. If you don't want to include subfolders in your search, clear the Include subfolders option.

4. Tell Find something about the file you're looking for, using any of the Search by methods described in the following sections.

5. When you're ready to conduct the search, click the Find Now button, and wait for the list of file names to appear.

Danger Zone Never assume a file has been deleted just because Find doesn't find it immediately. You may have searched for the wrong thing or inadvertently narrowed an unsuccessful search. More information on this subject appears under "If Find doesn't find your file" a little later in this chapter.

The following sections describe the various methods mentioned in Step 4.

Search by name

Suppose you're spearheading a luau for your upcoming convention in Hawaii and have already typed a partial list of people to invite. You must get back to that file now and add some more names, but you don't remember exactly what you named the file or what folder you put it in. All you know is you used the word *luau* somewhere in the filename (maybe it was `Luau people` or `Invitations for luau` or something like that).

Not to worry — all you must do is type the word **luau** in the Named text box and then click on the Find Now button. All the files that contain the word *luau* on the drive you're searching appear at the bottom of the list (see Figure 2-17).

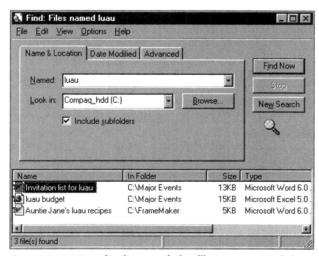

Figure 2-17: Result of a search for filenames containing the word *luau*

In this example, the file named `Invitation list for luau` probably is the one you're looking for. To open it and see, double-click its icon.

Search by date

Suppose you created and saved an important document yesterday. In your rush to get out of the office on time, you saved and closed the file without much thought. Today, you can't remember where you put the file or even what you named it.

To find the missing file, maybe a good starting point would be to look at all the files created or modified yesterday. In the Find dialog box, first click the Date Modified tab. If today is 6/2/97, you want to see all the files created on 6/1/97 (yesterday). So you would fill in the blanks as shown in Figure 2-18 and then click on the Find Now button.

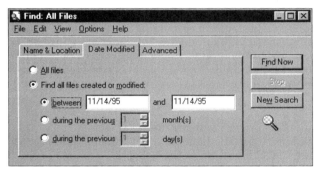

Figure 2-18: A search for files and folders created or modified on 6/1/97

Where are the filenames?

You may be wondering where the filenames are in Figure 2-17. Surprise, surprise — `Invitation list for luau` and the names below it *are* filenames. Windows 95 accepts filenames up to 255 characters in length, and spaces are allowed.

Be aware, though, only 32-bit programs (those designed for Windows 95 and Windows NT) allow you to save files with those long names and those programs are the only ones that let you view the long names.

When you're using a 16-bit program (one designed for DOS or Windows 3.x), you are still limited to eight-character filenames. In dialog boxes that display filenames, you'll see only the first six letters of long file-names, followed by a tilde (~) and a number. When viewing the filename `Invitation list for luau` in a 16-bit program, you see only `Invita~1.doc` as the filename.

The list at the bottom of the dialog box shows only the files and folders that were created or modified on that date. Double-click the one you want to open.

Search by contents

Suppose a month or two ago, you typed and saved a letter to a person named Wanda Bea Starr. You must find that letter now but cannot remember what folder it's in or even what you named the file. It stands to reason, however, that because the file is a letter, her name probably appears in the inside address or somewhere within the letter. You can search the entire disk for files that contain the text *Wanda* or *Starr*.

This method has one drawback: Windows 95 needs to read the contents of every file included in the search, and that procedure can take a very long time. You can speed things if you know what type of document you want. If you're sure the letter you want is a Microsoft Word document, for example, you can tell Find to search just Word documents.

For starters, click the Advanced tab in the Find dialog box. If you know what type of file you're looking for, choose that file type from the Of type drop-down list. Then type the word or phrase you seek in the Containing text box. In Figure 2-19, I want to search all the Microsoft Word document files for the word *Wanda*.

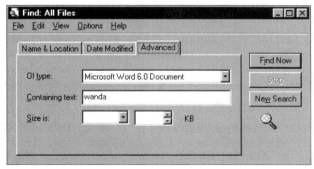

Figure 2-19: A search for Word documents that contain the text *Wanda*

To begin the search, click Find Now. The list at the bottom of the dialog box will (eventually) show all the Microsoft Word documents that contain the word *Wanda*. Remember, we're talking about the *contents* of the file here, not the name of the file; so the word *Wanda* may not appear in the list of filenames that appears. But rest assured, *Wanda* appears somewhere in each of those documents.

If Find lists too many files

In some cases, clicking Find Now produces more filenames than you care to sift through. Fortunately, you can narrow a search easily without starting over from scratch.

Suppose you searched for all files created or modified during the past week and the result was dozens of files — more than you care to peruse. So you want to narrow the list down to Word documents created during the past week. No problem: Click the Advanced tab, select Microsoft Word documents, and click Find Now again. The result will be only Word documents created or modified during the past week.

If Find doesn't find your file

If clicking Find Now does not help you find the file you're looking for, the first thing you should do is click the New Search button. Reason: if you don't do so before specifying a new search criterion, all you do is narrow down the previous unsuccessful search. When a search is unsuccessful, you want to *broaden* your search, not narrow it down. You must click the New Search button to dispense of the previous search (even if it resulted in no found files at all) before conducting a new search.

One of the reasons I emphasize this procedure is it's easy to forget this tidbit. No message will ever appear on the screen, saying, "Hey, Einstein, you'll never find what you're looking for by narrowing down the same old unsuccessful search!" So this whole business of searches being cumulative is just something you have to log into the "Don't Forget" department within your own brain.

As you'll learn in Part VII, you can use Find to search disks on other computers in your local area network, not just your own computer.

Whatever you do, don't panic if Find doesn't locate the file you're looking for. Don't wrongly assume the file has been deleted; instead, click the New Search button, and try some other means of locating the missing file.

If Find succeeds . . .

By default, the bottom of the Find dialog box displays folder and filenames in Details view. But just as you can in My Computer and Explorer, you can specify exactly how you want to view and arrange those icons and names. Use any of the following methods:

✦ Although no Options command exists in Find's View menu, you can still opt to hide or display file extensions. Open any My Computer window, choose View ➪ Options, click the View tab, and then check or clear the Hide MS-DOS file extensions check box.

✦ You can view files and folders as large icons, small icons, a list, or a detailed list by choosing an appropriate option from the <u>V</u>iew option on the Find menu bar.

✦ To see a detailed list of file/folder names in alphabetical order, choose the detailed view (<u>V</u>iew ➪ <u>D</u>etails). Then click the Name column heading.

✦ To bring the newest, oldest, largest, or smallest files into view at the top of the list, first go to the detailed view (<u>V</u>iew ➪ <u>D</u>etails). Then click the Size or Type column heading until the sizes or dates are arranged in either ascending or descending order — whichever you prefer. Then scroll up to the top of the list.

Cool tricks in Find

When the Find dialog box displays filenames, there are quite a few cool things you can do with those files and folders. I offer the quick overview below for you more experienced Windows users. If you're uncomfortable with the following discussion of "opening," "moving," and "copying," don't worry. All these topics are discussed in-depth in Chapters 3, 4, and 5.

Anyway, these are the cool tricks:

✦ To see the entire folder that houses a particular file, click the filename, then choose <u>F</u>ile ➪ Open Contai<u>n</u>ing Folder from Find's menu bar.

✦ To open a folder or file, double-click the filename. To open a document file with a particular program, right-click the filename, choose Op<u>e</u>n With, then double-click the name of the program with which you want to open the file (more on this topic in Chapter 3).

✦ To rename a file, right-click the filename, choose Rena<u>m</u>e from the shortcut menu that appears, type in the new filename, then click some other filename to save your change.

✦ To delete a file from the disk, click its name and press Delete. Or right-click the filename and choose Delete.

✦ To move or copy a file to another folder, or the desktop, hold down the right mouse button and drag the folder name to its new location. Then release the mouse button and choose <u>M</u>ove Here or <u>C</u>opy Here — whichever is appropriate at the moment.

✦ To create a quick desktop shortcut to a file, hold down the right mouse button and drag the filename out to the desktop. Then release the mouse button and choose Create <u>S</u>hortcut here.

✦ To view or change the properties of a file, right-click the filename and choose P<u>r</u>operties from the shortcut menu.

Hot Stuff
You can use the Properties dialog box to change a file that's been copied from a CD-ROM from Read-Only status to normal read/write status. Just clear the Read-Only checkbox. See Chapter 5 for more information.

Whew — I may be getting ahead of myself here. The purpose of this chapter was to show you how to get around your PC. And I started yappin' about "opening" and "copying" and such at the end. Let's put on the brakes for a moment and review the basic techniques for getting around on your PC. Then in the next chapter, I want to talk about launching programs and opening documents.

Summary

✦ Information in your computer is stored in *files*.

✦ Files are organized into *folders* and *subfolders*.

✦ The thing that stores the folders, subfolders, and files is called a disk drive, or just a *drive* for short.

✦ Windows 95 offers three tools for locating files: My Computer, Windows Explorer, and Find.

✦ My Computer offers a simple one-window-at-a-time method of exploring drives, where you can drill down through folders and subfolders to locate a file.

✦ Windows Explorer offers a two-pane method of exploration where a hierarchical tree of folders appears in the left pane, the names of subfolders and files within the selected folder appear in the right pane (much like the File Manager in Windows 3.x).

✦ Find will search an entire disk (all folders and subfolders) for a file based on whatever information you can provide about the file for which you're looking.

✦   ✦   ✦

Launching Programs and Documents

Opening programs and documents are two of those little tasks you're likely to do dozens of times a day, so Windows 95 offers many different ways to do them. There's no "right way" or "wrong way," of course. Choosing which method you want to use is simply a matter of deciding what's most convenient at the moment.

Understanding Programs and Documents

Before I get into how-to here, let me ensure we're speaking the same language. When I talk about a *document*, I'm generally referring to something you create, and save, by using a program. For example, you may use your word processing program to create a typed document or a spreadsheet program to create a spreadsheet document. Text files, such as the readme.txt or readme.doc file, that come with a program you purchase, also qualify as documents.

When I say "open a document," I mean bring the document to the screen so you can see it. In most cases, this statement implies you actually open whatever program is needed to create, change, and view a certain type of document before the document actually appears onscreen.

By *program*, I generally mean something you buy to run on your computer — for example, a game, a word processing program, or a graphics program. Programs also are called *applications* (or *apps*, for short). Small programs, such as the accessories that come with Windows, sometimes are called *applets*.

By *opening,* or *launching,* a program, I mean bringing the program to the screen (and, hence, into memory) so you can use it. Many terms exist for this process — including running, starting, and launching — but they all mean the same thing.

Opening Documents

In earlier versions of Windows, the typical method of opening a document was first opening the program you used to create the document, and then choosing File ⇨ Open within that program to open a specific document. In some programs, you can click the File menu and then click the name of the document you want to open. You can still use this technique in Windows 95. The only difference is you start the program with the Start button, rather than the Program Manager.

A great new feature of Windows 95 enables you to skip the step of opening the program first. Instead, you double-click the document's icon; the document opens immediately.

You can open documents in several ways, as discussed in the following sections.

Open a document from the Documents menu

If the desktop shows an icon for the document you want to open, just double-click that icon. Nothin' to it.

 I'll talk about how you put document icons on the desktop a little later in this chapter (and in more depth in Chapter 4).

If no icon for the document appears on the desktop, look at the Documents menu. This menu keeps track of the names of documents you've saved recently. This feature works only in Windows 95-aware programs, so the menu may not keep track of *every* document you create and edit, but it's worth a look nonetheless.

To get to the Documents menu, click the Start button and then point to Documents, as shown in Figure 3-1. If you see the name of the document you want to open, click that name. The appropriate program will launch and then automatically load the document on which you want to work. (If you don't see the document you want, move the mouse pointer off the Documents menu to eliminate the menus.)

Browse to a document's icon

If neither the desktop nor the Documents menu shows an icon for the document you want to open, you must do a bit more clicking to get to the icon. Use My Computer, Windows Explorer, or Find to get to the document's icon (refer to Chapter 2). When you see the icon, just double-click it. If the document doesn't open, the document type probably isn't registered. For details on what to do in this case, see the next section.

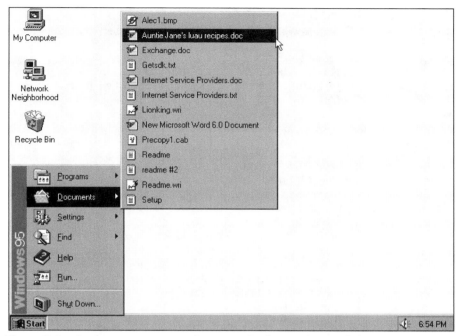

Figure 3-1: The Documents menu keeps track of recently saved documents.

Opening Unregistered Documents

In a perfect world, you could double-click any icon you come across, and the document would open. But in case you haven't noticed, this is not a perfect world. (Insights such as this are what separate the *real* authors from the amateurs.) The question is, what are you gonna do about it? One possible solution is to . . .

Register a file type on the fly

One way to deal with a document that won't open when you double-click it is to register the file type as you're trying to open the document. As an example, suppose I'm browsing around a disk and come across an icon named readme.wp. When I double-click that icon, I get the dialog box shown in Figure 3-2.

What this dialog box is telling me, in a roundabout way, is the document I'm trying to open is actually named README.WP and that no program on my PC is registered to open files automatically with the .WP extension. The dialog box is also showing me a list of programs that *are* on my computer. Now it's up to me to guess which of those programs is most capable of opening a .WP file.

What are ya — document-centric?

If you're an experienced computer user, you may think Microsoft has gone overboard by offering umpteen ways to open programs and documents. What you're really seeing is a shift from the program-centric operating systems of yesterday to the document-centric operating systems of tomorrow.

Let me explain. In the real world, when you hand a person a document printed on paper, she can start reading it. She doesn't need to know any special magic words to make the document readable. But this isn't true when you hand someone a document on a floppy disk. To the contrary, *this* person needs to know quite a bit to see the document: what program was used to create that document, how to start that program on his own computer, how to open files with that program, and, generally, how to operate that program. This is a lot to know.

The document-centric approach reduces some of this burden by making the operating system aware of what program is needed to open a document. The person who wants to read the electronic document just needs to know enough to get the document's icon on the screen and to double-click that icon. He or she needn't know what type or brand of program is required.

In the future, *documentcentricity* (I made up this word) will be the norm, rather than the exception. PC users may not even be aware things called programs and operating systems exist; instead, they'll see the PC as simply a machine for creating and reading documents stored on disks.

Figure 3-2: The .WP extension isn't registered to any program on my PC.

In this example, I guess .wp stands for WordPerfect. First, I could type a plain English description, such as **WordPerfect Documents**, in the Description of '.WP' files box. Then I could scroll through programs in the Choose the program you want to use list box. When I get to the WordPerfect program (WPWIN in the list), I can click that icon and then click OK. The document will open in WordPerfect for Windows.

Hot Stuff A simple way to open an unregistered document type is to open the program you normally would use to edit this type of file, and then choose File ⇨ Open in that program. This method, however, does not register this file type with that program.

Looking back at Figure 3-2, you may notice an option titled Always use this program to open this file. Because this option was selected as I proceeded through the dialog box, the .WP extension now is registered to the WordPerfect program. This means from here on, any time I double-click the icon for a file with the .WP extension, Windows 95 will automatically launch WordPerfect and open this document. I have created a registration on the fly.

By the way, I could have registered the .WP extension to any program capable of opening a WordPerfect document. If I had Microsoft Word on this PC instead of WordPerfect, I could have assigned the .WP extension to WINWORD rather than WPWIN.

Getting past a bad registration

The whole business of registering (also called *associating*) file types to programs is pretty automatic in Windows 95. But in this less-than-perfect world, you occasionally may have a hiccup. Consider an example in which double-clicking a document *almost* opens the document, and then something goes wrong. Suppose someone gives me a floppy disk and says, "Take a look at this." I put the floppy in drive A of my computer, open My Computer, double-click the icon for the A drive, and see a file named ClayAlan on the floppy. I double-click this icon. After a few seconds, my screen looks like Figure 3-3.

Although I can't see the document, the dialog box does give me three pieces of useful information:

✦ The file I'm trying to open has the extension .PCX (as in A:\ClayAlan.pcx).

✦ Apparently, .PCX files are registered to the Microsoft Paint program, because that's the program Windows 95 launched after I double-clicked the icon.

✦ For some reason, though, Paint can't read this particular .PCX file.

Figure 3-3: Can't seem to open this document on drive A

Before giving up hope, I think, "Hmmm. I wonder whether I have some other program that can open a .PCX file." It just so happens I *do* have a program, named HiJaak PRO, that's especially good at opening all kinds of graphics files. I'll try using this program to open the mysterious .PCX file.

For the moment, I have to forget all about documentcentricity and go back to the old way of doing things. In this example, I would fire up HiJaak PRO, choose File ➪ Open, specify a:\ClayAlan.pcx, and hope. Lo and behold, it works! I can see the contents of the file, as shown in Figure 3-4.

Trying to determine why Paint couldn't open this .PCX file probably would be more trouble than it's worth. A simpler solution is to change the Registry so files with the .PCX extension are associated with HiJaak, rather than with Paint.

Later in this chapter, I'll explain how to set — or change — manually, the program to which a particular file extension is registered.

Figure 3-4: HiJaak PRO opened the .pcx file.

Creating New Documents

In the past, the typical method of creating a new document was to start the program you needed to create that document, and then either start typing or choose File ➪ New to start a new piece of work. You can still use this method in Windows 95. But you also can use an alternative technique that enables you to create and name the document, give it a desktop icon, and launch the appropriate program, all in one fell swoop. Follow these steps:

1. Right-click the desktop and then click New.

   A menu of document types that you can create this way appears, as shown in Figure 3-5.

2. If you see an option for the type of document you want to create, click that option.

   If you don't see such an option, you can go back to the Start-button method to start the program and create the document.

3. An icon for the document appears on the desktop, along with a suggested name (for example, `New Microsoft Word Document.doc`).

4. If you want to change the name of this new document, type the new name.

If you want to change the icon name later, use the renaming method discussed in Chapter 5.

5. To launch the program needed to edit the new document, double-click the new desktop icon.

The program appears with a new, blank editing window, and the document is already saved under the name you specified in Step 4.

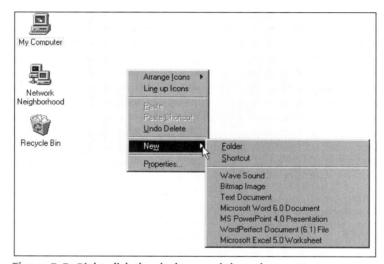

Figure 3-5: Right-click the desktop and then choose New.

You can just start using the program normally to create the document. When you finish, close the program (click its X button or choose File ➪ Exit). When you are asked about saving your changes, choose Yes. The icon for the new document stays on the desktop, as shown in Figure 3-6.

To resume work on this document, double-click its desktop icon. Optionally, you can right-click that icon to display a menu of options available for this document.

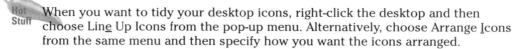

When you want to tidy your desktop icons, right-click the desktop and then choose Line Up Icons from the pop-up menu. Alternatively, choose Arrange Icons from the same menu and then specify how you want the icons arranged.

Initially, the new document is stored in a folder named C:\Windows\Desktop and appears only on the desktop. When you no longer need immediate access to the icon and you want to clear it off the desktop, you can move it into a regular folder. Follow these steps:

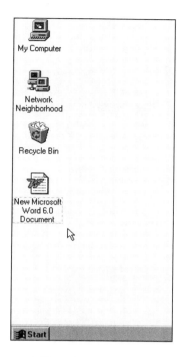

Figure 3-6: Desktop icon for a new document created by right-clicking the desktop

1. Use My Computer or Windows Explorer to open the folder in which you want to place the icon.

2. Position the folder window so you can see both the icon you want to move and the folder contents.

3. Right-drag the icon into the folder.

   By *right-drag*, I mean hold down the secondary mouse button (usually the button on the right side of the mouse) while moving the mouse.

More Info This right-dragging is a hint of things to come. Chapter 5 explains the many ways of moving and copying files.

4. Release the mouse button and then choose Move Here from the pop-up menu that appears.

Figure 3-7 shows an example in which I used My Computer to open the Winword folder. After sizing and positioning the open windows so I could see the desktop icons, I right-dragged the icon titled New Microsoft Word 6.0 Document from the desktop into that Winword folder. The figure shows the screen, just after I released the right mouse button, but before I chose Move Here to complete the move.

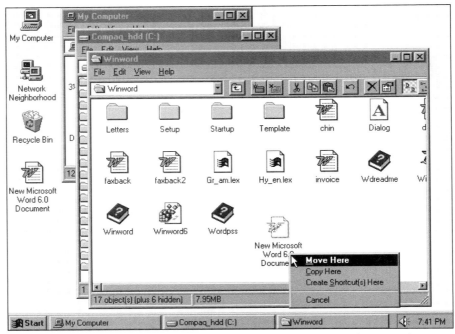

Figure 3-7: Moving an icon from the desktop into a folder named Winword

Launching Programs

Not all programs involve documents. Games and multimedia titles are two examples of programs that usually don't enable you to create and edit documents. Also, you sometimes may want to fire up a program without having any particular document in mind. In those situations, you can use any of the techniques discussed in the following sections to launch the program of your choosing.

Launching from the desktop

If you have already opened the program today, look at the taskbar to see whether the program is still open. If you see the program's icon, click that taskbar button to bring the program back to the forefront.

More Info In Chapter 4, you learn how to create your own shortcuts to frequently used programs.

Some programs have a *shortcut icon* on the desktop, even when the program isn't open. If you see such an icon, double-click it to start that program.

Launching from the Start menu

Chapter 1 showed you how to launch a program from the Start menu. For a quick review, here are the steps:

1. Click the Start button.

   If you see an icon for the program you want to start, click this icon instead, and skip the remaining steps.

More Info

Chapter 4 discusses techniques for creating and using shortcuts, including how to get a program's icon in the Start menu and how to create desktop shortcut icons for launching frequently used programs.

2. Point to (or click) Programs.

3. If you see the program's icon, click it.

   Alternatively, point to the program's group icon until you find the icon for the program you want to start, and then click the program's icon.

Figure 3-8 shows an example in which I'm about to launch the Hearts game. To get to this icon, I had to click the Start button and then choose Programs ⇨ Accessories ⇨ Games.

After you're in a program, you can use it normally. If the program enables you to create documents, you generally can use commands in the File menu to create, open, and save documents. Although some variation exists among programs, the usual commands are as follows:

✦ File ⇨ New: creates a new document within this program.

✦ File ⇨ Open: opens a document previously created and saved with this program.

✦ File ⇨ Close: closes (and, optionally, saves) the current document without leaving this program.

✦ File ⇨ Save: saves all recent changes to this document and leaves the document on the screen.

✦ File ⇨ Save As: saves the current document under a new name and possibly as a different type. This command often is used for exporting a document from one program (for example, Microsoft Word) to another (for example, WordPerfect).

✦ File ⇨ Print: prints the document currently onscreen in this program.

✦ File ⇨ Exit: closes (and, optionally, saves) the current document and closes the current program.

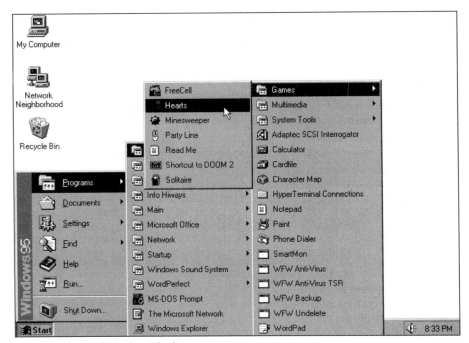

Figure 3-8: Ready to launch the Hearts program

Launching a program without the Start menu

If, when you go through the Start menu, you can't find an icon for the program you want to start, you can use any of the following techniques to start the program:

✦ Use My Computer, Windows Explorer, or Find to locate the program's icon; then double-click that icon.

✦ Click the Start button and choose <u>R</u>un; then type the command needed to start the program. You can include the DOS path. For example, type **c:\wp51\wp** to launch WordPerfect 5.1 for DOS, assuming the program is in the WP51 folder (directory).

✦ If you specifically want to run a SETUP.EXE or INSTALL.EXE program from a floppy disk or CD-ROM, try using the Add/Remove Programs wizard, as discussed under "Starting Programs on CD-ROM" later in this chapter, and in Chapter 9.

My instructions say to choose Run from the File menu

When you're running or installing a program designed for Windows 3.x, your instructions may tell you to go to Program Manager, choose Run from Program Manager's File menu, type something, and press Enter.

Windows 95 has no Program Manager per se. But all you must do to complete your instructions is click the Start button, choose Run from the Start menu, and then follow the written instructions for your Windows 3.x program.

Auto-Start Favorite Programs

You can have Windows 95 automatically start any program as soon as it finishes starting itself. If you have Microsoft Office, for example, you may want Windows to start the Office Manager program automatically so the Office toolbar appears onscreen.

To auto-start a program, follow these steps:

1. Click the Start button and then click Settings.
2. Click the Taskbar option in the menu.
3. Click the Start Menu Programs tab.

    You see the dialog box shown in Figure 3-9.

Figure 3-9: The Start Menu Programs tab of the Taskbar Properties dialog box

4. Click the <u>A</u>dd button and then click the B<u>r</u>owse button.

5. Browse (double-click your way to) the folder that contains the program you want to auto-start, and then double-click the startup icon for this program, as if you were going to start the program now.

   The path and program name for the program you want to auto-start appear in the <u>C</u>ommand line text box of the Create Shortcut wizard.

6. Click Next and then click the folder titled Startup (see Figure 3-10).

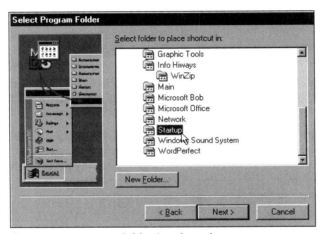

Figure 3-10: Startup folder is selected

7. Click Next, click Finish, and then click OK.

The program won't start right now; all you've done is put its icon in the Startup folder. To verify, click the Start button, point to <u>P</u>rograms, and then point to Startup. You should see the icon for your program in the submenu that appears.

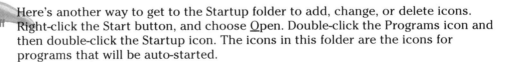 Here's another way to get to the Startup folder to add, change, or delete icons. Right-click the Start button, and choose <u>O</u>pen. Double-click the Programs icon and then double-click the Startup icon. The icons in this folder are the icons for programs that will be auto-started.

From now on, any program(s) listed in your Startup folder will run automatically as soon as Windows 95 starts.

Starting Programs on CD-ROM

CD-ROMs can be tricky, because different kinds are available. Some CD-ROMs can auto-start, whereas others require you to go through a setup procedure. Then again, some CD-ROMs are just collections of files, so you use them as though they were king-size, read-only floppy disks.

The easiest way to install and/or use a CD-ROM is simply to follow the instructions in the little manual that came with it. But if this isn't possible at the moment (or if you hate to read instructions), you can experiment with the methods discussed in the following sections.

Launching an auto-start CD-ROM

Many Windows 95-aware CD-ROMs include a hidden auto-launch feature. These CD-ROMs offer the ultimate in ease-of-use. To use one, follow these steps:

1. Stick the CD-ROM into the CD-ROM drive, per the drive manufacturer's instructions.

2. Sit back and watch the screen, and then follow any instructions that appear.

That's it. *Anyone* can do it — maybe even your boss.

Installing a CD-ROM

Many CD-ROMs include programs that must be copied to your hard disk before you can actually use the CD-ROM. In some cases, the CD-ROM is just a medium for getting the program to you. After you installed the programs, you don't really need the CD-ROM anymore, except as a backup. Either way, you usually can follow this procedure to install programs from a CD-ROM to your hard disk:

1. Put the CD-ROM in the CD-ROM drive, per the drive manufacturer's instructions.

   Remove any floppy disks from your floppy drives.

2. Click the Start button, click Settings, and then click Control Panel.

3. Double-click the Add/Remove Programs icon in Control Panel.

4. Click the Install button, and then follow the directions on screen.

Most likely, the installation procedure will create a program icon (and perhaps even its own program group). For example, I followed the preceding steps to install Microsoft Bob — which, in case you haven't heard, is a talking cartoon interface. Bob is sort of a Windows shell designed to make the PC easier and less intimidating for beginners, kids, the technically challenged, and business executives.

While I was installing Bob, the screen asked where I wanted to put its programs. I chose the default directory (folder), Microsoft Bob. I also opted *not* to auto-start Bob, because I personally don't need a talking dog to help me use a PC (humpf, humpf).

Anyway, when the installation was complete, I had a new program group and icon for starting Bob. In other words, to start Bob from now on, I just need to go through the standard ritual: click the Start button, click Programs, click the Microsoft Bob group icon, and then double-click the Bob icon (see Figure 3-11).

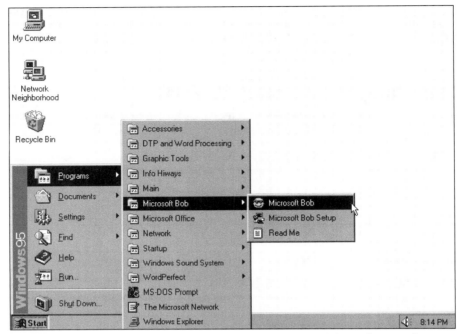

Figure 3-11: After installing a CD-ROM program, I can run it from the Start button.

The Bob example is one in which the CD-ROM is just a transport medium — that is, I don't need to put the disc in the CD-ROM drive to use Bob in the future. But that's not the case with most games and multimedia titles. For those programs, you need to put the CD-ROM in the drive and then launch the program from the Start menu. If you forget to load the disc first, a friendly message appears onscreen, telling you to put in the correct CD-ROM.

CD-ROMs that have no setup program

I suspect just about every consumer-oriented CD-ROM title will have some kind of auto-start or setup program you can run by using Add/Remove Programs. Some CD-ROMs, however, are simply collections of files with no single setup program. Clip art collections, fonts, demo programs, and shareware programs are often distributed in this manner.

If no single setup program is provided, you can browse the CD-ROM as though it were a hard disk. Put the CD-ROM in the CD-ROM drive, start My Computer or Windows Explorer, and then double-click the icon for the CD-ROM drive (typically, D) to see the folders and icons on that drive. Figure 3-12 shows an example in which I'm using My Computer to browse a CD-ROM that contains screens and wallpapers.

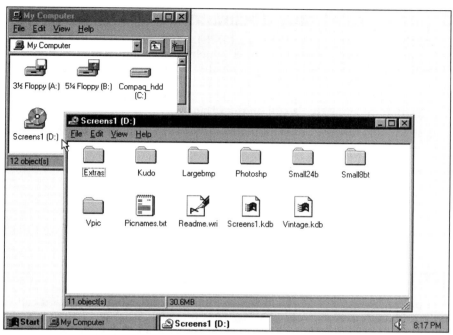

Figure 3-12: Using My Computer to browse the CD-ROM in drive D

You can open folders, view documents, and launch programs on the CD-ROM by using the standard technique: just double-click the icon you want to open. You also can copy stuff from the CD-ROM to your hard disk by using the various methods described in Chapter 5.

The *ROM* in *CD-ROM*

Don't forget, the *ROM* in *CD-ROM* stands for read-only memory. This means you can only read stuff from the disc; you cannot copy files *to* the disc or delete files *from* the disc. Neither can you change a file on a CD-ROM. You can, though, open a document on a CD-ROM, change the document, and then save the changed version to your hard disk. Exactly how you do this depends on the program you use to change the file. But in most cases, you just need to choose File ⇨ Save As and then specify a folder on your hard disk, rather than on the CD-ROM.

Changing read-only documents

Strangely, after you copy a file from a CD-ROM onto your hard disk, the file sometimes retains its read-only status, which makes it impossible to change the file with any of your programs. To eliminate this read-only status:

1. Use My Computer, Explorer, or Find to get to the file's icon on your hard disk (*not* to the copy that's still on the CD-ROM).

2. Right-click the file's icon and choose Properties from the shortcut menu that appears.

3. In the Properties dialog box that appears, click the General tab, then clear the Read-only check box.

4. Choose OK to close the dialog box.

Now you should be able to open and change the copy of the file on your hard disk.

Starting and Using DOS Programs

DOS programs may not show up anywhere in your Start menu, but you can start a DOS program in a couple of ways. Use My Computer, Windows Explorer, or Find to locate the icon for the DOS program; then double-click that icon, as usual, to launch the program.

Optionally, if you want to use the tried-and-true command-line method to start the program, follow these steps:

1. Click the Start button, click Programs, and then click MS-DOS Prompt.

2. At the C> prompt, enter the appropriate DOS command to start that program.

If you're trying to start WordPerfect 5.1 for DOS, for example, you would type **cd\wp51** to get to the appropriate directory (folder) and then press Enter. Then, to start the program, type **wp** and press Enter.

Using a DOS program

When you have your DOS program running, use it exactly as you use it in DOS. You should remember a few things, though. The toolbar that appears across the top of the DOS window (see Figure 3-13) belongs to Windows 95, not to DOS. If you don't see this toolbar, it may be turned off. Click the system icon in the upper-left corner of the DOS window; then choose Toolbar (if available) to display the toolbar. Buttons in that toolbar enable you to mark and copy text inside the DOS window. You then can paste this text into any DOS or Windows 95 window.

To switch between full-screen "windowless" DOS and windowed DOS, press Alt+Enter. Optionally, when you're in the windowed view, you can click the Full-Screen button in the toolbar to expand the DOS window to full screen.

Program won't run in a DOS window

Some DOS programs will refuse to run in a window. They'll insist you run from "plain DOS." This is a bit tricky in Windows 95, because no "plain DOS" mode exists to which you can exit. A mode that does a great job of mimicking plain DOS does exist, though. And even programs that refuse to run in a window will run there.

To get to this "plain DOS" mode you need to click the Start button, choose Sh_u_t Down, and then click the Restart the computer in MS-DOS mode? option. Click the _Y_es button, and you'll be taken to a C > prompt. From

there you can run any DOS program by entering its normal startup command. When you've finished with the DOS program and are back to the C > prompt, you can type **exit** and press Enter to return to Windows.

Be aware, you should use the Shut Down method _only_ when your DOS program refuses to run in a window. The Start ⇨ _P_rograms ⇨ MS-DOS Prompt method is preferred when you can use it, because this method offers your DOS programs more conventional, random access memory (RAM).

Figure 3-13: The Windows 95 toolbar near the top of a DOS window

Be aware, some graphics-intensive DOS applications can run only in full-screen mode. If the program you're trying to run falls into this category, you'll see a message indicating the DOS program will be suspended when you leave full-screen mode.

When you're in a DOS screen, you can do the following:

✦ Press Alt+Esc to return to Windows 95.

✦ Press Ctrl+Esc to get back to Windows 95 with the Start menu open.

✦ Press Alt+Tab to switch to another program.

Each of these techniques leaves a button for the DOS window in the taskbar. To return to your DOS program, click that taskbar button.

The toolbar also provides options for changing the font used in the DOS window. This procedure is not at all similar to the procedure for changing document fonts in Windows. In the DOS window, a font change affects the entire screen, rather than just the selected text, and it has no effect on anything you print from that window. A DOS-window font change is simply a way to size the screen text in a way that is comfortable for your eyes.

You can use the techniques described in Chapter 8 to add icons for starting DOS programs to your own Start menu. In fact, if you refer to Figure 3-8, which shows some Start menus, you'll see a Shortcut to Doom 2 icon in my Games menu. As you may know, *Doom* is a DOS program, so this is living proof you *can* add DOS programs to the Start menus.

Unlike earlier versions of Windows, Windows 95 does not require you to create a PIF (Program Interface File) for each DOS program you use. In fact, you should be able to run any DOS program you throw at Windows 95. If you do have problems or need to tweak the memory performance of a DOS program, you can change the program's properties.

First, get the DOS program running. If you're in full-screen mode, switch to windowed mode (press Alt+Enter). Then click the Properties button in the toolbar, or click the System menu in the upper-left corner of the DOS window and then choose Properties. Use the Memory and Misc tabs in the Properties dialog box to fine-tune your settings.

Closing a DOS window

You can use the standard title bar, the borders, and the Maximize, Minimize, and Restore buttons to size and shape the DOS window. You won't have as much freedom in sizing the window as you do with regular windows, however, and you may not be able to click the Close button on the window's border to close a DOS window. Instead, you may need to exit the DOS program by using whatever exit procedure is appropriate for that program.

Don't forget to save any unsaved work before you exit. Also, remember DOS can read and write only 8.3-character filenames; you cannot enter a longer filename in DOS. Doing a DIR at the command line shows the long filenames. When a DOS program does display a long filename, it shows only the first six characters (with any spaces removed), followed by a tilde and a number. A Windows 95 document named Morph me baby.txt, for example, would appear as morphm~1.txt to a DOS program.

If, after exiting your DOS program and saving your work, you end up at the C> prompt inside the DOS window, you can type exit and press Enter to close the DOS window and return to Windows 95.

Registering Documents with Programs

Enough of the "old DOS" stuff. Let's get back to the new document-centric Windows 95. As I've mentioned, many of your documents will already be registered to some program. For example, double-clicking a file name with the .doc extension automatically opens that document in Microsoft Word — because the .doc extension is registered to (or *associated* with) the Microsoft Word program. It's easy to create, change, and delete associations between documents and programs, as we'll discuss. You'll follow these steps to begin:

You can only associate a filename extension with one program. If you need to send a particular file type to different programs at different times, consider adding the programs to your Send To menu, as discussed in Chapter 4.

1. Double-click the My Computer icon.

2. Choose <u>V</u>iew ⇨ <u>O</u>ptions from My Computer's menu bar.

3. Click the File Types tab. You'll be taken to a list of registered file types.

4. To see how a specific file type is registered, click the appropriate document icon.

For example, in Figure 3-14, I clicked Microsoft Word Document. In the lower portion of the dialog box you can see the filename extension for Microsoft Word documents is DOC, and the program this file type opens with is WINWORD.

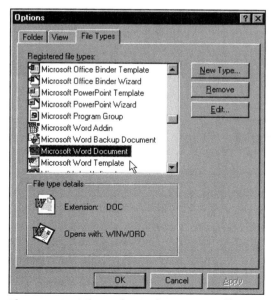

Figure 3-14: Microsoft Word Document file type's extension and associated program

In the following sections, I'll discuss how you can create new associations, edit existing associations, and delete associations. In each section, I assume you're starting from the dialog box shown in Figure 3-14.

Creating a new association

You can use the New Type button to create a new association. For example, let's say I want to assign the extension .LET to letters I write. But when I double-click a file with the .LET extension, I want that document to open in Microsoft Word. My job here, then, is to associate .LET with Microsoft Word, following these steps:

1. Click the New Type button.

2. In the Add New File Type dialog box that appears, type in a brief description for this type of document. And then type in the three-letter extension (without the leading period.)

For example, in Figure 3-15, I'm preparing to make an association to files with the LET.

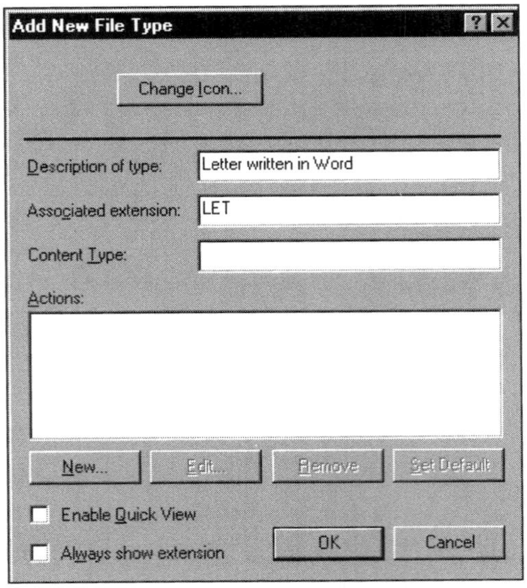

Figure 3-15: About to associate .LET extension with a program

3. Now before you invest any more time, I suggest you save what you have, just to see if the extension you type in is already registered. Click the OK button. If you see a warning message like the one in Figure 3-16, skip to Step 10.

4. Assuming you didn't get an error message, your new description will be in the list of registered types, with the highlighter on its name. Just click the Edit button.

Figure 3-16: Whoops, .LET is already registered.

5. Click the Change Icon button and choose an icon for this document type from the list that appears in the dialog box. If you have your own collection of icons, you can use the Browse button to choose an icon. You can also use the Browse button to go to the program's folder and look for icons in that folder. For example, I got the icon shown in Figure 3-17 from the c:\office95\winword\winword.exe file.

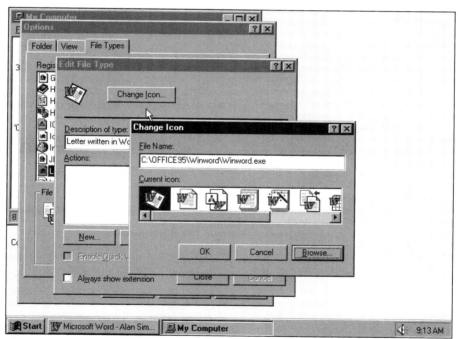

Figure 3-17: Icon I got from c:\office95\winword\winword.exe

6. Next, click the New button under Actions.

7. Type in the word **open** as the Action.

8. Then use the Browse button to select the program with which this extension will be associated.

For example, in Figure 3-18, I typed in **open** as the action, and chose c:\office95\ winword\winword.exe as the application used to perform the action.

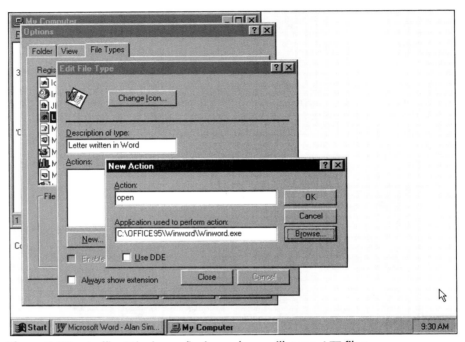

Figure 3-18: c:\office95\winword\winword.exe will open .LET files.

9. Choose OK and Close to work your way back to the desktop, and ignore Step 10.

10. If you got to this step, you're trying to create an association for an extension that already exists. Choose OK, and then choose Cancel. Now you'll need to delete or edit the existing association as discussed in the following sections.

From here on, when you save a Microsoft Word document, you can add the extension .LET to whatever file name you provide. Later, when you're browsing the folders and come across a .LET file, you can just double-click its icon to open that document in Microsoft Word.

Here's a shortcut to going through My Computer to associate a document type with a program. When you double-click a document file not associated with a program, you're automatically taken to the Open With dialog box. From there, you can type in a description of the file type, and select (check) the Always use this program to open this file option. Then, click the icon for the program you want to open the document, and click the OK button. Whichever program you chose will automatically be used to open that type of document in the future.

Changing an association

To change an existing association:

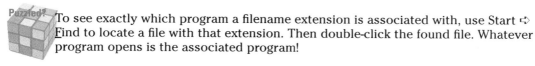

To see exactly which program a filename extension is associated with, use Start ⇨ Find to locate a file with that extension. Then double-click the found file. Whatever program opens is the associated program!

1. If you're not already in the list of registered file types, open My Computer, choose <u>V</u>iew ⇨ <u>O</u>ptions, and select the File Types tab.

2. Click the file type you want to change. (The program and extension for the currently highlighted file type appears under *File type details* at the bottom of the dialog box.)

3. When you get the highlighter to the file type you want to change, click the <u>E</u>dit button.

4. You can type in a new description for this file type in the <u>D</u>escription of type textbox.

5. To change an action, click the action you want to change, then click the <u>E</u>dit button. Use the Browse button to locate the program you want to initiate the current action.

   For example, in Figure 3-19, I changed what was originally called the Paintbrush file type (the program associated with the .PCX extension) to `c:\collwin\imgmgr.exe`, which is the Image Manager program I use for screen shots.

6. Choose OK and Close as necessary to work your way back to the desktop.

If you want to open a particular type of document with one of several possible programs, see "Customizing the Send To Menu" in Chapter 4.

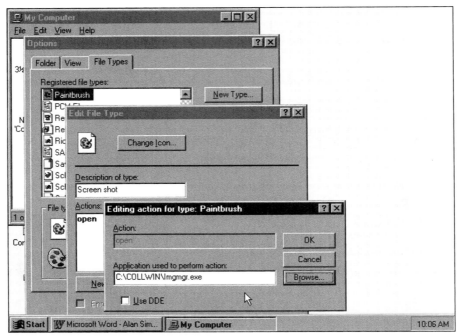

Figure 3-19: Changed the old Paintbrush file type to screen shot

Deleting an association

In some cases, you might want to delete an association between a filename extension and a program. For example, rather than editing an existing association, you may want to delete the existing association, and then build a new one from scratch. To delete an association:

1. If you're not already in the list of registered file types, open My Computer, choose View ➪ Options, and select the File Types tab.

2. Click the file type you want to delete. Remember, the program and extension for the currently highlighted file type appears under *File type details* at the bottom of the dialog box.

3. When you get the highlighter to the file type you want to change, click the Remove button.

4. You'll be prompted with a warning. Click Yes to proceed.

You can repeat Steps 2-4 to delete as many associations as you wish. When you've finished, click the OK button to return to My Computer.

Summary

✦ A program is typically something you purchase to run on your PC.

✦ A document usually is something you create yourself, using a program.

✦ The easiest way to start a program is to click the Start button, point to Programs, and then locate and click the icon for the program you want to start.

✦ If you're starting a program to resume work on a document you saved earlier, click the Start button, click Documents, then click the name of the document on which you want to work.

✦ If the Start menus don't offer an icon for the program you want to start, you can browse to the program using My Computer, Windows Explorer, or Find. Then double-click the icon for the program you want to start.

✦ You can use the DOS-like C> prompt to start DOS programs. Click the Start button, point to Programs, then click MS-DOS Prompt to get to the C> prompt.

✦   ✦   ✦

Shortcuts and Other Cool Tricks

Without a doubt, shortcuts are one of the best new features of Windows 95; they're easy to create and easy to eliminate. So you can make lots of shortcuts on the fly for whatever you're working on currently. Then, when new projects take precedence, you can dump the old shortcuts and create new ones.

As you'll see in this chapter, *drag-and-drop* is the easiest way to create a shortcut. And drag-and-drop, in turn, is useful for other handy features, such as *scraps*. When you carry these relatively simple techniques into other areas — networking, e-mail, editing, and so on — things get *really* interesting. You may want to put on your thinking cap and fasten your seat belt for this chapter; you're in for a wild ride.

How to Create a Shortcut

A shortcut offers quick double-click access to any folder, program, or document on your PC. Creating a shortcut is simple. All you have to do is follow these steps:

1. Use My Computer, Windows Explorer, or Find to get to the icon for the folder, program, or document to which you want to create a shortcut.

2. Hold down the right mouse button and drag the icon to the desktop (or to another folder or the Start button, as discussed later in this chapter).

3. Release the right mouse button, and choose Create Shortcut(s) Here from the menu that appears.

All you really need to know about shortcuts is you can get help creating them at any time by looking up *shortcut* in the online manual. Click the Start button, and then click Help. Click the Index tab, and type **shortcut**. You'll find many ways to create and manage shortcuts.

For the rest of this chapter, I'll mainly present examples of useful shortcuts, with specific instructions wherever possible. But if all you remember from this chapter is what I just told you, you're already on your way to being a true master of the Windows 95 shortcut.

Creating Desktop Shortcuts

You can put shortcuts to folders, programs, documents — and even to other computers right on your desktop. My favorite technique is putting a shortcut to a folder on the desktop, so I'll present an example of this first.

Desktop shortcut to a folder

My example creates a shortcut to the folder containing files I created while writing this book. Obviously, you don't have this folder on your PC, but you probably do have one or more folders of documents you need to access frequently. Anyway, here's how I create the shortcut to my Windows 95 Bible folder:

1. Using My Computer, Windows Explorer, or Find, I get to the icon for the folder to which I want to create a shortcut: Windows 95 Bible, as shown in Figure 4-1.

2. Next, I hold down the right mouse button and drag that icon to the place on the desktop where I want the icon to appear.

3. I release the right mouse button; a menu appears.

4. I choose Create Shortcut(s) Here.

   A copy of the icon, with a little shortcut arrow, appears on the desktop.

5. To tidy up, I close the My Computer windows.

   Or, I can right-click the desktop and choose Arrange Icons and by Name to put my desktop icons in alphabetical order.

What's really cool is, to get to any file in my Windows 95 Bible folder, I double-click that desktop icon. The files in this folder appear in a window, as shown in Figure 4-2.

Cooler still is, I can view or change any document in this folder just by double-clicking its icon (because Windows 95 is document-centric, remember?). I needn't go through the Start menu or launch any programs; a few double-clicks is all it takes.

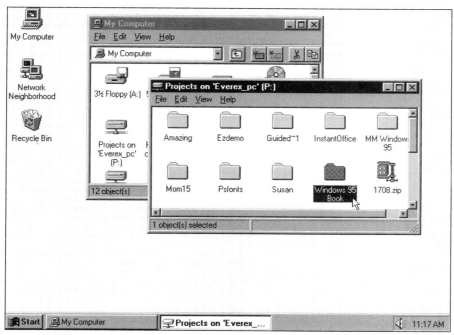

Figure 4-1: The Windows 95 Bible icon is visible in a My Computer window.

More Info   Chapter 5 discusses moving and copying files in detail.

Why the awful filenames?

You may look at Figure 4-2 and wonder why I came up with such weird, seemingly meaningless filenames, especially when Windows 95 enables me to use long filenames with spaces. Let me explain.

First, I sent the files to the publisher of this book as I completed my work. Because the publisher uses many 16-bit applications that don't support long filenames, I've stuck with the eight-character names. This is for the publisher's convenience.

As strange as the names look, they are meaningful. The w95b that starts every filename is a code for *Windows 95 Bible* — the title of this book. That latter part — 01as, 02as, and so on — identifies that chapter number and this is the copy I (Alan Simpson) submitted. The files with 0101, 0102, and so on, in the filename are figures. For example, w95b0101 is the file that contains Figure 1-1.

Finally, I can move and copy stuff to and from this shortcut as though it were the actual folder. Suppose I need to copy some files from a floppy disk to my Windows 95 Bible folder. I can drag the icon for those files from the My Computer window for drive A right to the shortcut on the desktop; I needn't go navigating down to the actual folder.

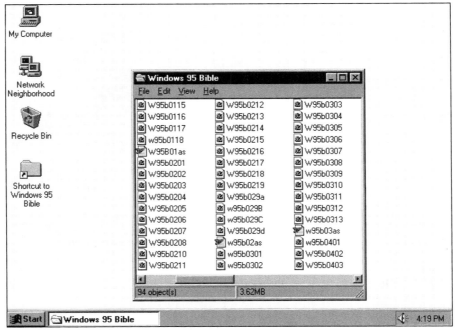

Figure 4-2: The Windows 95 Bible folder open on the desktop after its shortcut icon is double-clicked

If you're into local area networks (LANs), you may be interested in knowing, in this example, the Windows 95 Bible folder isn't even on my PC. Even though the shortcut to the folder is on my PC, the folder itself is on another PC in my LAN. I can go to any other PC in my LAN and create a shortcut to this folder. So no matter at what computer I'm sitting when I open my Windows 95 Bible folder, I'm sure to get to the original documents for this book. I needn't copy and move files from one PC to another via floppy disks.

More Info   Chapters 30 through 32 tell you how to set up and use a LAN. Scary as this procedure may sound, it's actually quite easy because networking capability is built into Windows 95.

Last, but not least, thanks to dial-up networking (Chapter 20), I can get to the files in the Windows 95 Bible folder via telephone lines. As long as I have my laptop and modem with me, I can get to those files from anywhere in the world. *Yowza!*

Program, document, and printer shortcuts

Using the same simple right-drag-and-drop procedure, I can create shortcuts to other items on my PC, as shown in Figure 4-3.

Figure 4-3: These are shortcuts to programs, documents, and a printer added to my desktop.

You create shortcuts in the following ways:

✦ To create a shortcut to a program, browse to the program's startup icon, and then drag that icon to the desktop. To launch the program, double-click its shortcut icon. (See the following "Desktop shortcut to a menu item" for an easy way to do this.)

✦ To create a shortcut to a document, browse to that document's icon. Right-drag the document to the desktop, release the right mouse button, and then choose Create Shortcut(s) Here. To open the document, double-click its shortcut icon.

✦ To create a shortcut to a printer, click the Start button, click Settings, and then click Printers. Right-drag the icon to the desktop, release the right mouse button, and choose Create Shortcut(s) Here. To print a document, drag that document's icon to the printer shortcut.

Not all programs enable you to print documents by dragging their icons to a printer-shortcut icon, but nearly any Windows 95-aware program will. Experiment, and if the procedure doesn't work, check that program's help file or manual to see whether you can implement drag-and-drop printing.

 More Info You also can print a document by right-clicking the document's icon, and then choosing Print from the shortcut menu that appears. Again, though, this procedure applies to Windows 95-aware programs. See Chapter 42 for ways to enable this feature.

Desktop shortcut to a menu item

Let's say you have some program you normally start by clicking the Start button, choosing programs, and then going through some additional menus. Because you use this program often, you'd prefer to open it from the desktop without going through the menus. Can do! First, go through the menu sequence needed to start the program (but don't actually start the program) and pay careful attention to how you got to the program's icon. For example, let's say you clicked the Start button and chose Programs ➪ Accessories to get to the icon for the Calculator applet.

Rather than starting the program, click outside the menus to return to the desktop. Then, to create the shortcut:

1. Right-click the Start button and choose Open.

2. Double-click the icons that match the menu sequence required to get to the program's icon. For example, I would double-click the Programs icon, and then double-click the Accessories icon to match the Programs ➪ Accessories sequence previously mentioned.

3. The final window will display a shortcut icon for the program. (For a good look, choose View ➪ Large Icons from the current window's menu bar.)

4. Now, rest the mouse pointer on the icon to which you want to create a desktop shortcut icon.

5. Hold down the right mouse button and drag the icon out to anyplace on the desktop.

6. Release the mouse button and choose Copy Here.

That's it, you're done! You can now close the open windows. If you want to rename your new shortcut icon, right-click it, choose Rename, and type in its new name. To get all your icons organized, right-click some empty area of the desktop and choose Arrange Icons ➪ by Name from the popup menu that appears.

Any icon you create in this manner will be a shortcut icon (showing the little shortcut arrow in its lower-left corner.) So if you decide you no longer need that shortcut icon on your desktop, you can right-click the icon and choose Delete. Only the shortcut icon — not the actual program or Start menu item — will be deleted.

What does "browse to" mean?

Saying "use My Computer, Windows Explorer, or Find to get to" something is going to get old. And now that you know how to create shortcuts, you have a whole new way to get to documents and other stuff.

So when I say "browse to," I mean *get to the icon so you can see it on your screen.* How

you get to the icon really doesn't matter; a folder shortcut is as acceptable as using My Computer, Windows Explorer, or Find. All that matters is you get to the icon, because you can't drag it until you can see it.

Putting Shortcuts in the Start Menu

You don't need to clutter your desktop with a zillion shortcuts. If you want to have single-click access to a program, folder, or document from the Start menu, drag the icon to the Start button instead of to the desktop. Before shooting Figure 4-4, for example, I did the following:

- ✦ I dragged the icon for a Word document named Fax Cover Sheet (Blank) to the Start button.

- ✦ I dragged the printer icon for my HP LaserJet from the Printers folder to the Start button.

- ✦ I dragged the icon for a folder named Major Events to the Start button.

- ✦ I dragged the icon for starting Microsoft Word to the Start button.

More Info Chapter 8 talks about other ways to customize the Start menu, as well as techniques to change and delete those shortcuts.

To open any of those items, I click the item's icon in the Start menu. The printer icon in the Start menu, however, is a little different from the one on the desktop. No way exists to drag an icon to the printer icon in the Start menu. When I click the printer icon in the Start menu, I'm taken directly to the print-queue window for that printer, so I can check the status of print jobs lined up for that printer.

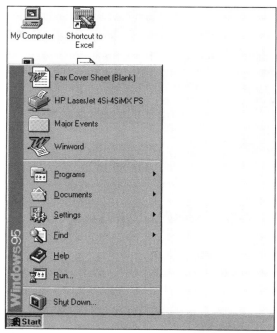

Figure 4-4: Shortcuts to a document, print queue, folder, and program in the Start menu.

Putting Shortcuts in the Programs Menu

You also can put shortcuts in the Programs menu (the menu that appears after you click the Start button and then click Programs). The procedure for doing so is a little different from the procedures I've discussed so far in this chapter, but it's still pretty easy.

Actually, you can put shortcuts and submenus in *any* menu accessible from the Start button, as you'll learn in Chapter 8.

To put shortcuts in the Programs menu, follow these steps:

1. Right-click the Start button, and choose Open from the menu that appears.

2. Double-click the icon for the Programs folder.

   The Programs folder window appears.

3. Choose File ➪ New.

4. Click Shortcut to get to the Create Shortcut wizard. Then use the Browse button to get to the icon for whatever item to which you want to create a shortcut.

5. When you get to this icon, double-click it.

   You return to the Create Shortcut wizard and the path to your icon appears in the Command line box.

6. Click Next>, and then type whatever word or phrase you want to appear in the Programs menu.

   The text can be a brief, plain-English description of your choice.

7. Click the Finish button.

Now you can close any open windows. Click the Start button, and then click Programs. You should see your shortcut in its proper alphabetical position below the icons that lead to folders.

More Info I talk about methods for changing and refining all these menus in Chapter 8.

Figure 4-5 shows an example in which I browsed to the startup icon for Microsoft Access in Step 4. In Step 6, I typed **Access**. Now, to run Access, I only need to click the Start button, click Programs, and then click Access.

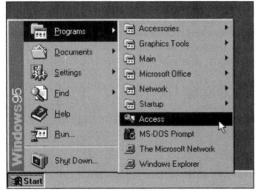

Figure 4-5: An icon for starting Microsoft Access in my Programs menu

Putting Shortcuts in Documents

Windows 95 enables you to put shortcuts in documents, as well. Simply drag the icon for the object to which you want to create a shortcut into your document. This procedure is great for writing notes to other users whose Windows 95 skills are sophisticated enough that they can double-click an icon. You can write such a user a note saying something like "Hey, click here to see [whatever]."

I can't give you exact step-by-step instructions for using this capability, because it may vary from one program to the next. You may need to check the help or manual for whatever program you're using to see whether it enables embedded shortcuts and how to implement them. I can, however, take you through an example using Microsoft Word 6 for NT and Excel 5 for NT, to illustrate how and why you might embed a shortcut in a document.

Suppose my name is Homer and I've been working on a spreadsheet for my boss, Marge. She's a great boss, but she can't work a computer worth beans. I'm sitting at her PC late at night because I'm the type of nerd who can't function when the sun is up.

I've finished the spreadsheet, and I want Marge to look at it when she comes to work in the morning. But I don't want to explain to her how to find the worksheet and open it, partly because Marge isn't interested in such technicalities, and partly because I'm too lazy. So here's what I do:

I save the spreadsheet in the usual manner (File ➪ Save), under the filename Homer's Spreadsheet. Then I exit Excel and fire up Microsoft Word. In Word, I type a document that says, "Good morning, Marge. I think I finally finished that spreadsheet. Double-click the icon to take a look."

Next, I use My Computer to browse to the icon for Homer's Spreadsheet. I right-click that icon, and then choose Create Shortcut(s) Here. Windows 95 immediately creates an icon titled Shortcut to Homer's Spreadsheet in the current folder. I drag that shortcut icon from its folder into my Word document. A few seconds later, a copy of that shortcut icon appears in my Word document.

Next, I save that Word document under the name MARGE Double-click me. Then I exit Word and use My Computer to browse to the icon for the MARGE Double-click me document. Next, I right-drag the icon for this Word document to the desktop to create a desktop shortcut to the Word document. At this point, I also can rename the shortcut icon by right-clicking it and choosing Rename. Finally, I close everything and go home.

When Marge comes into the office in the morning, she sees an icon on the desktop that says MARGE Double-click me (see Figure 4-6). When she double-clicks that icon, she sees my note (also in Figure 4-6).

To see the spreadsheet I created, Marge double-clicks the shortcut icon right there in the Word document. Bingo — up pops the spreadsheet. Cool, no?

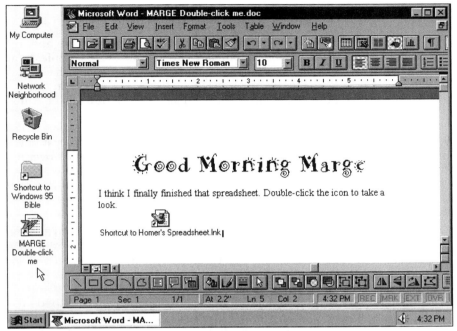

Figure 4-6: This is the note Marge sees in the morning, with its embedded shortcut.

This example is a preview of bigger and better things. Before long, you'll be embedding shortcuts to programs, folders, documents, and even Microsoft Network forums (see Chapter 21) in your documents. Then you'll e-mail those documents to other PC users all over the world so they can double-click your shortcut icon to get to wherever you want to send them. You won't need to wait until the twenty-first century, either. You can do these things right now, in Windows 95.

Shortcuts to Control Panel and Custom Icons

To create a desktop shortcut icon to Control Panel, or your Printers folder, open (double-click) My Computer. Hold down the right mouse button and drag an icon to the desktop. After you release the mouse button, choose Create Shortcut(s) Here.

To change the icon displayed by any shortcut, right-click the shortcut icon and choose Properties. Click the Shortcut tab, and then click the Change Icon button. If a message appears saying the exe file has no icons, don't worry. Click OK.

Under Current icon, use the horizontal scrollbar to find an icon you like. Then click this icon and choose OK (twice) to return to the desktop.

You'll Love These Scraps

I'm not so sure *scraps* belong in a chapter on shortcuts, but they are both real time-savers and too great to put off until later in the book. I must confess I'm walking on thin ice here because, even though Windows 95 supports scraps, it's up to the people who create the programs you'll use to use scraps in those programs. I suspect, though, all programs designed for Windows 95 or Windows NT eventually will support scraps.

 Not all pre-Windows 95 programs will support scraps. If in doubt, try it out. If the mouse pointer changes to an international NO symbol when you're hovering over the desktop, then the program you're using doesn't do scraps.

Scraps versus the Clipboard

If you're an ex-Windows 3.x user and familiar with the Clipboard, you'll especially appreciate scraps as being a great alternative to the Clipboard. If you're unfamiliar with the Clipboard in Windows 3.x, don't worry about it; skip this section and go to "Using scraps" later in this chapter.

To understand why scraps are such a great alternative to the old Clipboard, think about how you used the Windows 3.x Clipboard. Typically, you would select some text or some object and then choose Edit ➪ Copy to copy that item to the Clipboard. Then you would go to wherever you want to paste that object and choose Edit ➪ Paste. This method is not the most intellectually challenging feat in the world and it has two weaknesses, as follows:

✦ You can't see what's in the Clipboard at any given time unless you go to the trouble of opening the Clipboard Viewer.

✦ The Clipboard can (usually) hold only one thing at a time. To cut and paste several items, you need to cut or copy from the source, go to the destination and paste, come back to the source and cut or copy, and so on, cutting and pasting one object at a time.

Scraps make the process much easier because, rather than copying the selected text or object to the Clipboard, you drag it to the desktop (or a folder, or wherever). Whatever you dragged appears as a scrap icon. You can drag as many scraps to the desktop as you want and you can name the scraps. You're no longer working with an invisible Clipboard that can hold only one thing at a time.

Using scraps

To create a scrap, follow these simple steps:

1. Select the text or object you want to move or copy.

2. Drag that text or object to the desktop.

3. Repeat Steps 1 and 2 to create as many scraps as you want.

More Info Exactly how you select the object you want to move or copy depends on the program you're using. Typically, you drag the mouse pointer through text or click an object, such as a picture. If you have trouble, look up *select* in online help or the manual for the program you're using.

When you finish, each scrap appears on the desktop as an icon. You can name each scrap, if you want. Right-click the scrap's icon, choose Rena<u>m</u>e, type the name, and then click somewhere outside the scrap.

Figure 4-7 shows an example of scraps in action. Notice I have an Excel worksheet onscreen (I used Excel for NT in this example). I dragged the chart from the spreadsheet to the desktop and named the resulting scrap Scrap The Chart. Then I selected the range of numbers and dragged that range to the desktop to create a second scrap. I named that scrap Scrap The Numbers.

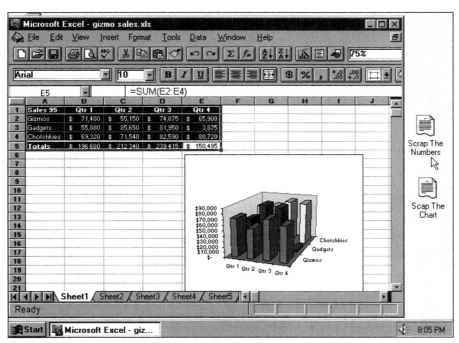

Figure 4-7: A few scraps from the Excel spreadsheet on the desktop

Now suppose I want to put those scraps in a Word document. I would close Excel (or leave it open — it doesn't matter) and launch Microsoft Word. Next, I would create or open the Word document in which I want to display the numbers and chart. Then I would drag each scrap from the desktop into the Word document.

Figure 4-8 shows an example with the two scraps from the desktop pulled into the Word document.

Obviously, the scraps don't look like scraps anymore. As soon as I dragged each scrap into the Word document, the scrap opened automatically, revealing its contents. Thus, the Word document now contains exact copies of the spreadsheet range and chart. Now I can print the Word document or e-mail it to anyone who has Microsoft Word on his or her computer.

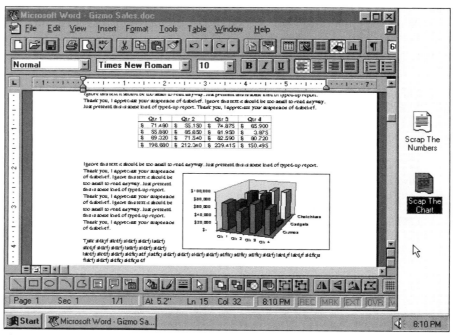

Figure 4-8: The scraps dragged into a Word 6 for NT document

Scraps are OLE-aware

I should point out that scraps are OLE-aware, which means each scrap knows where it came from. If you double-click a scrap on the desktop, the scrap opens in its proper program (assuming the program is on the current PC). You then can see, and even modify, the scrap's contents.

The scrap retains this awareness even after you drag it to some other document. Refer to Figure 4-8, in which you see an Excel spreadsheet range and chart in a Word document. If you were to double-click the spreadsheet portion of this document, you'd activate *in-place editing* — which means you would still be in Word, but Word's menu bar and toolbars would change to Excel's menu bar and toolbar. You'd suddenly have all the capabilities of Excel in your Word document, enabling you to make changes in the little spreadsheet, even though you're still in Word. For those of you who are familiar with OLE from earlier versions of Windows, you might realize now that scraps are actually linked OLE objects.

Hot Stuff If I e-mail the Word document shown in Figure 4-8 to someone who also has Word and Excel on his computer, he or she will have instant in-place editing capability.

If you change the numbers in the spreadsheet during in-place editing, the chart is updated instantly to reflect those changes. Yes, I'm talking about the copy of the chart in Word. To return to the normal Word menu bar and toolbars, simply click any "regular" portion of your Word document (outside the spreadsheet).

Please remember, like scraps, in-place editing is something Windows 95 supports, but it's up to the program you're using to take advantage of this capability. Many Windows 3.x programs already support in-place editing, and I suspect in-place editing will be built into virtually all programs designed for Windows 95 and NT.

Cutting and pasting to another PC

LAN users will love this little trick. If you want to move or copy an object on your PC to another PC on the LAN, drag the object from your program into a shared folder on the LAN. The scrap appears in this folder as an icon.

More Info Part VII of this book discusses LANs in detail.

When other LAN users open that shared folder, they, too, see your scraps. They can drag those scraps right to their own desktops or into whatever documents they are working on currently. In other words, you now have a simple way to cut (or copy) and paste multiple objects from one PC to another on a LAN.

More amazing feats

You can copy objects from one program to another without scraps, if you want, by dragging the object you want to embed to the destination program's taskbar menu.

Suppose I'm typing a Word document and I come to a place where I want to insert a chart from Excel. I can leave the insertion point at that spot and minimize Word's win-

dow, so it becomes a button in the taskbar. Next, I can open Excel and select the chart I want to put into the Word document. I drag this chart to the taskbar button for Word, and I'm done. To see my achievement, I click Word's taskbar button to reopen its window; I see my chart right where the insertion point was. Awesome!

Customizing the SendTo menu

The document-centric approach, which enables you to open a document by double-clicking it, is really cool. But, in some cases, you may want to use several different programs to work with a particular type of document. Here's an example. Let's suppose you create your own page for publishing on the Internet's World Wide Web. As you may know, these documents all have the filename extension .htm or .html. It would be nice if you could right-click the icon for a .htm or .html file and tell Windows to "open this in Internet Explorer, so I can see what it looks like there." Or, "open this in Netscape Navigator, so I can see what it looks like there." Or, "Open this in WordPad, so I can change the file's contents."

Well, you can do that. To make this happen you must customize the SendTo menu. And it's quite easy to do. To get started, follow these steps:

1. Starting at the Windows 95 desktop, double-click your My Computer icon, and then double-click the icon for your C: drive.

2. Double-click the Windows folder icon, then double-click the SendTo icon within the Windows folder. To give yourself some elbow room, leave the SendTo window open, but close the others behind it. You might also want to move the window aside and make it a little bigger, as in Figure 4-9.

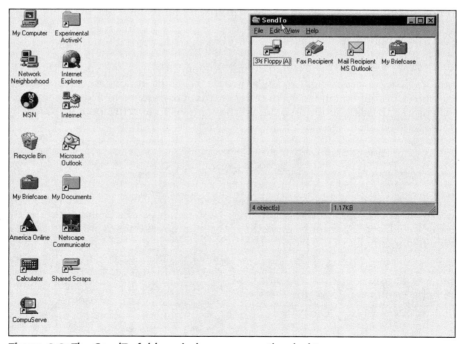

Figure 4-9: The SendTo folder window open on the desktop

Now, decide to which programs you want to send documents and create shortcut icons to those programs within the SendTo window folder. You can use the same technique I discussed under "Desktop shortcut to a menu item" earlier, but right-drag those icons into the SendTo menu folder, rather than to the desktop. If you already have a desktop shortcut to a favorite program, you can copy this shortcut icon into the SendTo menu. Let's look at a few examples.

In Figure 4-9, I already have shortcut icons to Internet Explorer and Netscape Communicator on the desktop. If I want to send documents to those icons, I can right-drag the icon from the desktop into the SendTo folder. (By right-drag I mean hold down the mouse button on the right, rather than the usual left mouse button, while dragging.) When you release the mouse button, choose Copy Here from the menu that appears. In Figure 4-10, I've copied the shortcut icons for Internet Explorer and Netscape Communicator from the desktop into the SendTo folder.

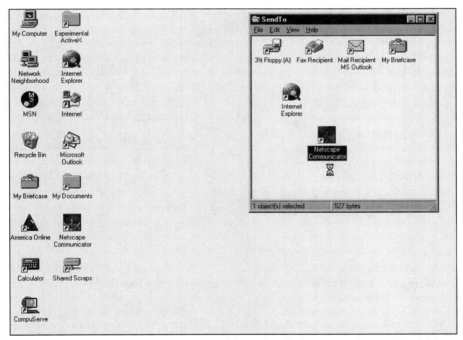

Figure 4-10: A few shortcut icons copied from the desktop into the SendTo folder

For programs that aren't on the desktop, you can copy the shortcut icons from the Start menu to the SendTo folder. For example, suppose I want to send documents to the Windows 95 WordPad program. Normally, to start WordPad, I click the Start button and choose Programs ➪ Accessories ➪ WordPad. Currently, though, I don't want to *start* WordPad. I just want to copy its startup icon from the menus. So I need to right-click the Start button, rather than click it, to get to those startup icons. That is:

1. Right-click the Start button and choose Open.

2. Double-click the icons necessary to get to the program's startup icon. (In this example, I would double-click the Programs and icon, and then double-click the Accessories icon because I normally choose Programs ⇨ Accessories to get to WordPad's startup icon.)

3. When you get to the icon for a program to which you want to send documents, right-drag that icon into the SendTo folder and, after you release the mouse button, choose Copy Here. For example, in Figure 4-11, I copied WordPad's startup icon into the SendTo menu.

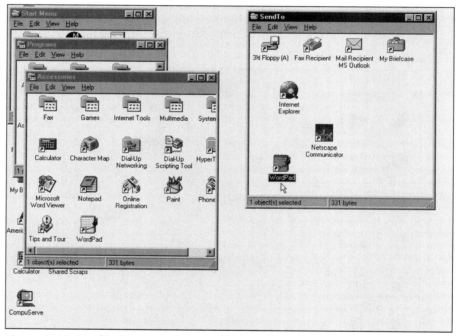

Figure 4-11: WordPad's startup icon copied into the SendTo folder

4. You can repeat the previous steps to add as many programs as you wish to the SendTo menu. (Make certain you only add programs capable of *accepting* documents — programs you use to create and edit documents.)

If you like, you can rename the shortcut icons in the SendTo folder in the usual manner. That is, right-click the icon you want to rename, choose Rename, and type in the new name. Whatever name you assign here will become the SendTo menu's item text.

When you finish, close all the open windows on the desktop. At any time in the future, when you want to open a document with one of those programs you added to the SendTo menu, just get to the document's icon. Then, right-click (rather than double-click) the icon, and choose Send To from the pop-up menu that appears, as in Figure 4-12. Then, choose the program you want to view or edit the document with and you're ready to roll!

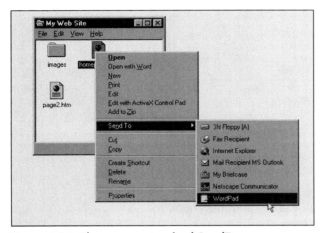

Figure 4-12: The new, customized SendTo menu

Remember, once you place a shortcut icon to a program in the SendTo menu, you can send documents to that program right from your Windows 95 desktop, by right-clicking the document's icon and choosing Send To. I think you'll find, overall, this is much better than the old method of starting the program first, and then choosing File ➪ Open to open a particular document. Personally, I think the SendTo menu is actually the *best* shortcut technique going!

It doesn't matter *how* you get to the document's icon. For example, let's say you use Start ➪ Find to locate a particular document. When you find the document, you can right-click it there in the Find window and send it to any program in your SendTo menu!

Tips and Tricks at Your Fingertips

If you like these time-saving tips and techniques I covered in this chapter, be sure to cruise through the tips and tricks in online help. Click the Start button, click Help, click the Contents tab, and then double-click the Tips and Tricks book to open it (see Figure 4-13.) Browse at your leisure and enjoy.

Figure 4-13: Browse through the Tips and Tricks book when you have some spare time.

Summary

✦ A shortcut offers quick double-click access to any folder, document, or program.

✦ To create a shortcut, right-drag its icon to the desktop, release the mouse button, and choose Create Shortcut(s) Here.

✦ A scrap is any "cutting" from a document, and can be text, a picture, sounds, or whatever.

✦ To create a scrap, drag the selection from your document onto the desktop.

✦ If you want to send a document from the desktop right into a favorite program, add a shortcut icon to that program to your SendTo menu.

✦ Knowing these tips will make your daily work at the PC much simpler!

✦   ✦   ✦

Have It Your Way

General Housekeeping (Copying, Deleting, and So On)

This chapter is all about the daily chores of managing files. That term *managing* includes copying, moving, deleting, and renaming folders and files. You should read Chapter 2 before you embark on this chapter. Be especially sure you understand the concepts of drive, folder, and file. And if you haven't already done so, get some experience with at least one of the three main browsing tools: My Computer, Windows Explorer, and Find. If you have no idea what I'm talking about, I recommend you go back and read Chapter 2.

Important Concepts for Ex-Windows 3.x Users

If you used Windows 3.x before learning Windows 95, you should be aware some important differences exist between Windows 3.x and Windows 95. (If you're not an ex-Windows 3.x user, you can skip this section.)

Icons in the Windows 95 browsing tools My Computer, Explorer, and Find are like the icons in the Windows 3.x File Manager. So when you move or delete an icon with a Windows 95 browsing tool, you're moving or deleting the actual file on the disk — not just a pointer to that file. Shortcut icons, on the other hand, are simply pointers, so you can move and delete those icons without disturbing the contents of the disk.

When you delete files from your local hard disk (that is, drive C), the files are moved to a thing called the Recycle Bin. Although they are invisible from outside the Recycle Bin, those files still occupy as much disk space as they did before you deleted them. The space won't become available until you empty the Recycle Bin, as discussed under "Recovering recycled disk space" later in this chapter.

Also, be aware the Recycle Bin keeps track of only the files you delete from your local hard disk (for example, C). Files you delete from removable media, including floppy disks and network drives, are *not* sent to the Recycle Bin and, therefore, cannot be undeleted.

Moving, Copying, and Deleting in a Nutshell

Drag-and-drop probably is the most intuitive way to copy, move, and delete files. Following is the general procedure in a nutshell:

1. Use My Computer, Windows Explorer, or Find to get to the drive and/or folder that contains the files you want to move, copy, or delete.

2. If you're moving or copying, use My Computer, Explorer, or Find to get to the drive and/or folder to which you plan to move or copy.

3. Size the windows so you can see both the *source* (the files or folders you want to move or copy) and the *destination* (the place to which you want to move or copy).

4. Select the folders or files you want to move, copy, or delete, using the techniques described in "Selecting Objects to Copy, Move, or Delete" in a moment.

5. To delete the folders or files, press the Delete key or drag them to the Recycle Bin; then skip the remaining steps.

6. To move or copy the files, point to any of the selected folders or files, hold down the right mouse button, and drag the selected items to the destination.

7. Release the right mouse button and then choose Copy Here or Move Here, depending on what you want to do.

These steps pretty much sum up the procedure. Figure 5-1 shows an example in which I have selected a few files in a folder named Learn to Sail, which I reached by using My Computer. The destination in this example is the floppy disk in drive A. Both the Learn to Sail folder icon and the icon for floppy drive A are visible onscreen. Now I can right-drag the selected files to the drive A icon.

The rest of this chapter focuses on specific parts of each step in the process and presents warnings to help you avoid mishaps.

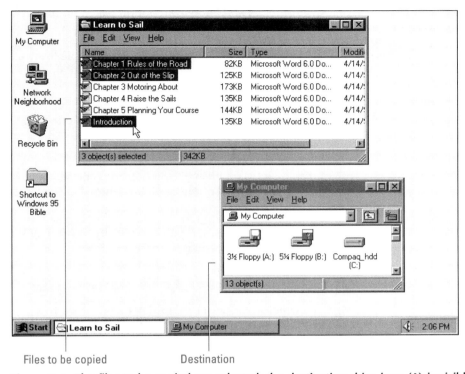

Files to be copied   Destination

Figure 5-1: The files to be copied are selected; the destination-drive icon (A) is visible.

Selecting Objects to Copy, Move, or Delete

When you want to move, copy, or delete more than one file, you can use the techniques described in the following sections to select those files. It doesn't matter which browsing tool you use to get to those icons: These techniques work the same in My Computer, Explorer, and Find.

First, pick your view...

You can decide how you want to view your icons. Your options (discussed in Chapter 2) are Large Icons, Small Icons, List, and Details. You can choose a view from the toolbar or from the View menu.

... then group things, if useful...

If you plan to manage a group of files that have something in common, you can save yourself some work by bunching those items in a list. Simply arrange the icons. Choose View ➪ Arrange Icons and choose an option based on the following examples:

✦ If the items you want to select have similar names (for example, they all start with the word *Chapter*), choose by Name to put the objects in alphabetical order by name.

✦ If the items you want to select are of a similar type (they all have the extension .BAK), choose by Type. Files with the same extension will be grouped in the list.

✦ If the items you want to select are the same size, choose by Size.

✦ If the items you want to select were created or modified on or near a particular date, choose by Date. Files with similar dates will be grouped in the list.

Remember, if you use Details view (choose View ➪ Details), you can see the name, size, type, and date modified for every file, and you can sort by any one of those columns simply by clicking the column heading.

... then select the items to move, copy, or delete

When you see the items you want to move, copy, or delete, you need to select the specific items. You can select items in the following ways:

✦ To select one item, click it. Any previously selected items are unselected instantly.

✦ To add another item to a selection, Ctrl+click it (hold down the Ctrl key while you click).

✦ To extend the selection to another item, Shift+click where you want to extend the selection.

Hot Stuff — To see how much space you'll need for all the selected files, look at the status bar at the bottom of the file list.

✦ To create another extended selection without disturbing existing selections, Ctrl+click the first item in the range and then Ctrl+Shift+click the last item in the range.

✦ To select all the items in the window, choose Edit ➪ Select All or press Ctrl+A.

✦ To deselect a selected item without disturbing the current selections, Ctrl+click the item you want to deselect.

✦ To invert the current selection (deselect all the selected files and select all the deselected ones), choose Edit ➪ Invert Selection.

Figure 5-2 shows an example in which I have selected several filenames. I started by clicking the topmost filename. The figure shows the keys I held down while clicking the mouse button to select other files in the list.

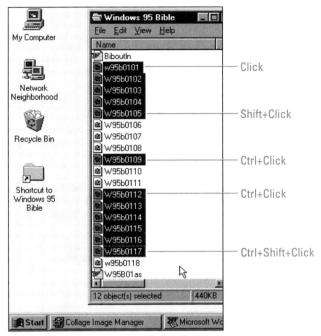

Figure 5-2: To select multiple items, use the Ctrl and Shift keys while clicking.

Yet another way to select multiple items is to drag a frame around them. This is especially handy when you're using the Large Icons view. Move the mouse pointer to just outside the first item you want to select. Then hold down the mouse button and drag a frame around all the items you want to select. The items will be selected as you drag and will remain selected after you release the mouse button.

Not sure what's in a file?

Many of your documents will support the Windows 95 Quick View feature, which enables you to peek inside a file without opening the document's program. To see whether this option is available for a certain file, right-click the file's icon. If you see a Quick View option, you can select that option to peek inside the file. To close the quick view, click the Close (X) button in its title bar.

Moving or Copying Selected Items

To move or copy selected items, point to one of them, hold down the right mouse button, and drag the mouse pointer to the destination's icon. When the mouse pointer is touching that icon, release the right mouse button. Then choose <u>M</u>ove Here or <u>C</u>opy Here, depending on what you want to do.

More Info If you ever need a reminder of how to do the things discussed in this chapter, click the Start button, click <u>H</u>elp, and then click the Index tab. The index includes the topic's files — copying, moving, deleting, renaming, selecting, Recycle Bin, drag-and-drop — and many others related to general file management.

If you want to save yourself one extra click, you can drag the selected files by using the regular (left) mouse button. When you release the mouse button, the files will either be copied or moved, depending on where the destination is in relation to the source, as summarized in the following list:

✦ If you drag to a different folder on the same disk, the selected items are *moved* to that location.

✦ If you drag to a different disk drive, the selected items are *copied* to that location.

If you drag the files with the left mouse button and aren't sure what Windows 95 intends to do with those items, look at the mouse pointer (without releasing the mouse button). The icon near the mouse pointer tells you what Windows intends to do, as follows:

✦ If you see a plus sign (+), Windows intends to copy the files (*add* them to the disk or folder).

✦ If you see a small arrow, Windows intends to create shortcut icons at the destination.

✦ If you see neither symbol, Windows intends to move the files to that location.

✦ If you see an international "prohibited" symbol, Windows intends to do nothing, because you're attempting a move that's not allowed.

If Windows 95 intends to do something you hadn't intended, you can force it to copy, move, or create a shortcut by pressing and holding down one of the following keys before you release the mouse button:

✦ Ctrl: copies the selected item(s)

✦ Shift: moves the selected item(s)

✦ Shift+Ctrl: creates a shortcut to the selected files or folder

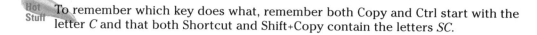

To remember which key does what, remember both Copy and Ctrl start with the letter *C* and that both Shortcut and Shift+Copy contain the letters *SC*.

Canceling a drag-and-drop

If you change your mind about a drag-and-drop procedure midstream, drag to any "illegal" destination — for example, the status bar at the bottom of the current window. When you see the international "prohibited" symbol, release the mouse button. Alternatively, tap the Esc key before you release the mouse button. Windows 95 will take no action on the dragged files.

Making a copy in the same folder

If you simply want to make a copy of a file within the current folder, click the file you want to copy, or use the techniques described earlier to select multiple files. Choose Edit ➪ Copy, press Ctrl+C, or click the Copy button in the toolbar. Then choose Edit ➪ Paste, press Ctrl+V, or click the Paste button in the toolbar. Each file is duplicated, with the filename *Copy of* followed by the original filename.

Figure 5-3 shows an example in which I selected the first three copies in the list, clicked the Copy button, and then clicked the Paste button. The last three files in the list now are copies of the first three files.

The new icons are added to the bottom of the list, so you may not see them right away. If you choose View ➪ Refresh or View ➪ Arrange Icons ➪ by Name, the new files fall into proper alphabetical place in the list.

How to squeeze more onto a floppy disk

A typical 3.5-inch floppy disk can hold about 1.4MB of stuff. But you can squeeze more than this onto a floppy in the following ways:

Use DriveSpace to double the capacity of the floppy before you put anything on it. (See Chapter 11 for information on DriveSpace.)

Use a compression program such as PKZip to compress the files before (or while) copying them. (See Chapter 27 for information on file compression.)

A third technique is to use Backup, rather than Copy, to copy the files to the floppies. Backup can split a single file or group of files across several floppies. If you use Backup, you then need to use Restore to copy the files from the floppies to a hard disk. See Chapter 11 for more information on Backup and Restore.

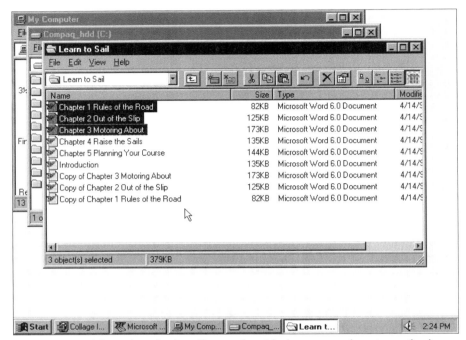

Figure 5-3: Quick copies of a few files made with the copy-and-paste method

An alternative to drag-and-drop

As an alternative to drag-and-drop, you can copy-and-paste to move and copy files. Select the items you want to use. To copy the selected items, choose Edit ➪ Copy, press Ctrl+C, or click the Copy button in the toolbar. To move the selected items, choose Edit ➪ Cut, press Ctrl+X, or click the Cut button in the toolbar.

Next, browse to the folder into which you want to put the moved or copied files. Open that folder and click within it; and then choose Edit ➪ Paste, press Ctrl+V, or click the Paste button in the toolbar.

Undoing a move or copy

If you complete a move or copy operation and then change your mind, you can undo this action as long as you don't do any more moving or copying. To undo a move or copy, choose Edit ➪ Undo Copy or Edit ➪ Undo Move. Alternatively, right-click the desktop and then choose Undo Copy or Undo Move from the menu.

Deleting Selected Items

Deleting stuff from a hard disk is always a bit of a risk, because undeleting something is not always easy — in fact, it's often impossible to undelete. So observe the following cautions:

✦ Make sure you look carefully at the files you're about to delete, and *never* delete a file unless you're sure you know what you are deleting.

✦ If you're deleting a program, try using Uninstall (see Chapter 9) first. Uninstall does a more thorough job than Delete and automatically cleans up the Registry.

✦ When you delete a folder, be aware you are deleting *everything* in that folder, including all subfolders.

Danger Zone Caution is the key to safe deleting. Always assume a worst-case scenario ("I *won't* be able to undelete this later") so you don't get cocky and careless. Also, never move things to the Recycle Bin just to get them out of the way temporarily; you may forget about them and permanently delete them later.

✦ Only items you delete from your local hard disk (typically, drive C) are sent to the Recycle Bin. Files on floppy disks and network drives are permanently deleted right on the spot and can't be undeleted.

✦ If you see the message `Are you sure you want to delete [whatever]?`, the files are going to be deleted immediately — *not* sent to the Recycle Bin. Think before you choose Yes.

✦ Remember, when you delete an icon, you are deleting everything on the disk the icon represents. The only exception is the shortcut icon, which you can delete without affecting the underlying disk files.

When you're sure you want to delete the selected items, do any of the following:

✦ Press the Delete key.

✦ Choose File ⇨ Delete.

✦ Drag the items to the Recycle Bin. (Once again, only files on your local hard disk will actually be sent to the Recycle Bin.)

Hot Stuff To delete a single item quickly, right-click it and then choose Delete, or click it and then press the Delete key.

Recovering trash from the Recycle Bin

If you move folders and/or files to the Recycle Bin, and then change your mind and decide to bring them back, you can *restore* them. Follow these steps:

1. Double-click the Recycle Bin icon on the desktop to view its contents (see Figure 5-4).

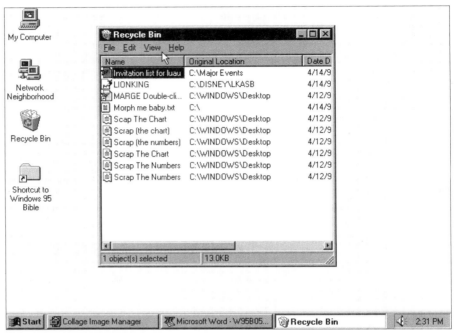

Figure 5-4: The Recycle Bin, with some files ready for deletion.

2. Select the items you want to bring back to the desktop, using the universal techniques described in "Selecting Objects to Move, Copy, or Delete" earlier in this chapter.

3. Choose File ⇨ Restore.

If you want to select all the files in the Recycle Bin for recovery, you can press Ctrl+A to select them all.

Another way to undelete

If you send a bunch of files to the Recycle Bin and immediately change your mind, you can take a shortcut to restore those files instantly. Right-click the desktop and choose Undo Delete from the menu that appears, or choose Edit ⇨ Undo Delete in the current window.

Recovering recycled disk space

Deleted files and folders in the Recycle Bin still occupy as much disk space as they did before you deleted them. In fact, the files are still on your hard disk; they're just hidden from all browsing tools except the Recycle Bin. To use the disk space occupied by those recycled files, you must delete those files permanently. This procedure is called *emptying the Recycle Bin*.

Remember, after you empty the Recycle Bin, you cannot restore the files.

To empty the Recycle Bin, follow these steps:

1. Double-click the Recycle Bin icon on the desktop.

2. Make certain *only* files you want to delete permanently are listed.

   (This is your last chance to change your mind and restore any files in the Recycle Bin.)

3. Choose File ➪ Empty Recycle Bin.

Danger Zone Microsoft should have named the Empty Recycle Bin command something like Burn Recycle Bin, because it permanently deletes the folders and files in the bin. Remember, the command does *not* empty the bin back onto the desktop.

Personalizing your Recycle Bin

You can customize the way the Recycle Bin works on your PC. To see your options, first close the Recycle Bin if it's open; then right-click the Recycle Bin icon and choose Properties. If you need help with an item, click the question-mark button in the menu bar and then click the item. Alternatively, click the item and then press F1.

Renaming a File or Folder

Before you rename an icon, remember you're actually doing two things: changing the name that appears below the icon and changing the name of the file on the disk. The only exception to this rule is the shortcut icon, which you can rename (or move, copy, or delete) without affecting files on the disk.

To rename an icon (and its file), follow these steps:

1. Use any of the following techniques to select the icon you want to rename and get the insertion point in place:

   • Right-click the icon you want to rename and then choose Rename.

   • Click the icon you want to rename and then choose File ➪ Rename.

- Click the icon (to select it), wait a second or two, and then click the text you want to change.

If you don't pause between the first and second click when clicking an icon to rename it, Windows 95 may interpret your action as a double-click — which, of course, opens the icon. This situation is not a big deal, just potentially confusing. If you open a window by accident, simply click its Close (X) button.

2. The text is selected, with the insertion point blinking, indicating Windows is ready to accept your changes.

3. Make your changes, using standard Windows text-editing techniques (see the following section).

4. To save your changes, click the area just outside the current icon, or click a different icon within the same window (before you close the current window).

Standard text-editing techniques

The standard text-editing techniques in Windows 95 are the same as they were in Windows 3.x. Notice you can use these techniques any time, anywhere, in any Windows program — in word processing programs, while filling in the blanks in forms, when filling a tiny text box, or while renaming something.

When text is selected, anything you type instantly replaces all the selected text. (If you do this by accident, just press Esc.) If you want to change, rather than replace, the selected text, click the place where you want to make your change, or press the Home, End, left-arrow, or right-arrow key.

The blinking insertion point (also called the *I-beam* or the *cursor*) indicates where any new text you type will be placed. You can press the Delete key to erase the character following the insertion point or press Backspace to delete the character to the left of the insertion point.

To select a chunk of text to change or delete, drag the mouse pointer through that text, or hold down the Shift key while you move the insertion point with one of the keyboard direction keys. Then type the replacement text or press Delete to delete the selected text.

If you select the wrong text and must make a change, drag the mouse pointer through some other text, click anywhere within the text, press Esc, or press any direction key without holding down the Shift key.

Changing the name of your C drive

If, for whatever reason, you want to rename your C drive, open My Computer and then right-click the icon for drive C. Choose Properties, and type the new name in the box titled Label. (This name can be no more than 11 characters long and cannot contain spaces.) Click OK when you finish.

You can use the same technique to name or rename a floppy disk in a floppy drive, but you can't rename read-only disks (including all CD-ROMs).

Selecting Across Folders and Drives

Both My Computer and Explorer work on sort of a narrowing-down principle — you start by picking a drive and then perhaps a folder on the drive, and you end up seeing files and other folders within that particular folder. Most of the time, this procedure is fine. But occasionally, you may want to do something to all the files on a particular drive, regardless of in which folder those files are located.

Suppose disk space is getting tight, and you want to get rid of old backup (.bak) files floating around on your hard drive. You don't really care what folder each file is in; you want to make the deletions on an entire-hard-disk basis. The solution is simple: use Find, rather than My Computer or Explorer, to isolate all the files. Follow these steps:

1. Click the Start button and then click Find.

2. Click Files or Folders.

3. In the Named text box, enter some word or phrase identifying the types of files you want to delete (or move, or copy).

4. In Figure 5-5, for example, I entered **bak** as the identifying portion of the name.

5. In the Look in drop-down list, select the drive you want to search (C, in my example), and make sure Include subfolders is selected if you want to search all the folders on the drive.

Hot Stuff If you want to move, copy, or delete files from all the folders in several drives, choose My Computer rather than a specific drive in Step 5. The resulting list shows files from all the folders from every drive physically connected to your PC, as well as from every drive on the LAN to which you have mapped a drive letter. Use caution, though — that's a lot of stuff.

6. Click Find Now.

   The bottom part of the dialog box shows all the matching files.

7. Select the files you want to delete (or move, or copy), and proceed as usual.

Danger Zone Don't be in too big a hurry when you're about to delete a group of files; look carefully before you leap. In the example shown in Figure 5-5, I chose View ➪ Arrange Icons ➪ by Type to group all the files that have similar extensions. Then I widened the Name column for the list of filenames so I could see the entire filenames. Using this method, I discovered one of the files actually is a Word document named Marcia Bombak Resume (note the *bak* embedded in the filename). To exclude this document from what I was about to do, I didn't select it.

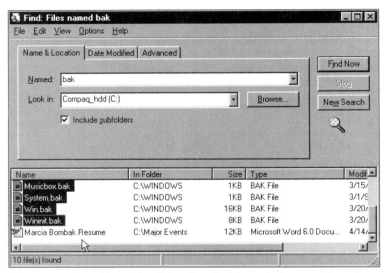

Figure 5-5: Searching drive C for files that have *bak* somewhere in the filename

Using DOS Commands to Manage Files

If you're familiar with DOS commands, you may be relieved to hear you can still use the CD, COPY, ERASE, DEL, MOVE, DELTREE, and RENAME commands to navigate and to move, copy, and delete files and folders.

First, click the Start button; then click Programs, and choose MS-DOS Prompt. You go to a C> prompt, where you can enter DOS commands. For brief help with a command, you can enter the command, followed by a space and /? — for example, **deltree /?**.

When you type folder (directory) and filenames at the C> prompt, use the shortened name — typically, the first six letters, followed by a tilde and a number. Also, spaces should be removed. To get to a folder named Major Events on the current drive, for example, type **cd \majore~1**, and then press Enter.

When you use the DOS DIR command, the leftmost column shows the shortened name of each folder and file; the rightmost column displays the long name. You can use this display to discover the short DOS name for any long Windows 95 name. Suppose you want to determine the short DOS name for a folder or file named Mathilda Misanthrope. You could enter the command **dir mat*.*** to search the current folder or **dir c:\mat*.*** **/s** to search all of drive C for names beginning with the letters *mat*. For a reminder of all the options you can use with DIR, enter **dir /?**.

To close the DOS window, enter the **exit** command at the C> prompt.

Where the file type comes from

When you look at a list of filenames in Details view, you'll notice some files have rather wordy descriptions in the Type column — for example, Microsoft Word Document or Paintbrush Picture. Files that have these wordy Type descriptions are registered files, as discussed in Chapter 3.

Other files will have less-glamorous descriptions, such as BAK file or OLD file. Those files are unregistered, and the Type column is simply showing you the file extension fol-

lowed by the word *file*. Therefore, a file described as the type BAK file is an unregistered file with .bak as its extension.

When you use the Advanced tab in Find, you may discover the Of type option allows you to isolate only registered file types. To isolate a nonregistered file type, click the Start button and choose Find ➪ Files or Folders. Then click the Name & Location tab. Then type the extension you're looking for into the Named box.

Summary

This chapter ends Part I of the book — the stuff you *really* must know to get along with your PC and Windows 95. If you've read from Chapter 1 to here, I thank you for your patience and I hope I've been of some help.

Remember, practice makes perfect. It takes time to become fluent in the many tricks and techniques that Windows 95 offers for getting around and using your system. And don't forget, whenever you need help, you can always look things up in the online help manual.

Each chapter that follows this part of the book is like an independent essay about a topic in which you may (or may not) be interested. Feel free to skip anything that doesn't interest you.

Here's a quick recap of the most important skills covered in this chapter:

✦ To select an object to move, copy, or delete, just click the object. To select several objects, you can drag a frame around them. Or use Ctrl+click, Shift+click, and Shift+Ctrl+click.

✦ To move or copy selected object(s), hold down the right mouse button and drag to the destination. Then release the mouse button and choose Copy Here or Move Here from the shortcut menu that appears.

✦ To delete selected objects, press the Delete key. Or right-click an object and choose Delete from the shortcut menu.

✦ Remember, objects you delete from your local hard disk (only) are sent to the Recycle Bin, and continue to use up disk space until you empty the bin.

✦ To rename an object, right-click the object and choose Rename from the shortcut menu.

✦ To "undelete" deleted items, open the Recycle Bin, select the items you want to restore, and then choose <u>F</u>ile ➪ <u>R</u>estore from Recycle Bin's menu bar.

✦ To permanently delete objects in the Recycle Bin and recover their disk space, choose <u>F</u>ile ➪ Empty Recycle <u>B</u>in.

✦   ✦   ✦

Personalizing the Screen

This chapter looks at all the ways that you can personalize your screen to suit your tastes and needs. Elements such as screen colors, the size of text and objects onscreen, and the appearance of dates, times, and numbers are discussed. But this chapter won't cover techniques for organizing your desktop. Those topics are discussed in Chapter 8, which covers topics such as arranging files in folders, personalizing the Start menu, and customizing the taskbar.

Customizing the Screen In a Nutshell

Personalizing your screen, wallpapers, and so on is easy in Windows 95. Just follow these simple steps:

Hot Stuff Always, always, *always* adjust the brightness, contrast, and sizing controls (if any) on your monitor to get the best possible picture before you mess with the Display Properties. Then, if you do adjust the onscreen display settings, adjust those controls again when you finish to get the best possible picture from your new settings.

1. Right-click on the desktop and choose Properties. Alternatively, click on the Start button, choose Settings ⇨ Control Panel, and then double-click on the Display icon.

   Either way, you see the Display Properties dialog box, shown in Figure 6-1.

2. Click on any tab near the top of the dialog box and then choose any options within that tab.

   The sample monitor in the middle of the dialog box gives you a preview of the way your current selection will look onscreen.

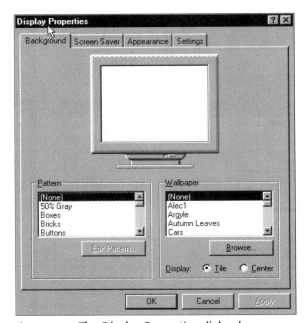

Figure 6-1: The Display Properties dialog box

3. To apply your selection to the screen without leaving the dialog box, click on the Apply button.

4. When you finish, choose OK to save all your selections, or click on Cancel to save only the settings that you've already applied.

The following sections describe in detail the various options in the Display Properties dialog box. You also can get instant help in the Display Properties dialog box by clicking on the question-mark button and then clicking on the option you need help with. Alternatively, click on the option you need help with and then press the Help key (F1).

Choosing color depth and resolution

The Settings tab in the Display Properties dialog box may be the most important of the four. Use the options in this tab to set up the general appearance of your screen, as discussed in the following sections.

Change display type

The first thing you want to do is make sure that Windows 95 is taking advantage of whatever features your graphics card and monitor have to offer. To do this, click on Change Display Type in the Settings tab. Windows 95 displays the Change Display Type dialog box, shown in Figure 6-2.

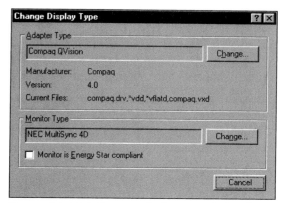

Figure 6-2: The Change Display Type dialog box

Chances are that Windows 95 has already detected your adapter card and monitor type and that those settings already appear in the dialog box. If that's the case, you can just click on Cancel.

More Info If you do purchase a new graphics adapter, use the Add New Hardware wizard (described in Chapter 10) to install it.

If you recently installed a new graphics card or monitor, the current settings may be incorrect. To choose the correct settings, first gather up your original Windows 95 floppy disks or CD-ROM. If your card or monitor came with disks, keep those disks handy, too. Then click on the Change button for whichever device you want to change. Read and follow the instructions that appear onscreen to install the software for that device.

Hot Stuff If you have a disk for the hardware that you're installing *and* your device appears in the list, choose the driver from the list to ensure that you get the 32-bit Windows 95 driver for your device.

Color palette

The Color palette option in the Settings tab lets you select whatever color depths your graphics hardware offers: 16-color, 256-color, High Color (16-bit), and True Color (24-bit). Only options that are available for your graphics hardware will appear in the list.

The difference among these settings is that the higher you go, the closer you get to true photographic-quality color. The downside, however, is that the higher you go, the longer it takes to repaint the screen when things change. So it's up to you to decide the best trade-off. I recommend that you not go below 256 colors, because most modern multimedia and graphics programs assume that you're using a 256 (or better) setting.

Desktop area (resolution)

What the Settings tab refers to as the desktop area is what the hardware manufacturers usually refer to as resolution. The terms really boil down to how many dots are onscreen (or, in plain English, how much stuff is displayed onscreen). The higher the resolution, the more stuff appears onscreen. The downside of resolution is that the higher the resolution, the *smaller* everything is onscreen.

To change the desktop area option, drag the slider to whatever setting you want. You are allowed to choose only settings that your graphics hardware supports. To get the best picture onscreen, it's especially important to adjust the brightness, contrast, and sizing controls on the monitor after changing the desktop area option.

Hot
Stuff
You also can change the appearance and size of the mouse pointer on the screen. See Chapter 7 for information.

Figure 6-3 shows three windows — one for Calculator, one for Cardfile, and one for CD Player — on the desktop at the low resolution of 640 × 480 pixels. I need to overlap the windows on this screen because of the small desktop area that I'm using.

Figure 6-4 shows the same three windows onscreen with the desktop area set to 1,024 × 768 pixels. Notice that I now have room to spread things out more, because each item on the screen is smaller.

Graphics-cards manufacturers often recommend that you choose a desktop area based on the physical size of your screen, as summarized in Table 6-1. It's really up to you, however, to decide what's comfortable for your eyes. Also, because changing the desktop area on the fly is so easy, you can choose whatever desktop area is most convenient for the work you happen to be doing at the moment.

Table 6-1
Physical Screen Size and Recommended Desktop Area

Screen Type/Size	Recommended Desktop Area
Laptop	640 × 480
15-inch diagonal	800 × 600
More than 15-inch diagonal	1,024 × 768

Hot
Stuff
You usually can magnify or shrink the document within a Windows program without fussing with the desktop area setting. Choose <u>V</u>iew ➪ <u>Z</u>oom in the current program or search the program's help system for the word *zoom*.

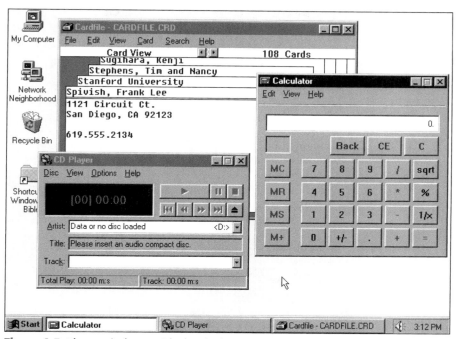

Figure 6-3: Three windows with the desktop area at 640 × 480

Font size

The Font size option in the Setting tab determines the size of text on the desktop. The name that appears below an icon, for example, is affected by this setting. The options available to you depend on your graphics hardware. Typically, you get to choose between Small Fonts and Large Fonts. If you have trouble reading that kind of text on your screen, try switching to large fonts.

More Info If you're not familiar with fonts, see Chapter 14 for the pertinent concepts and terminology. But keep in mind that in this chapter, I'm discussing only the fonts on the Windows desktop. Settings that you make here have no effect on printed documents.

Some graphics hardware even allows you to define your own custom screen font, as indicated by the button named Custom. If this option is available and none of the other settings work for you, try a custom screen font.

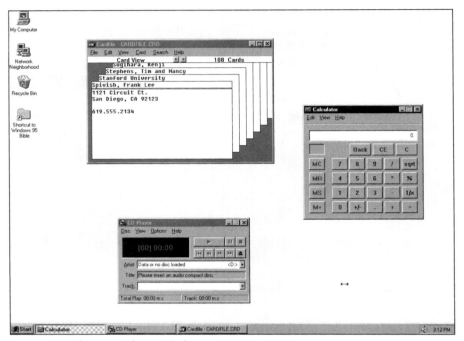

Figure 6-4: The same three windows at 1,024 × 768

Don't forget that within any program, you usually can change the size of the text on your screen by using Zoom. This method, which simply magnifies the text within the current window, is easy because you don't need to change the resolution for the entire screen.

Choosing a color scheme

You can choose a color scheme for your Windows 95 desktop or make up your own color scheme. In the Display Properties dialog box, click on the Appearance tab. To select one of the predefined color schemes, click on the down-arrow button in the Scheme drop-down list and then click on your preference.

To create your own color scheme, first choose any of the predefined schemes as a starting point. Then choose an option in the Item drop-down list to color individual portions of the screen. For example, you could choose Desktop as the area to color. Then choose a color from the Color drop-down list. Some options also let you choose a Size. If you opt for Icon Spacing (Horizontal), you see the Size rather than the Color option. Enter a size (in pixels).

If the item that you're coloring contains text, you also can choose a Font, Size, and Color for that text. In Figure 6-5, I chose 12-point Lucida Handwriting (a popular TrueType font) as the font for active title bars. You also can choose a color and a weight: Bold (**B**) or Italic (/).

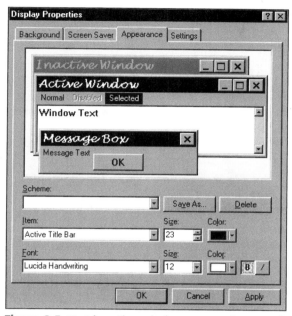

Figure 6-5: Text in active windows set to the 12-point Lucida Handwriting font.

Saving a custom color scheme

As soon as you start changing one of the predefined color schemes, the name for that scheme disappears from the Scheme text box. If you want to save the scheme you created, click on Save As and then enter a name.

Choosing a pattern or wallpaper

The Background tab of the Display Properties dialog box lets you add some texture to the desktop or put a picture (*wallpaper*) on the desktop. If your monitor is slow, you may want to use this option to remove patterns and wallpaper to speed things up. Either way, follow these steps:

1. Open the Display Properties dialog box, as discussed earlier, and click on the Background tab.

2. Do one of the following things:

- To add some texture (rather than a picture) to the background, choose an option from the Pattern list. To remove the current pattern, choose (None) from the top of that list. You also can click on Edit Pattern to change the currently selected pattern (if any).

- To add wallpaper to the desktop, choose a Wallpaper option. If you choose a small wallpaper pattern, you can select the Tile option to fill the screen with that picture.

3. Click on OK to save your selection.

If you choose a pattern and also tiled or full-screen wallpaper, the wallpaper will completely cover the pattern. In that case, you may as well set the pattern to (None).

Create your own wallpaper

You can use any graphic image that's stored on your disk in bitmap (.BMP) format as your wallpaper. If you have a scanner, you can scan a photo, company logo, or whatever into a file in the Windows folder and then set the filename for your wallpaper to that file.

If you want the scanned image to fill the screen as wallpaper, be sure to size and scale the scanned image to your screen before you save it. In Figure 6-6, I used the program for my HP DeskJet scanner to scan a photo of my wife. Using options within that scanning program, I scaled the cropped area to 637 pixels wide × 487 pixels high — a close fit for my current desktop area of 640 × 480.

Figure 6-7 shows how my Windows 95 desktop looks with that wallpaper onscreen.

Scanner tips

When you scan an image to use as wallpaper or a screen saver, you should set the unit of measurement to pixels. Then as you scan, crop, and scale the picture, set its size to that of the desktop area. The larger of the two numbers is always the width. If you use 640 × 480 resolution, for example, scan to about 640 pixels wide × 480 pixels high.

To keep the file size of the scanned image small, don't go for extremely high print quality. A setting of 75 *dpi* (dots per inch)

probably will do just fine.

If you don't have a scanner, check the phone book for desktop-publishing service bureaus in your area. Call around to see who can do the job and how much they'll charge. When you get there, show them this little sidebar to help explain what you want. Make sure that they save the image to a bitmap (.BMP) file. Warning: If the material you're scanning even *looks* like it's copyrighted, they may not be willing to scan it!

Figure 6-6: A photo scanned, cropped, and scaled for use as wallpaper.

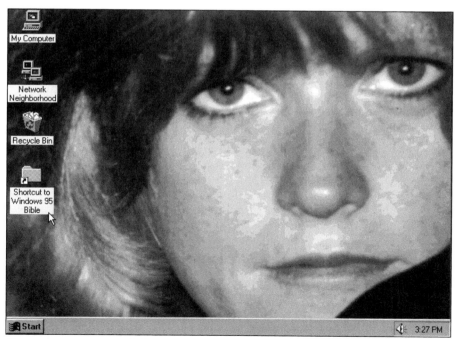

Figure 6-7: My scanned photo now is wallpaper.

Microsoft Plus!, discussed in Appendix F, includes an option to stretch a wallpaper image. So, if you scan a wallpaper image at 640 × 480, and then switch to a higher resolution on your screen, the wallpaper will stretch to fit the new resolution.

Paint a wallpaper

You also can use the Windows 95 Paint program to create wallpaper. To start Paint, click on the Start button, choose Programs ➪ Accessories, and then double-click on the Paint icon. You can use the Paint program's tools to create a picture from scratch. Alternatively, you can choose File ➪ Open within Paint to open an existing bitmap image and then use the program's tools to modify that image.

If you don't see Paint in your Accessories menu, maybe it isn't installed yet. See "Installing Missing Windows Components" in Chapter 9 for information on installing it.

To learn to use Paint, click on Help in Paint's menu bar and then click on Help Contents. Click on the Contents tab and then double-click on any book to learn about that topic.

When you're happy with the image that you created in Paint, save it, using the standard File ➪ Save command. After you save the image, you can set it as wallpaper by clicking on File and then choosing one of the following options:

✦ Set as Wallpaper (Tiled): fills the entire screen with your picture

✦ Set as Wallpaper (Centered): puts your picture in the center of the screen

Figure 6-8 shows an example in which I opened a clip-art image in Paint and used Paint's text tool to add the text *Under Construction* and *PLEASE DON'T TOUCH!*. Then I saved that image and chose File ➪ Save as Wallpaper (Tiled). The image fills the desktop behind Paint's window.

If you upgraded from Windows 3.x, you still may have the Paintbrush program on your system. You can use that program to create and modify bitmap images, but Paintbrush doesn't have the Set As Wallpaper commands described in this section.

To remove that wallpaper image or select another image, follow the steps described at the beginning of this section: right-click on the desktop, choose Properties, click on the Background tab, and then make your selections in the Wallpaper section.

Choosing a screen saver

A *screen saver* is a moving pattern that moves on your screen after some idle time. By *idle time*, I mean a period in which there has been no mouse or keyboard activity. The purpose of a screen saver is to prevent *burn-in*, a condition caused by keeping an unchanging image on the screen too long. Burn-in causes a screen to become blurry and lose some clarity.

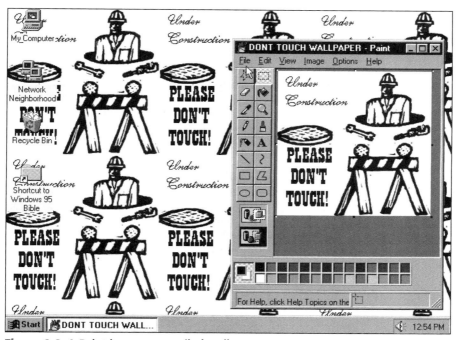

Figure 6-8: A Paint image set as tiled wallpaper.

Windows 95 gives you a few screen savers to choose among. To select a screen saver, follow these steps:

1. If you aren't in the Display Properties dialog box, right-click on the desktop and choose Properties.

2. Click on the Screen Saver tab.

3. Choose a screen saver from the Screen Saver drop-down list.

4. Do any of the following things:

   • To customize the screen saver that you selected, click on the Settings button and then choose among the options that appear.

   • To preview the currently selected screen saver and settings, click on the Preview button. (Move the mouse pointer a little to turn off the preview.)

   • Some screen savers, such as Flying Windows, support password protection. To use that feature, choose Password protected, click on the Change button, and enter a password as you are instructed onscreen.

Danger Zone If you password-protect your screen saver, make sure that you write your password on paper and store it in a safe place. Otherwise, if you forget the password, you won't be able to turn the screen saver off when you need to.

> ✦ To specify how long the PC needs to be inactive before the screen saver kicks in, specify the number of minutes in the Wait box.

Turning off the screen saver

When the screen saver kicks in, your Windows 95 desktop disappears, and a moving pattern or blank screen appears. To get back to your Windows 95 desktop, just move the mouse pointer a little or press any key. If you password-protected your screen saver, you will be prompted for your password. Type the correct password and press Enter to get back to the regular Windows 95 desktop.

Hacking the screen-saver password

I told a little white lie earlier when I said that after you enter a password for a screen saver, you're doomed if you forget it. Truth is, it's easy to hack (get around) a password-protected screen saver. I'm not telling you this to encourage computer break-ins; I just want to you to know what to do in case you forget your screen-saver password. (Or to get around the prank password left behind by some computer-store vandal.)

Create your own screen saver

Firefly Software Corporation (P.O. Box 782, Jericho, NY 11753, (516) 935-7060) sells a great program for making your own screen savers. The program is called PhotoGenix. It's not cheap (at least, it wasn't when I bought it), but it gets the job done, is simple to learn, and is fun to use. (Rumor has it that Microsoft may soon be releasing a similar program. Though I haven't seen it yet myself.)

First, you need to scan some photos (at least half a dozen, I'd recommend) into files. When you are scanning, scale and crop the photos to your desktop area, and then save them as bitmap files. In other words, create these images just as though you were going to use them as wallpaper (see "Create your own wallpaper" earlier in this chapter).

When you finish scanning, you can use PhotoGenix to assemble the photos into a slide show. You can even pick fancy transition effects from one picture to the next. That slide show then will become a screen saver, which you can select (like any other slide show) in the Screen Saver tab of the Display Properties dialog box. When the screen saver kicks in, you get to see a continuous slide show of your favorite photos.

To make a great computer gift for someone, steal his or her photo album temporarily — just long enough to scan that person's favorite photos — and then make a custom screen saver. Your friend will think that you're some kind of genius. (Don't tell him or her how easy it really was. And don't forget to return the purloined photo album.)

First, if you're stuck in the screen saver and can't get past the password request, you'll need to restart the PC. (I know this is a bummer, but you're stuck.) Either hit the Reset button on the PC, or turn the PC off then back on. Wait to get back to the Windows 95 desktop.

When Windows 95 has fully restarted, right-click the desktop and choose Properties. Click the Screen Saver tab, then click the Change button. Type in a new password, twice (preferably one you'll remember.). Or leave both password boxes blank. Choose OK. Optionally, if you want to get rid of Screen Saver password protection altogether, just clear the Password protected check box. Click on the OK button to return to the desktop. The original password is ancient history and won't bother you again.

Hot Stuff If you have a 486 or Pentium PC, and at least a 256-color monitor, you might want to purchase Microsoft Plus! (discussed in Appendix F). Plus! comes with some fun desktop themes that let you define a wallpaper, screen saver, colors — even sound events in one simple step.

Using Energy Star Features

Did you know that your computer monitor uses far more electricity than anything else in your computer? Even when the monitor is showing only a screen saver or blank screen, it's running up your electric bill. When you multiply your single monitor by the millions of computer screens out there, you've got a lot of screens sucking up a lot of energy, many of them doing nothing. To top it off, the monitors are putting out heat, even while they're doing nothing. According to some scientists, this contributes to global warming (I guess there are *a lot* of monitors out there!)

To curb this high-tech polluting waste of power, the Environmental Protection Agency (EPA) came up with a feature called Energy Star. Energy Star is a feature of many modern computer displays that automatically reduces power consumption — and even turns off the monitor automatically after the computer has been idle for some time. If your monitor complies with Energy Star standards, you'll see an Energy Star logo somewhere on the front or back of the monitor. You can use Windows 95 to put that feature into effect. Follow these steps:

Hot Stuff Even if you don't turn off your computer at night, you still should turn off the monitor.

1. If you're not already in the Display Properties dialog box, right-click on the desktop and choose Properties.

2. Click on the Settings tab and then click the Change Display Type button.

3. Make sure that the correct monitor type is selected in the Monitor Type list and that the Monitor is Energy Star compliant option is selected.

If your monitor is one of the generic types (such as Super VGA) and you're sure that your graphics hardware is Energy Star-compliant, choose the Monitor is Energy Star compliant option.

4. Click on Close (if you made a change) or Cancel (if you did not make a change) to get back to the Display Properties dialog box.

5. Click on the Screen Saver tab.

The Energy saving feature of monitor options become available for selection (see Figure 6-9).

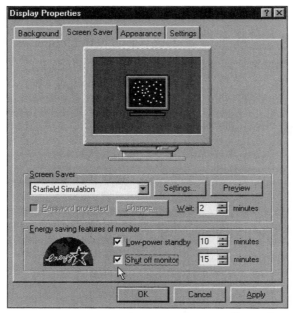

Figure 6-9: Energy Star's Low-power standby and Shut off monitor options are enabled.

6. Select Low-power standby, and then specify how long Windows 95 should wait (in minutes) to activate that feature.

7. Select Shut off monitor, and then specify how much idle time you require before that feature kicks in.

8. Click on the OK button.

In the example shown in Figure 6-9, I set up the screen saver to kick in after two minutes of idle time. I also activated the energy saving features as follows:

✦ After 10 minutes, the monitor will switch to Low-power standby mode.

✦ After 15 minutes of idle time, the monitor will shut itself off.

Changing the Date and Time

The time indicator in the lower-right corner of the screen shows the current time. When you click on this indicator, it shows the date. If either the date or time is wrong, you can follow these steps to correct it:

1. Click on the Start button and then click on Settings.

2. Click on Control Panel and then double-click on Date/Time to get to the Date/Time Properties dialog box.

3. In the Date pane (see Figure 6-10), choose the current month and year from the drop-down lists; then click on the current day in the calendar.

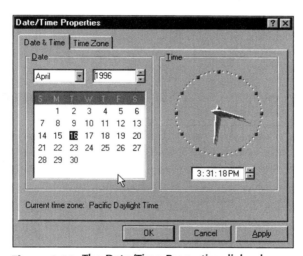

Figure 6-10: The Date/Time Properties dialog box

4. In the Time pane, click on the hour, minute, second, or AM/PM option; then use the spin box to set the appropriate time.

   Optionally, you can type the correct time.

5. Click on the Time Zone tab, and choose your time zone.

   You can click on your location on the map, or you can press the left-arrow and right-arrow keys to move the highlight to your time zone.

6. If you have daylight saving time in your time zone, select the Automatically adjust clock for daylight saving changes option (see Figure 6-11).

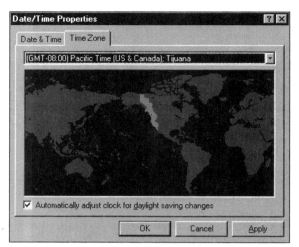

Figure 6-11: Map for telling Windows what time zone you're in.

7. Click on the OK button to save your settings.

Date, Time, Currency, and Number Formats

The world has many standards for displaying dates, times, numbers, and currency values. In the United States, we use a period as a decimal point, but Great Britain uses a comma. The Regional Settings dialog box in Windows 95 allows you to specify the formats that you want to use on your PC.

To choose regional formats, follow these steps:

1. Click on the Start button, point to Settings, and then click on Control Panel.

2. Double-click on the Regional Settings icon.

   You see the dialog box shown in Figure 6-12.

3. Click any green region on the map, or select a region from the drop-down list.

Hot Stuff   Most Windows programs use whatever date, time, currency, and number format you specify in the Regional Settings Properties dialog box. You don't have to pick the same settings for every program on your system.

4. To set the Number, Currency, Time, or Date format individually, click on the appropriate tab and then choose among the options provided.

5. Click on OK to save your changes.

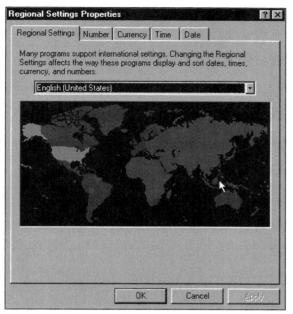

Figure 6-12: The Regional Settings Properties dialog box

Summary

All right, let's review the most important things discussed in this chapter:

✦ To personalize your screen settings, first right-click the desktop and choose Properties. Then...

✦ To change the background pattern or wallpaper, click the Background tab.

✦ To change the screen saver, click the Screen Saver tab.

✦ To change the screen colors, click the Appearance tab.

✦ To change the color palette, resolution, font, and display type, click the Settings tab.

✦ To change the date, time, and format of numbers and currencies, you need to go through the Control Panel (click the Start button, point to Settings, click Control Panel).

✦   ✦   ✦

Personalizing the Mouse, Keyboard, and Joystick

◆ ◆ ◆ ◆

In This Chapter

Tailor your mouse and keyboard to your own tastes

Fun with animated mouse pointers and cursors

Adding and calibrating a joystick

Using multiple languages and keyboard layouts

Accessibility options for physical impairments

◆ ◆ ◆ ◆

In this chapter I talk about techniques for tailoring your mouse and keyboard to your own personal work style and habits. If you use a joystick to play games on your PC, you'll find some tips for calibrating the joystick as well. This chapter will also discuss Window 95's accessibility options, which can make using a PC much easier for people with physical disabilities or impairments.

Customizing the Mouse/Keyboard In a Nutshell

It's easy to personalize your mouse and keyboard, as well as your joystick, if you have one. Following is the general procedure, no matter which device you want to personalize:

1. Click the Start button, and point to Settings.

2. Click Control Panel.

3. Do any of the following things:

   - To personalize the mouse, double-click the Mouse icon.

   - To personalize the keyboard, double-click the Keyboard icon.

   - To personalize the joystick, double-click the Joystick icon.

4. Make your selections in the tabs provided.

5. Choose OK to get back to the desktop.

As always, you can use the question-mark button (?) or the F1 key to get help with any option in a dialog box. You also can find information in the online manual. From the desktop, click the Start button, click <u>H</u>elp, and then click Index. Search for the word *mouse, keyboard*, or *joystick*, depending on your interest.

Personalize the Mouse

When you install Windows 95, it assumes you're using a standard mouse and a standard desktop monitor, that you're right-handed, and so on. This isn't always the case, though. If the mouse pointer is causing you eyestrain, or if you're just feeling a little klutzy with the mouse, perhaps you should change some of those assumptions.

Hot Stuff

If your work requires precise mouse pointing, consider using MouseKeys, which allows you to position the mouse with the numeric keypad. For information, see "Accessibility Options for Physical Impairments" later in this chapter.

To make changes, go to the Control Panel, as described in the preceding section. Then double-click the Mouse icon to get to the Mouse Properties dialog box, shown in Figure 7-1.

Tell Windows 95 which mouse you have

The first thing you want to do is tell Windows 95 which mouse you're using. Click the General tab. If the mouse displayed in the <u>N</u>ame text box is not the mouse you're using, you should install the appropriate mouse driver. Gather up your original Windows 95 disks or CD-ROM and the disk that came with your mouse (if any). Then click the <u>C</u>hange button, and click the Show <u>a</u>ll devices option button.

If you see the manufacturer and model of your mouse, select them, and then choose OK. If you *don't* see the manufacturer and model for your mouse but you *do* have a disk for that mouse, place the disk in the floppy drive, and click the Have <u>D</u>isk button. Then just follow the instructions onscreen. When you finish, the <u>N</u>ame text box in the General tab should show the correct name for your mouse.

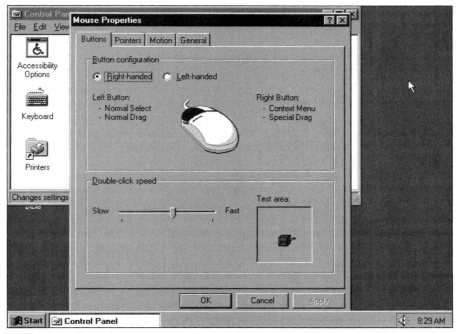

Figure 7-1: The Mouse Properties dialog box

Mice for lefties

If you're left-handed and want the main mouse button to be below your index finger, click the Buttons tab (Figure 7-1) and choose Left-handed. Now you must remember to use the mouse button on the right (the one below your index finger) to click, double-click, and drag. To "right-click" and "right-drag," you'll actually use the button on the left.

Take control of double-clicking

If you find double-clicking is a problem, you may want to speed or slow the double-click speed. If you can't seem to double-click fast enough, for example, you want to slow the double-click speed. On the other hand, if you often find yourself accidentally double-clicking when you really meant to make two separate clicks, you want to speed the double-click rate.

Mice and DOS programs

In Windows 3.x, using your mouse in both DOS and Windows programs was kind of a mess. You had to install a separate mouse driver in your CONFIG.SYS or AUTOEXEC.BAT file; even so, you may have found the mouse worked in a full-screen DOS session, but not in a windowed DOS session.

Windows 95 clears up this mess by having a single mouse driver for all occasions. That mouse driver is installed as soon as you start Windows 95. (In fact, if your mouse isn't plugged in when you start Windows 95 and you plug in the mouse later, the mouse *still* works — a handy arrangement when you forget to plug in your external mouse on a laptop).

Anyway, if you're familiar with DOS and drivers, you may want to peek at your C:\CONFIG.SYS and C:\AUTOEXEC.BAT files to see whether either still loads a mouse driver. If so, you can delete that command (or put a REM statement in front of it) to disable your driver. The next time you start Windows 95, that DOS driver won't be loaded (which saves a little precious RAM), and your mouse should still work fine in every program you use.

The <u>D</u>ouble-click speed option in the Buttons tab lets you determine how fast two clicks must be for interpretation as a double-click. To find the double-click speed that works best for you, try the following steps:

1. Drag the slider below <u>D</u>ouble-click speed to the Fast end of the scale.

2. Double-click on the jack-in-the-box, using your normal double-click speed.

3. If the jack-in-the-box doesn't open, drag the slider bar slightly toward Slow.

4. Repeat Steps 2 and 3 until you find a comfortable double-click speed.

Controlling the mouse motion

If you find it difficult to zero in on things with the mouse pointer, you'll want to slow the mouse-motion speed. Alternatively, if you must move the mouse too far to get from point A to point B onscreen, the mouse-pointer speed probably is set too slow. On laptop LCD screens (and some others), the mouse pointer may fade or even disappear when you move the mouse. To solve that irritating problem, you need to turn on the pointer trails.

When you use a projector to give a demonstration on the screen, turn on the pointer trails to make it easier for your audience to follow the mouse across the screen.

To control the mouse speed and trails, click on the Motion tab in the Mouse Properties dialog box (see Figure 7-2). To adjust the speed of the pointer, drag the slider in the Pointer speed slider bar toward the Slow or Fast end of the bar. To test your current setting, click on the Apply button, and try moving the mouse around. To see your full range of options, apply the slowest speed, and test the mouse. Then apply the faster speed, and try the mouse again.

To turn on pointer trails, select the Show pointer trails check box. The trails turn on immediately and will be visible as soon as you move the mouse. To control the length of the trails, drag the slider to the Short or Long end of the slider bar.

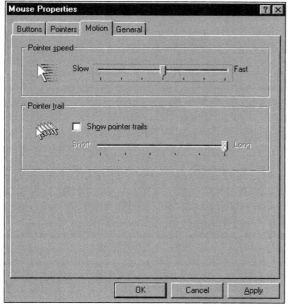

Figure 7-2: Options for controlling mouse speed and pointer trails

Choosing mouse pointers

If the mouse pointer is hard to see, try a larger pointer. If you get bored with the same old pointer, you can try some fancy 3D animated pointers, quite a few of which came with your Windows 95 program. If you haven't already installed these pointers, you can use the general technique for installing missing Windows components (described in Chapter 9) to install them at any time. When you get to the Windows Setup tab, click on Accessories, click on the Details button, and then click on Mouse Pointers.

After you install custom and/or animated mouse pointers on your hard disk, go back to the Mouse Properties dialog box, as described under " Customizing the Mouse/Keyboard In a Nutshell" earlier in this chapter. Then click on the Pointers tab to get to the dialog box shown in Figure 7-3. From there, you can select any predefined pointer scheme in the Scheme drop-down list or assign a custom pointer to any type of pointer. Double-click on the pointer that you want to change (such as Normal Select) to get to the Browse dialog box for pointers.

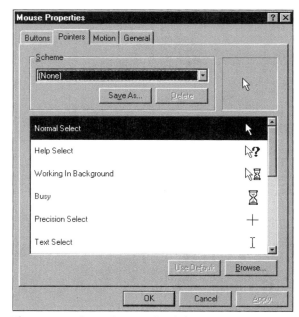

Figure 7-3: The Pointers tab of the Mouse Properties dialog box

In the Browse dialog box you can click on any cursor listed to get a closer look at that cursor. The Preview box shows you the pointer. The filename usually tells you something about the pointer. For example, ARROW_1 is the regular mouse pointer, ARROW_L is the large version of that cursor, and ARROW_M is the midsize one. After making your selection, click on the Open button.

If you have installed animated cursors in any other folder, you can use the Look in drop-down list to browse to the appropriate folder, where you can make your selections.

After you select one or more custom cursors, you can save your selections as a predefined cursor scheme. Click on the Save As button, give your scheme a filename, and then choose OK to return to the Control Panel. The cursors you selected will be in effect from that point on.

Finding animated cursors

If you have Internet access, you can download some cool collections of animated cursors. Microsoft offers a small collection under Accessories at their web site address http://www.microsoft.com/windows/common/aa2724.htm. Windows95.com offers a huge collection of shareware and freeware cursors at http://www.windows95.com/apps/cursors.html.

Files that contain an animated cursor have the extension .ANI. Files that contain a custom, nonanimated cursor have the extension .CUR. Types of files are displayed automatically in the Browse window in the Pointers tab of the Mouse Properties dialog box.

Personalize the Keyboard

You also can customize the way your keyboard operates in Windows 95. Follow the steps under "Customizing the Mouse/Keyboard In a Nutshell" at the start of this chapter to get to the Keyboard Properties dialog box (see Figure 7-4). Then use the options discussed in the sections that follow to fine-tune your keyboard.

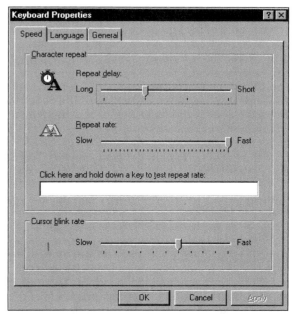

Figure 7-4: The Keyboard Properties dialog box

Tell Windows 95 what keyboard you have

To make sure you get the best performance from your keyboard, first make sure Windows 95 knows what keyboard you're using. Click on the General tab and then look at the Keyboard type setting. If your current keyboard isn't selected, follow these steps:

1. Gather up your original Windows 95 CD-ROM or floppy disks.

   If your keyboard came with a floppy disk of its own, keep that disk handy as well.

2. Click the Change button.

3. Click the Show all devices option.

4. If you see your keyboard listed, click its name and then click OK.

   Alternatively, put the floppy disk that came with the keyboard into a floppy drive and then click on the Have Disk button.

5. Follow any instructions that appear onscreen.

After you select the appropriate keyboard type, you can use the options described in the following sections to fine-tune your keyboard's performance.

Control the keyboard's responsiveness

Most keyboards are *typematic*, which means, if you hold down a key long enough, it starts repeating automatically. If you're a slow typist, you may find you accidentally type the same letter two or more times.

To correct the problem, click on the Speed tab of the Keyboard Properties dialog box. Then drag the slider below Repeat delay to the Long side of the slider bar. Click on the text bar below Click here and hold down a key to test the repeat rate; then hold down any letter key until it starts repeating.

To shorten the delay between the time when you hold down the key and the time when the key starts repeating, drag the slider toward the Short side of the slider bar.

You also can use the Repeat Rate slider bar to determine how fast the key repeats.

Control the cursor blink speed

The Speed tab of the Keyboard Properties dialog box also allows you to specify how fast the cursor (also called the *insertion point*) blinks. Drag the slider to the Slow or Fast end of the bar, and watch the sample blinking cursor. The idea is to find a speed that's in sync with your own cosmic biorhythms or, perhaps, the pace of life in your locale. In San Diego, for example, people probably like slow-blinking cursors; in New York City, they probably like their cursors blinking at full-on, high-anxiety speed (hurry! *hurry!*).

Multiple-language keyboarding

For people who work in multiple languages, Windows 95 offers some significant improvements over Windows 3.x, including the following:

✦ Easy switching from the keyboard layout used in one language to the keyboard layout for another language

✦ Automatic font substitution when switching among different languages (fonts are discussed in Chapter 14)

✦ Correct sorting and comparison rules for different locales and cultures

 You can set the format of dates, times, numbers, and currency values by using the Regional Settings icon in the Control Panel. Look near the end of Chapter 6 for more information.

The following sections examine techniques for installing multiple-language support and using multiple-language keyboard layouts.

Setting keyboard languages and layouts

The first step is to choose specific languages and keyboard layouts appropriate to your work. Follow these steps:

1. Windows 95 may need to install specific languages during this procedure, so first close all open programs and save your work; then gather up your original Windows 95 floppies or CD-ROM.

2. Click the Start button, point to Settings, and then click Control Panel.

3. Double-click the Keyboard icon.

4. Click the Language tab to display the options shown in Figure 7-5.

5. Click the Add button, and choose a language from the drop-down list.

6. Click the OK button, and follow any instructions that appear onscreen.

7. Click the Properties button, and choose a keyboard layout for the currently selected language.

8. Repeat Steps 5-8 to add as many languages as you want.

9. To select a default language, click the language you want and then click on the Set as Default button.

10. You also can choose a shortcut key for switching languages: Left Alt+Shift or Ctrl+Shift.

    Alternatively, choose None for no keyboard shortcut.

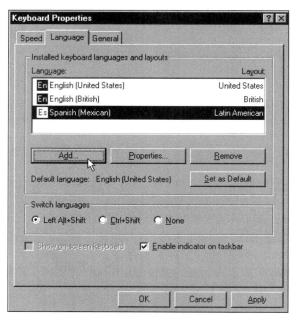

Figure 7-5: Options for selecting keyboard languages and layouts

11. Optionally, you can choose Show onscreen keyboard (if you plan to use a keyboard layout that differs from the physical layout of your keyboard) and Enable indicator on the taskbar (if you want to switch between languages simply by clicking an icon in the taskbar).

12. Choose OK when you finish making your selections.

As usual, if any additional instructions appear onscreen, be certain to read and follow them.

Switching among languages and layouts

After you select one or more foreign languages and layouts, switching among them is easy. If you selected the Enable indicator on taskbar option while you chose layouts, you'll see a two-letter abbreviation at the right end of the taskbar, indicating which language is in use at the moment — for example, you would see En if you're working in English.

To switch to another language and keyboard layout, do either of the following:

✦ Click the language indicator in the taskbar and then click the language you want to use (see Figure 7-6).

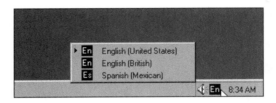

Figure 7-6: Clicking the En indicator to switch to another language

✦ Press the shortcut keys you indicated (for example, Left Alt+Shift) and then choose a language.

Now you can fire up your word processing program and type with the currently selected language and keyboard layout. In fact, you can switch to another language and layout on the spot; anything new you type will use the language, layout, and (if applicable) font for that language. In a true multilingually aware program, you can even move the cursor through existing text to change that text to whatever language and font you're using at the moment.

 Programmers: You can use the Win32 NLS APIs (National Language Support Application Program Interface) to build international-language support into all your Windows 95 and Windows NT applications.

Add and Personalize a Joystick

Joysticks are optional input devices used mainly for playing games. Joysticks range from an inexpensive movable stick with a button on top to elaborate steering-wheel and foot-control gizmos for playing simulation games (such as Microsoft's Flight Simulator). I'm more inclined to use my PCs as slave-labor devices than for entertainment, so I won't claim to be an expert on joysticks. I do know, though, that a joystick is fairly easy to install, use, and fine-tune in Windows 95.

To see a list of Windows 95-supported joysticks *before* you buy a joystick, click the Start button, choose Settings ➪ Control Panel and double-click the Joystick icon to get to the Joystick Properties dialog box. Click on the drop-down arrow under the *Joystick configuration* option, and scroll through the list using the scroll bar or arrow keys. After reviewing the list, choose Cancel to return to the Control Panel without actually installing a joystick.

You install the joystick as you would any other device (see Chapter 10 for instructions). If the joystick is a Windows 95 plug-and-play device, all you have to do is plug it in.

To test and calibrate the joystick, click the Start button, point to Settings, click Control Panel, and then double-click the Joystick icon. If you have several joysticks, select the one you want to calibrate now from the Current Joystick drop-down list.

Next (if you haven't already done so), assign a specific joystick to the option you selected. Click the Joystick Selection down-arrow button, and choose the type of joystick you have installed from the list that appears. The Rudder, Calibrate, and Test options then will be available, as appropriate.

Remember, if you need help with any option, you can click the question-mark button (?) and then click on the option you need help with, or click an option and then press the help key (F1).

Accessibility Options for Physical Impairments

More than half the corporations in the United States employ people whose disabilities can make using a computer difficult. In its never-ending battle to make computers easier for everyone to use, Microsoft included an enhanced version of its Access Pack in Windows 95. The features of the new Access Pack are called the Accessibility Options.

Installing accessibility options

If you've never used the Windows 95 accessibility options, you may need to install them. Use the standard technique for installing missing Windows components. Save any work in progress, and close all open programs. Gather up your original Windows 95 floppy disks or CD-ROM. Then click the Start button, point to Settings, and click Control Panel. Double-click the Add/Remove Programs icon and then click the Windows Setup tab. Click the Accessories option, and click the Details button. Finally, if the Accessibility Options item is *not* checked, select it and then click OK. Follow the instructions on the screen.

More Info For quick online information about accessibility options, click the Start button, click Help, then click the Index tab. Type **accessi** to get to the accessibility topic.

If you have any problems activating the accessibility options later, you may need to restart your PC. Remove any floppy disks, click the Start button, click Shut Down, choose Restart the computer?, and then click Yes. Wait for the Windows 95 desktop to reappear.

Activating accessibility options

When they are installed, you can activate the accessibility options through the Control Panel. Follow these steps:

1. Click the Start button, point to Settings, and then click Control Panel.

2. Double-click the Accessibility Options icon to display the Accessibility Properties dialog box, shown in Figure 7-7.

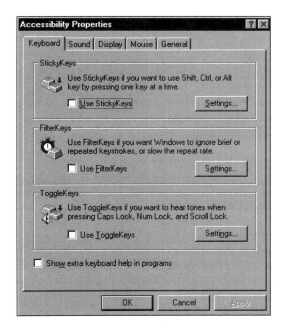

Figure 7-7: The Accessibility Properties dialog box

The following sections describe how to activate and use the various accessibility options. An alternative emergency hot key is available for activating and deactivating each option. Use the hot key if your impairment makes it difficult to get to the Control Panel. For future reference, Table 7-1 shows you how to turn each feature on and off (when the accessibility options are activated) by using the hot keys.

	Table 7-1	
Emergency Hot Keys for Turning Accessibility Options On and Off		
Activated Accessibility Feature	*Emergency Hot Key*	
FilterKeys	Hold down right Shift key for 8 seconds	
High-Contrast Mode	Left Alt + Left Shift + Print Screen	
MouseKeys	Left Alt + Left Shift + Num Lock	
StickyKeys	Press Shift 5 times	
ToggleKeys	Hold down Num Lock for 5 seconds	

 The accessibility options are available even when you're running a DOS program.

Easier mouse/keyboard interaction

Countless physical impairments can make operating the keyboard and mouse difficult. Some of the options for personalizing the mouse and keyboard, described earlier in this chapter, may help. In addition, you can activate options in the Keyboard tab of the Accessibility Properties dialog box, as described in the following sections.

StickyKeys

If you have difficulty pressing two keys at the same time, such as Ctrl+Esc, activate the StickyKeys feature. Choose that option in the Keyboard tab and then click on the Settings button to activate whichever StickyKeys features you want.

For example, you can set StickyKeys so that pressing any modifier key — such as Ctrl, Alt, or Shift — automatically locks down that key. The key stays locked down until you press the second (nonmodifier) key. Optionally, you can make a modified key even stickier, so pressing the key twice in a row keeps it locked down. To unlock the key, press the modifier key a third time.

When the feature is activated, you can turn StickyKeys on and off by tapping the Shift key five times.

FilterKeys

If you are double-pressing keys by holding them down too long or typing extra characters because your finger just brushes nearby keys, use the FilterKeys option to change the sensitivity of the keyboard. After you select the FilterKeys option, use the Settings buttons to specify which features you want to activate.

To turn FilterKeys on and off from the keyboard, hold down the Shift key on the right side of the keyboard for eight seconds.

ToggleKeys

The ToggleKeys option, when activated, uses high and low tones to tell you when the toggle keys Caps Lock, Scroll Lock, and Num Lock are on or off. To turn ToggleKeys on and off from the keyboard, hold down the Num Lock key for five seconds.

MouseKeys

If you want to control the mouse pointer from the numeric keypad, click on the Mouse tab of the Accessibility Properties dialog box and then activate Use MouseKeys. Click the Settings button to specify how you want to implement MouseKeys. For example, you can have the keys in the numeric keypad operate the mouse when the Num Lock key is on or when it's off.

When MouseKeys is activated, you can control the mouse as follows:

✦ *Move the mouse pointer.* Press (or hold down) the keys surrounding the number 5 in the numeric keypad.

✦ *Click.* Press the 5 key in the middle of the numeric keypad.

✦ *Double-click.* Press the plus-sign (+) key in the numeric keypad.

✦ *Drag (left mouse button).* Point to the object, press the Insert key to begin dragging, use the number keys to move the mouse pointer, and then press Delete to complete the operation.

✦ *Right-click.* To right-click, position the mouse pointer, and then press and release the minus-sign (-) key or the 5 key in the numeric keypad.

✦ *Right-drag.* To right-drag, point to the object you want to drag, press the minus-sign (-) key in the numeric keypad, and then press the Insert key to lock down that button. Use the arrow keys to drag; then press the Delete key to complete the drag.

✦ *Click both mouse buttons.* To click both mouse buttons, press and release the asterisk (*) key in the numeric keypad.

✦ *Jump the mouse pointer* in large increments across the screen. Hold down the Ctrl key while pressing a direction key in the numeric keypad.

✦ *Slow the movement of the mouse pointer* (as when you need to position it precisely). Hold down the Shift key as you move the mouse pointer with the numeric keypad.

Hot Stuff
Even if you're not physically impaired, you may find MouseKeys a handy option, especially if you need to position the mouse precisely in your work. It's easier to do that with the numeric keypad than with the mouse.

To turn MouseKeys on and off from the keyboard, hold down the left Alt key, hold down the left Shift key, and then hold down the Num Lock key.

Visual enhancements

If you have any difficulty seeing the screen, or if you find your eyes fatigue quickly, the first thing to do is adjust the knobs on the monitor and personalize the screen display, as discussed in Chapter 6. If your vision is impaired, you may want to select one of the predefined high-contrast color schemes, which are available when you follow the procedure in "Choosing a color scheme" in Chapter 6.

If your vision is impaired and you share a computer with another user, you may find it difficult to read the screen when that user leaves his or her settings behind. In such a case, you can set up some emergency hot keys to take you straight to high-contrast mode as soon as you sit down at the keyboard.

To activate the quick switch to high-contrast mode, display the Accessibility Properties dialog box (Start ⇨ Settings ⇨ Control Panel and double-click Accessibility Options). Click the Display tab, and choose Use High Contrast. Click the Settings button to select a scheme: Black on White, White on Black, or Custom (to choose a different color scheme). Make sure the check box for the emergency hot key is checked.

When this feature is activated, you can hold down the Alt key, hold down the left Shift key, and press the Print Screen key to turn high-contrast mode on and off.

Sound enhancements

Windows 95 offers visual cues as alternatives to the audio cues that alert the user to some condition. You can activate the sound enhancements by displaying the Accessibility Properties dialog box and clicking on the Sound tab (see Figure 7-8). Then you can activate either or both of the features provided.

If you activate the SoundSentry, you can choose the Settings button to assign visual cues to the warning beep that Windows 95 emits to call attention to the screen. When you activate ShowSounds, you actually activate the closed-captioned capability offered in many modern programs that offer speech or other audible cues.

Alternative input devices

Windows 95 also provides built-in support for alternative input devices, including eye-gaze systems and head pointers. Typically, you can plug any such device into any available serial port; you don't need to disconnect the mouse first.

To give an alternate input device its own serial port, install the device according to the manufacturer's instructions and then click the General tab in the Accessibility Properties dialog box. Turn on the Support SerialKeys devices feature, and use the Settings button to assign the device into which the serial port is plugged.

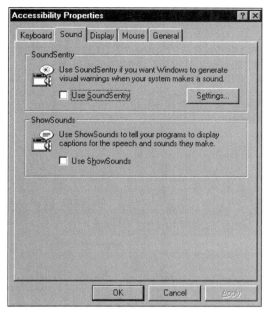

Figure 7-8: Accessibility options for hearing impairments

Accessibility time-out and status indicator

If disabled and nondisabled users share a PC, you may want to activate the time-out feature and status indicator. The time-out feature turns off the accessibility features and returns to the regular settings after the PC has been idle for a specified period.

The Accessibility Indicator lets all users see when the accessibility features are active and (optionally) can provide audio feedback when a feature is turned on or off. The indicator also tells MouseKeys and StickyKeys users when a key or mouse button is locked down.

To activate either of these options, click on the General tab of the Accessibility Properties dialog box. Then choose the options you want to use and the idle time (if any) for turning off the accessibility options.

Summary

All the techniques for personalizing your mouse, keyboard, joystick, and accessibility options are in the Control Panel. Here's a quick summary of the exact steps required to personalize each device:

✦ To personalize your mouse, click the Start button, choose Settings ➪ Control Panel, and double-click the Mouse icon.

✦ To personalize your keyboard, click the Start button, choose Settings ➪ Control Panel, and double-click the Keyboard icon.

✦ To personalize your joystick, click the Start button, choose Settings ➪ Control Panel, and double-click the Joystick icon.

✦ To activate accessibility options, click the Start button, choose Settings ➪ Control Panel, and double-click the Accessibility Options icon.

✦   ✦   ✦

Organizing Your Virtual Office

Earlier in the book, I said you can think of your computer's hard disk as being an electronic file cabinet where you keep everything in the computer. The screen is like your desktop, where you put the stuff you're working on at the moment. In a sense, every PC is like a small virtual office with a file cabinet and a desktop. And as in a real office, the better you organize those things in the virtual office, the easier you can find them.

Why Folders?

I'll talk first about file cabinets. Imagine a real file cabinet filled with documents (on paper), but no folders — just sheet after sheet of paper. What a pain trying to find a particular document would be.

Folders on a disk serve exactly the same purpose as folders in a file cabinet: to organize stuff so you can easily find it later. If you had no folders on your hard disk, you'd continually be digging through hundreds, maybe thousands of documents trying to locate whatever document you need.

Undoubtedly, your hard disk already is organized into folders; when you install a new program, the installation procedure (usually) creates one or more folders to put that program's files in. If you have Microsoft Word, for example, all the files that make up that program are stored together in a folder named (usually) WinWord.

Before I discuss creating and managing folders, I want to point out that, in general, it's *not* a good idea to move or rename any of the folders created by a program's installation procedure. Doing so usually is more trouble than it's worth.

First, the Windows 95 Registry keeps track of where various folders and files are, so when you start moving registered things around, you run the risk of fouling up the Registry.

Second, any shortcuts you create will continue to point to the original folder. The shortcut won't work anymore, because the folder it expects to find no longer exists. Older Windows 3.x programs become problematic, because they often put folder (directory) information in several places: initialization (INI) files, and perhaps in the DOS startup files C:\CONFIG.SYS and C:\AUTOEXEC.BAT.

To illustrate why it's not good to mess with the names or locations of a program's folders, let me tell you about two examples from my own experience. Of course, I'll tell you how I fixed the problems I'd created for myself.

Folder problem 1

One day, I was browsing around my hard disk and came across a folder named Waol15. I couldn't remember what was in the oddly-named folder. I did a little exploring and discovered it contained the programs I use to interact with America Online (an online information service). Thinking myself clever, I renamed the folder America Online so I wouldn't forget its contents in the future.

Whoops — that wasn't a good move. The next time I tried to use America Online, I had nothing but problems from the get-go — not because of anything that was wrong with America Online's program, but because I had renamed its folder. My America Online program still expected to find things in a folder named Waol15 (the C:\WAOL15 directory, in DOS terminology). But because I'd renamed that folder, I had no folder named Waol15 anymore.

Fixing the problem was simple, once I realized what was wrong. I changed the name of the America Online folder back to Waol15, and all was well again.

Folder problem 2

Another time, I moved a folder from its current location to a new location in a different folder. I'd made a slightly different mistake, but one that had the same unpleasant results.

Here's what happened:

I had installed Microsoft Access 2, and its installation procedure had put all the programs for Access in a folder named Access (C:\ACCESS, in DOS terminology). Later, I installed Microsoft Office. The installation procedure for Office created a folder named MSOffice; it also created two subfolders inside the MSOffice folder.

One of these subfolders was named WinWord (C:\MSOFFICE\WINWORD, in DOS terminology); Office used that folder to store Microsoft Word. The second subfolder, named Excel (C:\MSOFFICE\EXCEL), was where Office stored Microsoft Excel.

Then it dawned on me: Because Access is part of the Microsoft Office suite, I could move Access's folder into the MSOffice folder. So without much forethought, I dragged the Access folder into the MSOffice folder. Not smart. The next time I launched Microsoft Access, I immediately started having problems. As in the preceding example, when the Access program needed something from the disk, it went looking for a folder named C:\ACCESS.

You may think, "Yeah, but you didn't change the name of that folder." True. But by moving the folder, I automatically changed its name as well. In this case, I'd changed the name of the Access folder from C:\ACCESS to C:\MSOFFICE\ACCESS (looking at the names from a DOS perspective). Those names are not the same. So whenever Access needed something from C:\ACCESS, it would bomb.

Once again, the cure was simply to drag Access's directory back to its original location.

The moral of these stories is: When a program gets situated on your hard disk, it's best not to move or rename any of the folders. It's better to live with whatever organization and names the installation programs have created — even if they are the yucky old eight-character DOS names.

Why Create Folders?

After boring you to tears with stories of stupid things I've done, why would I tell you how to create (and manage) folders? Answer: Even though you don't want to mess with the folders your installation programs create, there are plenty of good reasons for creating folders to manage your document files, just as plenty of good reasons exist for managing your paper documents in folders in a file cabinet.

If I can provide a few more real-world examples, I think you'll see why folders are a good thing when it comes to organizing your documents.

As an author, I usually have a few projects going: a main project, some backburner projects in the idea stage, and perhaps some books still in production, which need occasional last-minute checks and changes.

To organize these various projects, I always keep a folder named Projects. Within that folder, I keep a subfolder for each project I'm working on. For example, right now my Projects folder contains a subfolder named Windows 95 Bible. That folder holds every file I created for this book. Another subfolder within Projects is called Susans Stuff. That subfolder contains some programs I've been creating for my wife.

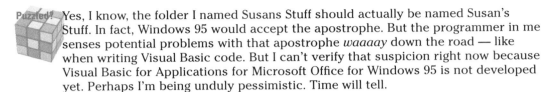 Yes, I know, the folder I named Susans Stuff should actually be named Susan's Stuff. In fact, Windows 95 would accept the apostrophe. But the programmer in me senses potential problems with that apostrophe *waaaay* down the road — like when writing Visual Basic code. But I can't verify that suspicion right now because Visual Basic for Applications for Microsoft Office for Windows 95 is not developed yet. Perhaps I'm being unduly pessimistic. Time will tell.

Figure 8-1 shows my Projects folder open on the desktop, with subfolders for all my ongoing projects (in their various stages of disarray).

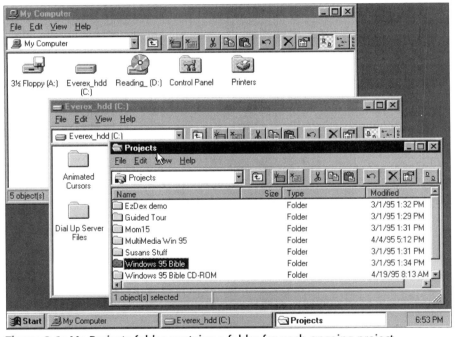

Figure 8-1: My Projects folder contains a folder for each ongoing project.

The beauty of this organization is when I need to open a document for any ongoing project, I just open the Projects folder and then double-click the appropriate project name to see all the documents associated with that project. When I find the document I'm looking for, I double-click it. No muss, no fuss, no trying to remember where things are or what program I used to create them.

When I start a new project, I always go right to the Projects folder and create a new subfolder for that project. Then it's just a matter of remembering to put each new document I create for the project in the appropriate folder so I can find it later, when I need it.

When I finish a project and don't need immediate access to its documents anymore, I move its subfolder to some obscure place on the disk. Eventually, I may reclaim all the disk space the folder is hogging by moving that folder to tape or some other storage medium.

Here's another example. I keep a folder named Clip Art that contains thousands of little pieces of royalty-free art. Within the Clip Art folder, I've categorized the files by theme. The Animals subfolder (see Figure 8-2), for example, contains picture of animals. The Business and Travel subfolder contains art related to business and travel, and so on, for the other subfolders.

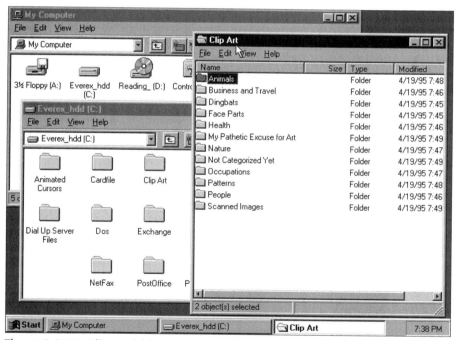

Figure 8-2: My Clip Art folder contains subfolders of art clips organized by theme.

More Info In case you're unfamiliar with publishing, *clip art* is small "filler" pieces of art you can put in newsletters, brochures, and other publications. Chapter 14 discusses clip art.

Whenever I need a piece of clip art, I know I can always start my search simply by opening the folder named Clip Art — a plain, simple, efficient process.

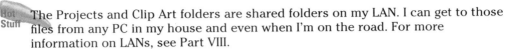

The Projects and Clip Art folders are shared folders on my LAN. I can get to those files from any PC in my house and even when I'm on the road. For more information on LANs, see Part VIII.

How to Create a Folder

After this preamble, you may think creating a folder is a big hassle. Not true — in fact, creating a folder is easy. The purpose of the preamble was just to give you some food for thought about how you might want to organize your own folders, as well as some tips on when not to mess with folders. You can create a folder with whichever browsing tool you prefer: My Computer or Windows Explorer.

Create a new folder with My Computer

To create a folder with My Computer, follow these steps:

1. Open (double-click) the My Computer icon.

2. Double-click the icon for the drive on which you plan to put the folder (usually hard disk drive C).

3. If (and *only* if) you want to put this new folder inside an existing folder, open (double-click) the folder in which you want to put the new one.

   You can repeat this step to drill down as far as necessary to get to the folder that will contain the new folder.

4. You may want to switch to Large Icons view to make it easier to see what you're doing.

   To do so, click the Large Icons button in the toolbar or choose View ➪ Large Icons.

5. Choose File ➪ New ➪ Folder.

   A folder titled New Folder appears, as shown in Figure 8-3. The insertion point is positioned for you to type a new name.

6. Type a name for this new folder.

7. To save the new folder, click some icon other than the new folder's icon.

If you want to move the folder to its proper alphabetical position within the current window, choose View ➪ Arrange Icons ➪ by Name. If you don't see the folder right away, try switching to Details view (choose View ➪ Details). Then click the Name button at the top of the first column to put the folders in alphabetical order. The folder icons will be grouped in alphabetical order.

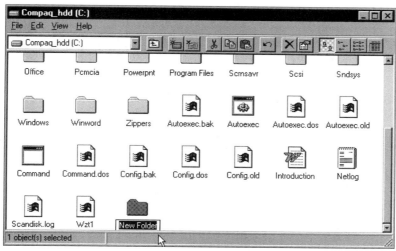

Figure 8-3: A new folder created on my hard drive (C).

Create a new folder with Windows Explorer

If you prefer to use Windows Explorer to browse your hard disk, you can create a folder from the Explorer window. Following is the basic procedure:

1. Click the Start button, point to Programs, and then click Windows Explorer. If you don't see a toolbar, choose View ⇨ Toolbar from Explorer's menu bar.

2. If you want to create the folder on some drive other than the one displayed in the *Go to a different folder* tool in the toolbar, use the drop-down list in that tool to navigate to the appropriate drive (normally A or C).

3. In the left column, click *one level above* where you want to create the new folder.

   If you want the new folder to be at the first level of drive C, for example, click the icon for the C drive. If you want to create a folder within a folder, click the folder that will contain the new folder.

Hot Stuff A subfolder that's inside another folder sometimes is called the *child folder*. The folder that contains the child is called the *parent folder*. To move from a child folder to its parent, you can click the Up One Level button in the toolbar.

4. Choose File ⇨ New ⇨ Folder.

   A new folder titled New Folder appears at the bottom of the list in the right-hand pane, as in the example shown in Figure 8-4. The insertion point is ready for you to type in a new name.

Figure 8-4: A new folder created with Windows Explorer.

5. Type a name for the new folder.

6. To save the folder with its new name, click some other folder or files icon.

If you want to shuffle the new folder into proper alphabetical position in the list, choose View ➪ Arrange Icons ➪ by Name.

Your new folder is just like any other; it's accessible from both the left and right panes of the Explorer window (when you have navigated to a place where you can see the folder). And, of course, it's accessible from My Computer as well.

Managing folders — a quick review

Earlier chapters discussed the many techniques for managing folders and files. Because we're on the subject of folders now, take a moment to review the main techniques, described in the following list:

✦ *To open a folder,* double-click it. If a folder is open but covered by other windows on the desktop, click the hidden folder's taskbar button to bring it to the forefront.

✦ *To close a folder,* click the Close (X) button in its window.

✦ *To rename a folder,* right-click it, choose Rename, and then use standard text-editing techniques to create a new name.

✦ *To move or copy items into a folder,* right-drag the selected objects to the folder's icon or the folder's open window, release the mouse button, and then choose Move Here or Copy Here.

✦ *To move or copy items out of a folder,* open the folder, select the items you want to move or copy, right-drag them to the destination drive and/or folder, release the mouse button, and then choose Move Here or Copy Here.

✦ *To move or copy an entire folder,* navigate to the drive and/or folder that will contain the folder. Then right-drag the folder's icon to that destination, release the mouse button, and then choose Move Here or Copy Here.

✦ *To view the DOS path name for a folder,* open the folder, choose View ⇨ Options, click the View tab, and select the Display the full MS-DOS path name in the title bar option. Then click OK.

✦ *To delete a folder,* click the folder's icon and then press Delete, or right-click the folder's icon and then choose Delete.

Danger Zone Don't forget, when you delete a folder, *you delete all the files and folders inside that folder, including any hidden files.* To bring hidden files into view before you delete a folder, choose View ⇨ Options, click the View tab, and choose Show all files. And remember, only deletions from your local hard disk are sent to the Recycle Bin. You cannot undelete folders deleted from removable media or network drives.

✦ *To create a shortcut to a folder,* drag the folder's icon to the desktop or to the Start button.

Find a lost folder

If you lose track of a folder, you can always look it up with Find. Click the Start button, point to Find, and then click Files or Folders. If you want to search the entire hard disk, make sure the C drive is selected in the Look in list and the Include subfolders option is checked. Type all or part of the folder name, and then choose Find Now.

Hot Stuff As discussed in Chapter 2, you can broaden the search beyond the local hard disk by choosing My Computer in the Look in list. As you'll learn in Part VIII of this book, you can even search other PCs in your local area network (if you're on a LAN).

Remember, Find is every bit as "live" as My Computer and Explorer. That is to say, Find is *not* like the old Windows 3.x, Program Manager that showed only iconic "pointers" to objects on the disk. Rather, Find is more like the Windows 3.x File Manager. If Find locates your folder, you can open the folder on the spot just by double-clicking it. You can even move or copy the folder to a new location just by right-dragging its folder from the Find window to the new location. And if you delete a folder in Find, you delete the folder from the disk as well.

Reorganizing Your Start Menu

The Start button is the easiest way to get documents from your virtual file cabinet onto your virtual desktop: the screen. The better you organize your Start menus, the easier it is to get things to the desktop when you need them. The following sections examine ways to organize your Start menu and its submenus.

Top o' the Start menu

We'll take it from the top. For lack of a better term, I'll refer to the options that appear at the top of the Start menu as being *Start-menu shortcuts*. Figure 8-5 shows two examples: one for opening a fax cover sheet and the other for starting Microsoft Word. As I discussed in Chapter 4, to create a Start-menu shortcut, you drag a program's, folder's, or document's icon right onto the Start button.

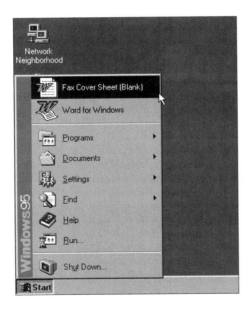

Figure 8-5: Menu shortcuts at the top of the Start menu

Even though you drag things *onto* the Start button to create shortcuts, you can't drag them back out if you change your mind. But changing or deleting those shortcuts is easy, nonetheless. Follow these steps:

1. Right-click the Start button and then choose Open.

   A window titled Start Menu appears. This window contains a program folder named Programs (discussed in the following section).

Also within the window is one shortcut icon for each item at the top of the Start menu. In Figure 8-6, I've opened the Start Menu window. Notice the names of the two shortcut icons inside that window match the options at the top of the Start menu.

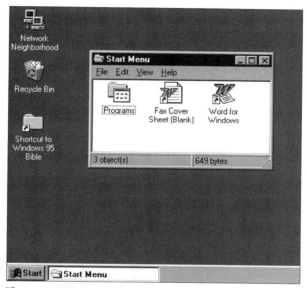

Figure 8-6: Icons in the Start Menu window represent Start-menu shortcuts.

Life Saver Remember, when you're working in the Start Menu window, you're working with shortcuts, as indicated by the little shortcut arrows in the icons. You can move, change, and delete shortcut icons without disturbing the underlying files on disk.

2. Do either of the following things:

- To delete a shortcut, click the icon and then press Delete, or right-click the icon and then choose Delete.

- To change the text of an icon, right-click the icon, choose Rename, and then use standard text-editing techniques to make your changes.

Hot Stuff The longer the name, the wider your Start menu will need to be to display that name. For best results, try to keep the name shorter than 25 characters.

3. Click some other icon after you change or delete an icon, because changes aren't saved until you move to a different icon.

4. When you're happy with your changes, click the Close (X) button in the upper-right corner of the Start Menu window.

To see the effects of your changes, click the Start button and then look at the top of your Start menu. The options in the menu are identical to the names you assigned to icons in the Start Menu window. That was easy, no?

Customizing the Programs menu

The Programs menu is your lead-in from the Start button to program folders and icons. Figure 8-7 shows an example in which you can see options leading from the Programs menu to program folders named Accessories, DTP and Word Processing, Graphic Tools, and so on. Also, some icons at the bottom of the Programs menu lead directly to programs (MS-DOS Prompt, The Microsoft Network, and Windows Explorer).

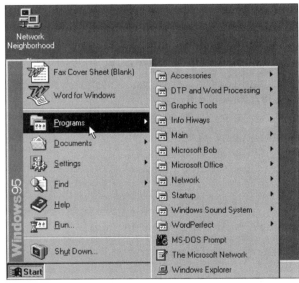

Figure 8-7: A sample Programs menu

You can arrange items in the Programs menu and all its submenus to your liking, as the following sections explain.

Adding folder options to the Programs menu

If you want to add a new program folder to the Programs menu, follow these steps:

1. Right-click the Start button and then choose Open.

2. Double-click the Programs icon.

A window named Programs appears, displaying an icon for each option in the Programs menu. Figure 8-8 shows an example. Compare that figure with Figure 8-7 to see how each icon in the Programs window relates to one option in the Programs menu.

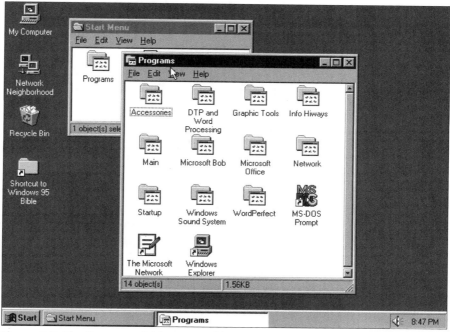

Figure 8-8: The Programs folder opened into a window.

3. To create a new program folder, choose File ➪ New.

4. Click Folder and then type a name.

The name you type is exactly what will appear as the option in the Programs menu, so you may want to keep the name fairly brief (fewer than 25 characters).

5. After typing the new name, click some other icon in the window to save the change.

To verify your work, click the Start button and then point to Programs to see your new folder as a menu item. In Figure 8-9, I just created a new folder named Multimedia Tools. That folder is the last icon in the Programs window. Then I clicked the Start button and pointed to Programs. Already, there's an option in the Programs menu with the same name. (The folder is empty because I just created it.)

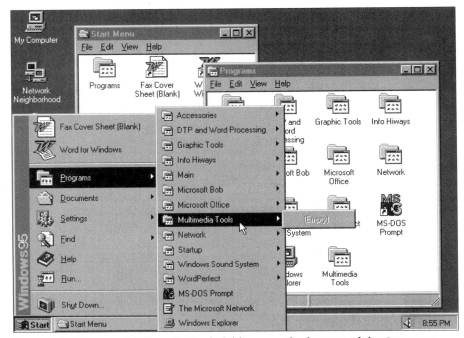

Figure 8-9: The new Multimedia Tools folder, near the bottom of the Programs window and also in the Programs menu.

When you finish adding your new folder, close all the open windows on the desktop by clicking their Close (X) buttons.

To put things in the new submenu, I can go back to the Programs window, open the Multimedia Tools folder, and then choose File ➪ New ➪ Shortcut to create shortcuts within that folder (see the following section).

Adding program options to the Programs menu

In addition to folders, your Programs menu can contain an icon to launch any program on your hard disk. As mentioned earlier, many programs' installation procedures automatically add a program folder and startup icon to the Programs menu. But if you need to create your own startup icon for a program already installed on your hard disk, follow these steps:

1. Right-click the Start button and then choose Open.

2. Double-click the Programs icon.

3. If (and only if) you want to put the icon in the Programs menu, rather than in a program file in that menu, skip to Step 5.

4. If you want to put the program icon in one of the program folders, open that folder by double-clicking its icon.

You can drill down as deep as you want to open a subfolder, sub-subfolder, or whatever.

5. In the current window, choose File ➪ New.

6. Choose Shortcut.

The Shortcut wizard appears. Follow the instructions onscreen to create a shortcut to whatever program you want to launch. The easiest way to do this is to click the Browse button and then navigate to the program's icon.

7. When you get to the last wizard screen, choose the Finish button.

To verify your work, close all open windows, click the Start button, and then point to Programs. If you skipped Step 4, your new shortcut appears in the Programs menu. If you put the icon in one of the program folders, point to the appropriate folder. (Repeat this procedure as necessary if you need to go deeper than one folder.) When you point to the folder containing your program icon, you'll see this icon as an option in the subfolder that appears.

Hot Stuff If you drill down to a folder via My Computer, you can close that window, and all the parent windows with one mouse click. Just hold down the Shift key while you click the Close (X) button of the last window you opened.

Changing the Programs menu

You can move, change, delete, and copy a program folder or program icon anywhere in the Programs menu by following these steps:

1. First, to minimize confusion, I suggest you close all open windows and start with a clean desktop.

2. Be sure you right-click the Start button and choose Open (*don't* try to use any of the other browsing tools, such as My Computer, because they have no effect on the Start button).

3. Double-click the Programs icon.

4. If you want to change an option in a submenu of the Programs menu, open (double-click) the icon representing that submenu.

You can repeat this step to drill down as far as necessary.

5. Now use the following techniques to make changes:

Life Saver Remember, because you started this procedure by right-clicking the Start button, your changes will affect the contents of the Start menu only — not the contents of the disk.

- To delete a menu item, click its icon and then press Delete, or right-click that icon and then choose <u>D</u>elete.

Life Saver If you delete or move an item by accident, or if you change your mind immediately after the fact, choose <u>E</u>dit ⇨ <u>U</u>ndo. To undo a deletion later open the Recycle Bin and look for the item there. The item's original location will be listed in c:\windows\start menu\programs.... Click the icon and then choose <u>F</u>ile ⇨ <u>R</u>estore.

- To rename a menu item, right-click its icon, choose Rena<u>m</u>e, and then type your changes. (Don't forget to click some other icon when you finish, to save your changes.)

- To move or copy an item to a different submenu, right-drag the item's icon to the icon representing that submenu item. Then release the right mouse button, and choose <u>M</u>ove Here or <u>C</u>opy Here.

6. When you finish, close all the open windows.

To verify the effects of your changes, click the Start button, point to <u>P</u>rograms, and explore the submenus.

Other ways to change the Programs menu

I would be remiss in my duty if I didn't tell you this: If you like Windows Explorer more than you like My Computer, you can use an Explorer-type window to make changes in your <u>P</u>rograms menu. To get started, right-click the Start button and choose <u>E</u>xplore. Then double-click the Programs icon in the right pane. You'll see icons for the program folders and icons in the <u>P</u>rograms menu.

You also can use a Find-style window to modify the <u>P</u>rograms menu. Right-click the Start button, and choose <u>F</u>ind. Type all, or part of, the menu option for which you're looking; then click F<u>i</u>nd Now. You move to the icon representing that item in the <u>P</u>rograms menu.

Confused?

You may think there's a similarity between the way you create and manage things in the Start menu and the way you create and manage things on disk. The techniques are exactly the same — which is good, because you don't need to learn new skills to manage options in the <u>P</u>rograms menu.

The downside is: If you don't keep track of where you started browsing, you may find yourself wondering, "Am I changing the Start menu now or am I changing the contents of the disk?" Here are some points to remember to minimize confusion:

✦ When you start browsing from My Computer, Windows Explorer, or Find, you are working directly with the contents of the disk. Anything you do affects the disk directly.

✦ When you start browsing by right-clicking on the Start menu, you are working strictly with the contents of the Start menu. Nothing you do affects the disk directly.

✦ The Programs folder is unique because it's only accessible from the Start button. The only way to modify the contents of the Programs folder is by starting off with a right-click the Start button. To use (not modify) the Programs folder, you click the Start button and choose P̲rograms. The menu that appears *is* the Programs folder, rearranged to look and act like a menu.

✦ If you're uncertain whether an icon represents something on the disk, look closely at that icon. If the icon is a program folder (a folder with a little program window in front) or a shortcut icon (with a little arrow in the lower-left corner, as shown in Figure 8-10), you're safe, because you're not working directly on the disk.

 — Program folder icon

Figure 8-10: Program folder and shortcut icons simply *point* to items on the disk.

 — Sample shortcut icon

To emphasize the last point, remember program, folder, and document icons essentially *are* the objects they represent. When you delete, move, or rename one of these icons, you delete, move, or rename the actual underlying folder or file on disk. Program-folder icons and shortcut icons, on the other hand, are just pointers to items on the disk.

I must confess it took me a while to get all this straight in my head, so don't feel bad if your brain feels a little fried. (My brain feels fried just *talking* about it.) But like anything else, practice makes perfect. Once you get into the habit of right-clicking that Start button whenever you want to make changes to the menu, it becomes second nature to you.

And the real bombshell is...

Now it's time for another confession. I've been saying that when you start a browse session by right-clicking on the Start button, your actions have no effect on the disk. That's virtually true, but with a slight twist. The program folders and icons you work with after a right-click the Start button are actually little files on the disk, but they're separate from all your regular folders and files. These files are lumped together in a subfolder named Start Menu in your Windows folder (c:\windows\start menu, in DOS path terminology).

The reason these files are on the disk at all is this: When you shut down your PC, Windows 95 has no way of remembering how you left your Start menu organized. When you restart your computer, Windows 95 reads the program folders in c:\windows\start menu to reassemble your Start button's menus.

It's important to remember c:\windows\start menu contains only program folders and shortcuts to items elsewhere on the disk. Your actual programs (such as Microsoft Word) are still stored in their real folders, not in the c:\windows\start menu folder.

Whew! Now I just have one more thing — a simple thing — to mention about the Start menu.

Using large or small Start-menu icons

You can choose between large, highly visible icons, or smaller space-saving icons, for your Start menus. Follow these steps:

1. Right-click the taskbar and then choose Properties.
2. Click the Taskbar Options tab.
3. To use smaller icons, select the Show small icons in Start menu check box; to use larger icons, clear that check box.
4. Click the OK button.

This procedure is easy. (Don't ask me why the icon-size option appears in the Taskbar Options tab rather than the Start Menu Programs tab. Perhaps no one at Microsoft noticed.)

Clearing the Documents Menu

As I mentioned earlier, the Documents submenu on the Start menu keeps track of recently saved document files (at least, for programs supporting that capability). So if you need to reopen that document in the near future, you can click the Start button, point to Documents, and then click the name of the document you want to open.

If your Documents menu gets cluttered with files you're not opening often anymore, follow these simple steps to clear the Documents menu and start with a clean slate:

1. Right-click the taskbar and then choose Properties.
2. Click the Start Menu Programs tab.

3. Click the Clear button.

4. Click OK.

That's all there is to that!

Personalizing the Taskbar

The second important tool on your desktop is the taskbar. The following list provides a quick review of the taskbar's purpose:

✦ Every open window has a button in the taskbar. To bring any window to the forefront onscreen, just click its taskbar button.

✦ To close or resize any open window (even one buried in a stack), right-click its taskbar button, and choose the appropriate option from the menu that appears.

✦ To tidy up (arrange) all the open windows, right-click the taskbar proper (not on a button in the taskbar), and then choose Cascade or one of the Tile options. You also can minimize all the windows from that menu.

✦ A little clock usually appears in the taskbar, showing you the current time. Point to the clock to see the current date; double-click the clock to change the current date and time.

✦ Some hardware devices (such as sound cards and printers) display an icon in the taskbar while they are running. Typically, you can click, right-click, or double-click that icon to get more information about — or even to control — the device.

Handy little gadget, that taskbar. The following sections explain some ways you can personalize it.

Size and position the taskbar

Sometimes, the taskbar covers the status bar of a program running at full-screen size. Fortunately, you can fix that problem simply by dragging the taskbar to some other edge of the screen. When you're using a word processing program, for example, you may want to drag the taskbar to the right edge of the screen so you can still see your program's title bar and menu bar (see Figure 8-11).

If you have many windows open, the window buttons in the taskbar can become pretty small. One way around this problem is to point to a taskbar button to see its tooltip. The other solution is to change the size of the taskbar. Place the mouse pointer on the inside edge of the taskbar (the edge closest to the center of the screen) so the pointer becomes a two-headed arrow. Then drag that edge in whatever direction you want to size the taskbar.

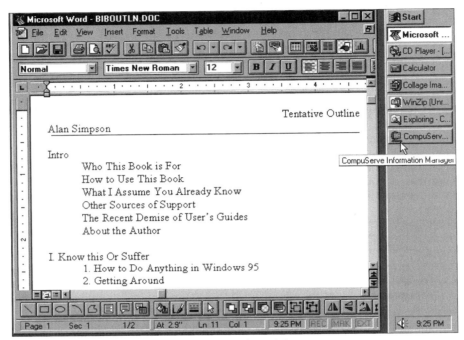

Figure 8-11: Taskbar dragged to the right edge of the screen.

Hide the taskbar

Another way to keep the taskbar out of the way is to hide it until you need it.
Follow these steps:

1. Right-click the taskbar and then choose Properties.

2. Click the Taskbar Options tab.

3. If you select Always on top, the taskbar never will be covered by a window; if
   you clear this option, open windows can cover the taskbar.

4. If you select Auto hide, the taskbar shrinks to a thin line along the edge of
   the screen when it's not in use. To redisplay the taskbar, point to that line. If
   you clear this option, the taskbar never shrinks to a thin line.

5. Choose OK.

If you want some advice, I suggest you leave the Always on top option selected;
there's no good reason to allow other windows to cover the taskbar. If you feel the
taskbar gets in your way, however, select the Auto hide option so it'll be tucked
away but within easy reach.

Show or hide the taskbar clock

I get to end this chapter with something really, really, *really* easy. If you want to get rid of or redisplay the clock in the taskbar, right-click the taskbar and then click Properties. Click the Taskbar Options tab, select or clear the Show Clock option, and then choose OK.

Summary

Windows 95 has lots of great stuff for organizing your desktop. The techniques involved take some getting used to — especially if you're familiar with the Windows 3.x Program Manager, which worked in completely different ways. Here are the main points to remember:

✦ When you want to change the Programs menu, or any submenu that follows it, *always* start off this way: right-click the Start button and choose Open.

✦ When you want to add a new submenu to the Programs menu, right-click the Start button, choose Open, and double-click the Programs icon. Then in the Programs folder that appears choose File ➪ New ➪ Folder and create your folder. Later, when you actually use the Start button, that new folder will become an option on the Programs menu.

✦ You can use the same technique as above to create a deeper-level submenu. Just drill down to where you want to create the folder before you choose File ➪ New ➪ Folder.

✦ To change the size of icons on the Start menu, right-click the taskbar, choose Properties, and then select, or clear, the Show small icons in the Start menu check box.

✦ To clear out the Documents menu, right-click the taskbar, click the Start Menu Programs tab, and click the Clear button.

✦ To customize the taskbar, right-click the taskbar (outside any buttons in the taskbar), and choose Properties.

✦ To size the taskbar, drag its inner edge (the edge nearest the center of the screen).

✦ To move the taskbar, drag the entire taskbar to any edge of the screen.

✦   ✦   ✦

Growth, Maintenance, and General Tweaking

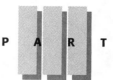

Installing and Removing Programs

Every Windows program, whether it is delivered to you on floppy disks or CD-ROM, comes with its own installation program. Installing the programs usually is a breeze, as you'll see in this chapter. Remember, the techniques described here will work with just about any DOS, Windows 3, Windows NT, or Windows 95 program you purchase. But if you have problems with a particular program or need more information during an installation procedure, you should refer to the installation instructions that came with the program for specifics. I can cover only the general procedures in this chapter.

Installing New Programs

Be aware, in this chapter, I'm talking specifically about installing *programs*. So consider the following guidelines before you begin:

◆ If you are trying to install fonts, you should use the techniques described in Chapter 14, rather than the techniques described in this chapter.

◆ If you are trying to install a driver for a new piece of hardware, use the Add New Hardware wizard discussed in Chapter 10.

◆ If you are trying to copy files, such as other people's documents or clip art, you should use the general copying techniques discussed in Chapter 5.

◆ If you are trying to install a program you downloaded from an online service, you need to follow the instructions that came with the program. Downloaded files usually require you to decompress them before you install them, and no general procedure applies to all downloaded programs. See Chapter 27 for more information.

So now, assuming you are indeed trying to install a program, you can use either the Add/Remove Programs wizard or the Run command. I suggest you try the wizard first.

Using the installation wizard

The Add/Remove Programs wizard makes installing new programs a cinch. To use the wizard, follow these steps:

1. Gather up the floppy disks or CD-ROM for the program you want to install.

2. Click the Start button, point to Settings, and then click Control Panel.

3. Double-click the Add/Remove Programs icon. The wizard starts up.

4. Click the Install button.

5. As instructed onscreen, insert the installation floppy disk in a floppy disk drive or put the CD-ROM in the CD-ROM drive.

Hot Stuff To make things quick and easy, empty or open the drives you're *not* going to use during installation.

6. Click the Next button.

The wizard searches the floppy and CD-ROM drives for a SETUP.EXE or similarly named file. If it finds such a file, the wizard displays the program, as shown in Figure 9-1.

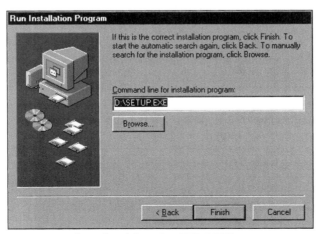

Figure 9-1: The wizard found a SETUP.EXE program on my CD-ROM drive (D).

7. If you're trying to run a setup program in a particular folder on the CD-ROM or floppy disk, click the Browse button and then navigate to that folder.

Life Saver If the wizard can't find a setup program, refer to "Programs that have no setup" later in this chapter.

8. Click the Finish button to launch the setup program.

Now you need to follow whatever instructions appear on the screen. I can't help you much with this part, because Windows 95 is out of the picture now. The setup program you ran is in control. Do pay attention to *where* the installation program plans to put the installed program, though, so you can find it later.

Be sure to complete all the installation instructions onscreen until you see a message indicating the installation was completed successfully. If you installed from floppy disks, remove the last floppy from the drive and put the floppies in a safe place for use as backups. If the screen tells you to restart the computer before trying to run the program, click on the Restart button (if any) onscreen. If no Restart button appears, get to the desktop, and choose Shut Down from the Start menu to shut down and restart your PC.

Using Run to install a program

The installation instructions for a Windows 3.x or DOS program probably will tell you to start by choosing File ➪ Run from Program Manager. Windows 95 has no Program Manager, of course, but you still can follow the program's installation instructions by making a detour to the Run dialog box, as follows:

1. Click the Start button.

2. Choose Run from the Start menu to get to the dialog box shown in Figure 9-2.

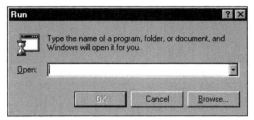

Figure 9-2: Click Run in the Start menu to get to this dialog box.

Now follow the instructions from your program, starting with the part that tells you what to type (for example, **a:\setup.exe** or **a:\install.exe**). If you have any problems, see the following section for suggestions.

Be sure to follow all the installation instructions until you see a message indicating the program was installed successfully. If the program requires you to restart Windows, click the Restart button (if available), or get back to the desktop and choose Sh_u_t Down from the Start menu to shut down and restart the PC.

Programs that have no setup

If the wizard or _R_un doesn't find a setup or install program — or finds the wrong one — don't panic. Just choose Cancel from the error message (then choose Cancel from the wizard window, if you're using the wizard.) Then try the following procedures:

✦ Empty or open all the drives _except_ the one from which you are installing the program, and make sure the installation disk is fully inserted into the appropriate drive. Then try again, using the Add/Remove Programs wizard.

✦ Check the program's documentation for the name of the program you need to run to start the installation. That program may not be named setup or install. When you find the name of the installation program, choose _R_un from the Start menu to run that specific program.

✦ If you are trying to run a setup or install program in a particular folder on the CD-ROM or floppy disk, you still can use either the wizard or _R_un. Either way, you'll get to a dialog box that offers a B_r_owse button. For example, you can click the Start button, click _R_un, and you'll come to a dialog box with a B_r_owse button in it. Click that B_r_owse button, and then navigate to the appropriate folder before you proceed.

✦ If you're having problems installing a DOS program, the Troubleshooter can help you. Click the Start button; then click on _H_elp. Click on the Contents tab; then double-click the Troubleshooting book. Double-click If you have trouble running MS-DOS programs; then choose I can't install the program.

✦ Review the list under "Installing New Programs" at the start of this chapter, and think about what type of files you're trying to install to your hard disk. Then proceed to the appropriate chapter.

Running the installed program

When a program is installed, you can use the following standard techniques to run it at any time:

1. Click the Start button and then point to _P_rograms.

2. Point to the program's folder (group) icon until you find the startup icon for the program.

3. Click the program's startup icon.

Consumer software alert

Consumer software for the home — including games, "edutainment" programs, and multimedia titles — is notoriously difficult to install and/or run. Some programs assume you're using a 256-color monitor and a 16-bit sound card. DOS-based programs assume you have plenty of conventional memory to spare. Those are big assumptions, of course, and plenty of home PCs don't measure up to the required specifications.

Sometimes, the problem is easy to fix. If the program complains you don't have a 256-color monitor, for example, you may need to activate that capability of your monitor

(refer to Chapter 6). Alternatively, you may be able to free some conventional memory. For help with that procedure, click on the Start button, click on Help, click on the Contents tab, double-click on the Troubleshooting book, and then explore the *If you run out of memory* and *If you have trouble running MS-DOS programs* topics. You also can examine your available hardware by using the Device Manager (see Chapter 10).

If all else fails, you may need to contact the manufacturer of the program. Or check out Michael Goodwin's *Making Multimedia Work*, also published by IDG Books.

If you can't find the program's startup icon, you can use My Computer, Windows Explorer, or Find (refer to Chapter 2) to locate the program's startup icon. When you do, just double-click that icon to launch the program. You also can create a shortcut to the program, as discussed in Chapters 4 and 8.

Installing Missing Windows Components

When you installed Windows 95 on your PC, the installation procedure made some decisions about which components to install and which not to install. You're not stuck with those decisions, however. If you can't seem to find one of the programs that supposedly comes with Windows 95, you can follow these instructions to install that program:

 If you purchased a computer that came with Windows 95 preinstalled, you might not need to bother with gathering up the floppies or CD-ROM. Many such machines can install missing Windows components right from your internal hard disk.

1. Gather up your original Windows 95 floppy disks or CD-ROM.

2. Click the Start button and then point to Settings.

3. Click Control Panel.

4. Double-click Add/Remove Programs.

5. Click the Windows Setup tab to get to the dialog box shown in Figure 9-3.

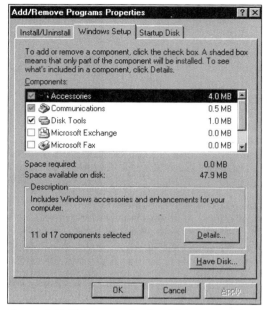

Figure 9-3: This property sheet lets you add and remove Windows 95 components.

Danger Zone Any component in the Windows Setup tab with a check mark is installed already. A check box that is both checked, and grayed, indicates some (but not all) of the components in that category are installed. (The Details button lets you see which are and which aren't.) Do not clear any check marks unless you're absolutely sure you want to remove those components.

6. Scroll through the list of available components; if you see the component you want to install, skip to Step 10.

7. If you don't see the component you want to install, check the component's details (that is, click any component, such as Accessories) and then click the Details button.

8. If you still don't see the component you want to install, click Cancel and then try a different component (for example, Communications).

9. Repeat Steps 7 and 8 until you find the component you want to install.

10. Click the component you want to install, so its check box is checked.

11. When you've finished choosing components, click OK to leave the Details box (if you're in it). Then click OK to close the Add/Remove Programs Properties dialog box. Then follow any instructions onscreen to install the component(s).

Things should go smoothly now. If the installation procedure looks for the components in the wrong place (for example, it looks for a floppy disk in drive A rather than for the CD-ROM in drive D), you can click the Browse button and navigate to the appropriate drive to begin the installation.

Removing Installed Programs

You may want to remove an installed program for many reasons. Maybe you decided you don't like the program and want to free the disk space it's using. Or perhaps you bought a competing program from a different vendor and now you need to make some room on the disk to install that program.

As a general rule, when you upgrade to a new version of an existing program, you do *not* want to uninstall the earlier version first. The upgrade program will expect the earlier version to be installed; it may even require that version to be installed. If you're in doubt, check the program's upgrade instructions.

Regardless of your motivation for removing a program, you need to exercise some caution. Deleting a program and its folder can have peculiar side effects on files *expecting* that folder and/or program to still be there, especially if you used the Delete key to delete the program's folder. A better practice is to uninstall (remove) the program formally, if possible, to prevent side effects.

Save your work first

Before you remove a program, stop to think about any documents you may have created and saved within that program's folder. If you're deleting Microsoft Word for Windows, for example, did you ever create and save documents in the c:\winword folder or in a subfolder, such as c:\winword\documents? If so, are you sure you want to delete those documents?

If the answer to the last question is no, create a new folder outside the program's folder (refer to Chapter 8); then move the documents you want to save to the new folder (refer to Chapter 5). Otherwise, when you delete the program's folder, you also delete any documents in that program's folder and subfolders.

Uninstalling with the Add/Remove Programs wizard

Most Windows 95-aware programs register themselves as programs that can be removed automatically. You should always try the following method of removing a program before resorting to one of the other methods:

1. Click the Start button and then point to Settings.

2. Click Control Panel.

3. Double-click Add/Remove Programs.

4. Click the Install/Uninstall tab.

5. If the program you want to remove appears in the list, click on that program's name; click the Remove button; and follow any instructions that appear on the screen.

If, in Step 5, you don't see the program you want to remove, check to see whether it's listed as a Windows component. Click on the Windows Setup tab; locate the component you want to remove, using the Details button if necessary; clear the check box for that component. Then choose OK and follow the instructions on the screen.

Uninstalling with setup.exe

If the Add/Remove Programs wizard doesn't find the program you want to remove, try the following method:

1. Click the Cancel button, if necessary, to return to the Control Panel.

2. Close the Control Panel to return to the desktop.

3. If the program you want to remove is open, close it.

4. Click the Start button, click Programs, and then find the folder for the program you want to remove.

5. Look for a Setup icon for the program you want to remove.

   In Figure 9-4, for example, I've located the Setup icon for Microsoft Office.

6. Open that setup program, and look for options that let you remove (or uninstall) programs.

   In Figure 9-5, I've found options that let me Add/Remove individual programs, as well as an option that lets me Remove All programs in Microsoft Office.

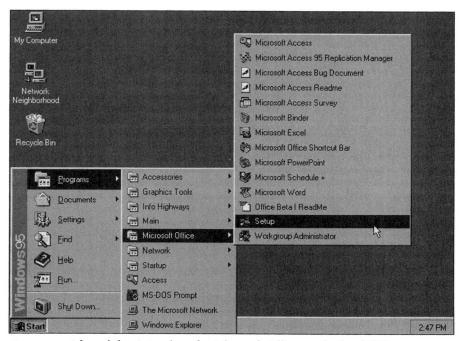

Figure 9-4: I found the Setup icon for Microsoft Office on the hard disk.

Figure 9-5: Microsoft Office's setup offers a couple of *uninstall* options.

7. From here on, the setup program is in control; follow instructions and choose options as appropriate to that program.

Remember, when Windows 95 moves files to the Recycle Bin, those files continue to take up disk space. The space doesn't become free until you empty the Recycle Bin.

If you can't find a setup program or uninstall option for the program you want to remove, terminate the current installation program and then use the last-resort method described in the following section.

If all else fails

If you can't find an uninstall option for the program you want to remove, you'll need to remove the program by deleting its folder. First, move anything you want to keep outside the program's folder and subfolders. Then you can delete the program's entire folder. Use My Computer, Explorer, or Find to get to that folder; select the folder; and then press Delete.

At this point, the deletion is finished, but you have not deleted references to that program. To tidy up and deal with any problems that arise, consider using the following methods:

✦ If you left behind any shortcuts to the program you deleted, browse to and then delete those shortcuts.

✦ If you left behind any Program menu options that lead to the deleted program, delete those options, using the techniques described in Chapter 8.

✦ If you experience problems with the Registry in the future, you may need to modify the Registry manually. For instructions, see Chapter 42.

✦ If you have startup problems in the future, your C:\CONFIG.SYS and C:\AUTOEXEC.BAT files may still contain references to the old program. You need to modify those files.

If you feel uneasy about taking any of the preceding actions, *don't* — there's little margin for error, especially when you're dealing with the Registry and with the CONFIG.SYS and AUTOEXEC.BAT files. I strongly recommend against the "wing it and hope for the best" approach here.

Making an Emergency Startup Disk

Keeping an emergency startup disk around is a good idea; you can use this disk in case some problem with your hard disk prevents you from starting your PC in the normal manner. Chances are you created this startup disk when you installed Windows 95. But if you didn't (or have forgotten where you put it), you can follow these steps to create a new one at any time:

1. Click the Start button and then point to <u>S</u>ettings.

2. Click <u>C</u>ontrol Panel.

3. Double-click Add/Remove Programs.

4. Click the Startup Disk tab.

5. Insert a blank floppy disk (or one containing files you're willing to trash for all eternity) into the floppy drive.

6. Click the <u>C</u>reate Disk button.

7. Follow the instructions onscreen.

Label the disk Windows 95 Startup Disk (or something to that effect); then put it in a safe place where you can find it. It's unlikely you'll ever need the startup disk, but if you do need it, you'll *really* need it.

Hot Stuff In a pinch, you can start your PC with a DOS startup disk. To create a DOS startup disk, type a command such as **a: /s** at the DOS prompt.

Summary

Here's a quick recap of the various ways you can install, and uninstall, programs on your Windows 95 PC:

✦ Click the Start button, choose <u>S</u>ettings ➪ <u>C</u>ontrol Panel. Double-click the Add/Remove Programs icon, click the <u>I</u>nstall button, and follow the directions on the screen.

✦ As an alternative to the above, you can click the Start button, click on <u>R</u>un, then use the B<u>r</u>owse button to locate the setup or install program that you need to run.

✦ To install missing Windows components (programs that come with Windows 95, but are not currently on your hard disk), click the Start button, choose <u>S</u>ettings ➪ <u>C</u>ontrol Panel. Double-click the Add/Remove Programs icon. Then click the Windows Setup tab.

✦ To remove a program from your hard disk, try the Uninstaller first (click the Start button, choose <u>S</u>ettings ➪ <u>C</u>ontrol Panel, double-click the Add/Remove Programs icon). If you see the program you want to remove, click its name and then click the <u>R</u>emove button.

✦   ✦   ✦

Installing New Hardware

First, I'll define my terms. *Hardware* refers to any physical device you plug into your computer — devices that plug in from the outside, as well as boards that must be installed inside the computer. Anything recorded on a disk is *software*. In this chapter, I'm talking specifically about installing hardware.

When to Skip This Chapter

Not all hardware installations require the elaborate procedures described in this chapter. Following are some tips that may simplify the task you're about to undertake:

+ If you're installing a PC Card in a PCMCIA slot, ignore this chapter and go straight to Chapter 19.

+ If you're installing a simple fax/modem (no voice-mail or multimedia sound capabilities), ignore this chapter and go to Chapter 15.

+ If you're installing a printer, plug in the printer, connect it to the PC, and then turn it on. Gather up your original Windows 95 disks or CD-ROM, as well as any disks that came with the printer. Then click the Start button and choose ➪ Settings ➪ Printers. Double-click the Add Printer icon, and follow the instructions onscreen.

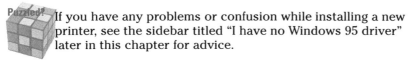
If you have any problems or confusion while installing a new printer, see the sidebar titled "I have no Windows 95 driver" later in this chapter for advice.

+ If you're replacing an existing keyboard, mouse, or monitor, shut down your equipment, remove the old device, plug in the new one, and restart the PC.

Chances are the new device will work fine. To select the new device, use the General tab of the Mouse or Keyboard Properties dialog box or the Settings tab of the Display Properties dialog box. You can use other tabs to fine-tune the device. See Chapters 6 and 7.

About Plug-and-Play

Historically, adding a new device to a PC was a somewhat haphazard ritual, often leading to hours or days of hair-pulling frustration. If, like most people, you don't know about — or care to learn about — such arcane subjects as IRQ lines, SCSI hosts, and DMA channels, those hours or days of frustration could be for naught. You'd give up and take the new device back to the store or put the device on the shelf, hoping time would make it easier to install the device later.

One of the most important new features of Windows 95 is support for plug-and-play devices. The idea behind plug-and-play devices is simple: Adding a new device to your PC should be as easy as plugging a game into a video-game player or hooking a pair of speakers to a stereo system. You just plug the device in and start playing.

A new breed of PCs and optional gadgets has followed Windows 95 to market, supporting the new plug-it-in-and-go concept. Millions of PCs and other devices, however, aren't plug-and-play-compliant. In this chapter, I'll discuss how to install both plug-and-play and *legacy* (nonplug-and-play) devices in your PC.

How to Install a Plug-and-Play Device

First, a word of caution: the term *plug-and-play* has been used for years, and not all products claiming to be plug-and-play truly are, in the sense I'm discussing here. The installation procedure discussed in this section works for devices whose cartons specifically display the "Designed for Windows 95 Plug-and-Play" logo.

To install a true plug-and-play device, follow these steps:

1. If you have any open program windows on your computer, close them.
2. Gather up your original Windows 95 floppy disks or CD-ROM, the device you want to install, and the disks that came with the device.
3. Check the instructions for the new device.

   If the instructions tell you to turn off the power to your PC, close Windows 95 and turn off the power.

4. Install the new device, per the manufacturer's instructions.

5. If you turned the PC off in Step 3, turn it back on.

6. The screen will notify you when Windows 95 detects the new device and probably will ask you to insert a Windows 95 disk or the disk that came with the device. Follow the instructions onscreen until a message indicates you are finished.

You're done. Windows 95 automatically notifies all other devices of the new device, and you should be able to start using that device.

If you need to install programs to use the device, do so now, using the Add/Remove Programs wizard discussed in Chapter 9. Then skip the rest of this chapter.

How to Install Legacy Hardware

The term *legacy hardware* refers to any device that doesn't bear the "Designed for Windows 95 Plug-and-Play" logo. This section discusses devices designed for DOS and Windows 3.x.

The procedure for installing legacy hardware goes something like this:

1. If necessary, use Device Manager to locate available resources for the device.

2. Follow the manufacturer's instructions for installing the device.

3. When you get to the part about installing DOS/Windows 3.x drivers, ignore them; use the Windows 95 Add New Hardware wizard instead.

4. Install any programs *other than drivers* that came with the device.

If you can complete these four steps on your own, great — you can ignore the following sections. If you need more support, read the following sections, which discuss each step in much greater detail. Please remember I cannot provide detailed instructions for installing every conceivable device on the market. Sometimes, you must do a little device-specific tweaking, and only the instruction manual that came with the hardware device can help you.

Step 1: Before you install the device

Before you actually put a hardware device in the PC, you must determine whether the device requires that you choose an interrupt request line (*IRQ*). To find out, browse through the device's instructions. If the device does *not* require you to specify an IRQ, skip to the section titled "Step 2: Put the device in the machine."

Virtual devices versus real-mode drivers

Windows 95 offers a new virtual method of device support unavailable in previous versions of Windows. To understand the advantages, you first must understand that Windows 3.x used real-mode drivers. These drivers were loaded into conventional or upper memory at bootup time via CONFIG.SYS and AUTOEXEC.BAT. The drivers were static, meaning, after they were in memory, you had no way to get them out, short of changing the configuration files and rebooting. Also, only one program at a time could use the device driver.

Windows 95 virtual device drivers offer significant advantages. For one, these drivers are loaded into extended memory, where they don't consume the conventional mem-ory DOS programs need. Also, the virtual drivers are dynamic, meaning they can be loaded and unloaded from memory on an as-needed basis. Finally, the virtual driver allows more than one program at a time to access the device.

Virtual device drivers on the disk can be identified by the .VXD file extension. These drivers are never loaded from CONFIG.SYS or AUTOEXEC.BAT; instead, the drivers are loaded after those two files have been processed. Any device driver included in CONFIG.SYS or AUTOEXEC.BAT is, by definition, a real-mode driver. When given a choice, you always want to use the virtual driver rather than the real-mode driver.

Finding an available IRQ

One of the biggest headaches in using legacy hardware is IRQ conflicts. An IRQ is sort of a voice for the device, telling the computer, "I'm doing something now; pay attention to me." Most PCs have 16 IRQs, numbered 00 to 16. Each device must have its own IRQ. If two devices attempt to share an IRQ, you have what's called an *IRQ conflict,* and neither device will work properly.

An IRQ conflict can have strange effects. Your floppy drive may no longer be able to read perfectly formatted floppy disks, for example, or your speakers may crackle madly as you move the mouse pointer across the screen.

The big problem was some hardware products expected you to specify an available IRQ. But earlier versions of DOS and Windows made it nearly impossible to determine which IRQs were available and which were already being used by some installed device. In some cases, you just had to guess. If your selections didn't work, you had to backtrack, pick another IRQ, and then try that one — on and on until you found one that worked. This situation was not good. (Whenever I hear news stories about some guy going berserk in public, I wonder whether he had been trying to find an IRQ just before the mania set in.)

Anyway, if the device's instructions tell you you're going to have to pick an IRQ at some point, you need not rely on trial and error. Follow these steps instead:

1. Click the Start button and then point to Settings.

2. Click Control Panel.

3. Double-click the System icon.

4. Click the Device Manager tab.

If your printer is already connected and ready to go, click on the Print button near the bottom of the System Properties dialog box, and then choose an option to get a printed summary of your current system settings.

5. Double-click on Computer at the top of the list in Device Manager.

6. Click the Interrupt request (IRQ) option at the top of the Computer Properties dialog box, as shown in Figure 10-1.

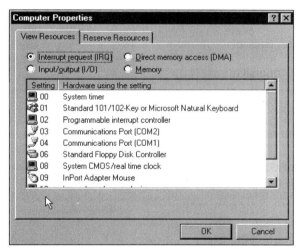

Figure 10-1: A list of used IRQs; any IRQ that's *not* listed is available.

7. Used (unavailable) IRQs are listed in the first column. On a piece of paper, jot down the IRQs that are *not* in the list: Those are available.

   In Figure 10-1, for example, 05 and 07 are missing from the sequence 00, 01, 02, 03, 04, 06, 08, and 09. Therefore, 05 and 07 are the available IRQs you would jot down. You can scroll through the list to see other available IRQs.

8. Although you may not need this information, it can't hurt to write down which DMA channels are in use. Click the Direct memory access (DMA) option, and write down the information you see in the list.

You needn't concern yourself with the other resources — Input/output (I/O) and Memory — unless you are familiar with those concepts and are certain you need that information.

9. After writing down the necessary information, click on Cancel to leave the Computer Properties dialog box. Then click on Cancel again to leave the System Properties dialog box. Close the Control Panel, and then proceed to the following section.

Setting jumpers and switches

The next thing you must determine is whether the board requires you to set jumpers or dip switches manually; check the device's instruction manual to find out. Three possibilities exist, as discussed in the three sections that follow.

If you have a jumperless device

Many modern cards are *jumperless*, which means you don't have to mess with any jumpers or switches on the board. If you have this type of board, skip to the section titled "Step 2: Put the device in the machine."

If your documentation includes written instructions for setting jumpers

If the device has jumpers or dip switches and the instruction manual includes instructions for setting them, follow those instructions now. Make sure you set the switches or jumpers to an available IRQ, and *write down the IRQ you decide to use*. Then skip to "Step 2: Put the device in the machine."

If you need to run a program to set jumpers

Some manufacturers do not provide written instructions on how to set jumpers or dip switches to pick an IRQ. Instead, these manufacturers require you to run a program that determines the best setting for your card; the program shows you, on-screen, exactly how to set the jumpers or switches. Typically, you can run the necessary program from the floppy disk that came with the hardware device. The device's instruction manual will tell you what program to run.

If you can run the program from Windows, insert the disk into a floppy drive, click on the Start button, choose Run, and type the appropriate startup command (for example, **a:\comcheck.exe**). Then press Enter.

If you need to run the program from DOS, click on the Start button, click on Shut Down, choose Restart the computer in MS-DOS mode?, and then click on Yes. When you get to the C prompt, type the command required to run the manufacturer's program (for example, **a:\comcheck.exe**), and then press Enter.

After you set the jumpers or dip switches according to the onscreen instructions, proceed to the following section.

Step 2: Put the device in the machine

Now you are ready to install the new device in (or on) the computer. Shutting down everything before you begin is important, so make sure you carry out this procedure carefully. Follow these steps:

1. Gather up the device you're installing, any disks that came with this device, and your original Windows 95 floppies or CD-ROM.

2. Close any open programs and then shut down Windows, using the Start button and the Shut Down option.

3. When the screen tells you it's safe, turn off the PC and any peripheral devices (for example, monitor, printer, modem, and CD-ROM drive).

4. Connect the device to the PC or install the card inside the PC, per the manufacturer's instructions.

   Just install the device; don't worry about installing any software right now.

5. When you finish connecting the device or installing the card, turn on all the peripherals, including the new device (if it has an on/off switch).

6. Make sure the floppy disk drives are empty.

   If you have a CD-ROM drive, you can put a CD-ROM in it now.

7. Turn on the PC.

If Windows 95 detects the new device as it starts, you go to the Add New Hardware wizard, described in the following section.

Step 3: Install the Windows 95 drivers

You should ignore any instructions for installing DOS/Windows 3.x drivers; the Add New Hardware wizard can install the Windows 95 drivers for you. As mentioned in the preceding section, that wizard may fire up automatically the first time you start the PC after installing the new hardware. If not, you can launch the wizard from the desktop. Follow these steps:

1. Click the Start button and then point to Settings.

2. Click Control Panel.

3. Double-click the Add New Hardware icon.

4. Read the first wizard window and then click Next.

5. In the second wizard window, choose the Automatically detect installed hardware option (see Figure 10-2) and then click Next.

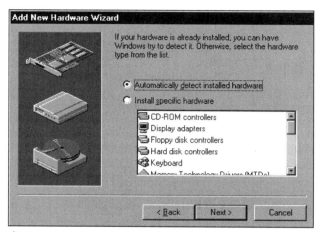

Figure 10-2: The Add New Hardware wizard

6. Follow the instructions that appear onscreen.

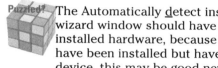 The Automatically detect installed hardware option in the Add New Hardware wizard window should have been called something like Automatically detect *newly* installed hardware, because the wizard concerns itself only with new devices that have been installed but have no drivers yet. If the wizard doesn't detect a new device, this may be good news; it could mean your new device is already installed and working fine.

How the wizard proceeds depends on the device you're installing. For example, if the wizard finds a device, it may install the appropriate drivers from the Windows 95 CD-ROM. If the wizard doesn't find a new device, you'll be given the option to install a specific device. Choose the type of device you're installing and then proceed through the wizard windows.

If Windows 95 has its own driver for the device, the wizard copies that driver from the Windows 95 CD-ROM or displays a message that tells you which floppy disk to insert. Be aware, if Windows 95 does have its own driver, it will never ask you to insert the manufacturer's disk; this is normal and nothing to be alarmed about. Just keep following every instruction that appears onscreen.

After the drivers have been copied to the hard disk, the wizard may ask you to shut down the computer. Again, do exactly what the wizard tells you to do. When the installation is complete and the drivers are installed, you should be able to go right to the Windows 95 desktop without a hitch.

I have no Windows 95 driver

In the worst-case scenario for installing legacy hardware, the device requires a driver, but no Windows 95 driver is available on your Windows 95 disks or on the manufacturer's disk. You may be tempted to try to force the DOS driver or Windows 3.x driver into the system. You can do that, but you won't like the result; most likely, the device won't work, and your whole system will behave strangely.

Your only real alternative is to contact the manufacturer of the device and ask where to get the Windows 95 driver for that device. If you already have access to the Internet and can browse the World Wide Web with Internet Explorer, here are several good sites to check for information on current drivers: Ken's Web Site at `http://www.cris.com/~Kmass` and Frank's Windows95 Driver Request Page at `http://www.conitech.com/windows/drivers.html`.

Step 4: Install nondriver programs

Many hardware devices come with their own programs. A fax/modem, for example, comes with a faxing program; a scanner may come with scanning and touch-up programs. If such programs came with your device, install those programs now, using the techniques described in Chapter 9.

Once again, make sure you install only the extra programs — not the DOS/Windows 3.x drivers.

If you accidentally install DOS/Windows real-mode drivers or need to eliminate old ones, see "Removing a Device" later in this chapter.

If you have any problems with your newly installed hardware, if a device that worked previously doesn't work anymore, or if you can't get Windows 95 started, try the troubleshooting techniques described in the following sections.

Troubleshooting Hardware Conflicts

Hardware conflicts occur when two or more devices try to use the same IRQ, or the same memory range, to get the computer's attention. The symptoms of a hardware conflict might be strange, erratic behavior of a device. Or, in many cases, one of the conflicting devices won't work at all. Fortunately, Windows 95 offers several tools for tracking down and resolving hardware conflicts.

Using the hardware Troubleshooter

If a new hardware device won't work, or if something that worked before has stopped working properly, you have a device conflict. The quickest and easiest way to resolve a conflict is to use the Troubleshooter. Follow these steps:

1. Click the Start button and then click Help.

2. Click the Contents tab.

3. Double-click the Troubleshooting book to open it.

4. Double-click If you have a hardware conflict.

5. Follow the instructions and suggestions onscreen.

As you proceed through the troubleshooting wizard, pay particular attention to any devices whose icons are covered by an exclamation point (!) inside a yellow circle. These devices are conflicting with some other device, and you need to reconfigure them to fix the problem.

If the Troubleshooter doesn't find any conflicts, something else is wrong. Check the manual that came with your new device for specific troubleshooting tips, or try some of the troubleshooting methods described in the following sections.

Getting around startup problems

If starting Windows 95 leads to a slew of error messages, and/or if Windows 95 hangs before you can get to the desktop, you can do many things to get around, diagnose, and fix the problem. Follow these steps:

1. Restart the computer.

2. When you see the Starting Windows 95 message onscreen, press F8.

3. Choose one of the following options:

   • *Normal:* starts Windows 95 in normal mode, as though you hadn't pressed F8.

   • *Logged* (\BOOTLOG.TXT): starts Windows 95 normally, but creates a C:\Windows\Bootlog.txt file containing a transcript of all the events that occurred during startup. Use BOOTLOG.TXT to locate failed startup events.

   • *Safe mode:* starts Windows 95 but bypasses many startup files; loads only the basic system drivers.

If Windows 95 starts with a blank or funky screen, choose Safe Mode to load only the standard VGA driver.

My mouse died

Sometimes, the mouse gets involved in a hardware conflict and stops working. To get to the Troubleshooter without a mouse, press Ctrl+Esc and then type **h** to choose Help. When you're in the Help Topics window, you can press Tab and Shift+Tab to move from one area of the window to another. Within an area, you can press the arrow keys to move from one option to another. When you get to the option you want to use, press Enter to select it. If the option you want to pick has a *hot key* (an underlined letter), you can hold down the Alt key and tap the underlined letter to select the option.

- *Safe mode with network support:* same as Safe mode, but also installs basic networking drivers.

- *Step-by-step confirmation:* lets you step through each command in the startup files so you can identify the commands causing problems.

Life Saver If Windows 95 displays error messages at startup or hangs before it starts, choose Step-by-step confirmation to identify the specific commands causing the problem.

- *Command prompt only:* processes all startup files and starts Windows 95 at the command prompt only. You can enter DOS commands, such as **edit** to change text files or **win** to start the Windows 95 GUI.

- *Safe mode with command prompt only:* same as Safe mode, but doesn't process startup files; loads only the bare-minimum drivers.

If you can't start Windows 95 because of a problem with the hard disk, you can boot from the Windows 95 startup disk, or from any DOS startup disk that has system tracks, in drive A.

Finding all references to a faulty driver

If you discover the problem is with Windows 95's loading a specific driver, you can delete references to that driver from all initialization files. Starting from the Windows 95 desktop, follow these steps:

1. Click the Start button and then click Find.

2. Click Files and Folders.

   In the Look in box, make sure all of drive C is selected; also make sure the Include subfolders option is checked.

3. Click the Advanced tab.

4. Enter the driver name (or some part of it) in the Containing Text box.

   If, for example, a driver named TSBA311.DRV is causing the problem, type **tsba311** as the text to search for.

5. Click Find Now, and wait for Find to locate every file containing the text you typed.

6. To edit a file that Find located, right-click on its icon or name at the bottom of the Find dialog box and then choose Open.

   You especially want to edit any file identified as being the Configuration Settings file type.

7. If you are prompted for a program to open the file with, choose Notepad.

8. Within Notepad, choose Search ➪ Find and press Find Next (F3) to locate and delete all references to the faulty driver.

9. When you finish, choose File ➪ Exit.

10. Repeat Steps 6-8 for each configuration file you want to edit.

11. Shut down and restart Windows 95 to test your changes.

Using Device Manager to resolve conflicts

If your system starts smoothly but you have problems with specific devices, a hardware conflict is the most likely cause. The Troubleshooter, described earlier in this chapter, takes you step by step through the procedure of finding and fixing the problem. Optionally, you can go into Device Manager yourself and change the settings. Follow these steps:

1. Click the Start button and then point to Settings.

2. Click Control Panel.

3. Double-click the System icon.

4. Click the Device Manager tab to get to the dialog box shown in Figure 10-3.

Danger! Edit only what you understand

In some of these troubleshooting procedures, I assume you understand the structure and purpose of initialization (.INI) and similar files (such as C:\CONFIG.SYS and C:\AUTOEXEC.BAT) and that you can use Notepad or DOS's EDIT command to change those files without making a mess of things.

If you are not familiar with those concepts and techniques, I strongly recommend you *not* make changes in those files. Get help from a more experienced user. There's not much margin for error when you are tampering at this depth; even the slightest mistake can make matters worse.

Figure 10-3: The Device Manager tab of the System Properties dialog box

Within Device Manager, you have enormous flexibility to explore — and change — specific settings for every device currently operating in your system. Following are some general guidelines for using Device Manager:

✦ The first items displayed are *classes* of devices. To see the specific devices within a class, click the class's plus button (+).

✦ If a specific device is conflicting with some other device, its icon is marked by an exclamation point within a yellow circle. If a specific device isn't working, its icon is marked by the international *prohibited* symbol.

✦ To view or change a device's properties, double-click on the device's icon or name, use whatever tabs and options are provided in the dialog box to resolve problems, and then click OK.

✦ To update the entire list of installed hardware, click the Refresh button.

✦ To remove a device, click its icon or name and then click the Remove button.

The Hardware Profiles tab of Device Manager is discussed under "Hot Docking and Flexible Configurations" in Chapter 17. The Performance tab is covered in under "Are We Optimized Yet?" in Chapter 12.

✦ To print a summary of the hardware list, click the Print button.

✦ To organize the devices by the way they're connected, click the View devices by connection button.

✦ To view devices by the resources they're using, double-click Computer at the top of the list to get to the Computer Properties dialog box, shown in Figure 10-4; then choose whichever option describes the way you want the list organized.

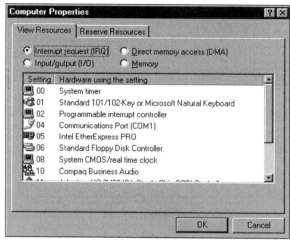

Figure 10-4: The Computer Properties dialog box

✦ For help with anything in Device Manager, click the question-mark button and then click whatever you need help with.

When you are finished with Device Manager, choose OK to close that window. You may need to shut down the PC and restart Windows 95 for your changes to take effect.

Removing a Device

Before you read this section, please be aware I'm discussing only devices you want to remove from your system permanently. You can ignore all this information if you're disconnecting a portable CD-ROM drive, modem, network card, or any other device you plan to plug back in and use later. On the other hand, if you're removing an internal PC card permanently, perhaps with the intention of replacing it with some new card, it's a good idea to remove all the drivers for that card first. Follow these steps:

1. If you have any open program windows on the desktop, close them.

2. Click the Start button and then point to Settings.

3. Click Control Panel.

4. Double-click the System icon.

5. Click the Device Manager tab.

6. Click the type of device you plan to remove.

7. Click the specific device you plan to remove.

Do yourself a favor and jot down any settings for the device you're going to remove, before you remove that device. This way, if you need to reinstall it later, you'll know what settings to choose.

In Figure 10-5, for example, I'm poised to remove the Gameport Joystick device.

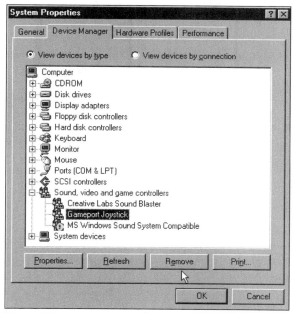

Figure 10-5: Poised to remove the Gameport Joystick virtual device driver

8. Click the Remove button, read the dialog box that appears to make sure you're removing the right device, and then click OK.

9. Repeat Steps 5-7 as necessary to remove all the drivers that support the device you plan to remove.

10. Click the Close button.

If you are instructed to restart your computer, do so. After the computer restarts, you can shut everything down and remove the device from your PC.

If you have any problems when you restart your PC, you may not have removed all the drivers for the device. Repeat the preceding steps, or use Find to find and remove all references to the device, as discussed under "Finding all references to a faulty driver" earlier in the chapter.

More Technical Stuff and Troubleshooting

As I've mentioned, my goal in this book is to empower people to take advantage of what Windows 95 has to offer, not to talk about design philosophy or architectural issues. The topics discussed in this chapter should allow you to install any hardware device successfully. If you encounter problems you can't solve, you can dig around in the online manual for more information.

 To find hardware-related topics and help in the online manual, click on the Start button, click Help, click the Index tab, and search for *hardware*.

If you want more advanced technical information or if you need to go deeper into hardware troubleshooting, you may want to purchase *Windows 95 SECRETS* by Brian Livingston (IDG Books Worldwide, 1995).

Summary

Here are the salient points about installing new hardware:

✦ A new breed of Designed for Windows 95 plug-and-play devices has followed Windows 95 to market. These devices are the easiest to install and use.

✦ Installing legacy (pre-Windows 95) devices is still a bit rough, but not as bad as it was in Windows 3.x.

✦ If a legacy device is going to ask for an available IRQ, you can easily see which are available. Click the Start button and choose Settings ➪ Control Panel. Double-click the System icon, then click the Device Manager tab. Double-click Computer at the top of the list to get to the Computer Properties dialog box. From there you can examine used (taken) IRQ's, I/O addresses, DMA channels, and Memory ranges.

✦ The typical scenario for installing a legacy device is to shut down everything, and install the device (but not the drivers) as per the manufacturer's instructions. Then....

✦ Restart the PC. If Windows doesn't detect the new device at startup automatically, click on the Start button, choose <u>S</u>ettings ⇨ <u>C</u>ontrol Panel, then double-click Add New Hardware to start the Add New Hardware wizard.

✦ If at all possible, use the Windows 95 driver for a legacy device, rather than the original DOS/Windows 3.x drivers. The Add New Hardware wizard will install the correct drivers for you, if they exist.

✦ If you end up with hardware conflicts, use the Troubleshooter to track them down and solve them. Click the Start button, choose <u>H</u>elp, and click the Contents tab. Double-click the Troubleshooting book, then double-click the If you have a hardware conflict topic.

✦   ✦   ✦

Routine Maintenance, General Management

As its title implies, this chapter is about routine maintenance tasks you can perform on a regular basis to keep your hard disk running smoothly and at top speed. For example, this chapter covers ScanDisk, which not only finds and repairs disk errors, but also frees wasted space. In addition, this chapter looks at the Disk Defragmenter, which keeps your disk running at top speed.

Under the topic of general management, the chapter looks at ways to back up your hard disk and to format floppy disks, as well as a tool called user profiles. *User profiles* are great when two or more people share the same PC because each user can have his or her own screen settings, desktop icons, and so on.

Finding and Repairing Disk Errors

The occasional unexpected power loss or fatal error that stops the PC dead in its tracks can leave behind trash on the hard disk, which does nothing but take up space. To keep your hard disk working at top speed, you should run ScanDisk occasionally to clean out the trash. You also can use ScanDisk to search for and repair damaged sections of the disk.

To use ScanDisk, follow these steps:

1. Click the Start button and then choose Programs ➪ Accessories ➪ System Tools.

2. Click ScanDisk to get to the dialog box shown in Figure 11-1.

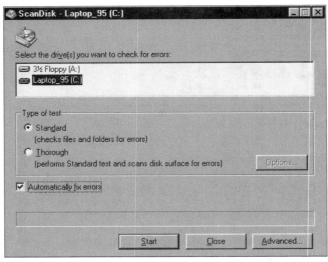

Figure 11-1: The ScanDisk dialog box

3. Click the drive you want to scan (for example, C for your hard disk).

4. If you're only performing routine maintenance, choose Standard, and make certain the Automatically fix errors box is checked.

5. Click the Start button.

6. Follow the instructions onscreen.

ScanDisk may take a few minutes to complete its job. When it finishes, you go to the ScanDisk Results dialog box. Review this information if you want; then click the Close button.

The optional Microsoft Plus! product comes with a program named *System Agent*, which enables you to schedule lengthy routine maintenance tasks. For example, you can have System Agent do a thorough scan of your drive and defragment it on, say, every Wednesday at 2 a.m. while you're sleeping. You'll need to leave the computer turned on, but you can turn off the monitor. See Chapter 39 for more information.

Finding lost files

I've often seen people lose a file and then go straight to ScanDisk to try to find it. These people assume the computer messed up somehow and the missing file is now floating around in lost fragments, which ScanDisk will reassemble into the missing file. But this isn't how it works. When you're looking for something that's missing, ScanDisk should be your *last* resort.

Most of the time, a "lost file" really is just a misplaced file. Perhaps you misspelled the intended filename when you saved the file. Or maybe you didn't specify a particular folder, so the file was saved in some folder other than the one you intended. You may even have inadvertently dragged the file, or its folder, to the Recycle Bin.

Before you assume the PC or hard disk messed up your file, try searching for the file by browsing. Check the Recycle Bin. Also, use Find (refer to Chapter 2) to search the entire hard disk for the missing file and/or for some text within the missing file. Chances are the file is still intact and you were confused about its exact name and/or location.

Remember, too, if you're missing a program that comes with Windows 95, you can use the Windows Setup tab of the Add/Remove Programs wizard (refer to Chapter 9) to reinstall that component.

The preceding procedure is fine for routine (say, weekly) maintenance. If you're having problems with your hard disk, however, you may want to perform a more thorough scan. Follow these steps:

1. Choose Thorough, rather than Standard, in the ScanDisk dialog box.

2. Click the Options button to specify further what you want to do.

3. Clear the Automatically fix errors check box.

4. Optionally, click the Advanced button and make additional choices.

Remember, for more information on any option ScanDisk presents, you can click the question-mark button, and then click the option in question. Or, click the option and then press the Help key (F1). When you're ready to begin the scan, click the Start button.

Keeping the Hard Disk at Top Speed

In time, files on your hard disk become fragmented, a situation that slows disk activity and, in turn, the entire system. To see how files become fragmented, consider an example: Suppose your hard disk is nearly full and you need to delete some stuff to make room for a new program. You drag some old files into the

Recycle Bin and then empty the bin. Now you have room. You don't really know, though, how that extra room is split up on the disk. Some of the files you deleted may have been near the outer edge of the disk, some may have been near the inner edge, and others may have been near the center of the disk. Therefore, you can say the empty space left by those deleted files is *fragmented* in different areas of the disk.

Now suppose you install the new program. Windows has to use whatever space is available, so part of your new program might be near the outside of the disk, part near the middle, and part near the center. Now your *program* is fragmented in different areas of the disk. Technically, this situation isn't a problem. Windows can find all the pieces automatically when it needs them; you won't ever know how fragmented the file has become.

But fragmentation has a downside. As time passes, more files become fragmented, and the drive head has to move more to get things off the disk. From your perspective, opening files and saving your work seem to take longer. If you're near the PC, you may even hear the heavy clickety-clack of the drive head moving frantically about the disk to get to all these fragments.

For best results, delete any unnecessary files, empty the Recycle Bin, and run ScanDisk before you start the disk-defragmentation process.

To get the hard disk back to top speed, you need to *defragment* the disk. The process takes a few minutes, but it's simple. Follow these steps:

1. Click the Start button and then choose Programs ➪ Accessories ➪ System Tools.

2. Click Disk Defragmenter.

3. Click the drive you want to defragment.

4. Choose OK.

Windows 95 first makes a quick pass on the disk to determine how fragmented the files are at the moment. If little fragmentation exists, you'll see a message to that effect, and you'll be given the option to Exit without defragmenting the drive.

Many laptops have a spin-down feature on the hard disk to minimize battery drain. If you're not dependent on batteries at the moment, you can disable that feature to speed operations — dramatically, in most cases. For instructions, see the user's guide for the laptop computer.

If the drive needs defragmenting or if you decide to defragment it anyway, you can click Start. A dialog box appears, keeping you posted on the defragmentation progress (see Figure 11-2). To see what's going on in more detail, click the Show Details button; to return to the smaller progress dialog box, click the Hide Details button.

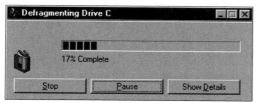

Figure 11-2: The Defragmenting dialog box

Danger Zone As you know, you should always shut down Windows before you turn off your PC, especially when the Disk Defragmenter is running.

You can use your PC normally while Windows is defragmenting your disk. Performance may be a little sluggish, however, because of all the disk activity. If you need to do something at normal speed, click the Pause button in the Defragmenting dialog box. When you finish doing whatever you needed to do, click the Resume button to resume defragmentation.

Backing Up Your Hard Disk

If you have hundreds, or thousands, of hours of work invested in the documents stored on your hard disk, or if the data on that disk is critical to operating your business, you really should keep a backup. I don't want to keep you up at night with worry, but you must remember that fire, flood, a hard disk crash, theft, or incompetence can wipe out those important files in an instant. In such a situation, an ounce of protection is better than tons of cure.

Danger Zone Keep your backups in a safe place off-site. After all, backup tapes and floppy disks also can fall victim to fire, flood, and theft.

Windows 95 comes with a program called Microsoft Backup, which greatly simplifies backing up your hard disk. You can back up to and from most media, including floppy disks, hard disks, removable hard disks, network drives, and tape drives.

Starting Microsoft Backup

The first step in making a backup (or restoring from a backup) is inserting a tape into the tape drive or a disk into the disk drive. Then follow these steps:

1. Click the Start button and then choose Programs ➪ Accessories ➪ System Tools.

2. Click Backup.

Trash the tape unit and get a Zip or Jaz Drive!

Tape backups are slow and laborious; they are quickly being supplanted by inexpensive Zip and Jaz drives. These drives simply plug into the back of the PC (via SCSI or parallel connection), and handle removable media that hold 100 megabytes (Zip) or up to a gigabyte of data (Jaz). Rather than going through this whole tape-backup routine, which can take a long time, you can just drag-and-drop files from your hard disk to a disk in the Zip or Jaz drive. Much simpler, and much faster! See your local computer dealer for information on Jaz and Zip drives.

More Info If Backup isn't available in your System Tools menu, use the Add/Remove Programs wizard to install the disk tools. See "Installing Missing Windows Components" in Chapter 9.

Read and progress through any information windows until you get to the window titled Microsoft Backup (see Figure 11-3).

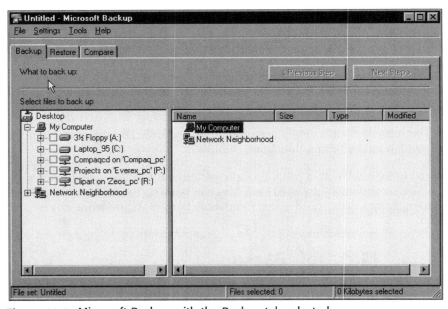

Figure 11-3: Microsoft Backup with the Backup tab selected

Microsoft Backup is its own little application with its own help file, so when you're looking for information on Backup, you should use the Help option in Backup's menu bar. The following sections look at the kinds of tasks you're most likely to do with Backup.

Backing up the entire hard disk

If you want to back up an entire hard disk, you should use anything *but* floppy disks. A tape backup unit may be a bit slow, but it's the most cost-efficient way to back up the hard disk. Regardless of which medium you back up to, you'll follow these steps:

1. In Microsoft Backup, select the Backup tab (if it isn't already selected).

   Notice the message What to back up just below the tabs (refer to Figure 11-3).

2. Click File; then click Open File Set.

3. Click Full System Backup, as shown in Figure 11-4.

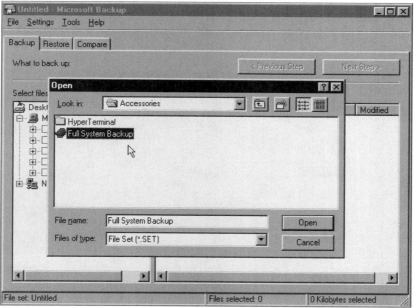

Figure 11-4: Full System Backup selected to back up the entire hard disk

4. Click Open, and wait a few seconds while Backup prepares the Registry and files.

   The name Full System Backup now appears in the title bar.

You can use commands in the Tools menu to format and erase tapes. You also can use the Tools menu to make Windows redetect the tape drive, in case you plugged it in recently.

5. Choose <u>S</u>ettings ⇨ <u>O</u>ptions.

6. Click the Backup tab.

7. Choose the Full backup of all selected files option.

8. Click the Next Step button.

   Notice the message below the tabs now is Where to back up.

9. Click the destination for the backup files.

   In Figure 11-5, for example, I clicked the cassette tape drive icon. That tape's electronic ID label (a long number in this example) is visible onscreen.

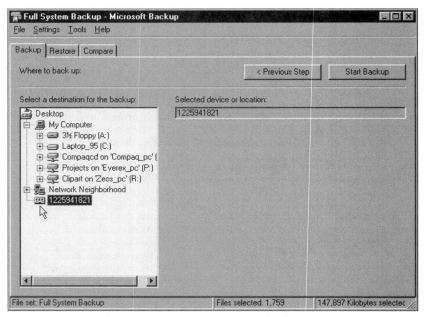

Figure 11-5: I selected the cassette tape icon to back up to.

10. Click the Start Backup button.

11. Follow the instructions onscreen.

You'll be asked to enter a label for the backup set. You can enter a plain English description — perhaps something like **Entire Hard Disk, January 1997**. After the backup process begins, you can go about your normal business on your PC. Operation may be a little sluggish, though, until the backup is complete.

LAN professionals: Windows 95 comes with updated versions of Cheyenne ARCServe agent and Arcada Backup agent for backing up to Windows NT Server and NetWare servers. For more information, search Windows 95 help (not Backup's help) or refer to the *Windows 95 Resource Kit*, published by Microsoft Press.

Backing up new or modified files

It isn't necessary to back up your entire hard disk every time you make a backup. In fact, you can save a great deal of time by backing up only the files you created or changed since the last backup. Follow these steps:

1. Start Microsoft Backup.
2. Click the Backup tab.
3. Choose File ➪ Open File Set ➪ Full System Backup.
4. Click the Open button, and wait a few seconds while Backup prepares to back up the Registry.
5. Choose Settings ➪ Options.
6. Click the Backup tab, and choose the Differential option.
7. Click the OK button.
8. Click Next Step, and select a destination for the backup (for example, the tape-drive icon).
9. Click the Start Backup button.
10. Follow the instructions onscreen.

Using Backup instead of Copy

When you want to copy some files from your hard disk to floppies, you can use Microsoft Backup rather than the Copy method described in Chapter 5. Using Backup has two advantages. For one, Backup compresses files as it copies them, so you can squeeze more onto the floppy. For another, Backup can split a large file across two or more floppies — something you can't do with the Copy method.

You can use DriveSpace (see Chapter 12) to increase the capacity of a floppy from 1.4MB to about 2.5MB.

If you're mailing the floppies to someone else, make sure the recipient has Windows 95, because he or she must use Restore (discussed later in this chapter) in Backup to copy the files you sent on to this person's hard disk. Anyway, here's how you use Backup with floppy disks:

A backup strategy

If backups are essential to your business, it's important to come up with a good strategy for making backups. One method many people use is to back up the entire disk once a week and then to back up only new and modified files for the rest of the week.

To do this on tape, you probably would want to use five separate tapes. If you do your full backup on Friday afternoon, for example, you could label that tape Friday: Full Backup. Label the other tapes Monday, Tuesday, and so on. On Monday through Thursday, you do a differential backup to the tape for that day; on Friday, you do a complete backup to the appropriate tape. Thereafter, if a major disk crash occurs, you can restore first from the Friday: Full Backup tape and then restore from the Monday, Tuesday, and other tapes up to the day of the most recent backup.

One disadvantage of this approach is if you need to restore a single file, you need to search all the tapes for the latest version of that file. Still, this procedure is faster than backing up the entire hard disk every day.

1. Start Microsoft Backup.

2. Click the Backup tab.

   You see the What to back up message.

3. Use either of the following methods to select the specific files and folders to browse:

   - Use the plus symbols (+) in the left pane to browse to the folder you want to back up, and then select that folder's check box.

     In Figure 11-6, for example, I'm about to back up a folder named Windows 95 Bible. You can select multiple folders, if you want.

   - Choose Settings ⇨ File Filtering to specify files to back up by date modified and type.

4. Optionally, you can use the right pane of the Backup window to clear the check marks next to files and subfolders you *don't* want to back up.

Hot Stuff The status bar shows you how much stuff is currently selected. In Figure 11-6, I've selected 6,585 kilobytes of data. That comes out to about 6.6MB, because a megabyte is about 1,000 kilobytes.

5. If you want to back up all the selected files, choose Settings ⇨ Options, click the Backup tab, choose the Full option, and then click OK.

6. Click the Next Step button to display the Where to back up options.

7. Click the destination for the backup (a floppy disk drive, in this example).

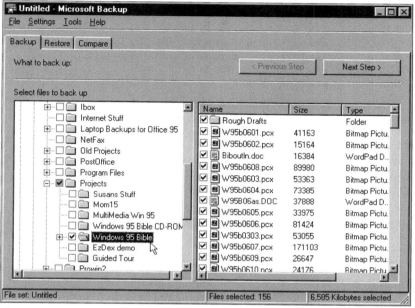

Figure 11-6: About to back up the folder named Windows 95 Bible

8. If you think you may back up the same set of files in the future, you can define the selected files as a set. Choose File ➪ Save As, enter a name, and then click the Start button.

9. Click the Start Backup button.

10. Follow the instructions onscreen.

Note, if you defined the selected files as a set in Step 8, you can back up the same set of files in the future without first selecting each file individually. Start Microsoft Backup and choose File ➪ Open File Set. Click the name of the file set you want to use, and then choose Open. Don't forget to check the options before you back up the set; choose Settings ➪ Options, click the Backup tab, and then choose the Full option (if you want to back up the entire set) or the Differential option (if you want to back up only files that have changed since the last backup).

Restoring from Backup

If you ever need to restore backed-up files from a tape or floppy disk, follow these steps:

1. Insert the tape or disk that contains the backed-up files into a drive.

2. Start Microsoft Backup.

3. Click the Restore tab.

4. In the left pane, click the icon for the drive that contains the files you want to restore.

5. In the right pane, click the name of the backup set you want to restore.

6. Click Next Step.

7. In the left pane, check each folder you want to restore.

8. To select subfolders or files within a folder, click the plus symbol (+) next to the folder, and then select subfolders and files in the right pane.

9. After you select all the files you want to restore, click Start Restore.

10. Follow any instructions that appear onscreen.

Comparing files with backups

If you need to compare files on the hard disk with copies on the backup tape or disk, follow the same general procedure as in the preceding section, but use the Compare tab. Follow these steps:

1. Insert the tape or disk that contains the backups into a drive.

2. Start Microsoft Backup.

3. Click the Compare tab.

4. In the left pane, click the drive that contains the files you want to compare.

5. In the right pane, click the backup set with which you want to compare the files.

6. Click the Next Step button.

7. In the left pane, check each folder you want to compare.

   You can expand the list by clicking the plus sign (+) and then selecting individual files in the right pane.

8. Click the Start Compare button.

9. Follow the instructions onscreen.

Formatting Floppy Disks

Floppy disks can be used to back up important documents and to transfer files from one PC's hard disk to another's. Programs you buy often are stored on floppies. Documents other people send to you also may be stored on floppies. In both cases, the floppy disk is already formatted, and *you do not want to format it again* — when you format a floppy disk, you also erase everything that's on it.

If you want to copy files to or from a floppy disk, see Chapter 5. If you want to install a program from a floppy disk or to create a bootable (startup) disk, see Chapter 9.

When you buy a box of floppy disks from your local Comput-O-Rama, those disks may be preformatted for PC use. Those floppies don't need to be formatted either. In fact, the only times when you *do* want to format a floppy are when the disk has never been formatted or when you want to erase everything on a floppy to make it a blank, formatted disk.

Formatting a floppy is easy. Follow these steps:

1. Put the floppy disk in drive A or drive B of your computer.

2. Open (double-click) My Computer.

3. Double-click the icon for the drive in which you put the floppy (usually drive A).

4. If the floppy disk has never been formatted, a message appears to inform you so; follow the instructions onscreen to format the floppy disk.

You can use ScanDisk to test and repair a floppy disk, and you can use DriveSpace (see Chapter 12) to increase the capacity of the floppy disk.

If you don't see a message indicating the floppy has never been formatted, then you needn't format it. If you really want to reformat the floppy and erase everything on it, however, close the window that displays the floppy's contents. In the My Computer window, right-click the floppy drive's icon and choose For<u>m</u>at. Then click the Start button to proceed.

Managing Multiple Users on One PC

Every user has personal preferences in screen colors, desktop icons, and the like. That's why you can personalize Windows 95 in so many ways, as discussed in Chapters 6 to 8. Historically, no way existed for people who shared a PC to set up their own preferences. If you sat down at the keyboard after someone else used the machine, you had two choices: Use whatever settings the other person left behind or go through the steps necessary to personalize the screen to your liking.

Those days are over. Thanks to user profiles in Windows 95, each person who uses a PC can have his or her own settings and can turn them on with just a few mouse clicks. To use this feature, every person who uses the PC must come up with a unique user name and password. (All users should write this information down and put it in a safe place in case they forget later and need to find that information to get their personal settings back onscreen.) Then one of the users must activate the user-profiles feature, discussed in the following section.

Enabling multiple user profiles

The first step in setting up user profiles is telling Windows 95 you plan to use that feature. Follow these steps:

1. If you have any work in progress onscreen, save all that work, and then close all open program windows.

2. Click the Start button, and then choose Settings ➪ Control Panel.

3. Double-click the Passwords icon.

4. Click the User Profiles tab to display the dialog box shown in Figure 11-7.

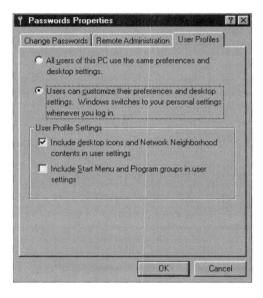

Figure 11-7: The User Profiles tab of the Passwords Properties dialog box

5. To activate user profiles, click the second option button.

   Each user now can save personal screen preferences, as described in the following section. In addition, you can allow or disallow individual desktop icons, Start menus, and so on.

   • If you want each user to have a personal set of desktop icons and Network Neighborhood contents, choose the first option.

   • If you also want each user to have a personal Start menu and Program menu options, choose the second option.

6. Click OK when you finish.

7. Click Yes to restart the computer.

When Windows restarts, you need to fill in your user name and password and, perhaps, answer additional questions onscreen. The following section explains how each user creates a personal profile.

Creating a user profile

Each user of a shared PC can create a personal user profile by following these steps:

1. To create a new user profile, the current user must log off by clicking the Start button, clicking Sh<u>u</u>t Down, clicking <u>C</u>lose all programs and log on as a different user?, and then clicking <u>Y</u>es.

   A dialog box appears, requesting a user name and password. The dialog box looks something like Figure 11-8.

Figure 11-8: The login dialog box asks for a user name and password.

2. The new user (the person who's creating the new profile) should type his or her user name and password, and then click OK.

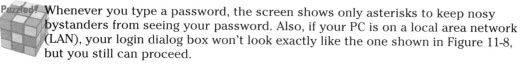

Whenever you type a password, the screen shows only asterisks to keep nosy bystanders from seeing your password. Also, if your PC is on a local area network (LAN), your login dialog box won't look exactly like the one shown in Figure 11-8, but you still can proceed.

3. The new user is asked to confirm the request and password; he or she should follow the instructions onscreen.

That's all there is to creating a user profile. Any personal preferences you set from now on are saved as part of your user profile — not as part of anybody else's profile.

If you need to connect and disconnect devices frequently, as you do on a laptop, look into hardware profiles (see Chapter 17). If you want to limit what other users can do on a PC, check out system profiles.

To keep other people from changing your settings, always remember to log off before you leave the PC, and also remember to log in under your own user name and password. If you sit down at the computer and someone else's settings are in effect, click the Start button, click Sh<u>u</u>t Down, click <u>C</u>lose all programs and log on as a different user?, and click the <u>Y</u>es button. Then log on as you normally would.

Changing your password

If someone discovers your password and you want to change it, follow these steps:

1. If you haven't already done so, log on as you normally do, using your current password.

2. Click the Start button and then choose <u>S</u>ettings ➪ Control Panel.

3. Double-click the Passwords icon.

4. Click the Change <u>W</u>indows Password button.

   The Change Windows password dialog box appears (see Figure 11-9).

   Follow the instructions onscreen.

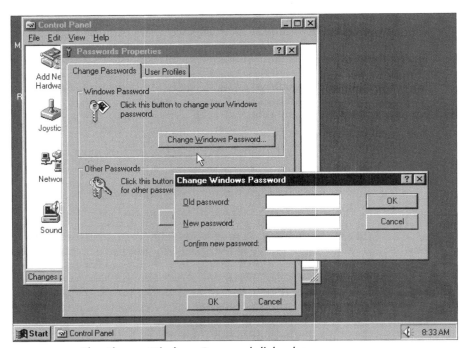

Figure 11-9: The Change Windows Password dialog box

You can change only your own password (the password for the user name under which you logged in). Also, you must type the old password before you can choose a new one — another good reason to keep a written copy of that password somewhere, in case you forget it.

Summary

This chapter has discussed tools and techniques to keep your PC tuned up and to deal with multiple users who need to share a single PC:

✦ To find and repair disk errors, click the Start button, point to Programs ➪ Accessories ➪ System Tools, and then click ScanDisk.

✦ Defragment your hard disk occasionally to keep it running at top speed. Just click the Start button, point to Programs ➪ Accessories ➪ System Tools, and then click Disk Defragmenter.

✦ You can use Microsoft Backup to make backup copies of your entire hard disk or just the files you've changed recently. To start Backup, click the Start button, point to Programs ➪ Accessories ➪ System Tools, and then click Backup.

✦ To format a floppy disk, put the floppy disk in drive A or B. Then open My Computer and double-click the drive's icon. If the floppy has never been formatted, you'll see a message to that effect. And you can just follow the onscreen instructions to format the floppy on the spot.

✦ If several people share one PC, you can activate user profiles so each user can save his/her own settings and preferences. To activate user profiles, click the Start button and choose Settings ➪ Control Panel. Double-click the Passwords icon and make your selections from the User Profiles tab.

✦   ✦   ✦

The Zen of Optimization

If there is a Zen of optimizing your PC via Windows 95, it's this: There ain't much to it. For the most part, Windows 95 is self-optimizing. If a particular component or process isn't optimized, Windows tells you so and even helps you fix the problem — kind of like having a nerdy technician type built right into your PC.

If you love to tinker and experiment, you may find all this rather disappointing. But as you'll see, you can do a few things on your own to make sure your programs are pumping out results as fast as the hardware allows.

Are We Optimized Yet?

The quickest and easiest way to check — and possibly improve — the performance of your PC is simply to have Windows 95 help you. Follow these steps:

1. Click the Start button and choose <u>S</u>ettings ➪ <u>C</u>ontrol Panel.

2. Double-click the System icon.

3. Click the Performance tab.

If you can do something specific to improve the performance of your system, a message near the bottom of the dialog box offers suggestions. In Figure 12-1, for example, the dialog box is telling me my PCMCIA cards are not using 32-bit drivers. For more information and instructions on resolving this problem, I click that message and then click the <u>D</u>etails button.

When all your components are tuned for optimal speed, no list appears, and the <u>D</u>etails button disappears. Both of these elements are replaced by the message Your system is configured for optimal performance.

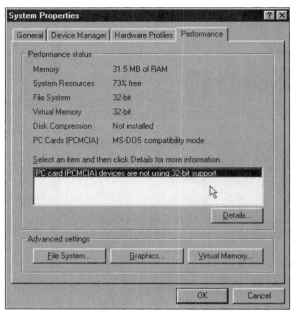

Figure 12-1: The Performance tab of the System Properties dialog box

If you love to tinker, however, you may be happy to know the message isn't always 100 percent correct. If you do a little exploring, you may squeeze a little more performance from your PC. But don't expect your tuning efforts to produce any dramatic results. You can't fine-tune a 386 into a Pentium any more than you can fine-tune a Ford Escort into a Ferrari. Such is life.

Careful!

I can't talk about optimizing the PC without getting somewhat technical. So throughout the rest of this chapter, I'll assume you have a bit of technical background. In particular, you should understand that a *real-mode* (16-bit) driver is one left over from DOS/Windows 3.x. Typically, the CONFIG.SYS and AUTOEXEC.BAT files load those drivers. If you want to remove such a driver, you must remove the appropriate command from CONFIG.SYS or AUTOEXEC.BAT, using a standard text editor, such as Notepad on the desktop or **edit** at the C:> prompt. If you're not experienced with editing those files, you should get some help from someone who *does* have that experience — or at least review the relevant information in a book about DOS.

What really dictates performance

The hardware, more than anything else, dictates how fast your PC runs. The most important factor is the processor. A Pentium (or 586) is faster than a 486, which in turn is faster than a 386. Period. Within a class of processor, clock speed determines how fast things go. A Pentium 120 is just flat-out faster than a Pentium 60.

The amount of RAM you have also plays a role in overall performance — a relatively minor role. But the amount of RAM matters, because accessing stuff in RAM is much faster than accessing stuff on a disk. When Windows 95 runs out of RAM, it starts using the disk as RAM. Given that the disk is slower than RAM, operations slow down.

It stands to reason the speed of the hard disk counts, too, especially if you have limited RAM, and Windows 95 often needs to spill data over to the disk. Performance-tuning your hard disk, then, can have a significant effect on overall speed. In this chapter, I will discuss techniques for optimizing performance in some detail.

The Need for Speed

In daily use, disk accesses tend to be the bottleneck in your PC's performance. The better tuned your hard disk is, the smaller that bottleneck. As I mentioned in Chapter 11, occasionally defragmenting your hard disk helps keep it running at peak speed. Telling Windows 95 how the hard disk is used on your PC also can help performance. To do that, follow these steps:

1. Click the Start button, and choose Settings ⇨ Control Panel.

2. Double-click the System icon.

3. Click the Performance tab.

4. Click the File System button and then choose one of the following options from the first drop-down list:

   - *Desktop computer:* for a normal stand-alone PC or a PC that's a client in a LAN

   - *Mobile or docking system:* for a portable or laptop computer

   - *Network server:* for a PC that plays the role of file server and/or print server in a peer-to-peer LAN

5. Click OK.

6. Click Close.

7. Follow the instructions onscreen.

Windows 95 automatically self-tunes to allocate resources according to your selection in Step 4. You may need to reboot to activate the new setting.

Disk caching

A *disk cache* (pronounced *cash*) serves as a sort of holding area between RAM and the disk; its purpose is to minimize disk accesses and thereby speed operations. Windows 95 uses a self-tuning cache named VCACHE (the *V* stands for *virtual*). Unlike the caches in earlier versions of Windows, VCACHE does not require you to set its size, because it's dynamic. When demand is high, VCACHE uses whatever resources it can find; when demand is low, VCACHE frees resources for other activities so they can run faster.

Caching is another reason why more RAM equates to faster performance: VCACHE automatically takes advantage of whatever RAM you have. The more RAM you have, the larger the cache. The larger the cache, the fewer disk accesses. The fewer disk accesses, the faster things go.

Caches are not additive. In fact, a cache within a cache slows operations. You should check your CONFIG.SYS and AUTOEXEC.BAT files to see whether either is loading a real-mode cache, such as SmartDrive (SMARTDRV). If so, remove the appropriate commands or at least comment them out with a **rem** command. While you're at it, you can remove any commands that load the old SHARE program, which is not needed in Windows 95 either. After making and saving your changes, don't forget to reboot the machine.

The swap file

When Windows 95 spills RAM data over to the disk, it uses what's called a *swap file*. In Windows 3.x, you could improve system performance by creating a permanent swap file. But it doesn't work that way in Windows 95. To the contrary, creating a permanent swap file may deteriorate Windows 95's performance.

Like VCACHE, the swap file in Windows 95 is dynamic, automatically using what resources are available, and freeing them when they're not needed. To ensure that you're using the dynamic swap file, double-click on the System icon and then click on the Performance tab. Click on the Virtual Memory button, and choose the first (recommended) option, as shown in Figure 12-2.

Then choose OK and follow the instructions onscreen.

Disk spin-down

Battery-operated laptops offer *disk spin-down* (also called *hard disk timeout*) to prevent the hard disk from running all the time and draining battery power. Unfortunately, spin-down also means slowdown — big-time slowdown. If you're not relying on batteries while you use your laptop, by all means disable spin-down (you may have to disable all the power-saving features to do so).

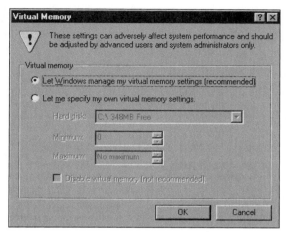

Figure 12-2: Virtual Memory (swap-file) options in Windows 95

Danger Zone Don't forget to reenable your laptop's power-management capabilities when you go back to battery power. Otherwise, you'll drain those batteries before the stewardesses serve the first round of drinks.

You'll need to check the manual that came with your laptop for specific instructions; the exact method varies from one machine to the next. Typically, however, you can control spin-down by using the CMOS setup. On my laptop, I have to shut down Windows and reboot the machine. After the memory test flashes onscreen, I press Del to run setup. Within that setup (called WinBIOS on my laptop), I can enable or disable all the power-management features. Turning all those features off disables disk spin-down and makes the machine run noticeably faster.

Maximize Your Disk Space

For most people, hard disk speed is not nearly as much a headache as hard disk capacity. Programs get bigger every year. Multimedia files are huge. A 200MB hard drive, which was a fantastic luxury just a few years ago, now is barely enough for your operating system and your favorite programs. It doesn't take long to run out of hard disk space. Luckily, Windows 95 comes with a program named DriveSpace that essentially doubles the capacity of your hard disk.

Disk space is cheap

Another solution to the hard disk-capacity problem is simply to buy a bigger hard drive. A bigger drive costs money, but perhaps less than you think. The day before I wrote this chapter, for example, I bought a 1.2GB (that's 1,200MB) hard drive for $355. That price works out to about 30 cents per megabyte — fairly cheap, especially compared with RAM, which costs anywhere from 30 to 50 *dollars* a megabyte.

Installation is fairly easy (for people who know what they're doing), so that part doesn't cost much. The store that performs the upgrade may even take your old drive as a trade-in, knocking the price down even further. It's worth a try to call your computer dealer and find out what it would cost to replace your current hard drive with a much larger one.

DriveSpace terminology

DriveSpace is easy to use but a bit mysterious until you get the hang of it. The way the program works is this: the folders and files on the drive you're compressing are squeezed into one big compressed file. Your PC doesn't know the compressed file is a file, however; it thinks the compressed file is a drive, such as C. In fact, your PC is so convinced the file is a drive, you won't even know such a file exists. When you go browsing through your C drive, everything will look normal.

The following buzzwords describe what DriveSpace creates:

✦ *Compressed volume file (CVF)*. The compressed volume file is the file that contains the compressed data. The CVF *acts* like a drive, *looks* like a drive (to Windows), and is *named* like a drive (such as C). In fact, the CVF is the file that holds all the compressed files.

✦ *Host drive*. The host drive is the actual drive that holds the CVF; it still has a drive letter name, but not the name it used to have. When you compress drive C, for example, the compressed file *becomes* drive C. The host drive, where that file is stored, will have some higher-letter name, such as H.

At first glance, this naming method may seem counterintuitive. You may think the host drive should get to keep its original name (C) and the CVF (the fake drive) should be assigned a new name. But it wouldn't work that way, because Windows needs to think the compressed file *is* the original drive. That's why the CVF gets the original drive name and the host drive takes on a new name.

More Info   Windows 95 DriveSpace is compatible with Microsoft's earlier DoubleSpace and DriveSpace programs. If you're using a disk compression tool from another vendor, such as STAC or AddStor, you should upgrade to the Windows 95 version of that product soon. You want to replace those products' original 16-bit real-mode drivers with 32-bit protected-mode drivers to get the best performance in Windows 95.

Compressing a disk

If you plan to compress your hard disk, be aware the process can take several hours. You can do other things while DriveSpace is compressing, but your system will seem sluggish — as slow as a slug in September snow. You may want to consider launching the compression program just before you go home or before you go to bed. When you see the Compress a Drive dialog box, turn off the monitor and call it a day. Your new double-capacity drive will be ready in the morning.

You follow these steps to compress a disk:

1. Close all open program windows, and save any work in progress.

2. Click the Start button, and choose <u>P</u>rograms ➪ Accessories ➪ System Tools.

3. Click DriveSpace to display the DriveSpace dialog box, shown in Figure 12-3.

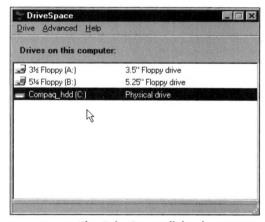

Figure 12-3: The DriveSpace dialog box

4. Click the drive you want to compress.

Puzzled? DriveSpace can't create a hard drive larger than 512MB; typically, it compresses only the first 256MB of a disk to a 512MB drive. If your drive is larger than 256MB, you'll probably end up with some free space on the host drive. You can use that free space to store normal (noncompressed) files. To create larger drives, use DriveSpace 3, which comes with the Microsoft Plus! product (see Chapter 39).

5. Choose <u>D</u>rive ➪ <u>C</u>ompress.

The Compress a Drive dialog box appears, showing you what to expect if you proceed with the compression. In Figure 12-4, for example, DriveSpace estimates it can increase my free space from about 46MB to 234 MB and my total disk capacity from about 323MB to 512MB.

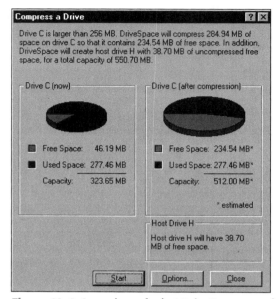

Figure 12-4: A preview of what DriveSpace can do.

6. If you want to proceed with the compression, choose <u>S</u>tart; otherwise, click <u>C</u>lose to back out and forget the whole thing.

The compression starts, and now it's a matter of waiting (and waiting).

Compressing floppy disks

Compressing a floppy disk takes only a few minutes. You can follow the steps in the preceding section to compress a floppy. When you get to Step 4, select the drive the floppy is in (for example, A). If the disk is empty, you'll end up with almost twice as much space as you had originally. A 1.44MB floppy disk, for example, ends up with about 2.5MB of space.

Recently, I put more than 10MB of graphic bitmap (.PCX) files on one floppy disk. I compressed the files, using PKZIP, and then copied the compressed .ZIP file to a 2.5MB floppy disk.

When the compression is done, you can use the floppy just as you would a normal (noncompressed) floppy disk; for example, you can copy other files to that disk. Just be aware, when you're browsing your system, you'll see two icons for the floppy disk: the original A icon and a new icon with some higher letter (such as E). The higher-letter name is for the host drive, which, for all intents and purposes, you can ignore. Be sure to copy files to and from the A: drive.

When you put the compressed floppy in another Windows 95 PC, you should be able to browse that floppy as you would any noncompressed floppy; for example, you can open My Computer and then double-click the A: drive icon. Again, an icon for the host drive appears in the My Computer window, but you can ignore the host drive.

If the PC can't read the compressed floppy, the browsing window probably will display an icon named ReadThis. Double-clicking on this icon displays text that explains the problem and gives you the solution. As the ReadThis file will suggest, you'll probably want to enable automatic mounting. Go back to the DriveSpace dialog box (choose Start ➪ Programs ➪ Accessories ➪ System Tools ➪ DriveSpace). Then choose Advanced ➪ Options, and select the Automatically mount option, as shown in Figure 12-5. Click on OK, and follow any instructions that appear onscreen.

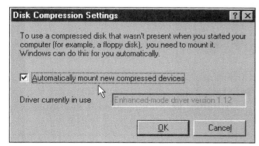

Figure 12-5: Choose this option to mount (read) compressed disks automatically.

Spelunking DriveSpace

The compressed volume file that DriveSpace creates is hidden from normal browsing modes. But you can do a bit of spelunking if you're curious about what's going on below the surface. All you need to know is the host-drive name (for example, H for a hard disk or maybe E for a floppy disk) and a little bit about the DOS DIR command. In the sample commands that follow, I assume you're exploring a compressed floppy in drive A whose host drive is named E.

If you pop out to the C:> prompt and enter a command such as **dir a:**, the result would be the same as looking at a noncompressed floppy: a list of files on the disk. The command **dir a: /c** would show the same list of files, but would include the compression ratio for each file. A file may show 2.0 to 1.0, for example, meaning the compressed file is half the size of the original file.

Danger Zone ▶ *Never, ever* try to open or modify the contents of the DBLSPACE.000 file. If you do, you're almost certain to lose everything within that file.

If you enter the command **dir e:** to look at the host drive, you see nothing other than (perhaps) the READTHIS.TXT file on a floppy disk. If you enter the command **dir e: /a** to include hidden files, however, you see a file named DBLSPACE.000. That file is the CVF. On a floppy, the CVF's size will be roughly equal to the capacity of the disk (because it fills the disk). On a hard drive, the CVF will be any size up to 512MB, which is the largest CVF that DriveSpace can create.

Tweaking DriveSpace

Like other miniapplications in Windows 95, DriveSpace has its own help file, which offers more options and settings than I need to discuss here. If you want to explore those options or learn about decompressing a disk, choose Help ➪ Help Topics. Alternatively, select an option in some menu other than Help and then click the question-mark button or press F1 for information about that option.

Optimizing Print Speed

Printing can be another bottleneck in overall PC performance. Even though you can do other things with your PC after the printer gets going, the print job takes up all system resources for a period right after you issue the Print command. All you can do is wait.

That waiting period, called *return-to-application time*, occurs when the PC is creating an image for the printer on the disk. Windows 95 offers a new format called EMF (Enhanced Metafile Format) for that disk image, which it can create quickly. The EMF can't make your printer go any faster than it was designed, but the time required to create the EMF is reduced, so return-to-application time is shorter.

EMF works only with non-PostScript printers and printer drivers. If you're not using a PostScript printer, follow these steps to ensure you're using the EMF format:

1. Click the Start button, and choose Settings ➪ Printers.

2. Right-click the icon for any non-PostScript printer driver.

3. Click Properties.

4. Click the Details tab.

5. Click the Spool Settings button and then choose EMF from the Spool data format drop-down list (see Figure 12-6).

6. Click OK twice to return to the Printers dialog box.

You can repeat Steps 2-6 for each non-PostScript printer driver in the Printers dialog box.

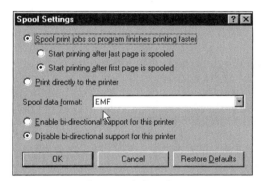

Figure 12-6: The Spool data format set to EMF

Parallel ECP Ports

Extended Capabilities Port (ECP) is a new standard for the parallel printer port. ECP supports high-speed printers and other devices connected to the printer port; it can even speed the performance of non-ECP devices. Remember, ECP is *hardware*. None of what's discussed in this section applies to a standard parallel printer port.

You need to refer to your computer manual to determine whether you have an ECP port (or whether you can upgrade your existing port to ECP). After you determine that you have an ECP port, follow these steps to enable ECP support in Windows 95:

1. Refer to the computer manual or add-in card documentation to determine the IRQ and DMA settings for each of the ECP ports you want to use.

   (This information is required, and there's no way to get it from Windows.)

2. Click the Start button, and choose Settings ➪ Control Panel.

3. Double-click the System icon.

4. Click the Device Manager tab.

5. Click the plus sign (+) next to Ports (COM & LPT) and then select Extended Capabilities Port (available only if you have an ECP).

6. Click the Properties button.

7. Click the Resources tab.

   The Input/Output range for the port should be listed under Resource Type.

8. Select Basic configuration 2 from the Settings based on options.

9. Under Resource Type, click on Interrupt Request; then click the Change Setting button.

10. Enter the IRQ value you determined in Step 1, and click OK.

11. Click Direct Memory Address.

12. Enter the DMA value you determined in Step 1, and click OK.

These steps configure only one ECP. If you have multiple ECPs, you need to repeat the steps to configure each port's IRQ and DMA settings. The ECP capabilities will be available after you shut down and restart the computer.

Using System Monitor

Windows 95 comes with a System Monitor feature that enables you to assess the speed of various components. System Monitor is sort of a debugger/oscilloscope that technicians and network administrators can use to analyze hardware performance and test for bottlenecks. But even if you don't work at that nitty-gritty level of detail, you may find it interesting to see how your system is actually working.

To start System Monitor, follow these steps:

1. Click the Start button, and choose Programs ➪ Accessories ➪ System Tools.

2. Click the System Monitor option.

The System Monitor window appears, probably nearly blank at first. But as you use your PC, the feature tracks the performance of various components, as shown in Figure 12-7.

More Info: If System Monitor isn't available in your Accessories menu, use the Windows Setup tab of the Add/Remove Programs dialog box to install it (refer to Chapter 9). System Monitor is with the Accessories programs.

Spikes in the chart indicate the amount of time or number of CPU cycles used by a component or process at this time. You can use buttons in the toolbar to select components to view and the type of graph to view. If your work requires this kind of detailed analysis of processes, you can learn more by browsing System

Monitor's <u>H</u>elp options. The *Windows 95 Resource Kit* (Microsoft Press) also describes System Monitor in some detail.

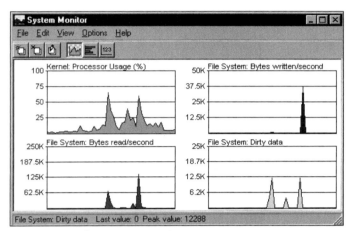

Figure 12-7: The System Monitor

Summary

This chapter is all about getting the best performance from your PC hardware and Windows 95. In a nutshell:

✦ To check/improve your system performance, click Start and choose <u>S</u>ettings ➪ <u>C</u>ontrol Panel. Double-click the System icon, then click the Performance tab.

✦ To maximize file system speed, click Start and choose <u>S</u>ettings ➪ <u>C</u>ontrol Panel. Double-click the System icon, click the Performance tab then click the <u>F</u>ile System button. Choose an option from the <u>T</u>ypical role of this machine drop-down list.

✦ To experiment with disk caching, disable SMARTDRV and SHARE in your AUTOEXEC.BAT and CONFIG.SYS files. Then shut down and restart the PC. VCACHE (Virtual Cache) that comes with Windows 95 will take over all caching, which might improve your overall disk performance.

✦ Windows 95 performs best when you *don't* set a fixed swap file (virtual memory) size.

✦ On a portable PC, disabling the disk spin-down feature when you're not relying on batteries will improve disk performance considerably.

✦ To squeeze more stuff onto a disk, use DriveSpace to compress the disk. For larger drives (up to 2 GB when compressed), use DriveSpace 3, discussed in Appendix F.

✦ To optimize return-to-application time after starting a print job, make sure you're using the EMF file format with any non-PostScript printers. To get to the file format, open My Computer, double-click the Printers folder and right-click a printer. Choose Properties ➪ Details ➪ Spool Settings and set the Spool Data Format to EMF.

✦   ✦   ✦

Takin' Care of Business

Brave New Officeware

This chapter is about the way things are evolving in PC business computing, in general. The trend, of course, is to keep giving users more and more power and, at the same time, to make the PC easier to learn and use. Windows 95 is certainly a big step in this direction.

But Windows 95 is only one gene in this evolutionary trend. Following in Windows 95's footsteps will be a whole new generation of office-productivity tools. In this chapter, I take the focus off Windows 95 and look at the parallel trends in officeware.

The Monoliths Are Fading

You may hear computer jocks refer to the great application programs of yesteryear as *monolithic apps*. The name comes from the fact that each of these programs was designed to do one thing. For example, a word processing program is for typing. A spreadsheet is for doing math calculations for forecasting and trying out "what-if" scenarios. And a database is for keeping records.

Those monolithic programs are, of course, still as great and as useful as they ever were; I'm not trying to discredit them by referring to them in the past tense. But some problems exist with the whole monolithic approach to creating programs.

One problem is, not everyone on the planet has a job description that can be facilitated with one application. In a huge corporation that has typists (word processors) and financial managers (spreadsheets) monolithic apps are OK. But the opposite of the corporation is the self-employed person who plays the role of president, janitor, and everything in between. This person probably needs the capabilities of many apps.

Monolithic apps tend to be overkill for the vast majority of users. Sure, it may be great that your word processing program can do columns, fonts, and typesetting. And, yeah, it's cool that your spreadsheet program can do the Einstein equations. But what if you only need *some* word processing capability (such as basic formatting and spelling check), *some* spreadsheet capability (such as basic calculations and preparing charts), and *some* database capability (such as managing customer lists and orders)?

 The 800+ page instruction manual accompanying each app represents another formidable problem. Newer programs provide much more onscreen support and access to help.

To complicate matters further, each app has its own commands and style, so no guarantee exists that *anything* you learned in the first app would apply to the next one! To top all this off, getting data from one application to another (especially in the DOS era), was often difficult, if not outright impossible.

Lack of interaction between the apps was even a problem for the more advanced programmers and power users. A WordPerfect and Lotus 1-2-3 macro maven, for example, could automate all kinds of things within one program or the other. But no in-between language existed that could take advantage of the capabilities of both programs. A WordPerfect macro couldn't open a 1-2-3 spreadsheet, yank out a chart, and put it in the current document; each macro language functioned only within its own environment.

The Birth of the Suites

All the problems with the monolithic apps are just now starting to fade away, as single apps become parts of integrated suites. Initially, a suite, such as Microsoft Office, was a way to bundle several programs together and sell them at a discount.

But there's a lot more to modern suites than shrink-wrapping. A new level of integration exists within those apps, which makes them behave more like a single app containing many tools. A "regular Joe" can use a pinch of word processing, a smidgen of spreadsheet, and a dash of database to get some work done.

New languages are evolving that enable power users to call upon the capabilities of all the apps in a suite. Using Visual Basic for Applications in Microsoft Office 95 and Office 97, for example, you can write a program that plots a graph from today's database data, places a copy of this graph in a word-processed written report, and places another copy in today's slide-show presentation. The person using this program only needs to click a button to accomplish all those tasks.

 The main difference between Office 95 and the newer Office 97 is the 97 product has a lot of Internet integration built in. When I refer to features both products support, I'll use the short name Office 95/97. As you may have guessed, no Office 96 product exists.

What I'm Showing You Here

In this chapter, I'll use the Microsoft Office 95/97 products to present some examples of several separate, independent applications that can work together as a single unit. Please understand this is neither endorsing Microsoft Office 95/97 nor, in any way, discrediting the competing products. I have the software for Office 95/97 right here, right now, as I'm writing this chapter. I'm sure the competing suites have many, if not all, these same features.

That Document-Centric Thang

Although Microsoft Office 95/97 still consists of several individual applications — Word, Excel, PowerPoint, Schedule +, and perhaps Access — the absolute beginner doesn't really need to know this because Office 95/97 is more document-centric than its predecessors. That is, the interface is geared toward documents rather than apps.

Perhaps you're familiar with the Office toolbar that appears in Microsoft Office 4.2 and 4.3. The toolbar contained a button for each application in the suite: a *W* for Microsoft Word, an *X* for Excel, and so on. The assumption of this toolbar was the person sitting at the keyboard knew what each button and each application were for — or he or she could figure everything out from the icon. (Yeah, right.)

The Microsoft Office toolbar, shown at the top of the screen in Figure 13-1, has no buttons for specific apps. In fact, the tooltips for the default buttons are simply Office, Start a Document, Open a Document, Make an Appointment, Add a Task, and Add a Contact. Hmmmmmmmm.

The window below the toolbar is called the *binder*. The binder enables you to stick all the documents for any given project into a single binder, or project. The binder is document-centric. At the left edge of the binder in Figure 13-1, you'll see icons for two documents I've added to this binder. One document, named Chart 1, shows an Excel icon. The other document, named Year End, displays a Word icon.

If I click a document's icon, this document appears inside the document area of the binder. For example, right now the Word document named Year End is selected in Figure 13-1, and the contents of this document are displayed in the binder's document area. The menu bar and the toolbar at the top of the binder are actually Microsoft Word's menu bar and toolbar.

Now suppose I click the Chart 1 document icon. No big application launch occurs, no new window, not many changes to the screen at all. Instead, the Excel document simply replaces the Word document in the binder, and Excel's menu bar and toolbar replace Word's (see Figure 13-2). Now I have access to all Excel's capabilities with only the smallest change of the menu bar and toolbar on the screen. This approach is much less confusing and intimidating to beginners and casual users.

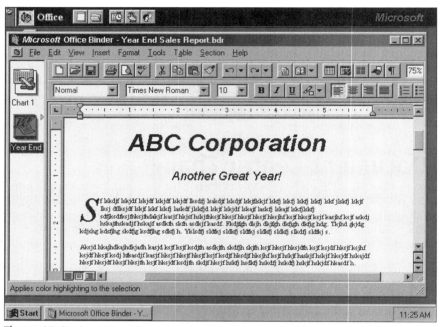

Figure 13-1: The Office 95 toolbar and the binder displaying a Word document

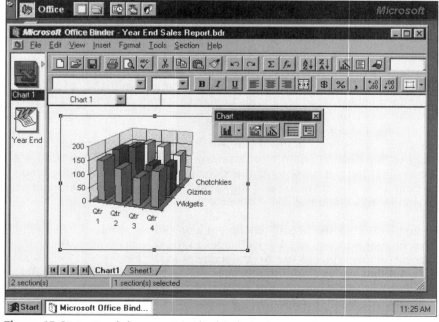

Figure 13-2: An Excel document in the binder's document area

Not so sure about that binder?

If you're an experienced Office user, this binder thing may seem more like an inconvenience rather than an aid. Not to worry — the binder is completely optional. You can work in Office 95/97 exactly the way you're accustomed to working in earlier versions of Office.

On the other hand, if you work with users who are less savvy than yourself, think what a great convenience the binder can be to them. You can pass a group of documents, neatly packaged in a binder, to another worker. That person can open the binder, and then open any document within the binder by clicking it. You'll spend much less time explaining what each document is and where to find it.

Also, you're not stuck with the default toolbar buttons described in this chapter. You can add whatever buttons you like, just as you can in the earlier versions of Office.

So managing documents in the binder is pretty darn easy. You needn't look around much at all. And when a document does come to the screen, it brings the appropriate tools.

Now you may be thinking, "Yeah, but if you can only see one document at a time, how can you drag-and-drop objects between documents?" Okay, Mr. Smarty Pants. Glad you asked.

Awesome Drag-And-Drop

As you've seen in earlier chapters, Windows 95 has made many inroads toward a universal drag-and-drop capability. For example, you can drag folders and files to the Recycle bin to delete them, and you can print many kinds of documents just by selecting their icons and dragging them to a printer icon.

Universal drag-and-drop is evolving in Office 95/97, as well. The goal is a general rule that says: "If you want to move object x to document y, drag the object to its destination." The person sitting there with mouse-in-hand shouldn't have to worry about a zillion rules defining whether this *particular* object can be dragged into that *particular* document. The person just does it, and it works.

Scraps

Scraps are the solution to the problem of dragging-and-dropping when only one document is visible on the screen at a time. For example, suppose I'm looking at my Excel chart in the binder and I want to put this chart into my Word document. To begin, I need to shrink the binder window a little to make room on the desktop. Then I can just click the chart and drag it to the desktop. A scrap appears on the desktop, as shown in the lower-left corner of Figure 13-3.

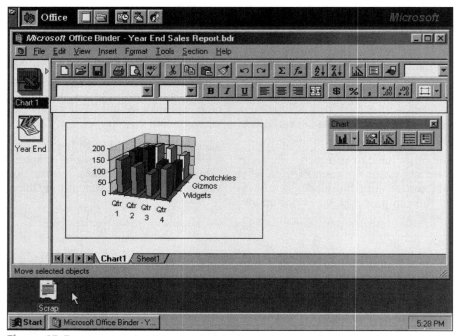

Figure 13-3: I dragged the chart to the desktop to create the little scrap.

Now I can simply click the icon for the Word document at the left side of the binder. My written document instantly appears in the binder's work area again, replacing the chart that was there. All I must do is drag the scrap from the desktop into my Word document, and my document now contains a copy of the chart, as shown in Figure 13-4.

If you think about it, this method is both natural and intuitive. No menu commands are involved; no window navigation is required; no mysterious invisible clipboard is used. This is more like the way you'd cut-and-paste between printed documents using real scissors and glue.

If you're wondering why my screen shots are so cluttered in this chapter, it's because I'm using 640 × 480 resolution; this resolution makes seeing small objects possible on these tiny black-and-white printed screens. In real life, I'd do this work at 800 × 600 or higher resolution, which would give me much more elbow room!

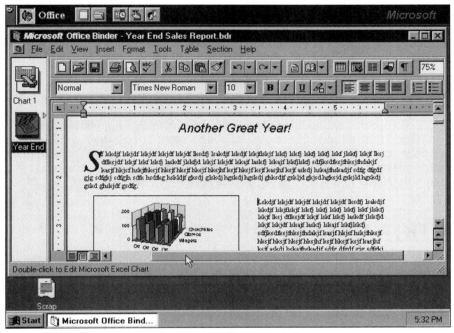

Figure 13-4: The Excel chart is now part of my Word document.

In-place editing

After an object is embedded in a document, you can edit this object in two ways: click the object's button in the binder bar at the left (that is, click the Chart 1 icon in Figure 13-3.) Or you can double-click the object in its container document to perform *in-place editing*. With in-place editing, the complete document remains on the screen, and tools from the other application (Excel in this example) simply appear in the document.

As you make changes to the object, you see exactly how the changes will look within the container document. To save the edited object, click anywhere outside the object in your document. The Excel tools disappear.

OLE ain't what it used to be

Some of you may be thinking "Hey, most of what you just described is called OLE, and we've had it since Windows 3.1." This is true. Only the scraps are new to Windows 95. But because I brought up the subject of OLE, I may as well discuss how it fits into the Windows95/Office 95 scheme of things.

As you may know, *OLE* stands for *Object Linking and Embedding* — at least it used to. If you were to ask a Microsoft employee what OLE stands for now, she'd probably say: "Nothing. It's just *olay*."

This could be a first — an acronym that doesn't stand for *anything*!

Why remove the meaning from an acronym? Because *object linking and embedding* no longer does justice to the many capabilities of OLE. Linking and embedding are only two end-user capabilities of OLE. We now have *OLE automation,* as well. As you'll see in the following section, OLE automation brings an enormous amount of power and flexibility to the folks on the high-end of the nerd scale: application developers and power users. In a nutshell, OLE automation enables you to manipulate an application's objects from *outside* the application.

One OOP Does It All

As I mentioned earlier, a big problem with the early monolithic apps for power users was that their macro languages could drive only one app. In Office 95/97, this has all been fixed with Visual Basic for Applications (VBA). The way this all works is elegant, simple, and very powerful.

You have one language, VBA, which *sees* Office 95/97 as if it were only one program. A single VBA program can contain commands that control Microsoft Word, Microsoft Excel, Microsoft Access, and Microsoft PowerPoint. VBA can use about any capability, no matter how large or small, from any single app, to get a job done. It can also move and copy things from one app to another.

Although the *one language drives all* itself is simple, mastering VBA is not so simple. You can't learn it overnight. There's a lot to know, and I certainly can't teach you everything in this one chapter. But I can give you an idea of how VBA works.

In a sense, VBA is like two languages in one. On one hand, the standard Visual Basic commands exist, which still resemble the BASIC commands of yesteryear. In the sample VBA code shown in Figure 13-5, you can see the If...Then...Endif, Sub, and Exit commands from traditional Visual Basic (if such a thing as *traditional* exists in this ever-changing industry). You use those commands to control what happens and when it happens.

On the other hand, VBA has an object-oriented programming (OOP) language. Unlike the regular Visual Basic commands, the OOP commands enable you to manipulate objects directly. The OOP commands all use a *dot* syntax, such as *ThisWorkbook.close* and *ActiveCell.Value= "Sheet Name"* as in Figure 13-5. (I'll talk about this syntax more in a moment.)

In some cases, the OOP commands are similar to earlier macro languages because you can create them by recording some action in a macro. Open the resulting macro and voila! — you have your OOP code right there, ready to put in your custom VBA program.

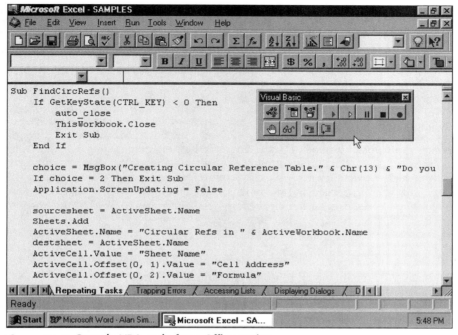

Figure 13-5: Sample VBA code from Office 95/97

Objects, properties, and methods

The key to understanding VBA is realizing nearly everything in Office 95/97 is an object. Excel is an object. A chart within Excel is an object. An Excel worksheet is an object. Even a single cell within a worksheet is an object. As a colleague eloquently put it after his moment of realization, "Every stinkin' thing is an object!"

Each object has its own unique set of properties and methods. An object's *properties* are things like its color and size — basically, how it looks on the screen or the printed page. An object's *methods* are things the object can do — or more specifically, things an outside program can make the object do. (For example, you can open, save, print, and close many objects using the Open, Save, Print, and Close methods.) In a sense, properties are nouns that describe the object, whereas methods are verbs that describe some action.

When you're doing daily work on the screen, you can right-click almost any object to display a pop-up menu listing several things you can do with this object. Most of the actions listed on that pop-up menu are methods. Typically, that pop-up menu also includes a Properties option. When you choose the Properties option, you're taken to a dialog box that enables you to change the properties of that particular object.

Object exposure

The objects that you can manipulate from outside an application are called this application's *exposed objects*. The idea is the application exposes certain of its objects to VBA, so programs outside the application can manipulate that object.

Probably the most formidable task in becoming a fluent VBA programmer is learning which objects each application exposes and what properties and methods each individual object offers. Learning these things is tough because Excel and Access each expose *hundreds* of objects, and every single object has its own unique set of properties and methods.

If you do start learning VBA, make certain you learn about the Object Browser early in your learning curve. The Object Browser is a big help in determining what objects are available and what properties and methods each object provides. For more information, search the help index in whichever application you're currently using for the phrase *object browser*.

Basically, VBA enables you to do those same things from within code. That is, VBA can do all those things automatically, behind the scenes, without your having to click anything. You don't need to see the pop-up menu, the object, or even the object's application onscreen.

The syntax for manipulating objects from within code is based on object names and actions, separated by dots. To make an object take some action, you use the following syntax:

```
objectname.method
```

In the following example, MyChart is the name of some object (most likely an Excel chart). When executed, the command copies this object to the Windows Clipboard:

```
MyChart.copy
```

To change one of an object's properties, you typically use this syntax:

```
objectname.property = setting
```

For example, the following command refers to an object named MyCell (which, presumably, is some cell in a spreadsheet). It sets the font of this cell's contents to boldface:

```
MyCell.font.bold = True
```

Notice no procedure exists, as in older languages. That is, you needn't go through a series of commands to make something happen to the object; rather, you name the object and specify what you want it to do or how you want it to look.

If you're steeped in traditional procedural programming languages, this new object-oriented approach feels strange at first, but once you get the hang of it, it's pretty slick.

What you need to create custom VBA programs

If you want to create custom VBA programs, you need several things: first and foremost is knowledge. Programming is not a skill you learn overnight. And, before you even think about programming, you must be familiar with the capabilities of all the Office 95/97 applications your programs will address.

In terms of tools, what you need depends on what you want to do. If you're developing a custom Office program for in-house use, you needn't do anything extra; Microsoft Office 95/97, by itself, is all you need. You can create your custom program within any Office app, such as Excel or Access, or you can spread your app's code across several objects. The app from which the VBA program starts doesn't matter because, once the program gets going, it has access to everything in all the Office 95/97 programs.

On the other hand, if you're thinking about developing a custom Office app to sell, then you'll probably want to buy Microsoft's Visual Basic for Applications. This product enables you to compile all your code into an .EXE file that you can easily distribute to anyone who has Office 95/97. Users treat your custom app like any other program. That is, they install it, and when they want to run it, they double-click its icon.

What is important to understand, though, is if your .EXE file calls upon Word, Excel, Access, or PowerPoint to do something, then this program must be on the user's machine. This isn't like distributing a standalone program.

The last little point is a bummer because it narrows your potential customer base to Office 95/97 users. But, remember, this is where we are currently in this evolving technology. Eventually, all this Office stuff will be built right into the operating system, along with multimedia, video, Internet access, and so forth. When we get to that point in the PC evolution, techno-artists will be able to create tiny programs that do huge and amazing things, just by calling upon built-in capabilities in new and interesting ways. The PC will be a household appliance, the custom programs you create simple plug-ins to make that appliance do great stuff.

Office Joins the Net Revolution

The new Microsoft Office 97 product offers several enhancements over Office 95, but nowhere are the changes more sweeping than in the way in which Office 97 has embraced the Internet. I realize we haven't really discussed the Internet yet in this book. So if you haven't surfed the Net yet, this discussion may not mean much. But, if you're already a Web/Internet guru, you'll definitely appreciate the new Internet integration offered by Office 97. In a nutshell, Office 97 enables you to create and edit documents ready for publication on the Web or a company intranet. Furthermore, you can be online and navigate the Web while you edit an Office 97 document.

Web pages and Microsoft Word

Office 97 makes it simple to edit a Web page much as you would create a page layout file, complete with text and graphics, but without needing to know complicated formatting codes. You can easily capture a page from the Internet, for instance, and edit it inside Microsoft Word 97. Exactly how you do this, though, depends on which Web browser you're currently using. You'll need to refer to the help screens or documentation that came with your Web browser to determine how to set up Word 97 as your HTML editor.

Loading a Web page into Word can be time-consuming. If you want to abort this operation after Word begins to convert the page, press the Escape key.

Once a Web page has been loaded into Word, the program becomes a WYSIWYG HTML editor. You'll notice a few new tools are in the toolbar, like the horizontal line tool, sometimes used to divide sections of a Web page visually. You can now actually use Word to navigate the Web like an ordinary browser; you simply need to add the Web toolbar. There are two ways to do this:

✦ Click a link on the Web page that is loaded in Word. The page is *hot,* and links work. Not only will you go to the location indicated by the link, but a new toolbar will appear that contains essential navigation tools.

✦ Choose <u>V</u>iew ➪ <u>T</u>oolbars ➪ Web. The toolbar will appear automatically, as seen in Figure 13-6.

The buttons on this toolbar should be familiar to any Web surfer. They are, from left to right:

✦ *Back*: Navigates backward through links you've visited.

✦ *Forward*: Navigates forward through links you've visited.

✦ *Stop Current Jump*: Halts Word from loading the current page.

✦ *Refresh Current Page*: Reloads current page.

✦ *Start Page*: Returns you to the home page specified in your preferences.

✦ *Search the Web*: Returns you to the search page specified in your preferences.

✦ *Favorites*: This drop-down menu lists all of the favorite or bookmarked Web sites specified in Internet Explorer.

✦ *Go*: This drop-down menu enables you to specify start and search pages, as well as manually type in a URL to visit.

✦ *Show only Web Toolbar.* If you want to reduce clutter, click this button to *roll up* all toolbars except the Web toolbar. Click it again to bring all the Word toolbars back.

✦ *Recent URLs*: Select recently visited URLs from this drop-down menu.

Figure 13-6: Familiar Web navigation tools are available in Office applications for surfing the Web.

Many tools are available to edit Web documents once you open a file in Word. In fact, so many Internet-specific tools are available, you can now create Web sites just with Word. Here are some things you can try.

Modify your view

Once you load a Web page into Word, a few ways exist to customize the view, depending on how you like to edit HTML. If you don't like to see the page as it appears onscreen but, instead, you'd rather roll up your sleeves and get into the guts of HTML code, choose <u>V</u>iew ➪ HTML <u>S</u>ource. A new window will open that displays the actual page's source code, just as if you were using a text editor. You can switch back at any time to the WYSIWYG view by choosing <u>V</u>iew ➪ Exit HTML <u>S</u>ource.

Likewise, you can switch between full graphics view and the HTML source code, even in the Normal or Page Layout view. Simply select the desired Web object, like graphic or link, and press Shift+F9. Shift+F9 will also toggle back to the previous view. You can make this change globally: First select the entire document, choose Edit ➪ Select All, and then Shift+F9.

A new view in the View menu, Online View, is the default setting for viewing and editing Web pages.

A new view mode in Word 97, shown in Figure 13-7, is called the *Document Map*. While the Document Map works on any kind of Word file, it is particularly helpful on documents featuring well-defined hierarchies, like outlined reports and Web pages with headlines and subheads. Enable the Document Map by choosing View ➪ Document Map. The screen will be divided into two regions; the region on the left shows an outline of the document with expandable and collapsible headings. The major features of the Document map are:

✦ The Document Map shows each major section and subsection in much the same way as the Outline view does.

✦ Click any line of text in the map and the document will scroll to the proper location.

✦ Collapse sections of the map by clicking the minus sign to the left of the text. Expand it again with by clicking the plus sign.

✦ Don't bother trying to change your text — you can't use the map to rearrange or directly edit the text in the document — it's just what the name implies: a map.

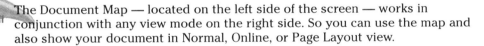

The Document Map — located on the left side of the screen — works in conjunction with any view mode on the right side. So you can use the map and also show your document in Normal, Online, or Page Layout view.

Creating a Web page

Word 97 has many tools for creating a Web page from scratch or for editing an existing one. To create a Web page from scratch, select File ➪ New and select the Web Pages tab from the New File dialog box. Then choose either the Blank Web Page template, or the Web Page Wizard. Either way, you needn't enter HTML codes by hand unless you want to do so. Once you're ready to work, follow these general procedures.

Entering text

Type text as you normally would onto the Web page. You can change the text size and justification in much the same way as in a normal Word document.

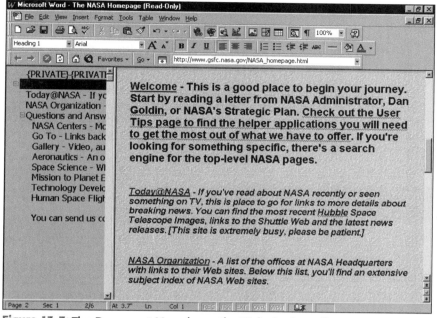

Figure 13-7: The Document Map shows the Web site in outline form.

Adding horizontal lines

Choose Insert ➪ Horizontal line... and a dialog box appears with a variety of choices. If you don't see the line style you like, click the button marked More, and an Open Picture dialog box offers additional choices.

Adding graphics

To add an image to your Web page, choose Insert ➪ Picture.... You'll have a few options available:

- ✦ *Clip Art*: Choose from the Microsoft Office clip art library.

- ✦ *From File*: Add any graphic from the hard disk, floppy, CD-ROM, or other locations to which you have access.

- ✦ *Browse Web Art Page:* Choose from art on a special Web page Microsoft has made available to expand the choices beyond those images on the CD-ROM.

- ✦ *From Scanner*: Scan an image and insert it directly from Word.

- ✦ *Chart*: Insert a business graphic.

After adding your graphic to the page, you can make it a link, which, when clicked, sends the user to another place on the Web. To do this, follow these steps:

1. Click the graphic with the right mouse button. A drop-down menu appears.

2. Select Hyperlink. An Insert Hyperlink dialog box appears as in Figure 13-8.

3. If you want to link to another Web site, enter the appropriate URL in the Link to file or URL box at the top of the dialog box. If you want to link to another location on the same page, enter the name of the bookmark in the Named location in the file box below. If you haven't yet created a bookmark, read on to learn how.

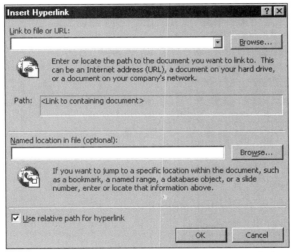

Figure 13-8: Use the Hyperlink dialog box to tell the link where to go.

Likewise, you can add video to your Web page by choosing Insert ➪ Video. Remember, video — even a short clip — consumes a lot of hard disk space and takes a while to download.

Adding bookmarks and hyperlinks

Often, you may need to let the user move between different parts of the same Web document, such as back to the very beginning or the end of a page, or to an article embedded in the middle. You can do this by assigning a *bookmark,* or *internal link,* to the desired section, and then linking to the bookmark from elsewhere. Note: If you're familiar with Netscape's bookmarks, this is a different definition of the same word. To use bookmarks, do the following:

1. Place the cursor at the start of the section you want to bookmark.

2. Choose Insert ⇨ Bookmark. A Bookmark dialog box appears like the one in Figure 13-9.

3. Enter a name for the bookmark and press Enter. Close the dialog box.

Figure 13-9: Bookmarks enable you to link different parts of a Web page together.

4. Place the cursor where you want to place a link to that bookmark. Choose Insert ⇨ Hyperlink. An Insert Hyperlink dialog box appears (see Figure 13-8).

5. Enter the name of the bookmark in the Named location in file box, or click the Browse button and select the bookmark from the list you created.

If you want to link to another Web page, simply choose Insert ⇨ Hyperlink and enter the name of the site in the Link to file or the URL box at the top of the dialog box.

Testing your page

You can test your work at any time by selecting File ⇨ Web Page Preview. This menu selection starts your default Web browser and displays the document as it would appear on the Internet.

Using Excel on the Internet

Like Word, Excel has a bunch of tools for vaulting your work onto the Web. And like Word, most of these tools are found in the Insert menu. Check out the previous section on using Word to learn how to tap into Excel's Internet capabilities.

Placing a spreadsheet on the Web

Thankfully, Microsoft has added a wizard to Excel 97 to simplify the task of adding a spreadsheet to a Web site. Using this tool, you can post detailed and timely data to intranets and the Internet with just a few mouse clicks. To create a Web page based on Excel data, follow these steps:

1. Select the range you want to depict on the Web page. You can actually include more than one range; if you plan to feature more than one, start with the first.

2. Choose File ➪ Save as HTML. An Internet Assistant Wizard like the one seen in Figure 13-10 appears. The first range you selected is already in the box; use the Add... button to include more cell ranges in your table.

3. Click Next when you're done adding ranges.

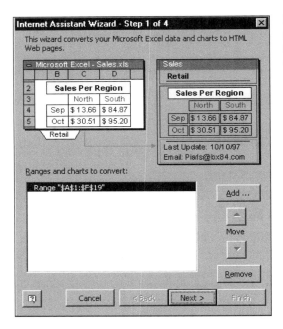

Figure 13-10: The Internet Assistant Wizard enables you to create an HTML-ready table from an Excel spreadsheet.

4. The next step enables you to include the specified range(s) in a Web page — either a new Web page or one you've already created. Click the appropriate button, and then click the Next button.

5. Add format and style information, like the title of the table and its creator. If you include the e-mail address, it will appear as a link connecting to the user's e-mail client. Click Next.

6. The final step specifies where the Web page will be saved on the hard disk. Click Finish to save your work. Figure 13-11 shows what the finished product looks like in Internet Explorer.

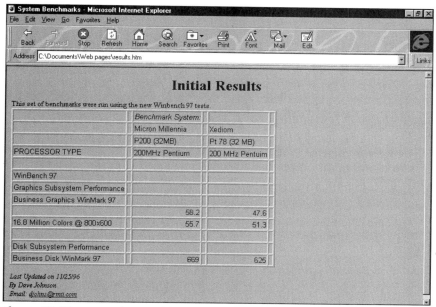

Figure 13-11: An Excel spreadsheet converted into a Web table

PowerPoint and the Internet

You probably know PowerPoint as a capable tool for creating presentations. PowerPoint can be used for 35mm, overhead, and computer-based slide shows. Now, though, PowerPoint has been beefed up to support the Internet as well. The interactive tools that appeared in PowerPoint 95 can now also be used to create Web pages.

Creating a Web page with PowerPoint

The tools we talked about in Microsoft Word are also available for PowerPoint. Visit the Insert menu for the opportunity to insert objects like hyperlinks, pictures, and text boxes.

If you don't know how to create a Web page, use the AutoContent Wizard (found under File ➪ New ➪ Presentations) to select one of the several Web pages in the PowerPoint library. Corporate and Personal Web page formats are there, for instance, that you can modify to your heart's content.

Adding navigation controls

Web pages need navigational tools and PowerPoint can help you make your site fully interactive. Add controls to a Web page by following these steps:

1. Click the AutoShapes button from the Drawing toolbar at the bottom of the screen.

2. Select the Action Buttons menu. A dozen buttons will be available.

3. Click any of the buttons, such as an arrow or the house.

Hot Stuff In hyperlink jargon, a house icon typically denotes *home,* as in the home — or start — page to which the user can return for navigation information or general information.

4. The cursor changes to a cross hair. Draw a box on the PowerPoint screen where you want to place the button.

5. An Action Settings dialog box appears as in Figure 13-12. This is where you tell PowerPoint what the button should do. Here are your choices:

   • *None*: The button does nothing. This isn't terribly useful as an Internet interactivity tool.

   • *Hyperlink to*: This drop-down menu enables you to jump to another page on your Web site or to another URL entirely.

   • *Run program*: Enables the user to run another program from the button.

   • *Run macro*: Enables the user to run a macro from the button. This is similar to the Run program option.

Hot Stuff Run macro will only be available if you have already created at least one PowerPoint macro. Create the macro first, and then build the button to execute it.

   ✦ *Object action*: This option is never available for action buttons. To use the Object action option properly, first insert an object like a Word document from the Insert ➪ Object menu. Then, right-click the object and select Action Settings. As you can see, the Object Action menu is now available and you can configure PowerPoint to launch the document's application when the object is clicked.

Hot Stuff Any of these actions, like Hyperlink or Run Program, can occur when the action button is clicked or simply when the mouse moves over the button. Add the desired action to the appropriate tab on the dialog box. Be careful with the *mouse-over* setting, though; this setting can be confusing for the user if things happen without a mouse click.

6. Make the desired settings and click OK.

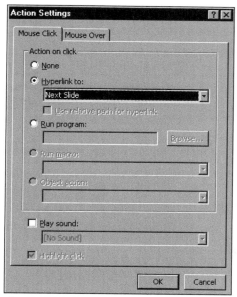

Figure 13-12: Action buttons can perform many different actions in PowerPoint.

Once you've set up an action button, you can customize its appearance. Here are more options:

✦ Click the button and a diamond appears above it. Click and drag the diamond to adjust the amount of 3D bevel the button displays.

✦ Right-click the button and select Format AutoShape. You can change the color of the button or make it semitransparent from the Fill section of the Colors and Lines tab. You can also click the Color menu to make the button display a textured background or a graphic image from your hard disk.

Conferencing via the Internet

You can take advantage of the Internet to deliver a PowerPoint presentation to one person or to a group of people, without having to meet with that person or group directly. This is called a *Presentation Conference.* To create a Presentation Conference, do the following:

1. Open the PowerPoint file you wish to present over the Internet.

2. Choose Tools ➪ Presentation Conference. The Presentation Conference Wizard appears.

3. Step through the wizard. Be sure to specify you will be the Presenter.

4. Enter the IP Address of each computer participating in the conference. (The addressees may have to give you this information.) As you can see in Figure 13-13, any number of people can participate.

5. When all the participants are online, you can click the Finish button on your own screen. PowerPoint will try to connect to each of the participants, and then you can begin the presentation.

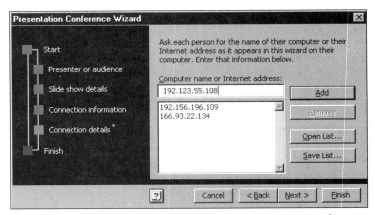

Figure 13-13: Add audience members to your Internet Conference via the wizard

A person's IP address may change each time he or she dials in to the Internet. An easy way to configure for a Presentation Conference is to ask participants to set up their PowerPoint session as audience members, and then ask them to e-mail their IP address to you immediately, just as it appears in their Presentation Conference Wizard. This way, you'll know their addresses and that they've completed their set-up, so you can proceed.

Keeping PowerPoint up-to-date

A new feature in PowerPoint is called *PowerPoint Central.* Start this tool by first connecting to the Internet, and then choosing Tools ➪ PowerPoint Central. You will be connected to the PowerPoint Web site where Microsoft maintains a wealth of PowerPoint tools, tips, and news. Use PowerPoint Central to download new clip art, learn about power user techniques, and stay current on ways to get the most out of PowerPoint. There is no cost to use this site.

Summary

Whew! In this chapter I tried to cover a lot of ground to explain how things are evolving and where we currently are in this evolution. Clearly, Office 95 takes advantage of Windows 95's document-centric approach and simplified cut and paste. Visual Basic for Applications provides a universal macro language, which can control all applications within Office 95/97, as though they were one large program. Office 97 brings all the resources of the Internet to your desktop, even while you create and edit documents. To summarize:

✦ Individual monolithic applications are being replaced by suites, where all programs are well-integrated and can act more as a unit.

✦ The document-centric approach to working is forcing the programs out of the limelight and into the background.

✦ Drag-and-drop is becoming the standard technique for doing just about anything and everything.

✦ In-place editing enables you to edit an object embedded in a document, without leaving that document.

✦ A single programming language can control all the data and programs in a suite of programs.

✦ The Internet figures prominently in Office 97. Create and edit Web pages from any of the major Office apps: Word, Excel, and PowerPoint.

✦ Use PowerPoint to conference on the Web and get updates to PowerPoint from PowerPoint Central.

✦   ✦   ✦

Printers, Fonts, and Pictures

Windows 95 comes with hundreds of new 32-bit printer drivers to make your print jobs faster and smoother than ever before. But more than the operating system, advances in printing technology, fonts, clip art, paper stock, and color have made printing something of an art form in and of itself. In this chapter, I discuss all the tools that enable you to do some awesome printing of your own.

Installing a Printer

Installing a printer is easy. Just follow these steps:

1. Gather up your original Windows 95 floppy disks or CD-ROM, as well as any disks that came with your printer.

2. If you are connecting to a network printer (a printer that has already been installed and shared on some other PC in the LAN), skip to Step 7.

3. Shut down Windows and shut down your PC.

4. Plug the printer into the computer and into the wall; then turn on the printer.

5. Restart your PC.

6. If your printer is Windows 95 plug-and-play-compatible, Windows detects this during startup and helps you install the drivers.

   Follow the instructions onscreen, and skip the remaining steps.

Whenever you're given the choice to install a Windows 95 driver or the manufacturer's driver, always try the Windows 95 driver first. Click on the Have Disk button only if the printer has no Windows 95 driver and you need to use the manufacturer's.

7. Click the Start button and choose Settings ➪ Printers.

8. Double-click the Add Printer icon.

You see the first page of the Add Printer Wizard (see Figure 14-1).

9. Follow the instructions onscreen.

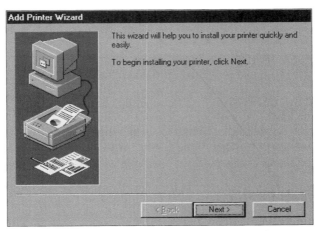

Figure 14-1: First page of the Add Printer Wizard

When you're given a choice between Local and Network printer installation, choose Local unless the printer is *not* physically attached to the PC. Use the Network option only to install shared printers on some other PC in the LAN. See Chapter 26 for more information on network printing.

To minimize return-to-application time when you use a non-PostScript printer, use the EMF data format; see "Optimizing Print Speed" in Chapter 12.

Every installed printer on your PC is represented by an icon in the Printers folder. To open the Printers folder, simply click on the Start button and choose Settings ➪ Printers.

Figure 14-2 shows a sample Printers folder from one of my PCs.

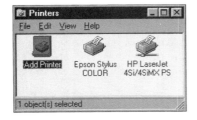

Figure 14-2: Sample Printers folder open on the desktop

Printing Documents

After your printer is installed, you can use any of these techniques to print most documents:

✦ *To print from a program:* Open the document by double-clicking on it or by choosing File ⇨ Open. When the document is open, choose File ⇨ Print.

✦ *To print from the desktop:* Browse to the document you want to print. Then right-click on the document's icon and choose Print from the pop-up menu that appears.

 More Info Not all document types support right-clicking and drag-and-drop printing, but you can use the Registry to add those methods to many document types. See Chapter 31 for details.

✦ *To print several documents:* Open the Printers folder; browse to and select the documents you want to print. Then drag the selected documents to the printer's icon in the Printers folder.

You can use the last technique to drag the selected documents to a printer's desktop shortcut icon. Figure 14-3, for example, shows a shortcut to my HP LaserJet printer, which I created by using the techniques discussed in Chapter 4. Then I browsed to the folder named Windows 95 Bible. Within that folder, I clicked on the Type column heading (in Details view) to group all the Microsoft Word documents. Then I selected all those Word documents. In the figure, I'm dragging the selected icons to the printer's shortcut icon to print them all in one fell swoop.

Managing Printers and Print Jobs

The icon for a printer doubles as the Print Manager for that printer. When you want to check the status of the printer or manage ongoing print jobs, double-click the printer's icon in the Printers folder or any shortcut icon for that printer. You go to a dialog box like the one shown in Figure 14-4.

You can choose options from the Printer menu to control the print queue. Choose Printer ⇨ Pause Printing to pause the entire print queue, for example, or choose Printer ⇨ Purge Print Jobs to clear all the documents waiting to be printed. To manage individual documents in the print queue, select a document by clicking it; then choose an option from the Document pull-down menu.

Puzzled? To view jobs sent to a network printer, you must go to the server (the PC physically connected to the printer) and double-click the printer's icon.

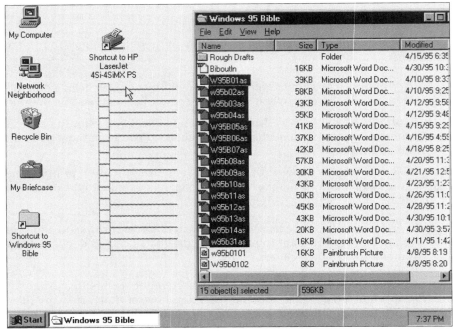

Figure 14-3: Dragging selected icons to a printer's shortcut icon

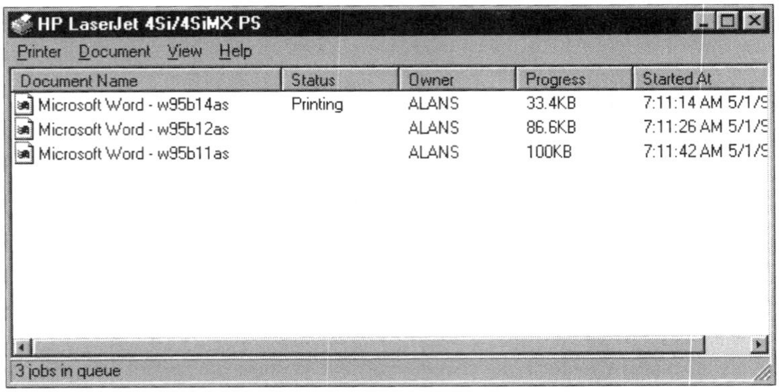

Figure 14-4: A queue of documents waiting to be printed.

Choosing a default printer

If you have access to several printers from your PC, you can specify the one you use most often as the default printer. That way, when you start a print job without specifying a particular printer, the job is sent to the default printer.

To define a default printer, follow these steps:

1. Click the Start button, and choose <u>S</u>ettings ⇨ <u>P</u>rinters.

2. Double-click the icon for the printer you want to make the default printer.

3. Choose <u>P</u>rinter ⇨ Set as De<u>f</u>ault.

Changing printer properties

Every printer has its own unique set of properties, which you can change. Regardless of what settings your printer offers, you can follow these simple steps to get to those properties:

1. Click the Start button, and choose <u>S</u>ettings ⇨ <u>P</u>rinters.

2. Right-click the icon for the printer you want to make the default printer.

3. Choose P<u>r</u>operties to get to the properties sheets.

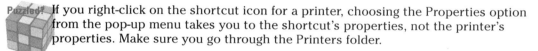 If you right-click on the shortcut icon for a printer, choosing the Properties option from the pop-up menu takes you to the shortcut's properties, not the printer's properties. Make sure you go through the Printers folder.

Figure 14-5 shows a sample properties sheet for a printer. Be aware, the properties that appear on your screen depend entirely on your printer. For more information about the available properties, refer to the manual that came with your printer.

Using Fonts

A *font*, simply stated, is a style of print. This text is in one font; the heading above this paragraph is in a different font. Any font can be printed in a variety of weights. What you're reading right now is the regular (or roman) weight. **This is the boldface (or bold) version of this font.** *And here is the italic weight for this font.*

The size of a font is measured in *points*: 1 point equals roughly 1/72 inch. Normal-size text (such as this) usually ranges from 8 to 12 points. Letters printed at 36-point size are around a half-inch tall, and letters printed at 72 points are around one-inch tall.

The three main classes of fonts are serif, sans serif, and decorative. *Serif* fonts have little curlicues at the end of each letter to minimize eyestrain when reading small print. This font and the Times New Roman font shown in Figure 14-6 are serif fonts.

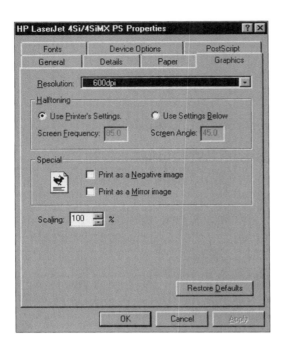

Figure 14-5: Properties for an HP LaserJet 4Si/4SiMX printer

Figure 14-6: Examples of fonts

Sans serif fonts don't have the little curlicues and generally are used for large text. The Arial font shown in Figure 14-6 is a sans serif font, as are the fonts that appear on most street signs.

Decorative fonts are used to call attention to something or to set a mood. Most of the fonts shown in Figure 14-6 are decorative. These fonts sometimes are used for headlines, advertisements, and signs, usually to call attention to a single word or short phrase. Some decorative fonts (for example, the last two in Figure 14-6) contain little clip-art images and symbols.

After a font is installed, the way you apply it to text depends on the program you're using. In most programs, you select the text to which you want to apply the font and then choose Format ➪ Font. In some cases, you can choose a font from the toolbar. Figure 14-7 shows a Microsoft Word document; I'm using the Font drop-down list in the formatting toolbar to apply a font to selected text.

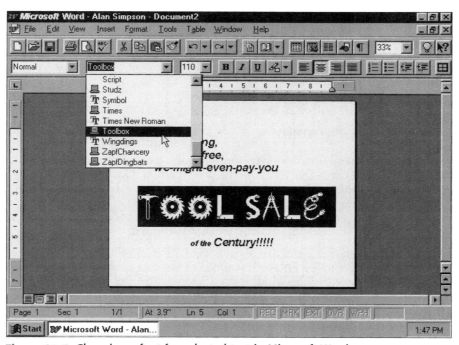

Figure 14-7: Choosing a font for selected text in Microsoft Word

Expanding your font collection

Thousands of fonts are available in the marketplace. When buying fonts, try to limit yourself to TrueType and PostScript Type 1 fonts, both of which are fully compatible with Windows 95. TrueType, however, offers a few advantages over

PostScript. For one thing, TrueType fonts are fully supported by virtually all Windows programs and utilities and by all printers that can print graphics. The tools for managing TrueType fonts are built into Windows 95.

The downside to TrueType is most professional typesetting and printing services support PostScript fonts, rather than TrueType. If your printing needs often take you beyond the desktop, you may want to ask your printing service which fonts it prefers; chances are the choice will be PostScript. If you lean more toward PostScript fonts, you'll need to buy a PostScript printer or add PostScript capability (if available) to your current printer.

You can find TrueType and PostScript fonts at computer stores; the fonts also are advertised in many computer and desktop-publishing magazines. One of my favorite sources of fonts is Image Club, which will gladly send you its catalog. Contact Image Club Graphics, Inc., c/o Publisher's Mail Service, 10545 West Donges Court, Milwaukee, WI 53224-9985. The phone number is (800) 387-9193; the fax number is (800) 814-7783.

Managing TrueType fonts

You can review, add, and remove TrueType fonts via the Fonts folder. To get there, follow these steps:

1. Click the Start button, and choose Settings ➪ Control Panel.

2. Double-click the Fonts icon.

An icon for each installed TrueType font appears, marked with a TT symbol. The folder also lists older raster fonts, which are included with Windows 95 to maintain compatibility with earlier versions.

   ✦ *To select a view,* pull down the View menu and choose any command, or click one of the view-option buttons in the toolbar.

   ✦ *To see what a font looks like,* double-click its icon. When the font's window appears (refer to Figure 14-8), you can click Print to print the font sample or click Done to close the window.

   ✦ *To delete a font,* click its icon and choose File ➪ Delete.

   ✦ *To view similar fonts,* choose View ➪ Fonts by Similarity. Then choose a font from the List fonts by Similarity to drop-down list.

   ✦ *To close the Fonts folder,* click its Close (X) button.

You don't use the Fonts folder to apply a font to text. Instead, you apply fonts to text within whatever program you are working with at the moment, as described earlier in this section.

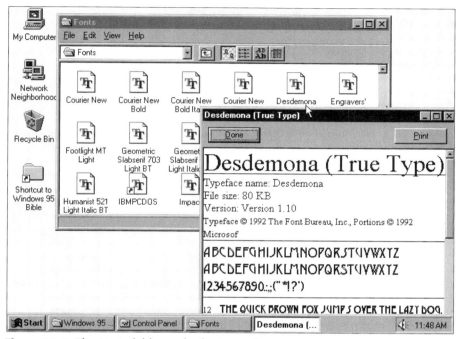

Figure 14-8: The Fonts folder and a font sample onscreen

Installing TrueType fonts

New TrueType fonts you purchase typically are delivered on floppy disk or CD-ROM. Before you can use a TrueType font, you must install it. Follow these steps:

1. Insert the floppy disk or CD-ROM that contains the font(s) into a drive.

2. Click the Start button, and choose Settings ➪ Control Panel.

3. Double-click the Fonts icon to display the Fonts folder.

4. Choose File ➪ Install New Font.

5. Use the Drives and Folders options to navigate to the disk that contains the fonts you want to install.

    In Figure 14-9, I've navigated to the floppy disk in drive A.

6. In the List of fonts box, select the font(s) you want to install.

    You can Shift+click and Ctrl+click to select multiple fonts. You also can click the Select All button to select all the listed fonts.

7. Click the OK button.

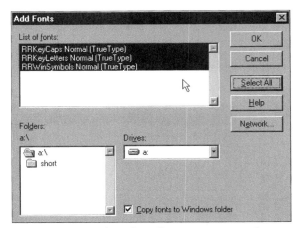

Figure 14-9: Ready to install a new TrueType font from a floppy disk

Copying the fonts to your hard disk takes a few moments. When that process finishes, you return to the Fonts folder; the new fonts will be listed there. To verify the font installation, close the Fonts and Control Panel windows, start any Windows program, and look at your font options within that program.

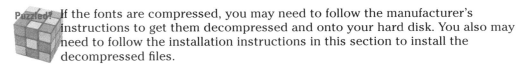 If the fonts are compressed, you may need to follow the manufacturer's instructions to get them decompressed and onto your hard disk. You also may need to follow the installation instructions in this section to install the decompressed files.

Managing PostScript Type 1 fonts

Windows 95 has no built-in capability to manage PostScript fonts; instead, you use Adobe Type Manager (ATM) to install and manage PostScript fonts. Typically, when you buy a set of PostScript fonts, a copy of ATM comes with the fonts on a disk labeled ATM Program Disk (or something to that effect). You have to install that program before you can use PostScript fonts.

Installing Adobe Type Manager

You install Adobe Type Manager as you would any other program; you need to install it only once. ATM is updated from time to time, however, so when you get a new copy of ATM, you may want to try installing it. If the version you are about to install is *not* newer than the version you already have installed, a message on the screen tells you so, and you can cancel the installation.

To install ATM, follow these steps:

  1. Save any work in progress, and close all open program windows.

2. Insert the Adobe Type Manager program disk or CD-ROM into the floppy or CD-ROM drive.

3. Click the Start button, and choose Settings ➪ Control Panel.

4. Double-click Add/Remove Programs.

5. Click the Install button.

6. Follow the instructions onscreen.

Life Saver If Add/Remove Programs doesn't find an INSTALL or Setup program, perhaps the disk you're using contains only fonts — not the ATM program. Look for the disk labeled Program Disk, and try again.

When the installation process starts, you go to a window that looks something like Figure 14-10 (depending on what version you happen to be installing). You can accept the suggested folders for storing the fonts (C:\PSFONTS and C:\PSFONTS\PFM) and then click on Install. After the fonts have been copied to your hard disk, you're prompted to restart Windows; do so. Remove the ATM disk from its drive after you restart Windows 95.

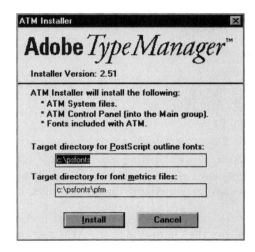

Figure 14-10: Ready to install Adobe Type Manager

From now on, ATM loads automatically whenever you start Windows 95. The Adobe icon will appear (briefly) in the lower-left corner of the screen while Windows 95 is starting.

Managing PostScript fonts

When you want to review, delete, or add PostScript fonts, you need to open the ATM Control Panel. Typically, you do this by following these simple steps:

1. Click the Start button, and point to Programs.

2. Point to Main, and click ATM Control Panel.

You are taken to the Adobe Type Manager Control Panel, shown in Figure 14-11. If you don't see a program group called Main, look through other program groups to see whether you can find the icon for the ATM Control Panel. If you still can't find the icon and are certain you have installed ATM, see the sidebar in this section titled "Where's my ATM Control Panel?"

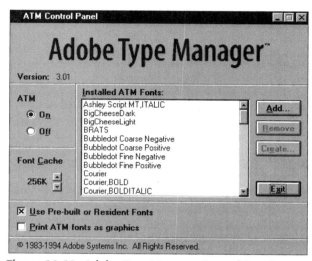

Figure 14-11: Adobe Type Manager Control Panel

The list in the center of the ATM Control Panel shows the PostScript fonts you already have installed. To remove a font, select the font name and then click on the Remove button. When you finish reviewing or deleting PostScript fonts, click on the Exit button.

Danger
Zone
In the ATM Control Panel, always make sure the On option in the ATM section is selected. If you select Off, ATM won't load at startup, and your PostScript fonts won't display onscreen.

Where's my ATM Control Panel?

If you are certain you have installed Adobe Type Manager but can't find its Startup icon anywhere in your <u>P</u>rograms menu, you can create a shortcut. Here's the basic procedure:

1. Right-click the Start button, and choose <u>O</u>pen.

2. Double-click the Programs icon.

3. Click the Start button again, and choose <u>F</u>ind ⇨ <u>F</u>iles or Folders.

4. Type **atmcntrl**, and click F<u>i</u>nd Now.

The icon you're looking for is represented by a lowercase *a*. Move and size the Find

and Programs windows so you can see the atmcntrl icon and the folders in the Programs menu.

5. Right-drag the atmcntrl icon into any folder in the Programs folder.

6. Release the right mouse button, and choose Create <u>S</u>hortcut(s) Here.

7. Close all open windows.

To start the ATM Control Panel in the future, click the Start button, point to <u>P</u>rograms, point to whatever program group you dragged the atmcntrl icon to, and then click the ATM Control Panel icon.

Installing PostScript fonts

When you purchase new PostScript fonts, they're delivered to you on floppy disk or CD-ROM. You need to use the ATM Control Panel to install those fonts on your hard disk before you can use them. Follow these steps:

1. Insert the floppy disk or CD-ROM that contains the fonts you want to install.

2. Start the ATM Control Panel, as described in the preceding section ("Managing PostScript fonts").

3. Click the <u>A</u>dd button.

4. Navigate to the drive and folder that contain the fonts you want to install.

   In many versions of ATM, you need to scroll to the bottom of the Directo<u>r</u>ies list, and then double-click on a drive letter, such as [-a-] for drive A. Then, if necessary, you choose the appropriate folder from the Directo<u>r</u>ies list.

5. Select the font(s) you want to install.

You can Shift+click and Ctrl+click to select multiple fonts.

6. Click the <u>A</u>dd button to begin the installation.

7. Follow the instructions (if any) that appear onscreen.

When installation is complete, you return to the ATM Control Panel. Click on the Exit button. To verify that the PostScript fonts are now available, start any program that supports fonts, and check out your selection of fonts within the program. If the PostScript fonts you just installed aren't available, you may need to restart Windows. Click on the Start button, and choose Shut Down ➪ Restart the computer? ➪ Yes. Then try again when you get back to the desktop.

Add a Little Art to Your Life

Clip art is a great way to spruce up newsletters, reports, brochures, and other printed material. You can buy clip-art collections at most computer stores, and also from mail-order houses that advertise in computer and desktop-publishing magazines. Figure 14-12 shows a few examples, ranging from the fun and funky images of Art Parts to the photographic realism of Oswego's Illustrated Archives.

Art Parts
Fax: (714) 633-9617

Oswego Illustrated Archives (eps)
Fax: (503) 274-9326

Presentation Task Force
(613) 727-8184

DigitArt (eps) from Image Club
Fax: (800) 814-7783

Figure 14-12: Sample clip art

Sharing PostScript fonts on a LAN

If you have a LAN, it's not always easy to ensure that every PC on the LAN has exactly the same set of fonts installed. Also, if your collection of fonts takes up a great deal of disk space, storing the same fonts on every PC in the LAN wastes disk space. You can solve both problems by installing fonts on only one PC in the LAN and then sharing the folder that contains the fonts.

To do this, first choose one PC in the LAN to hold the PostScript fonts. Install the PostScript fonts on that PC, using ATM as usual. After installing the fonts, share the folder that contains the fonts (typically, c:\psfonts).

Next, go to any other PC in the LAN, and use Network Neighborhood to map a drive letter to the shared folder that contains the PostScript fonts. Choose Reconnect at Logon, while you're at it. For example, suppose you decide to map the drive letter **t:** to that shared folder. (For more information on sharing folders and mapping drive letters, see Chapter 26.)

After mapping the drive letter, stay at this PC, and start ATM. Click on the Add button, and make sure Install without copying files is selected. Then use the Directories list to browse to the shared folder that contains the PostScript fonts (**t:**, in this example). Select the fonts you want to use, and click the Add button.

In the future, you can use the PostScript fonts normally from this PC, so long as you're connected to that shared folder (drive **t:**, in this example).

Windows 95 supports all popular PC clip-art formats including .CGM, .TIF, .PCX, .BMP, .WMF, and .GIF. The real compatibility issue, however, is between the program in which you plan to use the clip art and the format of the clip art. You should check the help file or documentation for your word processing, desktop publishing, or graphics program to see which formats are supported.

Danger Zone Some professional clip-art packages deliver their files in Encapsulated PostScript (EPS) format. You can print those images only on PostScript printers.

Many clip-art collections are delivered on CD-ROM, so you won't need to use a great deal of hard disk space to store them. I always keep a little collection of frequently used clip art on my hard disk. As I discussed in Chapter 8, I keep all the clip art in one folder and organize the art, by theme, in subfolders. That clip-art folder is shared on my LAN, so I can get to it from any PC in my LAN (or by phone, if I happen to be away).

A good clip-art browser is a tool worth having. One of these browsers, called the Microsoft Clip Art Gallery, is built into Office 95. The Gallery enables you to organize clip art by theme and displays thumbnails of each piece of art within a theme, as in the example shown in Figure 14-13.

Figure 14-13: Microsoft Clip Art Gallery comes with Office 95.

The Gallery is simple to use. When I want to pop a piece of art into a Word (or whatever) document, I choose Insert ⇨ Object ⇨ Microsoft Clip Art. The Gallery appears, and I choose a category from the left column. Then I double-click a thumbnail picture, and that picture pops into my document.

Printing the screen (screen dump)

If you're familiar with DOS, you may remember the days when you could press the Print Screen (Prt Scr) key to print a copy of whatever was onscreen. In Windows, pressing Print Screen sends a copy of the screen to the Clipboard, rather than to the printer, so you must take a few extra steps to print the screen. To take it from the top, follow these steps:

1. If you haven't already done so, arrange the screen so it looks as you want it to look in print.

2. To capture the entire screen, press Print Screen.

   To capture only the active window, press Alt+Print Screen.

   Some PCs require you to press Shift+Print Screen or Alt+Shift+Print Screen to capture the screen.

3. Click the Start button, and choose <u>P</u>rograms ⇨ Accessories.

4. Click the Paint icon.

5. Choose <u>E</u>dit ⇨ <u>P</u>aste or press Ctrl+V.

6. To print the image immediately, choose <u>F</u>ile ⇨ <u>P</u>rint ⇨ and then click the OK button.

This method is fine for the occasional screen shot. But if you need to manage many screen shots, or if you need to crop, size, add borders, and embed the screen shots in other documents, you'd do well to buy a program designed for that purpose.

To create the screen shots for this book, I used Collage for Windows, published by Inner Media Inc., 60 Plain Road, Hollis, NH (603) 465-3216.

Image Color Matching support

Windows 95 is the first version of Windows to support Image Color Matching (ICM). This technology, licensed from Eastman Kodak, enables programs to offer better consistency between the colors displayed onscreen and the colors that come out of the printer.

Because ICM is built in, there's nothing you, personally, must do to take advantage of it. Instead, when you purchase new software and hardware for printing color, you want to look for a product that supports ICM. When installed, the product creates a profile in the Windows\System\Color folder. When you use the product, Windows 95 automatically performs the appropriate color transformation to ensure consistent color representation across all display and printing devices.

Awesome Papers

Your printer can do much more than just print text and graphics on $8^1/_2 \times 11$-inch paper. The following sections examine ways you can expand your horizons by printing labels, cards, checks, and more.

Printing checks and business forms

You can use your printer to print on preprinted checks and business forms. Just remember, if you want to print on carbon-paper forms, you should use a *forms printer* (basically, a heavy-duty dot-matrix printer). Carbonless (single-sheet thickness) forms and checks can be printed on either a laser printer or a dot-matrix printer.

To check your options, request a catalog or brochure from the following companies:

Designer Checks
P.O. Box 13387
Birmingham, AL 35202
Phone: (800) 239-4087
Fax: (800) 774-1118

Nebs
500 Main Street
Groton, MA 01471
Phone: (800) 225-6380
Fax: (800) 234-4324

Cards, stickers, transparencies, and slides

Most laser printers can print on mailing labels, floppy disk labels, file-folder labels, and a wide variety of stickers. You can find stock for printing on those items, as well as for printing business cards, invitations, greeting cards, file cards, and gatefold mailers. Most laser printers even enable you to print on the transparencies used with overhead projectors. But don't trust just any paper or transparency to your laser printer; instead, find stock specifically designed to handle the high heat laser printers produce.

The Avery label company offers a large selection of laser-printer labels, stickers, and transparencies. You can find these products at most large office-supply and computer stores. Alternatively, contact Avery at the following address:

Avery Laser Products
P.O. Box 5244
Diamond Bar, CA 91765-4000
Phone: (800) 462-8379
FaxFacts: (818) 584-1681

For cards and predesigned labels, see the catalogs mentioned in "Color from black-and-white printers" later in this chapter.

Label printers

If you get tired of switching between regular stock and labels in your printer, consider purchasing a dedicated label printer. Typically, you can plug the label printer into a serial port, so it doesn't conflict with your main printer.

Seiko Instruments makes nice label printers, which you can find at most computer stores. I use a CoStar label printer, and I'm pleased with it. For more information on that label printer, contact the company at the following address:

CoStar Corporation
100 Field Point Road
Greenwich, CT 06830-6406
Phone: (800) 4-COSTAR or (203) 661-9700
Fax: (203) 661-1540

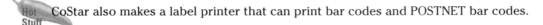

CoStar also makes a label printer that can print bar codes and POSTNET bar codes.

35mm slides

Printing on 35mm slides for a slide show requires special equipment. The most cost-effective means of creating and printing 35mm slides is presentation software such as Microsoft PowerPoint, which comes with the Office 95 suite. Within this program, you'll find instructions for sending your work to a service center that will create the slides for you.

Color from black-and-white printers

Even if you don't have a color printer, you still can use color to spruce up your letterhead, brochures, mailing labels, postcards, business cards, newsletters, and other items. Just purchase predesigned colored stock for laser printers. The selection of designs, paper sizes, and label formats is fantastic, and you can buy coordinated sets to give your documents a consistent, professional image. Contact the following companies, and ask them to send you a catalog. You'll be glad you did.

Image Street
P.O. Box 5000
Vernon Hills, IL 60061
Phone: (800) 462-4378
Fax: (800) 329-6677

On Paper
P.O. Box 1365
Elk Grove Village, IL 60009-1365
Phone: (800) 829-2299
Fax: (800) 595-2094

Premier Papers
P.O. Box 64785
St. Paul, MN 55164
Phone: (800) 843-0414
Fax: (800) 526-3029

Queblo
1000 Florida Ave.
P.O. Box 1393
Hagerstown, MD 21741-9893
Phone: (800) 523-9080
Fax: (800) 554-8779

Troubleshooting Printers and Fonts

If you have any trouble with printing or fonts, the Troubleshooter can help you. Follow these steps:

1. Click the Start button, and choose Help.

2. Click the Contents tab.

3. Double-click the Troubleshooting book.

4. Double-click If you have trouble printing.

5. Follow the steps onscreen.

If you have trouble with PostScript fonts, first make sure ATM is loaded. To do that, open the ATM Control Panel, and make sure ATM is on. Exit ATM, and restart the computer.

If PostScript fonts aren't included in your list of available fonts, check the program's help file or documentation for information on fonts. Some applications and utilities, such as Microsoft WordArt, do not support PostScript fonts. (I just hate it when that happens!)

Finally, if your PostScript fonts are on another PC in a LAN, use Network Neighborhood to map a drive letter to the shared folder. Be sure to use the same drive letter you used to install the fonts (such as T:) to reconnect to that shared folder.

Summary

Here's a quick recap of the important points about printing:

✦ To install a printer, connect it to your PC per the manufacturer's instructions. Then to install the Windows 95 drivers, click Start, choose Settings ➪ Printers, double-click the Add Printer icon, and follow the instructions on the screen.

✦ To print the document that's currently open and visible on the screen, choose File ➪ Print from the program's menu bar.

✦ To print a document that isn't open, right-click the document's icon and choose Print. Or drag the document's icon to a printer icon.

✦ To manage print jobs in progress, double-click the printer's icon. Use the Printer and Document commands in the menu bar that appears to manage print jobs.

✦ To install and manage TrueType fonts, click the Start button and choose Settings ➪ Control Panel. Then double-click the Fonts icon.

✦ To install and manage PostScript Type 1 fonts, you need to purchase and install the Adobe Type Manager program, available wherever fonts are sold.

✦ To apply a font to selected text, use commands in whatever program you're working with at the moment. Typically, you just need to select text, then choose Format ➪ Font from the program's menu bar.

✦ Clip art is a great way to spruce up printed documents. Learn to use a clip art browser, such as the ClipArt Gallery that comes with Microsoft Office to get the most from your clip-art collection.

✦ Remember, you're not limited to plain white 8.5 × 11-inch paper. There are hundreds of sizes and colors of papers from which to choose.

✦   ✦   ✦

Choosing and Installing a Modem

In the next chapter, I'll talk about PC faxing and telephony. In later chapters, I'll discuss using information services, transmitting files via phone lines, and dial-up networking. All these options require a modem. So this is a good time to discuss modems in general and how you install one on your Windows 95 PC.

Choosing a Modem

A *modem* is a gadget for hooking your computer to a telephone. Dozens of modems are on the market, each with its own strengths and weaknesses. Choosing a modem can be a little tricky, because you have so many options. The following sections explain the key features to consider.

Major features of modems

Before you buy a modem, you should consider which features you need. Some modems are strictly data modems; some modems have auto-answer capabilities; still other modems offer fax and voice-mail capabilities. Here, in a nutshell, are the reasons why you might want these features:

✦ *Data modem:* You use this basic modem to connect to cyberspace: the Internet, CompuServe, America Online, the Microsoft Network, bulletin-board systems (BBSs), and other PCs.

✦ *Auto-answer modem:* If you plan to use dial-up networking (see Chapter 19), you need a modem with auto-answer capability. You'll also need this capability if you want to accept incoming calls from other PCs.

✦ *Fax/modem:* A fax/modem enables you to send a fax directly from your PC, without printing it. The majority of fax/modems actually are fax/data modems; they can fax and do all the stuff that a data modem can do.

✦ *Cellular modem:* A cellular modem is a fax/data modem that fits into the PCMCIA slot of a laptop computer and connects to a cellular phone. This modem enables you to make fax/data transmissions on the road (that is, from your car or in a plane).

✦ *Telephony board:* A telephony board is a combination of a data modem and fax modem with sound that can act as an answering machine and/or voice-mail system. Some telephony boards even support fax on demand and fax back (see Chapter 16).

✦ *ISDN Terminal Adapter:* A special high-speed digital "modem" used to connect to the Internet and some of the online services. Requires special arrangements with the telephone company and the service to which you're connecting. See Chapter 23 for more information.

Internal, external, and PC Card modems

You can buy modems in three main configurations: internal, external, and PC Card. No real difference exists among the types in terms of performance. The following list summarizes the types of modem configurations:

✦ *External modem.* Up side: Easy hookup; you don't have to disassemble the computer. Down side: You must have a spare serial (COM) port, and the modem takes up a little space on your desktop.

✦ *Internal modem.* Up side: The modem stays inside your PC and doesn't take up any space. Down side: You need to disassemble the computer to install the modem and you may need to mess with IRQs and all that.

More Info For more information on IRQ settings and installing hardware, refer to Chapter 10. For more information on PCMCIA slots, see Chapter 19.

✦ *PC Card.* A PC Card (PCMCIA) modem fits into the PCMCIA slot. Most modern laptops have at least one PCMCIA slot. When you buy a PCMCIA modem, make sure it's compatible with your PCMCIA slot type. Chapter 19 discusses PCMCIA in depth.

Performance considerations

Modem speed determines how long it takes to send and receive files over telephone lines. The general rule of thumb is simple: The higher the baud rate, the less time you spend waiting. The going baud rate currently is 28.8K. Most online services support at least 14.4K. So, if you're going to buy a modem, 14.4 or 28.8 is the way to go.

So many gizmos, so few phone numbers

Pop quiz: Suppose you have several phone gadgets, such as an answering machine, fax machine, data modem, and regular voice telephone, but you have only one phone number. How do you handle incoming calls — that is, how do you keep the modem from answering when someone is calling you to talk? And how do you get the fax machine to pick up the call when someone is sending you a fax?

One simple answer is a telephone line-sharing device, such as the ComShare devices made by Command Communications Inc. A line-sharing device automatically determines whether an incoming call is a fax, a PC, or a human being, and then directs the call to the appropriate gadget. Check out these devices at your local computer store, or contact the manufacturer at (303) 751-5000 or fax (303) 750-6437.

Some modems also have what people call the *v-dot* standard. Again, the higher the number, the faster and more capable the model is. Currently, v.34 is the latest standard.

A fast modem may pay for itself quickly if you download files from services that charge for connect time. A file that takes 60 minutes to download at 9600K baud, for example, might take 30 minutes to download at 14.4K. Half the connect time means half the cost.

Most modems are downwardly compatible — that is, if you buy a state-of-the-art 28.8K, v.34 modem, you can still access older (slower) modems. You can, for example, use your 28.8K modem to dial in to a service that only supports speeds up to 14.4K. A good modem detects the slower speed of the modem at the other end of the line and adjusts itself accordingly. This feature is called *auto-negotiation*.

Choosing a modem based on performance is simply a matter of deciding how much money you want to spend. A state-of-the-art modem always costs more than yesterday's model, but the return on your investment is less waiting time (and, usually, better reliability).

Windows 95 compatibility

Modems that bear the Designed for Windows 95 plug-and-play logo are the easiest to install; you just plug in the modem and go. Windows 95 also comes with built-in 32-bit drivers for many nonplug-and-play modems. If you want to see which nonplug-and-play modems Windows 95 has drivers for, follow these steps:

1. Click the Start button.

2. Choose <u>S</u>ettings ➪ <u>C</u>ontrol Panel.

3. Double-click the Modems icon.

4. Do one of the following:

- If — and *only* if — you see a dialog box rather than the Install New Modem wizard, a modem already is installed on your PC.

- If you want to look at drivers for other modems, click the Add button.

5. In the Install New Modem wizard, select the check box for the option Don't detect my modem; I will select it from a list.

6. Click Next.

You are taken to the window shown in Figure 15-1.

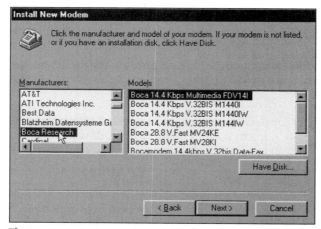

Figure 15-1: Makes and models of modems supported by Windows 95

7. Click any modem manufacturer in the left column.

The right column shows you the specific models Windows 95 supports directly. Browse at your leisure.

8. When you finish, click Cancel.

Be sure to click Cancel in Step 8 because, at this point, you're just looking at makes and models of supported modems, not actually installing the modem. If you already have a modem installed, click the Close button in the dialog box that displays that modem name to return to the Control Panel without disturbing the existing modem installation.

Installing the Modem

The first step in installing a modem is actually installing the modem hardware. Follow the modem manufacturer's instructions to do this. But *don't install any DOS or Windows 3 drivers.* Just physically install the modem in your PC or connect it to a serial port, and then connect the modem to a telephone wall jack.

If your modem has a jack labeled Phone, use that jack *only* if you are using one wall jack and one telephone number for both your modem and voice telephone. The jack labeled Phone always connects to a voice telephone — never to the wall jack.

When your modem is installed, turned on, and connected to the phone jack, and your PC is up and running, you're ready to install the modem drivers. If Windows 95 detects the new modem at startup, it may install the correct drivers automatically. But even if the modem appears to be installed, there's no harm in checking to make certain. Even if you think the modem drivers are already installed, complete at least the first four of the following steps:

1. Gather up your original Windows 95 floppies or CD-ROM.

   Keep any disks that came with the modem handy, too, in case you need to install the manufacturer's drivers. (You install those drivers only if Windows 95 has no driver for your modem.)

2. Click the Start button.

3. Choose <u>S</u>ettings ⇨ <u>C</u>ontrol Panel.

4. Double-click the Modems icon.

   If your modem is already installed, the Modem Properties window appears. Click the Cancel button — you don't need to reinstall the same modem.

   If your modem is not installed, you see the Install New Modem wizard, shown in Figure 15-2.

5. Click the Next button.

6. Follow the instructions on the screen.

The wizard guides you through the process of installing your modem. When you finish, you return to the Windows 95 desktop.

If your modem has a built-in sound card for voice, the Add New Hardware wizard may install everything without activating the modem. Follow the preceding steps to verify installation or, if necessary, to install the modem.

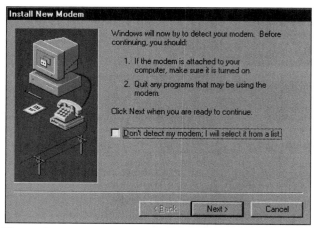

Figure 15-2: The Install New Modem wizard

Using Your Modem for Speed Dialing

Windows 95 comes with a handy little phone dialer. Like the speed dialer on some phones, this device enables you to keep a list of frequently called numbers and to dial those numbers with the click of a button. Phone Dialer is especially handy if your modem shares the same phone number as your voice phone, because you can use Phone Dialer to dial out. When the connection is made, an onscreen message tells you to pick up the receiver and click the Talk button.

More Info If Phone Dialer isn't in your Accessories menu, you can install it now. See "Installing Missing Windows Components" in Chapter 9. When you get to the Windows Setup tab, click the Communications component, and then click the Details button to find Phone Dialer.

To use Phone Dialer, follow these steps:

1. Click the Start button.

2. Choose Programs ➪ Accessories.

3. Click Phone Dialer to display its dialog box (see Figure 15-3).

Figure 15-3: The Windows 95 Phone Dialer

Phone Dialer is fairly self-explanatory after you're in it. But I'll discuss the basic options in the following sections.

Adding numbers to the speed dialer

Adding a new phone number to the speed dialer is easy: Just click any blank button and fill in the blanks that appear. Include the area code, even if the phone number is within your own area code. Suppose your phone number is (619) 555-4321 and the number you want to speed dial is (619) 555-1234. You would type the number as follows:

```
(619)555-1234
```

When you speed dial the number, Phone Dialer automatically omits the area code. So why include it in the first place? You'll see when you get to "Changing Phone Dialer's dialing properties" later in this chapter.

The only time you need to omit the area code from a phone number is when you're predialing some number to get a discounted local rate. For example, my phone company promises that if I dial 10+ATT before I dial a local number, the call will cost me less. I can use 10+ATT only when I'm dialing a number within my area code, so I must omit the area code. If I want the speed dialer to dial, say, 10+ATT, and then 555-9876, I would type the number to dial like this:

```
10288,555-9876
```

The comma is optional; it causes a slight pause in the dialing sequence. I include the comma just so I can hear the pause when the modem is dialing, as a reminder that 10+ATT is activated. This way, if I use the speed dialer on my laptop from another area code, and the call doesn't go through, the pause reminds me I must dial 1 and the area code, rather than 10288, from my current location.

You can add up to eight speed dial numbers. If you need to change an entry later, choose Edit ➪ Speed Dial from within Phone Dialer, and follow the simple instructions onscreen.

Changing Phone Dialer's dialing properties

Phone Dialer's properties sheet enables you to define where you're dialing from and how to dial. This feature is especially handy if you use Phone Dialer on the road because you need to change only the dialing properties — not all your speed dial numbers — to dial each number correctly. But even if you don't take your PC traveling, you should set up the dialing properties for your permanent location. Follow these steps:

1. If you haven't already done so, open Phone Dialer.

2. Choose Tools ➪ Dialing Properties.

3. Fill in the blanks for your default location.

   If you need more information about an option, click the question-mark button, and then click the option.

Danger Zone
Don't use the options in the How I dial from this location section to dial a 1 before dialing an area code; that procedure is taken care of behind the scenes. I'll show you when those options are useful in a moment.

4. Choose OK when you finish.

Figure 15-4 shows the options in the Dialing Properties dialog box set up for me to use at my default location (home) in San Diego, which is in the 619 area code.

Using Phone Dialer

To use Phone Dialer, follow these steps:

1. Open Phone Dialer, as described earlier in this chapter.

Hot Stuff
If you use Phone Dialer often, create a desktop shortcut icon for it (refer to Chapter 4).

On the road with Phone Dialer

When you're using Phone Dialer on a laptop, and you're outside your own area code, you can set up a new set of dialing properties for your current location. Open Phone Dialer (if you haven't already), and choose Tools ⇨ Dialing Properties. Click the New button, and enter a name for your new location. (The name of the city would do, or perhaps even a hotel name and city.) Choose OK, and fill in the dialog box for your current location.

In Figure 15-5, I set up properties for dialing from a hotel in the San Francisco area. Notice the area code is shown as 415. The instructions on the hotel room's phone told me I must first dial 8 to dial a local number or 9 to dial a long-distance number, so I set the How I dial from this location options accordingly. I also opted to use my calling card from the new location.

The cool thing is when you return home, you don't need to mess with all the dialing properties. Instead, open the Dialing Properties dialog box again, and select your current location from the I am dialing from drop-down list. If you go back to that hotel in San Francisco, simply choose your San Francisco-area properties from the same drop-down list.

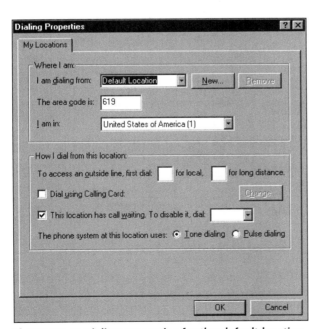

Figure 15-4: Dialing properties for the default location

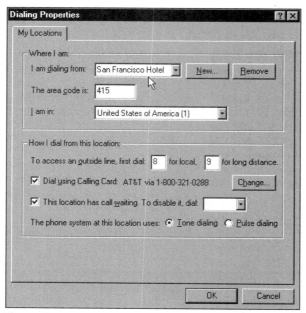

Figure 15-5: Dialing properties set for a San Francisco hotel room

2. If you've changed your location since the last time you used Phone Dialer, choose (or create) dialing properties for your current location.

3. To speed dial a number, click its speed dial button.

   If you don't have a speed dial button, use any of the following techniques:

   • If you dialed the number recently, you may be able to select it from the <u>N</u>umber to dial drop-down list.

   • In the <u>N</u>umber to dial text box, type the number you want to dial.

> **Hot Stuff** You can omit parentheses, hyphens, and spaces in Phone Dialer numbers. You can type 6195551234, for example, rather than (619)555-1234.

   • Click the dialing buttons as though you are dialing on a touch-tone phone.

4. Click the <u>D</u>ial button.

5. Follow the instructions onscreen.

Using Phone Dialer is easy and convenient, after you get the hang of it. But you can do more with your modem than just dial the phone, as you'll learn in upcoming chapters.

Troubleshooting a Modem

If you have any problems with your modem, use the Troubleshooter to track down and correct the problem. Follow these steps:

1. Click the Start button.
2. Click Help.
3. Click the Contents tab.
4. Double-click the Troubleshooting book.
5. Double-click the If you have trouble using your modem option.
6. Follow the instructions onscreen to diagnose and solve the problem.

If you're using a PC Card (PCMCIA) modem, see Chapter 19 for more information.

Removing a Modem

If you plan to remove an external or internal modem, you should first remove its driver and free whatever resources the driver is using. To do so, repeat Steps 1–4 in "Installing the Modem" earlier in this chapter to display the Modem Properties dialog box. Click the name of the modem you want to remove; then click the Remove button. Shut down Windows and turn off the PC before you remove the modem.

Summary

Here are the main points to remember when choosing and installing a modem:

✦ The most important factor in choosing a modem is speed. The faster the better. If you plan to purchase a modem, be sure to get one that supports at least 14.4Kbps transmission speeds.

✦ When installing a modem, follow the manufacturer's instructions for installing the hardware only. Don't install any DOS or DOS/Windows 3 drivers for the modem.

✦ After you physically install the modem, install the Windows 95 drivers. To do so, click the Start button and select Settings ➪ Control Panel. Double-click the Modems icon and follow the onscreen instructions.

✦ Once your modem is installed, you can use the Windows 95 Speed Dialer. Click the Start button, point to Programs ➪ Accessories, and then click Phone Dialer.

✦   ✦   ✦

PC Faxing and Telephony

The capability to send faxes directly from your PC has several advantages over sending faxes on a standard fax machine. First, if you compose the fax on your PC, you don't have to print it and feed it through the fax machine. Second, you can broadcast the fax to several people at the same time, if you want.

And third, you can receive faxes on your PC without a fax machine. Documents sent from a regular fax machine are stored as "photographs" that you can view on your screen and print at your convenience. As you'll learn in this chapter, if both the sending and receiving machines use Microsoft Fax, you also can send an editable file via fax. For example, you can fax a Microsoft Word document (.DOC) to someone. The recipient can open the faxed document, edit it normally with Word, and then fax it back to you.

In this chapter, I'll discuss Microsoft Fax, the faxing tool built right into Windows 95. I'll also discuss general telephony, such as voice mail and fax-on-demand. While these features are not actually built into Windows 95, you can add them to your Windows 95 PC by purchasing the appropriate hardware and software.

Is Microsoft Fax Installed Yet?

If you've never used Microsoft Fax, it may not yet be installed on your PC. Following is a quick and easy way to determine whether you need to install Microsoft Fax:

1. Click the Start button.
2. Choose <u>P</u>rograms ➪ Accessories.

3. If you see a Fax option in the Accessories menu, you're in luck. Click anywhere outside the menus, and then go straight to the section "Setting Up Your Fax Properties."

If you did not see a Fax option in your Accessories menu, you need to install Microsoft Fax, as described in the following section.

Installing Microsoft Fax

Be sure to install your fax/modem, as discussed in Chapter 15, before you install Microsoft Fax. Testing the modem with Phone Dialer first is a good idea, to make certain you get a dial tone. When your modem is installed, you can follow the steps to install Microsoft Fax. Note: Microsoft Fax uses Microsoft Exchange to handle incoming and outgoing faxes. But don't worry. If you've never installed Microsoft Exchange, these steps will install and set up Exchange for you, as well.

Puzzled? Microsoft Exchange is a program that handles all your incoming and outgoing messages and faxes. But you don't need to know anything about Exchange to use Microsoft Fax. Windows 95 automatically sets up Exchange for you and makes it available when you need it. For now, it's best to stay focused on Microsoft Fax and those aspects of Exchange discussed in this chapter.

1. Gather your original Windows 95 floppy disks or CD-ROM; then put Disk #1 in the floppy drive or the CD-ROM in the CD-ROM drive.

2. Click the Start button.

3. Choose <u>S</u>ettings ⇨ <u>C</u>ontrol Panel.

4. Double-click Add/Remove Programs.

5. Click the Windows Setup tab.

6. Select Microsoft Fax (so it has a check mark ✔).

7. If you've never installed Microsoft Fax *or* Microsoft Exchange, you'll see a message indicating you need to install both. That's OK; choose <u>Y</u>es to proceed.

8. Click the OK button.

9. Follow the instructions onscreen.

If you are installing Exchange for the first time, the installation wizard asks which information services you want to install. For now, you only need to choose Microsoft Fax, as shown in Figure 16-1; then click the Next button. You can install other information services later, at your convenience.

The installation wizard may ask some questions about your modem, fax number, and so on. If you see this wizard, proceed through the dialog boxes and answer questions until you get to the Congratulations! screen. Then click the Finish button.

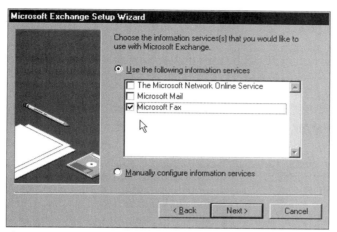

Figure 16-1: Installing both Microsoft Exchange and Microsoft Fax

Don't worry if the installation wizard doesn't appear; you'll be checking and refining all your fax settings. When you return to the Control Panel, close it. You should see a new shortcut icon, named Inbox, on your desktop. As you'll see later in this chapter, Inbox takes you to Microsoft Exchange, where you can see all your received messages, including faxes.

Setting Up Your Fax Properties

Before you use Microsoft Fax for the first time, take a few minutes to shape up all your settings. As you do for most items on your PC, you go through the Settings menu and Control Panel to set up your fax. You may be surprised to see you actually must go through yet another program — Microsoft Exchange — to get to your fax settings. This occurs because Microsoft Fax actually is an information service within Microsoft Exchange. The arrangement is a bit confusing at first, but if you can remember Microsoft Fax *is* an information service, like e-mail, you'll get used to going through Exchange to handle faxes.

To set up your fax properties, follow these steps:

1. Click the Start button.

2. Choose Settings ➪ Control Panel.

3. Double-click the Mail and Fax icon.

    You see a dialog box titled MS Exchange Settings Properties.

The Mail and Fax icon in Control Panel is strictly to configure your information services. To send and read messages, you use the Inbox icon.

4. To tweak your fax settings, click the Microsoft Fax service, and then click the Properties button.

You go to the Microsoft Fax Properties dialog box, shown in Figure 16-2. Notice this dialog box has four tabs. The following sections explain how to set up your options within each tab.

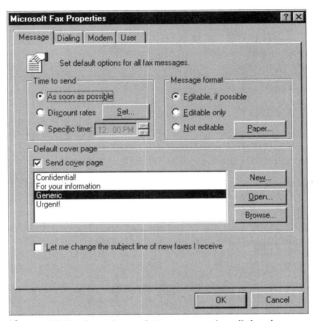

Figure 16-2: The Microsoft Fax Properties dialog box

Remember, you are choosing default settings for all future faxes here. You're choosing the most likely settings for each future fax, so you needn't make the same selections with each fax you send. When you actually send a fax, you have ample opportunity to override any of the default settings for that fax, if you want.

 As always, you can get more information about an option onscreen. Click the question-mark button and then click that option.

The Message tab

The Message tab describes how your faxes will be sent. The Time to send option enables you to determine when to send faxes. You can send each fax as you complete it or you can opt to have Exchange hold on to all outgoing faxes until the phone company's discount rates kick in (or until a specific time of your choosing).

In the Message format section, you almost certainly will want to choose Editable, if possible. This setting enables you to send editable documents to other PCs by using Microsoft Fax (or any version of Microsoft At Work). If the receiving device is a fax machine, you obviously can't send the document as an editable file; Microsoft Fax automatically sends it as a regular fax, which prints on the recipient's fax machine.

In the Default cover page section, select (check) the Send cover page option if you want each fax preceded by a cover page. For starters, use the Generic cover page. Under "Creating a Custom Cover Page" later in this chapter, I'll show you how to create your own cover page.

If you want to change the subject line appearing in the faxes you receive on the PC, choose the corresponding option. As you'll see later in this chapter, you can arrange received faxes in alphabetical order, by subject, so having the freedom to change the subject line can help you organize your faxes.

The Dialing tab

The Dialing tab records important information needed to send your faxes. Click the Dialing Properties button and choose the default location from which you send faxes. Fill in any other information, as appropriate; then choose OK to save your new settings.

Faxing editable files

Windows 95 supports Microsoft At Work fax capability, meaning it can send a file in its native format. By *native format,* I mean the format on your PC — for example, a .DOC file for a Microsoft Word document. For this reason, you want to choose the Editable, if possible option as a default.

When you attach a file to a fax message, Windows automatically detects what type of device is receiving the fax. If this receiving device supports Microsoft At Work (as Windows 95 does), the attached file is sent in its native format. When the recipient opens your fax message, he sees an icon in the body of the message. The recipient can double-click that icon to open the document in the appropriate program, ready for editing, printing, or whatever.

If the receiving device is a fax machine or a PC that does not support Microsoft At Work, Windows detects this as well. In either case, Windows automatically renders and sends a standard "photographic" fax image of your document. The recipient can open, view, and print this document with her Fax Viewer, but she cannot edit the document (unless she then uses OCR software to convert the faxed image to text, as described in the "Converting bitmaps and paper to editable text" sidebar later in this chapter).

If any prefixes within your own area code require long-distance dialing, click the Toll Prefixes button and add those prefixes to the list.

In the Retries section, define how many times you want Microsoft Fax to try sending a fax in case an attempt fails (if Microsoft Fax gets a busy signal after dialing the fax number, for example). You also can specify how long you want Microsoft Fax to wait between attempts.

The Modem tab

The Modem tab enables you to specify which modem to use for sending faxes. This capability is especially useful if you have two or more modems installed on your PC. Click the name of the modem you want to use for faxing, and then click the Set as Active Fax/modem button.

You also can set your answering options, speaker volume, and other preferences in the Modem tab. Click the Properties button and make your selections in the Fax Modem Properties dialog box, shown in Figure 16-3. Note: If you prefer to receive faxes on your fax machine, you need to set Answer mode to Don't answer. When you finish, choose OK to return to the Microsoft Fax Properties dialog box.

If you're on a LAN, you can use the Modem tab to share your fax/modem with other LAN members. Chapter 32 covers sharing resources on a LAN in depth.

The User tab

The User tab enables you to set up the information that will appear on each fax cover page. In the blanks, type whatever information you want the fax recipient to see.

Remember, after you make your selections in each of the four tabs, you can click the OK and Close buttons to work your way back to the desktop. If you decide to change any of the default settings, repeat the steps in "Setting Up Your Fax Properties" earlier in this chapter.

Setting Up Your Personal Address Book

You probably will send many faxes from your PC. Wouldn't it be convenient to have a list of fax numbers you call frequently? When you want to send a fax to someone, just select that person's name from a list; you don't have to look up the fax number or even dial the phone.

The Personal Address Book feature in Microsoft Exchange gives you this capability. This feature is your "little black book," storing the names, addresses, and phone numbers of people whom you contact often. You can use Personal Address Book in many settings — to send a fax or an e-mail message, for example, and (in some programs) even to write a letter.

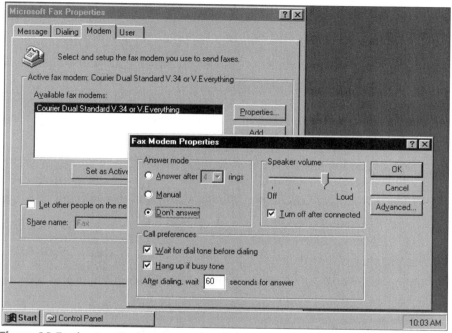

Figure 16-3: The Fax Modem Properties dialog box

Personal Address Book is accessible from many areas in Windows 95, not just from Microsoft Fax. You can get to your Personal Address Book from many Office 95 programs.

Like Microsoft Fax, Personal Address Book is an information service within Microsoft Exchange, so to get to it, you must first go into Microsoft Exchange. Follow these steps:

1. Double-click the Inbox icon on the desktop, or click the Start button and then choose Programs ➪ Microsoft Exchange.

   You see the Inbox for Microsoft Exchange, shown in Figure 16-4.

2. Click the Address Book button, or choose Tools ➪ Address Book from Exchange's menu bar.

   You go to the Address Book window.

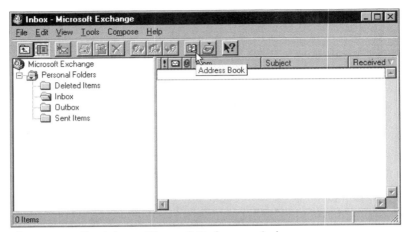

Figure 16-4: The Inbox - Microsoft Exchange window

3. To add a new name and address, click the New Entry button in the toolbar or choose <u>F</u>ile ➪ New <u>E</u>ntry.

The New Entry dialog box appears.

4. In the Microsoft Fax section, click Fax, and then click OK.

The New Fax Properties dialog box appears, as shown in Figure 16-5.

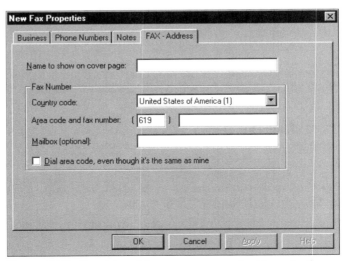

Figure 16-5: About to add a new name and address to the Address Book

5. Fill in the text boxes, as appropriate.

   Optionally, you can enter some notes about the person in the Notes tab.

6. After you fill in as much information as you have for the person, click the OK button.

7. Repeat Steps 3-6 for each name and address you want to add now (you can add more names and addresses at any time).

8. When you finish adding names and addresses, close the Address Book by clicking its Close (X) button or by choosing File ⇨ Close.

In the next section, you'll see how you can look up people in your Personal Address Book. For now, remember any time you need to add more names and addresses, you can repeat the preceding steps. You also can add names and addresses on the fly as you compose faxes and other messages; simply click the Address Book button wherever you happen to see it.

Composing and Sending a Fax

When you have all your fax stuff set up, you're ready to begin sending faxes. Follow these steps:

1. If you're at the desktop, click the Start button, choose Programs ⇨ Accessories ⇨ Fax, and then click Compose New Fax.

   If you're in the Inbox - Microsoft Exchange window, choose Compose ⇨ New Fax.

   Whichever method you use, the Compose New Fax wizard starts.

2. First you'll be given the option to choose the location from which you're dialing. If you're not on the road, just click the Next button. Then you'll come to the wizard screen shown in Figure 16-6. Type the recipient's name and fax number.

   Or click the Address Book button, click a name, click the To button, and then click OK.

   Hot Stuff To send your fax to several people who are listed in the Address Book, Shift+click or Ctrl+click each name and then click the To button. Or click a name, click To, click another name, and so on. Optionally, you can create a list of people to whom to send a fax, as discussed under "Create Your Own Distribution Lists" later in this chapter.

3. After you select one or more recipients, click the Next button to display the next wizard screen, and specify whether you want to use a cover page by choosing Yes or No cover page (see Figure 16-7).

If, for this particular fax, you want to override the default properties you set earlier, click the Options button and make additional selections.

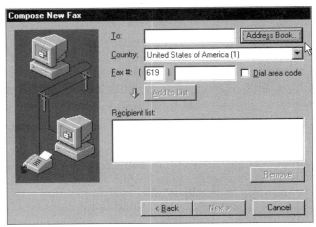

Figure 16-6: The Compose New Fax wizard

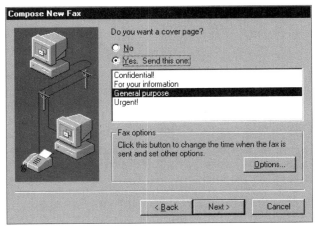

Figure 16-7: Select a cover page and other options.

4. Click the Next button and type a Subject and your Message.

5. Click the Next button and select any files you want to send with your fax.

   If you want to include a file, click Add File, browse to and select the file(s) you want to include with your fax, and then click Next.

The documents you attach in Step 5 are the ones that will be sent in editable format, if possible. When the recipient opens your fax message, he or she sees an icon representing each attached document. Double-clicking the icon opens the document, ready for editing or printing.

6. In the last wizard screen, select the location from which you're dialing (if it's different from the location shown), and then click Finish.

You're done. Exchange takes a little time to put the fax together, and then, to send it. When Exchange actually sends the fax, a little telephone icon appears in the lower-right corner of the screen, perhaps with a message box. If you choose As soon as possible as your default Time to send option, you may not see any activity immediately. You can always check the current status of a fax you sent, as discussed under "Checking the status of outgoing faxes" later in this chapter.

A few cool fax shortcuts

This section describes a few quick and easy alternative ways to fax a document to someone. First, you create a shortcut icon for the Microsoft Fax printer. Follow these steps:

1. Click the Start button.

2. Choose Settings ➪ Printers.

3. Right-drag the Microsoft Fax printer icon to the desktop.

4. After you release the right mouse button, choose Create Shortcut(s).

Now you can browse to the document(s) you want to fax, using the My Computer, Windows Explorer, or Find browsing tool. When you find the file you want to send, simply drag its icon to the Shortcut to Microsoft Fax icon (shown near the lower-left corner of Figure 16-8). The Compose New Fax wizard starts to help you address and send the fax.

An even easier route is available for some document types. Use My Computer, Explorer, or Find to get to the document's icon. Then right-click that icon and choose Send To ➪ Fax Recipient (refer to Figure 16-8). The Compose New Fax wizard starts.

Sending a fax from a program

If you're in a program and want to fax the document on which you're working, you can use this method:

1. If you plan to send the document on which you're currently working, choose File ➪ Save to save that document.

2. Pull down the File menu in your program, and then do one of the following:

   • If you see a Send option in the File menu, select it, and then follow the instructions onscreen to send your fax.

   • If you don't see a Send option, choose Print from the File menu. When you get to the Print dialog box, select the Microsoft Fax (or similarly named) printer, click the Print button, and then follow the instructions onscreen.

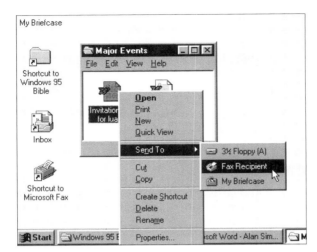

Figure 16-8: Drag a document to the Microsoft Fax icon or right-click and choose Se**n**d To.

If you're wondering, the Microsoft Fax icon was put in your Printers folder automatically when you installed Microsoft Fax.

Notice the latter method is exactly like printing to a printer. But, because you chose the fax printer icon, the document gets "printed" to the fax card. The document isn't actually put on paper until it reaches the recipient's fax machine, so you're using the other person's printer instead of your own.

Checking the status of outgoing faxes

If you want to see the status of your outgoing faxes, follow these simple steps:

1. If you're not already in Microsoft Exchange, double-click the Inbox icon on the desktop or click the Start button, and then choose Programs ➪ Microsoft Exchange.

If you don't see a left pane in your Microsoft Exchange screen, choose View ➪ Folders.

2. In the left pane, click the Outbox folder.

The right pane lists all the outgoing faxes (and other messages), as in the example shown in Figure 16-9.

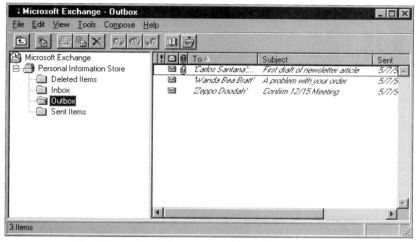

Figure 16-9: The Microsoft Exchange - Outbox window

While you're in the Outbox, you can do any of the following to manage your outgoing messages:

✦ If you don't see a toolbar, choose View ➪ Toolbar.

✦ To sort messages by priority (!), recipient name (To), or whatever, click the appropriate column heading in the right pane of the window.

✦ To select a message, click it. You can Ctrl+click and Shift+click to select multiple messages.

✦ To deliver selected message(s) immediately, choose Tools ➪ Deliver Now.

✦ To delete selected messages(s), click the Delete (X) button in the toolbar or press the Delete key.

> **More Info** You can get onscreen help with Microsoft Exchange, Fax, and Mail by choosing Help from Exchange's menu bar (not from the Start button).

✦ To view the contents of, and full list of recipients for, an outgoing fax message, double-click it in the right pane. Close the window when you finish viewing the message.

Creating a Custom Cover Page

Windows 95 comes with the Fax Cover Page Editor, which enables you to view, change, and even create fax cover pages. To begin with the cover page editor, follow these steps:

1. Click the Start button.

2. Choose <u>P</u>rograms ➪ Accessories ➪ Fax ➪ Cover Page Editor.

3. To open an existing cover page, click the Open button in the toolbar or choose <u>F</u>ile ➪ <u>O</u>pen.

4. Browse to the Windows folder on your C drive (or wherever you keep fax cover pages).

5. Double-click the name of the fax cover page you want to open.

Figure 16-10 shows an example in which I opened the GENERIC.CPE cover page. Notice some of the information on the page is inside curly braces, such as {Recipient Name} and {Recipient's Company}. Those items are placeholders that are filled in automatically when a fax is sent. The information comes from entries you made when you defined your fax properties and from the selections you made in the Compose New Fax wizard.

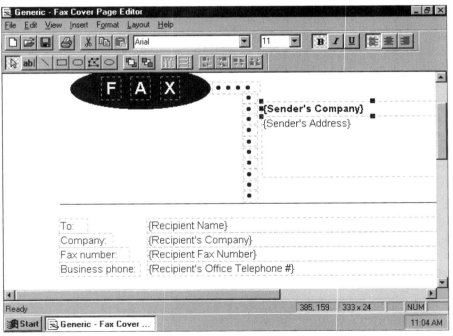

Figure 16-10: The Generic cover page in the Fax Cover Page Editor

You can modify the cover page on your screen. First, you save your version under some new name (in case you mess up, the original cover page will be available under its original name). Choose <u>F</u>ile ➪ Save <u>A</u>s and enter your own name for the cover page (such as **My Fax Cover Page**). If you want to start from scratch, you can choose <u>F</u>ile ➪ <u>N</u>ew.

Next, set up the window for editing. Use the options in the View menu to hide or display toolbars, the status bar, and grid lines (useful for aligning things on the page). Then you can use the techniques described in the following sections to add, delete, and change elements of the page.

Changing and deleting objects

If you're creating your custom cover page by modifying an existing page, you probably will want to start by changing and deleting information already on the page. Use these standard editing techniques:

✦ To select an item, click it. To select multiple items, Ctrl+click them or drag a frame around them. To select every object on the page, choose Edit ➪ Select All or press Ctrl+A.

✦ To delete the selected item(s), press Delete. If you do this by accident, choose Edit ➪ Undo.

✦ To move the selected item, point to its frame until you see the four-headed mouse pointer, and then drag the item to its new location.

✦ To size the selected item, drag one of its sizing handles.

✦ To change the text in the selected item, click wherever you want to put the insertion point. Then type your new text and/or delete old text with the Backspace and Delete keys. Click outside the box to save your changes.

✦ To change the font and/or size of the text in a selected box, select a font and/or size from the drop-down lists in the formatting toolbar.

✦ To align selected items, click one of the alignment buttons in the toolbar, or choose Layout ➪ Align Objects, and then choose an alignment option.

✦ To space the selected objects evenly, choose Layout ➪ Space Evenly, and then choose Across or Down.

✦ To center the selected item on the page, choose Layout ➪ Center on Page.

Inserting new objects

You can add new objects to your cover page at any time. To insert new text, click the Text (ab|) button in the toolbar. In the body of the document, create a frame that indicates the space you want the text to occupy; then type your text. To change the font of the text, select a font and size from the drop-down lists in the toolbar or choose Format ➪ Font.

To insert a placeholder, click approximately where you want the placeholder to appear, choose Insert from the menu bar, select the type of information you want to insert (Recipient, Sender, or Message), and then select a placeholder for specific information (such as Fax Number).

Scan your signature without a scanner

If your fax/modem is set up to receive faxes, you can use any fax machine as a simple black-and-white scanner. This method is an inexpensive way to scan your signature into a bitmap file that you can import into word processing and other documents. To begin, sign your name, using a black felt-tip pen, on plain white paper; then fax that page from any fax machine to your PC's fax/modem. When you get back to your PC, open your Inbox, and double-click the fax you sent yourself. You'll see your signature in Fax Viewer. Rotate and zoom the image until your signature (roughly) fills the Fax Viewer screen. Then press Alt+Print Screen to capture the entire Fax Viewer window in the Clipboard.

Next, start Microsoft Paint (choose Start ⇨ Programs ⇨ Accessories ⇨ Paint). Maximize the Paint window, and then choose Edit ⇨ Paste. In Paint, use the Select tool to drag a frame around your signature. Choose Edit ⇨ Cut to cut out your signature, choose File ⇨ New ⇨ No to start a new document, and then choose Edit ⇨ Paste to paste in your signature.

Now choose Edit ⇨ Copy To, and choose a monochrome bitmap format for the picture. Enter a folder and file name you'll remember later, and choose OK. Then exit Paint without saving the rest of the image (choose File ⇨ Exit ⇨ No). You also can exit Fax Viewer and Exchange.

Now your signature is a bitmap file you can import into any document. To bring your signature into a Microsoft Word document, for example, choose Insert ⇨ Picture, browse to the folder and file containing the signature, and double-click. Your signature appears in your document.

For more information and related topics, see "Printing the Screen (Screen Dump)" in Chapter 14, the help screens in Microsoft Paint, and your word processing documentation (for information on importing pictures and graphics).

To insert a picture, such as a scanned bitmap image of your company logo, click about where you want the object to appear in the cover sheet. Then choose Insert ⇨ Object ⇨ Create from File. Browse to the filename of the object you want to insert. Click that filename and then click the Insert and OK buttons.

When you finish, exit the Fax Cover Page Editor and save your work. The next time you send a fax, the Compose New Fax wizard will include your new cover page for selection. To make your new cover page the default, use the methods described in "Setting Up Your Fax Properties" earlier in this chapter.

Creating Your Own Distribution Lists

If you need to send a fax to the same group of people often, you can save time by creating a distribution list. This way, when the time comes to send the fax, you can choose the list, rather than individual recipients.

The easiest way to create a distribution list is first to put everyone in your Personal Address Book, using the method described in "Setting Up Your Personal Address Book" earlier in this chapter. Then follow these steps:

1. If you aren't already in Microsoft Exchange, open it (double-click the Inbox icon or choose Start ➪ Programs ➪ Microsoft Exchange).

2. Open the Address Book (click its toolbar button or choose Tools ➪ Address Book).

3. Click the New Entry button or choose File ➪ New Entry.

4. In the Microsoft Fax section, choose Personal Distribution List; then click OK.

5. In the Name text box, type a descriptive name for the entire group.

   In Figure 16-11, I named my group Agents and Publishers.

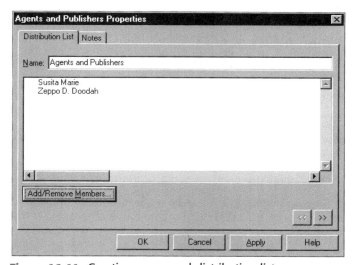

Figure 16-11: Creating a personal distribution list

6. Click the Add/Remove Members button.

7. In the left column, select the names of the people to include in the list.

   You can Ctrl+click and Shift+click, as usual, to select multiple names.

8. Click the Members button to copy the selected names to the right column.

9. Choose OK twice.

10. Close the Address Book and Microsoft Exchange.

When you want to send a fax to everyone in the list, begin by composing your fax in the usual manner. When the Compose New Fax wizard asks to whom you want to send the fax, click the Address Book button, select your distribution list, click the T<u>o</u> button, and then click OK. You can leave the Fax # option blank and proceed through the wizard in the usual manner.

Receiving Faxes

If you want to use your PC to receive faxes, make certain your fax/modem answers incoming calls. Follow these steps to check (and, optionally, change) the modem settings:

1. Click the Start button.

2. Choose <u>S</u>ettings ➪ <u>C</u>ontrol Panel.

3. Double-click the Mail and Fax icon.

4. Click Microsoft Fax; then click P<u>r</u>operties.

5. Click the Modem tab; then click the name of the modem you're using to answer incoming calls.

6. Be sure to click Set as Active Fax/modem; then click <u>P</u>roperties.

7. In the Answer mode section, choose one of the following options:

   • *Answer after x rings.* If you choose this option, the fax/modem always answers the phone after the number of rings you specify. This option is good if your modem is connected to a dedicated fax number that never will receive voice calls.

   • *Manual.* The fax/modem never answers, but a dialog box appears onscreen when the phone rings. You must click the Answer Now button in that dialog box to answer the phone.

8. After making your selection, choose OK to work your way back to the desktop.

You're done. Your PC now can receive incoming faxes. You'll probably hear some modem activity when a fax comes in, and a small dialog box will tell you what's happening. You can read the fax at any time after it's been fully received and the phone has disconnected.

All the faxes you receive will be stored in your Microsoft Exchange Inbox. Remember, to open the Inbox, you double-click the Inbox icon on your desktop or you click the Start button, and then choose <u>P</u>rograms ➪ Microsoft Exchange. If you don't see incoming messages, perhaps you're looking in the wrong box. Click the Inbox icon in Exchange's menu bar.

To print a message, click it and then choose File ⇨ Print. Select a regular printer (not your fax printer) in the Name section. If you want to print any files attached to the message, choose the Print attachment option, and then click the OK button.

To look at a fax, double-click it. If the fax was sent from a regular fax machine, it appears in Fax Viewer, as in the example shown in Figure 16-12. You can choose File ⇨ Print within Fax Viewer to print the message.

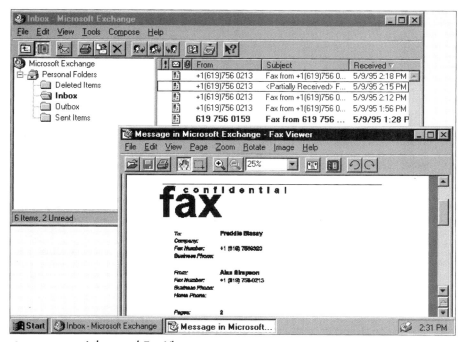

Figure 16-12: Inbox and Fax Viewer

If the fax was delivered as an editable document, it automatically opens in a different window used for messages. Any document attached to that fax appears as an icon within the message portion of the fax. To open the document, double-click its icon in the message. The appropriate program starts and displays the document. Now you can use that program to print or edit the document. You also can choose File ⇨ Save As to save the document to a folder and file of your own choosing.

You can use all the tools Microsoft Exchange offers to manage your incoming faxes along with other messages you receive. Chapter 30 discusses the full range of Exchange's capabilities in more depth.

Converting bitmaps and paper to editable text

Any fax sent to you from a fax machine or non-Microsoft At Work PC is stored in a noneditable bitmap file. You can, however, get the text of that message into a document file you can edit. Instead of typing the text into the file from scratch, you can use an optical character recognition (OCR) program. An OCR program converts the text that's hidden in a bitmap "photograph" file to a document you can edit with your favorite word processor.

If the text you want to get into your PC is on paper, you need both OCR software and some kind of scanner. A flatbed scanner is best. You also can buy a device that allows your fax machine to act as a simple scanner.

For a simple all-in-one method of turning printed text into editable text, look at Visioneer's PaperPort, a full-page scanner small enough to fit between your monitor and keyboard. The device comes with OCR software. You just feed in a sheet of a paper and PaperPort copies it to a document file you can edit. The cost is less than $400. Ask your computer dealer for a demo, or contact Visioneer at (800) 787-7007, Division PM.

Fax Troubleshooting

If you have problems with faxes, the troubleshooter in Microsoft Fax (not the desktop troubleshooter) can help you. Follow these steps:

1. Start Microsoft Exchange by double-clicking the Inbox icon or choosing Start ➪ Programs ➪ Microsoft Exchange.

2. From Exchange's menu bar, choose Help.

3. Choose Microsoft Fax Help Topics.

4. Click the Contents tab.

5. Double-click the Troubleshooting book to open it.

The troubleshooter will guide you the rest of the way through the troubleshooting process.

 More Info Both Microsoft Exchange and Microsoft Fax have their own online help systems, which are not immediately accessible from the desktop. To get to the help systems for those programs, start Microsoft Exchange, and then click the Help option in Exchange's menu bar.

If the Microsoft Fax Troubleshooter and help screens don't help, the problem may be in Microsoft Exchange. In Exchange, choose Help ➪ Microsoft Exchange Help Topics to explore the possibilities.

Secured Faxing

If you need to fax a "for your eyes only" message to someone, you can encrypt your faxes so only the intended recipient can open the fax. Be aware, though, you can secure only faxes sent to another PC. If you send a secured fax to a regular fax machine, the recipient sees your fax cover sheet and subject, but the message section will be blank. (No way exists for someone to enter a password on a sheet of fax paper.)

Simple password protection

The quick and easy way to protect a faxed message is to use a password. Follow these steps:

1. Start composing your fax message to get into the Compose New Fax wizard.

2. When you get to the screen that asks about a cover page, click the Options button in the Fax options section.

3. Click the Security button (see Figure 16-13).

4. Choose Password Protected, and then click OK.

5. Type a password, and then type it again to confirm.

   Pay careful attention to whether you're using uppercase or lowercase letters (especially because you can't see them onscreen).

Passwords are case-sensitive. The recipient must use the exact uppercase and lowercase letters you used when you typed your password. To avoid confusion, always use a particular case — type all passwords in lowercase letters, for example.

6. Choose OK twice.

   Proceed through the rest of the wizard screens as usual.

Remember to tell the recipient the password. When the recipient receives your fax, his or her Inbox will display the message `<Encrypted>Password protected!` When the recipient tries to open the message, a dialog box pops up, requesting the password. The recipient has no way to open or print the document without typing the proper password.

Advanced fax security

Microsoft Fax also offers more advanced security measures: key encryption and digital signatures. This type of security requires some time to implement, because the sender and receiver must swap *public keys* — computer-generated passwords that enable you to read other's faxes. You never actually see the public key: It's a string of 154 characters you typically swap via floppy disk.

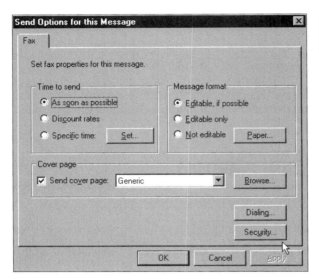

Figure 16-13: The Security option in the Compose New Fax wizard

Advanced security works only for faxes transmitted to and from Microsoft Fax and Microsoft At Work-compatible fax programs. You can't use advanced security with a regular fax machine.

You'll also create a *private key* — a password you keep to yourself to ensure no one else can alter your public keys. The private key gives you the capability to create a new set of public keys at any time. If you don't want Johnny D. Crook to read your key-encrypted faxes anymore, just change your public key and send the new key to everyone except Johnny D. Crook.

Step 1: Creating your keys

The first step to implement advanced key-encryption security is getting everyone who will participate to create a set of keys. To create the keys, follow these steps:

1. Stick a label on a blank, formatted floppy disk.

2. Start Microsoft Exchange by double-clicking the Inbox icon or choosing Start ⇨ Programs ⇨ Microsoft Exchange.

3. Choose Tools ⇨ Microsoft Fax Tools ⇨ Advanced Security.

   You go to the dialog box shown in Figure 16-14.

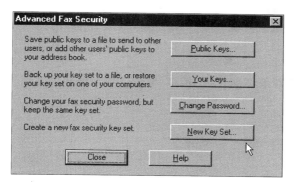

Figure 16-14: Advanced Fax
Security dialog box

4. Click the New Key Set button.

5. Follow the instructions onscreen to type and confirm your password; then choose OK.

   Remember to keep the password private, because it enables you to manage both your public and private keys.

Danger Zone Remember, passwords are case-sensitive — watch your Ps and Qs. Also remember the password is *not* the key: The password is your secret code to create, change, and delete your automatically generated public and private keys.

6. To create a set of public keys to exchange with recipients, insert a floppy disk into drive A or B.

7. Click Save, click To, and then click OK.

8. When you are prompted, enter a location and filename (with the .AWP extension) for your public-key set.

   I would name mine `A:\Alan Simpson.Awp`, for example.

Hot Stuff The extension .AWP stands for *at-work public password.* The advanced security features discussed in this section are part of the entire Microsoft At Work product line, which is supported by Windows for Workgroups and Windows NT as well as Windows 95.

9. Click the Save button.

10. Follow any instructions onscreen.

When copying is complete, repeat Steps 6 through 10 to create more public-key disks (one for each recipient). When you finish, click Close and exit Exchange to work your way back to the desktop.

On each disk's label, write a discription of the contents of that disk. I might label my disks *Alan Simpson's Public Key Set,* for example.

Now you can mail a copy of your public-key set, on floppy disk, to each of your intended recipients and wait to receive their public keys, also on floppy disk, in the mail.

Step 2: Installing other people's public keys

When you receive another person's public-keys floppy disk, you must import those keys into your copy of Microsoft Exchange. Follow these steps:

1. Put the floppy disk containing the other person's public keys in a floppy drive.

2. Start Microsoft Exchange by double-clicking the Inbox icon or by choosing Start ➪ Programs ➪ Microsoft Exchange.

3. Choose Tools ➪ Microsoft Fax Tools ➪ Advanced Security.

4. Choose Public keys.

5. As you are prompted, type your private-key password and choose OK.

   This step prevents just anyone from messing with your keys.

6. Choose Add.

7. Choose the Look in option to browse to the floppy drive containing the other person's public keys.

8. Click the .AWP file name.

9. Choose Open.

10. Follow the instructions onscreen to install the other person's public keys.

When both people have installed each other's public keys, you're ready to start using advanced security.

Step 3: Sending secured faxes

After two or more parties install each other's public keys, anyone can send an encrypted fax to any (or all) parties. Follow these steps:

1. Start composing your fax, using whatever technique you want.

2. When you get to the wizard screen that asks whether you want to include a cover sheet, click the Options button in the Fax options section.

3. Click the Security button.

4. Choose either or both of the following options:

   • *Key-encrypted.* This option ensures only people who have your public key can read the fax message.

Danger Zone Digital signatures are legally binding. Use them with care.

- *Digitally sign all attachments*. This option enables the recipient to verify that the purported sender is the actual sender and the fax has not been altered during transmission. The digital signature is created automatically from your public and private keys.

5. Choose OK.

6. Proceed normally through the Compose New Fax wizard screens.

   If you need to change your keys, make a new set, or whatever, then return to the Advanced Security dialog box, as described in previous sections. This dialog box contains options to add, change, and delete keys.

Retrieving Faxes from Online Services

Microsoft Fax can retrieve documents, software updates, drivers, and images from any information service that supports Group 3 poll-retrieve capability. If you know of such a service, follow these steps to download (retrieve) from it:

1. Open Microsoft Exchange by double-clicking the Inbox icon or choosing Start ➪ Programs ➪ Microsoft Exchange.

2. Choose Tools ➪ Microsoft Fax Tools ➪ Request a Fax.

3. Follow the instructions presented in the wizard.

   Any documents you retrieve will be stored in your Inbox.

Hot Stuff If you want to offer fax-on-demand to your customers, you need a telephony board that supports this capability. See the following section.

Telephony

One of the big buzzwords in PC-land is *telephony*, which is a general term for all kinds of computer/telephone integration. You've probably been on the calling end of telephony before. Perhaps you called a phone number, and a computerized voice started giving you options, such as "If you know your party's extension . . ." and "If you want to check on your order. . . ." This kind of telephony is called *voice mail*.

Another form of telephony that's become popular recently is fax-on-demand (also called fax back, fast facts, fax facts, and so on). As a caller, you use such a service to get more information about a product or answers to frequently asked questions (FAQs). The information then is sent to your fax machine automatically.

How do you pronounce *telephony*?

Telephony is such a new technology, people haven't come to a consensus about how to pronounce the word. Some people pronounce it *TELL-a-phony*; others pronounce it more like *te-LEH-phone-ee*. If the Official Board of Pronunciations for New Technical Terms has not already stamped its blessing on one or the other, I vote for the latter. The *TELL-a-phony* pronunciation sounds weird to me.

To confuse things, of course, some people refer to the whole thing as CTI, for computer/telephone integration. I'm not so sure we need yet another three-letter acronym in the PC world, so I'm still holding out for the *te-LEH- phone-ee* pronunciation. Maybe I should set up a 900 number and put it to a vote.

Historically, telephony has been the turf of huge corporations with complex PBX systems. A few years ago, for example, I inquired about buying a voice mail/fax-on-demand system for my little office. The price was a mere $10,000. (Obviously I stuck with my $100 answering machine.)

More recently, I bought a modem that supports all the voice mail and fax-on-demand capabilities the $10,000 machine offered. The modem even came with the necessary software, and it works in just about any PC. A single phone line is all you need, and your existing phone number will do. The price of this board and the software was less than $200 — a considerably more wallet-friendly figure.

The reason I'm telling you this is I know confusion exists about telephony. You may hear Windows 95 supports telephony and the Telephony Applications Programming Interface (TAPI). You may be overwhelmed by discussions of telephony in some of the literature. But as a consumer, you really don't need to know any of the technical stuff.

As a consumer, you can just think of TAPI as a tool for modem manufacturers and programmers who write communications programs; this tool makes it much simpler for them to create modems and programs that you, the consumer, can install and use on your own PC. And because TAPI is easier for the manufacturers and programmers, it is both cheaper and easier for you.

The hardware you need goes by two names. Some manufacturers call the hardware *telephony boards*; others call their products *modem+voice* boards. Basically, the necessary hardware is a modem with sound-card capability that can record and play back human speech.

If you have a full-function telephony board, you don't need a fax machine, an answering machine, or even a telephone. The board will send and receive faxes and take voice messages. Many boards also enable you to plug in a headset or speakerphone for normal telephone conversations.

Why DSP Costs More

When you're shopping for a telephony board, you might notice there's a price hike of at least $100 when going from an ASIC (application-specific integrated circuit) board to a DSP (digital signal processing) board. ASIC boards cost less but have a distinct disadvantage. When new and better modem standards come along, you either have to throw away the modem and get a new one or, at least, upgrade the chips on the modem.

DSP boards and Mwave boards (IBM's version of DSP) enables you to upgrade to new standards through software. So when new, faster modem standards and better voice compression schemes come along, you just have to run a program to update your existing hardware.

Performance-wise, the ASIC boards are better able to handle multiple sound tasks concurrently, because they use separate chips for separate functions. So, for example, if you use your PC to answer the phone and play multimedia titles, you'll get better performance from the ASIC board.

New boards are appearing on the market all the time, so you may want to check your local computer store to see what's available.

If you can find a Windows 95 Plug-n-Play telephony board — great. This will be the easiest to install. (I don't want to mislead you, though. Installing telephony boards can be a major challenge!) Many new PCs come with telephony boards built in, which saves you the trouble of installing and configuring the board. But I must confess, even a built-in board can be difficult to set up.

Telephony boards are not hugely popular, probably because of the difficulties people have encountered in setting them up. Also, many of the alternatives are more attractive and simpler. For example, a Web site is a terrific alternative to fax-on-demand and Internet e-mail is a great alternative for trying to send files from PC to PC through fax boards and such. For more information on the Internet and Web sites, see Part VII.

Summary

You may have read this chapter and wondered how a topic as simple as faxing could become so complicated when you throw a PC into the works. Most of the headaches occur during installation and setup. Once this is done, just remember these important points:

✦ To send a fax, click the Start button and choose Programs ➪ Accessories ➪ Fax ➪ Compose New Fax, and let the wizard guide you.

✦ To check on received faxes, double-click the Inbox icon on the desktop.

✦ To change your fax/modem properties, click the Start button, choose Settings ➪ Control Panel, double-click the Mail and Fax icon, click Microsoft Fax, and then click the Properties button.

✦ To determine whether you want your fax/modem to answer the phone and accept incoming faxes, go to the fax/modem properties, choose the Modem tab, click the name of the modem you want to use, and then click Set as Active Fax/modem. Then click the Properties button and choose an option under Answer mode.

✦ To check on the status of an outgoing message, double-click the Inbox icon. Then click the Show/Hide Folder List or choose View ➪ Folders until you see the list of folders. To review faxes waiting to be sent, click the Outbox folder. To check on faxes you've already sent, click the Sent folder.

✦   ✦   ✦

Mobile Computing

Road Warrior Tools and Techniques

Hardware for mobile computing has evolved tremendously over the past few years. Laptop computers now rival desktops in storage and processing capability. *PC Cards* (PCMCIA) are credit card-size boards you can install and remove on the fly. Docking stations make it easy to use a laptop as both a desktop and a mobile PC.

On the software side of the coin, things didn't change quite so much. Operating systems didn't offer anything new to take advantage of the advances in portable hardware. Things do change (eventually), however. And as you'll see in this chapter and the next few chapters, Windows 95 offers many goodies to help you get the most from your portable PC.

Summary of Mobile-Computing Features

Many features in Windows 95 make mobile computing much easier. Some of the features are specifically designed for newer laptops with the special plug-and-play BIOS and power-management capabilities. But if you're one of the many millions who bought a laptop before these hardware options became available, don't fret — plenty of features help you compute on the road, regardless of what type of laptop PC you own.

Following is a summary of these features:

   ✦ Hot docking and flexible configurations
   ✦ Power management

✦ Deferred printing

✦ Dial-from settings you can change on the fly

✦ The Briefcase (see Chapter 18)

✦ Improved PC Card (PCMCIA) support (see Chapter 19)

✦ Dial-up networking (see Chapter 20)

✦ Direct cable connection to a LAN or PC (see Chapter 20)

Many of these features are installed automatically when you install Windows 95 and choose Portable as your computer type. If you don't find a particular component, you may be able to install it via Windows Setup, as discussed in Chapter 9. If you can't find a particular component, your hardware may not support it. For more information, check the documentation that came with your laptop computer.

Hot Docking and Flexible Configurations

A *docking station* (more recently also called a *port replicator*) is an optional device that connects a laptop to a desktop PC or to a desktop-size monitor, keyboard, mouse, and other peripherals. The idea is to give you the storage, display, and extensibility options of a desktop PC without sacrificing portability. For example, a docking station or port replicator might connect to a CD-ROM drive, multimedia device, a large monitor, a LAN, and so forth.

Hot Stuff
Consider packing these items whenever you take your laptop on the road: your power cord and extension cord, a two-prong to three-prong adapter, extra batteries, and two phone cords with RJ-11 jacks. If you'll be connecting to other PCs on the road, be sure to bring your network card, network connector cables, and/or direct connect cable.

If you are traveling abroad, you need a plug adapter for the power cord (often best purchased on arrival) and an adapter for local phone jacks. You should also carry a phone cord fitted with alligator clips on one end to attach to wires inside a telephone's mouthpiece. (Better yet, get an acoustic coupler for the handset. Hotels in London usually do not provide phone jacks and accessible handsets.)

To become mobile, the user simply needs to disconnect his or her PC from the docking station. Unfortunately, disconnecting hasn't been as easy as it sounds. The job required manually changing configuration files, such as CONFIG.SYS and AUTOEXEC.BAT, before disconnecting or reconnecting — a time-consuming and technically challenging endeavor for many laptop users. Windows 95 offers two features that simplify the process: hot docking and flexible configurations.

Hot docking

Many laptops that ship with Windows 95 support *hot docking*, which enables you to dock and undock the laptop without even turning it off. This capability is both a hardware and software thing, so you probably should check the manual that came with your laptop computer for specific instructions.

In general, though, you should be able to undock your laptop by clicking the Start button and choosing Eject PC. Windows 95 automatically detects the impending hardware changes, takes care of any potential problems with open files on an external drive, and loads or unloads any appropriate drivers.

To redock, simply put the laptop back into the docking station. Windows 95 once again loads the appropriate drivers automatically. If you used deferred printing while your laptop was undocked, Print Manager starts automatically and prompts you to print any documents you "printed" while the laptop was undocked.

Not-so-hot docking

If you have a pre-Windows 95 laptop, you can't count on hot docking; you must power down your PC before connecting to, or disconnecting from, the docking station. You can simplify matters, however, by creating two separate hardware configurations: one for docked status, and the other for undocked status.

In this section, I show you how to create these configurations, starting with the laptop already docked to a port replicator. Figure 17-1 shows how the screen of my laptop looks while the machine is docked. Notice, the My Computer window shows my laptop is connected to a CD-ROM drive (D) and to drives E, P, and W on my local area network.

While the laptop was in this docked state, I created two hardware configurations: one named Docked Configuration and the other named Undocked Configuration. Following is the quick and easy way to create these configurations:

1. Click the Start button.
2. Choose Settings ➪ Control Panel.
3. Double-click the System icon.
4. Click the Hardware Profiles tab.
5. Click the Original Configuration option, and then click the Copy button.
6. Name the new configuration Docked Configuration.
7. Click the Original Configuration option again, and then click the Copy button again.

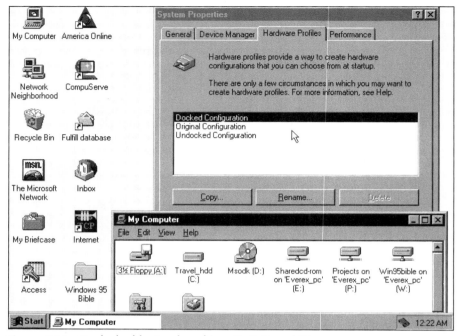

Figure 17-1: My docked laptop has drives D, E, P, and W.

8. Name this new configuration Undocked Configuration.

9. Choose OK to leave the System Properties dialog box.

Now you have three identical hardware configurations, named Original Configuration, Docked Configuration, and Undocked Configuration. (You can delete Original Configuration, if you want; I keep it around as a safety net.) I'll show you how to make each configuration unique soon. First, however, you must know the proper way to dock and undock your laptop.

Cold docking and undocking

Whenever you want to dock or undock your laptop, follow these steps:

1. Click the Start button.

2. Choose Sh<u>u</u>t Down.

3. Choose <u>S</u>hut down the computer?, and then click <u>Y</u>es.

4. When the screen says it's safe to do so, turn off the laptop.

5. Dock or undock the laptop.

When you restart the PC later, keep an eye on the screen. You'll see something like the following before the Windows 95 desktop appears:

```
Windows cannot determine what configuration your computer is in.
Select one of the following:
1. Original Configuration
2. Docked Configuration
3. Undocked configuration
4. None of the above
Enter your choice:
```

Type the appropriate item number (2 if you're docked, 3 if you're undocked, and so on), and then press Enter.

The first time you use Undocked Configuration, Windows 95 may complain about some missing hardware, but you should be able to work your way through any error messages until you get to the Windows 95 desktop.

The following section shows you how to customize your configurations.

Customizing hardware configurations

Much of the work needed to customize your docked and undocked configurations may have been done automatically when you restarted your PC and chose Undocked Configuration.

Examine the My Computer window in Figure 17-2, which shows how my PC looks when I start it with Undocked Configuration. The icon for drive D is gone; that drive is a CD-ROM drive that hooks into my docking station and is unavailable when my laptop is undocked. Icons for network drives E, P, and W still appear, but a big red *X* through each icon reminds me my laptop is not hooked up to the drives (because I removed my network card before undocking).

You can refine your hardware settings for a particular configuration by following these simple steps:

1. Click the Start button.

2. Choose Settings ➪ Control Panel.

3. Double-click the System icon.

4. Click the Device Manager tab.

5. Click the plus sign (+) next to any device type to see devices within that category.

6. Double-click a specific device to see its properties.

7. At the bottom of the dialog box that appears (see Figure 17-3), select the hardware configurations you want to use for the device and deselect configurations you don't want to use for the device.

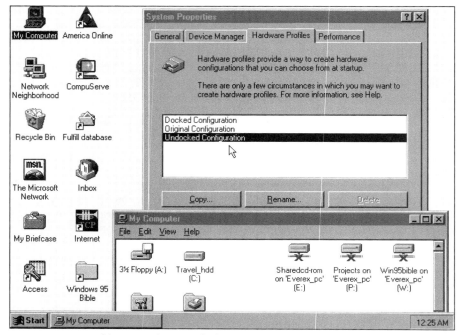

Figure 17-2: No drive D and network drives unavailable when undocked

8. Repeat Steps 5-7 for as many devices as you want.

9. Choose OK and Close to work your way back to the desktop.

The preceding steps work only with virtual-mode drivers — the 32-bit Windows 95 drivers discussed in Chapter 10. Real-mode drivers (namely, those loaded via CONFIG.SYS) attempt to load, regardless of which configuration you chose. If such a driver causes a problem, you can use the techniques in the following section to bypass the driver at startup.

Bypassing real-mode drivers

Eventually, you'll want to replace all your DOS/Windows real-mode device drivers with Windows 95 virtual drivers. But if you're stuck with a real-mode driver and can't get through startup without having problems with it, follow these steps to load drivers individually at startup:

1. Start your PC as usual, but keep your eyes on the screen.

2. When you see the `Starting Windows95` message, press the F8 key.

3. Choose 5: Step-by-step confirmation.

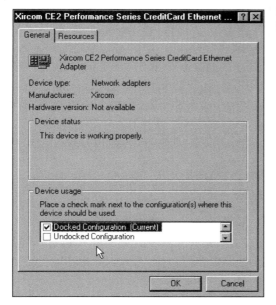

Figure 17-3: Docked Configuration selected for a device

You'll see options that enable you to process the Registry and to step through CONFIG.SYS and AUTOEXEC.BAT. Choose Yes at each prompt. When you get to a real-mode driver that you don't want to install, press Esc to bypass it.

Comfort settings

The hardware configurations discussed so far in this chapter work for hardware devices. You also may want to carry more-refined "comfort settings" from one configuration to another — for example, you may want to use one set of screen colors and mouse properties when your laptop is docked and another set when the machine is undocked.

The hardware configurations don't keep track of personal preferences. But you can create multiple user profiles for yourself, perhaps named Docked and Undocked. Thereafter, when you log in, you can choose whichever user profile is currently appropriate. For more information, see "Enabling Multiple User Profiles" in Chapter 11.

Power Management

Battery life is a major concern for many mobile-computer users. Windows 95 supports Advanced Power Management (APM) 1.1, a standard for modern laptop computers. If — and only if — your laptop hardware supports APM, you can use the following features of Windows 95:

✦ Battery indicator in the taskbar

✦ Capability to put your laptop in Suspend mode by clicking the Start button and choosing the appropriate option from the menu

✦ Capability to configure power management to shut down your PC when you shut down Windows 95

To configure power management (assuming your laptop supports the AMP 1.1 standard), follow these simple steps:

1. Click the Start button.

2. Choose Settings ➪ Control Panel.

3. Double-click the Power icon (if available).

4. Select your options.

Hot Stuff The disk spin-down power-saving feature can slow your PC. Consider disabling this feature when you're not relying on battery power. See your laptop manual for directions.

There's more to APM 1.1 than meets the eye. APM enables software developers to design programs that are sensitive to the power state and remaining battery life. Soon, you'll be installing battery-aware programs that can make smart decisions about whether to undertake a demanding task based on the amount of battery power left. You won't need to worry about sudden power-downs.

Hot Stuff If possible, use nickel metal hydride (NiMH) rather than nickel cadmium (NiCad) batteries. NiMH batteries charge faster and hold more power than NiCad batteries, and they are immune to memory loss caused by premature charging.

Deferred Printing

Deferred printing is a great feature for computer road warriors. This feature enables you to "print" a document even when your laptop is not connected to a printer. More specifically, the feature does everything necessary to prepare a file for printing.

Hot Stuff If you're in a hotel room with your laptop and fax modem, but you don't have a printer, send a copy of the document to yourself via the hotel's fax machine — instant hard copy. You also can use the hotel's fax machine to scan documents into your PC. Fax the hard copy to your hotel room and have the portable PC answer the phone.

Suppose you aren't currently connected to a printer, but you want to be certain to print a document when you get to a printer. No problem — go ahead and print the document, using any of the techniques discussed in Chapter 14. A message appears, telling you the printer isn't available, but that you can work in offline mode. When you choose OK, the document is prepared for printing and sent to the selected printer's queue.

When a printer is available offline, its icon is dimmed in the Printers folder, but you still can drag icons to that dimmed icon for printing.

Now you can forget about that document. You can do all your other work normally, exit Windows, turn off the computer, whatever. When you reconnect to the printer later, you see a message, something like the example shown in Figure 17-4. To start printing, choose <u>Y</u>es.

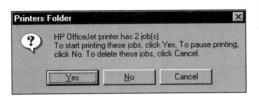

Figure 17-4: Deferred print jobs are ready to be printed.

Managing Multiple Dial-From Locations

Another traditional headache associated with mobile computing is dialing out from the PC. When you're dialing from outside your own area code, you must dial 1 plus the area code for numbers that used to be local. When you're in a hotel room, you may need to dial 8 to get an outside line or to dial 9 before dialing long distance.

The Windows 95 modem properties greatly simplify matters by enabling you to change dial-out settings on the fly. You need to install your modem first, as discussed in Chapter 15. Then, whenever you want to change the location from which you're dialing, follow these steps:

1. Click the Start button.

2. Choose <u>S</u>ettings ➪ <u>C</u>ontrol Panel.

An alternative to the Control Panel route is to double-click My Computer, and then double-click the Control Panel icon.

3. Double-click the Modem icon.

4. Click the <u>D</u>ialing Properties button to display the dialog box shown in Figure 17-5.

5. To set new dialing properties, click the <u>N</u>ew button, and type a name for the settings you're about to create.

If you're dialing from the 714 area code, for example, you can name the settings 714 Area Code. If you're dialing from a specific hotel, you can enter a name, such as Honolulu Hilton.

6. Choose OK.

7. Fill in the Dialing Properties dialog box with information that describes where you're dialing from and how to dial.

   If you're outside your normal area code, for example, type the current area code. If you need to dial a special number to get an outside line, set the appropriate options for local and long-distance dialing.

8. When you finish, choose OK.

After you create the dialing settings, you needn't recreate them; the settings you choose stay in effect until you go back into the Control Panel and choose different dialing properties.

To use the dialing settings again, open the Control Panel, double-click the Modems icon, click the Dialing Properties button, select your current location from the I am dialing from drop-down list, and choose OK to begin working your way back to the desktop.

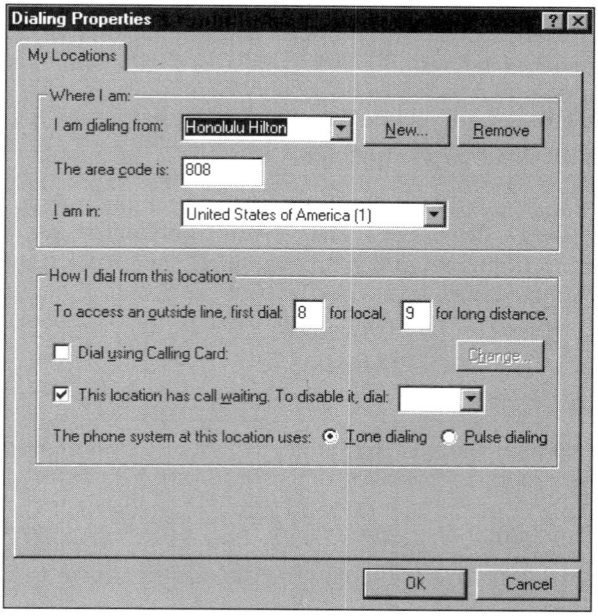

Figure 17-5: Dialing properties

Portable voice mail

Near the end of Chapter 16, I mentioned some data/fax/voice cards that can turn your desktop PC into a complete voice-mail and fax-on-demand communications center. By the time you read this book, many credit card-size modems with the same capabilities (or similar capabilities) undoubtedly will be available. You can pop such a modem into your PCMCIA slot and convert your laptop to a voice-mail system.

Microsoft's Windows Driver Library contains drivers for at least two Data-Fax-Voice

PCMCIA modems: NovaLink Technologies' *Novamodem 28.8 Data-Fax-Voice* modem, and NTT Intelligent Technology's *Thunder-Card AVF288 Data-Fax-Voice* modem. If you have access to the Internet you can download either driver from the Windows Driver Library. Point your Web browser to `http://www.microsoft.com/isapi/hwtest/Hsearch.idc` to begin.

Even More Great Goodies

In the next three chapters, I'll talk more about the mobile-computing features of Windows 95. First, I want to point out a few built-in gems and general ideas:

✦ When you change configurations, Windows 95 automatically detects and activates whichever mouse is available in that configuration.

✦ When you take your laptop to a meeting, get to the conference room early and sit next to a wall outlet, so you can plug in your laptop, rather than rely on its batteries.

✦ When you disconnect from an external monitor at 800×600 or higher resolution, Windows 95 automatically reverts to 640×480 resolution, which is ideal for most laptop screens.

✦ Quick Viewers enables you to view a document even if the appropriate application isn't installed. Right-click the document name, and choose Quick View (if it's available for that document) from the pop-up menu.

More Info For more information on Quick Viewers and on customizing the pop-up menu, see Chapter 31.

✦ You can buy a cellular modem to fit in a PCMCIA slot, which, in turn, connects to a cellular phone. This arrangement enables you to send and receive faxes and e-mail and to connect to online services even when you're not near a phone line (when you're on a plane or a boat, for example).

✦ Don't forget, when you're on the road, you still have access to Microsoft Exchange, which, in turn, gives you access to Microsoft Fax (Chapter 16), information services (Chapters 21-23), and even the PC you left at the office (Chapter 20).

✦ A new set of wireless infrared drivers are being developed for release with future versions of Windows 95. These drivers will be a great boon to mobile computing, because they'll provide immediate access to other people's hardware. To hook up to some other company's printer, modem, or local area network, you'll simply put your laptop in the same room as that device.

Summary

Hardware for mobile computing has evolved beautifully over the past few years. But, until now, not much was happening in the software world to take advantage of those developments. Windows 95 is the first operating system to offer special features for mobile computerists:

✦ Hot docking lets PCs with the plug-and-play BIOS connect and disconnect from a docking station or power replicator without powering down.

✦ Even if your portable PC doesn't have the plug-and-play BIOS, you can use flexible hardware configurations to simplify startup after docking or undocking.

✦ If your portable PC supports APM 1.1 power management, you can use Windows 95 to manage battery power.

✦ Deferred printing enables you to "print" a document while you're away from the printer (so you don't forget to do so later.) When you re-connect to a printer, the actual print job will begin automatically.

✦ To use your modem on the road, you just need to define your current dialing location. Windows 95 will take care of the "details," such as when, and when not, to dial 1 and an area code before dialing a number.

✦   ✦   ✦

The Virtual Briefcase

Many people use their portable PC as sort of a virtual briefcase. Perhaps you generally do your work on a desktop PC. To take your work on the road, you copy the appropriate files from the desktop PC to your laptop. For a while, you edit those files on your portable PC. When you get back to the office, you copy the updated files from the portable PC back to the desktop PC.

The one problem is things can get confusing. After a while, you may lose track of which PC — the desktop or the laptop — contains the latest version of a file. Before long, you're comparing dates and times of files, trying to keep track of which file to copy where and when. Fortunately, the Windows 95 Briefcase helps reduce the confusion and simplify the entire process. Briefcase keeps tracks of the dates and times of multiple copies of a file and tells you which files must be copied and where. In fact, Briefcase even copies the files for you.

Preparing for Briefcase

Before you use Briefcase, you must have the My Briefcase icon on one of the computers. If neither computer shows the My Briefcase icon on the desktop, use the techniques described in "Installing Missing Windows Components" in Chapter 9 to install Briefcase on one of your PCs. If your portable is attached to the desktop PC via a docking station or cable, install Briefcase on the portable PC. If the two computers are not connected by any kind of cable, install Briefcase on the desktop PC.

When you're in Windows Setup, you'll find Briefcase in the Accessories set of components.

Briefcase relies entirely on your computer's internal calendar and clock to determine which version of a document is the most current version, so make sure your clocks are in sync. Double-click the little time indicator in the lower-right corner of the screen, and set the date and time on both the desktop and laptop PC.

 If you don't see the time indicator on your desktop, you can search the online Help index for the word *date*. The Help window for changing the system date takes you to the Date/Time Properties dialog box.

The general idea behind using Briefcase is simple, as the following list explains:

✦ When you want to take work on the road, you simply drag that work into Briefcase.

✦ To use a Briefcase document on the road, open Briefcase and double-click the document name. Then perform your work, close, and save the document normally.

✦ When you get back to the office, unpack Briefcase by opening My Briefcase and choosing <u>B</u>riefcase ➪ Update <u>A</u>ll.

Using Briefcase is simple if your portable and desktop PCs are connected with a cable or LAN cards. The procedure gets a bit more complicated if the machines aren't connected, because you must use a floppy disk to move files from one PC to the other. To prevent any unnecessary confusion for those of you who have achieved floppy-free living, I've broken the instructions for using Briefcase into the following sections:

✦ If the portable and desktop PCs are physically connected via a LAN, direct-cable connection, or dial-up networking, skip to "Using Briefcase Without Floppies" now.

✦ If the portable and desktop PCs are not physically connected by a cable, you need to use a floppy disk to transport the My Briefcase icon between the desktop and portable PCs. Skip to "Using Briefcase With Floppies" now.

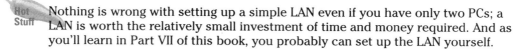 Nothing is wrong with setting up a simple LAN even if you have only two PCs; a LAN is worth the relatively small investment of time and money required. And as you'll learn in Part VII of this book, you probably can set up the LAN yourself.

Using Briefcase Without Floppies

As mentioned, if the desktop and portable PCs are connected via a LAN or some other cable connection, you can use Briefcase without fumbling with floppies. When you're about ready to hit the road, all you must do is pack your Briefcase.

When you're ready to hit the road

To pack Briefcase, drag the files you want to take on the road into the My Briefcase icon on your portable PC. Follow these steps:

1. On the portable computer, use Network Neighborhood, My Computer, Explorer, or Find to locate any document you want to put into Briefcase.

2. If you want to put several documents into Briefcase, select them by Ctrl+clicking and/or Shift+clicking.

3. Drag the documents to the My Briefcase icon.

   Alternatively, right-click the selected documents, choose Send To, and then choose My Briefcase.

Figure 18-1 shows an example in which I browsed to and selected three files to put in my Briefcase. I could drag those files over to the My Briefcase icon, near the left edge of the screen. Alternatively, I could right-click a selected file and then choose Send To ⇨ My Briefcase.

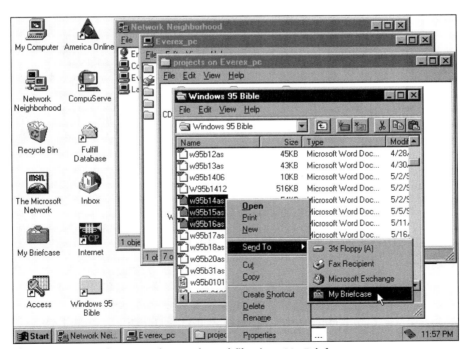

Figure 18-1: Ready to put three selected files into My Briefcase

When Windows 95 finishes copying files, the hard disk in the portable PC will have its own copies of the files you want to take on the road. Then you can shut down the portable and disconnect it from its docking station or network card.

While you're on the road

While you're on the road, remember one simple thing: Whenever you want to work on a Briefcase document, get it from Briefcase. You can retrieve the document in either of the following ways:

✦ Double-click the My Briefcase icon on the desktop and then double-click the document with which you want to work (see Figure 18-2).

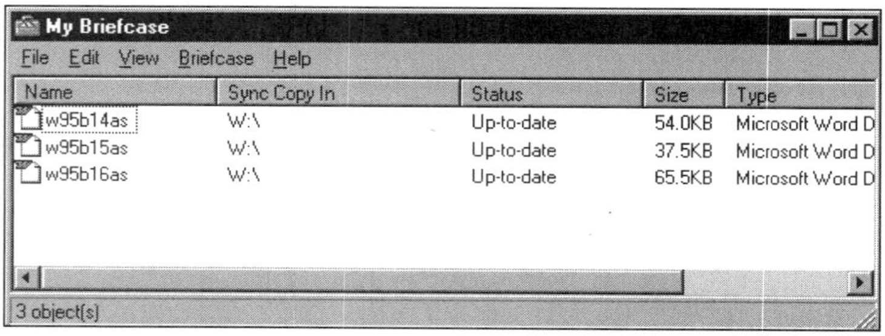

Figure 18-2: My Briefcase open on the desktop

✦ If you're already in a program, choose File ⇨ Open to display the Open dialog box. In the Look in drop-down list, select My Briefcase (see Figure 18-3). Then double-click the name of the file you want to open.

Now you can go about your business normally. When you finish, close the document and exit the program normally. The edited copy of your document is stored in Briefcase automatically.

When you return from the trip

When you get back from your road trip, you want to unpack Briefcase — that is, get the documents you left behind in sync with the newer copies on your portable PC's hard disk. Follow these steps:

1. Redock (or reconnect) the portable PC to the docking station, LAN, or cable that hooks it to the desktop PC.

If your laptop supports hot docking, My Briefcase may launch automatically as soon as you reconnect to the docking station.

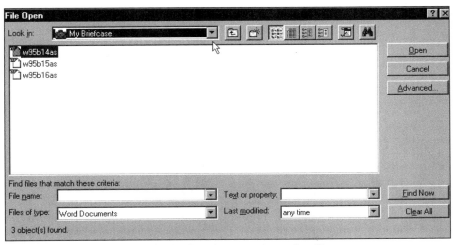

Figure 18-3: The File Open dialog box from a Microsoft Office 95 program

2. Start Windows 95, and double-click the My Briefcase icon.

3. Choose Briefcase ➪ Update All.

   You see a dialog box like the one shown in Figure 18-4, with an arrow pointing from the new version of the file to the old version.

4. To update, click the Update button.

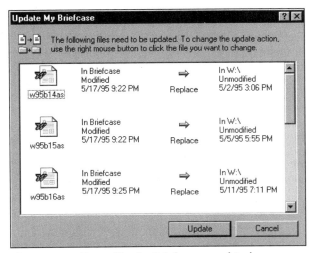

Figure 18-4: Three files in Briefcase need to be synchronized.

When you finish, the files still are in Briefcase, and the copies of those files on the desktop PC match them. If you think you'll soon be working on the same documents off-site again, you can leave them in Briefcase. Just remember, if you change the documents on the desktop PC, you need to update Briefcase before you hit the road again. Follow the preceding steps, and Windows 95 automatically copies the latest versions of the files back into Briefcase.

If you don't think you'll be working with the same files again off-site, you can delete them from Briefcase. Select the files you want to delete, and then press Delete or choose File ➪ Delete.

Using Briefcase With Floppies

You can use Briefcase even if the portable and desktop computers are not connected by any sort of cable. The downside to this approach is you have to use a floppy disk as your virtual briefcase, which means your storage is limited to 1.4MB (or 2.5MB). If you work mainly with word processing and spreadsheet documents, however, that limit may be plenty roomy.

Hot Stuff As mentioned in "Maximize Your Disk Space" in Chapter 12, you can use DriveSpace to increase the capacity of a 1.4MB floppy to about 2.5MB.

What if both copies change?

Suppose you load a document into Briefcase and edit that document on the road. While you're away, somebody (let's say Harry) opens the document you left behind and changes it. When you return, Harry may not be too thrilled at the prospect of your replacing his copy of the document with the one in your Briefcase. You and Harry may have to figure out who did what while you were away and then reconcile the differences. If you're lucky, the program both of you used to edit the document can reconcile the differences automatically.

Windows 95 supplies programmers with a set of tools called *Reconciliation APIs*. This means the people who create your favorite programs now can hook into Briefcase, and their programs automatically reconcile the differences between two copies of a document that changed while one document was away in Briefcase. When you start upgrading to Windows 95 versions of your favorite programs, check the manuals or online help systems for information on reconciling documents. Your days of negotiating with Harry may be over.

Before you begin

Before you launch into the sections that follow, peek at the Windows 95 desktop on your larger (desktop) PC. If you see the icon named My Briefcase, grab a floppy disk and label it My Briefcase. Then skip to "Packing the floppy Briefcase" later in this chapter.

If My Briefcase is on your portable PC, read the next two sections to learn how to create your virtual briefcase and move it from the portable to the desktop PC.

Creating a My Briefcase floppy disk

Step 1 in using Briefcase with floppies is creating a floppy disk that acts as your virtual briefcase. Follow these steps:

1. Grab a blank floppy disk, and label it My Briefcase.

2. Go to the portable PC, which has the My Briefcase icon on its screen, and put the floppy disk in drive A.

3. Open My Computer so you can see the icon for drive A.

   Move and size the My Computer window, if necessary, so you also can see the desktop icon for My Briefcase.

4. Drag the My Briefcase icon to the icon for drive A.

The briefcase moves to the floppy disk, and its icon disappears from the Windows desktop. Don't worry; you're just going to move the icon to the desktop PC.

Putting Briefcase on the desktop PC

Now you need to put Briefcase on the desktop PC (the one containing the files you plan to take on your trip). Follow these steps:

1. Take the floppy disk labeled My Briefcase to the desktop PC (which, presumably, contains the latest versions of the documents you want to take with you).

2. Put the floppy disk in drive A.

3. Double-click My Computer.

4. Double-click the icon for drive A.

   You should see the My Briefcase icon in the window that opens.

5. Drag the My Briefcase icon from drive A to the Windows 95 desktop.

At this point, Briefcase is on the desktop PC only. The floppy disk is empty, because you moved Briefcase — you didn't copy it. This is good, because this will be your starting point whenever you plan to use Briefcase. Take a break. Go to lunch. Forget all about that little floppy-disk shuffle you just did; you won't need to do it again.

 I realize moving Briefcase can be confusing, but you have to do this only once. Still, the real solution is to set up a little LAN between the two computers, as you'll learn in Part VII.

Packing the floppy Briefcase

Suppose you're about to go on a trip and want to take a few documents from the desktop PC with you. Follow these steps:

1. At the desktop PC, use My Computer, Explorer, or Find to get to any document you want to put into Briefcase.

2. Select the documents you want to take by Ctrl+clicking and/or Shift+clicking them.

3. Drag the documents to the My Briefcase icon.

Now the My Briefcase icon on your desktop PC contains copies of the files you want to take on your trip. You need to take those copies with you, so now you need to move the filled Briefcase from the desktop PC to a floppy disk. Follow these steps:

1. Insert the floppy disk you labeled My Briefcase into drive A of the desktop computer.

2. Open My Computer, and move and size its window so you can see both the icon for drive A and the icon for My Briefcase.

3. Drag the My Briefcase icon from the Windows 95 desktop to the icon for drive A.

Windows 95 moves Briefcase to the floppy disk, so you won't see the My Briefcase icon on the desktop computer's screen anymore. Don't worry. Just pack that floppy disk with your portable PC; you'll be using that floppy as your virtual briefcase while you're on the road.

On the road with a floppy Briefcase

When you're on the road with your portable PC and floppy Briefcase, follow these steps to work on your documents:

1. Insert the My Briefcase floppy into drive A of your portable PC.

Hot Stuff If you don't want to work from floppies on the road, you can drag the files from My Briefcase on the floppy disk to your portable PC's hard disk. Then you can edit directly from the hard disk. When you finish editing, put the My Briefcase floppy disk in drive A, open My Briefcase on that floppy, and choose Briefcase ➪ Update All.

2. Double-click the My Computer icon.

3. Double-click the icon for drive A.

4. Double-click the My Briefcase icon.

5. Double-click the name of the document with which you want to work.

Now you can work on the document normally. Just don't take that floppy out of its drive while you're working.

When you finish working with the document, exit the program and save your work normally. Windows automatically saves the modified version in its original location: My Briefcase on drive A.

Unpacking the floppy Briefcase

When you return to the home office, your best bet is to move the My Briefcase icon back to the Windows 95 desktop of your desktop PC, and then update files from there. Follow these steps:

1. Insert the My Briefcase floppy into drive A of the desktop PC.

2. Double-click My Computer.

3. Double-click the icon for drive A.

4. Drag the My Briefcase icon to the Windows 95 desktop.

At this point, the floppy disk is empty again, and Briefcase is back on the desktop PC. You can see the My Briefcase icon on the Windows 95 desktop.

To get the documents on the desktop PC in sync with the copies in Briefcase, follow these steps:

1. Double-click the My Briefcase icon on the desktop.

2. Choose Briefcase ➪ Update All.

3. To update all the files, click the Update button, and follow the instructions onscreen.

When you finish, you can go back to editing the files outside Briefcase. You need to use the files inside Briefcase only when you're on the road. If you don't think you'll be editing the same files on the road again, you can regain some space by deleting them from Briefcase. Double-click the My Briefcase icon, select the files you want to delete, and then choose File ➪ Delete.

When you're ready to go on another road trip, you can repack Briefcase and move it to a floppy by repeating the steps in "Packing the floppy Briefcase" earlier in this chapter.

Other Briefcase Goodies

Briefcase has most of the same capabilities My Computer has. The View menu within Briefcase, for example, offers many common options for changing your view of files. The File and Edit menus offer commands for deleting, renaming, and copying files within Briefcase. You also can do the following handy-dandy things with files inside Briefcase:

✦ To check the status of a file, select its name in My Briefcase, choose File ➪ Properties, and then click the Update Status tab. You can click the Find Original button in that dialog box to locate the original version of the file.

✦ You can get help with My Briefcase in either of two ways. If you're at the desktop PC, click the Start button, choose Help, click the Index tab, and search for *briefcase*. If you're already in My Briefcase, click the Help command in its menu bar.

✦ To update only a few files in Briefcase, select the files you want to update and then choose Briefcase ➪ Update Selection.

✦ To split a file off from Briefcase, select its name in My Briefcase and then choose Briefcase ➪ Split from Original. The original copy of the file becomes an *orphan*, meaning it no longer will be altered when you synchronize files from Briefcase.

Summary

Briefcase is a handy tool for road warriors, because it helps you keep track of which document is which when you're taking copies of your work on the road:

✦ Briefcase is automatically copied to your hard disk when you install Windows 95 and choose Portable as the installation method.

✦ If your portable PC is attached to your desktop PC via a LAN card or cable, keep the My Briefcase icon on your portable PC at all times. When you're ready to go on the road, just drag the files you want to take with you from My Computer into the My Briefcase icon.

✦ If your portable PC is not attached to the desktop PC, it makes more sense to keep the My Briefcase icon on the desktop PC. When you're ready to go on the road, drag documents into the My Briefcase icon. Then drag the entire My Briefcase icon onto a floppy disk.

✦ While you're on the road, edit documents that are in the My Briefcase icon. For example, you can double-click the My Briefcase icon then double-click the document you want to edit. Or you can choose File ⇨ Open from your program's menu bar, and specify My Briefcase as the place to Look In.

✦ When you've finished editing a Briefcase document, just close and save the document normally.

✦ When you return from your trip, you need to update Briefcase on your desktop PC. If you used a floppy disk while on the road, first move the My Briefcase icon from the floppy disk onto the Windows 95 desktop of the desktop (stationary) PC.

✦ To update (synchronize) the files, double-click the My Briefcase icon and choose Briefcase ⇨ Update All.

✦   ✦   ✦

The Dreaded PCMCIA Slot

Some of you probably read this chapter title and wondered, "What's a PCMCIA slot, and what did it do to deserve my dread?" So I'm going to start this chapter with a brief history lesson.

If you're into computer hardware, you probably know what the boards you add to your computer are like. The boards usually are anywhere from 4 to 12 inches long, and they have all their little circuits and chips exposed. These boards have a few negatives: to the technologically timid, they're kinda scary-looking; they're usually hard to install; they come with instruction manuals that assume you have a Ph.D. in electrical engineering; perhaps worst of all, they don't fit into portable computers. But zillions of these boards are on the market nonetheless.

Enter PCMCIA — a clever idea in which the board actually is a credit card-size card called, simply, a PC Card. The circuits aren't exposed, so the card looks like a fat credit card. The card's size makes it much more portable than the older boards. And you install the card from outside the computer. You don't have to take the PC apart to install the thing; you can pop it in when you want to use it and yank it out when you're done. Sounds great, no?

The PC Card *is* a great idea but, until recently, it's been a poorly realized idea. People who have been using their PCMCIA slots have had to contend with many problems. Standards changed (Type I, then Type II, and then Type III). You never were quite sure whether a particular card would work in your system. You had to jump through all kinds of hoops involving card drivers and socket services to get the thing to work. Inserting, installing, configuring, and even removing cards usually was a headache. For many portable-PC users, the thought of sliding a PC Card into the PCMCIA slot was scary.

But the procedure has become fairly easy. The plug-and-play architecture of Windows 95 really shines in the PCMCIA department. You can insert and remove true plug-and-play cards without powering down the PC. And even cards that don't bear the "Designed for Windows 95" plug-and-play logo are easier to get along with than ever before. (I know this sounds like a sales pitch, but it's not. The truth is I hated messing with PCMCIA slots before Windows 95. Now I hardly give it a second thought.)

Types of PC Cards

You can put a wide variety of cards and devices into a PCMCIA slot, including the following:

✦ *Fax/modems*. If your portable PC doesn't have a built-in fax/modem, you can pop one into the PCMCIA slot. Most of these devices provide full faxing and data support for e-mail.

✦ *Cellular modems*. Same as fax/modems, except these devices plug into a cellular phone for wireless communications.

✦ *Digital-video boards*. These boards enable you to hook your portable PC to a VCR or video camera to view, capture, and edit video.

✦ *Sound cards*. If your system has no built-in sound card, you can add a sound card via the PCMCIA slot.

✦ *Network cards*. Ethernet and Token Ring PC cards enable you to connect your portable PC to an existing LAN (local area network) so you can share files, printers, modems, and other resources.

✦ *CD-ROM drives*. Many portable CD-ROM drive units are available, including some with built-in sound for full multimedia capability. You can attach one of these devices to the PCMCIA slot of your portable.

✦ *Flash memory, ATA drives, and SRAM*. These cards enable you to add more memory and more disk storage to your portable PC via the PCMCIA slot.

 More Info If you plan to install SRAM or flash memory, search the Windows 95 Help index for *SRAM* or *flash*, as appropriate, for more information.

Some portables allow you to insert two or more PCMCIA cards at a time, so you're not limited to one. Remember, many CD-ROM and hard disk drives can be driven from the parallel port as well. When I'm at home, I keep an Ethernet card in my PCMCIA slot to connect my portable to my desktop PCs. I also plug a CD-ROM drive into the portable's parallel port.

Installing PCMCIA Support

PCMCIA support is available only if your PC has a PCMCIA slot. When you installed Windows 95, the software would have detected a PCMCIA slot automatically. To install PCMCIA services, follow these steps:

1. Click the Start button.

2. Choose Settings ➪ Control Panel.

3. Double-click the PC Card (PCMCIA) icon.

   If you haven't already installed PCMCIA services, a wizard appears to help you replace any existing real-mode drivers with the new 32-bit virtual drivers.

4. Follow the instructions presented by the wizard.

5. After you install the 32-bit drivers, double-click the PC Card icon.

   The PC Card (PCMCIA) Properties dialog box appears, as shown in Figure 19-1.

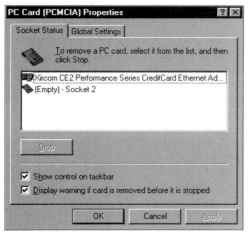

Figure 19-1: The PC Card (PCMCIA) Properties dialog box

As you see in Figure 19-1, the dialog box is simple. If you want to remove a PCMCIA card from your system, click its name and then click the Stop button.

The following sections discuss inserting and removing cards.

Hot Stuff If you already have a card in the PCMCIA slot, you can double-click the little PC Card indicator near the lower-right corner of the screen to display the PC Card (PCMCIA) Properties dialog box.

Adding a PCMCIA slot to a desktop PC

You can add a PCMCIA slot to your desktop computer. This slot can be handy if you buy a PC Card you want to use in both your desktop and portable PCs. You may want to use a digital-video card in both PCs, or you may want to use a PCMCIA hard disk to transfer files between your portable and desktop PC without the need for floppies.

Several companies manufacture PCMCIA slots for desktop PCs. I recently purchased one called the SwapBox, manufactured by SCM Microsystems (phone (408) 395-9292). Installation was a breeze. I installed the hardware per the manufacturer's instructions. Then I ignored the instructions for installing DOS/Windows drivers (called card services and sockets). Instead, I fired up Windows 95 and ran the Add New Hardware wizard (refer to Chapter 10). Windows found the device and installed it correctly.

When the Add New Hardware wizard finished, I opened the Control Panel and double-clicked the PCMCIA icon to load the Windows 95 PCMCIA drivers. The process was surprisingly easy.

Inserting and Removing PC Cards

With the release of Windows 95 came a new breed of PC Cards that support hot swapping. But you should perform hot swapping only if the manufacturer's instructions specifically tell you it's OK to do so. In this situation, you must check the instruction manual that came with the PC Card for specific instructions. The following sections summarize the general procedures for hot and not-so-hot swapping.

 The first time you install a PC Card, have your original Windows 95 disks or CD-ROM and the manufacturer's disks (if any) handy. The Add New Hardware wizard may ask for one of those disks — bad news if you're on the road and didn't bring the disks with you.

Hot swapping

PC Cards specifically designed for Windows 95 support hot swapping. This means you can simply pop in a PC Card while the computer is running. Windows 95 detects the card and loads the appropriate drivers automatically for true plug-and-play compatibility.

If you're removing a hot-swappable card, you should stop the card before you yank it out of the slot so Windows has a chance to gear up for the coming hardware change. To stop a device, click the PC Card indicator in the lower-right corner of the screen and then choose the Stop option. Alternatively, double-click the PC Card icon, choose a device from the list, and then click the Stop button. Wait for the instruction that tells you when it's safe to remove the card.

Not-so-hot swapping

If you're uncertain a particular card supports plug-and-play compatibility, you should power down before inserting the card. If you're replacing a card already in the slot, stop that card first. Follow these steps:

1. If you are removing a card, first click the PC Card indicator in the lower-right corner of the screen; then click the appropriate option to stop that card.

   Alternatively, you can double-click the PC Card indicator and then use the PC Card (PCMCIA) Properties dialog box to stop the card.

2. When you see the message You may safely remove this device, click OK.

3. To play it extra safe, click the Start button and choose Shut Down; when you are asked whether you want to shut down the computer, choose Yes.

4. When you're told it's safe to do so, shut down the PC.

5. Remove the PC Card from its slot.

6. Insert into the PCMCIA slot the PC Card you want to use.

7. Turn the power back on.

   Most likely, Windows will detect the new device at startup, and install the appropriate drivers for it.

If Windows does not detect the new device, or if you have problems using the device when you get to the Windows 95 desktop, use the Add New Hardware wizard (refer to Chapter 10) to install the driver for that particular PC Card. You also may need to shut down Windows, power down the PC, and restart.

Using the installed device

After you successfully install the PC Card, Windows treats the device for this card like any other device in that category. If you installed a CD-ROM drive or hard disk drive, for example, an icon for this drive appears when you open My Computer, Windows Explorer, or any other dialog box that allows you to browse through drives.

If you installed a modem, it should be available wherever the dialing properties are available. If you want to make sure (or if you have trouble with the modem), click the Start button, choose Settings ⇨ Control Panel, and then double-click the Modems tab. If you don't see the new modem, click the Add button and use the wizard to install the modem. After installation, the modem will be listed like any normal modem, but it will have a PC Card icon rather than a telephone icon, as shown in Figure 19-2.

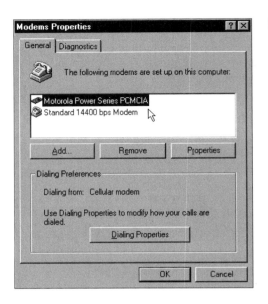

Figure 19-2: The Modems Properties dialog box recognizes a Motorola PCMCIA cellular modem.

More Info If you have a regular built-in modem and later install a cellular modem, you need to tell programs which modem you want to use. To tell Microsoft Fax which modem to use, open the Control Panel, double-click Mail and Fax, click an information service, and then click Properties. Choose Set as active fax/modem in the Modem tab to choose one of your available modems. If you need more information, refer to Chapters 15, 16, and 23.

Remember, if you change hardware configurations on your PC frequently, you may want to create multiple hardware configurations, as discussed in "Not-so-hot docking" in Chapter 17. In that section, I described docked and undocked configurations. But you can create as many configurations as you want.

Summary

This chapter has been about the PCMCIA slot featured on most portable PCs and some desktop PCs. Following are the main points:

✦ The card you can slide into a PCMCIA slot is sometimes called a *PC Card*, a *credit-card sized adapter*, or perhaps a *PCMCIA Card*.

✦ To ensure you're using the 32-bit Windows 95 PCMCIA drivers, click the Start button, choose Settings ➪ Control Panel, and double-click the PC Card (PCMCIA) icon. If you need to update your drivers, a wizard will help you.

✦ Many new "Designed for Windows 95" PC Cards will support hot-swapping, which means you can pop a PC Card into the PCMCIA slot without powering down the PC.

✦ To insert a card that doesn't support hot swapping, shut down Windows, power down the PC, insert the card, then restart the PC.

✦ To remove a PC Card, double-click the PC Card indicator in the taskbar, click the card you plan to remove, then click the Stop button. Then you can physically remove the card from the slot.

✦   ✦   ✦

Dial-Up Networking and Direct Cable Connection

Direct cable connection is a way to connect your portable PC to a desktop PC, or even to a network of PCs, by using just a cable (no network cards). You use this method to connect to a PC that's within a few feet of your portable PC, even if you don't have LAN (local area network) cards in either PC. When the PCs are connected, you can transfer files back and forth without using floppy disks.

Dial-Up Networking is a way to connect your portable to a desktop PC or LAN anywhere in the world. For this type of connection, both computers must have a modem. The stationary PC must be configured as a dial-up server, and the portable must be configured as a dial-up client. To set up a PC as a Dial-Up Networking server, you must purchase and install the Microsoft Plus! program. You can buy this program at any computer store. For information on hardware requirements of Plus!, and other program features, please refer to Chapter 39.

Direct cable connection and Dial-Up Networking, and all the associated "how-tos," are the topics of this chapter. (Which is a good thing, because if I suddenly started writing about some unrelated topic instead — say, a clambake — I bet you'd be displeased.)

I'm going to be using my trusty laptop to illustrate some things in this chapter. Be aware, in this chapter, I use my laptop without its LAN card. Network cards are *not* required to make these kinds of connections.

Before You Do Anything Else Network Neighborhood

Whether you plan to use dial-up or direct cable connection, you need to ensure that Network Neighborhood is installed on both PCs. Look at the Windows 95 desktop. If you do not see Network Neighborhood on the desktop, you must install it, as described in the following section.

When you're certain both PCs have Network Neighborhood installed, you can skip to the "Direct Cable Connection" or "Dial-Up Networking" section later in this chapter.

Installing Network Neighborhood

Network Neighborhood is installed automatically if your PC has a network card or if you install a network card and then run the Add New Hardware wizard (refer to Chapter 10). But if the PC you plan to use has no network card, you must install Network Neighborhood by following these steps:

1. Gather up your original Windows 95 floppy disks or CD-ROM.
2. Open Control Panel by choosing Start ➪ Settings ➪ Control Panel.
3. Double-click the Network icon.
4. Click the Add button.
5. Click Protocol, and then click the Add button.
6. In the Manufacturers list, choose Microsoft.
7. In the Network Protocols list, choose IPX/SPX-compatible Protocol.
8. Click OK.
9. When you are asked to select a device, choose OK.
10. Choose Client for Microsoft Networks from the Primary Network Logon drop-down list.
11. Click the File and Print Sharing button.
12. If you want the other PC to copy files to or from this PC, choose the first option, I want to give others access to my files.

I suggest you always select both checkboxes in the File and Print Sharing dialog box. By doing so, you give yourself the option to share resources later, if you want; you're not giving other computers free rein over your PC.

13. If you want the other PC to use this PC's printer, choose the second option, I want to allow others to print to my printer(s).
14. Choose OK.

15. If you plan to share a CD-ROM drive between two or more computers, check to make sure Client for Netware Networks is listed in the installed components list. If that component is NOT installed, install it now by using the Add button to install Client ⇨ Microsoft ⇨ Client for NetWare Networks.

Puzzled? The client for Netware Networks must be installed if you plan to share a CD-ROM drive. This is true even when you're not using Novell Netware software.

16. Click the Identification tab in the Network dialog box.

17. In the Computer name box, type a name of up to 15 characters, with no blank spaces.

You can use any name you want, but each PC must have a unique name. You could name this PC Office_PC, for example, and name the other Travel_PC.

Hot Stuff On a piece of paper, write the exact name you type in the Network dialog box. You may need to know this name later when you try to connect.

18. In the Workgroup box, type a name of up to 15 characters, with no spaces.

If you don't belong to a workgroup, you can make up a workgroup name. For example, I use the workgroup name ALANS_OFFICE on my PCs.

Danger Zone Only PCs with the same workgroup name can share resources. Make up a name you will remember easily and make sure you spell it the same way each time you type it.

19. Optionally, you can type a brief description of this computer.

Figure 20-1 shows how I identified one of the computers I'll be using in this chapter.

20. Choose OK.

21. Follow the instructions onscreen.

When you finish, your Windows 95 desktop displays the Network Neighborhood icon near the My Computer and Recycle Bin icons. Remember, both computers in the planned connection must have Network Neighborhood installed.

Hot Stuff Make up one arbitrary password — such as *pinkcat* — that you'll never forget. Never tell the password to anyone. Use this password in every situation in which you create your own password. Remember to use all lowercase letters (or all uppercase letters), because passwords often are case-sensitive.

You probably will be instructed to restart the computer; follow that direction. When the computer restarts, you'll be asked to provide a user name and password. Use a separate user name for each PC. You can use the same password for each PC; just don't forget that password. Remember always to use the same case letters, so you don't get confused as to which letters are uppercase and which are lowercase.

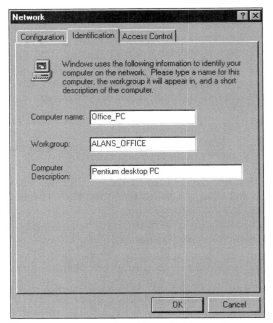

Figure 20-1: Example of identifying a PC

Changing Network Neighborhood

If you need to view or change your network protocol or identification settings, follow these steps:

1. Right-click the Network Neighborhood icon.

2. Choose Properties. .

3. Make your selections in the tabbed dialog boxes.

4. Choose OK.

5. Follow the instructions (if any) that appear onscreen.

Sharing resources

Whether you plan to use direct cable connection or Dial-Up Networking, you need to decide which resources will be shared (If you don't share any resources, the connection won't be worth making). In general, you need to share resources only on the stationary PC.

✦ If you're setting up direct cable connection, share resources on the host.

✦ If you're setting up Dial-Up Networking, share resources on the dial-up server (the PC that will answer the phone).

The following sections show you how to share resources:

If you want to share a printer

If you want both PCs to be capable of using one printer, you first need to share that printer. Follow these steps:

1. On the PC to which the printer is physically connected, choose Start ➪ Settings ➪ Printers.

2. Right-click the icon for the printer you want to share.

3. Click Sharing.

4. Click Shared As.

5. Type a name (or accept the suggested name).

6. Choose OK.

   In the Printers folder, a little hand appears below the icon for that printer, indicating the printer is shared.

7. Close the Printers folder.

If you want to share files

If you want to move or copy files from one PC to the other, you first need to share the disk drive, or at least specific folders, on the stationary PC. Follow these steps:

1. On the stationary PC, double-click the My Computer icon.

2. Right-click the icon for hard disk drive C.

3. Click Sharing.

Hot Stuff You can share a CD-ROM drive, as well. You also can open a drive and choose specific folders to share on that drive. Right-click the device you want to share, click Sharing, and complete Steps 4-7 for that drive or folder.

4. Click Shared As.

5. In the Share Name box, type a short name, using no spaces.

   Optionally, type a longer descriptive name.

6. If you want to move and copy files in both directions (to and from the portable PC to this PC), select Full in the Access Type section.

   If you accept the default Access Type setting, Read-Only, the guest/client PC can only copy files from this PC.

Life Saver If you plan to permit others to connect to this PC, but you don't want them to put things on or take things off your PC, you may want to choose Read-Only or Full with a password.

7. Choose OK.

Now that you've set up Network Neighborhood and defined something to share on the stationary PC, you can set up direct cable connection, Dial-Up Networking, or both. The following sections discuss each topic independently.

Direct Cable Connection

Direct cable connection is the type you use when (1) you want to connect two PCs without using network cards, (2) the PCs are close enough to each other to connect by a cable, and (3) you already have the appropriate cable for the job. Before you connect the PCs, you must do some setup on both PCs. You only need to go through this setup procedure one time, so if you've already done that, skip to "Making the direct cable connection" later in this section.

Installing the direct cable connection

The following sections outline the steps involved in getting set up for a direct cable connection.

Step 1: Get the right cable

First, you need the appropriate type of cable for direct cable connection. Specifically, you want the type of cable named file-transfer cable, null-modem cable, LapLink cable, InterLink cable, or Serial PC to PC File Transfer cable. Trust me — you really want to get the right cable. Otherwise, you're likely to spend hours trying to get the connection to work, with no positive result.

Direct cable connection also supports ECP and UCM parallel cables. But the ECP cable works only with ECP parallel ports enabled in BIOS.

Before you buy the cable, check to see what kinds of serial ports are available (or can be made available) on both PCs. These ports often are labeled COM 1 and COM 2, or perhaps Serial Port 1 and Serial Port 2. The ports should be male (the prongs stick out) and may be 9-pin or 25-pin. When you buy the cable, make sure it has the correct-size plug on each end.

Try to get a two-headed file-transfer cable — one with both a DB-9 and DB-25 plug on each end — so you can plug the cable into whichever port is available. You also can buy gender changers to convert male ports to female ports (and vice versa).

Step 2: Connect the PCs

Second, connect the two PCs. I strongly suggest you shut down Windows and power down both PCs before you make the connection. Pay attention to which port you're using on each PC; you can use COM 1 on one PC and COM 2 on the other. After the PCs are connected, power up each PC.

While you wait for the PCs to power up, decide which one will be the host and which one will be the guest, based on the following criteria:

✦ *Host.* The computer with the resources you want to use, that is, an attached printer or shared folder) is the host. Usually, the larger, stationary computer plays the role of host.

✦ *Guest.* The computer that wants access to resources is the guest. Typically, this computer is the portable PC.

When both PCs are running, you're ready to complete the connection.

Step 3: Set up the host

Third, get the host PC ready to connect. Go to the computer that will act as the host and follow these steps:

1. Choose Start ➪ Programs ➪ Accessories ➪ Direct Cable Connection.

   Assuming Direct Cable Connection has been installed, go to the Direct Cable Connection wizard. The first time you use direct cable connection, that wizard looks like Figure 20-2.

   More Info If Direct Cable Connection isn't available in your Accessories menu, you need to install it. For instructions, refer to "Installing Missing Windows Components" in Chapter 9. The Direct Cable Connection component is in the Communications group.

2. Click Host.

3. Click the Next button.

4. Follow the instructions presented by the wizard, clicking Next after you complete each screen.

5. In the last wizard screen, you can set a password, if you want.

6. Click the Finish button when you finish.

The host PC displays a message, telling you it's ready for the guest PC to drop in, but there's no hurry (I think the question Is the guest computer running? is a rhetorical one. Don't answer). If you want, you can close the dialog box for now; first, you need to decide what this host PC is going to share.

Hot Stuff Remember, you also need to define what you will share on the host PC. If you haven't done this, refer to "Sharing resources" earlier in this chapter.

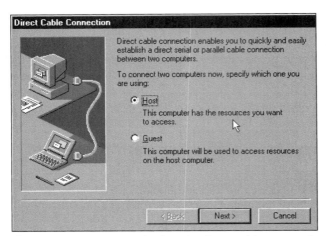

Figure 20-2: Setting up the host in direct cable connection

Step 4: Set up the guest

Fourth, when the host PC is set up and you've shared the items to which you want the guest to have access, you're ready to set up direct cable connection on the guest. Go to the guest (portable) PC and follow these steps:

1. Choose Start ➭ Programs ➭ Accessories.

2. Click Direct Cable Connection.

More Info If Direct Cable Connection isn't available in the Accessories menu, you need to install it. Bummer, I know, but you must do it only one time. Refer to "Installing Missing Windows Components" in Chapter 9.

3. Click Guest.

4. Click the Next button.

5. Follow the instructions onscreen to complete the wizard.

When you finish, you see a message indicating the guest is trying to make a connection. You can close this dialog box for now, if you want.

The following sections show you how to connect the two PCs from now on (after you complete all this setup business).

Making the direct cable connection

Fortunately, after you finish the setup and your cable is in place, connecting the two PCs is easy. Follow these steps:

1. On the host PC, choose Start ➪ Programs ➪ Accessories.

2. Click Direct Cable Connection.

3. If Windows needs more information, you'll be asked to fill in some wizard screens; do this.

4. When you get to the wizard screen shown in Figure 20-3, click the Listen button.

5. On the guest PC, choose Start ➪ Programs ➪ Accessories ➪ Direct Cable Connection, and complete the wizard screens.

6. When you get to the wizard screen shown in Figure 20-4, click the Connect button.

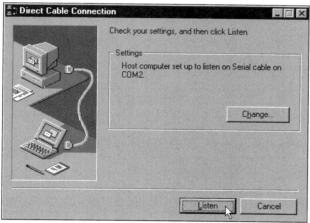

Figure 20-3: Click Listen to prepare the host PC.

You see some activity in the dialog boxes onscreen as the two PCs connect. If the guest PC complains it can't display the shared folders of the host computer and asks for a computer name, provide that name. If you don't remember exactly what you named the host PC, go to the host, right-click Network Neighborhood, click Properties, click the Identification tab, and look at the entry in the Computer name box. Click Cancel to close the Network Properties dialog box. Now go to the guest PC, type the name, and choose OK.

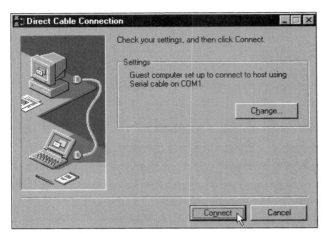

Figure 20-4: Click Connect on the guest PC.

When the connection is made, the small Direct Cable Connection status dialog box appears on both screens, displaying the message Connected via Serial cable on COMx. The computers remain connected until you click the Close button on either the host or guest PC.

Some people opt for this method of connecting two PCs because they assume setting up a LAN is too complicated. In truth, setting up a LAN probably is easier, and a LAN connection definitely is easier to work with than a cable connection is.

The guest PC displays a window of shared drives or folders available on the host PC (if not, click the View Host button on the guest PC). Figure 20-5 shows the screen of my guest PC (my portable PC) after the connection was made.

Notice the window titled Office_pc. The folders in that window represent two resources I shared on the host: a hard disk drive (Office_hdd) and a CD-ROM drive (Office_cd), each represented as a folder on this PC (the guest). So even though I'm looking at the screen on my portable PC, I have full access to the hard drive and CD-ROM drive on the larger desktop PC (the host).

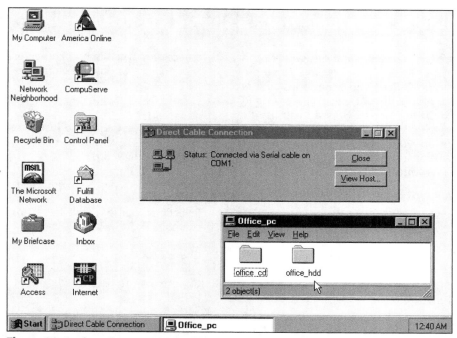

Figure 20-5: Shared resources on Office_pc appear on the guest PC's screen.

Transferring files via direct cable connection

To transfer files between connected PCs, use exactly the same techniques you always use. Follow these steps:

1. On the guest PC, use the host PC window (Office_pc, in my example) to browse to the folder containing the files you want to move or copy.

2. Also on the guest PC, use My Computer, Windows Explorer, or Find to browse to the folder on this PC containing the files you want to move or copy.

3. In either window, select the files you want to move or copy, and right-drag those files to the destination window.

4. Release the mouse button, and then choose <u>M</u>ove Here or <u>C</u>opy Here, depending on what you want to do.

Hot Stuff
If you find the connection is too slow, you can crank up the baud rate on both PCs, as described in "Troubleshooting a direct cable connection" later in this chapter.

Installing programs from a shared CD-ROM drive

Here's an all too-common scenario for many portable PC owners. You buy a program on CD-ROM and want to install it on your portable PC, but only your desktop PC has a CD-ROM drive. How do you use the desktop PC's CD-ROM drive to install a program on your portable PC's hard disk? Installation is easy if you can connect the two PCs with a cable.

On the host PC, follow these steps:

1. Insert the CD-ROM into the CD-ROM drive.

2. Double-click the My Computer icon.

3. Right-click the icon for the CD-ROM drive.

4. Click Sharing.

5. Click Shared As, and type a name (such as CDROM).

6. Choose OK.

7. Close My Computer.

8. Choose Start ➪ Programs ➪ Accessories ➪ Direct Cable Connection ➪ Listen.

On the guest PC, follow these steps:

1. Choose Start ➪ Programs ➪ Accessories ➪ Direct Cable Connection ➪ Connect.

2. If necessary, type the host computer's name (Office_pc, in my example).

3. Choose OK.

4. When you see the shared resources on the host PC, click the icon for the shared CD-ROM drive.

5. Choose File ➪ Map Network Drive.

6. Select any available drive letter (for example, D).

7. Choose OK.

8. Choose Start ➪ Settings ➪ Control Panel.

9. Double-click Add/Remove Programs.

10. Click the Install button.

11. Click the Next button to start the search.

If the wizard doesn't find an install program, click the Browse button in the wizard, select the shared CD-ROM drive (D, in my example) from the Look in drop-down list, and double-click the name of the install or setup program you need.

When you locate the install program, click the Finish button and proceed through the installation normally.

 If you have any trouble sharing a CD-ROM drive, check to make sure Client for Netware Networks is installed on both PCs. To do so, right-click the Network Neighborhood icon on the Windows 95 desktop, and choose Properties. If Client for NetWare Networks is not listed as an installed component, use the Add button to add Client ➪ Microsoft ➪ Client for Netware Networks.

Using a shared printer via direct cable connection

If you want to use the host PC's printer to print something from the guest PC, follow these steps:

1. On the guest PC, go to the window showing shared resources from the host PC.

2. Click the name of the shared printer from the host PC.

3. Choose File ➪ Install.

4. Work your way through the wizard to make the connection.

Now the host PC's printer is just like any other printer. If you want to print from a particular program on the guest PC, run that program, load the document you want to print, and choose File ➪ Print. When you're asked to choose a printer, select the name of the printer on the host; then choose OK.

Optionally, you can use drag-and-drop printing if the documents you want to print support that feature. On the guest PC, choose Start ➪ Settings ➪ Printers. Arrange the printer icons in the window so you can see the icon for the printer on the host. Then, staying on the guest PC, browse to and select the files you want to print, and drag those files to the host PC's printer icon, just as though you were printing on a local printer.

Closing the connection

To close the direct cable connection between two PCs, click the Close button in the Direct Cable Connection status dialog box on either PC.

Troubleshooting a direct cable connection

Many factors are involved in making a successful direct cable connection between two PCs. The built-in troubleshooter offers some help. If you have any problems making the connection, however, I suggest you first go through the following process:

1. On both PCs, right-click Network Neighborhood and then choose Properties.

2. Make sure both PCs have at least one network protocol in common (such as IPX/SPX-compatible Protocol).

   If not, click the Add button to add a common protocol.

3. On the host PC, click the File and Print Sharing button in the Network dialog box; make sure the PC can share printers and files; and then choose OK.

4. On both PCs, click the Identification tab in the Network dialog box; make sure each PC has a unique computer name; make sure both PCs have the same workgroup name; and choose OK to close the Network dialog box.

5. On both PCs, choose Start ➪ Settings ➪ Control Panel; double-click the System icon; click the Device Manager tab; and click the plus sign (+) next to Ports (COM and LPT). Double-click the icon for the port to which the cable is

connected on this PC (COM1 or COM2), click the Port Settings tab, and make sure each port uses the same settings (Bits per second = same, Data Bits = 8, Parity = None, Stop Bits = 1, Flow Control = Xon/Xoff). Then close the Communications Port and System Properties dialog boxes on both PCs.

Hot Stuff

You can crank the baud rate (Bits per second) up to 115,200 on both PCs to maximize the speed of transfers across the cable.

6. On the host PC, use My Computer to verify the drives (or folders) and printers you want to share have been shared (a little hand appears below the icon for a shared resource). If a resource you want to share is not shared, right-click this resource, click Sharing, and share the resource.

7. On both PCs, close all open windows, and choose Start ➪ Shut Down ➪ Shut down the computer ➪ Yes. When you are told it's OK to do so, turn off each PC.

8. Make sure the cable is properly connected to each PC, and make sure you know which port each computer is using (COM1 or COM2). Losing track of which PC is using which port is a common (and frustrating) mistake.

9. Power up both PCs again.

10. When you get to the Windows 95 desktop, try the connection again, as described in "Making the direct cable connection" earlier in this chapter.

If you still have problems, try using the Windows 95 Troubleshooter. Choose Start ➪ Help, click the Contents tab, double-click the Troubleshooting book, and then double-click If you have trouble using Direct Cable Connection.

Also check for and resolve any hardware conflicts, as described in "Using the Hardware Troubleshooter" and "Using Device Manager to Resolve Conflicts" in Chapter 10.

Dial-Up Networking

Dial-Up Networking enables you to connect to a PC via a modem. When you go on a trip, you can use Dial-Up Networking to access files you left behind on your office or home PC. Dial-Up Networking requires the following:

✦ Both PCs must have a modem installed.

✦ Both PCs must display the Network Neighborhood icon on the Windows 95 desktop.

✦ Both PCs must have the Windows 95 Dial-Up Networking component installed.

✦ The PC that answers the phone must have Microsoft Plus! (see Chapter 39) installed so it can be configured as a dial-up server.

✦ Any device you want to access over the phone lines must be shared on the dial-up server PC.

✦ The PC that places the call must be configured as the dial-up client.

In the following sections, I'll assume the first two items are taken care of on both PCs. If you haven't installed modems on both PCs, install them now, following the directions in Chapter 15. If the Network Neighborhood icon isn't visible on the Windows 95 desktop, install it as described in "Installing Network Neighborhood" earlier in this chapter. Remember, both PCs must display the Network Neighborhood icon.

The theory behind Dial-Up Networking

Dial-Up Networking can be confusing if you don't understand its theory. To illustrate the theory, here's an example from my home office: I keep all my current, ongoing projects in one folder, named Projects, on one PC. I share this folder so other PCs in my local area network (LAN) can have access to all the files in this folder. This way, regardless of which PC I happen to be currently using, I always know I'm working with the original files in the Projects folder. I don't need to move and copy files from one PC to another — a procedure, as you may know, which can be confusing and subject to errors.

While I'm in the home office, my portable PC is connected to this LAN via a network card that lives in the PCMCIA slot, so my portable has all the resources of the LAN. Namely, I can access the Projects folder to work on current projects.

When I take the portable PC on the road, I can't take my network card with me because it's connected to the LAN with cables. So when I open My Computer on my portable PC, I see what you see in Figure 20-6. The icon for drive P (the Projects folder on the Pentium PC) is marked out with an *X*. I don't have access to this shared folder because I'm disconnected from my LAN.

The theory behind Dial-Up Networking is simple. While I'm traveling with my portable PC, I can use my modem to dial up the LAN I left behind. As soon as the dial-up connection is made, I once again have access to any shared folders. In Figure 20-7, I've completed a dial-up connection. I have access to the shared Projects folder (P), so I can work with my original files even though I may be several thousand miles away. Notice the icon for that drive no longer is marked out with an *X*. Within this chapter, I'm focusing on just one aspect of dial-up networking — using telephone lines to connect your portable computer to some PC you've left back at the office or home. You can also use Dial-Up Networking to connect your PC to the Internet and some other services, such as MSN. I'll talk about those uses of Dial-Up Networking in Part VI of this book.

Mind you, the modem and phone lines aren't as fast as LAN cables, so operations are a little slower. But slow access to my Projects folder (and any other shared resources) is better than no access.

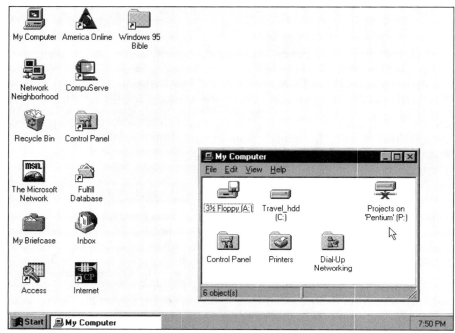

Figure 20-6: I can't use the Projects folder (P) when I'm disconnected from the LAN.

To make the original connection to the Projects folder, I chose File ⇨ Map Network Drive in Network Neighborhood on the portable PC while the computer was physically connected to the LAN with a network card. Chapter 32 explains in detail how to map a drive letter to a shared folder.

I realize some of you will want to use Dial-Up Networking to connect to an office PC from your portable, even if those PCs normally are not connected via a LAN at the office. If so, you should know the Universal Naming Convention (UNC) for the resource to which you want to gain access. I'll explain how you determine that name when I show you how to share a resource on the dial-up server PC.

Installing Dial-Up Networking

To use Dial-Up Networking, both PCs must have the Dial-Up Networking component installed. If you're not sure whether this component has been installed, choose Start ⇨ Programs ⇨ Accessories. If you see an icon for Dial-Up Networking, the component is installed, and you don't need to reinstall it. Skip to the following section, "Configuring the dial-up server."

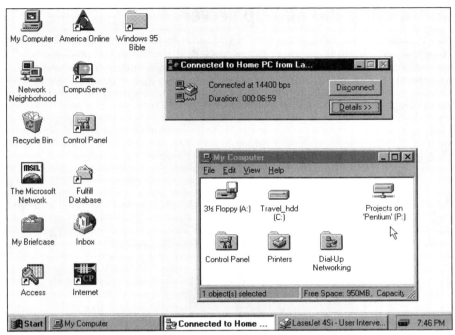

Figure 20-7: Dial-Up Networking gives me access to the shared folder.

To install the Dial-Up Networking component, follow these steps:

1. Gather up your original Windows 95 floppy disks or CD-ROM.

2. Choose Start ⇨ Settings ⇨ Control Panel.

3. Double-click Add/Remove Programs.

4. Click the Windows Setup tab.

5. Click Communications.

6. Click the Detail button.

7. Click the Dial-Up Networking checkbox (so it has a ✔ check mark).

8. Choose OK twice to begin the installation.

9. Follow the instructions onscreen.

You may need to restart the computer after Add/Remove Programs completes the installation. Don't forget the Dial-Up Networking component must be available on both PCs.

Configuring the dial-up server

As I've mentioned, configuring one of your PCs as a Dial-Up Networking server requires you to purchase the optional Microsoft Plus! program and to install Plus! on the computer that will act as the dial-up server. Remember, you can refer to Chapter 39 for more information on Plus! After you install Plus! on the PC that will answer the phone, you can follow these steps to configure that computer as the Dial-Up Networking server:

1. Double-click My Computer.

2. Double-click Dial-Up Networking.

   The Dial-Up Networking dialog box appears.

 If a wizard screen appears, click Cancel to close it; the wizard isn't designed to help you set up the server.

3. Choose Connections ⇨ Dial-Up Server (see Figure 20-8).

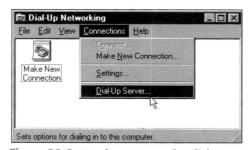

Figure 20-8: Ready to set up the dial-up server

4. Click Allow Caller Access.

   Optionally, click Change Password, and then enter a new password and confirmation. (Don't forget that password!)

If you choose Allow Caller Access, the modem will answer all incoming calls to this phone number. If you want to channel voice calls to an answering machine or telephone, you need a sharing device. See the sidebar titled "So many gizmos, so few phone numbers" in Chapter 15.

5. Click the Server Type button.

6. From the drop-down list, select PPP: Windows 95, Windows NT 3.5, Internet.

7. Set up the other options as shown in Figure 20-9.

8. Choose OK twice to return to the Dial-Up Networking dialog box.

9. Close that dialog box by clicking its Close button.

Figure 20-9: Configuring the dial-up server

The Point-to-Point Protocol (PPP) for networking over phone lines is built right into Windows 95. You don't need any extra software to use PPP with Dial-Up Networking.

Remember, when you dial into the computer, you have access only to shared resources. In a moment, I'll show you how to access the entire hard disk of this PC while you're away. First, you need to set up the other PC, as described in the following section.

Configuring the dial-up client

Now go to the portable PC (the dial-up client) and define the connection you'll make to the dial-up server (the PC that will answer the phone). Follow these steps:

1. Double-click My Computer.

2. Double-click Dial-Up Networking.

3. Double-click the Make New Connection icon.

4. In the first wizard screen, enter a name for this connection (see Figure 20-10).

   If you have more than one modem installed, select that modem in the Select a modem drop-down list.

5. Click Next.

6. Type the number you'll use to phone the dial-up server's modem.

7. Click Next to go to the last wizard screen.

8. Click Finish.

   The Dial-Up Networking dialog box now includes an icon for the connection you just defined (see Figure 20-11). Before you use it, though, you need to check some other settings.

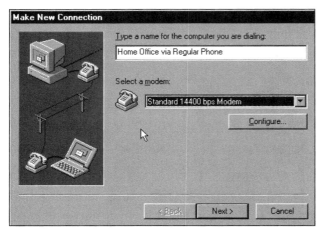

Figure 20-10: First screen of the Make New Connection wizard

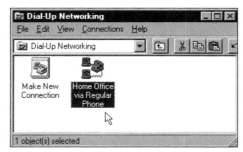

Figure 20-11: The Dial-Up Networking
dialog box with some connections defined

9. Right-click the icon for the connection you just created.

10. Click Properties.

11. Click the Server Type button.

12. In the Dial-Up Server drop-down list, select PPP: Windows 95, Windows NT 3.5, Internet.

13. Set the other options as shown in Figure 20-12.

14. Choose OK twice to save your settings.

15. Close the Dial-Up Networking dialog box.

Everything is set up to make connections. Before you go anywhere, though, don't forget you can connect only to shared resources while you're away. I've talked about this topic already, but a new issue, called Universal Naming Conventions (UCN), may come into play with Dial-Up Networking. The following section shows a new example of sharing a resource with Dial-Up Networking.

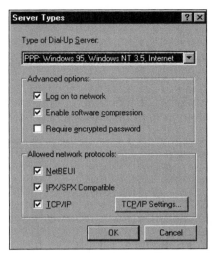

Figure 20-12: The dial-up client needs some information about the server you will call.

Sharing resources on the dial-up server

When you make a connection with Dial-Up Networking, you do not have free rein over the computer into which you dialed; you have access only to shared resources on that PC. So before you leave town, make sure you have shared the resources to which you'll need access while you're away.

With Dial-Up Networking, you can't simply browse the server and make connections on the fly. To connect to a shared resource while you're away, you may need to enter the UNC for that resource. This section shows you how to share a resource on the dial-up server and how to determine that resource's UNC.

Suppose you're going on a trip and want access to every file on the entire hard disk of the PC you'll leave behind. You need to define this hard disk as a shared resource and also determine the UNC for this resource. Follow these steps:

1. On the dial-up server (the computer you're leaving behind), right-click the Network Neighborhood icon.

2. Click Properties.

3. Click the Identification tab.

4. Write down the Computer name entry, preceded by two backslashes.

   The computer name of my PC is Office_pc, so I would write \\Office_pc.

5. Choose OK to close the Network dialog box.

6. Double-click My Computer.

7. Right-click the resource you want to share.

8. Click Sharing.

9. Click Shared As.

10. Type a name up to 15 characters long, with no spaces.

    I used Office_hdd (hdd is an abbreviation for hard disk drive).

11. Beside the computer name you wrote down in Step 4, write the name you entered in Step 10, preceded by one backslash.

    I would write \\Office_pc\Office_hdd.

    What you wrote is the UNC for the resource you shared.

12. If you want to read from and write to that drive while you're away, select Full as the Access Type, as shown in Figure 20-13.

13. Choose OK.

    You return to My Computer, where you see a little hand below the icon for the item you just shared. The share name you assigned does not appear; the original local name stays intact. You use the share name when you access the shared resource from another PC.

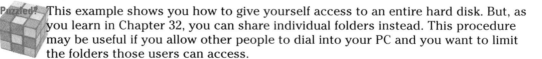 Simply stated, the UNC for a device is *computer name**share name*. To find the computer name, right-click Network Neighborhood, click Properties, and click the Identification tab. To find a shared resource's share name, right-click the icon for the shared resource, and then click Sharing.

Of course, you can repeat Steps 7-13 to share other resources — for example, the entire CD-ROM drive, so you have access to whatever CD-ROM is in this drive while you're away.

This example shows you how to give yourself access to an entire hard disk. But, as you learn in Chapter 32, you can share individual folders instead. This procedure may be useful if you allow other people to dial into your PC and you want to limit the folders those users can access.

When you go on the road, don't forget to take the UNC you jotted down; you may need it to connect to the shared resource when you dial in.

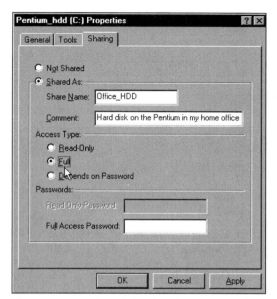

Figure 20-13: Giving myself full access to the hard disk that I'm leaving behind

Making the dial-up connection

By the time you get to this section, you should have installed Dial-Up Networking on both the server (the PC that answers the phone) and the client (the portable PC). You also should have shared the resources you need to access while you're away. Leave that PC running and its modem on, of course, so the PC can answer the phone when you dial in. (You can turn off the monitor on the server, if you want.) Now you're far away with your portable PC, all hooked up to a modem and ready to dial out.

Follow these steps to make the connection:

1. Double-click My Computer.

2. Double-click the Dial-Up Networking icon.

3. Double-click the icon for the connection you defined for dialing in to your dial-up server.

   You can leave the Password box blank unless you assigned a password when you set up the dial-up server.

4. If you need to dial the area code, country code, or whatever from this location, click the Dialing from button and/or the Dial Properties button to define from where you're calling.

5. Click the Connect button.

You should see some activity onscreen and may hear the modem as your portable PC connects to the dial-up server. When you're connected, you see a message like the one shown in Figure 20-14.

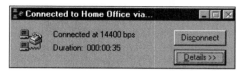

Figure 20-14: The dial-up connection to the home-office PC is successful.

If you return to My Computer, any connections you made previously via the LAN (or whatever) will be restored, as in the examples shown in Figures 20-6 and 20-7. If so, skip the rest of the steps and resume work normally. You are, for all intents and purposes, back on the LAN. (You just happen to be using a modem rather than a LAN card at the moment.)

6. If you need to connect to a shared resource, double-click Network Neighborhood and wait for the Entire Network option to appear.

7. In Network Neighborhood's toolbar, click the Map Network Drive button.

8. Select any available drive letter (I'll use *D* in this example).

9. In the Path box, type the UNC for the resource to which you want to connect.

In my example, I would type **\\Office_pc\Office_hdd**.

 When you're physically connected to your LAN with a network card, you can double-click Entire Network to browse around the LAN. Dial-Up Networking doesn't support this capability, however, because the modem connection is too slow. For this reason, you must know the UNC for the resource to which you want to connect.

10. Choose OK.

Most likely, a window for browsing that drive appears immediately, just as though that hard disk was part of the PC you're using currently.

To see things from the My Computer perspective, you can close the browsing window that just opened (if any), and go back to the My Computer window. In that window, choose View ➪ Refresh and perhaps View ➪ Arrange Icons ➪ By Drive Letter. You should see an icon for the shared drive.

Figure 20-15 shows an example in which I dialed in to my home-office PC. The My Computer window now shows an icon for the shared resource I left at home: Office_hdd on 'Office PC' (D:).

Preflight checklist for Dial-Up Networking

When you're away from your dial-up server PC, you can't easily change any settings you forgot to change before you left. You'll be high and dry until you return unless someone at the home office can set everything up for you. Your best bet is to make the necessary changes on the PC you'll be leaving behind. Check the following things:

✦ Make sure you can get a dial tone on the PC answering the phone. Start Phone Dialer (choose Start ➪ Programs ➪ Accessories ➪ Phone Dialer), type any phone number, and click Dial. If the modem can dial out, it can answer your incoming calls.

✦ Open My Computer, double-click Dial-Up Networking, close the wizard, and choose Connections ➪ Dial-Up

Server. Make sure Allow Caller Access is selected. Check your password (if any) and server type (it should be PPP for dialing in from a Windows 95 client). Then choose OK twice.

✦ Use My Computer to make certain all the resources you'll need are shared; if they're not, be sure to share them before you go. Remember to write down the UNC names; you may need them on the road.

✦ Close all open windows, and leave the server PC running with just the Windows 95 desktop showing. You can turn off the monitor, if you want, but don't turn off the PC or the modem.

While you're connected, you can treat that drive as though it really is a hard disk drive named *D* on your portable PC. To browse the shared drive, double-click its icon in My Computer. To copy things to and from folders in that shared drive, select items and drag them to or from whatever folders you want. You can use the shared resource for as long as you want.

Disconnecting a dial-up connection

When you finish using a dial-up connection, you can click the Disconnect button. To play it safe, though, I suggest you go through the following ritual to make certain you don't leave any unfinished work behind:

1. Save all work in progress.

2. Close all windows, except the Connected To dialog box.

3. Click the Disconnect button in the Connected To dialog box.

When you are disconnected, you can shut down the portable PC, if you want. All your work is safe and sound on whichever drive you stored it.

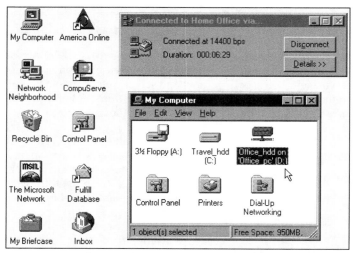

Figure 20-15: The icon for Office_hdd is available in My Computer during dial-up connection.

Disabling Dial-Up Networking

When you return from your trip, you may want the modem on the dial-up server to stop answering the phone. Follow these steps:

1. On the dial-up server, double-click My Computer.

2. Double-click the Dial-Up Networking icon.

3. If a wizard screen appears, click Cancel to bypass it.

4. In Network Neighborhood, choose Connections ➪ Dial-Up Server.

5. Select No Caller Access, as shown in Figure 20-16.

6. Choose OK.

7. Close the Dial-Up Networking dialog box.

After you perform these steps, no one (including you) can dial in to the dial-up server. If you want to regain access to this PC on your next trip, remember to complete the entire procedure described in the "Preflight checklist for Dial-Up Networking" sidebar earlier in this chapter.

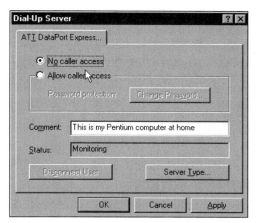

Figure 20-16: Modem won't answer incoming calls anymore

Troubleshooting Dial-Up Networking

Many factors go into Dial-Up Networking; unfortunately, this means many little things can go wrong and make the whole thing unworkable. If you have two phone lines in your office, I strongly suggest you plug the dial-up server into one line and the portable PC into the other. Then dial the server from the portable right there in the office. This way, you'll have access to both PCs while you troubleshoot.

Following are some basic troubleshooting tips for Dial-Up Networking:

✦ If you didn't complete the checklist on the server, you can do absolutely nothing until you return to the server and prepare it to answer the phone and share resources.

✦ If you're on the road, make sure you're using the correct dialing properties. See Chapter 15 for more information on this topic.

✦ If you're certain the server is prepared, but you still can't connect from the client, try using the Windows 95 Troubleshooter. Choose Start ⇨ Help, click the Contents tab, double-click the Troubleshooting book, and select If you have trouble using Dial-Up Networking.

If you can't solve the problem through these means, try the following procedures when both computers are within immediate reach:

✦ On both PCs, right-click Network Neighborhood, and click Properties. Make sure both PCs have at least one network protocol in common (for example, IPX/SPX-compatible Protocol); if not, click the Add button to add a common protocol.

✦ On the host PC, click the File and Print Sharing button in the Network dialog box. Make certain this PC can share printers and files. Then choose OK.

✦ On both PCs, click the Identification tab of the Network dialog box. Make sure each PC has a unique computer name and both PCs have the same workgroup name. Then click the OK button to close the Network dialog box.

✦ On both PCs, choose Start ➪ Settings ➪ Control Panel, double-click the Modems icon, and make sure the modem is installed properly. See Chapter 15 for more information on installing modems and setting up your dialing properties.

Dialing into non-Windows 95 servers

Throughout this chapter, I assume both the dial-up client and the server (the one that answers the phone) are using Windows 95. A Windows 95 dial-up client can, however, dial in to any of the following:

✦ Windows for Workgroups Version 3.11 Remote Access Services (RAS)

✦ Windows NT 3.5

✦ Windows NT 3.1 with RAS protocol

✦ Novell NetWare connect server

✦ Shiva LanRover or NetModem/E remote access servers

Techniques for setting up both the server and the client for these other operating systems are included in the *Windows 95 Resource Kit*, published by Microsoft Press (800-MS-PRESS). I don't want to repeat all this information here, because if you're working in an environment that supports those systems, you probably need this resource kit anyway. The book is written specifically for corporate users and others who have a large investment in big-time legacy hardware and software.

You also can find more information on Dial-Up Networking in the help screens. For the broadest selection of topics, choose Start ➪ Help, click the Find tab, and search for *dial-up*.

Summary

Dial-Up Networking and direct cable connection enable you to share resources on two PCs without fumbling with floppy disks. To recap:

✦ Both direct cable and dial-up connections require that both PCs in the LAN have Network Neighborhood installed.

✦ In direct cable connection, the PC with the resources to share is called the host. The PC that wants access to those resources is called the guest.

✦ In Dial-Up Networking, the PC with the resources and that answers the phone is called the *dial-up server*. The PC that dials in is called the *dial-up client*.

✦ The guest or client PC can gain access to *shared resources* on the host/server PC only.

✦ In Dial-Up Networking, it's important to share resources on the server *before* you leave town. Otherwise, you cannot get at those resources while you're on the road.

✦   ✦   ✦

Hopping on the Info Superhighway

Cruising the Microsoft Network (MSN)

The Microsoft Network (MSN) is Microsoft's commercial online service where you can mingle with other Windows 95 users, ask questions, meet people with similar interests, send and receive Internet e-mail, catch up on the news, get free software, and much more. Now I don't mean to imply MSN itself is free; MSN is an extra service you can join if you like. But joining MSN is by no means mandatory.

If you're not exactly sure whether you want to start paying for an online service, I suggest you read this chapter to get a sense of what MSN is all about. Then, you can begin the sign-up procedure if you're interested and review Microsoft's billing rates, terms, and conditions that will appear on your screen. If you're still interested at this point, you can proceed with the sign-up procedure. If you don't like the rates, terms, and conditions, you can cancel the sign-up procedure. This is up to you.

What Is MSN?

Let's look at what you'll get if you do become a member of MSN.

When you're connected, you'll find most of MSN is organized like the rest of Windows 95, with folders and icons. As you cruise MSN, you'll come across the following kinds of services:

- ◆ *Bulletin boards.* Bulletin boards (BBSs) offer discussions and postings of recent information from specific companies that act as *content providers*.

- ◆ *Chat rooms.* Chat rooms offer online conversations with other users, as well as special events featuring celebrities and captains of industry.

✦ *File libraries.* These libraries contain freeware and shareware programs, add-in utilities, and drivers you can download (copy) to your own PC.

✦ *Electronic mail (e-mail).* You can send e-mail messages to anyone else on MSN, and those people can send messages to you. E-mail is especially good for mobile computing, because you can pick up your messages from wherever you currently are.

✦ *Internet access*: If you don't have any other means to connect to the Internet, you can use your MSN account as your connection to many services, including the World Wide Web, e-mail, and newsgroups.

You may find all or some of these services within a single topic area, be it art, business, games, or whatever. Figure 21-1 shows an example of the Computer Games folder on MSN.

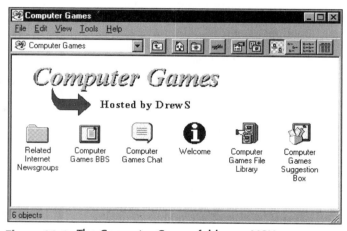

Figure 21-1: The Computer Games folder on MSN

Establishing an Account

Before you can use MSN, you need to establish an account. Before you do this, however, do the following:

✦ If you haven't already done so, install a modem, as described in Chapter 15.

✦ Think up a member ID (also called an *alias*) to identify you to other users on the network. No spaces are allowed. You can use your real name with no spaces (for example, *WilmaWangdoodle*). If you want to be anonymous, make up a *handle*, such as *WildWoman* or *Godzilla_Breath*.

✦ Think up a password for logging in and keep it secret to prevent other people from logging in under your user ID. The password can be up to 15 characters long, with no spaces. If you have a universal password for all your PC access, you can use that password.

✦ Grab your local phone book and find the page that tells you which prefixes you can dial for no charge.

✦ Grab a credit card.

To establish your account, follow these steps:

1. Double-click the MSN icon (titled The Microsoft Network) on your desktop.

   Or, choose Start ⇨ Programs ⇨ Microsoft Network.

More Info If you can't find an icon for the Microsoft Network, first choose Start ⇨ Programs ⇨ Accessories ⇨ Online Registration. If this procedure doesn't work, you need to install the Microsoft Network from Windows Setup in Add/Remove Programs. See Chapter 9.

2. Follow the instructions onscreen to set up your account and to choose a phone number for dialing in.

Danger Zone If possible, choose a phone number with a prefix you can dial free.

You need to establish an account only one time. After you complete the necessary steps, you can log in at any time by following the steps in the next section.

Getting in to MSN

When you have an account with MSN, logging in to the service is kind of a no-brainer. Follow these steps:

1. Double-click the MSN icon on the desktop.

   The Sign In dialog box appears (see Figure 21-2).

2. Type in your member ID and password.

   If you don't share your PC with other people and you aren't concerned other people will log in under your member ID, you can check the Remember my password option. Then you needn't type the password every time you log on.

   If you're calling from someplace other than your normal location, or if you're using a different modem (such as your cellular modem), click the Settings button, and then select the local Access Number, Dial Helper, and Modem Settings appropriate for your current situation.

Figure 21-2: The Microsoft Network Sign In dialog box

4. Click the Connect button and wait for the connection.

5. If any instructions appear onscreen, follow them.

If you have any new mail waiting, a message informs you of this. Click Yes to check your mail now or No to check it later. If you choose Yes, Microsoft Exchange starts; then you can double-click any message you want to read. (Microsoft Exchange is a central repository for all incoming and outgoing messages and faxes, as you'll learn in Chapter 30.) When you finish reading your mail, you can close the Inbox and access the other features of MSN.

When you're connected, a small MSN indicator appears in the taskbar, most likely near the lower-right corner of your screen. This indicator stays there as long as you're connected. You can right-click the indicator to jump to someplace special within MSN.

Getting Around MSN

The Microsoft Network is sort of an extension to Windows 95. The MSN interface has the same elements as the desktop: toolbars, shortcuts, command buttons, menus, and a Close (X) button in the upper-right corner of Windows. When you first log on, you probably will see MSN Today and MSN Central (see Figure 21-3).

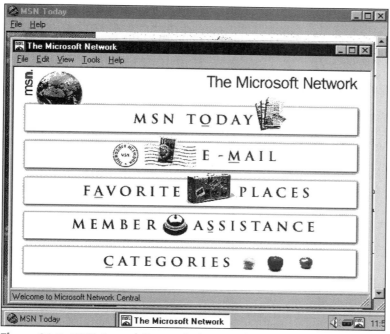

Figure 21-3: MSN Central (front window) and MSN Today

The following are the basic skills you need to go exploring:

✦ To go someplace that looks interesting, click its name or button, or double-click its shortcut icon.

✦ If you feel stuck at any point, click Member Assistance, The MSN Lobby, or the Go To MSN Central button (whichever is available at the moment), to display more options.

✦ While you'reconnected to MSN, you can right-click the MSN indicator in the taskbar (near the lower-right corner of your screen), and choose a destination from the pop-up menu that appears.

Hot Stuff Toolbars are useful in MSN. If you don't see a toolbar in the current window, choose View ➭ Toolbar (if available).

✦ To exit, click the window's Close (X) button or the Up One Level button in the toolbar.

✦ To exit a series of windows, hold down the Shift key and click the Close button of the last window you opened.

✦ If you find a place you want to revisit later, click the Add to Favorite Places button in the toolbar.

✦ To return to a place that you sent to Favorite Places, click the Go To Favorite Places button in any toolbar, in MSN Central, or in the pop-up menu that appears when you right-click the MSN button in the taskbar.

Using Find on MSN

The basic skills listed in the preceding section get you on the path to discovering what's available in MSN. If you have a specific goal in mind, you can use Find. Choose Tools ➪ Find ➪ On The Microsoft Network in any window that offers a Tools menu. Or, click Start ➪ Find ➪ On The Microsoft Network. Then fill in the blanks as instructed onscreen. In Figure 21-4, I typed **chat** as the topic I want to check.

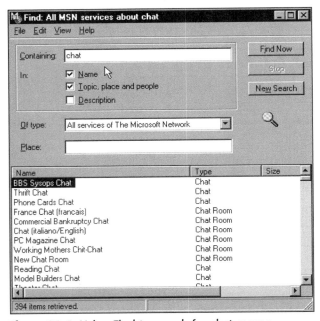

Figure 21-4: Using Find to search for chat rooms

After clicking Find Now, I see a long list of chat rooms. I can double-click one of those rooms to go there. Notice that Find in MSN works much like Find on the desktop (refer to Chapter 2) — that is, searches are cumulative unless you click New Search to cancel the preceding search.

When Find locates all the topics for the word(s) for which you searched, you can click Name at the top of the column to alphabetize the list.

What's with the fade-in pictures?

You may notice when you get into MSN, there are certain pictures (especially photos) that appear terribly out of focus. But if you wait, the picture sort of fades in and becomes clear. The reason is, sending a picture from one PC to another over telephone lines takes a long time. Telephone lines were, after all, invented to transport voices, not pictures. So MSN sends a little bit of the picture at a time.

The advantage to you is if you don't feel like waiting around to see a picture, you needn't. Just go about your business and forget the picture. As soon as you jump to another window, MSN stops spending time and resources getting the picture to you.

Using MSN E-Mail

The Microsoft Network's e-mail service is tightly integrated with Microsoft Exchange, which means all your messages coming from MSN are listed along with your incoming faxes and local e-mail. In addition, you can compose new messages within Exchange, and then use your Personal Phone Book or the MSN Phone Book to address those messages.

Creating an MSN e-mail message

Suppose you want to write an e-mail message to someone else on MSN. Follow these steps:

1. If you haven't already done so, connect to MSN.

2. Right-click the little MSN indicator in the taskbar, and then choose Send Mail.

   Hot Stuff
   To reply to a message you received, click the Reply to Sender button in Microsoft Exchange's toolbar.

3. In the To box, type the recipient's name.

   Or, click the To button, and choose a name from your Personal Address Book. Within the Address Book, choose Microsoft Network from the Show Names drop-down list. Then, where indicated, start typing the name of the person to whom you want to send the message so you can jump to that part of the list (see Figure 21-5).

4. If you want to send the same message to several people, select the appropriate names from the list, or type the names, separated by semicolons (;).

5. Type a brief subject (to appear in the recipient's Inbox) and the main body of your message.

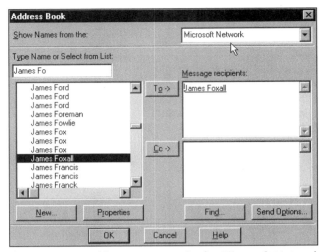

Figure 21-5: Looking up a name in the Microsoft Network Address Book

Figure 21-6 shows an example.

6. Click the Send button in Exchange's toolbar, or choose File ➪ Send.

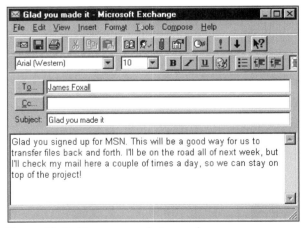

Figure 21-6: Message ready to send

Your message is sent immediately and appears in the recipient's Inbox the next time he or she opens Microsoft Exchange. If you want to verify the message was sent, turn on the folder list in Microsoft Exchange (click Show/Hide Folder List or choose View ➪ Folders); then select the Sent Items folder. If your message isn't listed there, click the Outbox folder, click your message, and then choose Tools ➪ Deliver Now.

Sending a file via MSN

If you want to send a document to someone on MSN, you can attach it to a message by completing the steps in the preceding section. But before you send your message, click the Insert File button in Exchange's toolbar or choose Insert ➪ File. In the Look In drop-down list, browse to the drive, folder, and filename of the document you want to send. Then double-click the document's filename. The file appears as an icon in your message, as shown in Figure 21-7. The recipient simply double-clicks that icon to open the attached file.

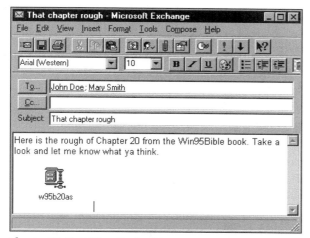

Figure 21-7: A file attached to a message appears as an icon.

In Exchange's Inbox, messages marked with a little paper-clip icon are the ones that contain attached files.

Sending a message to other services

When you want to send an e-mail message to someone who isn't on MSN, you can use that person's Internet, CompuServe, America Online, or Prodigy account. Compose your message normally within MSN and Microsoft Exchange. In the To box, address the message, using the appropriate format listed in Table 21-1.

Notice in Table 21-1, when you type a CompuServe ID, you use a period (.) where you normally would type a comma. If you forget that period, your message won't be delivered.

Table 21-1
Formats for Addressing Messages to Other Services

Service	Format of To Address	Example
America Online	username@aol.com	SimpsonAC@aol.com
CompuServe	nnnnn.nnnn@compuserve.com	72420.2236@compuserve.com
Internet	username@domainname	alan@coolnerds.com
Prodigy	userID@prodigy.com	JohnDoe@prodigy.com

If you ever need a reminder on how to address a message to another service, choose Help ➪ The Microsoft Network Help within Exchange, and then use the Index tab to search for the service in which you're interested (America Online, CompuServe, Internet, or Prodigy).

Your new e-mail address

If you want someone to send you an e-mail message from MSN, that person must look up your name in the Microsoft Network Address Book. You also have an Internet address now; that address is your user ID followed by @msn.com. If your user ID in MSN is WildWoman, for example, your Internet address would be wildwoman@msn.com.

A person who sends you mail from the Internet or America Online uses that address. A person who sends you e-mail from CompuServe uses that service's standard Internet addressing scheme (INTERNET:WildWoman@msn.com). Regardless of from where the sender sends the message, it ends up in your Microsoft Exchange Inbox.

MSN and the Internet

While we're on the topic of the Internet, I should point out that MSN offers access to the Internet's World Wide Web, e-mail, and newsgroups. For more information on getting Internet access via MSN, follow these steps:

1. If you're no longer at the MSN Central screen, right-click the MSN indicator down near the lower-right corner of your screen, and choose Go to MSN Central from the pop-up menu that appears.

2. In MSN Central, click Categories.

3. Double-click the Internet Center icon.

You'll be taken to the MSN's Internet Center, as shown in Figure 21-8. The icons titled Getting on the Internet, Shareware for the Internet, and Internet Info Center are good places to explore first. Of course, I'll also discuss various ways you can get connected to the Internet in Chapter 23. Then in Part VII, I'll teach you everything you need to become an Internet guru. If you want to skip the Internet stuff right now and stay focused on MSN, just continue reading.

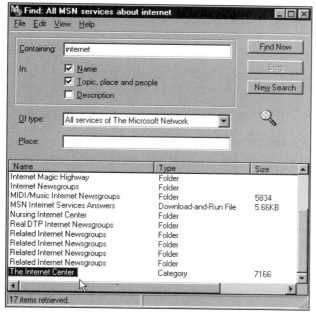

Figure 21-8: The MSN's Internet Center creating MSN shortcuts

One of MSN's best features is its capability to create shortcuts. Just as you can create a shortcut to any file, folder, or program on your PC (refer to Chapter 4), you can create a shortcut to any place on MSN. Shortcuts are great because sometimes you find something you want to share with other people, but you forgot how you got there. No problem — just drag an icon to that place on your desktop, or drag the icon into an e-mail message to whomever you want to share your discovery.

The Favorite Places described earlier are shortcuts, in a sense, but they're accessible only from the Favorite Places area of MSN. The shortcuts I describe in this section can go right on your desktop or into e-mail messages you send to someone else.

Suppose you're on MSN, and you come to some place you want to find again easily and/or share with other users. Follow these steps:

1. If you're in the area to which you want to create a shortcut, click the Up One Level button in the toolbar, or choose File ➪ Up One Level.

   Now you see the icon that took you to where you are.

2. Move and size windows so you can see any portion of the Windows 95 desktop.

3. Drag the icon to your desktop.

Figure 21-9 shows an example in which I dragged the icon for the Computer Games File Library file from its folder in MSN to my desktop.

Figure 21-9: Desktop shortcut to the Computer Games File Library on MSN

If you want to send a shortcut to someone else, you can drag it from its original location or drag a copy of the shortcut from your desktop to an e-mail message. In Figure 21-10, I created an e-mail message by right-clicking the MSN indicator in the taskbar and choosing Send Mail. Then I addressed and typed the message normally. Finally, I dragged the Shortcut to Computer Games File Library icon from my desktop into the body of the message.

Now I can send that message, using the usual techniques. When the recipient gets the message, he or she can double-click the shortcut icon to go right to the Computer Games File Library on MSN or drag that icon to his or her desktop to create a permanent shortcut.

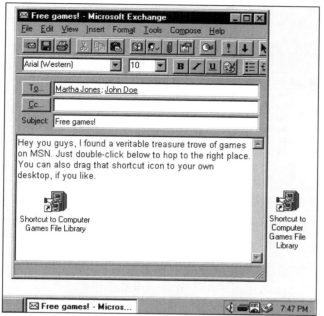

Figure 21-10: MSN shortcut dragged into an e-mail message

Downloading Files from MSN

You can download programs and other files from any MSN file library or BBS. *Downloading* means copying something from the host PC (MSN) *down* to your personal computer. *Uploading* means the opposite: copying something from your PC *up* to the host PC.

This section demonstrates how to download a file named WinZip for Windows 95. (You can use the steps to download any file from MSN.) Suppose you have cruised through Categories to Computers and Software to Computer Games to Computer Games File Library to Utilities. You find WinZip for Win95 & NT near the top of the list shown in Figure 21-11.

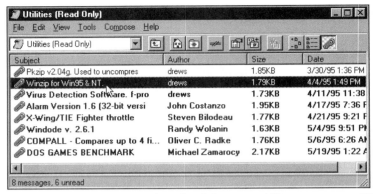

Figure 21-11: You want to download the second file to your own PC.

To download that file to your own PC, follow these steps:

1. Choose <u>V</u>iew ➪ Attached <u>F</u>iles to limit the list to files you can download.

2. Double-click the name of the file you want to download.

   You should see some instructions and an icon for the file you want to download, as shown in Figure 21-12. If you want to print the instructions, click the Print button in the toolbar.

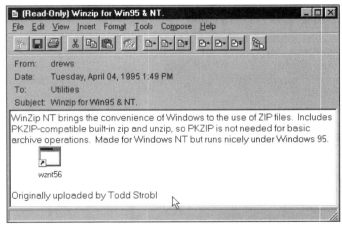

Figure 21-12: After double-clicking the Winzip for Win95 & NT message

3. Click the icon for the file you want to download.

   A border appears around the icon to indicate you selected it.

4. Choose File ➪ Save.

5. Click the Attachments radio button.

6. In the Folders section, browse to the drive and folder on your own PC where you want to save the file.

   In Figure 21-13, I chose a folder named Zippers on my drive C.

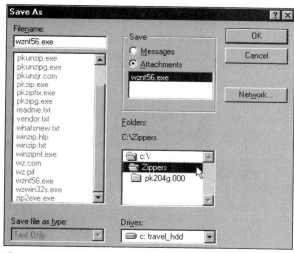

Figure 21-13: Ready to download file to C:\Zippers

7. Choose OK.

   The File Transfer Status dialog box appears. The odometer and timer at the bottom of that dialog box indicate how long the transfer will take.

You needn't wait for the entire transfer; you can minimize that window and go about your business. Just remember not to disconnect from MSN until all the downloads are completed. The little modem indicator probably will flash red and green while the download is in progress. To check the progress of the download at any time, click the File Transfer Status button in the taskbar.

 More Info If you need a reminder on how to copy a file to your PC, search MSN's help system for *download*.

Dealing with Zipped Files

Files on information services, such as MSN, often are compressed, or *zipped*. Files are zipped for two reasons: The sender can combine many files in one zipped file and a zipped file is compressed to speed its transfer over phone lines. When you download a zipped file to your own PC, you can get several files in one comparatively brief transfer.

The catch, of course, is the downloaded zipped file is useless until you decompress it. Exactly how you decompress depends on the format of the zipped file. The two most likely formats are .EXE and .ZIP (based on the extensions assigned to the filenames). The following list explains the difference:

✦ *.EXE.* If a compressed file is self-extracting, it has the .EXE file extension. To decompress this type of file, you must run the .EXE file just as you would run any other program. Choose Start ➪ <u>R</u>un, and browse to the .EXE file.

✦ *.ZIP.* These files are not self-extracting. You must have — and know how to use — an unzipping utility such as WinZip.

The latter files are a bit of a problem if you don't own and know how to use an unzipping utility. Unfortunately, I can give you only rough instructions, because WinZip is a third-party shareware program, and could change by the time you read this book. In general, most people get an unzipping utility such as WinZip by downloading a copy from an information service. (I used the downloading of WinZip as the example in "Downloading Files from MSN" earlier in this chapter.)

Hot Stuff
If you have a CD-ROM drive, you can get the WinZip shareware from the companion CD-ROM in the back of this book.

I can't even say for certain where you'll find WinZip; the owners of BBSs are free to organize and reorganize files however they want. But I will tell you where I found the copy I used in the MSN example. Starting at MSN Central, I used the following buttons and icons, in this order:

<u>C</u>ategories ➪ *Computers and Software* ➪ *Computer Games* ➪ *Computer Games File Library* ➪ *Utilities folder*

WinZip itself usually is stored as a self-extracting (.EXE) file. After you download the file to your PC, you need to run that .EXE file, and then follow the instructions onscreen to decompress it. Then you can open the file named ReadMe on the floppy disk for installation instructions.

When you get WinZip running on your PC, you can press F1 to get help information for it.

After you successfully install WinZip, you can launch the program by choosing Start ➪ <u>P</u>rograms ➪ WinZip ➪ WinZip for Windows (or whatever it's called). Typically, you see a sign-on screen; then WinZip starts on your PC.

To unzip a .ZIP file, use My Computer, Find, or Windows Explorer to get to the icon for the .ZIP file, and then drag that file into the WinZip window. You see the names of the files inside the zipped file. In Figure 21-14, I used Find to locate a .ZIP file, and then dragged that file into the WinZip window. The README.TXT and RNASERV.DLL files shown inside WinZip's window are the compressed files inside RNA456.ZIP.

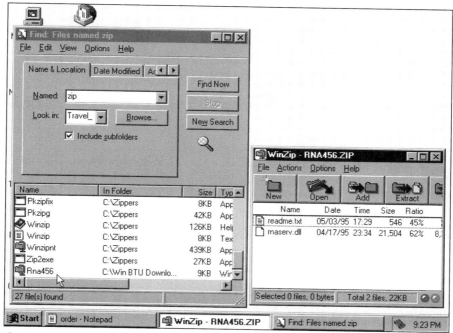

Figure 21-14: Ready to decompress a .ZIP file on my PC

To decompress the files, I would click the Extract button in WinZip's toolbar, select a destination, and then click Extract again. The extracted files would reside in whatever folder I specified after clicking Extract, and would be normal (uncompressed) files.

To compress files, you do pretty much the same thing. Use My Computer, Find, or Windows Explorer to get to the files you want to compress. Press Ctrl+click or Shift+click to select those files, run WinZip, and drag the selected files into the WinZip window. Click the New button, type a folder and filename for the .ZIP file, and then click Add to put the files into the .ZIP file. When WinZip finishes, you can attach that .ZIP file to any e-mail message you send.

As mentioned earlier, I can give only rough instructions here. By the time you read this book, a completely new and different WinZip 95 may be available from MSN. Remember, after you get WinZip running, you can press the F1 key for help at any time.

Disconnecting from MSN

As long as you see the MSN indicator in the taskbar, you're connected to MSN. (You may be racking up connect time and Ma Bell charges until you disconnect.) To disconnect from MSN, do any of the following:

✦ Right-click the MSN indicator in the taskbar, and choose Sign Out.

✦ Click the Sign Out button in any MSN toolbar.

✦ Choose File ➪ Sign Out in any MSN window.

You'll be given an opportunity to change your mind. Click the Yes button to sign off and disconnect from MSN.

Summary

Microsoft Network (MSN) is a great online service for newbies and experienced Internauts alike. Here are some salient points to mull over:

✦ Before you can connect to MSN, you must install a modem, as discussed in Chapter 15.

✦ Your first trek into MSN requires you to establish an account. Grab a credit card, click the Start button, choose Programs ➪ The Microsoft Network. Follow the onscreen instructions that appear.

✦ While you're connected to MSN, a tiny MSN indicator appears in the taskbar (perhaps to remind you you're spending money!).

✦ If you get lost in MSN, right-click the tiny MSN indicator in the taskbar and choose a more familiar location.

✦ To create and send an e-mail message in MSN, right-click the MSN indicator in the Taskbar and choose Send Mail.

✦ Establishing an MSN account automatically gives you an Internet e-mail address — your Member ID followed by @msn.com.

✦ To disconnect from MSN, right-click the MSN indicator and choose Sign Out.

✦ Consider purchasing Microsoft Plus! to explore and use the Internet fully from your MSN account.

✦   ✦   ✦

Connecting to a Bulletin Board System (BBS) or PC

All the big commercial online services offer custom front ends. When you sign up with America Online, CompuServe, or the Microsoft Network (MSN), for example, you use a program specifically designed for interacting with that service. A smaller bulletin board system (BBS) has no custom front end. Instead, you communicate with the small BBS by using general communications software. This chapter discusses HyperTerminal, the general communications program that comes with Windows 95.

How to Connect to a BBS

When you see an ad or a listing for a BBS, the least information you'll find is the phone number you use to dial in. You may (or may not) see a string of other numbers after the bulletin board's name. Following is an example:

Everybaudy's BBS   (610) 668-2983   28.8 n-8-1

The phone number is probably all you need to know. The 28.8 part is the fastest possible baud rate you can use with that BBS. The n-8-1 part stands for the settings Parity = None, Data Bits = 8, and Stop Bits = 1. You usually needn't concern yourself with those settings. Your modem will automatically use the fastest baud rate the BBS allows. And n-8-1 is the default setting for HyperTerminal and most BBSs.

So, in most cases, all you must know is the phone number of the BBS. To set up a connection to the BBS, follow these steps:

1. Choose Start ⇨ Programs ⇨ Accessories ⇨ HyperTerminal.

   You go to the folder for the HyperTerminal program.

2. Double-click the Hypertrm icon.

   You see a wizard screen titled New Connection.

3. Type the name of the BBS you're going to contact, and choose an icon for that service, as in the example in Figure 22-1.

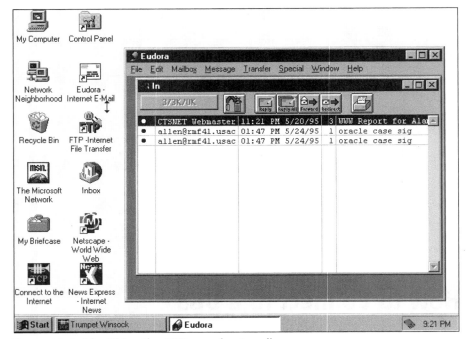

Figure 22-1: Identifying the BBS you plan to call

4. Choose OK.

5. In the next wizard screen, enter the country code, the area code, the phone number, and the modem you plan to use to make the connection (see Figure 22-2).

6. Choose OK.

7. In the next wizard screen, modify the number you're calling or select your own dialing properties, if necessary; then click the Dial button.

   You should hear the modem dial in, and you'll be connected.

If no activity occurs onscreen after you hear all the dialing and buzzing sounds, press the Enter key once or twice (the universal, "Hey, you; I'm here," signal in modem communications).

If you still have trouble connecting, check out all your settings. To do this, click File in HyperTeminal's menu bar, and choose Properties. Click the Configure button in the dialog box that appears to get to more advanced settings, such as baud rate, parity, data bits, and so forth. Make any changes the BBS requires, and then try again.

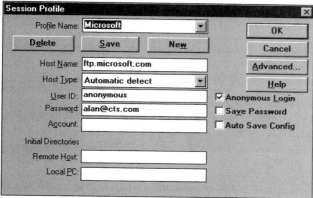

Figure 22-2: Phone number and other information for the BBS you want to call

After you're connected, you're on your own. Every BBS is different, so you must rely on the screen to navigate the BBS.

If you see weird characters onscreen when you connect to the BBS, try using a different font. Choose View ➪ Font, and try the Terminal font first. If that font doesn't work, try some others.

Capturing and printing BBS text

Most BBSs are *text-based*, which means, after you connect to a BBS, you interact with it by reading text and answering questions, or by choosing items from menus (perhaps typing the letter or number of the option you want, and then pressing Enter).

Often, the text from a BBS scrolls by quickly. Even if the text scrolls by a screen at a time, the document may contain too much information for you to absorb at one sitting. To give yourself time to think, you can capture text as it goes by onscreen, either straight to your printer or into a file you can open and print later.

Use either of the following techniques:

✦ To capture incoming text in a file, choose Transfer ➪ Capture Text, and then type a filename, or choose Start to use the suggested filename (CAPTURE. TXT). The Capture indicator lights in HyperTerminal's status bar.

✦ To capture incoming text to the printer, choose <u>T</u>ransfer ➪ Capture to <u>P</u>rinter. The Print Echo indicator lights in HyperTerminal's status bar.

Now you can go about your business normally. But be aware, only new text that scrolls by after this point will be captured. Your printer may not start printing until its buffer is filled. You may scroll through several screens of text before you hear any printer activity. When you want to stop capturing text, do either of the following:

✦ To stop capturing to the file, choose <u>T</u>ransfer ➪ <u>C</u>apture Text ➪ <u>S</u>top.

✦ To stop capturing to the printer, choose <u>T</u>ransfer ➪ Capture to <u>P</u>rinter ➪ <u>S</u>top.

The file capturing your text closes. To see the contents of this file later, simply browse to it. If you used the default name, the file will be in the same folder as HyperTerminal; if you don't find the file there, use Find to search for CAPTURE.TXT (or whatever filename you used). Double-click the icon to open the file. To print the file, choose <u>F</u>ile ➪ <u>P</u>rint in the program that opens. You also can open and edit the file in any text editor or word processing program.

When you stop capturing to the printer, your printer probably will eject all captured text.

Downloading files from a BBS

The exact steps you follow to *download* (copy a file from) from a BBS to your own PC depend on what type of BBS you're connected to currently. The typical scenario is to work your way to the BBS's file area or file library, and then use whatever tools are available to locate the file you want.

When you find the file you want, follow these steps to download it:

1. Choose Download from the BBS's menu system, and follow any instructions.

   You may, for example, be told to type the number (onscreen) of the file you want to download.

2. If you are asked which protocol to use, choose Zmodem, Kermit, or Xmodem.

   HyperTerminal supports the Xmodem, Ymodem, Zmodem, and Kermit protocols. Zmodem generally is the fastest protocol for modern modems, but you can use any protocol available. *Both PCs must be using the same protocol or the transfer will fail.*

3. Keep following the instructions onscreen until you see an instruction, such as Receive, Receive Files, or Download.

4. What you do next depends on what happens onscreen, as follows:

   • If you see a dialog box like the one shown in Figure 22-3, HyperTerminal started the download automatically. You needn't do anything (except wait).

- If HyperTerminal doesn't kick in automatically, choose Transfer ➪ Receive File, fill in the requested information, and make sure you select the same protocol you chose in Step 2. Then click the Receive button.

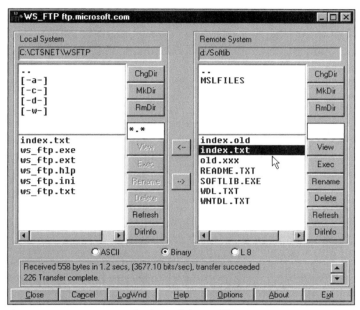

Figure 22-3: HyperTerminal receiving a file

The indicator in the dialog box gives you a sense of how long the download will take. If you have a long wait ahead and you want to do something else, minimize — but don't close — the HyperTerminal window. Then you can use some other program(s), occasionally reopening HyperTerminal's window to check the progress of your download.

When you finish downloading, the BBS is back in control and you need to choose options from its menus. The file you downloaded is stored in the same folder as HyperTerminal, unless you specified some other folder for the download. If the file is zipped (has a .ZIP extension), you must unzip it before you can use it. If you don't have a clue as to what I'm talking about here, refer to "Dealing with Zipped Files" in Chapter 21.

WinZip is included on the companion CD-ROM in the back of this book.

Uploading to a BBS

Whether you can *upload* (send files to) to a BBS and, if so, exactly how you do it depends on the BBS. If the BBS's menu system contains an upload option, you typically select this option and follow any instructions onscreen. Then, when the BBS is ready to receive, you choose one of the following options from within HyperTerminal:

✦ If you're sending a program or document, or if you're unsure how the file is formatted, choose Transfer ➪ Send File, and follow the instructions onscreen.

✦ If you're certain the file you're sending is pure ASCII text, choose Transfer ➪ Send Text File, and follow the instructions onscreen.

Any problems you encounter are most likely on the receiving (BBS) end. You must send a message to, or page, the *sysop* (system operator) for assistance.

Disconnecting from a BBS

When you finish exploring the BBS and/or downloading files, follow these steps to disconnect:

1. Exit or log off, as the BBS instructs.

2. Click the Disconnect button in the toolbar or choose Call ➪ Disconnect (to make sure you hang up the phone on your end).

3. Choose File ➪ Exit from within HyperTerminal.

   If you just connected to the BBS for the first time, you have a chance to save those settings. Choose Yes if you think you'll contact the same BBS in the future.

When you return to the HyperTerminal folder, you see an icon for the BBS you just dialed, as shown in Figure 22-4. To contact this BBS in the future, all you must do is double-click that icon.

Create Your Own BBS

Creating and managing your own BBS is no small undertaking. The job is expensive, time-consuming, and (as most entrepreneurial sysops have discovered) a labor of love rather than profit — all of which is fine if that's what you expect.

If you're thinking about starting your own BBS, the first thing you'll want to do is shop around for BBS software. I suggest you go to your local computer store and pick up the latest issue of *Boardwatch* magazine or *BBS* magazine. You'll learn about the latest products and get the inside scoop on the BBS industry.

When you look for BBS software, be aware most of it still is text-based DOS stuff. Frankly, this kind of BBS isn't going to attract many users anymore — not when you have to compete with the likes of the Microsoft Network, America Online, and other graphical systems. (I hate to sound like a curmudgeon, but I must tell the truth as I see it; that's my job.)

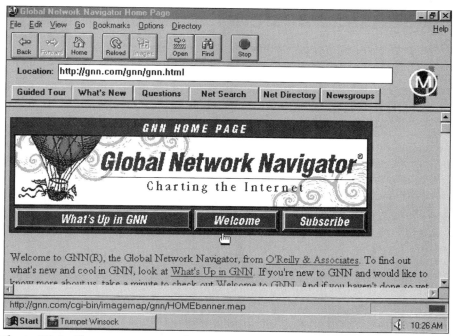

Figure 22-4: After you save a BBS's settings, double-click its icon to reconnect.

By far the easiest — and probably the least expensive — way to gain an online presence is to set up your own Web site on the Internet, a topic we'll discuss in Chapter 29.

I know of only four Windows-based BBS software packages currently on the market (or close to release). Those packages are:

Excalibur BBS
Excalibur Communications, Inc.
4410 East 80th Place
Tulsa, OK 74136
Voice: (800) 392-2522
        (918) 488-9801
Modem: (918) 496-8113

Power BBS
Power Computing
35 Fox Court
Hicksville, NY 11801
Voice: (800) 242-4775
        (516) 938-0506
Modem: (516) 822-7396

MediaHost
MediaHouse Software, Inc.
32 Eardley Road
Aylmer, Quebec, Canada J9H 7A3
Voice: (819) 682-9737
Modem: (819) 682-3330
Fax: (819) 685-0994

WorldGroup
Galacticomm
4101 S.W. 47th Avenue, Suite 101
Fort Lauderdale, FL 33314
Voice: (800) 328-1128
Modem: (305) 583-7808
E-mail: sales@gcomm.com or
        http://www.gcomm.com

PC-to-PC File Transfers

The easiest way to send files from one PC to another is through an information service to which both PCs can connect. When I finish writing a chapter, for example, I zip the text and figures for the chapter into a file, and I e-mail the file — via the Internet — to the publisher. The publisher unzips the file, makes editorial and technical passes through the material, zips it all back up and e-mails the file back to me. I then review the changes and suggestions, zip everything back up and e-mail it back to the publisher. We send files back and forth this way until the publisher actually starts printing galleys, at which point we have to start sending paper back and forth.

You can, of course, get into a situation in which the two parties who want to transfer files don't have a common online service. In this case, you can send files directly from one PC to the other by using HyperTerminal. This kind of transfer can be tricky, however, because one of the PCs must answer the incoming call, and getting a modem to do this isn't always easy. Nonetheless, the following sections lay out the basic procedure and then leave you to your own devices.

Step 1: Get your modems in sync

The sender and receiver must get their modems on the same wavelength. Each user must install a modem (refer to Chapter 14 for instructions), and then choose similar settings. To synchronize modem settings, follow these steps:

1. Choose Start ➪ Settings ➪ Control Panel.

2. Double-click the Modems icon.

3. Select the modem you'll be using for this transfer, and then click the Properties button.

4. Click the Connection tab.

5. Set the Connection preferences as follows: Data bits = 8, Parity = None, and Stop Bits = 1.

6. Choose OK to return to the Control Panel.

7. Close the Control Panel by clicking its Close button (X).

Now proceed to the appropriate Step 2 section, depending on whether your PC will dial out or answer the incoming call.

Step 2: If your PC will be dialing out . . .

If your PC is the one that will dial out, follow these steps to set up your end of the connection:

1. Choose Start ➪ Programs ➪ Accessories ➪ HyperTerminal.

2. Double-click the Hypertrm icon.

   The first New Connection wizard screen appears.

3. Type a descriptive name (for example, **Elizabeth's PC**), select any icon, and then choose OK.

4. In the next wizard screen, type the area code and phone number of the PC you want to dial; then choose OK.

5. In the last wizard screen, click the Modify button, click the Settings tab, and then click the ASCII Setup button.

6. Select Send line ends with line feeds so its check box is checked.

7. Select Echo typed characters so its check box is checked (see Figure 22-5).

8. Choose OK twice.

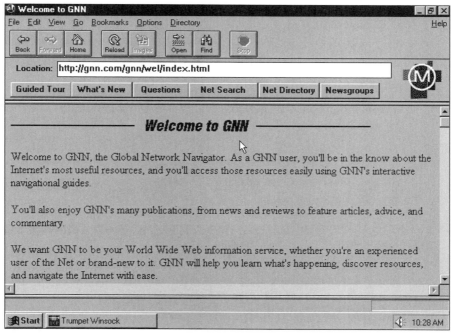

Figure 22-5: ASCII settings for connecting to another PC

Proceed to "Step 3: Make the connection."

Step 3: If your PC will be answering . . .

If your PC will be answering the phone, you must set up bogus dial-out settings so you can get your settings in sync with the caller's PC. Follow these steps:

1. Choose Start ➪ Programs ➪ Accessories ➪ HyperTerminal.

2. Double-click the Hypertrm icon.

   The first New Connection wizard screen appears.

3. Type **Answer incoming calls** as the descriptive name, select icon, and then choose OK.

4. In the next wizard screen, type your own area code and phone number (the number of the phone line your modem uses), and then choose OK.

   (I know this step sounds strange, but you must specify some kinds of settings, and HyperTerminal won't let you leave the phone number blank.)

5. In the last wizard screen, click the Modify button, click the Settings tab, and then click the ASCII Setup button.

6. Select Send line ends with line feeds so its check box is checked.

7. Select Echo typed characters so its check box is checked (refer to Figure 22-5).

8. Choose OK twice.

9. Click the Dial button.

   Because you're dialing your own phone number, you get a busy signal.

10. Click Cancel and wait.

    You should see a dialog box titled Answer incoming calls — HyperTerminal.

Proceed to the following section, but start with Step 2, rather than Step 1.

Step 4: Make the connection

By this time, the two parties are in sync. To proceed, follow these steps:

1. If your PC is the one that will be dialing out, give the other PC a minute or so to prepare; then click the Dial button.

2. If your PC is the one that will be answering, wait for the phone to ring, for the words RING RING to appear onscreen, or for the AA (Automatic Answer) indicator light on the modem to blink. When one of those things happens, type **ata** and press the Enter key.

   After some modem yelping, you should see a message indicating you are connected.

3. If your PC answered the call, type a message (such as **Are you there?**), press Enter, and wait a few seconds.

4. If your PC dialed out, wait to see the message from the person at the other end. When you see the message, type a message back (something like **Yeah, I'm here. I can't believe this worked!**), and press Enter.

If you can see each other's messages, your PCs are connected, and you can type messages back and forth for as long as you want. I suspect, however, that your real motivation for making the connection was to transfer files from one PC to another. To do this, follow these steps:

1. The person who will send the file should type a message to the recipient, telling him or her the name of the file, and then press Enter.

   The sender may type a message like the following:

   I am going to send mydocument.zip.

2. The sender should choose <u>T</u>ransfer ⇨ <u>S</u>end File, <u>B</u>rowse to the file to be sent, choose Zmodem as the protocol, and then click the <u>S</u>end button.

   You should see a dialog box like the one shown in Figure 22-6.

Zmodem file send for Elizabeth's PC		
Sending:	C:\COLLWIN\CAPTURE.EXE	
Last event:	Sending	Files: 1 of 1
Status:	Sending	Retries: 0
File:	▮▮▮▮▮▮▮	47k of 229K
Elapsed: 00:00:26	Remaining: 00:01:42	Throughput: 1823 cps
	Cancel	cps/bps

Figure 22-6: The sender is sending a file.

3. The recipient should wait to see whether the dialog box for receiving the file appears automatically.

   If the dialog box appears, the recipient simply waits for the transfer to complete.

   If the dialog box doesn't appear, the recipient must choose <u>T</u>ransfer ⇨ <u>R</u>eceive File and fill in the dialog box that appears.

You can send as many files back and forth as you want. When you're ready to disconnect, both parties must click the Disconnect button or choose <u>C</u>all ⇨ <u>D</u>isconnect.

The recipient should be aware that unless he or she specified a different directory when receiving, the files received will be in the HyperTerminal folder. To get to this folder via My Computer, double-click your hard-drive's icon; then choose Program Files ⇨ Accessories ⇨ HyperTerminal.

Remember, the method described in the preceding sections is sort of a *kludge* (something thrown together quickly). If you must transfer files often, you should use an intermediary online service, such as CompuServe or MSN. Use a compression program to compress files before you send them (refer to Chapter 21).

If you must connect to your home PC while you're on the road, you'll want to use dial-up networking (refer to Chapter 20) rather than HyperTerminal.

Summary

Most of the big commercial online services have their own custom *front ends*, programs you use to connect to and interact with the service. To connect to a smaller "local" bulletin board, you must use a generic communications program.

✦ HyperTerminal, which comes with Windows 95, is a good general communications program for connecting to small BBSs and other PCs.

✦ To get to HyperTerminal click the Start button and choose Programs ➪ Accessories ➪ HyperTerminal.

✦ If you want to reconnect to a BBS you've previously connected to, double-click the icon for the BBS for which you've saved settings.

✦ To create a new connection, double-click the HyperTrm icon. Then follow the instructions onscreen to describe the BBS. When you reach the end of the questions, click the Dial button.

✦ Once you connect, you must follow whatever instructions the BBS presents onscreen to get around and to download files.

✦ To disconnect from a BBS, enter the BBS's "Quit" or "Goodbye" command (often **Q** or **G**) and press Enter. Then click the Disconnect button in HyperTerminal's toolbar, or choose Call ➪ Disconnect from HyperTerminal's menu bar.

✦   ✦   ✦

Connecting to the Internet

Y ou've undoubtedly heard of the Internet — the huge network that connects millions of computers from around the world. I'm sure many of you are already connected to the Internet — perhaps some of you without even knowing it. For example, if you have an account with one of the large commercial online services like CompuServe, America Online, Prodigy, or the Microsoft Network (MSN), you already have access to the Internet through that service. To get to the Internet through that service, just hunt for the word *Internet* within that service for more information.

Many new PCs, and recent releases of Windows 95, come with Microsoft's Internet Starter Kit and Internet Connection Wizard, which offers yet another way to connect to the Internet. The wizard will take you step-by-step through connecting to the Internet through MSN or an Internet Service Provider (ISP) of your choice.

If you don't have the Internet Connection Wizard (inetwiz.exe) on your PC, but you know someone who has access to the Internet, you can have that person download a copy of the wizard, free-of-charge, from http://www. microsoft.com/windows95.

If you work for a large organization, you may be able to access the Internet through your computer at work. If you're in doubt, ask your network administrator or the person in charge of granting network access to workers, for more information.

Yet another means of getting access to the Internet involves setting up an account through a local ISP, and then using the Windows 95 Dial-Up Networking program to dial into the Internet at your leisure. This last approach requires you to go through some specific steps to configure a Dial-Up Networking connectoid; those steps are what this chapter covers.

What You Need to Connect to the Internet

If you don't have any access to the Internet or an online service, you'll need to do some things before you can get connected to the Internet. Specifically, you must:

✦ Install and set up a modem, as discussed in Chapter 15.

✦ Set up an account with an ISP.

✦ Install a Web browser program, such as Microsoft Internet Explorer, which comes with newer versions of Windows 95. You can also download Internet Explorer from MSN or purchase it at most computer stores.

Unfortunately, I can't help you much with the second item. Thousands of ISPs exist in the world and choosing one that's good for you is something you must do on your own. Here's how you can conduct your search:

✦ Check your local Yellow Pages (under *Internet*) or newspaper for local Internet services.

✦ Or, call your local phone company and ask if they offer a service.

✦ Or, call 1-888-ISP-FIND for an automated referral service.

✦ Or, if you have access to the Internet through work or a friend, visit ISP FIND at http://www.ispfind.com.

✦ Or, go to your local computer store or book store and ask for *Boardwatch* magazine's book on SPs.

You'll probably be presented with a ton of options when you contact an ISP. For starters, you can get a basic account that offers e-mail and access to the World Wide Web. As you gain experience with the Internet, you may want to upgrade your account to include more options, such as your own Web site. Upgrading an account after the fact is usually easy, though, so there's no harm in starting with the basic services.

When you set up an account with an ISP, you will be provided with a lot of information about your account. Save this information — permanently — and keep it handy as you work through this chapter. You can fill in the blanks in Table 23-1 right here in the book, if you like. If your ISP doesn't provide you with all the information presented in Table 23-1, you may want to send them a copy of Table 23-1 and ask them to fill in the blanks.

Hot Stuff For obvious security reasons, you may not want to write your password in Table 23-1, especially if other people could peek at your answers.

Table 23-1
What You Need to Know to Set Up a Dial-Up Connection
Your IP address:
Your subnet mask:
Your gateway IP address:
Your computer's user host name:
Your ISP's domain name:
Your ISP's primary DNS server IP address:
Your ISP's secondary DNS server IP address (if any):
Your ISP's domain suffix:
Your ISP's telephone number:
Your login name:
Your password:

Setting Up Dial-Up Networking

Now let's suppose you have a modem that you know is properly installed and working. And, you also have the information needed in Table 23-1. Your next step is to get onto your PC and set up a Dial-Up Networking connectoid to put you in touch with the Internet.

Before you can configure Dial-Up Networking, it must be installed on your PC. Gather your original Windows 95 CD-ROM or floppy disks (unless your PC came with Windows 95 pre-installed and you don't have either of those items). Then follow these steps to install this component:

1. Starting at the Windows 95 Desktop, open the My Computer icon.

2. If you see an icon named Dial-Up Networking, as in Figure 23-1, then you needn't install anything. Skip to the section titled "Installing TCP/IP Networking."

3. To install Dial-Up Networking, click the Start button, point to Settings, and choose Control Panel.

4. Double-click the Add/Remove Programs icon.

5. Click the Windows Setup tab.

6. Click the Communications component, and then click the Details button.

7. Select Dial-Up Networking, so its check box is checked, and then click the OK button.

8. Click the OK button, and then follow the instructions on the screen to install Dial-Up Networking.

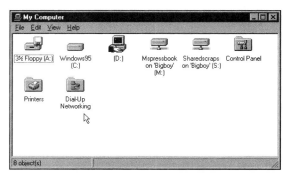

Figure 23-1: Icon for the Dial-Up Networking component in My Computer

When you finish all the instructions on the screen, you can get to your Dial-Up Networking folder at any time, simply by opening your My Computer icon.

Installing TCP/IP Networking

The Internet is based on a communication protocol named TCP/IP, which stands for *Transmission Control Protocol/Internet Protocol.* Windows 95 has TCP/IP built right in, but it may not be installed on your PC. To find out, and to install TCP/IP, if necessary, follow these steps:

1. Click the Windows 95 Start button and choose <u>S</u>ettings ➪ <u>C</u>ontrol Panel.

2. Double-click the Network icon.

3. Click the Configuration tab, and scroll down through the list of installed components. If you see the TCP/IP protocol listed already, as in Figure 23-2, you needn't install that now. Click OK, close the Control Panel, and skip down to "Configuring TCP/IP for Dial-Up Networking."

4. Click the <u>A</u>dd button below the list of installed network components. Then select Network Component Type dialog box. Click Protocol, as in Figure 23-3.

5. Click the <u>A</u>dd button to open the Select Network Protocol dialog box.

6. In the Manufacturers list in the left panel, click Microsoft. In the Network Protocols list in the right panel, click TCP/IP, as shown in Figure 23-4.

7. Click the OK button and follow the instructions that appear on the screen.

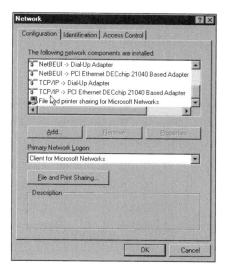

Figure 23-2: In this example, TCP/IP protocol is already installed.

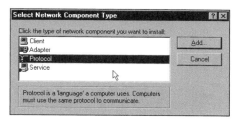

Figure 23-3: Now we're ready to install a new network protocol.

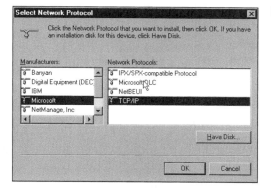

Figure 23-4: Here is the Select Network Protocol dialog box, with Microsoft and TCP/IP selected.

Click the OK button as necessary to work your way back to the Windows 95 desktop and reboot, if requested to do so. When you get back to the Windows 95 desktop, you're ready to proceed with the next main step, configuring TCP/IP for a dial-up connection to the Internet.

Configuring TCP/IP for dial-up networking

Once the TCP/IP network protocol is installed, the next step is to bind that to the Dial-Up Networking component. You'll need much of the information you jotted down in Table 23-1 here, so have it ready. Then follow these steps:

1. Click the Windows 95 Start button, and then click Settings ➪ Control Panel.

2. Double-click the Network icon, and then click the Configuration tab.

3. Scroll down to and click *TCP/IP ➪ Dial-Up Adapter* in the installed components list, and then click the Properties button. You'll see the TCP/IP Properties dialog box shown in Figure 23-5 (though a different tab might be visible when you first get there).

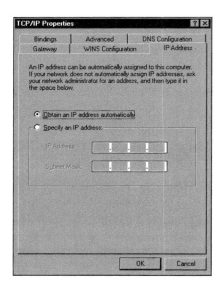

Figure 23-5: The TCP/IP Properties dialog box

4. Click the IP Address tab.

5. If your ISP assigns IP addresses dynamically, select the Obtain an IP address automatically option button, and skip to Step 6. Otherwise, click the Specify an IP address option button, and enter your IP Address and your Subnet Mask in the appropriate fields.

6. Click the Gateway tab. Next enter your gateway IP address in the New Gateway box, and click the Add button.

7. Click the DNS Configuration tab, and then click the Enable DNS option button. Fill in the following items, so your screen resembles Figure 23-6, but with information from your copy of Table 23-1.

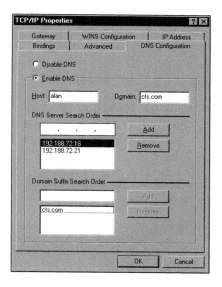

Figure 23-6: The DNS Configuration tab of the TCP/IP Properties dialog box

- In the Host box, enter your computer's user host name.
- In the Domain box, enter your ISP's domain name.
- In the DNS Server Search Order box, type your ISP's primary DNS server IP address, and click the Add button.
- If your ISP has provided a secondary DNS server IP address, type this address in the DNS Server Search Order box, and click the Add button.
- In the Domain Suffix Search Order box, type your ISP's domain suffix, and click the Add button.

8. Click OK to return to the Configuration tab of the Network dialog box.

9. Click OK again to exit the Network Properties dialog box. Windows 95 will ask whether you want to reboot your system. Click Yes.

After your PC reboots, you'll be back to the familiar Windows 95 desktop. The worst is over, so you can relax a little. The next step — creating a Dial-Up connectoid — is relatively easy.

Creating a Dial-Up Connectoid

If you've followed along since the beginning of this chapter, you're now ready to create a simple connectoid that will connect you to the Internet with a few mouse clicks. Here are the steps to follow:

1. Double-click My Computer on the Windows 95 desktop, and then double-click the Dial-Up Networking icon. The Dial-Up Networking window will open.

2. Double-click the Make New Connection icon to start the Make New Connection Wizard, shown in Figure 23-7.

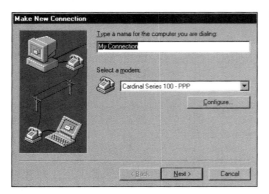

Figure 23-7: The Make New Connection Wizard dialog box

3. Type the name of your ISP in the Type a name for the computer you are dialing text box. You can type *Internet* if you like, or the name of your ISP — whichever will help you easily identify the icon in the future.

4. Be sure the name of your modem appears in the Select a modem drop-down list box. If it doesn't, select your modem's name from the drop-down list.

5. Click the Configure button to display the Properties dialog box for your modem. If necessary, you can adjust the options shown on the General tab, though you probably won't need to do this.

6. Click the Options button in the Properties dialog box.

7. On the Options tab, select (check) *only* the following two options, as shown in Figure 23-8:

   • Bring up terminal window after dialing (checking this option enables you to supply your user name and password when logging on to your ISP).

   • Display modem status (checking this option displays a status window that shows the progress of your connection and makes troubleshooting connection problems easier).

8. Click OK to return to the Make New Connection dialog box, and then click Next to continue.

9. In the phone number page, shown in Figure 23-9, type the correct information for dialing your ISP, and then click Next.

10. Follow any other instructions that appear, and then click the Finish button.

A new connection icon appears in your Dial-Up Networking window, looking something like the example in Figure 23-10.

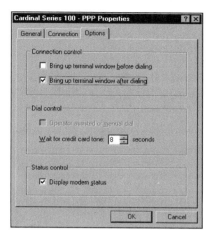

Figure 23-8: This is the Options tab, with the required options checked.

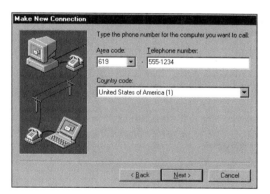

Figure 23-9: Fill in the phone number from your version of Table 23-1.

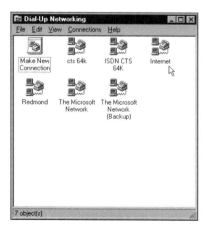

Figure 23-10: Here is the Dial-Up Networking window, with a new connection.

Configuring the dial-up connection

A few finishing touches will make your Internet connection go more smoothly. With your version of Table 23-1 handy, follow these steps:

1. In the Dial-Up Networking window, right-click the dial-up connection icon you just created, and choose Properties from the shortcut menu that appears. You're taken to that connectoid's Properties dialog box.

2. Click the Server Types tab in the dialog box that appears.

3. From the Type of Dial-Up Server drop-down list, choose *PPP: Windows 95, Windows NT 3.5, Internet* (unless your ISP specifically told you to select some other option).

Hot Stuff *Point-To-Point Protocol* (PPP), which is built into Windows 95, is the most common way to connect to an ISP via phone lines. *Serial Line Internet Protocol* (SLIP) is an older connection protocol that isn't built into Windows 95 and is unnecessary for most ISPs.

4. In the Advanced options area, select (check) only Enable software compression. (If you have problems with communications later, ask your ISP whether to clear this option.)

5. In the Allowed network protocols area, make sure TCP/IP is selected. At this point, your dialog box should look like Figure 23-11.

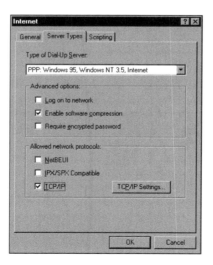

Figure 23-11: The Server Types tab of a connectoid's Properties dialog box

6. Click the TCP/IP Settings button to open the TCP/IP Settings dialog box.

7. Choose the Specify an IP address option button, and fill in the IP address from your version of Table 23-1. (Unless your ISP tells you to choose the Server assigned IP address option.)

8. Choose the Specify name server addresses option button. Then enter your ISP's primary DNS server IP address in the Primary DNS box. If your ISP has a secondary DNS server IP address, enter it in the Secondary DNS box. (Ignore the Primary WINS and Secondary WINS boxes.)

9. Assuming your ISP hasn't given you other instructions, be sure to check the bottom boxes (Use IP header compression and Use default gateway on remote network). At this point your dialog box looks something like Figure 23-12, but with information filled in from your version of Table 23-1.

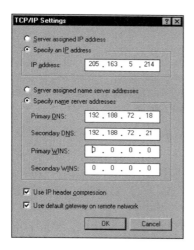

Figure 23-12: The completed TCP/IP Settings dialog box for fixed IP and DNS addresses

10. Click OK until you return to the Windows 95 desktop.

Whew! Aren't you glad you only have to go through this hassle once? You're almost ready to go online.

To make your connection icon even more convenient, create a shortcut to the connection icon on your desktop. Hold down the Ctrl key and drag the new connectoid's icon to the desktop. When you release the mouse button and the Ctrl key, the shortcut appears on the desktop.

Connecting to the Internet

Now that the connectoid exists, getting onto the Internet should be easy. If you followed the previous tip and made a desktop shortcut to your new connectoid icon, you can just double-click that icon. Or, follow these steps:

1. On the Windows 95 desktop, open My Computer.

2. Open the Dial-Up Networking icon, and then double-click the icon for your new Internet connectoid.

3. The Connect To dialog box will appear (see Figure 23-13).

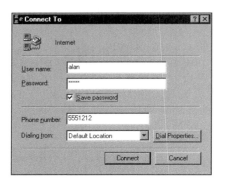

Figure 23-13: The Connect To dialog box

4. Type your Underline{U}ser name and Underline{P}assword from Table 23-1. Optionally, you can click the Underline{S}ave password button so you needn't retype your password in the future.

5. Click the Connect button. A Connecting To... message will appear, and your modem will click and clack away. Soon you'll see a Post-Dial Terminal Screen window where the computer you're dialing into asks for your login name.

6. Type your computer's login name, and press Enter. Then type your computer's password, and press Enter. You may be prompted for other information as well. If the host system assigns you an IP address or displays other important information, be sure to write it down. (Don't worry if you see some gobbledygook on the screen; that's normal.)

7. Click the Continue button or press F7.

8. If your ISP dynamically assigns you a different IP address each time you log in, you may be asked either to verify or enter your IP address. Enter the IP address you just jotted down, and click OK to continue.

After a few moments, you'll see the Connected To dialog box, which looks something like Figure 23-14. This means you're on! You can now start any modern Internet-aware program, such as Microsoft Internet Explorer or Netscape Navigator, and start using the Internet.

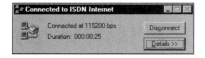

Figure 23-14: The Connected To dialog box

Disconnecting from the Internet

Disconnecting from the Internet is a breeze — just click the Disconnect button in the Connected To dialog box. The Connected To dialog box will disappear, and you'll be disconnected from your ISP. Your Internet-aware programs won't work normally until you reconnect again in the future.

Automating A Connectoid

If you find you must type in your user name and/or password each time you connect to the Internet, you may want to create a dial-up script that can do this for you. Before you create this, though, you must install the SLIP and Dial-Up Scripting component, which comes with the Windows 95 CD-ROM. Here's how:

Hot Stuff If you don't have the CD-ROM version of Windows 95, you can download the SLIP and Dial-Up Scripting component from http://www.microsoft.com/windows/ software/admintools.htm. You can use Internet Explorer, discussed in Chapter 24, to get to this address.

1. Insert the original Windows 95 CD-ROM into your CD-ROM drive.

2. Click the Windows 95 Start button and choose Settings ⇨ Control panel.

3. Double-click the Add/Remove Programs icon.

4. Click the Windows Setup tab.

5. Click the Have Disk button.

6. Click the Browse button and on the CD, browse down to the folder admin\apptools\dscript.

7. In that folder, click the rnaplus.inf filename.

8. Click the OK button(s) to work your way back to the Have Disk dialog box. Then click the check box next to SLIP and Scripting for Dial-Up Networking as in Figure 23-15.

9. Click the Install button and follow the instructions on the screen.

Once you complete the installation, you can follow the procedures in the following sections to create your own custom script for connecting to your ISP.

Figure 23-15: About to install SLIP and Scripting for Dial-Up Networking

Creating a dial-up script

Creating the dial-up script is the only tricky part of this whole business. To make life as simple as possible, grab some paper and a pencil, then log on to the Internet manually. Write down *exactly* what appears on your screen, including any blank spaces, just before you type your user name and password, and jot down *exactly* what you type in response — including any presses of the Enter key. For example, when I log in manually, I first see this (the underline character represents a blank space):

```
Login:_
```

I type my login name and press Enter.

Then I see

```
Password:
```

I type my password and press Enter.

When I'm successfully connected, a message that ends with the word *enabled* appears on my screen.

To create a script, you need to tell the script what prompt to wait for, and then what text to type in response to the prompt. For example, the first prompt that appears when I try to log in is Login: followed by a blank space. When the script sees this prompt, it needs to type in my user ID, and press Enter.

Next, the prompt Password: appears on my screen. So the script will need to wait for that, type in my password, and then press Enter. The script can stop paying attention when it sees the word *enabled* appear on the screen.

There is one little trick to all of this. The computer you're logging into may have some attribute assigned to the first character it sends, such as an underscore or boldface. The program waiting for prompts may not recognize that first character. So, as a general rule, having your script wait for just the last few characters of a prompt is a good idea. For example, in my case I'd have the script wait for *ogin:* (including the colon and space) before I type my user name. And I'd have the script wait for *word:* before I type my password, as in the example shown in Figure 23-16.

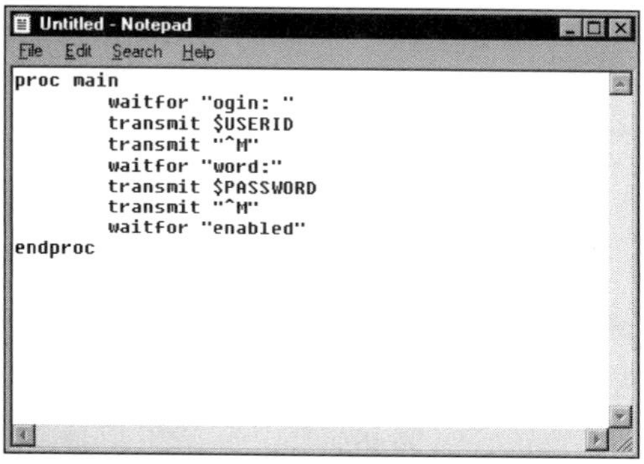

```
proc main
        waitfor "ogin: "
        transmit $USERID
        transmit "^M"
        waitfor "word:"
        transmit $PASSWORD
        transmit "^M"
        waitfor "enabled"
endproc
```

Figure 23-16: A sample dial-up script

To create the script, you'll need to use some simple text editor like Notepad. To start Notepad:

1. Click the Start button.

2. Choose <u>P</u>rograms ➪ Accessories ➪ Notepad.

3. In the blank document window that appears, type your login script.

While typing the script, you can use these special words:

✦ **proc main** starts the scripts.

✦ **waitfor** tells the script player what characters to wait for.

✦ **transmit** tells the player what character to send.

✦ **^M** represents a press on the Enter key.

✦ **$USERID** tells the script to use the User Name from the Connect To dialog box.

✦ **$PASSWORD** tells the script to type the password from the Connect To dialog box.

✦ **endproc** ends the script.

> **Hot Stuff** You must select the Save password check box in the Connect To dialog box if you want the script to type your password automatically for you.

To save your script in Notepad:

1. Choose File ⇨ Save As from Notepad's menu bar.

2. Navigate to the \Program Files\Accessories folder.

3. Type in a filename such as *myscript*.scp (where *myscript* is any valid filename you want).

4. Close Notepad by clicking its Close (X) button, or by choosing File ⇨ Exit from Notepad's menu bar.

The next step requires you to attach the script to your Dial-Up Networking connectoid.

Hooking up the script to your Dial-Up Networking icon

Now you need to tell your Dial-Up Networking icon to use the new script. Here's how:

1. Double-click My Computer on the Windows 95 desktop, and then double-click the Dial-Up Networking icon.

2. In the Dial-Up Networking window, right-click the icon you use for dial-up networking and choose Properties.

3. In the dialog box that appears, click the Server Type button.

4. In the Advanced options area, make sure the Log on to network option is selected (checked) as in Figure 23-17.

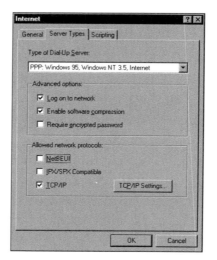

Figure 23-17: Log on to network option is selected

5. Click the Scripting tab, and then use the Browse button to locate the name of the scripting file you just created (for example, c:\Program Files\Accessories\ myscript.scp in my example).

6. Clear the Step through script option, and select the Start terminal screen minimized option, as in Figure 23-18.

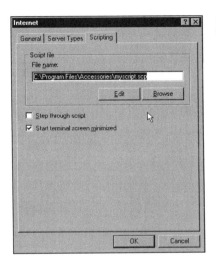

Figure 23-18: Script is selected for this connectoid.

7. Click the General tab.

8. Click the Configure button, and then click the Options tab, and make sure both the first two check boxes are clear, as in Figure 23-19.

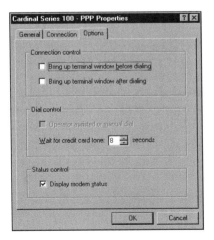

Figure 23-19: The first two check boxes are cleared.

9. Click OK (twice) to return to the Dial-Up Networking window.

That's it! The dial-up script setup is complete and will automatically kick in the next time you use that connectoid to connect to the Internet. Don't forget, though, the user name and password will come from the Connect To dialog box. So, the first time you use the connectoid with the dial-up script, the routine will go something like this:

1. If you created a shortcut for your Internet connectoid, double-click it. Otherwise, open My Computer, open Dial-Up Networking, and then double-click your Internet connectoid. The Connect To dialog box will appear.

2. If the correct Underline name and Password for your Internet connection aren't already in the box, type them in. Also, make sure the Save password check box has a check mark in it.

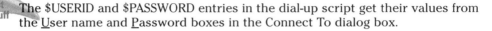

The $USERID and $PASSWORD entries in the dial-up script get their values from the User name and Password boxes in the Connect To dialog box.

3. Click the Connect button.

The rest of the logon process takes place automatically — no more going through that text screen where you need to type in your user name and password manually.

The ISDN Connection

Integrated Services Digital Network (ISDN) is an alternative to using a standard, or analog, modem to connect to the modem. Whereas the top-end speed for a standard modem is about 56K, and ISDN connection can communicate at 128K — more than twice as fast.

Connecting a LAN to the Internet

If you're looking for an inexpensive way to connect a LAN workgroup to the Internet, without giving each person an Internet account and phone line, consider an IDSN Router. Two popular products in this category include Farallon's Netopia Internet Router (http://www.farallon.com) and Ramp Networks' WebRamp IP Router (http://www.rampnet.com).

Another alternative, though considerably more expensive, is to build a *proxy server*. You can learn more about proxy servers at http://www.microsoft.com/proxy.

Unfortunately, ISDN isn't as readily available as the regular phone lines modems use. Many cities don't even have ISDN yet. Furthermore, ISDN isn't easy to set up, and it doesn't come cheap. Many steps are involved in setting up an ISDN connection to the Internet:

✦ Find out whether your ISP supports ISDN. If the answer is no, stop right here, or get an account with an ISP that does supports ISDN. If the answer is yes, make sure you can get a true 128K connection and ask how much it will cost. A monthly ISDN connection may cost you more than a standard telephone connection.

✦ Find out whether your telephone company supports ISDN. If the answer is no, stop right here. If the answer is yes, make sure you can get a 128K connection, and then ask how much the installation and monthly service will cost.

✦ Find out what hardware your ISP has tested with its ISDN connection. It's essential for you to choose hardware that is compatible with your ISP's equipment and can perform at 128K speeds.

✦ Order ISDN service from your local telephone company.

✦ Purchase the hardware — an ISDN modem or ISDN adapter — needed to connect your PC to an ISDN line.

✦ If you plan to use an internal ISDN adapter, you must install the ISDN Accelerator Pack from Microsoft. You can download that program from `http://www.microsoft.com/windows/getisdn/dload.htm`.

✦ Set up your ISDN account with your ISP.

✦ Install the ISDN adapter hardware and software, as per the manufacturer's instructions.

Unfortunately, I can't help you much with these items because so many different brands of ISDN adapters and ISPs exist. But I can offer a few alternatives that might save you some headaches:

✦ Search for local ISPs who offer a complete ISDN package, where *they* come to your home or office and set up everything for you.

✦ If you already have some kind of Internet connection, read about current events and products in the ISDN arena at `http://www.microsoft.com/windows/getisdn` (see Figure 23-20).

From my own personal experience, I can tell you 128K ISDN access to the Internet offers a *major* speed improvement over standard analog modems. But I must confess, getting it all working was one of the biggest headaches of my computer career (and believe me, I've had my share of headaches). My advice to anyone contemplating ISDN is: Try to find a service that offers both the connection *and* the installation!

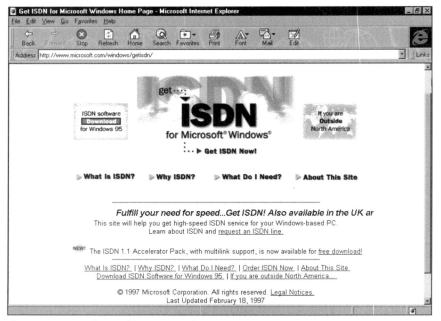

Figure 23-20: Microsoft's ISDN Web page

Summary

In this chapter we've looked at all the steps required to connect your personal computer to the Internet. To recap the main points:

✦ To use the Internet, first you must get a modem, a Web-browsing program, such as Microsoft Internet Explorer, and some kind of account that gives you access to the Internet.

✦ Some of the large online services like Microsoft Network (MSN), America Online, CompuServe, or Prodigy offer Internet access. Search your service for information on the Internet.

✦ Another way to access the Internet is through a local Internet Service Provider (ISP), which you can find in your Yellow Pages (under *Internet*), or local newspaper ads, or by calling 1-888-ISP-FIND.

✦ To access the Internet through a local ISP, you'll probably need to install and configure the Windows 95 Dial-Up Networking component and TCP/IP networking protocol.

✦ Once you have account information from your ISP, you can create a Dial-Up Networking connectoid to make accessing the Internet as simple as opening an icon.

✦ ✦ ✦

Becoming an Internet Guru

Exploring the World Wide Web

The Internet offers many services. But none is as popular as the Word Wide Web (aka *the Web*). The Web provides an easy and fun point-and-click interface to a vast amount of information, free software, technical support, and just plain fun. Even if you haven't actually been on the Internet yet, you've undoubtedly seen Web site addresses — those www.whatever.com things — in ads, letterhead, or elsewhere. To get to those addresses you need a connection to the Internet, as discussed in the previous chapter. And you also need a Web browser — a program that provides access to the Web.

Several Web browsers are on the market, the two most popular being Netscape Navigator and Microsoft Internet Explorer (MSIE or IE, for short). In this book, I'll focus on Internet Explorer because I suspect most of you already have it. Internet Explorer comes with many new PCs and with current versions of Windows 95. In particular, I'll focus on Internet Explorer Version 4. This product is still in the early beta-testing phase. But, currently, over a million people have downloaded this product and are using it today. Nonetheless, some features might change slightly between now and when the final product is released. But chances are, everything I discuss in this chapter will work fine for you, no matter when you get your copy of Internet Explorer 4.0.

If you have Internet access already, you can download Version 4 of Internet Explorer from http://www.microsoft.com/ie. You can then install IE 4 by following the instructions that come with the program — or the instructions provided at the download Web site. If you don't already have a Web browser, you might want to purchase Microsoft's Internet Starter Kit. You'll get a great Web browser, and lots of useful information for Internet *newbies* (people just getting started on the Internet).

Getting on the Web

Getting onto the World Wide Web is usually fairly easy. How you go about it depends on your Internet connection. For example, if you work for a company that provides a permanent connection to the Internet, you probably only have to start up your Web browser. If you're going through America Online, CompuServe, or Prodigy, you'll need to look up information on the Web within that service to learn how to connect. I suspect most of you, however, will have some kind of dial-up account like the ones we focused on in the previous chapter. If that's the case, getting on the Web is simply a matter of firing up your connectoid, and then starting your Web browser. Here are the exact steps:

1. If you created a desktop shortcut to your Internet connectoid, as discussed in Chapter 23, double-click it. Otherwise, open My Computer, and open Dial-Up Networking, and then double-click your Internet connectoid's icon.

2. Fill in the <u>U</u>ser name and <u>P</u>assword, if necessary, and then click the Connect button.

3. Wait for the Connected To message to appear, as in Figure 24-1.

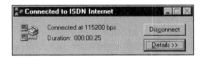

Figure 24-1: Connected to the Internet through my ISP

4. Start your Web browser (for example, Microsoft Internet Explorer 4).

Your Web browser will start and connect to its default home page. For example, the home page for Microsoft Internet Explorer is Microsoft's Web site at `http://www.microsoft.com`. While there's no telling how this page will look when you get there, because Web pages change daily, you will probably see something that looks like Figure 24-2.

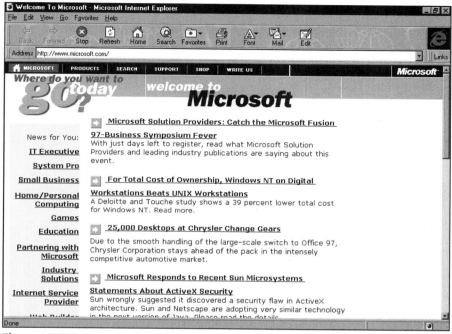

Figure 24-2: Internet Explorer showing Microsoft's home page

Visiting a Web Site

Suppose now you want to go to a specific Web site you've heard of. Say, my Web site at http://www.coolnerds.com. How would you get there? Simple:

1. Click in the address bar near the top of the Web browser window.

Hot Stuff If you don't see an address bar, choose View ➪ Toolbar from Internet Explorer's menu bar.

2. Replace the address currently shown with the address to which you want to go.

3. Press Enter.

4. Wait for the page to appear.

While you're waiting, the globe near the upper-right corner will spin to let you know the browser is working. And the left side of the status bar at the bottom of the screen will present messages to inform you of progress. When the Done message appears in the left side of the status bar, as in Figure 24-3, the entire page has been downloaded to your PC.

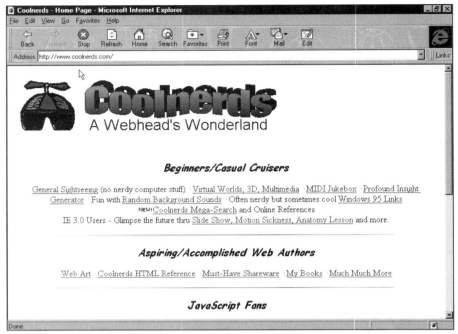

Figure 24-3: Now viewing the page at `http://www.coolnerds.com`

Typing the entire Web site address into the Address box of the browser isn't necessary. You can select just the part you want to change, and type in the new part. For example, when the address bar is showing `http://www.microsoft.com` and you want to go to `http://www.coolnerds.com` you can drag the mouse pointer through the word *microsoft*. Then type **coolnerds** which changes the address to `http://www.coolnerds.com` and then press Enter.

Also, Internet Explorer keeps track of sites you visit and tries to fill in the blanks of any partial Web site addresses you type. For example, say you visited Coolnerds in the past. And now you want to revisit that site. You could click to the right of whatever address is currently shown in the Address box, which will select that entire address. Then start typing **www.coolnerds**. Chances are, Internet Explorer will finish typing the correct address for you, at which point you can press Enter to go. If Internet Explorer tries to complete the address for you, but gets the wrong address, don't worry. Keep trying the address you want. If you end up with some extra stuff to the right of the address you typed, press Delete (Del) to delete it.

Point your Web browser to . . .

You'll often come across an instruction to "Point your Web browser to *(some address)*." What this means is simply to type the suggested address into the Address box on Internet Explorer (or whatever Web browser you are using), and press the Enter key. Some mysterious terms you might encounter include *URL*, which stands for Uniform Resource Locator and is the fancy term for a Web address like http://www. whatever.com. There are also less technical terms, such as *newbie* (someone new to the Internet) and *Webhead* (someone who's a Web "addict," also know as a *Webaholic*).

Using hyperlinks

One of the best features of the Web is its use of *hyperlinks* — hot spots on the screen — which, when clicked, take you to images, videos, audio clips, or other Web pages. Most hyperlinks appear as blue underlined text, although any text, or even part of a picture, can actually be a hyperlink. You can tell when the mouse pointer is resting on a hyperlink because the pointer turns to a little pointing hand. In Internet Explorer 4, you might also see a tooltip showing the address to which the hyperlink will take you. To follow the link to its destination, click the left mouse button, and wait for the new page to download to your screen.

Creating a favorites list

As you follow links and explore the Web, you'll find sites you may want to revisit in the future. You can make the return trip easier by adding the site to your favorites list while you're there. Here's how:

1. While viewing the page you want to add, choose Favorites ⇨ Add to Favorites from Internet Explorer's menu bar.

2. You can type in a name for this favorite item or just accept the suggested name.

3. Click the OK button.

When you want to revisit that site in the future, you needn't type in its address. Instead, click Favorites in Internet Explorer's menu bar, and choose the site's name from the menu that appears.

Other navigation tools

The toolbar across the top of Internet Explorer's window provides some additional, simple navigation buttons. If the toolbar isn't visible, choose <u>V</u>iew ➪ Toolbar from Internet Explorer's menu bar. Then you can use the buttons as summarized in the following:

✦ **Back**: Goes back to the previous page you visited (if any).

✦ **Forward**: Goes to the page from which you just backed up (if any).

✦ **Stop**: If a download takes too long, you can click the Stop button to end the download. This frees the browser so you can visit elsewhere.

✦ **Refresh**: Ensures you are viewing the absolute latest version of the current page.

✦ **Home**: Returns you to your default home page — `http://www.microsoft.com` — in our example.

✦ **Search**: Takes you to Microsoft's Search page, described later in this chapter.

✦ **Favorites**: Displays your bookmarks menu.

✦ **Print**: Prints the Web page you're viewing.

✦ **Font**: Increases or decreases the size of the text on the page.

✦ **Mail**: Takes you to Internet E-Mail, as discussed in Chapter 25.

✦ **Edit**: Enables you to change the current page, assuming it's *your* page (see Chapter 29).

Every Web site you visit is bound to have hyperlinks to take you to other sites. So the few skills you've learned already in this chapter will enable you to explore the Web forever! But, at some point, you might get tired of being led around the Web, and you may start asking "How do I find information on *such-and-such*?" The *such-and-such* part can be any topic that interests you. And I do mean *any* topic because the Web is loaded with millions of pages of information.

Well, fortunately for all of us, some Web sites exist whose sole purpose is to help you find information on the Web. These sites are often called *search sites*, and you can choose from several different kinds. In the following few sections, we'll look at the various types of search sites you can use to find what you need in a jiffy.

Kinds of Search Sites

Three basic kinds of Web sites exist that help you find things on the Internet: *indexes, directories,* and *search engines*, and many of them combine aspects of the three.

An *index* is generally a simple list of Internet sites, although it might be quite a long or well-organized list. Indexes may or may not be annotated; some describe the sites in the index, while others don't. An index is generally comprised of sites on a single topic, although anybody's *hotlist* of favorite sites could be called an index. A *meta-index*, on the other hand, is an index of indexes.

A *directory* is a large index that divides the sites listed into categories by subject. Most directories include some sort of description or extra information about the site. Some of them, called *guides*, include some sort of rating system that directs you toward the "best" sites in a specific category (or on the Web in general). Many directories and indexes are searchable.

Search engines are sites that use computers to search the Web and compile a miniature version of its contents in a database on a central computer. When you use a search engine on the Web, you're searching that computer's database. Search engines collect varying amounts of information about other Web sites, including the URL, the title, and keywords from the page. And some search engines include their own indexes, directories, or guides to enhance their editorial content. (This is what *value added* means — you get bonus content that makes the site more informative or useful.)

Directories and indexes

As mentioned, directories and indexes select Web sites, sort them into categories, and describe them. Human beings do all this work, so some kind of editorial slant is inherent in any directory. Some directories focus on particular topics, while others take on the task of indexing the whole Web. Directories are necessarily not as big as search engines, but they're more likely to point you to quality sites rather than a bunch of garbage.

Yahoo!

Yahoo!, one of the more popular directories, is actually an acronym for Yet Another Hierarchically Organized Oracle. To get to Yahoo! (the exclamation point is part of their name), point your Web browser to `http://www.yahoo.com`. You'll come to a page that looks something like Figure 24-4.

Yahoo! is a searchable index of Web sites that also has some qualities of a directory. There isn't much in the way of description at Yahoo!, but the sites are sorted into hundreds of categories. You can browse through Yahoo!, clicking the names of categories until you find a selection of sites that looks appealing, or you can use the search box to look quickly for a list of Web sites on specific topics.

To search Yahoo!, type a word or two into the text box, and then click the Search button. Yahoo! only indexes the titles of sites and, sometimes, a brief description. Your search results will include any Yahoo! categories, Web sites, or news headlines related to the word(s) you typed.

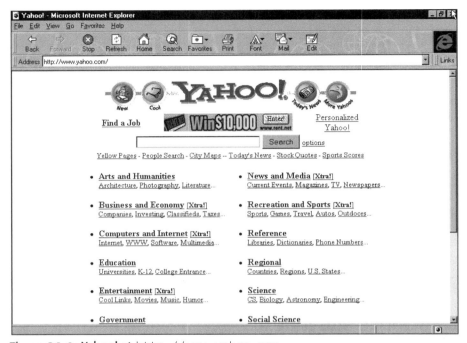

Figure 24-4: Yahoo! at `http://www.yahoo.com`

Yahoo! is best for looking up a quantity of sites on a particular subject. You might not find much about something specific, such as *gypsy moth caterpillars*, but you will find many sites about insects, entomology, or pest control. Another cool thing about Yahoo! is, if it doesn't find a site related to your query in its own database, it automatically rolls over and asks AltaVista — a large search engine described later in this chapter — to look up the topic for you.

Other Yahoo! features include subject-specific directories for kids' sites, selected countries, and selected cities. Listings also exist for live events online, current headline news stories, and picks for cool sites of the week.

Many search sites combine some aspects of a directory (ratings, reviews, and categories you can browse) with a search engine. Some Web sites tout their Web-wide search engine as their key feature, while others call the editorial (human-run) directory aspect of the site the main attraction. You can get tips on searching and browsing these sites by clicking words like "Help" or "Tips" on the site's home page.

NetGuide Live

NetGuide Live is like the Web's equivalent to *TV Guide*. The site includes many feature articles and columns, but the star of the site is the Best of the Web directory, shown in Figure 24-5. To get to this page, point your Web browser to `http://www.netguide.com`.

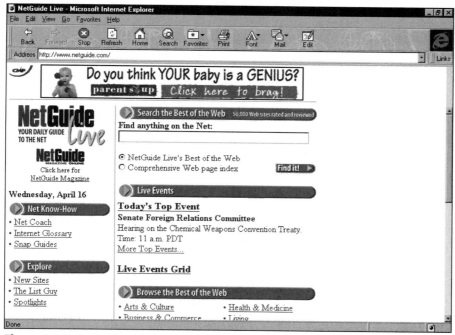

Figure 24-5: NetGuide Live features the Best of the Web and more.

You can search or browse these listings of all kinds of Web sites, each of which includes a short review and a one- to four-star rating of the content. Like other rated-and-reviewed directories, NetGuide Live is best for when you're looking for high-content sites. The searches are moderately fast, but the site is rather graphics-intensive.

Magellan

The first-ever site to review and rate Web sites based on their content, Magellan (see Figure 24-6) includes other features such as a Green Light rating for child-safe sites and lengthy reviews that describe the site in detail. To get to Magellan, point your Web browser to `http://www.mckinley.com/`. When you search Magellan, your results will be a combination of rated-and-reviewed Web sites and other sites Magellan's search engine has found. (More on search engines later in this chapter.) Magellan is best for finding high-quality sites on broad topics, but you can search for more specific topics and the search function will come to the rescue.

Figure 24-6: Magellan offers lengthy reviews and child-safe sites.

Excite

Excite, at `http://www.excite.com`, combines aspects of a directory and a search engine, but for now the two are kept separate. Look at Figure 24-7 for a glance at some of Excite's features. Click Excite Web Reviews in the pull-down menu for sites that have been reviewed by the editorial staff, or click World Wide Web to search a larger database of the Web found by Excite's search engine. Excite searches are called *concept searches*, which means they try to simulate natural English language usage, including synonyms, into the search function. Click Help or Advanced Search to read more about concept searching.

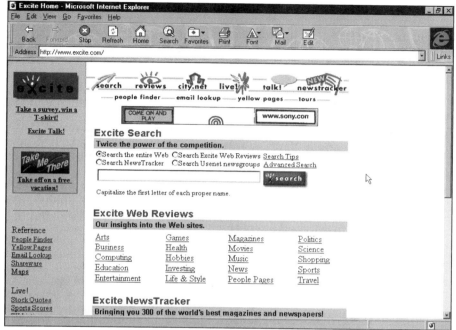

Figure 24-7: Excite features both a search engine and a Web directory.

Point

Point is a directory service that tries to find good Web sites and grant them a "Top 5 Percent of All Web Sites" status. While this isn't exactly a real Web directory — it's more of an arbiter of taste than a cross-section of the Web — you can still find many good sites with Point, especially if you're looking for popular topics, such as UFOs or kids' stuff. Point your browser to `http://www. pointcom.com` to check it out.

Search engines

Pure search engines make little or no attempt to have editorial content or reviews of Web sites. They realize what you want is to find something specific *you know is out there somewhere.* Search engines send little computer programs, called *robots,* out over the Internet sniffing for text. When they find a page that looks useful, they make a copy and send it back home. They scour the Web this way, link by link. Back home, they compress the data and make an index of all, most, or some of the words found on the chunk of the Web they've visited. When you *query* a search engine (ask it to look something up for you), you're asking the robot's kid brother to search the database of all the words on the Web.

Search engines are best for those times when you want to find something specific, such as your own name, or a specific business name or product name. Some search engines, like AltaVista, store the entire text of every Web page they keep on file. What this means is, if you type in a bunch of specific data, like a lyric from a song, or the Latin name of a flowering cactus, the search engine will make every effort to find exactly what you asked for, no matter how obscure.

AltaVista

Folk wisdom on the Internet says if it's out there, you can find it in AltaVista (http://www.altavista.digital com), shown in Figure 24-8. Of course, no matter how big and powerful AltaVista is, it doesn't contain an index of the whole Internet. Yet. AltaVista is run by Digital Equipment Corporation, one of the big guns in UNIX computing. Their search engine is renowned for its speed, because it has the power of a whole bunch of computers strung together, each of which contributes a little energy to every request for data that comes its way. *Parallel computing,* as this is called, is also known as throwing more computers at the problem. All you must worry about is that AltaVista is big, fast, and adept at handling specific queries.

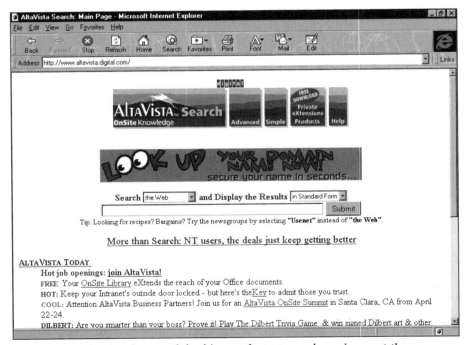

Figure 24-8: AltaVista is one of the biggest, fastest search engines out there. (Reproduced with the permission of Digital Equipment Corporation.)

To search AltaVista, type some words, as many as you like, in the search box. Note, common words like *the* and *some,* and common Internet words, like *Web* and *service,* will be ignored. When you're ready, press the Submit button, and your results will appear on the screen. Click the titles or URLs of the documents displayed to visit them; you can always return to the search results page by using the Back button or the Go menu.

Getting precise results

If you want to fine-tune your search, you can use the following symbols shown in Table 24-1 to make your query more specific. Table 24-2 presents examples of using these special symbols.

	Table 24-1
	Special Symbols Supported by AltaVista

Symbol	Meaning
+	The word must be included
-	The word must be excluded
""	Phrases in quotes will return only exact matches
*	Wildcard
N/n	Capitalization of search terms will retrieve only capitalized references

	Table 24-2
	Examples of Using Special Symbols in AltaVista Queries

Rocket+science	Results might include *rocket* and must include *science*
rocket science-model	Results must not include the word *model*
"rocket science"	Results will include the exact phrase *rocket science*
rocket*	Results can include words such as *rocketing, rocketeer, rockette,* and so forth
"Rocket Science"	Results will only include incidences of *Rocket Science* as a capitalized phrase
rocket+science -"video games"	Results may include the word *rocket*, must include the word *science* and will not include the phrase *"video games"*

Note, no spaces are between the symbols and the words they're used with; that is, it's "+rocket," not "+ rocket". For more search tips, click the word Help on any of AltaVista's pages.

AltaVista Advanced Search

AltaVista's Advanced Search page, which you can get to by clicking the Advanced Search icon, enables you to conduct searches using a different query language that might enable you to manipulate your query even more precisely. You can see the Advanced Search page in Figure 24-9. Table 24-3 summarizes special words you can use in the Advanced Search Query Language to get the search results you want. Table 24-4 presents some examples of how these terms will influence the outcome of a search.

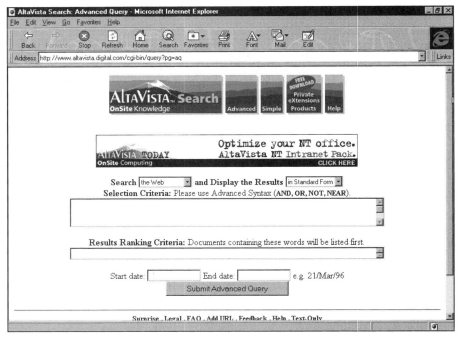

Figure 24-9: AltaVista's Advanced Search page enables you to exercise even more control over your search. (Reproduced with the permission of Digital Equipment Corporation.)

Table 24-3 Terms Supported by AltaVista's Advanced Query Language	
AND	both terms should appear in the search results
OR	either term can appear in the search results
NEAR	terms should appear within a few words of one another
NOT	the term should be excluded from the search results

Table 24-4
Examples of Advanced Query Language Results

Hope AND diamond	Search results will include both *Hope* and *diamond*
diamond OR ruby	Search results may include either *diamond* or *ruby*
diamond NEAR mine	The words *diamond* and *mine* should appear within a few words of one another (in either order) in the search results
diamond NOT baseball	Results will include *diamond*, but not *baseball*
"Hope diamond" NEAR luck NOT Bob	The phrase *"Hope diamond"* should occur near the word luck and should not include the word *Bob* (as in *Bob Hope*)

Things such as quotation marks for exact phrases and asterisks for wildcards still work with the Advanced Search language. For more help and tips on using AltaVista's Advanced Search for finding things on the Web, simply click Advanced Search and then Help.

Lycos

Started at Carnegie Mellon University, Lycos is famous for size and speed. Two of its other features, Point and a2z, incorporate a large directory of rated-and-reviewed sites with other editorial features you may find interesting. You can find Lycos at http://www.lycos.com.

Hotbot

Hotbot, at http://www.hotbot.com, is a joint effort between the University of California at Berkeley's computer science department and *Hotwired/Wired* magazine. Hotbot, as seen in Figure 24-10, includes lots of zippy extra features the other search engines don't have, such as searching by country and media type (Java, VRML, and so forth). Plus it looks really cool.

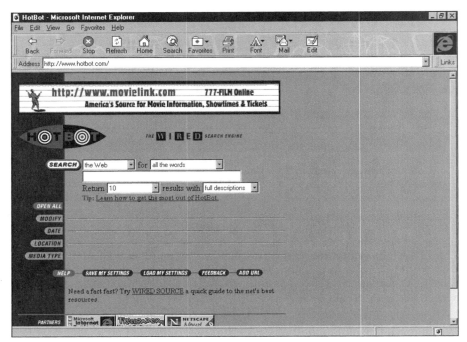

Figure 24-10: Hotbot — the high-tech search engine

Infoseek

With a nice and fast search engine and a really user-friendly interface, Infoseek's search engine would be enough on its own. But the folks at Infoseek also maintain a directory of sites indexed by category. Check it out at `http://www.infoseek.com`.

Webcrawler

One feature of Webcrawler (`http://www.Webcrawler.com`) many people like (and many people hate) is the search results include only the title of the Web page, leaving out the sample text from the top of the page. While this means you may have to guess at which pages are worth visiting, it also means the results page loads much faster. Webcrawler has its own Web directory listings, too.

Internet Explorer's Search Bar

A super-handy feature on Internet Explorer 4.0 is its built-in Search Bar. To use Search Bar, click the Search button in the toolbar. The viewing area splits into two frames, as in the example shown in Figure 24-11. Whatever page you were viewing goes over to the frame on the right. The new frame on the left acts as your Search Bar.

Finding what you found

Every so often, you'll search for something in your favorite search engine, and a page will pop up in the results list that doesn't seem to belong there. Say, for example, you're looking for Mikhail Baryshnikov, and up pops a page about football. You can't for the life of you figure out what Baryshnikov and football have in common. When you visit the page, you still have no idea. This is where the familiar Find feature you may have used in other programs will come in handy. Just choose Edit ➪ Find from Internet Explorer's menu bar, type in the specific word you're looking for, and click the Find Next button. The Find feature will try to locate the word you're looking for *on the Web page that's currently in the Internet Explorer window.* In the case of the ballet-football mystery, we did a Find for *Barysh,* (just part of the word will often do) and found the sports writer said the quarterback "leapt with the grace of Baryshnikov." There's nothing a search engine can do about synonyms, homonyms, and creative metaphors, but at least now we know what our pal Mikhail was doing in the end zone.

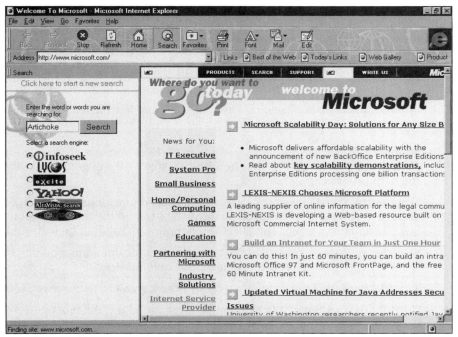

Figure 24-11: Click the Search button to get to the Search Bar on the left side of the screen.

To search for a word or phrase, type it into the space provided — where I've typed the word *Artichoke* in the example. Then, choose a service to perform the search, Infoseek, Lycos, Excite or whatever, and click the Search button.

The left frame will change to list Web sites relevant to the word for which you searched. Click any link, the frame on the right will show you that page! If you want to see the page full-screen, click the Search button in the toolbar again to hide the Search Bar. When you want to return to the Search Bar, click that Search button again.

If you don't find what you're looking for, you can try another search engine. Just click where it says "Click here to start a new search," choose a different search engine, and click the Search button again. Very convenient!

Microsoft Support Online

One of the great things about the Internet is Web sites and other documents online can be updated daily, or even more frequently. Microsoft's Web site, particularly its support documents and online Knowledge Base, uses this to great advantage. If Microsoft finds a bug in its software or updates a software component, it (and you) no longer must wait for the next release to get a fix or an upgrade. The most recent versions of the help files are a major part of the Knowledge Base, as are problems reported by users (and how to fix them). Microsoft's support area starts at the Support home page at `http://www.microsoft.com/support/mtshome.htm`, shown in Figure 24-12.

The Support site consists of several key areas you can familiarize yourself with by browsing around. These include:

✦ **Support Wizard**: Works like the Windows 95 Help Wizards. Choose a product from the pull-down menu, and the Web-based wizard will guide you through the help process.

✦ **Frequently Asked Questions**: A frequently asked questions file, or *FAQ,* is a popular tool used to provide one handy place to find the most common questions about a topic. The Microsoft Support FAQ should be your first stop.

✦ **Knowledge Base**: A searchable database of technical documents, bug fixes, software updates, and lots more questions and answers.

✦ **Troubleshooters**: Take a step-by-step tour through a problem-solving scenario.

✦ **Downloads**: Download a Driver, Patch, or Sample File. The most current versions of Microsoft software components can be found in this section. If you need one of these, chances are you'll learn this while you search for your answer in the Knowledge Base.

✦ **Newsgroups**: Read through real-life questions from fellow users like yourself, and answers from both Microsoft employees and amateur experts. Rather than just reading stock answers to your question, you can post your own questions and follow discussions that reflect varying opinions.

✦ **Web Response**: This service for Microsoft developers and customers requires purchasing chunks of Microsoft's time to get feedback from support technicians.

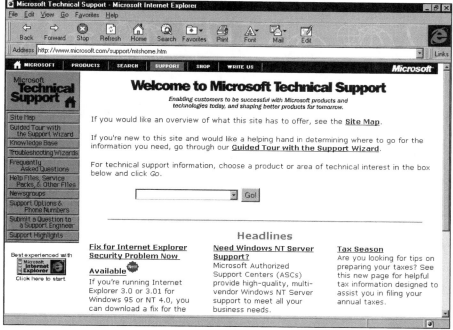

Figure 24-12: You'll find an array of choices for technical support at Microsoft's Support page.

Navigating the Knowledge Base

The Knowledge Base, so named because it's a database of knowledge, contains so much information it can be daunting to browse through or difficult to find the answers you seek. This makes it a miniversion of the Internet, with one exception: The Knowledge Base was developed by a single entity, Microsoft, so all the documents in it have been filed according to a single governing body. This means it's more consistent throughout, so once you learn the ins and outs of the organization scheme, you'll have an easier (and faster) time finding what you want.

How to use the Knowledge Base

You can navigate straight to the Knowledge Base by pointing your Web browser to http://www.microsoft.com/kb. The first thing you want to do there is choose a

Microsoft product from the pull-down menu, as seen in Figure 24-13. If you don't choose a product (Step 1), you'll be searching the entire thing, aka "Any Product." This may be useful if you're searching for a general topic, such as *virus* or *Internet*, and you're not sure to which application it applies. But your search will return many records this way. Also note, the list is alphabetical, and a large number of the products start with the word Microsoft, which is not counted in the alphabetization. If you want to search for information about the Windows 95 operating system, therefore, select Microsoft Windows 95 from the pull-down menu under *W*.

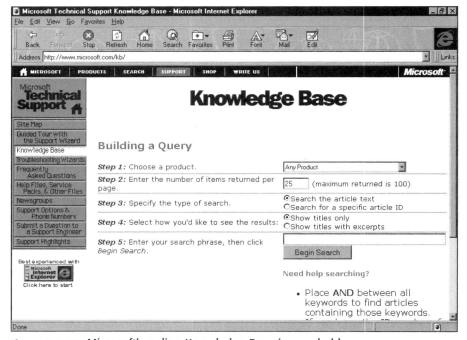

Figure 24-13: Microsoft's online Knowledge Base is searchable.

Now you're going to pick something to type in the box. Generally what you type depends on what you're looking for. Things such as *crash, memory leak, disk error,* or other problems you may have had will be what you seek. Or, if you want to find out more about an application's graphics capability, pick your application from the pull-down menu, and then type **graphics** in the text box.

Hot Stuff You must type something in the text box to use the Knowledge Base or you will get an error. You cannot leave the text box blank and simply read *all* the entries about an application.

Your next step is to choose a radio button under Step 4. Click the "Show titles only" button if you want to fit more document titles per page, or click the "Show titles with excerpts" button if you want these titles accompanied by an excerpt from the document itself. The latter can help you discern which documents may be more useful to you even before you visit them.

When you're ready to go, click Next. You'll be sent to a page containing the results of your query. The document titles are links, and clicking them will retrieve the entire document. The number of titles you get depends on whether any articles are in the Knowledge Base that apply to your question. If nothing shows up, press the Back button or the New Query button and try again.

Phrasing your questions

The Microsoft Knowledge Base, like any other search engine, has its own quirks that, once learned, will make it easier for you to find what you want. For instance, you may not find what you want if you search for *crash,* but you might get the results you want if you search for *error message.* If you get too many results, try adding more words to make your query more specific. For example, if you're looking for information about Microsoft Word, use the word *Word* as one of your search terms. If you don't get any results, you may need to be more general. Try both plural and singular variations of your search terms. In general, the documents in the Microsoft Knowledge Base do not duplicate the help files so, remember, your answer may be found in the program itself.

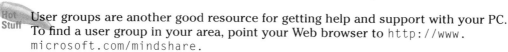 User groups are another good resource for getting help and support with your PC. To find a user group in your area, point your Web browser to `http://www.microsoft.com/mindshare`.

Web Sites for Windows 95 Fans

You're probably aware you're not the only person in the world who uses Windows 95. And you probably guessed other folks are out there who are, at times, intrigued, frustrated, and confused by the array of functions this operating system can perform — or the things it doesn't seem to want to do. But what you may not have found yet is many of these Windows users have not only mastered all the tricks, they've put up Web pages so anyone who's wired can share their knowledge. Some of these pages focus on learning the system, while others help you customize it either within Windows itself, or by downloading free and cheap software that enhances Windows' capabilities. We'll look at both kinds.

Rather than typing in all the lengthy Web addresses that follow, you can stop by the Windows 95 area of my own Web site at `http://www.coolnerds.com`. You'll find simple one-click links to all the following sites, and more.

Windows95.com

Windows95.com, located at http://www.windows95.com and shown in Figure 24-14, is put together by fellow Windows users. It isn't entirely a labor of love, however — Windows95.com does sell some stuff, most notably a CD-ROM collection of freeware and shareware for optimizing your computing experience. But you needn't buy the CD to get the software — Windows95.com is renowned as a software site. A good deal of the software they recommend is archived locally, and links galore exist to nearly everything else you might want. Windows95.com isn't just a shareware archive, either — its help files, tutorials, and glossaries are extensive. Navigating this site is a snap, because it's decorated with versions of the familiar graphics Windows 95 uses.

Figure 24-14: Windows95.com is a labor of love by users like you.

> **More Info** Of course, Microsoft has an area for Windows 95, as well. Its address is http://www.microsoft.com/windows95.

Angela Lilleystone's Windows 95 and NT Resources

Angela Lilleystone's site at http://www.cs.umb.edu/~alilley/win.html, shown in Figure 24-15, offers a page chock full of tips for users — things you might not even think to look up in a book like this. The rest of her info is mainly comprised of links to other sites, but her links are quite well-organized. Lilleystone is one of many Windows 95 users on the Net who form a volunteer user group called *Club Win.* These folks are recognized by Microsoft as having something extra to contribute to the online world.

Figure 24-15: Angela Lilleystone's Windows 95 page is full of good links.

TUCOWS

Looking for some freebie Windows 95 software? Point your Web browser to TUCOWS at `http://www.tucows.com`. TUCOWS is pronounced *two cows,* and it stands for The Ultimate Collection of Winsock Software. Don't worry if you're unsure whether you need Winsock applications. TUCOWS includes lots of Internet apps that work with Windows 95 and Dial-Up Networking, as well as software for Windows 3.x and the Mac.

The first thing you'll see when you visit TUCOWS is a huge list of places around the world. Click the place *closest* to you — these places are *mirror sites,* which means they duplicate the Web site in different places around the world so everyone can have relatively fast access (rather than trying to make everyone in the world download software from one little server). Once you're in, you can browse the software listings by category, you can search for what you want, or you can read a fantastic set of help files for general help with the Internet. Moo!

Frank Condron's World O' Windows

Frank's site at `http://www.conitech.com/windows` goes beyond the regular old help-and-software formula to include more news about Windows 95 than you'll find on any other Web page — and that might include Microsoft's own site. This includes lots of rumor investigation and links to official MS documents. But that isn't to say Frank's site doesn't include help or downloads, because it does. Frank's section on tips is quite good and he's written his own guide to Microsoft's site, which is sort of an alternate map of the site designed so inexperienced Net users can understand it. More is here than I can discuss in a quick review, but one more section worth noting is a set of newsgroups in which you can post questions and read answers about the various aspects of Windows 95.

The Windows QAID

QAID stands for Question Answer Information Database, and that's exactly what it is. You can get QAID in two different formats: the Web site at `http://www.kingsoft.com/qaid` or you can download the same set of files and read them without being logged on to the Net. This option should especially appeal to people who use a per-minute online service as their primary means of connecting to the Net. What you'll find here are dozens of pages of help, from troubleshooting hardware problems to configuring modems. QAID also includes Visual Basic help files, for anyone who gets into creating their own Windows 95 products.

The O'Reilly Windows Center

Once you have a handle on Windows 95 and you want to get down to the nitty gritty, run — don't walk — to the O'Reilly Windows Center at `http://www.ora.com/ centers/windows`. O'Reilly and Associates, a publishing company, is renowned for computing books at the expert and administrator level. Its Web site isn't complete *geekeldygook,* but it is more advanced than a straight-up intro site. Big features here are a guide to the Windows 95 Registry, fixes for TCP/IP connections, and more. If your interest in Windows 95 includes the computing industry as a whole, you'll love this site.

Winstuff

Packed with information and downloads, Winstuff includes a Backstage section, in which you can learn how to customize your desktop and learn the Registry. The file downloads and uploads sections, which comprise a sort of "best of" Windows 95 freeware and shareware. You can submit files for inclusion you find in your Internet travels. Point your browser to `http://www.winstuff.de` if you want to peek.

Windows 95 Annoyances

Windows 95 Annoyances at `http://www.creativelement.com/win95ann` is useful for people who are coming to Windows 95 from some other operating system, such as the Mac OS or X Windows. Tuning in to the Windows 95 Annoyances site connects you with dozens of articles that help you customize the interface, turn off unneeded animations and warning messages, and learn how to tackle the Windows 95 Registry. I found articles, such as "What to Do if You Hate the Start Menu" and "Rename Files Without Being Hassled by the 'Man'" both informative and highly entertaining. But this site isn't just for advanced fine-tuning — it also has a good beginners' FAQ. Last, but not least, the archive of Windows 95 humor is a good place to laugh your frustrations away.

Downloading from the Web

Downloading is copying a file from the Internet to your own PC. Tons and tons of things exist on the Web to download — mostly in the form of free programs, updates to existing programs, and shareware (try-before-you-buy) programs. Downloading from the Web is remarkably easy, almost effortless. Typically, you'll find a link to the program or file you want to download, like many shown in Figure 24-16 available at `http://www.microsoft.com/msdownload`. To perform the download:

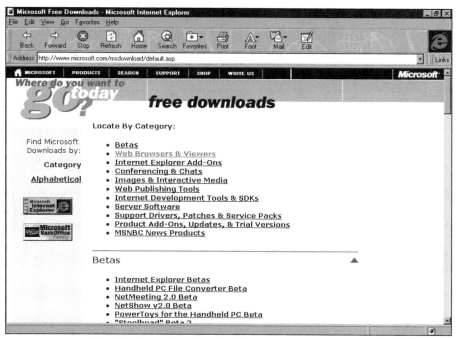

Figure 24-16: Links like these, for downloading files, are available in many Web sites.

1. Click the link that offers to enable you to download the file. (Eventually) you'll see a dialog box like the one shown in Figure 24-17.

Figure 24-17: This dialog box asks what you want to do with a Web file.

2. Choose <u>S</u>ave it to disk and click the OK button. The Windows 95 Save As dialog box, shown in Figure 24-18 appears.

Figure 24-18: Tell Internet Explorer where to put the file you're downloading.

3. In the Save As dialog box, choose the disk drive and folder in which you want to store the file you're downloading. Take a quick look at the filename too, so you'll remember what file to look for later.

4. Click the <u>S</u>ave button.

The download will begin and you'll see a progress meter. You can do other work while waiting for the download to complete. If you interact with the Internet a lot, however, you'll slow down the download. If you can find something to do *locally* (on your own PC, rather than on the Internet), you won't compete with the download. (Of course, if the file you're downloading is a large one, going out to lunch isn't a bad idea!)

A note on Zip files

Some of the files available for download on the Web are compressed, or *zipped,* so they'll download more quickly. These files typically have the extension .zip on their file names. Before you can use such a file, you must decompress, or *unzip* it. To do this, you need to use a decompression program like WinZip. You can download a free evaluation copy of WinZip from `http://www.winzip.com.`

Downloading when no link exists

In some cases, you might see a picture in a Web page, or some other item that offers no real download option. Chances are, you can still download a copy of that item right to your own PC by following these steps:

1. Right-click the link or the item you want to download to your own PC.

2. From the pop-up menu that appears, choose Save Target As or Save Picture As (or whichever option implies you can save the item you just right-clicked).

3. When the Save As dialog box appears, choose the disk drive and folder in which you want to store the file, and remember to take a quick look at the filename, as well.

4. Click the <u>S</u>ave button to begin the download.

As with any download, you'll see a dialog box keeping you informed of the download's progress. When the download is complete, that dialog box will close and disappear from the screen.

Summary

This chapter has been something of a whirlwind tour of the World Wide Web. But the techniques you learned already represent the most important everyday skills you need to use the Web successfully. To recap:

✦ To browse the World Wide Web, connect to the Internet, and then start your Web browser program.

✦ Every site on the World Wide Web has a unique address, or URL, often in the format `http://www.whatever.com.`

✦ To go to a specific Web site, type its address (URL) into the Address text box near the top of the Web browser window, and then press Enter.

✦ You can browse the Web by following hyperlinks — hot spots that appear on the various pages you visit.

✦ To search for specific information on the Web, use a directory or search engine such as Yahoo! (`http://www.yahoo.com`) or AltaVista (`http://www.altavista.digital.com`).

✦ Many sites offer programs and information of interest to Windows 95 users. To get to some links, stop by the Windows 95 area at `http://www.coolnerds.com`, or visit Microsoft's site at `http://www.microsoft.com/windows95`.

✦ To download a file means to copy from the Internet to your own PC.

✦ To download a file from the Web, click the download link and choose Save to Disk from the pop-up menu. Or, right-click the link or item you want to download and choose Save...As from the pop-up menu.

✦   ✦   ✦

Doing Internet E-Mail

Perhaps the busiest feature of the Internet is electronic mail, *e-mail* for short. And no wonder. Unlike regular *snail mail,* which takes days to reach its destination, e-mail usually takes only a few seconds no matter how far the message has to travel.

In the e-mail world, every person has a unique address. You've probably seen dozens of Internet e-mail addresses, which all tend to look something like *someone@someplace.com*. For example, my e-mail address is alan@coolnerds.com.

In this chapter, you'll learn to send and receive Internet e-mail messages. The program you'll use to do all this is called Microsoft Outlook Express Mail, and is built into the Internet Explorer 4 program discussed in the previous chapter. Do remember, though, I'm only using Internet Explorer and Outlook Express as examples. The basic concepts presented in this chapter will work with nearly any e-mail program (or e-mail *client*, as it's called). You need to explore the menus and help system of whatever e-mail client you choose to determine where to plug in the information required for your e-mail addresses and servers.

What You Need for Internet E-Mail

To send and receive Internet e-mail, you need the following:

- ✦ Some kind of connection to the Internet, as discussed in Chapter 23.
- ✦ An e-mail client (a program for managing Internet e-mail).
- ✦ An e-mail address and other information about your mail server, which you get from your Internet Service Provider (ISP).

On the last item, you'll especially need the information presented in Table 25-1. The second column in that table is blank so you can fill in your own information. The only place to get this information is from your ISP — the company or organization providing you with access to the Internet.

Table 25-1 **Information You Need from Your ISP to Send and Receive E-Mail**	
Information to Get	*Write It in This Column*
Outgoing (SMTP) Mail Server Address	
Incoming Mail Server Type (POP3 or IMAP)	
Incoming Mail Server Address	
Your E-Mail Address	
Your E-Mail Account Name	
Your E-Mail Password	

Once you gather the information you need from your ISP, setting up nearly any e-mail client should be a breeze.

Starting Outlook Express Mail

The Internet Explorer 4 component used for sending and receiving e-mail is called *Outlook Express Mail.* Three main ways exist to start this program and you can use whichever method is most convenient:

✦ Click the small Outlook Express Mail icon just to the right of the Windows 95 Start button on the taskbar.

✦ Click the Start button and choose <u>P</u>rograms ➪ Outlook Express Mail.

✦ If you're in Internet Explorer 4, click the Mail button on the toolbar, and then click the Read Mail option.

When Outlook Express Mail starts, you'll probably be viewing its Inbox, which looks something like Figure 25-1. From this one window you can compose, send, and read Internet e-mail messages, as we'll discuss throughout this chapter.

> **More Info** You can customize the Outlook Express window in many ways, as explained later in this chapter under "Personalizing Outlook Express Mail."

Folder list   Message list   Preview pane

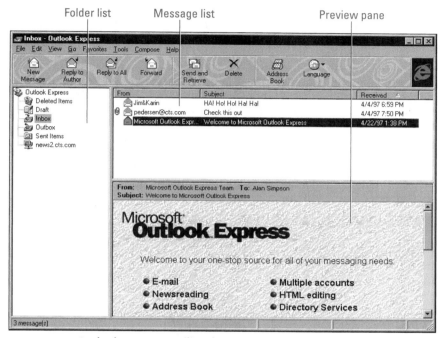

Figure 25-1: Outlook Express Mail's Inbox

If this is the first time Outlook Express Mail has ever been started on your PC, you may be taken straight to the Internet Connection Wizard, which will help you configure the program using your own information from Table 25-1. If you don't get the wizard, or if you need to make changes to your configuration after going through the wizard, you can use the technique described in the next section.

Setting Up Outlook Express for E-Mail

Before you can send and receive Internet e-mail, you must configure Outlook Express to communicate with your Internet e-mail server. Here's how to do that:

1. Start Outlook Express Mail using any of the techniques described in the previous section.

2. If the Internet Connection Wizard starts, skip to Step 5.

3. From the Outlook Express menu bar, choose Tools ➪ Accounts. You'll see the Internet Accounts dialog box.

4. Click the Add button and choose Mail from the small menu that appears (see Figure 25-2).

5. When the Internet Connection Wizard kicks in, fill in the blanks and options on each dialog box, and click the Next button to move on to the next dialog box. When you reach the last dialog box, click the Finish button.

The Internet Connection Wizard will ask you to supply a descriptive name for the account, the name that should appear in the From field of your outgoing messages, your e-mail address, and other information you've jotted down in Table 25-1. You also must specify the type of connection you'll use for this account (phone line or local area network).

If you have multiple e-mail accounts with one service provider or you have e-mail accounts with several service providers, you can use the Internet Connection Wizard to configure each e-mail account.

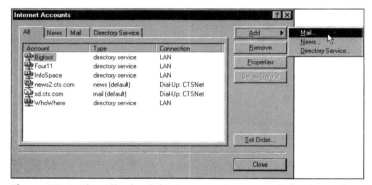

Figure 25-2: The All tab of the Internet Accounts dialog box after clicking the Add button

Changing an e-mail account setting

It's easy to view or change the settings for any e-mail account after you use the Internet Connection Wizard to set it up:

1. Go to the Internet Accounts dialog box if you're not there already (choose Tools ➪ Accounts from the Outlook Express menu bar).

2. Click the Mail tab if you want to focus on your e-mail accounts without the added clutter of news and directory service accounts (see Figure 25-3).

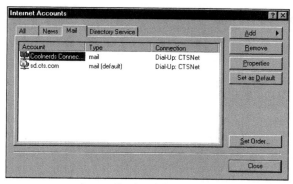

Figure 25-3: The Mail tab of the Internet Accounts
dialog box

3. Click the account name you want to view or change, and then do one of the
following:

   • To make the highlighted account your default e-mail account, choose Set
     As Default.

   • To delete the highlighted account, click Remove, and then click Yes to
     confirm.

   • To change the settings for the selected account, click the Properties
     button (or double-click the account name). Then, fill in or change the
     fields on the General, Servers, Connection, and Advanced tabs of the mail
     account Properties dialog box as needed. For example, to have Outlook
     Express disconnect automatically after sending and receiving messages,
     click the Connection tab, and then select Disconnect when finished
     sending and receiving (see Figure 25-4). When you finish changing the
     account properties, choose OK.

4. Choose Close to return to Outlook Express.

Anytime you need help with one of the options in an Outlook Express dialog box,
simply click the question-mark button at the upper-right corner of the dialog box,
and then click the field or option puzzling you. A pop-up description appears near
the mouse pointer. Press the Esc key to hide the description again. Try it, you'll
like it!

Hot
Stuff

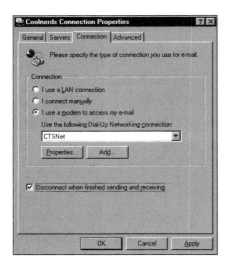

Figure 25-4: The mail account Properties dialog box for an e-mail account named Coolnerds Connection

Composing a Message

Once you start Outlook Express, typing an e-mail message is easy. Three ways can get you started; choose whichever is most convenient:

✦ Click the New Message button in the Outlook Express toolbar.

✦ Choose Compose ➪ New Message from the Outlook Express menu bar.

✦ Press Ctrl+N.

To find out the purpose of any toolbar button, point to the button with your mouse and wait a moment. A pop-up description appears near the mouse pointer.

Regardless of how you start, the New Message window for composing your e-mail message will appear on the screen, looking something like Figure 25-5. To compose your message, first fill in the address portion of the window as explained in the following steps.

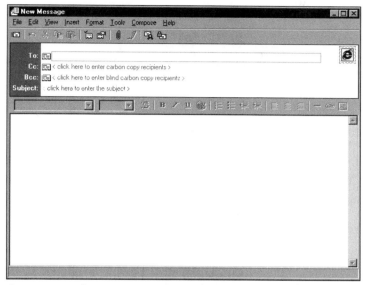

Figure 25-5: The New Message window for composing an e-mail message

1. In the To: box, type the complete mailing address of each recipient. For example, the hypothetical message in Figure 25-6 is addressed to me. To send the message to multiple recipients, type in each e-mail address separated by a semicolon(;).

> **More Info** Instead of typing in an e-mail address, you can choose one from your Windows Address Book by clicking the little Rolodex card icon. More about this topic is under "Using the Windows Address Book" later in this chapter. (By the way, sending messages to yourself is a good idea when you're trying new features in your e-mail program.)

2. In the Cc: box, type the e-mail address of anyone to whom you want to send a carbon copy of this message. Again, you can type multiple recipients as long as you place a semicolon between each address.

3. In the Bcc: box, type the e-mail addresses of anyone who is to receive blind carbon copies. Separate multiple addresses by a semicolon.

> **Hot Stuff** A carbon copy of an e-mail address shows the recipient who else received a copy of the message. A blind carbon copy does not display the names of other recipients.

4. In the Subject: box, type a brief subject description. This part of the message appears in the recipient's Inbox and is visible prior to opening the message.

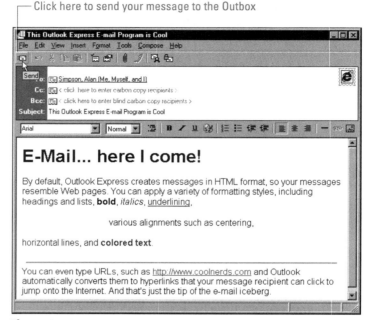

Figure 25-6: An e-mail message addressed to alan@coolnerds.com

5. If you'd like to set the priority or importance of the message, choose Tools ➪ Set Priority, and then choose High, Normal, or Low. Or, click the little stamp icon at the upper-right corner of the address area and choose the priority you want. The stamp icon changes to reflect the priority you chose. The default priority is Normal.

6. Type your message in the larger editing window below the address portion. The next section offers some basic editing techniques.

If you want to take a break while composing your message, choose File ➪ Save from the New Message menu bar and click OK when you see the dialog box informing you the message has been saved in your Draft folder. Then close the New Message window and answer Yes when asked about saving changes. When you're ready to finish composing the message, click the Draft folder in the folder list, and then double-click the message in the message list. Finish editing your message and send it as the following explains.

When you finish composing your message, click the Send button near the upper-left corner of the New Message window toolbar (see Figure 25-6) or press Alt+S. If you have multiple service providers, the message will be sent using your default service provider. (To specify which service provider to use, choose File ➪ Send Message Using, and then click the name of the service provider you want.)

What happens next depends on how Outlook Express is set up on your computer:

✦ If Outlook Express is set up to spell check your messages automatically, the spell checker will kick in and help you to fix any spelling errors it finds in the message (you also can check your spelling manually before sending the message). I'll explain more about spell checking later in this chapter under "Spell checking your message."

✦ If Outlook Express is set up to stack your outgoing messages in the Outbox, you see a message like the one shown in Figure 25-7. This is a healthy reminder that clicking the Send button doesn't actually send the message over the Internet. Rather, it just puts the message in your Outbox so you can send it later (as discussed under "Sending and Retrieving Messages").

Figure 25-7: A reminder that clicking the Send button stores a new message in your Outbox

Basic editing techniques

If you know how to use Microsoft Word, WordPerfect, WordPad, or some other Windows word processing program, you already know the basic skills you need to type and edit a message in Outlook Express. In case you're unfamiliar with word processing, you should know a few key things.

First, the text will automatically wrap to the next line when the insertion point (or cursor) reaches the right edge of the editing window. So when you type a paragraph, press Enter only to end the paragraph or to end a short line. When you press Enter, a blank line will appear and the insertion point will move to the next line. (If you do not want a blank line to appear between short lines or paragraphs in a formatted message, press Shift+Enter rather than Enter.)

Outlook Express can create messages in either HTML format (the default format) or plain text format. If you're editing a plain text message, you must press Enter twice to get a blank line between short lines or paragraphs. See "Formatting your messages" for more information.

As you type, you can use the buttons in the Formatting Toolbar (shown just above the message) to format your text, insert a horizontal line, or add a picture to your e-mail. More on these topics under "Formatting your messages" a little later in this chapter.

If you need to change the text in your message, use either of the following techniques:

✦ Position the insertion point where you want to make the change (for example, click your mouse or press the arrow keys on your keyboard). Then type new text, or press Backspace or Delete to delete text, or press Enter to break the paragraph or line in two.

✦ Select a chunk of text (for example, drag the mouse pointer through it). Then, delete the chunk by pressing Backspace or Delete, or format it by choosing buttons on the Formatting Toolbar. (If you select the wrong chunk of text, click the mouse outside the selection or press an arrow key to deselect it.)

Hot Stuff To select all the text in the message, choose Edit ➪ Select All from the New Message menu bar or press Ctrl+A.

You can use standard Windows Clipboard techniques or drag-and-drop to copy or move text and objects in the message. To begin, select the chunk of text or click an object you want to move or copy. Then do any of the following:

✦ To copy the selection using the Windows Clipboard, choose Edit ➪ Copy (or press Ctrl+C or click the Copy button on the toolbar). Position the insertion point where the copied item should appear and choose Edit ➪ Paste (or press Ctrl+V or click the Paste button on the toolbar).

✦ To move the selection using the Windows Clipboard, choose Edit ➪ Cut (or press Ctrl+X or click the Cut button on the toolbar). Position the insertion point where the moved item should appear and choose Edit ➪ Paste (or press Ctrl+V or click the Paste button on the toolbar).

✦ To copy the selection with drag-and-drop, hold down the Ctrl key while dragging your selection to a new place in the message.

✦ To move the selection with drag-and-drop, drag your selection to a new place in the message without pressing any keys.

Attaching a file

You can attach one or more files to an e-mail message. The attachment can be virtually any kind of file on your PC — a word processing document, a graphic image, a program, whatever. If the attached file is large, and both you and the recipient have a compression/decompression program such as WinZip (available at http://www.winzip.com), you'd be wise to compress (zip) the file(s) before attaching them. Doing so will shrink the files so they transfer more quickly and with less chance of damage during the transfer.

Anyway, to attach one or more files to your e-mail message, click the Insert File toolbar button (the little paper clip) or choose Insert ➪ File Attachment from the New Message menu bar. When the Insert Attachment dialog box appears, browse to the file you want to attach; then click the filename and click the Attach button (or double-click the filename). You can attach as many files as you wish. Each attached file will be represented by an icon at the bottom of the New Message window, as in the example shown in Figure 25-8.

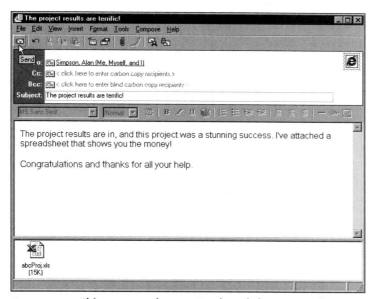

Figure 25-8: This message has an Excel worksheet named abcProj.xls attached.

 If you change your mind about an attachment, you can right-click its icon at the bottom of the New Message window and choose Remove from the shortcut menu that appears.

Formatting your messages

By default, Outlook Express sends messages in rich text (HTML) format rather than as plain text. With rich text format, your messages can resemble full-fledged Web pages complete with headings, images, fancy fonts, hyperlinks, cool background colors, and more. Your decorative options are almost unlimited. Figure 25-9 illustrates some of the possibilities by showing the greeting message that appears after you install Microsoft Outlook Express.

Of course, not everyone is lucky enough to own Outlook Express or another e-mail program that understands rich text HTML. But that's OK. If the recipient's program can't deal with HTML formatting, your message appears as plain old text with an HTML file tacked onto the bottom. The recipient can still view the formatted HTML file by saving the attachment and opening it in any Web browser.

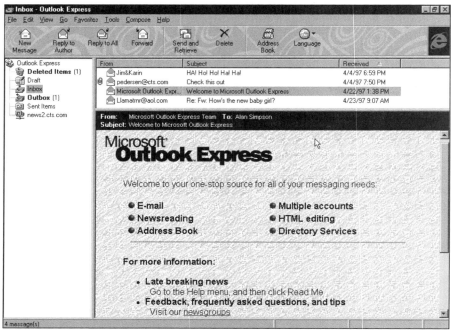

Figure 25-9: The Microsoft Outlook Express greeting message

If you'd rather create your message as plain text, without any HTML formatting, choose Format ↻ Plain Text from the New Message menu bar. You can change the default message format if you want, as explained later under "Customizing the default mail options."

Using the Formatting Toolbar

When you begin composing a new message, the Formatting Toolbar usually appears between the message header section (To:, Cc:, Bcc:, and Subject:) and the message editing area, as shown in Figure 25-10. You can use buttons on the toolbar to help you decorate your message in many ways. The basic steps for using the Formatting Toolbar are simple:

1. Position the insertion point where you want to make a change or select a chunk of existing text to format.

2. Click a button on the toolbar. (To find out the purpose of any Formatting Toolbar button, point to it with your mouse. After a moment, a descriptive tooltip will appear near the mouse pointer.)

3. If a drop-down menu appears below the button, click the option you want. If a dialog box opens, fill in the dialog box and choose OK.

4. If necessary, type new text. (Be careful! If you selected text in Step 1, your typing will *replace* the existing text.)

Life Saver If you don't see the Formatting Toolbar, open the View menu in the New Message window and be sure the Formatting Toolbar option is checked. If it isn't, choose the option; if it is, press the Alt or Esc key to close the menu. If you still don't see the Formatting Toolbar, choose Format ➪ Rich Text (HTML) from the New Message menu bar.

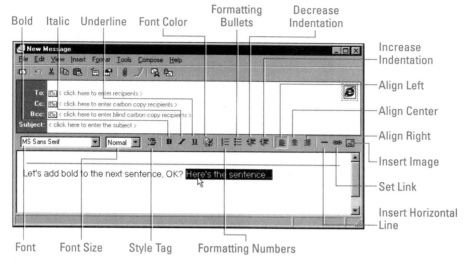

Figure 25-10: The Formatting Toolbar across the middle of the window makes it easy to format a message.

By the way, most of the options on the Formatting Toolbar are available on the Insert and Format menus in the New Message window. You also can choose formatting options from the shortcut menu that appears when you right-click within selected text or at a particular spot in the message.

Changing the Font, Style, Color, and Size

You can use any of the first seven buttons on the Formatting Toolbar to change the appearance of text in the message. Here's how:

1. Position the insertion point where you're about to type new text or to select a chunk of existing text.

2. Click the drop-down arrow on the Font or Font Size button or click the Style Tag, Bold, Italic, Underline, or Font Color button. If you chose Font, Font Size, Style Tag, or Font Color, click the option you want from the drop-down menu that appears. Repeat this step as needed.

3. If necessary, type new text (assuming you didn't select text in Step 1).

Figure 25-11 shows a sample message after I went crazy with the first seven buttons on the Formatting Toolbar. This figure resembles a ransom note, but it's not.

Figure 25-11: A message with several types of text formatting

If you want to apply a formatting style to text you've already typed, just select the text by dragging the mouse pointer through it, or by holding down the Shift key while pressing the arrow keys. When the text you want to format is highlighted, choose your format.

The Bold, Italic, and Underline buttons are *toggles*. Click them once to turn on the effect and click them again to turn off the effect. You also can press shortcut keys to turn the effects on and off: use Ctrl+B for bold, Ctrl+I for italic, and Ctrl+U for underline.

Instead of using buttons on the Formatting Toolbar or shortcut keys, you can choose Format ➪ Font from the New Message menu bar, and then choose the font name, style, size, underlining, and color from one convenient Font dialog box (see Figure 25-12). After making your selections, click OK to save your changes.

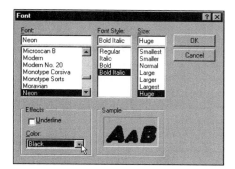

Figure 25-12: The Font dialog box

Aligning text

Your text usually is left aligned, but you can center or right align text if you want (see Figure 25-13). To alter the text alignment, click in the paragraph or short line you want to change or click where you're about to type a new paragraph or line. If you want to adjust several paragraphs or short lines at once, select them. Now click the Align Left, Align Center, or Align Right button on the Formatting Toolbar or choose Format ➪ Align from the New Message menu bar, and then choose Left, Center, or Right.

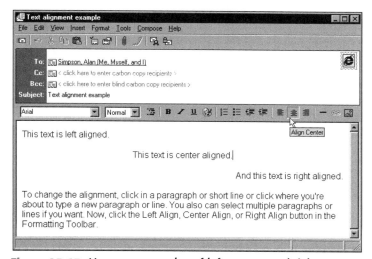

Figure 25-13: Here are examples of left, center, and right text alignment.

Indenting and outdenting text

You can indent a paragraph by moving it in one tab stop (about five spaces) toward the right or outdent a paragraph by moving it out one tab stop toward the left, as shown in Figure 25-14. This is an excellent way to make certain paragraphs — such as quotations — stand out. The steps should be familiar by now:

1. Click in the paragraph or short line you want to indent or outdent, or click where you're about to type a new paragraph or line. If you want to adjust several paragraphs or short lines at once, select them.

2. Click the Increase Indentation or Decrease Indentation button on the Formatting Toolbar or choose Format ➪ Increase Indent or Format ➪ Decrease Indent from the New Message menu bar.

That's all there is to it. As you'll see next, indenting and outdenting is also useful when you're typing lists.

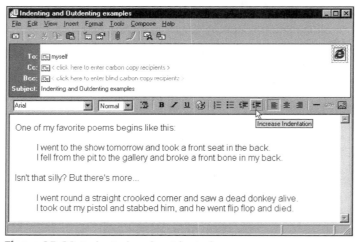

Figure 25-14: Indented and outdented text

Typing lists

I'm a great fan of bulleted and numbered lists because they make it easier to understand a series of choices or a logical sequence of steps. You can create lists like the ones shown in Figure 25-15 with a few keystrokes and mouse clicks. When you create a numbered list, new items are numbered automatically in their proper sequence. If you delete an item in the list, the numbering adjusts accordingly, as you would expect.

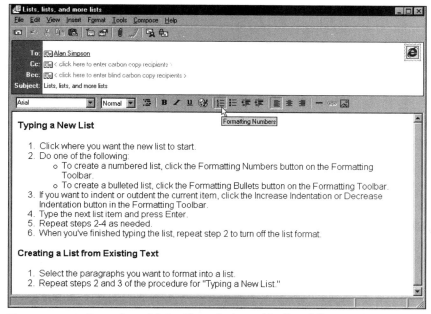

Figure 25-15: A numbered list with an indented bulleted list

Typing a new list

Here's how to type a new list:

1. Click where you want the new list to start.

2. Do one of the following:

   - To create a numbered list, click the Formatting Numbers button on the Formatting Toolbar or choose Format ➪ Numbers from the New Message menu bar. A number appears at the insertion point and the Formatting Numbers button will appear pushed in.

   - To create a bulleted list, click the Formatting Bullets button on the Formatting Toolbar or choose Format ➪ Bullets from the New Message menu bar. A bullet appears at the insertion point and the Formatting Bullets button will appear pushed in.

3. If you want to indent or outdent the current item, click the Increase Indentation or Decrease Indentation button in the Formatting Toolbar (or choose the equivalent options on the New Message menu bar).

4. Type the next list item and press Enter. A new number or bullet will appear.

5. Repeat Steps 2–4 as needed.

When you finish typing the list, follow the steps given under "Removing numbers and bullets." (Basically, you repeat the previous Step 2 to turn off the list.)

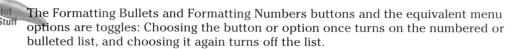

The Formatting Bullets and Formatting Numbers buttons and the equivalent menu options are toggles: Choosing the button or option once turns on the numbered or bulleted list, and choosing it again turns off the list.

Creating a list from existing text

If your message already includes some paragraphs or short lines that would work better as a list, converting them is easy:

1. Select the paragraphs or lines you want to format into a list.

2. Repeat Steps 2 and 3 of the procedure for typing a new list.

Creating a list within a list

You can even create a list within a list, like the bulleted list within the numbered list shown in Figure 25-15. As usual, you can make the change while you're typing a new list or by selecting text first. Here are the steps:

1. Position the insertion point where you want the indented list item to appear or select the existing paragraphs or lines you want to indent.

2. Click the Increase Indentation button on the Formatting Toolbar or choose the equivalent menu options until you get the indentation level you want.

3. If you want to change the type of list, click the Formatting Numbers or Formatting Bullets button or choose the equivalent menu options. An appropriate number or bullet to the indentation level will appear.

4. If you did not select text in Step 1, type your list items, pressing Enter after each one.

Of course, you can return list items to their previous levels by outdenting. Simply repeat the previous four steps *except*, in Step 2, click the Decrease Indentation button on the Formatting Toolbar as needed.

Removing numbers and bullets

You can remove the numbers or bullets from list items at any time. Simply select the items or position the insertion point anywhere in the item from which you want to remove the number or bullet. Then click the Formatting Numbers button (if it's a numbered item) or the Formatting Bullets button (if it's a bulleted item) in the Formatting Toolbar until the number or bullet disappears. If necessary, increase or decrease the indentation level.

You can remove numbers and bullets *and* return the text to its leftmost position by clicking the Decrease Indentation button repeatedly.

Inserting an image

A great-looking picture of your pet, spouse, kid, or newest possession can spice up an e-mail message. You can insert many types of pictures, including scanned images and clip art, by using the following steps :

1. Click in the message editing area where you want the image to appear.

2. Click the Insert Image button in the Formatting Toolbar or choose Insert ⇨ Picture from the New Message menu bar. You'll see the Picture dialog box shown in Figure 25-16.

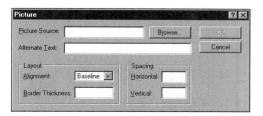

Figure 25-16: The Picture dialog box

3. In the Picture Source box, type the complete filename of the picture. Or, click the Browse button, and then locate and double-click the picture's filename in the dialog box that appears (see Figure 25-17).

Figure 25-17: The Picture dialog box after clicking the Browse button

4. If you want to specify alternate text (text that appears in place of the picture) when the recipient is using a program that can't display pictures or various layout and spacing options, fill in the appropriate Alternate Text, Layout, and Spacing fields.

5. Choose OK.

Your picture appears at the insertion point. Recipients who don't have rich-text e-mail clients will see the image as a regular attachment, not inline. Recipients who have no graphics capability will see only the alternate text.

Outlook Express can import images in GIF, JPEG (JPG), bitmap (BMP), Windows metafile (WMF), XBM, and ART formats. The default import formats are GIF and JPEG. You can choose a different format from the Files of type drop-down list shown at the bottom of Figure 25-17.

Inserting a hyperlink

By now, you've probably had experience browsing the World Wide Web and you know you can click *hyperlinks* on a Web page to jump to another place on the Internet or to perform some action, such as sending electronic mail or downloading a file. Well, guess what? You can insert your own hyperlinks into any e-mail message (see Figure 25-18).

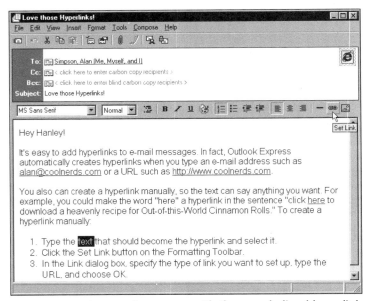

Figure 25-18: An e-mail message with three underlined hyperlinks — *alan@coolnerds.com, http://www.coolnerds.com,* and the word *here).*

Outlook Express automatically creates hyperlinks from valid e-mail addresses and URLs as soon as you type them into a message and press the spacebar or Enter key. For example, after I type my e-mail address (alan@coolnerds.com) or the URL of my home page (http://www.coolnerds.com) and press the spacebar or Enter key, Outlook Express automatically converts the text to an underlined blue hyperlink. The message recipient simply clicks the hyperlink to send me an e-mail message or to jump to my home page on the Web.

You also can create hyperlinks manually, using any text you want. For example, you might want your message to include a sentence, such as:

```
Click here to send me an e-mail message or click here to
          download a heavenly recipe.
```

In this example, the first word "here" is a hyperlink that sends me an e-mail message; the second word "here" is a hyperlink that sends my favorite recipe for cinnamon rolls to your computer (just kidding, I don't cook).

To create a hyperlink manually from any existing text, follow these steps:

1. Type in and select the text you want to use as a hyperlink.
2. Click the Set Link button on the Formatting Toolbar. You'll see the Link dialog box, shown in Figure 25-19.
3. Click the drop-down arrow in the Type box and select one of the types listed in Table 25-2. The type you selected is filled in as the prefix in the URL box.
4. Click after the prefix in the URL box and type the rest of the URL.
5. Click OK.

The selected text becomes a hyperlink in your message.

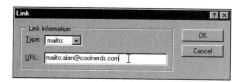

Figure 25-19: The Link dialog box after choosing a link type and entering the URL for sending me an e-mail message

To change a hyperlink you created manually, repeat the preceding Steps 1 through 5. To change a manual hyperlink to plain text, select the hyperlink text, delete it, and then retype it.

Try as you might, you can't change an automatic hyperlink, such as an e-mail address or a Web page URL, to plain text unless you format the *entire* message as plain text. (To format the message as plain text, choose Format ➪ Plain Text from the New Message menu bar.)

	Table 25-2	
	Types of URLs You Can Use to Create Hyperlinks	
Link Type in the Type Drop-Down List	**Description**	**Sample Entry in the URL Box**
file:	Opens the file specified in the URL box.	`file://c:/windows/desktop/wrinkled_paper.bmp`
ftp:	Downloads the file specified in the URL box.	`ftp://ftp.winzip.com/winzip/winzip95.exe`
gopher:	Goes to the Gopher site specified in the URL box.	`gopher://gopher.well.com`
http:	Goes to the Web page specified in the URL box.	`http://www.branchmall.com`
https:	Goes to the secure Web page specified in the URL box.	`https://www.branchmall.com`
mailto:	Sends a new message to the e-mail address specified in the URL box.	`mailto:alan@coolnerds.com`
news:	Goes to the newsgroup specified in the URL box.	`news:news.newusers.questions`
telnet:	Establishes a Telnet link to the computer specified in the URL box.	`telnet:compuserve.com`

Changing the background color or picture

Normally your e-mail message will have whatever background color is the default for the recipient's e-mail program or browser. You can, however, specify the background color or even use a picture as the background, as I did in Figure 25-20.

Specifying a colored background

To specify a colored background, choose Format ⇨ Background ⇨ Color from the New Message menu bar, and then choose a color from the menu that appears. You should try to pick a color that won't obliterate the message text (or reformat the text if you must). For example, your recipient will have a hard time reading a message typed with black text on a purple background. The text might look rather cool, though, if you reformat it in boldface, a larger size, and the color white. (See "Changing the Font, Style, Color, and Size" earlier in this chapter.)

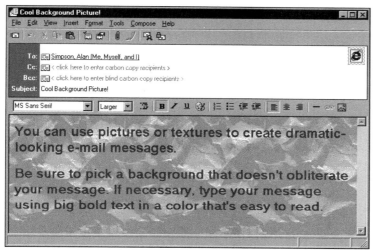

Figure 25-20: This message uses a textured picture as a background and big bold text for added readability.

Specifying a picture background

To use a favorite picture or texture as a background, follow these steps:

1. Choose Format ➪ Background ➪ Picture from the New Message menu bar. The Background Image dialog box appears.

2. In the URL box, type the URL of a file on the Internet or the path of a file on your own computer. Here's the format to use:

   • To enter the URL of a picture stored on the Internet, type **http://** followed by the URL. For example, type **http://www.users.cts.com/sd/e/eolson/llama2.gif** in the URL box.

   • To enter the URL of a file stored on your local computer, type **file://** followed by the complete path of the file name. For example, if you stored a texture graphic named wrinkled_paper.bmp on your Windows desktop (c:\windows\desktop), type **file://c:\windows\desktop\wrinkled_paper. bmp** in the URL box.

3. Choose OK.

The picture or texture you chose will be repeated as needed to fill up the background, as in Figure 25-20. Again, be careful to choose a picture that won't obscure the text in your message and type the message in an easy-to-read format.

Inserting a text file or an HTML file

Let's suppose you already put together a plain text file containing your message (perhaps using Notepad) or you have an HTML Web page prepared. Now you want to e-mail the text or Web page to someone else. No sweat. Here's what you should do:

1. Click in your message where you want the text or HTML page to appear.

2. Choose Insert ➪ Text from File from the New Message menu bar. The Insert Text File dialog box appears (see Figure 25-21).

Figure 25-21: The Insert Text File dialog box

3. Choose the type of file you want to insert from the Files of type drop-down list near the bottom of the dialog box. You can choose either Text Files (*.txt) to insert a plain text file or HTML Files (*.htm,*.html) to insert an HTML file.

4. Locate and double-click the file that contains your text.

The plain text or HTML page appears in your message.

HTML stands for *HyperText Markup Language,* a language Web browsers and some e-mail programs interpret to display Web pages. You can create HTML pages from scratch, using Windows Notepad or other simple word processors, or you can use fancier word processors and specialized Web page design programs to create what-you-see-is-what-you-get (WYSIWYG) Web pages. Microsoft Word and Corel WordPerfect are two word processors that can create Web pages; Microsoft FrontPage, Microsoft Publisher, and Netscape Composer are just three examples of Web page design programs.

Fixing "broken" HTML images and links

If the HTML file you inserted is at all fancy, it may have broken image icons like the "x low-budget logo" shown in Figure 25-22; the hyperlinks probably won't work when the recipient clicks them.

Try the following methods to solve these problems:

✦ To fix a broken image icon, click the icon, and then click the Insert Image button on the Formatting Toolbar (or right-click the icon and choose Properties). Now complete the Picture Source box as explained earlier under "Inserting an image." Figure 25-23 shows the page from Figure 25-22 after I fixed the low-budget logo image at the top.

✦ To fix a broken hyperlink, select the hyperlink text, click the Set Link button on the Formatting Toolbar, and complete the Link dialog box as explained earlier under "Inserting a hyperlink."

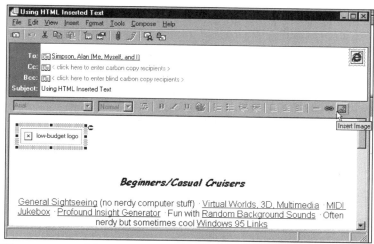

Figure 25-22: This is an HTML page that includes broken image icons and links. I've selected the low-budget logo in this example.

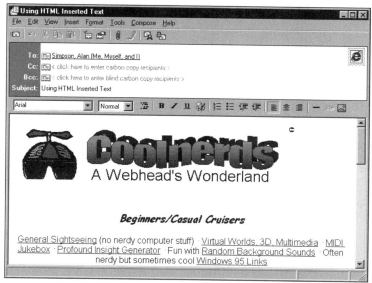

Figure 25-23: Here is the HTML page from Figure 25-22 after I fixed the broken image icon and links.

Spell checking your message

No one wants to seem careless or ignorant, especially when using e-mail to communicate with other people. One way to avoid bad impressions is to send messages free of embarrassing spelling errors. Outlook Express has a built-in spell checker that makes spell checking a breeze, and it usually kicks in automatically as soon as you click the Send button in the New Message toolbar.

If the spell checker doesn't start automatically (or you want to spell check the message while you're composing it), choose Tools ➪ Spelling from the New Message menu bar or press F7. The spell checker will start. If it doesn't find any errors, a dialog box informs you the spelling check is complete (click OK to clear it). If the spell checker does find an error, you'll see a Spelling dialog box like the one in Figure 25-24. The unrecognized word appears in the Not In Dictionary box just below the title bar.

If the Spelling dialog box is covering part of the message, simply drag the dialog box by its title bar to move it out of the way.

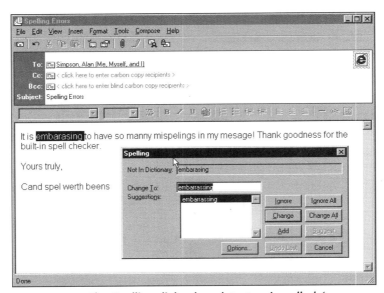

Figure 25-24: The Spelling dialog box detects misspelled (or unrecognized) words.

Be aware, the spell checker isn't all-knowing. Sometimes it fumes about a perfectly acceptable word. As I'll explain in a moment, you can add unrecognized (but properly spelled) words to the spell checker's custom dictionary and you can change the spelling options so the spell checker doesn't complain so much.

The buttons in the Spelling dialog box are as follows:

✦ **Ignore**: Click Ignore to ignore this error and move on to the next one.

✦ **Ignore All**: Click Ignore All to ignore this error throughout the entire message.

✦ **Change**: Click the word you want to use as a replacement in the Suggestions list (if it's not highlighted already) or edit the word in the Change To box. Then click the Change button to change the misspelled word to the word shown in the Change To box.

✦ **Change All**: Click the word you want to use as a replacement in the Suggestions list (if it's not highlighted already) or edit the word in the Change To box. Then click Change All to change the same misspelled word throughout the entire message to the word shown in the Change To box.

✦ **Add**: Click this button to add the unrecognized word to the spell checker's custom dictionary.

✦ **Suggest**: Type a word into the Change To box, and then click Suggest to look up the word and display other possible spellings in the Suggestions list.

✦ **Options**: Click Options to open the Spelling Options dialog box (shown in Figure 25-25), which enables you to customize the current spelling options. You can check or clear the check boxes, choose a language from the Language drop-down list, and even edit the custom dictionary, which contains words you've added via the Add button, plus any words you type in manually.

✦ **Undo Last**: Click Undo Last to undo your most recent change (if any) and skip back to the previous misspelled word.

✦ **Cancel** (or **Close**): Click Cancel or Close to stop spell checking immediately.

A message appears when the spell check is complete. Click OK to clear the message.

Hot Stuff Your choices in the Spelling Options dialog box affect the current spell check session only. You can change the spelling options for all future spell checking sessions, however, as explained later in "Customizing the default mail options."

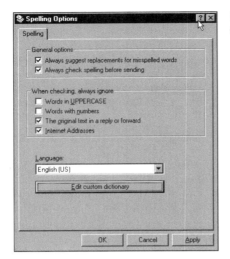

Figure 25-25: Use the Spelling Options dialog box to customize the spell check.

Sending and Retrieving Messages

When you have some messages ready to go, follow these simple steps to send them:

1. Open Outlook Express Mail using whichever method you prefer (see "Starting Outlook Express Mail").

2. If you want to see a list of messages waiting to be sent, click the Outbox folder in the folder list (left pane of the window). A list of messages waiting to be sent appears in the upper-right pane, as in the example shown in Figure 25-26.

3. If you want to send all the current messages and also retrieve any messages that are waiting for you, click the Send And Retrieve button in the toolbar or choose Tools ⇨ Send And Retrieve (or press Ctrl+M). Or, if you'd rather send the pending messages without retrieving new ones, choose Tools ⇨ Send from the menu bar.

A "Sending Mail" dialog box will keep you posted on the progress and your computer will dial your service provider (if you use a modem to connect). When all the messages have been sent, the Outbox will be empty. Copies of the sent messages will be stored in the Sent Items box.

You can change any message waiting in your Outbox. Simply click the Outbox icon in the folder list, double-click the message you want to change in the message list, change the message as needed, and click the Send button in the toolbar (or press Alt+S).

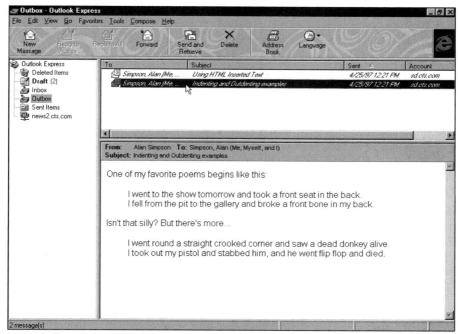

Figure 25-26: Outlook Express's Outbox

If you close Outlook Express while unsent messages are still in your Outbox, you'll see a box telling you:

```
You have unsent mail in your Outbox. Do you want to send it
      now?
```

This is a friendly reminder in case you composed a message and forgot to send it. You can choose Yes to send the message immediately or No to leave it in the Outbox for sending later.

> **More Info** You can customize Outlook Express so it sends each e-mail message immediately, instead of putting each message in the Outbox. For more information, see "Customizing the default mail options" later in this chapter.

Reading Your Messages

Retrieving and viewing new Internet e-mail messages is easy. Just follow these steps:

1. Open Outlook Express Mail using any of the techniques described under "Starting Outlook Express Mail" earlier in this chapter.

2. Click the Send And Retrieve button (or press Ctrl+M). Or, if you just want to retrieve mail, choose <u>T</u>ools ➩ <u>R</u>etrieve ➩ All Accounts from Outlook Express's menu bar.

You'll see some progress dialog boxes as Outlook Express sends any messages in your Outbox and then copies new messages from your e-mail server on the Internet to your PC.

To view the new messages, click the Inbox folder in the folder list (a number appears next to the Inbox to indicate the number of unread messages it contains). New messages you haven't read yet are listed in boldface in the message list (right pane), and are preceded by a closed envelope icon as in the example shown in Figure 25-27. The number of unread messages appears in parentheses next to the Inbox folder. Messages containing attached files are preceded by a paper-clip icon and those with a high or low priority are preceded by an exclamation point (!) or a down arrow, respectively.

Life Saver Don't panic if the boldface attribute suddenly disappears from the message line. This means you viewed the message for about five seconds (an interval you can adjust, as explained later in "Customizing the default mail options").

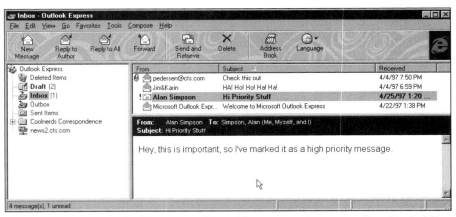

Figure 25-27: The Outlook Express Inbox with an unread message listed in boldface

To read a specific message, click it. The preview pane at the bottom shows the contents of the e-mail message. If you prefer to open the message in a separate window, double-click it.

Hot Stuff If you already have messages stored in one of the more popular e-mail programs, you can import them into Outlook Express. Importing old messages can be especially handy when you're switching from some other e-mail program to Outlook Express. See "Importing and Exporting Messages" for details.

When you finish reading the message, you can do any of the following:

✦ **Reply To Author**: To send a reply to the author of the e-mail, click the Reply To Author toolbar button or press Ctrl+R. Type your reply and click the Send toolbar button.

✦ **Reply To All**: To reply to everyone who received the message (including those who received carbon copies), click the Reply To All toolbar button or press Ctrl+Shift+R. Type your reply and click the Send toolbar button.

✦ **Forward**: To forward the message to someone else, click the Forward toolbar button or press Ctrl+F. Type the new recipient's name, type a message describing the forwarded information (optional), and then click the Send toolbar button.

✦ **Forward As Attachment**: To forward the message to someone else as an attachment to a message you've written, choose Compose ➪ Forward As Attachment. Type the new recipient's name, type a message describing the forwarded information (optional), and then click the Send toolbar button.

✦ **Delete**: To delete the message, click the Delete toolbar button or press Ctrl+D. Outlook moves the message to the Deleted Items folder.

✦ **Print**: To print the message, choose File ➪ Print from the menu bar, or press Ctrl+P, or click the Print toolbar button if it's available.

✦ **Mark As Unread**: To mark the message line with boldface as a reminder to reread it later, choose Edit ➪ Mark As Unread from the menu bar.

✦ **Mark As Read**: To remove the boldface and mark a message as read, choose Edit ➪ Mark As Read or press Ctrl+Q.

✦ **Mark All As Read**: To mark all the messages as read, choose Edit ➪ Mark All As Read.

✦ **View the Next Message**: To view the next message in the folder, click the Next button on the toolbar (if it's available) or press Ctrl+> (Ctrl+greater than), or choose View ➪ Next ➪ Next Message from the menu bar.

✦ **View the Previous Message**: To view the previous message in the folder, click the Previous button on the toolbar (if it's available) or press Ctrl+< (Ctrl+less than), or choose View ➪ Next ➪ Previous Message from the menu bar.

More Info Instead of using the toolbar buttons to reply to or forward the message, you can choose options from the Compose menu. And if you're viewing the message in the message list (rather than in a separate window), you can right-click the message and decide its fate by choosing an option from the shortcut menu that appears. More about replying to messages, forwarding them, and deleting them is in the later sections on "Replying to a Message," "Forwarding a Message," and "Deleting Messages."

Working with several messages at once

Working with several messages at once is often handy. For example, you might want to delete several messages, mark them as read (or unread), move them to another folder, open them in separate windows, and more. The first step is to click the folder containing the messages with which you want to work. Next, select (highlight) the messages with which you want to work, using any of the following techniques:

✦ To select one message, click it in the message list.

✦ To select all the messages, choose Edit ➪ Select All or press Ctrl+A.

✦ To select several adjacent messages, click the first message you want to select, and then hold down the Shift key, while clicking the last message you want to select (this technique is called *Shift+click*).

✦ To select several nonadjacent messages, click the first message you want to select, and then hold down the Ctrl key, while clicking each additional message you want to select (this technique is called *Ctrl+click*). If you select a message by accident, Ctrl+click it.

Now you can work with all the selected messages at once. Here are some things you can do with them:

✦ Right-click any of the selected messages and choose an option from the shortcut menu that appears. Right-clicking is perhaps the easiest way to work with multiple messages.

✦ Choose File ➪ Open or nearly any option from the Edit menu.

✦ Click the Forward or Delete button on the toolbar.

✦ Drag any of the selected messages to another folder in the folder list (all the selected messages are *moved* to the new folder).

✦ Hold down the Ctrl key while dragging any of the selected messages to another folder in the folder list (all the selected messages are *copied* to the new folder).

More Info   You can create your own folders to organize your e-mail messages and you can have the Inbox Assistant automatically move or copy incoming messages to specific folders. See "Creating your own folders" and "Using the Inbox Assistant" for more information.

Finding and sorting messages

Eventually, you might end up with a huge number of messages in your Inbox and other folders within Outlook Express. Finding a particular message in that pile of mail could be like looking for the proverbial needle in the haystack. But thanks to the Find Message feature, it's easy to search for messages. Follow these steps to find the message(s) you want:

1. Starting from the main Outlook Express window, click the folder you want to search.

2. Choose Tools ➪ Find Message from the menu bar or press Ctrl+Shift+F. You'll see the Find Message dialog box, shown in Figure 25-28.

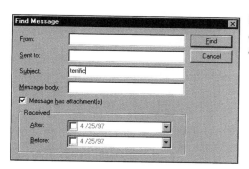

Figure 25-28: Use the Find Message dialog box to search for messages in any of your Outlook Express folders.

3. Fill in as much information about the messages you want as you need to narrow down the search. (It doesn't matter whether you type uppercase or lowercase letters.)

4. Click the Find button to begin the search.

In Step 3, you can specify partial words or names in the From, Sent To, Subject, and Message body fields. If you enter information into more than one field, Outlook treats each field as an "and." For example, Outlook Express interprets the find in Figure 25-28 as "Find any message that contains the word *terrific* in the subject line and that also has an attachment."

If there's a match, Find will highlight it in the message list of the selected folder. If there isn't, you'll see a "No messages found" dialog box; click OK to close the dialog box.

To search for the next match in the folder, choose Tools ➪ Find Next from the menus or press F3 as needed. When no more matches exist, Outlook Express asks whether you want to start over from the top of the list; click Yes to begin the search again or click No to quit the search.

Sorting the message list

Another quick way to find a message is to sort the message list. You can sort the list by any column in either ascending (A to Z) or descending (Z to A) order. To begin, click the folder you want to sort. Then, use any of the following methods to sort the message list:

✦ Click the column button at the top of the message list. For example, click the Subject column button to sort the messages by subject. If you click the column button again, the sort order is reversed. A small up-pointing triangle on the button indicates an ascending sort and a down-pointing triangle indicates a descending sort.

✦ Right-click the column button at the top of the message list and choose either Sort Ascending or Sort Descending.

✦ Choose <u>V</u>iew ⇨ Sort <u>B</u>y from the menu bar, and then choose the column by which you want to sort. If you want to toggle the current sort order between ascending and descending order, choose <u>V</u>iew ⇨ Sort <u>B</u>y ⇨ <u>A</u>scending. If the Ascending option is checked, the list is sorted in ascending order. If it isn't checked, you get a descending sort.

More Info You can add and remove columns in the message list, as explained later in "Customizing the Outlook Express window."

Finding text within a message

In addition to searching for a specific message, you can search for text *within* the message you're currently viewing in the message list or in a separate window. To do this, choose <u>E</u>dit ⇨ <u>F</u>ind Text from the menu bar, or press F3. Type the text you're looking for in the Find what box and choose any options you want. You can decide whether to match the whole word only, whether to match the uppercase and lowercase letters you typed, and the search direction. Click the Find Next button to start the search. Find will highlight the next match it finds. You can continue clicking Find Next and highlighting matches until you find the match you want. When you finish searching, click Cancel.

Viewing and saving attachments

If a message includes an attachment, a paper-clip icon appears next to the message in the message list and also at the upper-right corner of the message in the preview pane. The icon for the actual file appears at the bottom of the message anytime you view it in a separate window. Figure 25-29 illustrates the same message opened in both the preview pane (left side of figure) and in a separate window (right side of figure).

Viewing or saving the attachment is easy:

✦ If you highlighted the message in the preview pane, click the paper-clip icon at the upper-right corner of the message, and then click the filename of the attachment you want to open.

✦ If you opened the message in a separate window, double-click the attachment icon near the bottom of the message. Or, for even more processing options including Open, Print, and Save As, right-click the attachment icon and choose an option from the shortcut menu.

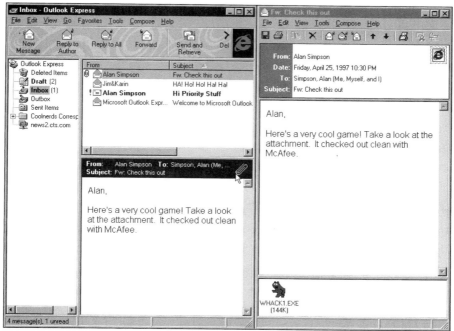

Figure 25-29: This message has an attachment, as shown in the preview pane and in a separate window.

What happens next depends on the type of information the attachment contains. If the attachment is an e-mail message, it'll open in a separate window. If it's a compressed file (such as a .zip file), it may open in your file compression program (such as WinZip or PKUNZIP). If it's a program or data file (such as a spreadsheet or word processing document), you'll usually see the Open Attachment Warning dialog box shown in Figure 25-30. Now take either of the following actions:

✦ To open the attachment, click O<u>p</u>en it, choose OK, and then respond to any dialog boxes that appear.

✦ To save the attachment to disk, choose <u>S</u>ave it to disk, and choose OK. When the Save Attachment As dialog box appears, specify a filename in the File name box (optional), choose a disk drive and folder location in the Save in: area near the top of the dialog box, and then click the Save button or press Enter.

Danger Zone Be careful about opening a file if you haven't yet checked it for viruses. It's okay to save a file to disk and then check it for viruses, but once you open the file (by choosing O<u>p</u>en it in the Open Attachment Warning dialog box or by double-clicking it in My Computer or Windows Explorer), you can expose your computer to any viruses the file contains.

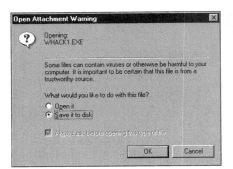

Figure 25-30: This dialog box enables you to open the attached file or to save it to disk.

Replying to a Message

You can reply to any message you highlighted in the message list or that you're viewing in a separate window. First, do one of the following:

✦ To send a reply to the author of the e-mail, click the Reply To Author toolbar button or press Ctrl+R (or choose Compose ➪ Reply To Author).

✦ To reply to everyone who received the message (including the people who received carbon copies), click the Reply To All toolbar button or press Ctrl+Shift+R (or choose Compose ➪ Reply To All).

A Reply window will open, as shown in Figure 25-31. Notice the To: box in the address area is already filled in with the recipient's e-mail name and the Subject line displays Re: (for reply) followed by the original subject. The insertion point is positioned above the original message, which appears in the lower portion of the editing area. (If the message originally contained an attachment, the attachment *is not* included.)

Type your reply using any of the editing and formatting techniques discussed under "Composing a Message." Although you shouldn't need to, you also can change any items in the address and subject areas. When you finish typing your reply, send the message as usual (for example, click the Send toolbar button in the Reply window or press Alt+S).

You can choose whether to include the original message in the reply, as explained under "Customizing the default mail options." For the best reminder about what you're replying to, include the original message. You can always delete any extraneous text from the original message using standard editing techniques.

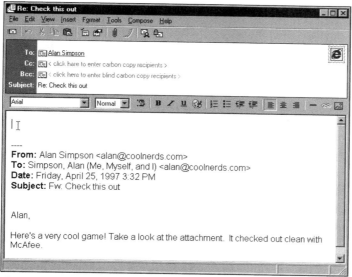

Figure 25-31: Preparing to reply to this message

Forwarding a Message

You also can forward any message to someone other than the original author or carbon copy recipients. Forwarding a message is similar to sending a reply, although some differences exist, namely that attachments are included in the forwarded message, the To: box in the address area is not filled in automatically, and the Subject: line is filled in with Fw: (for forward) followed by the original subject or it is blank.

To forward a message, follow these steps:

1. Highlight the message you want to forward in the message list or open it in a separate window.

2. Do one of the following:

   • To forward the message exactly as it originally appeared in your Inbox, click the Forward toolbar button or press Ctrl+F (or choose Compose ➪ Forward). A Forward (Fw) window opens and shows the original message and its attachments, if any.

   • To forward the message as an attachment, choose Compose ➪ Forward As Attachment. A New Message window opens with the original message appearing as an attachment icon at the bottom of the window.

3. Type the recipient's e-mail address in the To: box or use your Windows Address Book to fill in the address (see "Using the Windows Address Book" later in this chapter). If you want to forward the message to more than one recipient, type a semicolon between each recipient's e-mail address.

4. If you forwarded the message as an attachment, type a subject in the Subject: box.

5. Click in the message editing area and type an introduction to the message you're forwarding. This introduction is optional, but it's helpful to tell recipients why you're forwarding the message.

6. Send the message as usual (for example, click the Send toolbar button or press Alt+S).

Deleting Messages

Deleting an unwanted message from any folder is easy. First, click the folder containing the message and open the message or select it in the message list. Then, click the Delete button on the toolbar or press Ctrl+D. If you selected messages in the message list, two more ways exist to delete them: either press the Delete (Del) key on your keyboard or drag the selection to the Deleted Items folder.

 You can empty your Deleted Items folder automatically as soon as you exit Outlook Express, as explained later under "Customizing the default mail options."

When you delete a message from any folder *except* the Deleted Items folder, you actually move it to the Deleted Items folder. So if you ever need to "undelete" a message, you can move it to another folder. To do so, click the Deleted Items folder in the folder list and select the message(s) you want to undelete in the message list. Then right-click the selected message(s), choose Move To from the shortcut menu, and double-click Inbox or whatever folder to which you want to move the message(s). Or, you can select messages in the Deleted Items folder and drag them to another folder in the folder list.

 When you delete a message from the Deleted Items folder, the message is removed from your hard disk and it cannot be undeleted.

Backing Up Your Messages

Backing up your Outlook Express message folders to a floppy disk, Zip disk, or network drive occasionally is a good idea. Backups can protect you against the loss of all your saved messages in the event of a hard disk crash and they provide some extra insurance just before or after you do a major cleanup in your message folders.

Each Outlook Express message folder is actually composed of two files on your hard disk: one message file with a .mbx extension and one index file with a .idx extension. These files usually appear in a folder named C:\Program Files\

`InternetExplorer\Outlook Express\username\Mail`, where *username* is your
e-mail name or network user name. (The files might be in a different folder on your
hard disk, depending on how you set up Outlook Express.)

Life Saver For safety's sake, go ahead and back up *everything* in the `C:\Program Files\Internet Explorer\Outlook Express\username\Mail` folder, not just the .mbx and .idx files.

The general steps for backing up your messages are as follows:

1. Open the folder that contains your Outlook Express messages using Find,
   Windows Explorer, or My Computer. See the following "Finding your Outlook
   Express messages" for some tips on locating this folder.

2. Compress the files you want to back up with a file compression program,
   such as WinZip (available at `http://www.winzip.com`). This step is
   optional, but it will help to conserve space on your backup disk. There's just
   one hitch: If you ever need to restore the compressed messages from your
   backup disk, you'll also need to *decompress* them with your file compression
   program before Outlook Express can use them.

3. Copy the message files (or the compressed file you created in Step 2) to a
   backup folder on your computer, to a floppy disk or Zip disk, or to a network
   drive. Note, some message files might be too large to fit on a floppy disk.

Finding your Outlook Express messages

You can use the Windows Find command to find and open the folder quickly that
contains your Outlook Express message files. Here's how:

1. Click the Start button on the Windows taskbar and choose Find ➪ Files Or
   Folders.

2. In the Named box of the Find: dialog box, type ***.mbx; *.idx** and then click
   the Find Now button.

3. When the search is complete, point to one of the files shown near the bottom
   of the Find dialog box (for example, point to Draft.idx) and then choose File ➪
   Open Containing Folder from the Find menu bar.

The folder containing your Outlook Express messages opens on the Windows
desktop.

Danger Zone Other programs besides Outlook Express create .idx and .mbx files. Therefore, in the previous Step 3 , be sure to choose files in the `C:\Program Files\Internet Explorer\Outlook Express\username\Mail` folder rather than some other folder that doesn't have "Outlook Express" in its name.

Compacting a folder

Outlook Express occasionally may ask for permission to compact your message folders to eliminate wasted space. Choose Yes when prompted because compacting takes only a few moments and conserves your hard disk space.

You also can compact a folder manually at any time. First, click the folder in the folder list of the Outlook Express window. Then choose File ➪ Folder ➪ Compact and wait a moment while the compactor cleans up the wasted space.

Hot
Stuff
Compacting is not the same as compressing. Outlook Express can directly use any folders it has compacted; you needn't decompress them in any way.

Importing and Exporting Messages

If you recently switched from Eudora Pro, Eudora Light, Microsoft Exchange, or Netscape Mail to Outlook Express Mail, you might have a bunch of messages you want to import for use in Outlook Express. Conversely, you may want to export your Outlook Express Mail messages for use in Microsoft Outlook or Microsoft Exchange, predecessors of Outlook Express. As the following sections explain, importing and exporting messages between Outlook Express and other e-mail programs is easy.

Importing messages

To import messages from another e-mail program into Outlook Express, use the following steps:

1. Open Outlook Express and choose File ➪ Import ➪ Messages from the menu bar. An Import Messages dialog box appears.

2. From the Select e-mail client to import drop-down list, choose the type of file to import. Your choices are Eudora Pro or Light, Microsoft Exchange or Outlook, Netscape Mail v1.22, and Netscape Mail v2.0x or v3.0x.

3. Click OK.

4. Respond to any prompts that appear. The prompts will depend on your choice in Step 2.

When importing is complete, the messages will appear in the appropriate Outlook Express folders. Simply click the folder you're interested in to view the imported messages.

Hot
Stuff
If necessary, Outlook Express will create new folders to hold messages from the original e-mail program. For example, if the old e-mail program contained messages in a folder named "Good Stuff," a Good Stuff folder will appear in the Outlook Express folder list and will contain messages from the Good Stuff folder in your old program.

Exporting messages

Use the following steps to export your Outlook Express Mail messages to either Microsoft Outlook or Microsoft Exchange:

1. Open Outlook Express and choose File ➪ Export ➪ Messages from the menu bar.

2. When you see the message This will export messages from Outlook Express Mail to Microsoft Outlook or Microsoft Exchange, **click** OK.

3. When the Choose Profile dialog box appears, choose a Microsoft Outlook or Microsoft Exchange profile from the Profile Name drop-down list, and then click OK. (If you have no idea what profiles are all about, click the Help button in the Choose Profile dialog box.)

4. When prompted to select the folders to be exported, choose All Folders or choose Selected Folders, and then click, Shift+click, or Ctrl+click the folders you want to export.

5. Choose OK to export the messages.

Using the Windows Address Book

Outlook Express has a handy address book you can use to record, maintain, and find peoples' addresses, phone numbers, and, of course, e-mail addresses. You also can use the address book to fill in the e-mail addresses of your recipients automatically when you compose a new message or when you reply to or forward a message.

To get to the Windows Address Book, use any of the following approaches:

✦ From the Windows 95 desktop, click the Start button and choose Programs ➪ Windows Address Book.

✦ From Outlook Express, click the Address Book toolbar button, or choose Tools ➪ Address Book from Outlook Express's menu bar, or press Ctrl+Shift+B.

✦ From the New Message window, the Reply window, or the Forward window, choose Tools ➪ Address Book or press Ctrl+Shift+B.

The Windows Address Book window opens, perhaps empty if you've never used it before, as in Figure 25-32. Now you can add new contacts and new groups, change the properties of, or delete any existing entry, search or print the address book, send mail to anyone in the address book, and more. When you finish using the Windows Address Book window, click its Close (X) button in the upper-right corner or choose File ➪ Close from its menu bar.

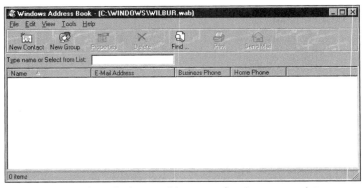

Figure 25-32: The Windows Address Book prior to entering any names and addresses

Adding names and addresses

Adding peoples' names and addresses to the Windows Address Book is simple. First open the address book. Then, click the New Contact button on the toolbar, or choose File ➪ New Contact from the menu bar, or press Ctrl+N. The Properties dialog box shown in Figure 25-33 will appear.

Anytime you're viewing an e-mail message in a separate window, you can quickly copy any underlined address in the From:, To:, Cc:, or Bcc: area to your Windows Address Book. Simply right-click the address and choose Add To Address Book from the shortcut menu. You'll be taken to the Personal tab of a Properties dialog box and you can complete the contact information as explained in this section. (You cannot enter duplicate addresses.)

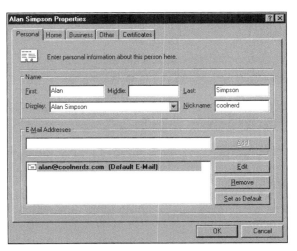

Figure 25-33: Sample entry for the Personal tab of the Windows Address Book

You can type in any person's name and (if applicable) e-mail address. For example, in Figure 25-33, I've typed a sample using my own name and e-mail address.

If the person has several e-mail addresses, you can type one at a time, clicking the Add button to record each one. The first address you enter is automatically assigned as the default e-mail address. You can change that, however, by clicking the e-mail address you'll send to most often, and then clicking the Set As Default button. If you want to remove an e-mail address from the list, click it, and then click the Remove button. To change an e-mail address, click it, click the Edit button, change the address, and press Enter.

The Home, Business, Notes, and Certificates tabs enable you to record additional information about this person. For example, in Figure 25-34, I've typed some sample information into the Home tab.

As explained under "Customizing the default mail options," you can have your address book updated automatically with the address of every e-mail message to which you respond. And if you already have an address book in Eudora Light, Microsoft Exchange, Microsoft Internet Mail for Windows 3.1, Netscape, or a comma-separated text file, you can import it into your Windows Address Book and save yourself a bunch of time as explained in "Importing and exporting address books."

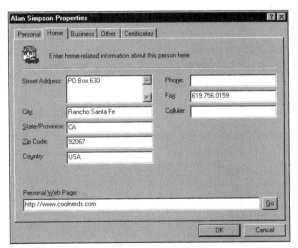

Figure 25-34: More sample information for one person in the Windows Address Book

Creating groups and mailing lists

Suppose you have a group of friends who like to receive jokes by e-mail, or you're organizing a family reunion, or maybe you're a project leader. When sending e-mail to all these folks, you certainly won't want to specify each person's e-mail address individually. Instead, you'll want to enter the name of a group — such as *Joke list*, or *Reunion list*, or *Project team* — and have Outlook Express automatically know to send your message to each address on the list. Creating a group of e-mail addresses is easy. As always, begin by opening the Windows Address Book. Then follow these steps:

1. Click the New Group button on the Windows Address Book toolbar, or choose File ➪ New Group from the menu bar, or press Ctrl+G. A Properties dialog box will appear (Figure 25-35 shows a completed example).

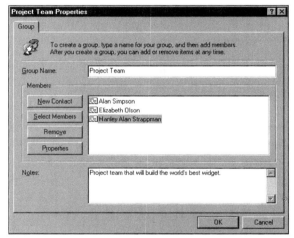

Figure 25-35: A completed group in the Windows Address Book

2. In the Group Name box, type the name for your group (for example, **Project Team**).

3. Do any of the following, as needed:

   • To select addresses already in your Address Book, click the Select Members button, and then double-click the names of the people or groups you want to add to your group. When you finish, click OK.

   • To create a new address book entry on the fly and add it to the group, click the New Contact button, fill in the Properties dialog box (shown back in Figure 25-33), and click OK.

   • To remove an entry from the group, click it, and then click the Remove button. This does not remove the entry from your address book, just from the group itself.

   • To update the details about any group member, click the member's entry, and then click the Properties button (or double-click the member's entry). Edit the entry as needed and click OK.

4. If you want to add some notes about the group, click in the Notes box and type away.

5. When you finish creating the group, click OK in the Properties dialog box.

The group name will appear in the Windows Address Book in boldface text, with a little project icon beside it. If you point to the project name with your mouse, a list of the group members will appear near the mouse pointer.

You can point to any entry in the address book and Outlook Express will display the name and e-mail address near the mouse pointer. Very cool!

Changing and deleting address book entries

Of course, you'll probably need to change the entries in your address book occasionally. It's easy. First, open the Windows Address Book and click the entry you want to change. Then, click the Properties button on the Windows Address Book toolbar, or choose File ➪ Properties from the menu bar, or press Alt+Enter. As a shortcut, you can double-click the entry you want to change. Now change the entry using the same techniques you used to create it in the first place. When you finish, click OK to return to the Windows Address Book window.

To delete an entry, highlight it in the Windows Address Book. Or, if you want to delete multiple entries, select them by using the same Shift+click or Ctrl+click techniques discussed earlier under "Working with several messages at once." Then, click the Delete button on the Windows Address Book toolbar, or choose File ➪ Delete from the menu bar, or press the Delete key. When prompted for confirmation, click Yes. Poof, the entries are gone.

Searching the address book

As your address book grows, you might have trouble finding a particular entry simply by scrolling up and down. But it's no problem at all because several ways exist to search for entries. The easiest method is to click in the Type name or Select from List box, and then type any part of the name or e-mail address for which you're looking. As you type, Outlook Express selects and displays matching entries. The more information you type, the narrower the search. In Figure 25-36, for example, I typed **son** and Outlook Express matched the names Simp**son** and Ol**son**. To restore the entire list, simply delete the text in the Type name or Select from List box.

You can also find entries quickly by sorting your address book. The techniques are similar to those already discussed under "Sorting the message list." To sort by a particular column, click the column heading button (click it again to reverse the sort order). You also can choose options from the View ➪ Sort By menu.

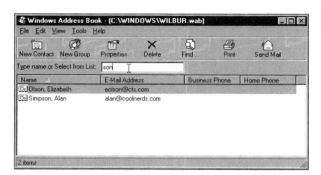

Figure 25-36: Searching for people whose names contain "son"

Doing fancy Find People searches

You can do an even fancier Find People search of your Windows Address Book or various online directory services. To begin, click the Find button in the Windows Address Book toolbar, or choose Edit ⇨ Find from the menu bar, or press Ctrl+F. When the Find People dialog box appears, click the name of the address book or directory you want to search in the Search list, fill in the blanks with the text you want to look for in the Look for list, and then click Find Now. (If you chose an online directory service, you may be prompted to connect to the Internet.) Figure 25-37 shows the results of searching for Alan Simpson in the Four11 online directory.

More Info You'll learn more about online directory services in the later section "Using online directory services."

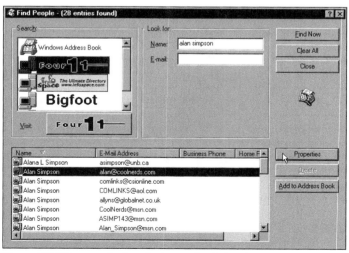

Figure 25-37: Here is the Find People dialog box after choosing the Four11 directory, typing "alan simpson" in the Name box, and then clicking Find Now.

You can work with any address shown at the bottom of the Find People dialog box. First, click the entry to highlight it. Then . . .

✦ To view or change the entry, click the Properties button or double-click the entry.

✦ To delete the entry, click the Delete button or press Delete, and then choose Yes to confirm the deletion (available only if you're searching the Windows Address Book).

✦ To add the entry to your Windows Address Book, click the Add To Address Book button (available only if you're searching an online directory service).

If you want to do a new search, click the Clear All button, and then choose an address book or directory to search, fill in the boxes under Look for, and click Find Now. When you finish using the Find People dialog box, click Close and you'll return to the Windows Address Book.

Choosing recipients from your address book

Several ways exist to choose recipients from your address book when you're composing a new message, replying to a message, or forwarding a message.

If you're starting from the Windows Address Book, select the addresses you want to include in the To: box of a new message. You can use the click, Shift+click, and Ctrl+click selection methods discussed earlier. Now click the Send Mail button on the toolbar or choose File ➪ Send Mail. A New Message window will open and the To: box will include the addresses you selected.

If you're starting from the New Message window, the Reply window, or the Forward window, click the little Rolodex card next to the To:, Cc:, or Bcc: box. You'll see a Select Recipients dialog box like the one shown in Figure 25-38. From here you can take any of the following actions as needed:

✦ To select the name(s) you want from the Name list, use the click, Shift+click, and Ctrl+click methods described earlier under "Working with several messages at once." Then, click the To—>, Cc—>, or Bcc—> button depending on whether you want to add the names to the To:, Cc:, or Bcc: address boxes in your message.

✦ To narrow the Name list, click in the Type Name or Select from List box and type any part of the name or e-mail address (see "Searching the address book"). Now select the names you want, and then click the To—>, Cc—>, or Bcc—> button as appropriate.

✦ To do a fancy Find People search, click the Find button and do a Find People search (see "Doing fancy Find People searches). Select the names you want, and then click the To—>, Cc—>, or Bcc—> button as appropriate.

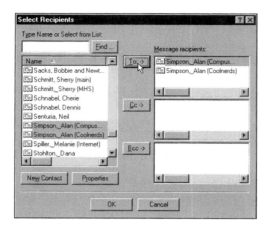

Figure 25-38: The Select Recipients dialog box after selecting two recipients and clicking the To—> button

When you've finished using the Select Recipients dialog box, click OK. The e-mail recipient names you selected will appear in the address boxes of your message. (If you added a name by accident, simply click the name in the address box to select it and then press the Delete key.)

Now that you're an ace with your address book, why not try this great shortcut for specifying e-mail recipients? It works anytime you're using the New Message window, the Reply window, or the Forward window.

1. Click in the To:, Cc:, or Bcc: box of the message as usual.

2. Type any part of a name or e-mail address that you know is in your address book. For example, type **alan** or **simpson** or **coolnerds** if you've entered my name and e-mail address in your address book. If you want to enter more than one recipient, type a semicolon, and then type the next name or e-mail address.

3. Repeat Steps 1 and 2 as needed.

4. When you finish entering names, click the Check Names button on the toolbar, or press Ctrl+K, or choose Tools ⇨ Check Names from the menu bar.

Outlook Express will do its best to match and fill in the names you chose. If it needs your help to decide which address to include, you'll see a Check Names dialog box, as shown in Figure 25-39. Click the address you want to use and then click OK (or click Show More Names, highlight the name you want, and then click OK).

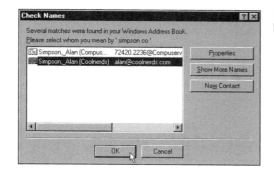

Figure 25-39: The Check Names dialog box

Printing your address book

Who ever said you can't take it with you? If they were talking about the Windows Address Book, they were wrong. You can easily print a paper copy of your address book to take on a trip or drop into your little black book by following these steps:

1. Open the Windows Address Book (click the Address Book button on the main Outlook Express toolbar).

2. If you just want to print certain addresses, select them with the usual click, Shift+click, or Ctrl+click methods (or type any part of a name or e-mail address in the Type Name or Select from List box, and then select the entries you want).

3. Click the Print button on the Windows Address Book toolbar, or choose File ➪ Print from the menu bar, or press Ctrl+P.

4. In the Print dialog box (see Figure 25-40), choose a printer, a print range, a print style, and the number of copies to print as needed.

5. Click OK to start printing.

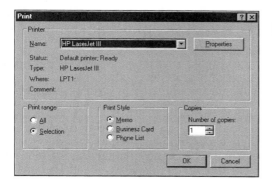

Figure 25-40: The Print dialog box for your Windows Address Book

Using online directory services

The Internet is swarming with online directory services that enable you to look up e-mail addresses. Outlook Express can automatically access four of the most popular online directory services — Bigfoot, Four11, InfoSpace, and WhoWhere — but you can add others, if necessary. Once a directory service is added to the list, you can search that directory from Outlook Express, as explained earlier in "Doing fancy Find People searches."

To view or change the directory list Outlook Express can search, choose File ➪ Directory Services from the Windows Address Book menu bar (or choose Tools ➪ Accounts from the main Outlook Express menu bar, and then click the Directory Service tab in the Internet Accounts dialog box).

If you want to add a new directory service to the list, click the Add button (or click Add, and then choose Directory Service). You'll be taken to the Internet Connection Wizard, which will prompt you for information including the name of the Internet directory service, the Light Directory Access Protocol (LDAP) server, whether the server requires you to log on, and whether you want to check e-mail addresses using this directory service. Fill in each box and click Next or Finish to continue (you may need to contact the directory service if you're uncertain how to fill in the dialog boxes). When you finish adding the service, you'll see it in the list, as shown in Figure 25-41.

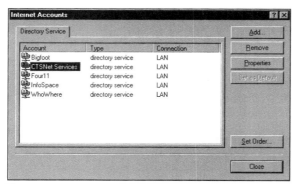

Figure 25-41: The Directory Service tab after adding a new online directory service

Updating the directory service list is easy. First, click the name of the directory service you want to change. Then, click Remove to remove the service from the list, Properties to view or change the settings you assigned in the Internet Connection Wizard, or Set as Default to make this your default account. If you want to change the order used to check names when you send e-mail, click Set Order, move the directory services up or down in the list that appears, and choose OK. When you finish using the Internet Accounts dialog box, click Close.

Although you can have Outlook Express check names against the online directory service when you're sending e-mail, everything will go faster if you search the online directory occasionally and add selected addresses to your local Windows Address Book (as explained in "Doing fancy Find People searches").

Backing up your address book

Just as you'll want to back up your message folders, you'll also want to back up your Windows Address Book. The Windows Address Book is stored in two files named `c:\windows\`*username*`.wa~` and `c:\windows\`*username*`.wab`, where *username* is your e-mail name or network user name.

Even a large address book like mine will fit conveniently on a floppy disk, so compressing the address book files before backing them up isn't important. Simply use My Computer, Windows Explorer, or Find to open the C:\Windows folder. Then select the two address book files and copy them to your backup disk.

Importing and exporting address books

If you used another e-mail program before switching to Outlook Express Mail, you probably already have a bunch of addresses stored in an address book. Back in the bad old days, switching to a new e-mail program was a major pain; you had to re-enter all your contact information from scratch. There was no way to import existing addresses into the new address book. Fortunately, those bad old days are over, at least where Outlook Express is concerned. You can import address books from several different e-mail programs into the Windows Address Book. Likewise, you can export your Windows Address Book to a file many other e-mail programs can import and use in *their* address books.

Importing an address book

To import an address book from another e-mail program into your Windows Address Book, follow these steps:

1. Choose File ➪ Import ➪ Address Book from the main Outlook Express menu bar. Or, open the Windows Address Book and choose Tools ➪ Import ➪ Address Book.

2. When the Windows Address Book Import Tool dialog box appears, click the import format you want. Your choices are shown in Figure 25-42.

3. Click Import.

4. Respond to any dialog boxes that appear next. The prompts will depend upon your choice for the import format in Step 2.

5. When you see the message `Address book import has completed successfully`, click OK, and then click Close to exit the Windows Address Book Import Tool dialog box.

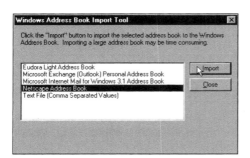

Figure 25-42: The Windows Address Book Import Tool dialog box

When you import address books (or vCards), Outlook Express will check to see whether an address you're importing already exists in your Windows Address Book. If it does, you'll be asked whether you want to replace the old entry with the new one. Choose Yes to replace the old entry or No to keep it.

The next time you open your Windows Address Book, it will include any addresses you had before, plus all the addresses you imported.

Exporting your Windows Address Book

Exporting your Windows Address Book to a format another e-mail program can use is equally easy:

1. Choose File ⇨ Export ⇨ Address Book from the main Outlook Express menu bar. Or, open the Windows Address Book and choose Tools ⇨ Export ⇨ Address Book.

2. When the Windows Address Book Export Tool dialog box appears, click the export format you want. Your choices are Microsoft Exchange (Outlook) Personal Address Book, and Text File (Comma Separated Values). Most e-mail programs can import comma-separated value text files if they can import any files at all. Click Export.

3. Respond to any additional dialog boxes that appear. The prompts will depend on your choice for the export format in Step 2.

4. When you see the message `Address book export has completed successfully`, click OK, and then click Close to exit the Windows Address Book Export Tool dialog box.

By default, Outlook Express creates the Microsoft Exchange (Outlook) Personal Address Book in the file `C:\Exchange\Mailbox.pab` and it exports the Text File (Comma Separated Values) address book to the C:\Windows folder. When exporting to a text file, be sure to specify the .csv file extension.

Importing and exporting vCards

vCards are a standardized electronic business card that can be exchanged between e-mail, address book, communications, personal planner, and other types of programs. vCards can even be exchanged between different types of devices and platforms, including desktop computers, laptops, personal digital assistants (PDAs), and telephony equipment. Thus, vCard files (which have a .vcf file extension) offer a flexible, universal format, something like Esperanto for the computerized address book world.

Outlook Express can import and export vCard files with ease. (Unfortunately, you can import or export just one vCard at a time, not an entire address book. Oh, well.)

Importing from vCards

Follow these steps to import an address from a vCard file into your Windows Address Book:

1. Open the Windows Address Book and choose Tools ➪ Import ➪ vCard from the menu bar.

2. When prompted for a filename, locate and double-click the vCard file you want to import.

The selected address appears in a Properties dialog box like the one you use to create new e-mail addresses. Enter any additional information you want on the Personal, Home, Business, Other, or Certificates tab, and then click OK. Voila! The new address appears in your address book.

Exporting to vCards

To export an address from your Windows Address Book to a vCard file, follow these steps:

1. Open the Windows Address Book.

2. Select the address you want to export. You can select only one address and groups aren't allowed.

3. Choose Tools ➪ Export ➪ vCard from the menu bar.

4. When prompted for a filename, type a filename for the address (for example, Alan.vcf) and choose a drive and folder location, if you wish.

5. Click Save.

The selected address is saved in vCard format to the location you specified in Step 4.

Personalizing Outlook Express Mail

Many ways exist to personalize both the appearance and behavior of Outlook Express Mail to your liking. First we'll look at ways to customize the Outlook Express window. Then we'll explore ways to change the program's behavior, to create folders, and to filter incoming messages using the Inbox Assistant.

Customizing the Outlook Express window

Throughout this chapter, I've shown you examples of the default Outlook Express window in which the toolbar, status bar, folder list, and message header are visible, the text appears in a medium-sized font, and the preview pane appears horizontally across the bottom of the window. You'll probably find the default setup easiest to use, but you certainly can change things, if you like.

Choosing what appears in the window

You can use options on the View menu of the main Outlook Express window to choose which features appear onscreen. The following options on the View menu are toggles: When checked, the feature appears on the screen; when unchecked, the feature is hidden:

✦ **View** ➪ **Toolbar**: Shows or hides the toolbar.

✦ **View** ➪ **Status Bar**: Shows or hides the status bar at the bottom of the window.

✦ **View** ➪ **Folder List**: Shows or hides the list of folders at the left side of the window.

✦ **View** ➪ **Preview Pane** ➪ **Header Information**: Shows or hides the preview pane's header information (the gray strip just above the message). This option isn't available when the preview pane is hidden.

Arranging the preview pane

The preview pane enables you to preview your message by clicking it in the message list. You can hide the preview pane altogether or display it in a vertical or horizontal fashion.

✦ To hide the preview pane, choose View ➪ Preview Pane ➪ None from the main Outlook Express menu bar. When the preview pane is hidden, you must double-click a message in the message list to read it.

✦ To split the window so the preview pane is arranged vertically (see Figure 25–43), choose View ➪ Preview Pane ➪ Split Vertically.

✦ To split the window so the preview pane is arranged horizontally (as shown throughout this chapter *except* in Figure 25-43), choose View ➪ Preview Pane ➪ Split Horizontally.

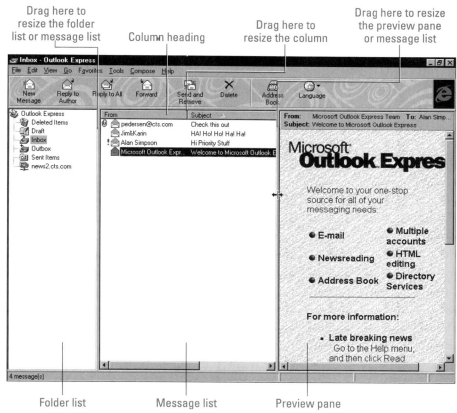

Figure 25-43: The Outlook Express screen with the preview pane arranged vertically and the mouse pointer poised to resize the preview pane

Resizing the lists, panes, and columns

You can resize the lists, preview pane, or columns for easier viewing of the information they contain. Here's how:

1. Move the mouse pointer to the dividing line for the pane or the column you want to resize. The mouse pointer changes to a two-headed arrow or to a two-headed arrow and crosshair (see Figure 25-43).

2. Drag the mouse in the direction of the arrows. As you drag, you'll see a dotted outline.

3. When the dotted outline indicates the size you want, release the mouse button.

That's it! If you don't like the results, simply repeat these three steps.

Configuring columns in the message list

In addition to resizing the columns, you can add or remove columns in the message list or reposition them by following these steps:

1. Choose <u>V</u>iew ⇨ <u>C</u>olumns from the main Outlook Express menu bar. You'll see the Columns dialog box, shown in Figure 25-44.

2. Do any of the following:

   - To add a column to the message list, click the column you want to add under A<u>v</u>ailable columns, and then click <u>A</u>dd (or double-click the column name under A<u>v</u>ailable <u>C</u>olumns).

   - To remove a column from the message list, click its name under Di<u>s</u>played columns, and then click <u>R</u>emove (or double-click the column name in the Di<u>s</u>played columns list).

   - To reposition a column in the message list, click its name under Di<u>s</u>played columns, and then click Move <u>U</u>p or Move <u>D</u>own as needed (this moves the column heading to the left or right, respectively, in the actual message list.)

   - To return to the default columns for the message list, click the R<u>e</u>set button.

3. Click OK.

The new list of columns will appear in the Outlook Express message list. If necessary, you can resize the columns as explained in the previous section.

Hot Stuff If you only want to reposition an existing column, you can skip the Columns dialog box altogether and use the drag-and-drop technique. That is, drag the column button left or right along the top of the message list until the column is where you want it, and then release the mouse button.

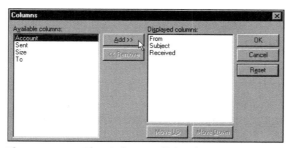

Figure 25-44: The Columns dialog box

Customizing the toolbar

The main Outlook Express toolbar is customizable. You can add or remove its buttons, change its position, and choose whether to display its text labels and background swirls. To begin, go to the main Outlook Express window and choose Tools ➪ Customize Toolbar or right-click the toolbar, and then choose options from the submenu that appears. Figure 25-45 shows the Tools ➪ Customize Toolbar menu and submenu. You can experiment with the alignment options and turn the text labels and background on and off by clicking the submenu option you want.

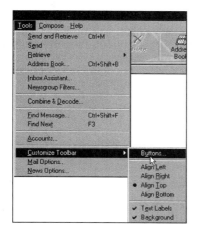

Figure 25-45: The Tools ➪ Customize Toolbar menu and submenu

If you want to add, remove, or reorganize the toolbar buttons, choose the Buttons option on the submenu. You'll see the Customize Toolbar dialog box shown in Figure 25-46. The techniques for customizing the toolbar buttons are similar to those for customizing the columns in the message list. You can double-click a button under Available buttons to add it to the toolbar or double-click a button under Toolbar buttons to remove it. To reposition a button, click it under Toolbar buttons, and then click the Move Up or Move Down button, as needed. Anytime you want to return to the default toolbar, click Reset. When you've finished making changes, click Close.

Hot Stuff As a shortcut, you can drag the items from the Available buttons list to the Toolbar buttons list, and vice versa. You also can drag items in the Toolbar buttons list up or down to reposition them.

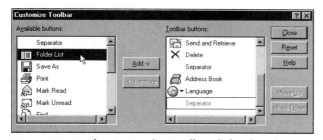

Figure 25-46: The Customize Toolbar dialog box

Customizing the default mail options

Tons of options exist for customizing the way Outlook Express behaves, and they're all available from the Mail Options dialog box. To open this dialog box, choose Tools ➪ Mail Options from the main Outlook Express menu. Next, click the tab you want to use, change the settings as needed, and then click OK to save your changes. In the following sections, we'll look at the Send, Read, Spelling, and Signature tabs in the Mail Options dialog box.

You can learn more about any option in the Mail Options dialog box. Simply select the tab you want to use, click the ? button at the upper-right corner of the dialog box, and then click the option for which you need help. A description will appear near the mouse pointer. To clear the description, press Esc.

Send options

Figure 25-47 shows the Send tab of the Mail Options dialog box. As you can see, the Mail sending settings area on this tab controls what happens when you send a message. Check or clear the boxes as needed.

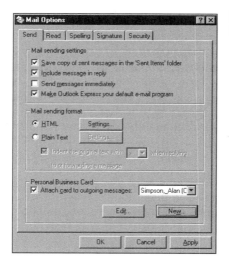

Figure 25-47: The Send tab of the Mail Options dialog box

The default format for sending mail is HTML, but you can select either HTML or Plain Text in the Mail sending format area, and then click the appropriate Settings button to change the settings as needed.

If you want to change the format of a message in which you're currently working, choose Format ➪ Rich Text (HTML) or Format ➪ Plain Text from the menu bar on the New Message, Reply, or Forward window.

If you want to attach a personal business card to each message you send, check the Attach card to outgoing messages option, and then select a contact from the drop-down list in the Personal Business Card area. You can edit the selected contact or create a new one by clicking the Edit or New button, respectively.

Read options

The options on the Read tab of the Mail Options dialog box (see Figure 25-48) control what happens when Outlook Express delivers new mail from your e-mail service provider. You can choose whether to play a sound when new messages arrive, whether to mark previewed messages as read and how long to wait before marking them, whether to check for new messages automatically and how often to check, whether to empty deleted messages from the Deleted Items folder when you exit Outlook Express, and whether to put e-mail addresses of people you reply to in your Windows Address Book automatically. You also can choose the font used to display your messages.

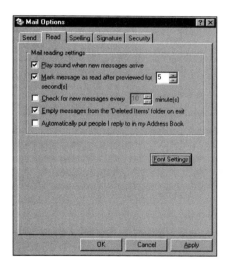

Figure 25-48: The Read tab of the Mail Options dialog box

Spelling options

If you want to customize the default spell checking options, flip to the Spelling tab of the Mail Options dialog box (see Figure 25-49). Here you can choose whether to suggest replacements for misspelled words always, and whether to check spelling before sending your messages. You also can choose the types of words to ignore during spell checking and the language to use for spell checking.

To add your own words to the custom Outlook Express dictionary or to delete words you added during a spell check, click the Edit custom dictionary button, and then click OK. The file named `C:\Windows\Msapps\Proof\Custom.dic` will appear in a Notepad window and you can add and remove words as needed. When you finish editing the dictionary, choose File ➪ Exit from the Notepad window or click the Close (X) button on the Notepad window.

More Info See "Spell checking your message" earlier in this chapter for more information about using the spell checker and changing its options.

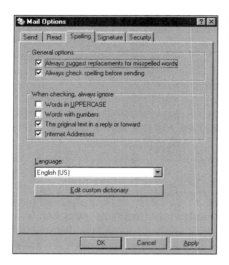

Figure 25-49: The Spelling tab of the Mail Options dialog box

Automatic signature options

Outlook Express can automatically insert a signature at the bottom of your messages, which will save you time and trouble. To use the automatic signature options, switch to the Signature tab in the Mail Options dialog box. Now choose one of these Signature options:

✦ **No signature**: Do not use an automatic signature. You'll have to sign the messages yourself.

✦ **Text**: Automatically sign messages using text you typed in the box next to the Text option (see Figure 25-50).

✦ **File**: Automatically sign messages using text in the file specified next to the File option. (You can use the Browse button to help locate and insert the filename.) The signature file can be a text file (.txt) or an HTML file (.htm or .html).

Finally, choose whether to add the signature to the end of all outgoing messages and whether to include or omit the signature in replies and forwards.

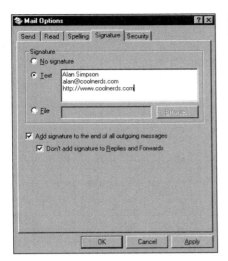

Figure 25-50: The Signature tab of the Mail Options dialog box

If you set up a signature text or file, you can manually insert your signature in a message. Starting from the New Message, Reply, or Forward window, position the insertion point where the signature should appear in the editing area of your message. Then click the Insert Signature button on the toolbar or choose Insert ⇨ Signature from the menu bar.

Leaving mail on the server

You already know how to customize your e-mail account settings by changing the settings in the mail account Properties dialog box, which opens when you choose Tools ⇨ Accounts and double-click the name of the account you want to change. The Advanced tab in this dialog box offers a Leave a copy of messages on server option (see Figure 25-51). Most e-mail client programs have a similar option. As a general rule, if you use only one e-mail program, you'll want to leave that option deselected (unchecked) to keep mail from building up on your mail server.

If you use more than one program to check your e-mail, however, you should allow only *one* of those programs to remove the mail from the server. Otherwise, you may end up with some e-mail messages in one e-mail client program and some messages in another, which makes keeping track of messages difficult. If you choose to leave a copy of messages on the server, you also can choose when to delete the messages as Figure 25-51 shows.

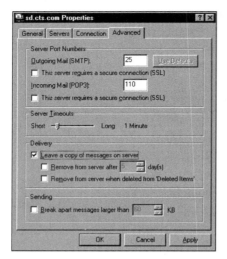

Figure 25-51: The Advanced tab of the mail account Properties dialog box enables you to choose whether to leave mail on your server and when to remove it.

Creating your own folders

Outlook Express Mail automatically comes with the following folders for storing your e-mail messages:

✦ **Deleted Items**: Stores your deleted messages until you delete them manually or Outlook Express deletes them for you.

✦ **Draft**: Stores draft messages you've saved with the File ➪ Save command while composing them.

✦ **Inbox**: Stores your incoming messages.

✦ **Outbox**: Stores messages waiting to be sent.

✦ **Sent Items**: Stores messages you already sent.

Chances are, though, you'll want to create some folders of your own to store copies of messages regarding specific projects or people. Folders offer a great way to organize your messages so you can find them easily.

Creating folders is a breeze. Here are the steps to follow:

1. Starting from the main Outlook Express window, choose File ➪ Folder ➪ New Folder from the menu. Or right-click any folder except the "news" folder and choose New Folder from the shortcut menu. You'll see a Create Folder dialog box, as shown in Figure 25-52.

2. In the Folder name box, type a name for the new folder.

3. Click the folder that should contain the new folder (that is, click the parent folder). If the parent folder is hidden within a higher-level folder, click the plus sign (+) next to the higher-level folders until you see the parent folder you want; then click the parent folder.

4. Choose OK.

In Figure 25-52, I've already created one folder named Coolnerds Correspondence under the Outlook Express folder and another E-Mail Project folder inside Coolnerds Correspondence. To add a folder named News Project inside the Coolnerds Correspondence folder, I typed the new folder name into the Folder name box, and then I clicked the Coolnerds Correspondence folder and chose OK.

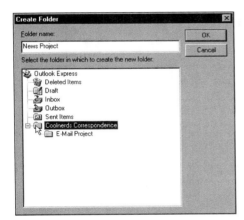

Figure 25-52: I'm about to create a new folder just below the Coolnerds Correspondence folder.

Using folders and subfolders

Any folders you create will appear in the folder list at the left side of the main Outlook Express window. Here's how to expand, collapse, and open a folder in the folder list:

✦ To expand a folder so its folders or subfolders are visible in the folders list, double-click the folder icon (for example Coolnerds Correspondence, in Figure 25-53) or click the + sign next to the icon.

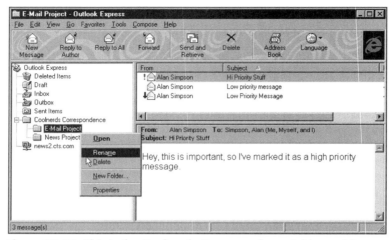

Figure 25-53: This is the Coolnerds Correspondence folder and its two subfolders. I right-clicked the E-Mail Project folder to display the shortcut menu.

✦ To collapse a folder so its folders or subfolders are hidden, double-click the folder icon or click the - sign next to the icon.

✦ To open a folder so you can see its contents in the message list, click the folder icon (or right-click it and choose Open).

You can rename, delete, move, and copy any folder you create. Use these techniques:

✦ To rename a folder, open the folder. Then right-click it and choose Rename, or choose File ➪ Folder ➪ Rename from the menu bar. Type a new folder name and choose OK.

✦ To delete a folder and the messages it contains, open the folder. Then, press the Delete (Del) key on your keyboard or right-click the folder and choose Delete. You also can choose File ➪ Folder ➪ Delete from the menu bar. When prompted for confirmation, choose Yes.

✦ To move a folder and its contents to another folder, click the folder you want to move and choose File ➪ Folder ➪ Move To. When prompted, click the new parent folder and choose OK. You also can move a folder by dragging it to the desired parent folder in the folder list.

✦ To copy a folder and its contents to another folder, click the folder you want to copy and choose File ➪ Folder ➪ Copy To. When prompted, click the new parent folder and choose OK.

More Info See "Working with several messages at once" earlier in this chapter for information about moving and copying messages between folders.

Using the Inbox Assistant

Suppose someone has been sending you annoying e-mail messages and you want to delete that person's messages without reading them. Or perhaps you want to move or copy certain messages automatically to specific folders. Or maybe you want to send an automatic reply, such as

```
Gone fishin' and I won't be back until the twelfth of never.
```

to some or all of the messages you receive. All this and more is possible with a little help from the Inbox Assistant, a tool that enables you to set up rules and actions to take when Outlook Express delivers your incoming mail. Once you get the hang of using the Inbox Assistant (and it won't take long!), you'll appreciate the amount of time it saves you.

To add a new rule, follow these steps:

1. Choose <u>T</u>ools ➪ <u>I</u>nbox Assistant from the main Outlook Express menu bar.

2. Click the <u>A</u>dd button in the Inbox Assistant dialog box (shown later). You'll be taken to a Properties dialog box that resembles Figure 25-54 when filled in.

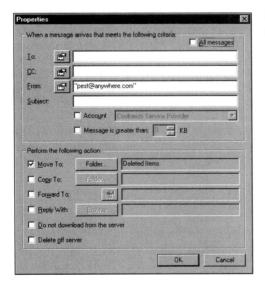

Figure 25-54: Setting up the criteria and actions for incoming messages

3. In the upper portion of the dialog box, specify one or more criteria a message must meet for the Inbox Assistant to take an automatic action. In Figure 25-54, the Inbox Assistant will match messages from pest@anywhere.com.

4. In the lower portion of the dialog box, specify one or more actions to take when retrieving new messages that satisfy the criteria. The example shown in Figure 25-54 will automatically move any messages from pest@anywhere.com to my Deleted Items folder so I never have to see them.

5. Click OK. You'll be returned to the Inbox Assistant dialog box and your new rule will appear in the Description list, as in Figure 25-55.

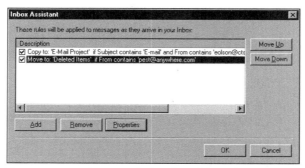

Figure 25-55: The Description list of the Inbox Assistant after setting up some rules

You can repeat Steps 2–5 to set up as many rules as you need and you can adjust the rules, as I will explain in a moment. When you're happy with the list as it is, click OK. The next time you receive new messages, the Inbox Assistant will process any messages that match the criteria you set up.

Here are some points to remember about the Inbox Assistant:

✦ The Inbox Assistant processes only the rules checked in the Description list. It ignores rules that appear in the Description list, but aren't checked.

✦ If an incoming message matches more than one rule, the Inbox Assistant will process it according to the first rule it matches and ignore the others. (Of course, if you've set up multiple actions in a single rule, the Inbox Assistant will take all the actions you requested.)

You can adjust the rules in the Inbox Assistant dialog box at any time:

✦ To turn off a rule temporarily, deselect (clear) the check box next to the rule. To turn the rule back on again, check the box once more. Turning off a rule and turning it back on is easier than removing the rule and recreating it later.

✦ To remove a rule permanently, click it in the Description list, and then click the Remove button. Watch out! No prompt exists for confirmation. The rule is history the moment you click Remove.

✦ To change a rule, click it in the Description list, and then click the Properties button (or double-click the rule's description). The Properties box will open and you can change any criteria or actions you want.

✦ To move a rule up or down in the Description list (and thus change the order in which the Inbox Assistant processes the rules), click the rule you want to move, and then click the Move Up or Move Down button as needed.

Summary

Well, folks. That's about it for using Outlook Express Mail. As you've seen, it's a powerful program that can simplify your electronic correspondence in dozens of ways. In the next chapter, we'll explore some more Internet goodies. But first, let's review the salient points covered in this chapter:

✦ Outlook Express Mail comes with Microsoft Internet Explorer 4 and is installed automatically with that program.

✦ To start Outlook Express Mail from the Windows 95 desktop, click its icon just to the right of the Windows 95 Start button, or click the Start button and choose Programs ➪ Outlook Express Mail.

✦ To start Outlook Express Mail from within Microsoft Internet Explorer 4, click the Mail button in its toolbar and choose Read Mail or New Message.

✦ To configure Outlook Express Mail to your own e-mail account(s), start Outlook Express Mail and choose Tools ➪ Accounts and click the Mail tab. Use the Add button to add a new account.

✦ To compose a new mail message, click the New Message button in its toolbar, or press Ctrl+N, or choose Compose ➪ New Message from the menu bar. You'll be taken to a New Message window where you can compose your message.

✦ To send a composed message, click the Send button in the New Message window, or choose File ➪ Send Message from its menu bar. The message will be placed in the Outbox, but not actually sent yet.

✦ To send all new messages to their recipients, choose Tools ➪ Send from Outlook Express Mail's menu bar. Optionally, choose Tools ➪ Send and Retrieve, or click the Send and Retrieve button in the toolbar, to send all pending messages, and to download (receive) any new incoming messages you haven't seen yet.

✦ To check for new incoming mail in Outlook Express Mail, click the Send and Retrieve button in its toolbar, or choose Tools ➪ Retrieve from its menu bar. Make sure to select the Inbox folder in the left column.

✦ To read a message, click it. The message content appears in the lower-right pane of Outlook Express Mail's window.

✦ Two ways exist to reply to the message you're currently reading. If you want to reply to only the author, click the Replay To Author button in the toolbar or choose Compose ➪ Reply to Author from the menu bar. Or, to reply to everyone who received this message, choose Reply to All.

✦ To delete the message you just read, click the Delete button in the toolbar or choose Edit ➪ Delete.

✦ To create and use an address book, click the Windows 95 Start button and choose Programs ➪ Windows Address Book. Or, if you're already in Outlook Express Mail, click the Address Book button in the toolbar.

✦   ✦   ✦

Participating in Usenet Newsgroups

Usenet, like the World Wide Web, is a service provided by the Internet. To take advantage of Usenet, you need an Internet account with access to Usenet newsgroups and a newsreader program, such as Microsoft Express News, which comes with the Internet Explorer 4 Suite. Usenet is divided into many electronic bulletin boards, or *newsgroups*, where people gather to discuss a particular topic. The term *newsgroup,* however, is a little strange, because they're not about news. Instead, a newsgroup is sort of a forum where people with similar interests can share ideas, exchange information, ask questions, and post answers. Each newsgroup consists of messages written by members using software that's similar to an e-mail program.

Newsgroup Factoids and Buzzwords

Newsgroups and e-mail are similar in many ways. For example, both are used to send messages electronically between networked computers. The techniques for composing, reading, and replying to e-mail and newsgroup messages are almost identical. Still, there are some important differences and a few newsgroup facts and buzzwords you should know.

More Info Please be sure to read Chapter 25, which explains how to send and receive electronic mail with Outlook Express. Once you know the basics of using e-mail, you'll know how to use newsgroups practically by osmosis.

First, some differences between e-mail messages and newsgroup messages:

✦ Unlike e-mail messages, which go to specific electronic mailboxes, newsgroup messages go to specific newsgroups and stay there so visitors can read past correspondence between members to find information and get a feel for discussions in progress. Anyone in the newsgroup can read its messages.

And now some buzzwords:

✦ Each message in a newsgroup is sometimes called an *article*, though I'll stick with the term *message* in this book. A series of messages on the same subject is called a *thread*. For example, if I post a message with the subject *Llama Wanted*, I've started a new thread. If anyone replies to my original message or if anyone replies to that reply, all those messages will be part of the same thread. If I later post a new message with the subject *Angora Rabbit Wanted*, I've started a new thread.

✦ Many newsgroups are *moderated* by people who screen messages for suitability to the newsgroup; however, most newsgroups are *unmoderated* and messages pass through unscreened.

✦ *Lurking* is hanging around a newsgroup to see what's being said, without actually contributing anything. When you're new to a newsgroup, lurking for a while is a good idea — to get a feel for what's going on — before you start making contributions.

✦ *Flaming* is sending nasty messages to people in the group. If you don't lurk to find out what's going on in a group and, instead, start making irrelevant contributions, you're likely to get flamed. Also, anything that smacks of advertising in a newsgroup will surely result in a lot of flame mail directed at you!

✦ *Spamming* is sending advertisements to a newsgroup. Highly unacceptable!

✦ *Netiquette* is observing proper newsgroup etiquette by *not* sending irrelevant comments and not spamming the group. A good *netizen* (network citizen) follows proper netiquette.

And finally, some factoids:

✦ Newsgroups come and newsgroups go, and some aren't accessible on every newsgroup server. So don't be concerned if a newsgroup you read about in this book has disappeared by the time you sign on or simply is unavailable.

✦ Some newsgroups contain offensive material. Please do not let your kids wander newsgroups (or any other part of the Internet) unsupervised!

Newsgroup categories

Each newsgroup discusses topics in a specific category. For example, the *alt.humor.puns* newsgroup covers *pun*ishing humor of this ilk:

```
Q: Why were the baby ants confused?
A: Because all their uncles were ants.
```

By contrast, the *rec.food.chocolate* newsgroup discusses the dark, gooey, fat-inducing sweet that has destroyed many a New Year's resolution to shed excess weight.

Danger Zone

Before you post messages to a newsgroup for the first time, spend a while lurking in the newsgroup and absorb the local culture. If you post messages that are inappropriate for the category or the culture, newsgroup members may send you insulting messages in return (flaming). (Never send flame mail to anyone; it's just plain rude!)

Newsgroup categories reflect a hierarchy, starting with the least specific category and ending with the most specific one as you read from left to right. A period (.) separates each subcategory from the next. Using *alt.humor.puns* as an example, the newsgroup name goes from the broad category *alt* (for *alt*ernative topics), to the more specific subcategory of *humor* to the still more specific humor subcategory of *puns*. Table 26-1 presents some examples of top-level categories. Later in this chapter, you'll find out how to display the complete list of newsgroups on your server and how to join any available newsgroup.

Table 26-1
Some Newsgroup Main Categories, Descriptions, and Names

Main Category	Description	Sample Newsgroup Names
Alt	Alternative topics and lifestyles. Some material in this category may be offensive.	alt.humor.puns alt.pets.rabbits alt.test
Bionet	Biology	bionet.microbiology bionet.mycology
Bit	Bitnet, redistribution for BitNet Listserv mailing lists	bit.listserv.autism bit.listserv.movie.memorabilia
Biz	Business	biz.comp.hardware biz.comp.software
Comp	Computers	comp.human-factors comp.jobs
Humanities	Arts and humanities	humanities.classics humanities.music.composers.wagner
Misc	Miscellaneous	misc.books.technical misc.computers.forsale misc.test
News	Usenet news network and software	news.announce.newusers news.answers news.newusers.questions

Main Category	Description	Sample Newsgroup Names
Rec	Arts, hobbies, recreation	rec.food.drink.coffee rec.food.chocolate
Sci	Science	sci.agriculture.beekeeping sci.bio.food-science
Soc	Social topics and socializing	soc.culture.punjab soc.geneology.surnames
Talk	Debates, opinions, and general *yakkety-yak*	talk.environment talk.politics.medicine

A little advice for the newcomer

If you're a newcomer to newsgroups (that is, a newsgroup *newbie*), you should be aware that the Usenet world, like the real world, is something of a jungle, which is home to both benign and malevolent critters. To avoid being bitten by the bad guys and to make your newsgroup safaris as fun as possible, consider these tips:

✦ Learn to use the newsreader software (Outlook Express News) with help from this chapter.

✦ Read the FAQs (frequently asked questions) in the newsgroups you visit and lurk in a newsgroup for a while before posting any messages.

✦ Learn more about how newsgroups work in *news.announce.newusers* and *news.newusers.questions*. If you're still unsure about how to use newsgroups, post a question in *news.newusers.questions*.

✦ Post some test messages in *alt.test* or *misc.test*.

Here's some advice on network etiquette (or *netiquette*) which, if heeded, will make you a better network citizen (or *netizen*) as you post messages to newsgroups:

✦ Post your message to the most appropriate newsgroup only.

✦ Do not ask questions that already are answered in the newsgroup's FAQ message.

✦ Make the Subject line of your message concise, but descriptive, like a headline in a newspaper or magazine.

✦ Keep the message text brief, but don't omit important details or background information that other newsgroup members might not know.

✦ When responding to newsgroup messages, consider responding directly to the author by e-mail if your answer requires some privacy or if it won't interest the entire group.

✦ Never send flames (insulting messages), advertisements, offensive material, chain letters, jokes (unless you're writing for a humor newsgroup), or *anything* illegal to a newsgroup.

✦ If someone is sending you flames or other unwanted messages via the newsgroup or e-mail, ignore them or complain to the author's system administrator.

Spams and scams

Unsolicited e-mail (or spam) that advertise goods or services or are downright scams is a big problem on the Internet. Sooner or later, you're likely to get spammed if you post messages to a bulletin board on an online service or the Internet, post to a Usenet newsgroup, visit chat rooms (as discussed later in this chapter), or are listed in an online service's member directory.

Although you probably can't avoid spam entirely, some ways exist to minimize it. First, you should never respond to the e-mail address of the spammer or to any e-mail address the spammer claims you can use to get yourself off the spam list. Instead, send an e-mail complaint along with a copy of the original spam message to the spam-stopper e-mail address at the *spammer's* Internet service provider. Typically, this e-mail address is `postmaster@spammersDomain`, where you replace `spammersDomain` with the domain of the person sending the spam.

The spammer's domain name is often buried in the header of the message you receive. Look on the From:, X-Sender:, or Sender: line, one of the Received: lines, or other headers that carry machine identification including Message-ID: or Comments. Suppose you receive a message from `slime@spammers-are-us.com` and you're pretty certain `spammers-are-us.com` is the real domain name of the spammer's Internet service provider. In this case, you'd send your complaint and attached spam message to `postmaster@spammers-are-us.com`.

Responding to the demand for less spam in the world, America Online, Netcom, Earthlink, and InterRamp have set up special e-mail addresses for handling complaints about spam originating from their machines. These e-mail addresses are `abuse@aol.com`, `abuse@netcom.com`, and `abuse@interramp.com`, respectively.

To learn more about reading message headers and avoiding spam, point your browser to this finger-twisting URL:

```
http://www.yahoo.com/Computers_and_Internet/Communications_and_
      Networking/Electronic_Mail/Junk_Email/
```

You also can search for *spam* in your favorite search engine, including Yahoo! at `http://www.yahoo.com` or Microsoft's all-in-one search page at `http://home.microsoft.com/access/allinone.asp`.

Starting Outlook Express News

All righty! We're ready to explore newsgroups. Getting started is a breeze, especially if you've already set up your e-mail client as explained in Chapter 25. For the examples in this chapter, I'll assume you've done this already and you're using Microsoft Outlook Express as your e-mail client, Microsoft Internet Explorer 4.0 as your browser, and Microsoft Outlook Express News as your news reader. Of course, you can use any e-mail client, browser, and news reader you want, but the setup will be a little different.

Starting for the first time

Before starting Outlook Express Mail for the first time, you need the same information you needed to set up your Outlook Express Mail e-mail client (see Chapter 25). You also need the name of your Internet news (NNTP) server. You can get all this information from your Internet service provider (ISP).

Hot Stuff For the acronymically aware, NNTP stands for Network News Transfer Protocol, the method your ISP's news host uses to communicate with your news reader. If you don't know the name of your ISP's news server, try Microsoft's news — `servermsnews.microsoft.com` — which offers newsgroups that provide help with Microsoft products.

Now you're ready to start the Outlook Express Mail news reader and set it up. Follow these steps:

1. Connect to the Internet as explained in Chapter 23. Or, if you've set up your computer to dial into the Internet automatically, skip this step and let your computer dial up whenever it needs to (see Chapter 20).

2. Use any of the following methods to start Outlook Express Mail:

   - Starting from the Windows 95 taskbar, click the Start button, and then choose Programs Í Outlook Express News.

   - Starting from Outlook Express (see Chapter 25) or Internet Explorer (see Chapter 24), choose <u>G</u>o ➪ <u>N</u>ews from the menu bar.

   - Starting from Outlook Express, click the Outlook Express icon at the top of the folder list (in the left side of the window), and then click Read News.

   - Starting from Internet Explorer, click the Mail button on the Internet Explorer toolbar, and then choose Read <u>N</u>ews.

3. Because you haven't set up your news server yet, the Internet Connection Wizard will kick in, just as it did when you set up your e-mail account in Outlook Express Mail. Simply read the instructions in each dialog box and answer the questions presented. Click the Next or Finish button to move to the next dialog box. When you finish the last step, the Connection Wizard will download the list of newsgroups available on the server. This may take a while, but you only have to do it once.

4. If you see the message shown in Figure 26-1, click <u>Y</u>es and continue with Step 5. If you don't see the message, you'll be taken to the main Outlook Express News window (shown later) and you can start browsing the newsgroups immediately.

Figure 26-1: This message appears if you haven't subscribed to any newsgroups yet.

5. The Newsgroups dialog box will open (see Figure 26-2). If more than one news server appears in the <u>N</u>ews servers list in the left side of the dialog box, click the name of the server you want to use.

6. In the display <u>N</u>ewsgroups which contain box, type the name (or any part of the name) of the newsgroup you want to join, as shown in Figure 26-2. The list under News groups will match your typing. To start over again with the full list of newsgroups, simply delete the text in the box (for example, by pressing the Backspace key repeatedly).

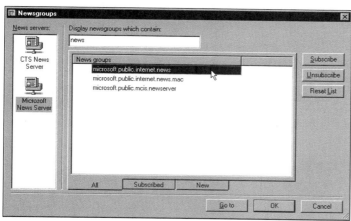

Figure 26-2: The Newsgroups dialog box with Microsoft News Server selected and the word *news* typed in.

7. Scroll through the News groups list until you find the newsgroup you want to join, and then click its name. Now, do one of the following:

- To subscribe to the selected newsgroup, so you can get to it more quickly in the future, click <u>S</u>ubscribe. Then click <u>G</u>o to to open the newsgroup.

- To open the selected newsgroup without subscribing to it first, click <u>G</u>o to.

You'll see the main Outlook Express News window, shown in Figure 26-3. Notice it's almost identical to the Outlook Express Mail window; however its toolbar and menus are for use with newsgroups rather than e-mail. Now you're ready to browse the newsgroups, as explained later under "Browsing Newsgroup Messages."

Anytime you click any of the e-mail folders (for example, Inbox, Outbox, or Sent Items), the toolbar and menus automatically switch to those for Outlook Express Mail and you can use Outlook Express Mail as explained in Chapter 25. To return to the Outlook Express News toolbars and menus from Outlook Express Mail, simply click the name of your news server (or any newsgroup) in the folder list or choose <u>G</u>o ⇨ <u>N</u>ews from the menu bar.

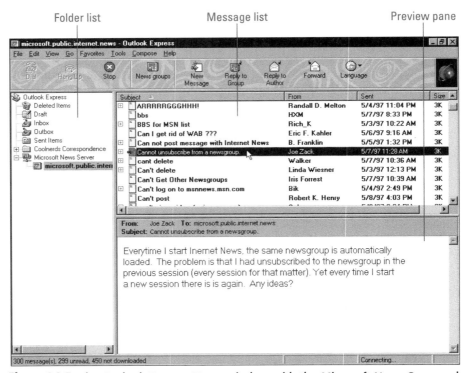

Figure 26-3: The Outlook Express News window with the Microsoft News Server selected and a newsgroup visible

Starting later

Once you set up Outlook Express News, you can start it the same way you started it the first time. That is, connect to the Internet (if you haven't set up your computer to dial automatically) and use any of the methods given in Step 2 of the "Starting for the first time" procedure to fire up the program.

If you subscribed to any newsgroups, you'll be taken directly to the Outlook Express Mail window, shown in Figure 26-3. If you haven't subscribed, simply follow Steps 4–7 of the first-time procedure to choose and/or subscribe to a newsgroup. Like the Outlook Express Mail window described in Chapter 25, the Outlook Express News window usually is divided into three parts:

✦ **Folder list** (at the left): Displays your e-mail folders, your newsgroup server(s), and any newsgroups you've subscribed to or opened during the current session.

✦ **Message list** (at the right): Displays the headers (summary information) of messages in the currently selected newsgroup.

✦ **Preview pane** (below the message list): Displays the contents of the currently selected message.

Browsing Newsgroup Messages

Browsing the newsgroup message is easy. To begin, you must choose the newsgroup you want to read, as explained here:

1. Connect to the Internet and start Outlook Express News, as explained earlier.

2. If you have set up more than one newsgroup server, click the name of the server you want to use in the folder list.

3. Do one of the following, depending on your setup and your whims:

   • If you haven't subscribed to any newsgroups yet, repeat Steps 4–7 of the procedure under "Starting for the first time."

   • If you subscribed to the newsgroup you want to view, click its name in the message list or in the folder list under the server you selected. If the subscribed newsgroups are hidden in the folder list, click the plus sign (+) icon next to the server name, and then click the name of the newsgroup. (The plus sign changes to a minus sign, which you can click to hide the list of newsgroups again.)

   • If you want to view a newsgroup that isn't on your subscription list, return to the Newsgroups dialog box by clicking the News Groups button on the Outlook Express Mail toolbar or choosing Tools ⇨ Newsgroups from the menu bar. Now repeat Steps 5–7 of the procedure under "Starting for the first time."

Once you select the newsgroup you want to read, reading a message is basically the same as reading an e-mail message. Simply click the message you want to view in the message list and the message will appear in the preview pane at the bottom of the screen (see Figure 26-3).

If you prefer to view the message in its own window, simply double-click it in the message list. Figure 26-4 shows an example of a newsgroup message opened in a separate window. When you finish viewing the message, click the Close (X) button in the upper-right corner of the message window, or choose File ➪ Close, or press Alt+F4 to return to the main Outlook Express Mail window.

In the message list, unread messages are boldface and preceded by plain yellow *paper* icons. After you read a message, the boldface is turned off, and the icon turns white with a little pushpin on it (see Figure 26-3).

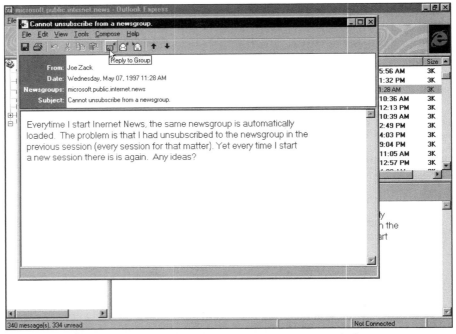

Figure 26-4: A newsgroup message is opened in a separate window.

Replying to newsgroup messages . . . the short of it

Anytime you're viewing a message, you can reply to it in any of the following ways:

✦ Post a reply to this message that anyone in the newsgroup can read. To get started, click the Reply To Group button on the toolbar, or choose Compose ➪ Reply To Newsgroup, or press Ctrl+N.

✦ Post a reply, via e-mail, to the author of the message. Only the author will see your reply. To get started, click the Reply To Author button on the toolbar, or choose Compose ➪ Reply To Author, or press Ctrl+R.

✦ Forward the message to someone else, via e-mail. Only the recipient will see your forwarded message. To get started, click the Forward button on the toolbar, or choose Compose ➪ Forward (or Compose ➪ Forward As Attachment), or press Ctrl+F.

After choosing any of the reply options, you reply to the message as you would any standard e-mail message. When you're ready to send your reply, click the Post Message button on the toolbar (or choose File ➪ Send Message or press Alt+S). See "Replying to newsgroup messages" later in this chapter for more details.

Customizing the Outlook Express News window

The procedures for customizing the Outlook Express News window are identical to those discussed in Chapter 25, "Doing Internet E-Mail." Here are some reminders:

✦ To turn the toolbar, status bar, or folder list on and off, open the View menu and choose Toolbar, Status Bar, or Folder List, respectively.

✦ To position or hide the preview pane, choose options on the View ➪ Preview Pane submenu. Your choices are None, Split Vertically, and Split Horizontally (the default setting).

✦ To show or hide the message header information above the preview pane, choose View ➪ Preview Pane ➪ Header Information.

✦ To reposition the columns in the message list, simply drag the buttons at the top of the message list to the left or right. Or, choose View ➪ Columns from the menu bar and complete the Columns dialog box.

✦ To sort the columns in the message list, click the buttons at the top of message list or right-click a button and choose Sort Ascending or Sort Descending from the shortcut menu. Or, choose View ➪ Sort By from the menu bar and choose an option from the submenu that appears.

Hot Stuff

After sorting the messages by the Subject or From column, you can type the first letter of the Subject or From item you're looking for and quickly highlight the next message that matches that letter.

Limiting the current view and finding messages

If you're viewing a newsgroup that contains many messages, you may become daunted by the sheer number of messages you must wade through and have trouble finding those you really want to read. One way to find messages more quickly is to sort them, as explained previously.

You also can limit the current message view by choosing options on the View ➪ Current View submenu. Here are your submenu choices:

✦ **All Messages:** Displays all messages in the newsgroup.

✦ **Unread Messages**: Displays only the messages you haven't read yet.

✦ <u>**D**</u>**ownloaded Messages**: Displays only the messages you've read so far.

✦ **Replies To My Posts**: Displays replies to messages you have posted.

✦ <u>**F**</u>**iltered Messages:** Displays or hides messages that match group filters you've set up. When Filtered Messages is checked, the headers of messages that match your filters appear in blue and you can easily identify (and ignore) them; when it isn't checked, filtered messages are hidden. See "Filtering Out Unwanted Newsgroup Messages" for details on setting up filters.

You also can use the Find command to find a message. This command works basically the same as it does for e-mail:

1. Go to the newsgroup you want to search.

2. Choose <u>T</u>ools ⇨ <u>F</u>ind Message or press Ctrl+Shift+F. You'll see the Find Message dialog box, shown in Figure 26-5.

3. Specify the From:, Subject, and Posted criteria for which you want to search. In Figure 26-5, I'm searching for messages containing *can't* in the Subject line and posted after May 6, 1997.

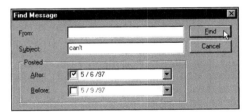

Figure 26-5: The Find Message dialog box in Microsoft Outlook Express News

4. Click <u>F</u>ind.

Find will highlight the first matching message (if it finds one). If you want to look for the next match, choose <u>T</u>ools ⇨ Find Nex<u>t</u> or press F3. You can repeat this step until Outlook Express reports no more messages were found and asks if you want to start over from the top of the click. Click Yes to search again or click No to stop searching.

Viewing, expanding, and collapsing threads

Although the term *threads* might make you think I'm giving a sewing lesson or discussing the latest fashions, I'm not. A *thread* is simply an original message and any posted replies, as shown in Figure 26-6.

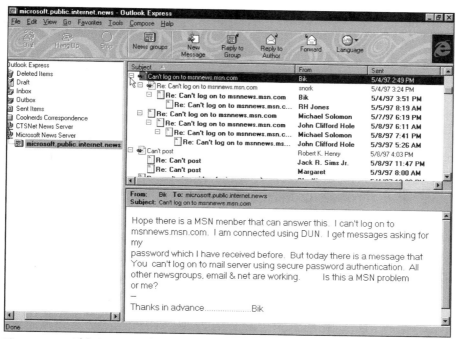

Figure 26-6: This message list is organized in a hierarchy of threads.

Notice the threads are sorted and grouped according to the original title (or *subject*). The top level of each thread shows the original message. Below that, you see responses to the original message and any responses to the responses. As a simple example, suppose I post a message with this subject:

```
Wanted — Purple People Eater
```

My message will be at the top of a new thread. All replies to this message will have the subject:

```
RE: Wanted — Purple People Eater
```

and they'll appear below my original message in the thread.

If someone replies to my message and changes the subject to:

```
Wanted — Purple People Eater. Let's end this thread now! PPEs
        don't exist.
```

that message automatically starts a new thread.

Although it's easiest to work with newsgroups if you group messages into threads, you can flatten out the hierarchy, as shown in Figure 26-7. This way, the message list looks more like the one for Outlook Express Mail.

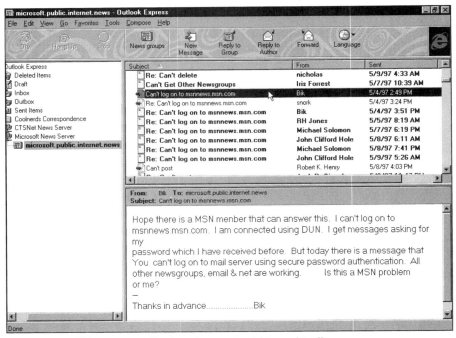

Figure 26-7: This message list is not organized hierarchically.

It's easy to turn the threading display on or off. Just choose <u>V</u>iew ➪ <u>S</u>ort By ➪ <u>G</u>roup Messages By Thread. When the Group Messages By Thread option is checked, the messages appear in a hierarchy, as in Figure 26-6. When it isn't checked, the messages appear in a long flat list, as in Figure 26-7.

When threading is turned on, you can expand or collapse any thread or subthread:

✦ To expand a thread, click the plus sign (+) next to the message icon in the message list. The plus sign changes to a minus sign (-) and the subordinate messages appear in the message list.

✦ To collapse a thread, click the minus sign next to the message's icon in the message list. The minus sign changes to a plus sign and the subordinate messages are hidden in the message list.

Keeping track of what you've read

Remember, unread messages appear in the message list in boldface text and are preceded by yellow icons; read messages are not bold and have a white icon with a pushpin. You can manually stick the pushpin into a message (that is, mark the message as *read*) or remove the pushpin (marking the message as *unread*). You can even mark an entire newsgroup, thread, or selected messages as read or unread. Here's how:

✦ To mark one message as read, click (select) the message and choose Edit ➪ Mark As Read from the menu bar or press Ctrl+Q.

✦ To mark several messages as read, select those messages using the click, Ctrl+click, and Shift+click techniques explained in Chapter 25 (see "Working with several messages at once"). Then, choose Edit ➪ Mark As Read or press Ctrl+Q.

✦ To mark an entire thread as read, select any message in the thread and choose Edit ➪ Mark Thread As Read or press Ctrl+T.

✦ To mark all messages in the newsgroup as read, choose Tools ➪ Mark All As Read.

✦ To mark messages in the newsgroup as unread, select the message or messages. Then choose Tools ➪ Mark As Unread. This option might come in handy if you accidentally marked a message as read or you want to remember to read a message again later.

Instead of using the menu options, you can select one or more messages, right-click the selection, and choose Mark As Read, or Mark Thread As Read, or Mark As Unread from the shortcut menu.

Messages usually are marked as read after you preview them for five seconds. To change this, choose Tools ➪ News Options, click the Read tab, change the setting for the Message Is Read After Being Previewed For *n* Second(s) option, and choose OK.

Replying to newsgroup messages . . . the long of it

You can reply to a newsgroup message you're viewing in several ways as the following sections explain. As you'll see, replying to a newsgroup message is similar to replying to an e-mail message.

Replying to the group

Normally you'll want to send your reply to the original newsgroup, so everyone who visits the group — including the person to whom you're replying — can benefit from your gems of wisdom.

To reply to the group, first make sure you're viewing the message to which you want to reply, either in the message list or in a separate window. That is, make it the current message. Now, follow these steps:

1. Click the Reply To Group button on the toolbar, or choose <u>C</u>ompose ➪ Reply To Newsg<u>r</u>oup from the menu bar, or press Ctrl+G, or right-click the message and choose Reply To Newsgroup from the shortcut menu. A new newsgroup Reply window will appear and the insertion point will be poised above the original message text, ready for you to type your answer (see Figure 26-8).

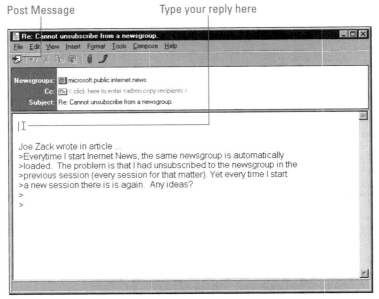

Figure 26-8: Here is a new newsgroup reply window, ready for you to type in your reply.

2. Type the reply as you'd type any standard e-mail reply (see Chapter 25). You also can use the techniques discussed later under "Posting new newsgroup messages" to update the Newsgroups:, Cc:, or Subject: information at the top of the reply and to attach a file, add a signature, or format your message.

3. When you're ready to send the message, click the Post Message button on the toolbar, or choose <u>F</u>ile ➪ <u>S</u>end Message, or press Alt+S.

Eventually your reply will make its way to all servers that carry your newsgroup and you'll see it under the thread for the original message.

Danger Zone Remember, if you change the text in the Subject: box, your reply will start a new thread, and it will be impossible to find for the person who posted the original message.

Replying to the author

Perhaps you'd like to keep your reply a secret from the other members of the newsgroup or maybe the author of a message has specifically asked that you reply via e-mail. In this case, you'll want to reply by e-mail. The steps are similar to those for replying to the newsgroup. As usual, make sure you're viewing the message to which you want to reply. Then, follow these steps:

1. Click the Reply To Author button on the toolbar, or choose <u>C</u>ompose ➪ <u>R</u>eply To Author from the menu bar, or press Ctrl+R, or right-click the message and choose Reply To A<u>u</u>thor from the shortcut menu. A new e-mail Reply window will appear (see Figure 26-9).

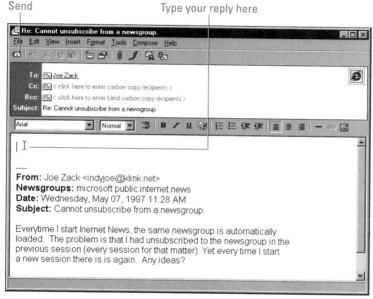

Figure 26-9: This is a new e-mail Reply window, ready for you to type in your reply.

2. Type the reply as you'd type any standard e-mail reply (see Chapter 25). You also can use the techniques discussed in Chapter 25 to update the To:, Cc:, Bcc:, or Subject: information at the top of the reply and to attach a file, add a signature, or format your message.

3. When you're ready to send the message, click the Send button on the toolbar, or choose <u>F</u>ile ➪ <u>S</u>end Message, or press Alt+S.

Your reply will be plopped into your e-mail Outbox (unless you've changed your e-mail settings so messages are sent immediately). To send the messages in your

Outbox, choose <u>T</u>ools ➪ <u>S</u>end And Retrieve or <u>T</u>ools ➪ S<u>e</u>nd from the menu bar, or press Ctrl+M. Your reply will go to the electronic mailboxes of the recipients listed in your message.

Forwarding the message

Perhaps you have a buddy who's an expert in the topic a newsgroup member is asking about, but you doubt your buddy is a member of the newsgroup. In this case, you might want to forward the message to your friend's electronic mailbox and ask him or her to reply directly to the original author. To do this, select the message to which you want to reply, and then . . .

1. Do one of the following, depending on how you want the message to look:

   - To forward the message as it appears in the newsgroup window, click the Forward button on the toolbar, or choose <u>C</u>ompose ➪ <u>F</u>orward from the menu bar, or press Ctrl+F, or right-click the message and choose <u>F</u>orward By Mail from the shortcut menu. A new e-mail Forward window appears. It looks just like the reply window except the To: box is empty and the Subject: box says Fw:... instead of Re:....

   - To forward the message as an attachment, choose <u>C</u>ompose ➪ For<u>w</u>ard As Attachment from the menu bar, or right-click the message and choose Forward As <u>A</u>ttachment from the shortcut menu. A new e-mail forward attachment window appears, as shown in Figure 26-10.

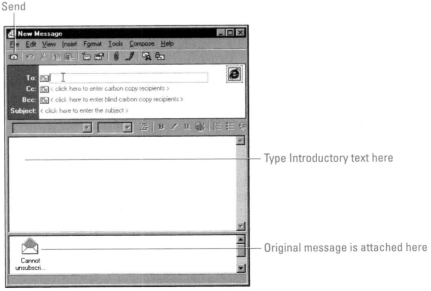

Figure 26-10: A new e-mail Forward window is ready for you to specify recipients and to type in your reply.

2. In the To: box, specify the e-mail address of the recipient using any of the techniques discussed in Chapter 25. You also can fill in the Cc: and Bcc: boxes if you want.

3. Click in the message editing area and type text that introduces your forwarded message. As usual, you can attach a file, add a signature, or format your message as needed.

4. Click the Send button on the toolbar, or choose File ➪ Send Message, or press Alt+S.

Again, your forwarded message is stored in your e-mail Outbox (if it isn't sent automatically). To complete the job, choose the usual Tools ➪ Send And Retrieve or Tools ➪ Send options from the menu bar, or press Ctrl+M.

Posting new newsgroup messages

Sometimes you'll be the one with a question or an opinion and you'll want to post it to the newsgroup of your choosing. This is easy to do, but please remember the two points of netiquette I mentioned earlier:

✦ Lurk in a newsgroup to absorb its culture before posting for the first time.

✦ Post *only* to the most relevant newsgroups. Do not post to multiple newsgroups unless it's absolutely necessary.

OK, now I'll get off my soapbox and list the steps for posting a new message to a newsgroup:

1. Go to the newsgroup where you want the message to appear.

2. Click the New Message button on the toolbar, or choose Compose ➪ New Message from the menu bar, or press Ctrl+N. You'll see a New Message window, as shown in Figure 26-11.

3. Although this probably won't be necessary, you can choose a different newsgroup or specify additional newsgroups in the Newsgroups: box, as explained under "Posting to multiple newsgroups" in a moment.

4. If you want to send a copy of your message to an e-mail address, specify it in the Cc: box using any of the techniques discussed in Chapter 25.

5. In the Subject: line, specify the subject for your message. This subject will appear in the Subject column of the message list. Make it descriptive so other newsgroup members will want to read it.

6. Click in the message editing area and type your message (again, be sure to follow the network etiquette advice given earlier in this chapter).

7. If you want, you can attach a file, add a signature, or format your message as explained under "Spiffing Up Your Newsgroup Messages," also in a moment.

8. When you're ready to post the message, click the Post Message button on the toolbar, or choose File ➪ Send Message from the menu bar, or press Alt+S.

Post Message   Insert File

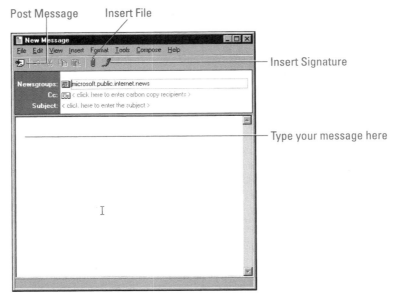

Insert Signature

Type your message here

Figure 26-11: The New Message window for a new newsgroup message

After a while, your message will be propagated to all the servers that carry your newsgroup and it'll start a new thread in the message list.

Posting to multiple newsgroups

You can post your new newsgroup message or your reply to more than one newsgroup, if necessary. There are two ways. First, you can type each newsgroup name, separated by a semicolon, in the Newsgroups: box as shown in Figure 26-12.

Figure 26-12: Two newsgroup recipients specified in the Newsgroups: box

If finger-twisting newsgroup names aren't exactly your cup of typing tea, you can pick the newsgroups you want. To begin, click the newspaper icon next to the Newsgroups: box or choose Tools ➪ Select Newsgroups from the menu bar. You'll see the Pick Newsgroups on... dialog box, shown in Figure 26-13.

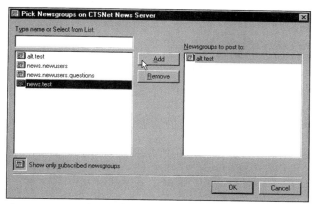

Figure 26-13: The Pick Newsgroups on... dialog box

Do any of the following to select the newsgroups to which you want to post:

✦ To show all the newsgroups for this server in the list below Type name or Select from List, click the button next to Show only Subscribed newsgroups (in the lower-left corner of the dialog box). To limit the newsgroups to those you've subscribed to, click the button again.

✦ To display a subset of the newsgroups, type all or part of the name of the newsgroups you want to match into the Type name or Select from List box. For example, if I typed **test** into the box, the list below Type name or Select From List in Figure 26-13 would include only the alt.test and news.test newsgroups.

✦ To add a newsgroup to the Newsgroups to post to list, click that newsgroup name in the left side of the dialog box, and then click Add (or double-click the name).

✦ To remove a newsgroup from the Newsgroups to post to list, click that newsgroup name in the right side of the dialog box, and then click Remove (or double-click the name).

When you've placed all the newsgroups you want to post to in the right side of the dialog box, click OK. The selected newsgroups will appear in the Newsgroups: box of your message (see Figure 26-12).

Remember, it's considered bad netiquette to post messages to multiple newsgroups. Do this *only* if it's absolutely necessary.

Spiffing Up Your Newsgroup Messages

Normally your newsgroup messages are sent as plain text, without a predefined signature, and without any attached files. You can change all this if you want.

Formatting your messages

Remember, e-mail messages can come in two flavors: plain text and fancier rich text (HTML) that allows for special formatting like boldface, italics, and so forth. In e-mail, the rich HTML text is the default setting. Newsgroup messages also can come in the same two flavors; however, plain text is the default because most newsgroup readers do not support the fancier rich text (HTML) format that Outlook Express does.

To change the format of a new newsgroup message or one to which you're replying, choose Format ➪ Rich Text (HTML) or Format ➪ Plain Text. If you chose Format ➪ Rich Text (HTML), you'll see the dialog box shown in Figure 26-14. Choose Yes to switch to the HTML format (remembering not everyone will be able to read your message) or choose No to stick with plain text format everyone can read.

Figure 26-14: This dialog box reminds you using rich text (HTML) format for your newsgroup messages may be risky.

If you do opt to use the rich HTML format, you'll see the Formatting Toolbar shown in Figure 26-15, and you can use any of its buttons to dress up your message. Chapter 25 explains how to use the Formatting Toolbar and equivalent options on the menu bar.

To change the default format used for all newsgroup messages, choose Tools ➪ News Options, click the Send tab, choose the appropriate HTML and plain text options in the News Sending Format area, and click OK.

Inserting predefined signature text

If you set up some predefined signature text, you can add it to your message with one click of a button. First, position the insertion point where the signature text should appear. Then, click the Insert Signature button on the toolbar (see Figure 26-11), or choose Insert ➪ Signature from the menu bar.

If you haven't set up a predefined signature yet, see the later section on "Automatically signing newsgroup messages" for instructions.

Figure 26-15: The Formatting Toolbar for a rich text (HTML) format message

Attaching a file

You can attach files to a newsgroup message just as you attach them to e-mail messages (see Chapter 25). Here's a quick review of what to do:

✦ To insert plain text from a file, position the insertion point where the text should appear and choose Insert ➪ Text From File. When the Insert Text File dialog box appears, locate and double-click the filename you want to insert. The text appears at the insertion point, just as though you had typed it in yourself.

✦ To attach a text file or a nontext file (which will appear as an icon in the message), click the Insert File button on the toolbar (see Figure 26-11) or choose Insert ➪ File Attachment from the menu bar. When the Insert Attachment dialog box appears, locate and double-click the filename you want to insert. An icon appears at the bottom of the message, as shown in Figure 26-16. The reader usually can just double-click the icon to display, open, run, or save the attached file.

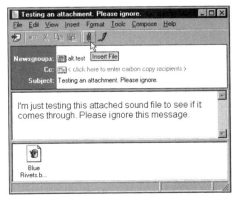

Figure 26-16: A newsgroup message that contains an attached file

Automatically signing newsgroup messages

The section titled "Automatic signature options" in Chapter 25 explains how to set up automatic signature text so Outlook Express will sign your messages automatically (or so you can insert the signature text manually whenever you want). These options work the same way in Outlook Express News. Here's how to begin:

1. Choose Tools ➪ News Options and click the Signature tab in the News Options dialog box.

2. Specify one of these Signature options:
   - **No Signature**: Do not sign the messages.
   - **Text**: Display the text you type into the box next to the Text option.
   - **File**: Display the contents of the file listed next to the File option (you can click the Browse button to locate and fill in the filename).

3. Specify whether to add the signature manually by selecting or deselecting Add Signature To The End Of All Outgoing Messages and Don't Add Signature To Replies And Forwards. If you deselect the Add Signature... option, you can insert the signature manually as explained earlier.

4. Choose OK.

Filtering Out Unwanted Newsgroup Messages

Suppose you're tired of viewing old messages or you don't want to read any messages containing the word *spam* or *adult* in the Subject: line. No problem! You can filter out unwanted newsgroup messages using the Group Filters feature. Your filters can weed out messages by sender, subject, length in lines, or length of time they've hung around in the newsgroup. Like the Inbox Assistant in Outlook Express Mail, the Group Filters is a tool for defining rules for weeding out messages in one or more newsgroups.

To add a new rule, follow these steps:

1. Choose Tools ➪ Newsgroup Filters from the Outlook Express News menu bar.

2. Click the Add button in the Group Filters dialog box (shown later). You'll be taken to a Properties dialog box that resembles Figure 26-17 when filled in.

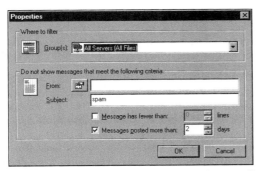

Figure 26-17: Setting up the criteria for weeding out newsgroup messages

3. In the Group(s) drop-down list, specify which newsgroups you want to filter. You can filter All Servers (All Files), a particular server, or a particular newsgroup you've subscribed to (as explained in the section "Subscribing and Unsubscribing," coming up soon).

4. In the do not show messages that meet the following criteria area, specify one or more criteria a message must meet for the Group Filters to hide it. In Figure 26-17, the Group Filters will hide messages with the word *spam* anywhere in the Subject: line and that have been posted for more than two days.

5. Click OK. You'll return to the Group Filters dialog box and your new rule will appear in the Description list, as in Figure 26-18.

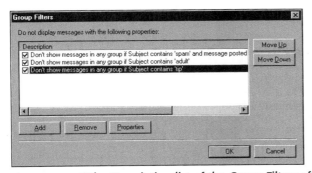

Figure 26-18: The Description list of the Group Filters after setting up some rules

You can repeat Steps 2–5 to set up as many rules as you need and you can adjust the rules, as I'll explain in a moment. When you're happy with the list, click OK. The next time you access the newsgroup, the Group Filters will process any messages that match the criteria you set up.

Here are some points to remember about the Group Filters:

✦ The Group Filters process only the rules checked in the Description list. It ignores rules that appear in the Description list, but aren't checked.

✦ If an incoming message matches more than one rule, it's processed according to the first rule it matches and the others are ignored.

You can adjust the rules in the Group Filters dialog box at any time:

✦ To turn off a rule temporarily, deselect (clear) the check box next to the rule. To turn the rule back on again, check the box once more. It's easier to turn off a rule and turn it back on than it is to remove the rule and recreate it later.

✦ To remove a rule permanently, click it in the Description list, and then click the Remove button. Be careful! No prompt exists for confirmation. The rule evaporates the moment you click Remove.

✦ To change a rule, click it in the Description list, and then click the Properties button (or double-click the rule's description). The Properties box will open and you can change any criteria you want.

✦ To move a rule up or down in the Description list (thus changing the order in which the rules are processed), click the rule you want to move, and then click the Move Up or Move Down button as needed.

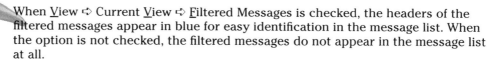

When View ➪ Current View ➪ Filtered Messages is checked, the headers of the filtered messages appear in blue for easy identification in the message list. When the option is not checked, the filtered messages do not appear in the message list at all.

Subscribing and Unsubscribing

After a while, you'll discover some favorite newsgroups you'll want to return to again and again. That is, you'll want to *subscribe* to those newsgroups. Any newsgroup to which you've subscribed will appear below the appropriate newsgroup server name in the folder list; you can click the newsgroup in the folder list or message list to pay it a visit.

If you don't see the subscribed newsgroups below the server in the folder list, click the plus sign (+) next to the server name. If you want to display the subscribed newsgroups in the message list instead, simply click the server name in the folder list.

It's easy to subscribe to (or drop a subscription from) any newsgroup your server offers. Follow these steps:

1. Starting from Outlook Express News, click the News Groups button on the toolbar or choose Tools ➪ Newsgroups. You'll see the Newsgroups dialog box, shown in Figure 26-19.

2. In the News servers list at the left side of the window, click the server you want to use (optional if only one server name appears).

3. Or, click the Reset List button if you want to download the latest list of newsgroups your server offers.

4. Choose whether to show all newsgroups, only the newsgroups to which you've subscribed, or new newsgroups on the server by clicking the All, Subscribed, or New tabs, respectively. Most often, you'll want to stick with the All tab so you can see all the available newsgroups.

5. In the News groups list, locate the newsgroup you want to subscribe to or unsubscribe from (newsgroups are listed in alphabetical order). You can use any of these techniques:

   • Use the vertical scroll bar to scroll up and down in the News groups list.

   • Click in the Display newsgroups which contain box and type all or part of the newsgroup name, as shown in Figure 26-19. The News groups list will display only the matching newsgroup names.

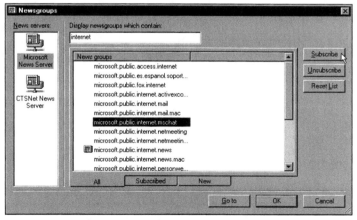

Figure 26-19: The Newsgroups dialog box with *internet* newsgroups selected

   • Click in the Display newsgroups which contain box and delete or edit the text it contains to redisplay the entire list or correct a typing error.

6. Click the name of the newsgroup you want to subscribe to or unsubscribe from. Then do one of the following:

- To subscribe to the selected newsgroup, click the Subscribe button. A newspaper icon will appear next its name (see Figure 26-19) and the newsgroup will appear in the folder list of the Outlook Express News window.

- To unsubscribe from the selected newsgroup, click the Unsubscribe button. The newspaper icon disappears and the newsgroup won't appear in the folder list.

- To subscribe or unsubscribe quickly to the newsgroup, double-click its name. The newspaper icon appears if it wasn't there before and disappears if it was there.

7. Repeat Steps 2 through 6 as many times as you want.

8. If you want to close the Newsgroups dialog box and jump to the currently selected newsgroup, click the Go to button. Otherwise, click OK.

That's it! When you return to the Outlook Express News window, the folder list will show the newsgroups to which you've subscribed. If you clicked Go to in Step 8, but you didn't subscribe to the newsgroup you went to, that newsgroup also will appear in the folder list, but only during the current Outlook Express Mail session. It'll disappear from the folder list the next time you start Outlook Express Mail.

You can bypass the Newsgroups dialog box if the newsgroup you want to subscribe to or unsubscribe from already appears in your folder list. Simply right-click the newsgroup name in the folder list and choose Subscribe To This Group (if you haven't subscribed to it yet) or Unsubscribe From This Group (if you have). Or, click the newsgroup in the folder list and choose Tools ➪ Unsubscribe From This Group from the menu bar.

Connecting to Multiple News Servers

You're not limited to viewing the newsgroups on your own ISP's news server. No indeed! Many publicly accessible news servers are all over the Internet. To connect to them, you just have to find out the server name and plug it into your list of Outlook Express Mail accounts (as explained shortly).

One handy server for getting help and information on Microsoft products is named `msnews.microsoft.com` and I recommend you add it to your news server account list. For a list of other public access NNTP servers on the Internet, point your Internet browser to the following URLs and explore the hyperlinks they offer:

✦ `http://www.reed.edu/~greaber/url-servers.html`

✦ `http://www.geocities.com/Hollywood/2513/news.html`

Or, search in Yahoo! (http://www.yahoo.com) or another favorite search engine for *newsgroup server* or *NNTP*. Not all the servers listed will be valid or useful, of course, but many will be. Whether you want to subscribe to a particular news server will depend on several factors, such as the groups the server offers and how much censorship, if any, the server imposes.

Once you find a newsgroup server in which you're interested, you can plug it into Outlook Express News in two ways:

✦ By clicking the hyperlinks to those servers in the lists at the URLs mentioned previously. You'll be taken to Outlook Express News and asked if you want to download the list of newsgroups for the server. This method adds the server to the folder list of the Outlook Express News window during the current session only.

✦ By plugging the server names into the Internet Accounts dialog box in Outlook Express, as the following explains. This method adds the server to the folder list of the Outlook Express News window permanently (until you delete it).

To add a newsgroup server to your Internet Accounts, follow these steps:

1. Starting from Outlook Express News or Outlook Express Mail, choose Tools ⇨ Accounts from the menu bar. The Internet Accounts dialog box appears.

2. To limit the account list to news servers only and reduce the clutter in the dialog box, click the News tab.

3. Click the Add button and choose News.

4. The Internet Connection Wizard will kick in just as it did when you first set up Outlook Express News and you can follow the prompts to add the news server. As usual, fill in the dialog boxes that appear and click Next and Finish to continue.

5. When the Wizard finishes, you'll be returned to the Internet Accounts dialog box, shown in Figure 26-20.

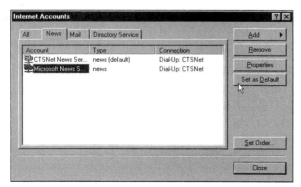

Figure 26-20: The Internet Accounts dialog box with two news servers added

The first server you set up will be the default server, but you can change this. Starting from the News tab in the Internet Accounts dialog box, click the name of the account you want to use as the default account, and then click Set as <u>D</u>efault. When you finish using the Internet Accounts dialog box, click Close. See Chapter 25 for more details about using the Internet Accounts dialog box and the Internet Connection Wizard.

The basic steps for setting up News accounts in the Internet Accounts dialog box are the same as for setting up Mail accounts, except you choose the News tab to display only the news accounts and you choose <u>N</u>ews from the <u>A</u>dd button, rather than <u>M</u>ail, to set up more news servers.

Speeding Up Outlook Express News

Outlook Express News usually copies message headers and body text from the newsgroup to your local hard disk automatically. It also deletes read messages when you exit the program and it only keeps unread messages for a limited time. You can customize this default behavior to make the program work more efficiently for your hardware setup.

If you're working with newsgroups over a slow connection, such as a 14.4Kbps modem, you might want to avoid downloading much information from a newsgroup onto your computer's hard disk until you're sure you want to read it. Outlook Express News offers two ways to serve up your newsgroup information in smaller bites:

✦ Download fewer message headers at once. By default, Outlook Express News downloads 300 message headers.

✦ Download only the headers and avoid downloading the body of the message unless you actually want to read it. By default, Outlook Express News downloads both the header and the body of each message. The body appears in the preview pane when you click its associated header in the message list.

To adjust the settings for downloading message headers and body text, choose <u>T</u>ools ➪ <u>N</u>ews Options from the Outlook Express News menu bar, and then click the Read tab (see Figure 26-21). Now change the following options as needed:

✦ **<u>D</u>ownload *n* headers at a time**: Select this option, and then specify the number of headers you want to download at once — between 50 and 1,000. If you deselect this option, Outlook Express News will download *all* the headers when you select a newsgroup, which can be time consuming.

✦ **Automatically show messages in the Preview Pane**: Deselect this option to avoid displaying the body of the messages in the preview pane when you click their headers in the message list. Select this option to show the messages in the preview pane.

Choose OK to save your settings. They'll take effect the next time you visit the newsgroup.

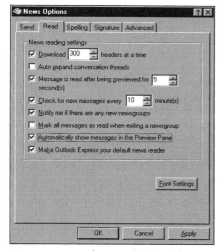

Figure 26-21: The Read tab of the News Options dialog box

If you limited the number of headers downloaded at once, you can display the next group of message headers. First, get online and connect to the newsgroup (if you haven't already). Then choose Tools ➪ Synchronize ➪ Get Next *n* Headers (where *n* is the number you entered in the News Options dialog box).

If you chose not to display messages in the preview pane, you'll see the following message when you click the header of a message:

```
Press <Space> to display the selected message.
You can also choose to automatically show messages in the
        preview pane from the News Options command.
```

To display the body of the message, get online and connect to the newsgroup (if you haven't already). Then, press the spacebar to view the associated message in the preview pane.

Downloading Messages for Later Viewing

If you're like most netizens nowadays, you pay a nominal flat rate for your Internet usage, regardless of how many hours you're actually connected to the Internet. But even if you do have unlimited flat-rate Internet access, it's best to disconnect from the Internet when you aren't using it and to read and compose newsgroup (and e-mail) messages offline whenever possible.

Outlook Express News offers many ways to read newsgroups offline and to copy (or *download*) messages to local files on your own computer, so you don't tie up valuable Internet resources (phone lines, LAN connections, and the like) while you read the daily news.

Dialing and hanging up

If you set up the Dial-Up Networking program to dial your ISP automatically, it'll connect to the Internet anytime it must. You can manually connect and disconnect from the Internet anytime you like, though:

✦ To disconnect from the Internet, click the Hang Up button on the Outlook Express News toolbar or choose Tools ➪ Offline ➪ Hang Up.

✦ To connect to the Internet, click the Dial button on the Outlook Express News toolbar or choose Tools ➪ Offline ➪ Dial.

Marking messages for retrieval

Suppose you're not connected to the Internet, you click a message header in the message list, and you see the following message in the preview pane:

```
This article is not cached. Please connect to your server to
        download the article.
```

This message tells you you're not connected and no local copy of the message exists on your hard disk for you to review. You have two choices:

✦ Go online now and view the message. You already know how to do this: Click the Dial button on the toolbar and wait to connect; then click or double-click the message header of the message you want to view.

✦ Mark all the messages you want to view while you're offline. Then connect and download all the marked messages at once.

Follow these steps to mark the messages you want to download (you don't have to be online):

1. Select the newsgroup you want to work with (if you haven't already).

2. Select the headers of the messages you want to download. You can use the standard click, Ctrl+click, and Shift+click techniques to highlight the messages in the message list. To select all the messages at once, click any message in the message list and choose Edit ➪ Select All, or press Ctrl+A. (Chapter 25 explains more about selecting multiple items in the message list.)

3. Choose one of the following options from the Tools ➪ Offline submenu:

   • **Mark For Retrieval**: Marks the selected messages for retrieval.

   • **Mark Thread For Retrieval**: Marks the selected thread for retrieval.

   • **Mark All For Retrieval:** Marks all messages in the newsgroup for retrieval.

The messages you selected are marked with a little down arrow icon, as shown in Figure 26-22. You can repeat these steps for as many newsgroups as you want.

As a shortcut, you can mark one message for retrieval by right-clicking it and choosing Mark Message For Download from the shortcut menu or by clicking it and pressing Ctrl+M.

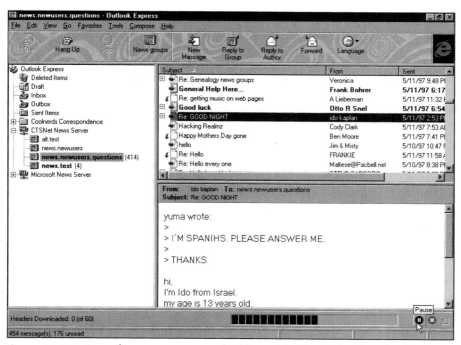

Figure 26-22: Several messages are marked for retrieval and the download is in progress.

Unmarking messages for retrieval

If you change your mind about marking a message header for retrieval, it's easy enough to unmark it. First, select the messages you want to unmark using the usual click, Ctrl+click, Shift+click, or Ctrl+A methods given in the previous Step 2. Then choose Tools ➪ Offline ➪ Unmark.

Downloading marked messages

Downloading marked messages is a breeze. Do either of the following:

✦ To download marked messages in all newsgroups, choose Tools ➪ Offline ➪ Synchronize All.

✦ To download marked messages in the currently selected newsgroup only, choose Tools ➪ Offline ➪ Synchronize This Newsgroup.

✦ To download marked messages in the currently selected newsgroup, choose Tools ➪ Offline ➪ Get Marked Messages.

Outlook Express News will connect to the Internet and download the messages to your hard disk. When downloading is complete, you can click the Hang Up button on the toolbar if you want. Now you can view the messages by clicking (or double-clicking) their headers in the message list.

Getting new messages and headers

If you usually work offline, it's a good idea to connect to the Internet occasionally and refresh the list of headers and messages in the newsgroups. Here's how:

1. Select the newsgroup you want to work with as explained earlier in this chapter.

2. Do any of the following:

   • To download new headers for the newsgroup, choose Tools ➪ Synchronize ➪ Get New Headers.

   • To download new headers *and* messages for the newsgroup, choose Tools ➪ Synchronize ➪ Get New Messages.

   • To download all headers and messages for the newsgroup, choose Tools ➪ Synchronize ➪ Get All Messages.

Outlook Express News will connect to the Internet and download the headers or messages you requested.

While downloading takes place, a progress bar appears at the bottom of the screen, along with a Pause and Stop button (see Figure 26-22). You can click the buttons as needed to pause (or resume) or to stop the downloading. When downloading is complete, the progress bar and buttons will disappear.

Cleaning Up Your Local Files

Outlook Express News does a lot of cleanup on its own, so it doesn't leave a flotsam of unnecessary messages and headers floating around on your hard disk. You can control how often the program does garbage collection and you can manually clean up unnecessary files in a few ways.

To customize how often Outlook Express News does its automatic cleanup, follow these steps:

1. Choose <u>T</u>ools ➪ <u>N</u>ews Options and click the Advanced tab in the News Options dialog box (see Figure 26-23).

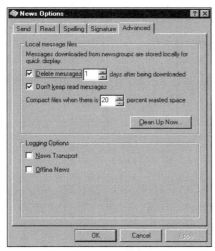

Figure 26-23: The Advanced tab of the News Options dialog box with the default options set

2. Choose options in the Local message files area of the dialog box, as the following describes:

   • **Delete messages *n* days after being downloaded**: Select this option to delete downloaded messages automatically after they are *n* days old (where *n* is a number in days). Deselect this option if you never want to delete downloaded messages.

   • **Don't <u>k</u>eep read messages**: Select this option to toss out read messages when you exit Outlook Express News. Deselect this option to keep read messages when you exit.

   • **Compact files when there is *n* percent wasted space**: Specify the amount of space that can be wasted before Outlook Express News compacts the files automatically.

3. Choose OK.

You also can clean up messages manually by following these steps:

1. Choose <u>F</u>ile ➪ Clean <u>U</u>p Files from the Outlook Express News menu bar (or click the <u>C</u>lean Up Now button on the Advanced tab of the News Options dialog box, shown in Figure 26-23). You'll see the Local File Clean Up dialog box, shown in Figure 26-24.

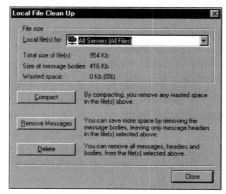

Figure 26-24: The Local File Clean Up dialog box

2. From the <u>L</u>ocal file(s) for: drop-down list, choose which news server messages to clean up. You can choose All Servers (All Files) or you can select a specific news server or newsgroup.

3. Click any of the following buttons as needed:

   • **<u>C</u>ompact**: Reclaims disk space by eliminating old unwanted messages.

   • **<u>R</u>emove Messages**: Removes only the message bodies downloaded from the location you selected in Step 2 without removing any message headers.

   • **<u>D</u>elete**: Removes all message headers and bodies from the location you selected in Step 2. When asked for permission to delete all of your cache files, click <u>Y</u>es.

4. Repeat Steps 2 and 3 for as many news servers as you want.

5. Click Close and OK (if necessary) to return to the main Outlook Express News window.

Other ways to customize Outlook Express News

You've already learned several ways to customize the behavior and appearance of Outlook Express News. Of course, many more exist and they'll be mighty familiar if you read Chapter 25, especially the sections on "Customizing the default mail options," "Sorting the message list," and "Customizing the Outlook Express window."

If you'd like to experiment a little, choose Tools ➪ News Options and explore the Send, Read, Spelling, Signature, and Advanced tabs in the News Options dialog box. Also check the options on the View menu. I'm sure you'll find the options available to you are easy to understand and use.

Summary

In this chapter you've learned about Usenet newsgroups, yet another popular service provided over the Internet. To summarize the main points:

✦ A newsgroup is a collection of messages sent to and from people who share an interest.

✦ You can use Outlook Express News to participate in Usenet newsgroups.

✦ To subscribe to a newsgroup in Outlook Express News, click the News Groups button on the toolbar. Then click any newsgroup you want to join and click the Subscribe button.

✦ To read an article (message) within a newsgroup, just click the article's subject line.

✦ To view replies to a message, click the plus sign (+) to the left of the message subject line.

✦ To reply to a newsgroup message, click the Reply to Group button (to reply to the entire group) or Reply to Author button (to reply to only the message author). Type your reply and click the Post Message button.

✦ To unsubscribe from a newsgroup, click the News Groups button in Outlook Express News, click the newsgroup you wish to leave, and then click the Unsubscribe button.

In the next chapter we'll look at yet another powerful Internet capability — the ability to conduct meetings. There, you'll learn about the Microsoft NetMeeting program.

✦   ✦   ✦

Using Microsoft NetMeeting

With Microsoft NetMeeting, you can converse and conduct meetings on the Internet. During a meeting, you can speak to and see others, send them files, work with them in shared applications, draw on a shared Whiteboard, and type messages back and forth using Chat. You can even use NetMeeting as a means of bypassing long distance charges from Ma Bell because all your communications take place over the Internet.

In this chapter, I'll discuss Version 2.0 of Microsoft NetMeeting. If you don't already have this program, you can download a copy from http://www.microsoft.com/NetMeeting.

NetMeeting Basics

To use Microsoft NetMeeting with Windows 95, you need the following:

+ At least a 486/66 processor with 8MB of RAM, though a Pentium with 12MB of RAM is recommended.

+ Internet access (at least a 28.8K modem is recommended.)

+ To communicate by voice via NetMeeting, you need a sound card, speakers, and a microphone.

+ To use the video features of NetMeeting, you need either a video-capture card and camera, or a video camera that connects through your computer's parallel printer port. A Pentium computer is highly recommended.

Hot Stuff For the best results, all persons attending a meeting should be using Microsoft NetMeeting 2.0.

How many people?

As a general rule, you can have up to 32 people collaborating in a meeting. All can have access to chat (typed messages), the Whiteboard, and file transfers. Only three people in the group, however, can have access to shared applications. I'll discuss these and how you work them later in this chapter. It's important to understand, though, that in a meeting, only two people at a time can communicate by voice and/or video. But, as I'll also discuss a little later, it's easy to connect to and from any member in a meeting using voice or video.

Finally, you should be aware, the more people who are in a meeting, and the more services they're using, the slower things go. Even when only two people are in a meeting, things can move slowly because so many factors contribute to how fast things move across the Internet. The amount of traffic on the Internet and/or on the *directory server* (discussed in a moment), and the speed of each member's PC, modem, and Internet connection can all be bottlenecks that slow communications

Directory servers

NetMeeting communications take place through a directory server, which is a place on the Internet where NetMeeting users gather. Directory servers are also called *Internet White Pages*, *Internet Locator Services* (ILS), and *User Locator Services* (ULS). Most directory servers have Web sites you can visit with Internet Explorer or any other Web browser. The address you use in NetMeeting to get into a directory, however, is different from that Web address. For instance, here are the addresses of some of the freebie directory servers offered by Microsoft:

✦ ils.microsoft.com

✦ ils1.microsoft.com

✦ ils2.microsoft.com

✦ ils3.microsoft.com

✦ ils4.microsoft.com

✦ ils5.microsoft.com

✦ uls.microsoft.com

These directory servers come in two flavors — the basic list of participants, as in the example shown in Figure 27-1. You can also access these directory servers through pages that look like Web sites, like the example shown in Figure 27-2. I'll explain how to use both, and how to switch between the two presentations as we go. You may want to experiment for a while to decide which type of presentation you prefer.

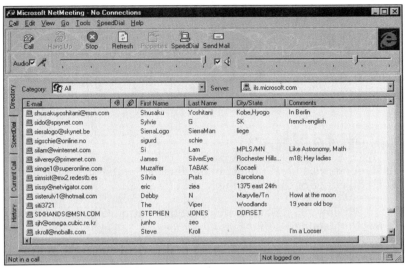

Figure 27-1: Directory server list view

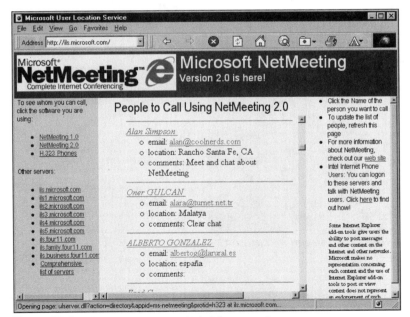

Figure 27-2: Directory server — Web Directory view

Many other directory servers are also out there. Most require some kind of registration, however, perhaps even sign-up fees. If you want to explore some of the other directory servers, using your Web browser, take a look at Bigfoot (http://www.bigfoot.com), Four11 (http://www.Four11.com), InfoSpace (http://www.InfoSpace.com), Internet Address Finder (http://www.iaf.net), Switchboard (http://www.switchboard.com), or WhoWhere (http://www.whowhere.com).

Starting NetMeeting

Starting NetMeeting is simple. Connect to the Internet in the usual manner for your PC. Then do either of the following:

✦ From the Windows 95 desktop, click the Start button and choose Programs ⇨ Microsoft NetMeeting.

✦ Or, if you're already in Outlook Express or Internet Explorer 4, choose Go ⇨ Internet Call from the menu bar.

The first time you start NetMeeting you'll be taken to a wizard that gets you started in choosing a directory server, identifying yourself, and configuring your audio gear. The first page of the wizard is shown in Figure 27-3.

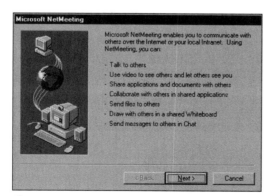

Figure 27-3: First wizard screen in Microsoft NetMeeting

The wizards will take you through some options. For example, clicking the Next> button in the first wizard screen takes you to the screen where you can choose a default. If you don't know what directory server you want to use, try some general server, such as ils.microsoft.com and click the Next> button.

Additional wizard screens will enable you to fill in information about yourself. This information will be visible to others in the directory server. You'll also be taken to a wizard that helps you fine-tune your audio settings for voice communication. After you complete the wizard screens and click the Finish button, you'll come to the Microsoft NetMeeting window, which will look something like Figure 27-4.

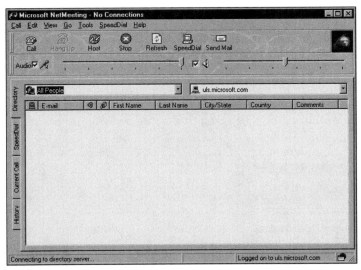

Figure 27-4: Microsoft NetMeeting window

Depending on how fast the Internet is running that day, the window will eventually fill up with names, e-mail addresses, and comments of other people logged into that same server, like the example shown back in Figure 27-1. Your own name will be included in this list.

If you can't find your own name in the directory, you might not be logged on to that server, or you may have set your options to keep yourself invisible. If you do, indeed, want to be listed on the current server . . .

1. Choose Tools ➪ Options and click the Calling tab.

2. Make sure the second check box, Do not list my name... is clear (does not contain a check mark).

3. From the Server Name drop-down list, choose the name of the server you want to log on to.

4. Click the OK button.

5. Choose Call ➪ Log On To (*directory server*).

If you want to change your identification information after you start NetMeeting, choose Tools ➪ Options and click the My Information tab. To change the default server name, choose Tools ➪ Options and click the Calling tab.

If you want to switch to the Web Directory view of the directory server, choose Go ➪ Web Directory from NetMeeting's menu bar. Your Web browser will pop up and show you some names and addresses in the format I showed you in Figure 27-2. To return to the directory server list view, close your Web browser.

Placing a Call

You can contact any person listed in the directory server. In fact, you can contact up to 32 of them and conduct a meeting. To call someone from NetMeeting:

1. Click the name of the person you wish to call, and then click the Call button in NetMetting's toolbar. You'll be taken to a dialog box like the one in Figure 27-5.

Figure 27-5: About to place a call through NetMeeting

2. Click the Call button, and then wait.

Actually, you can place a call to anyone in the Directory, SpeedDial, or History tab of NetMeeting by double-clicking the name of the person you want to call.

If you're in the Web Directory, rather than in NetMeeting, you can click the name of the person you want to call. If you get a dialog box asking what to do next, choose Open it.

If the other person answers, you'll be taken to the Current Call tab of NetMeeting. Your name, and the person you called (or the people you've called), will be listed in that pane, as in the example shown in Figure 27-6. That pane lists everyone connected in a call. This means everyone listed in your Current Call tab is in a meeting together and can chat, talk, view each other on video, share applications and the Whiteboard, and transfer files to one another, using any of the techniques described in the later sections of this chapter.

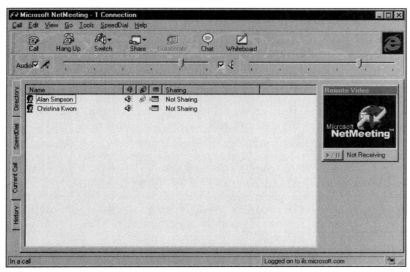

Figure 27-6: In the Current Call tab of NetMeeting

Incidentally, if the person you called doesn't answer, you'll see the message shown in Figure 27-7. If you want to leave this person an e-mail message, choose Yes and type your message. Otherwise, choose No to hang up without leaving a message.

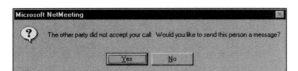

Figure 27-7: The person you called did not answer your call.

Receiving a Call

If someone calls you for a NetMeeting conference, you'll hear a sound like a telephone ringing (if you have a sound card) and see the message shown in Figure 27-8. If you want to meet with that person, click Accept and that person will be added to people in your active meeting listed in the Current Call tab of NetMeeting. You can then chat, talk, or whatever, just as though you had called that person.

Figure 27-8: Message that appears when someone calls you in NetMeeting

Should you choose <u>I</u>gnore, the person calling will receive a message indicating you're unwilling to accept the call and will be given the option to send you an e-mail message.

 Unlike Ma Bell, which is very fast, communications on the Internet are very slow. Expect to spend a fair amount of time waiting for things to happen when you place calls, accept calls, send messages, and so forth. Messages in NetMeeting's status bar will keep you apprised of progress. While writing this chapter, I found the server at ils.business.four11.com quite speedy and reliable.

If you don't want to be bothered with incoming calls, yet you want to stay logged on to a directory server, hang out your Do Not Disturb sign. To do so, choose <u>C</u>all ➪ <u>D</u>o Not Disturb from NetMeeting's menu bar. Your phone won't ring, and anyone trying to contact you will be given the option to leave you an e-mail message. When you do want to receive calls again, be sure to choose <u>C</u>all ➪ <u>D</u>o Not Disturb again to disable this feature.

Hosting a Meeting

The techniques for placing and receiving calls are often used by people who simply want to meet new people over the Internet. If you want to host a real meeting with specific people on the Internet, you need to plan ahead. Each potential participant in the meeting needs to know:

✦ What time the meeting will start

✦ What directory server will be used — ils.microsoft.com for example

✦ The e-mail address of the person hosting the meeting

Send this information to each of the potential participants in this meeting, so they can easily find you in the directory server. When the agreed-upon time arrives, log on to the agreed-upon directory server and choose <u>C</u>all ➪ <u>H</u>ost Meeting from NetMeeting's menu bar. You may see the message shown in Figure 27-9. Choose OK if you see this message.

You'll be taken to the Current Call tab with your own name listed as a participant in your own meeting, as in Figure 27-10.

Figure 27-9: Someone is about to host a meeting in NetMeeting.

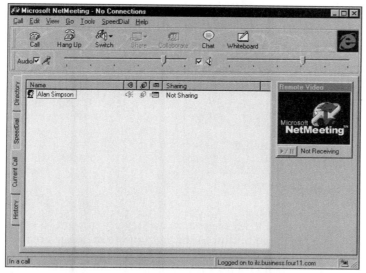

Figure 27-10: One person is hosting a meeting. Others haven't joined yet.

Other people who plan to join the meeting must place a call to you from their PCs. As they call in, accept their calls to add them to the Current Call list on your PC. As more people call in, each will see your name and other participants' names in NetMeetings's Current Call tab on their own PCs.

As the host of a meeting, you can automatically accept incoming calls by choosing Tools ➪ Options and selecting Automatically Accept Incoming Calls from the General tab. Choose OK after making the selection.

So the bottom line on conducting a meeting is simply: Whoever is listed in the Current Call tab of NetMeeting on your PC is in your current meeting. It doesn't matter who called whom. People listed there in the Current Call tab can communicate using Chat, the Whiteboard, audio, video, and so forth, as discussed in the following sections.

Typing Messages with Chat

Chatting is a quick and easy method of communicating with others in a meeting. To chat, click the Chat button in the toolbar above the list of people in the Current Call. Or choose Tools ➪ Chat from the menu bar. The Chat window opens, as in Figure 27-11; its title bar indicates how many other people in your Current Call are using the same Chat window. Other peoples' messages will automatically appear in the largest window.

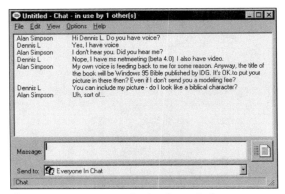

Figure 27-11: NetMeeting's Chat window

To send out a message, type in the Message area whatever you want to say, and then press Enter or click the large button to the right of the message area. If you want to whisper (send a chat message to just one member of the meeting), choose that person's name from the Send to: drop-down list before you send the message.

You can also control how chats are displayed on your screen using the Options menu in Chat. Choose Options ➪ Font to pick a font, size, and color for your text. Choose Options ➪ Chat Format to decide what information you want to display in your Chat window.

To save a chat session, choose File ➪ Save from Chat's menu bar. Choose a folder and filename for the chat, and then click the Save button. The chat is saved as a text (.txt) file you can open later using Notepad, WordPad, or any word processing program. You'll also be given an opportunity to save the current chat session when you exit the Chat program.

Talking on the Internet

If you have a sound card, speakers, and a microphone installed in your PC, you can use NetMeeting to talk to other people on the Internet. Make sure your sound card, speakers, and microphone are installed correctly, as per the manufacturer's instructions. (You can also use Chapter 38 in this book to help you.) Once you're in a call, the audio capabilities will turn on automatically. So all you must do is to start talking into your microphone.

Two kinds of sound cards are out there: half-duplex and full-duplex. If your sound card supports full-duplex, you can use both your microphone and speakers at the same time. Thus, you can carry on a regular telephone conversation (or videophone conversation, if both members have video cameras). With a half-duplex sound card, though, the speakers must take turns talking and listening. Kind of like a walkie-talkie or older-style speakerphone.

If you have any problems with audio, you can use Chat to type messages back and forth while you try to resolve those problems. In the meantime, adjust the volumes on the audio toolbar in NetMeeting Figure 27-12). If that toolbar isn't visible, choose View ⇨ Toolbar. Make sure the check boxes next to the microphone and speaker are selected (checked). Clearing the check box next to the microphone mutes the microphone, so no one can hear you talk. Clearing the check box next to the speaker mutes the speakers, so you can't hear anyone else (if you want to bark orders at people and not hear any feedback!). You can also adjust your microphone's sensitivity and other audio features by choosing Tools ⇨ Options and clicking the Audio tab.

Figure 27-12: Use the scroll bars to adjust your microphone sensitivity and speaker volume.

If problems persist, run the Audio Tuning wizard. You can do so even while you're connected to someone in a meeting. Choose Tools ⇨ Audio Tuning Wizard from NetMeeting's menu bar, and follow the instructions that appear. You might also want to check the volume on your speakers. For more information on using your sound card, please refer to the manufacturer's instructions and to Chapter 38 in this book.

Finally, be aware you can converse with only one other person at a time. If three or more people are in the current call, you can decide which person you want to speak to by clicking the Switch button in the toolbar, or by choosing Tools ⇨ Switch Audio and Video. Choose which person you want to speak with, and then start speaking. The little speaker icon that appears to the right of everyone's name will darken to indicate this is the person to whom you're talking.

To stop sending audio to someone, go to the Current Call tab, click the speaker icon next to the name of the person to whom you want to stop sending audio, and then click Stop Sending Audio and Video. You'll still be in a meeting with this person and you can use Chat and the other communication options discussed in this chapter. But you will no longer have voice/video contact with this person.

Videoconferencing

Like audio, video generally kicks in automatically when a connection is made. If the person you're connected to has video equipment, his or her image will appear in the small Remote Video window in NetMeeting. Likewise, if you have video, your image will appear in the same window on their screen. You can see only one person at a time in video, as in the example shown in Figure 27-13. To choose which person you want to view, click the Switch button in the toolbar, or choose Tools ➪ Switch Audio and Video and the name of the person with whom you want to do video.

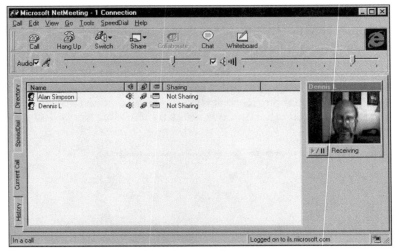

Figure 27-13: Receiving video from a caller

If you don't want to send video automatically when you place or receive a call, choose Tools ➪ Options. On the Video tab, clear the check box next to the Automatically Send Video… option. Likewise, if you don't want to receive video automatically, clear the check box next to the Automatically Receive Video… option.

You can also preview your own video image prior to placing a call. Go to the Current Call tab and click the button at the bottom of the My Video window to see the image you are sending.

As with audio, you can stop sending video to someone without hanging up. Go to the Current Call tab, click the video camera icon next to the name of the person to whom you want to stop sending video, and then click Stop Sending Audio and Video. You can also stop sending video by choosing Video ➪ Detach my Video. To stop receiving video, choose Video ➪ Detach Remote Video.

Danger Zone As a general rule, video works best with computers that have a 133MHz (or better) Pentium processor. Running video in a busy meeting can slow down all the computers in the meeting. Opening a video window while sharing an application can make it difficult for others to take control of the application. Detaching video at such a time will help speed things again.

Video quality can vary a lot. Depending on your equipment, you can control certain aspects of video quality using options on the Video tab of the Options dialog box (choose Tools ➪ Options from NetMeeting's menu bar.) Also, if you are experiencing "choppy" video, you might get better performance by switching to half-duplex. You must hang up to disconnect from any call you're in currently. Then choose Tools ➪ Options. On the Audio tab, clear the Enable Full Duplex Audio... check box.

If you don't have videoconferencing, but you're intrigued by the idea, you might want to look at the Connectix Corporation's videoconferencing camera, Color QuickCam 2. It plugs into the parallel printer port on your PC, so no internal cards exist to mess with. This camera retails for about $250 (but don't quote me on this — it's a ballpark figure and prices can change at any time). For more information, check your local computer store or stop by http://www. connectix.com on the Web.

Intel Corporation, makers of the Pentium chip, also offers several products for video conferencing via NetMeeting, including the Intel Internet Video Phone. For more information stop by their Web site at http://www.connectedpc.com.

Using the Whiteboard

The *Whiteboard* is similar to chat, but enables you to communicate with pictures rather than text. All the members of the current call can draw simultaneously. And everyone sees whatever is placed in the Whiteboard. Think of the Whiteboard as the regular chalkboard or white board often used in classrooms and meeting rooms. But in this case, one person, or several people, can draw and write on the board at the same time. To start the Whiteboard:

✦ Go to the Current Call tab in NetMeeting and click the Whiteboard button on the toolbar.

✦ Or choose Tools ➪ Whiteboard from NetMeeting's menu bar. The Whiteboard pops up on your screen, as well as on the screen of everyone else in the current call. With the Whiteboard on the screen, you can draw using the various tools, such as Pen, Line, Unfilled Rectangle, Filled Rectangle, Unfilled Ellipse, and Filled Ellipse. Click the appropriate button and drag across the large drawing area. Choose Options ➪ Line Width to select a line width for drawing.

Typing text in the Whiteboard

You can also type text using the Text button. Choose a color and font for the text by clicking a color or the Font Options button, or by choosing Options ➪ Font from the Whiteboard's menu bar. To highlight text you've already typed, click the Highlighter button in the Whiteboard (the yellow pen), and then click a line width below the buttons. Drag the mouse pointer through the text you want to highlight.

Pasting pictures into the Whiteboard

To paste an image of a window from your desktop into the Whiteboard, click the Select Window button, and then choose OK when the message appears. The Whiteboard will disappear, and the mouse pointer will change to a little square with crosshairs. Click the window you want to copy. The Whiteboard will reappear displaying a copy of the window on which you clicked.

To paste an image of part of your screen into the Whiteboard, click the Select Area button in the Whiteboard, and then click OK when the next message appears. The Whiteboard disappears and the mouse pointer turns into a pair of crosshairs. Drag a rectangle around the area you want to place into the Whiteboard. When you release the mouse button, the Whiteboard will reappear with an image of the area you selected displayed.

You can also cut and paste a picture into the Whiteboard. For example, say you open or create some picture in a graphics program like Paint Shop Pro. Within Paint Shop Pro you could select the whole picture or part of the picture, and then choose Edit ⇨ Copy. Next, click the Whiteboard and choose Edit ⇨ Paste. Figure 27-14 shows an example of a photograph I copied from Paint Shop Pro and pasted into the Clipboard.

Figure 27-14: A photo pasted into the Whiteboard

Erasing from the Whiteboard

You can erase materials from the Whiteboard two ways . To erase a drawn object or block of text, click the Eraser tool. Then click the object or chunk of text you want to erase. Or, to delete individual letters rather than a whole block of text, choose Tools ➪ Text, select the letters you want to erase, and then press the Delete (Del) key.

Other Whiteboard features

The Zoom button in the Whiteboard enables you to double the size of the image in the Whiteboard. The Lock Contents button locks the Whiteboard's contents, so other meeting members can't change it. The Pointer button puts a pointing hand on the screen, which you can drag around with your mouse pointer to call attention to parts of the screen. All members will see exactly where your pointer is pointing.

You can store multiple pages in the Whiteboard. To add a new page, click the Insert New Page button down near the lower-right corner of the Whiteboard. Or choose Edit ➪ Insert Page Before or Insert Page After. A new, blank Whiteboard appears on which you can draw, type, or paste pictures. To scroll through pages, use the First Page, Previous Page, Next Page, and Last Page buttons near the bottom-right corner of the Whiteboard. Or, type a page number into the Page text box, and then press Enter. You can also view thumbnails of multiple pages and rearrange pages by choosing Edit ➪ Page Sorter.

Sharing Applications

One of the most amazing features of NetMeeting is the capability to share applications. And it's easy to do. The only bummer is it's all slow. Nonetheless, if you want to try it:

1. Start any program on your PC, or open any document.

2. Go to NetMeeting, click the Share button, and click the name of the application you want to share.

Everyone in the current call can see your program and document. The name of the person who shared the application appears in a tab at the upper-right corner of the application's window. For example, in Figure 27-15, Elizabeth Olson has shared a document in the Windows WordPad application.

Initially, only the person who shared the document can make changes. If you want others to work in the same document, click the Collaborate button. Other members who want to work in the program must also click their Collaborate buttons. Then things get kinda weird.

Basically, any collaborator can take over the application simply by clicking his or her mouse button. When someone else takes over the application, the mouse pointer shows that person's initials. You can watch the person work and see the changes he or she makes. Those changes, however, are taking place on your machine (assuming you're the person who initially shared the application) — even though the person making those changes may be thousands of miles away!

Figure 27-15: Elizabeth Olson has shared a document in her WordPad application.

Danger Zone If you share an "explorer" window like My Computer or Windows Explorer, you essentially give other collaborators free reign over your entire computer system! In addition, any other programs you open after opening such a window will also be shared. So be careful!

To regain control over the shared application, click your mouse button. When you're in control, the mouse pointer returns to normal and you can work normally. To stop allowing others to work in the application:

✦ Click the Collaborate button again.

✦ Or press ESC.

The application will still be shared (visible to others), but no one else can take control of the application. If you want to stop sharing altogether, click the Share button again, and then click the name of the application you want to stop sharing.

Puzzled? Only the person who originally shared the application can stop sharing it. Only that person can save any changes made to the shared document.

Remember, any and all changes made to the document are saved only if you save the changes (using File ⇨ Save in that application). Furthermore, the changes are saved only on your computer. If you want others in the meeting to have copies of the completed document, you must send them copies as discussed in the next section.

Transferring Files

Sending a file to members of a net meeting is easy:

1. In NetMeeting choose Tools ➪ File Transfer ➪ Send File.
2. Browse to and click the name of the file you want to send, and then click the Send button.

You'll see a message indicating the file is being sent. All net meeting members will be given the option, on their own screens, to accept or reject the file. Should they accept, you'll see a message as the file is being sent, and another message indicating when the send is complete. If someone else sends a file to you, you'll see a message box giving you the choice to accept or reject the file.

When the transfer is complete, recipients can choose Tools ➪ File Transfer ➪ Open Received Files. Or, browse to the Received Files (typically `c:\Program Files\ NetMeeting\Received Files`) using My Computer, Windows Explorer, or Find.

Sharing the Clipboard Contents

As you probably know, choosing Edit ➪ Copy or Edit ➪ Cut in an application copies or moves the current selection on the screen into the Windows Clipboard. In a meeting, copying or pasting to the Clipboard puts the same contents in *all* recipients' Clipboards. This is true even if those members aren't sharing an application.

For instance, let's say you copy a picture or a section of a picture from some program like Paint Shop Pro. If anyone in the meeting chooses Edit ➪ Paste in some program that can accept pictures from the Clipboard (say, Microsoft Word), this person will paste *your* selection into their document on their machine. Funky!

Perhaps this goes without saying, but if there's anything on your machine you don't want others to see, make sure it isn't in the Windows Clipboard when you're in a net meeting.

More on NetMeeting

What you've learned here is probably more than enough to keep you busy with NetMeeting for a long time. But if you're looking for more information or you have any problems, you can explore other places to get more details, including:

✦ NetMeeting's online help (choose Help ➪ Help Topics from NetMeeting's menu bar)

✦ NetMeeting's readme file (choose Help ➪ Readme from NetMeeting's menu bar)

✦ Microsoft's NetMeeting Web site at `http://www.microsoft.com/ NetMeeting`

✦ The Intel Connection Advisor (while NetMeeting is running, double-click the Intel Connection Wizard icon in the Windows taskbar)

✦ Intel's ConnectedPC site at `http://www.connectedpc/com`

Summary

Microsoft NetMeeting is an Internet tool that enables you to communicate with other people in real time. Once connected to others, you can communicate by typing messages (Chat), by voice and video, and by drawing pictures in a Whiteboard. You can also share applications, and transfer files and Windows Clipboard contents. The main points to remember are:

✦ To get started with NetMeeting, connect to the Internet, and then click the Start button and choose Programs ➪ Microsoft NetMeeting.

✦ If you're not logged into a directory server automatically at startup, choose Call ➪ Log On To *directory server* from NetMeeting's menu bar.

✦ If you don't see a list of e-mail addresses when you've logged into a directory server, click the Refresh button in NetMeetings's toolbar.

✦ To place a call, go to the Directory, SpeedDial, or History tab of NetMeeting, click the e-mail address of the person you want to call, and then click the Call button in the toolbar.

✦ When two or more people are in a meeting, their names appear in the Current Call tab of NetMeeting.

✦ To chat with people in your current call, click the Chat button in the toolbar above the Current Call list.

✦ To communicate via voice and/or video, click the Switch button in the toolbar, and then click the name of the person to whom you wish to speak.

✦ To share pictures on a Whiteboard, click the Whiteboard button in the toolbar above the Current Call list.

✦ To share an application, open the document you want to share or start the program you want to share. Then click the Share button.

✦ When you first share an application, others can see it, but cannot change it. To enable others to work on a document, you must click the Collaborate button. Members wishing to collaborate must also click their own Collaborate buttons.

✦ To send files to others in the current call, choose Tools ➪ File Transfer ➪ Send File from NetMeeting's menu bar.

In the next chapter we'll look at yet another way to communicate over the Internet — Microsoft Comic Chat.

✦   ✦   ✦

Fun with Microsoft Chat

Microsoft Chat, also known as *Comic Chat*, is a fun program that enables people on the Internet to chat with one another by typing messages. Microsoft Chat is similar to the Chat feature of NetMeeting, discussed in the previous chapter. Unlike NetMeeting's Chat, however, Comic Chat members can choose characters, also known as *avatars*, to represent themselves and can assign facial expressions to those characters.

Microsoft Chat is an easy program to use, so this will be a short, easy chapter for most of you (hooray!). Let's get started. . . .

Getting Microsoft Comic Chat

I'll discuss Version 2.0 of Microsoft Chat. If you have Microsoft Chat already, you might want to make certain you have Version 2. To do this, start up Microsoft Chat and choose Help ⇨ About Microsoft Chat from the menu bar. If you aren't using Version 2.0, or you don't have Microsoft Chat on your system at all, you can easily download a copy — free of charge — from Microsoft's Web site. If you did open Microsoft Chat, go ahead and close it now by clicking its Close (X) button, or by choosing File ⇨ Exit from its menu bar. Then, if you need to download a new copy, follow these steps:

1. Connect to the Internet in the usual manner for your PC.

2. Start your Web browser (Microsoft Internet Explorer 4) and point it to `http://www.microsoft.com/ie/download`.

3. Choose Windows 95 and Windows NT 4.0 as the first option, and then click the Next button.

♦   ♦   ♦   ♦

In This Chapter

Connecting to chat rooms with Microsoft Chat

Choosing a cartoon character and name for yourself

Talking, whispering, and showing emotion in Chat

Playing sounds in Chat

Transferring files in Chat

Hosting your own chat room

♦   ♦   ♦   ♦

4. When you're asked to select a product, choose Microsoft Chat 2.0 for Internet Explorer for Windows 95 & NT 4.0. Then click the Next button.

5. Choose a language from the next screen, and then click the Next button.

6. Choose a server near you from which to download.

7. When asked, choose <u>S</u>ave it to Disk, and then click the OK button.

8. Choose a drive and directory to put the file on, and then click the <u>S</u>ave button.

This file — mschat2.exe — is over 1MB in size, so it will take a few minutes to download. When the download is complete, you can follow these steps to install Microsoft Chat on your PC:

1. Close all open programs and disconnect from the Internet.

2. Open the folder that contains the mschat2.exe file you just downloaded. (If you forget where you put that file, use Find to locate mschat2.exe).

3. Double-click the mschat2.exe filename.

4. Choose <u>Y</u>es when asked if you want to install Microsoft Chat 2.0 and follow the instructions onscreen.

Microsoft Chat will install like any other program, and you'll see a message telling you when the installation is complete.

Starting Microsoft Chat

To start Microsoft Chat and get on a chat server, follow these steps:

1. Connect to the Internet.

2. On the Windows 95 desktop, click the Start button and choose <u>P</u>rograms ⇨ Microsoft Chat.

3. In the Connect dialog box that appears (see Figure 28-1), you can click the OK button to choose the suggested server and chat room (more on those later in the chapter).

After a brief delay, the status bar will show a message like Now chatting in Room #Comic_Chat2. And you'll see conversations among the members of that chat as shown in Figure 28-2.

Figure 28-1: Chat's Connect dialog box

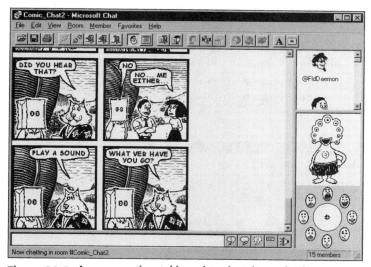

Figure 28-2: A conversation taking place in Microsoft Chat

Chatting Basics

When you first enter a chat room, you may want to sit back and watch the conversations taking place to get a sense of what's happening. Then you can jump in and start talking at any time. Here are some basic skills you'll need:

✦ To see who is in the current chat room, scroll through the list in the upper-right corner.

✦ To see which character just spoke in a comic pane, point to the character. That character's name will appear in a tooltip near the mouse pointer.

✦ To say something, click in the text box at the bottom of the window and type your message. Then, choose an expression from the emotional wheel in the lower-right corner and click the Say button next to the message you typed.

✦ You can refine an expression by dragging the black dot from a facial expression to the crosshairs in the center of the circle.

✦ To switch between comic view and text view, click the Comics View or Text View button in the toolbar, or choose View ⇨ Comic Strip or View ⇨ Plain Text from the menu bar.

✦ To try a different chat room, click the Chat Room List button in the toolbar, or choose Room ⇨ Room List from the menu bar. Click any room, and then click the Go To button.

While viewing the list of chat rooms, you can click any column heading to sort the list. For example, to see which rooms are least or most crowded, click the Members heading once or twice to sort the rooms into ascending or descending order by size.

✦ To change anything (background, character, personal info, and so on) choose View ⇨ Options and explore the various tabs.

✦ To change your character, choose View ⇨ Options and click the Character tab. Choose your character from the list that appears (see Figure 28-3) and click the OK button.

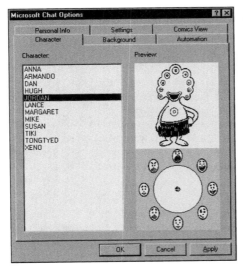

Figure 28-3: Characters available in Microsoft Chat

✦ Chatters use some acronyms and abbreviations of their own. *LOL* means Laughing Out Loud. *BRB* means Be Right Back. *NP* means No Problem. *K* means OK. *LMAO* means Laughing My A*s Off, *CYA* means See Ya.

✦ If you find a chat room you like, choose Favorites ⇨ Add to Favorites. To return to this chat room in the future, choose Favorites ⇨ Open Favorites and double-click the appropriate file name.

✦ To create a desktop shortcut to a favorite chat room, choose File ➪ Create Shortcut.

✦ As with any Windows program, you can get quick help by choosing Help from Chat's menu bar, or by pressing the F1 key.

The few things in this list will cover about 95% of what you'll see and do in Chat. Remember, in addition to the regular online help, you can probably get human help from other chat members, especially if you go to the Newbies chat room. Just type a message like "I need help" and another member will probably come to your aid.

Now, let's look at some of the fancier things you can do in Chat.

Identifying Yourself (or Not)

You can divulge as much, or as little, about yourself as you like in Chat. To create or change your personal information:

1. Choose View ➪ Options and click the Personal Info tab. You'll come to the dialog box shown in Figure 28-4.

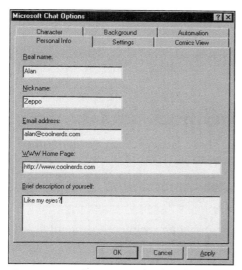

Figure 28-4: The Personal Info tab in Options

2. Type in whatever information you care to about yourself.

3. Click the OK button.

Other chat members can see some of this information; they can send you stuff by right-clicking your character, as we'll discuss next.

Identifying Others

To get more information on someone in the chat, right-click the person's character. You'll see a pop-up menu, like the example in Figure 28-5. You can choose Get Profile to see the person's brief description. Or choose Get Identity to view this person's Internet identity. As you can see in Figure 28-5, you can send this person an e-mail or file, visit his home page on the Web, or call him in NetMeeting. These options will work only if the person put the appropriate addresses into the Personal Info tab in Options.

Figure 28-5: Pop-up menu appears when you right-click a character

Speech, Thought, Whisper, Action

Five ways exist to send a message. These are indicated by the tooltip that appears when you point to one of the buttons to the right of where you type your message:

✦ **Talk:** Message appears in a comic talk bubble.

✦ **Think:** Message appears in a comic thought bubble.

✦ **Whisper:** Message is visible to only one recipient — the intended one, the one you clicked before typing — in a broken-line bubble.

✦ **Action:** Message is sent as a caption at the top of the frame. Used to describe some action or emotion, such as `Flip is blushing`, as opposed to saying something aloud.

✦ **Sound:** Message is sent as a caption at the top of the frame and a sound file is played.

Figure 28-6 shows how the various messages look.

Figure 28-6: Different types of messages

To send a message, type your message in the text box at the bottom of the Chat window, and click the appropriate button to the right. If you want to speak to a specific character, click her name in the member list near the upper-right corner, before you send the message. That character will appear in the same cartoon frame as your message. You can select multiple characters using Ctrl+Click.

To send a whisper, in the upper-right corner click the character to whom you want to whisper. To whisper to more than one person, hold down the Ctrl key and click their characters. Then type your message and click the Whisper button. Only the selected character(s) will see the whispered message. It will be invisible to other people in the chat room.

You can use the Whisper box to chat outside the rest of the group. Click the character to whom you want to whisper, or Ctrl+Click on multiple characters. Then choose Member ➪ Whisper Box, or right-click a character icon and choose Whisper Box. You're taken to a box that looks like the example in Figure 28-7. You can type messages in the long text box and click the Whisper button to send them.

If you receive a Whisper Box, but you don't want to be involved in it, you can click the Ignore User button. If several people are in the Whisper Box and you want to eliminate one, click that person's name button, and then click the Delete Tab button. To close the Whisper Box, click its Close (X) button.

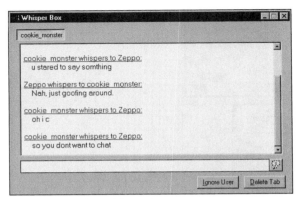

Figure 28-7: The Whisper Box

Controlling your emotions

The emotion wheel near the lower-right corner of the Chat window (see Figure 28-8) enables you to choose an emotion for your character. If you point at each face in the wheel, starting at the top, you'll see they're labeled Shout, Laugh, Happy, Coy, Bored, Scared, Sad, and Angry. Click any face to assign that emotion to your character. To lessen the intensity of the emotion, drag the little dot toward the center of the wheel.

Figure 28-8: Sample character showing different emotions

Note, not all characters can display the full range of all emotions. You must experiment to see what's available for the character you've selected. Remember, if you haven't already done so, you need to type a message, as well. And, if you want to speak directly to another character, you need to click that character's nickname in the list above the emotion wheel before you click the Say, Whisper, Think, or Action button.

If you press Enter just after sending your message, your character will move slightly within the frame. Don't press Enter too much, though, as this floods the chat server.

Sending sound

To send a sound, click the Play Sound button, choose a sound, type an accompanying message, and then click the OK button. Only people with that sound file in their sound search path will actually hear the sound. To choose a sound search path for your own computer:

1. Choose <u>V</u>iew ➪ <u>O</u>ptions.

2. Click the Settings tab.

3. Type the path to your sound (.wav files) in the bottom text box, and then click the OK button.

The search sound path you specify will be used to play sounds other people send. For example, if someone plays the sound called `aoogah.wav`, and this sound file isn't in your sound search path, you won't hear the sound. If `aoogah.wav` is in that folder, you will hear the sound.

The search sound path is also used for picking sound files to send. That is, when you click the Sound button, the Play Sound dialog box that appears will show sound files from your sound search path. You can send sound files, as well as any other files, to chat members. And other chat members can send files to you, as I'll discuss in the next section.

Sending and receiving files

To send a file to someone, right-click the person's character and choose <u>S</u>end File. Choose the file you want to send and click the <u>S</u>end button. You'll see a dialog box indicating the file is about to be sent, just waiting for the recipient to approve, as shown in Figure 28-9.

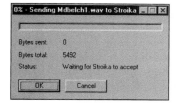

Figure 28-9: Waiting for recipient to accept file

The recipient will receive a message like the one shown in Figure 28-10. Of course, if someone tries to send you a file, you'll see that same message. The file will be transferred only if the intended recipient accepts it by clicking the <u>Y</u>es button.

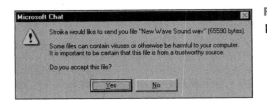

Figure 28-10: Waiting for permission to send file

Sending links

If you type a link into a message, it will automatically become "hot" when it's displayed in Chat. That is, the link will turn blue and anyone who clicks it will be taken to that link. For example, if you type:

```
Stop by http://www.coolnerds.com
```

into a message, then the http://www.coolnerds.com part will be blue, and clicking it will fire up the reader's Web browser and send him to this Web site.

Creating boilerplate messages

If you type the same message over and over again, you can save this message as a *macro,* so to type it in the future, you only have to press a few keys. Here's how:

1. Choose <u>V</u>iew ➪ <u>O</u>ptions and click the Automation tab.
2. Under Macros, select a key combination that will trigger the macro, such as Alt+0 (Alt plus a zero), next to <u>K</u>ey combination. You're limited to 10 macros — 0-9.
3. Type in a short name for the macro next to Nam<u>e</u>.
4. Type the message you want the macro to type, and then click the Add <u>M</u>acro button.
5. Click the OK button.

Figure 28-11 shows an example where I've created a macro named PlaySound. Pressing Alt+0 will type out the macro. Just above the Add <u>M</u>acro button, you can see the message the macro will type.

After you choose OK, you'll be returned to Chat. When it's time to send the boilerplate message, choose <u>V</u>iew ➪ M<u>a</u>cros and the name of the macro you want to play. Or just press the shortcut key combination you assigned to the macro.

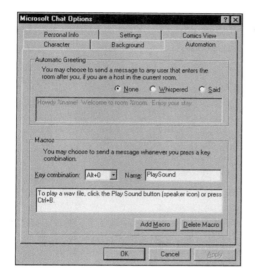

Figure 28-11: Sample macro to type a typical message

Downloading More Characters

You can download some extra characters for Chat from Microsoft's Web site. Here's how:

1. Connect to the Internet and start your Web browser (Internet Explorer 4, for example).

2. Point the Web browser to `http://www.microsoft.com/ie/download`.

3. Choose Windows 95 and Windows NT 4.0, and then click the Next button.

4. From the Please select product here list, choose Additional Chat Characters Pack, and then click Next.

5. Choose a server, select Save it to Disk, and save the file in the usual manner.

When the download is complete, close your Web browser. Then use My Computer, Windows Explorer, or Find to locate the file you downloaded (`cchatpack.exe`). Double-click the filename and follow the instructions onscreen.

Creating Your Own Chat Room

You can create your own chat room, if you like. This is handy if you want to have some kind of private online meeting. Or, perhaps, try to gather up a group of people with similar interests. To create a new room:

1. Choose Room ➪ Create Room. The dialog box shown in Figure 28-12 appears.

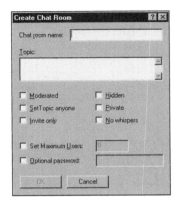

Figure 28-12: The Create Chat Room dialog box

2. Type in a name and topic for the chat room.

3. Select other options as the following describes:

- Moderated: If selected, only the room host and host-designated speakers can talk. All other participants are only spectators.

- Set Topic anyone: If selected, anyone can set the room's topic. If left clear, only the room host can set the topic.

- Invite Only: If selected, only people to whom the room host sends an invitation can join the room.

- Hidden: If selected, room does not appear in the Chat Room List.

- Private: If selected, people outside the room can't look to see who is inside the room.

- No whispers: If selected, no whispers can be used in this room.

- Set Maximum Users: Specifies the maximum number of people who can be in the room at one time.

- Optional password: If selected, only people who type the password you supply can enter the room.

Danger Zone

Passwords are case-sensitive. So, if you create a password-protected chat room, be sure to tell all potential participants to use correct upper/lowercase letters when typing the entry password.

As the host of a chat room, you also have access to some, or all, of the following options under Member ➪ Host in the menu bar. Exactly which options you have access to depends on how you defined the room in the Create Chat Room dialog box.

✦ Kick: Removes a participant from the room.

✦ Ban/Unban: Bans a user from the room or lets a previously banned user back into the room.

✦ Sync Backgrounds: Makes everyone in the room see the same background as the host.

✦ Host: Makes a person the host.

✦ Speaker: Defines a participant as a speaker.

✦ Spectator: Defines a participant as a spectator.

4. Click the OK button.

If you change your mind after you define the room, choose Room ⇨ Properties to change the room's settings.

Creating a welcome message

As host, you can also define a message that appears automatically to anyone new who joins the group. You might use this to display a message or to tell them the rules. To create a custom message:

1. Choose View ⇨ Options and click the Automation tab.

2. In the Automatic Greeting pane, choose whether you want the message to be Whispered only to the newcomer or Said aloud, so all members of the room can see it.

3. Type your message using regular text and, optionally, these special variables (placeholders):

   • **%name%:** Replaced by the newcomer's Chat nickname.

   • **%room%:** Replaced by the name of the current room.

4. Click the OK button.

Figure 28-13 shows an example where the greeting will be whispered to newcomers. For example, if the newcomer is named Judy, and the name of the room is Wave Traders, this person will see the message `Hey there Judy! Welcome to Wave Traders where we exchange and play wave files.`

Inviting people to your room

To invite people into a chat room, you can choose Member ⇨ User List. All people currently in chat rooms will be listed. (Click the Update List button to make sure the list is current). To invite someone to your chat room, click the person's name, and then click the Invite button. Or, if you know a chat room member's nickname already, you can choose Member ⇨ Invite, type the nickname (or several nicknames) into the dialog box that appears, and then click the OK button.

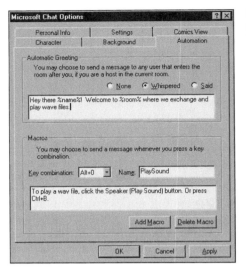

Figure 28-13: Use the Automatic Greeting pane to define a welcome message.

Summary

Microsoft Chat is a fun tool for conversing with others over the Internet. These are the main points to remember . . .

✦ To create a Chat character, start Chat, choose View ➪ Options, and use the Personal Info and Character tabs to define your own persona.

✦ When you're online with Chat you can choose Room ➪ Room List to see all the active chat rooms. Click the Members column heading if you want to sort by how crowded the rooms are.

✦ To join a chat room in the list, click the name of the room you want to join, and then click the Go To button.

✦ To send a message in Chat, choose an emotion from the emotion wheel, type your message, and then click the Say, Think, or Action button.

✦ To direct your message to a specific member, click the member's name in the list of participants before you send the message. You can select multiple members using Ctrl+Click.

✦ To whisper a private message, select the name(s) to whom you want to talk from the list of members' names. Type your message, and then click the Whisper button.

Next we'll look at the *Active Desktop* — a feature of Internet Explorer 4 that combines the power of your Windows 95 desktop with the resources of the Internet.

✦   ✦   ✦

Using the Active Desktop

The *Active Desktop* is actually a part of Internet Explorer 4 that changes your Windows 95 desktop, taskbar, and Start menu to integrate your PC better with the Internet. In addition, the Active Desktop can automatically check the Internet for changes and updates to favorite material, so you needn't check constantly.

The new Active Desktop is a feature of the Internet Explorer 4.0 suite. Currently, the specific product to be downloaded from Microsoft's Web site (http://www.microsoft.com/ie/ie40) is the Internet Explorer 4.0 with Shell Integration, abbreviated as Browser + Integrated Shell. Although it's still in the beta test phase, over a million people have downloaded, and are using, the product!

What Is the Active Desktop?

The Active Desktop is many things. But from a Windows 95 perspective, it's a new way of interacting with your PC and the Internet. For starters, the Active Desktop changes your Windows 95 desktop so it has two *layers* instead of one. First, there's a transparent *icon layer* (you're already accustomed to this layer). The icon layer displays all the desktop icons with which you're familiar.

Behind the icon layer, however, is the new *Active Desktop layer* (also called the *HTML layer*), on which you can place new Desktop Components — items we'll discuss later in this chapter. You may think of this new Active Desktop layer as a replacement for wallpaper. But unlike wallpaper, which is only a picture, the Active Desktop is a dynamic, interactive environment that can provide information from the Internet and can have live hot spots which, when clicked, perform some function for you.

When you install Internet Explorer 4 with Shell Integration, the Active Desktop is installed automatically. You can do several things to control the behavior and appearance of your screen when the Active Desktop is installed. We'll talk about those things first, so you can find your way around this new desktop.

Turning the Active Desktop on and off

Like most things, the Active Desktop is an option. You can easily hide, or display, the Active Desktop layer. Just right-click the desktop, and you'll see a new option at the top of the pop-up menu, as in Figure 29-1.

Figure 29-1: Once installed, the Active Desktop becomes an option on the pop-up menu.

If the Active Desktop menu option has a check mark next to it, this means it's currently visible and available. If no check mark is next to it, the Active Desktop is currently invisible and unavailable. To switch from one state to the other, click the Active Desktop menu option. To leave the option in its current state, click outside the pop-up menu to remove it without changing the option. Figure 29-2 shows how the screen in Figure 29-1 looks with the Active Desktop turned off.

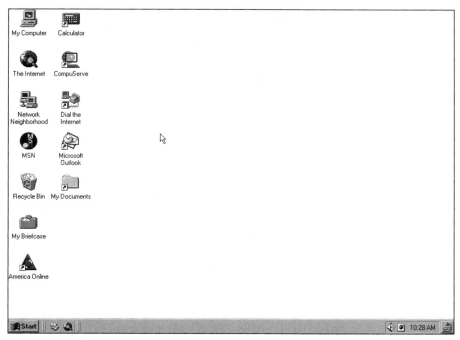

Figure 29-2: The Active Desktop (layer) is off (hidden).

Also on the new pop-up menu is an option titled S<u>h</u>ow Icons. When clear (not checked), the entire icon layer becomes invisible and only the HTML layer is visible. To redisplay the icons, right-click the desktop again and choose S<u>h</u>ow Icons from the pop-up menu. As you gain experience, you may find hiding the desktop icons occasionally is handy, so you can focus on the underlying HTML layer. Figure 29-3 shows how the desktop looks with the Active Desktop turned on, and S<u>h</u>ow Icons turned off.

Figure 29-3: A̲ctive Desktop is turned on; S̲how Icons is turned off.

Hiding/showing application windows

As you probably know, when you start a new program (application), it comes to the desktop and, perhaps, covers the desktop icons. For example, if you open the Windows Calculator and Paint programs, they will cover the desktop and icon layers as in Figure 29-4.

A cool new feature of the Active Desktop is the ability to hide those open programs, which are in a transparent *application layer,* so you can quickly get to the underlying icons and desktop. Just click the Surface/Restore button way down in the lower-right corner of the screen (or at the right edge of the taskbar if your taskbar is elsewhere.) The applications disappear, but they are still open. In fact, their buttons still appear in the taskbar, as shown in Figure 29-5. So, basically, when you hide the application layer, you minimize, in one fell swoop, all the open application windows on your desktop.

To bring the applications back into view, click the Surface/Restore Desktop button again. Or, you can bring back a single application by clicking its button in the taskbar. Very cool!

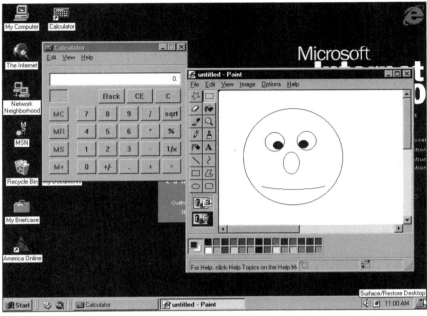

Figure 29-4: Programs cover the desktop and icons.

Figure 29-5: The application layer is invisible now.

New desktop properties

The Active Desktop also brings some new properties to the Windows 95 desktop. As you may recall, two ways exist to get to the desktop properties:

✦ Right-click the desktop and choose Properties.

✦ Or, click the Start button and choose Settings ➪ Control Panel, and then open the Display icon.

Once you get to the Display Properties dialog box, click the Desktop tab to view the new properties, shown in Figure 29-6. Here's a quick rundown of what the various options in the Desktop tab give you:

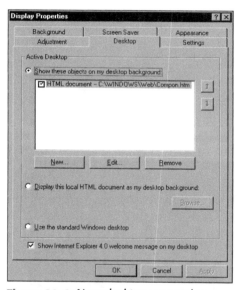

Figure 29-6: New desktop properties

✦ **Show these objects on my desktop background:** Enables you to hide/display desktop components listed beneath the option. If you choose this option, you can specify which objects are visible by selecting them in the list below the option.

I'll explain Desktop Components in detail a little later in this chapter. For now, you need to get a sense for what the new Desktop tab in Display Properties is all about.

✦ **Display this local HTML document as my desktop background:** If you know how to create Web pages (HTML files), you can use this option to choose an HTML file as your Active Desktop background.

✦ **Use the standard Windows desktop:** Completely disables all Active Desktop features bringing "classic Windows 95" back to life.

✦ **Show Internet Explorer 4.0 welcome message on my desktop:** If selected, the large Microsoft Internet Explorer 4.0 message is visible on the desktop. You can choose this option only when *Show these objects*... is selected.

Note, your selections do not take effect until you click the OK button or the Apply button. (The difference being: OK makes the changes and closes the Display Properties dialog box; Apply makes the changes without closing that dialog box.)

To single-click or double-click?

Perhaps the hardest thing to get used to with the Active Desktop is you no longer need to double-click to open a desktop icon. Instead, you only have to click once. The idea behind this is to have the Windows desktop act more like a Web page, where you just have to click a link once to go to some new destination.

When single-clicking on the desktop is active, the icons and mouse pointer even take on a slightly different appearance. Pointing to a desktop icon changes the mouse pointer to a little pointing hand. And the text beneath the icon turns to underlined blue, like a hyperlink in a Web page. Figure 29-7 shows an example with the mouse pointer resting on the My Computer icon.

Figure 29-7: Pointing to My Computer with an Active Desktop

Actually, underlined blue is the default color for icon text on the desktop. You can control the color via the Display Properties dialog box, which you reach by right-clicking the desktop and choosing Properties.

So now, some of you might be thinking "Yeah, but I used to single-click a desktop icon to select it, and double-click that icon to open it. How do I select now?" The answer is *pointing* to an icon in Active Desktop selects it. In essence, the Active Desktop subtracts one left click from the classic Windows way of doing things. The right mouse button is unaffected, as summarized in Table 29-1.

Table 29-1 Classic Windows vs. the Active Desktop		
Action	*Classic Windows*	*Active Desktop*
Select icon	Click	Point
Open icon	Double-click	Click
Display shortcut menu	Right-click	Right-click

As in classic Windows, you can select multiple icons by dragging a lasso around them. With the Active Desktop, however, you must make sure you click outside some icon first, so no icon is selected. Then start dragging your lasso outside any icon, as well.

 If you continue to double-click desktop icons, from habit, you'll often find yourself in some unexpected window because the second click applies to the next icon that appears. As I'll discuss in a moment, you can use the new Back button to "undo" that second click.

But I hate single-clicking!

If many months, or years, of double-clicking make it hard for you to get accustomed to single-clicking on the desktop, you can easily go back to a more classic double-clicking routine. Here's how:

1. Right-click the desktop, choose Properties, and click the Desktop tab.

2. Make sure <u>U</u>se the standard Windows desktop is *not* selected (choose either of the two option buttons above it.)

3. Click the OK button to close the Display Properties dialog box.

4. Open your My Computer icon.

5. Choose <u>V</u>iew ➪ <u>O</u>ptions from My Computer's menu bar.

6. Click the View tab.

7. In the Web View pane, choose <u>D</u>ouble-click to open any item as shown in Figure 29-8.

8. Click the OK button.

You'll be returned to classic Windows clicking. You still can use all the other features of the Active Desktop, however, which I discuss later in this chapter.

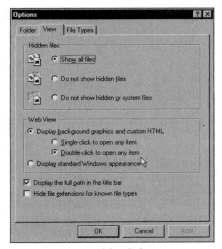

Figure 29-8: Double-click to open any item is selected here.

But I hate Active Desktop!

If you, or someone with whom you share the computer, hate the whole single-clicking and Active Desktop scenario, here's a simple way to deactivate both without uninstalling anything:

1. Go to the Display Properties dialog box (right-click the desktop and choose Properties.)

2. Click the Desktop tab and choose the Use the standard Windows desktop option.

3. Click the OK button.

Remember, this approach disables all features of the Active Desktop, returning you to the classic Windows 95 discussed throughout this book. You can easily reinstate the Active Desktop features, though, by repeating the steps, but choosing some option other than Use the standard Windows desktop.

New Folder Goodies and Toolbars

As though changing the Windows desktop weren't enough, Active Desktop even changes your individual folders. In particular, when the Active Desktop is active, you'll see some major changes to your My Computer and Windows Explorer folders, as in the examples shown in Figure 29-9.

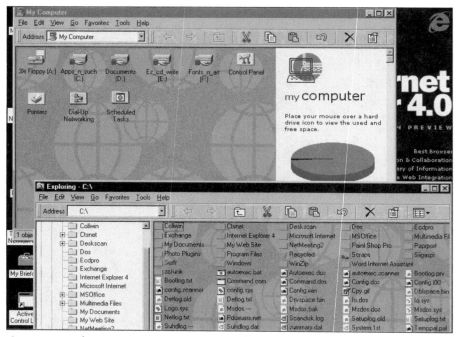

Figure 29-9: The My Computer and Windows Explorer folders in an Active Desktop

Probably the first thing you'll notice is the new baby-blue wallpaper within each folder. Also, My Computer has a large graphic to the right. When you point to (not click!) a drive in My Computer, the pie chart and text beneath show how much space is available on that drive. You can further customize these folders, as I'll discuss a little later in this chapter. For now, however, I'd like to call your attention to the new toolbars in these folders.

If you can't see the toolbar in a folder, choose <u>V</u>iew ➪ <u>T</u>oolbar from that folder's menu bar.

New folder toolbars

Many of the new toolbars (and the taskbar, as well) have pairs of raised vertical lines. When multiple sets of these lines are across a toolbar, you can drag the lines left and right to widen or narrow that part of the toolbar. Also, you can drag toolbars up or down to stack, or unstack, them. For example in Figure 29-10, I've stacked the Address toolbar over the buttons portion in My Computer.

Figure 29-10: Toolbar in My Computer split into two and stacked

To determine which button is which in a toolbar, point to a button and wait a second or two for the tooltip to appear. Common buttons in the toolbars are now like the buttons used in Web-browsing programs. For example, many folder toolbars contain the following buttons:

✦ **Back:** Returns you to what was previously displayed in this window (if anything).

✦ **Forward:** Returns you to the display you just backed out of (if any).

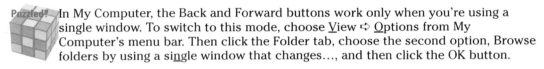

Puzzled? In My Computer, the Back and Forward buttons work only when you're using a single window. To switch to this mode, choose <u>V</u>iew ➪ <u>O</u>ptions from My Computer's menu bar. Then click the Folder tab, choose the second option, Browse folders by using a si<u>n</u>gle window that changes…, and then click the OK button.

✦ **Up:** Moves up a level, if possible, when navigating through folders.

✦ **Cut:** Moves the currently selected item into the Windows Clipboard.

✦ **Copy:** Copies the currently selected item(s) into the Windows Clipboard.

✦ **Undo:** Undoes your most recent action, if any.

✦ **Delete:** Deletes the currently selected item(s).

✦ **Properties:** Displays the currently select item's properties (if any).

✦ **Views:** When available, enables you to choose a format for displaying the folder's contents.

New desktop toolbars

In addition to the changed toolbars within folders, Internet Explorer 4 adds four new toolbars to the Windows 95 desktop:

✦ **Quick Launch Toolbar:** Provides shortcuts to all programs in the Internet Explorer Suite.

✦ **Address Toolbar:** Type a URL to open a Web page right from the desktop.

✦ **Links Toolbar:** Provides shortcuts to important Web sites, right from your desktop.

✦ **Desktop Toolbar:** Provides shortcuts to favorite files, folders, documents, and programs on your PC.

These toolbars can be sized, displayed in the taskbar or on the desktop, and docked to any edge of the screen. To add one of these toolbars to the desktop:

1. Right-click the taskbar and point to <u>T</u>oolbars as in Figure 29-11.

Figure 29-11: To find new toolbars, right-click the taskbar.

2. Click the name of the toolbar you want to add.

When you first add a toolbar, it will appear in the taskbar with the two vertical lines that enable you to widen and narrow the toolbar. All these new free-floating toolbars share some noteworthy characteristics:

✦ To make a toolbar free-floating, like the example shown in Figure 29-12, drag its two vertical lines onto the desktop.

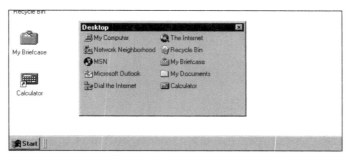

Figure 29-12: Free-floating Desktop toolbar

✦ To dock a free-floating toolbar to an edge of the screen, drag it by its title bar to where you want to dock it.

✦ When a toolbar is docked, you can right-click it and choose Auto-Hide to hide it when not in use. To bring it out of hiding, move the mouse pointer to the edge where the toolbar resides.

✦ When a toolbar is docked, you can also right-click the toolbar and select or clear the Always on Top option, which determines whether the toolbar covers overlapping application window.

✦ To show or hide the text under toolbar icons, right-click the toolbar and choose Show Text.

✦ To show or hide the toolbar's title, right-click the toolbar and select Show Title.

✦ To size the toolbar's icons, right-click the toolbar and choose View ➪ Large or View ➪ Small.

✦ To put a free-floating toolbar back into the taskbar, drag it by the vertical lines back into the taskbar.

✦ To close a toolbar, right-click some neutral gray area on that toolbar and choose Close.

✦ If the toolbar is free-floating, you can also click the X button in its upper-right corner to close it.

Creating a new custom toolbar

You can also create your own custom toolbar, which acts as sort of a shortcut to any folder on your PC. To do this:

1. Right-click the taskbar or any desktop toolbar and choose Toolbars ➪ New Toolbar. You'll come to the dialog box shown in Figure 29-13.

Figure 29-13: Dialog box for creating a new toolbar

2. Select, or browse to, a folder you want to display as a toolbar.

3. Click the OK button.

The new toolbar squeezes into the available space on the taskbar. As with any other desktop toolbar, however, you can drag it out to the desktop using those two little vertical lines. For example, in Figure 29-14, I created a toolbar version of my Network Neighborhood folder.

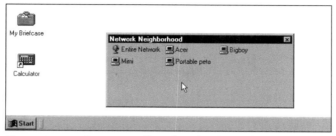

Figure 29-14: Custom toolbar showing icons from my Network Neighborhood folder

As an alternative to creating a custom toolbar, you can add new icons to the Quick Launch toolbar. Right-drag any icon into the Quick Launch toolbar, and when you release the mouse button, choose Create Shortcut(s) Here.

The new Address toolbar

The new Address toolbar is unique among toolbars. For one thing, it's almost ubiquitous. It appears in Internet Explorer, as well as in most folders. Furthermore, you can add the new Address toolbar to the desktop or taskbar using the Toolbars menu, which is accessible when you right-click the taskbar. For example, if you look around the screen in Figure 29-15, you'll see an Address toolbar in Internet Explorer, My Computer, floating on the desktop, and in the taskbar.

The Address toolbar is a pretty wild one, in that it can take you anywhere on your own computer, as well as anywhere in the world via the Internet! For example, if you open the Address box drop-down list in My Computer, as in Figure 29-16, you can easily choose a local drive or folder to cruise to by clicking your choice.

You can also type a destination into the Address box. For example, if you type C:\ into any Address toolbar, you'll be taken to a display of all the folders in your hard drive, drive C:\. If you're connected to the Internet and type `http://www.coolnerds.com` into any Address box, you'll be taken to my Web site!

So the idea here is, regardless of what program you are in currently, you can get to any local resource (something on your own computer) as well as to any remote resource (something on the Internet) without switching programs. Just type the desired address into the Address box and press Enter. Wow!

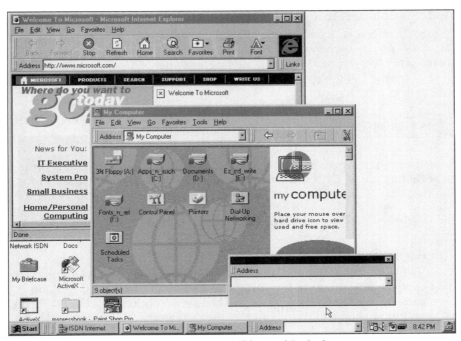

Figure 29-15: Four Address toolbars are visible on this desktop.

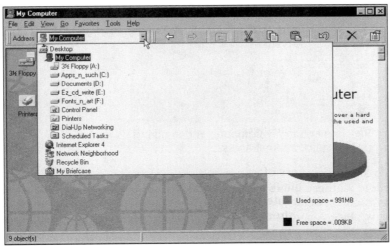

Figure 29-16: This is the Address toolbar drop-down list in My Computer's toolbar.

Address toolbar AutoComplete

The Address box is "smart" because it will try to complete whatever you're typing currently. As you type in some new address, the box will extend your text to match an earlier entry, as in the example shown in Figure 29-17, where I typed `http://www.mi` and the Address box filled in the rest for me.

Figure 29-17: I typed `http://www.mi` and the address box filled in the rest, by guessing.

Sometimes the Address box will guess right, and all you need to do is press Enter to accept its guess. Of course, sometimes the Address box will guess wrong, too. But that's no problem. Just continue to type in whatever you want. Or, if the Address box adds too much extra text to whatever you're typing, you can press the Delete key (Del) to delete the highlighted text the Address box added.

The Go menu

The Go menu in My Computer and Windows Explorer, shown in Figure 29-18, also offers some quick access to Internet capabilities, right from your desktop. If you aren't already on the Internet when you choose an option from the Go menu, you'll be prompted to connect to the Internet through your dial-up connection.

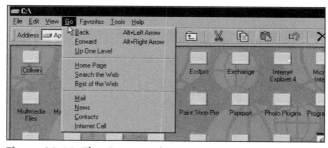

Figure 29-18: The Go menu in My Computer and Windows Explorer also provides quick Internet access.

The idea behind all these handy-dandy new features we've discussed so far is tighter integration between Windows 95 and the Internet. You can hop to a Web site from many places on your desktop — it isn't necessary to fire up Internet Explorer or any other Web browser first.

For the rest of this chapter I'd like to focus on some other, optional, features that make staying in touch with the Internet easier for you, namely Desktop Components, subscriptions, and smart favorites.

Desktop Components

Desktop Components are one of the best new features of the Active Desktop. These components exist on the Active Desktop layer, behind the icons layer. Like icons, you can move Desktop Components around. Unlike icons, though, Desktop Components can be sized and Desktop Components can contain multiple hot spots which, when clicked, take you to a Web page. In fact, Desktop Components can be linked to Web sites giving you up-to-the-minute information on news, stock prices, sports scores, and other useful information.

Manipulating Desktop Components

When you put the mouse pointer on a Desktop Component, little gray controls appear in the upper-left and lower-right corners of the component, as in the example shown in Figure 29-19.

Figure 29-19: The mouse pointer is resting on a Desktop Component.

To move the component, put the point to the upper-right corner of the component until the mouse pointer turns to a four-headed arrow. Then drag the component to its new location. To size a component, drag its lower-right corner.

When you point to a hot spot on the component, the mouse pointer will turn to a small hand with the index finger pointing upward. If you click that hot spot, its action will be carried out. Some hot spots will actually take you to a site on the Internet. If you point to such a spot for a few seconds, without clicking or moving the mouse, a tooltip will appear showing the address to which the hot spot will take you. If, indeed, you want to go to that address, go ahead and click the hot spot.

The hot spot in a Desktop Component can take you to an Internet site only if you're actually connected to the Internet already.

Unlike the sample "Hey! I'm a desktop component" component that comes with Internet Explorer 4, most components are actually live links to information on the Internet or a corporate intranet. Desktop Components are generally used to give you up-to-the-minute, perhaps time-critical, information. Examples include stock prices, current news headlines, sports scores, and weather.

Adding a Desktop Component

As the popularity of Internet Explorer 4 grows, more and more companies will be releasing Desktop Components. While I can't describe in any detail every component that exists now and will exist in the future, I can give you some general guidelines on installing those components. I'll use some examples here from Microsoft's Desktop Component Gallery to teach you the basics. To download and install a component from the Gallery:

1. Get online and point your Web browser to `http://www.microsoft.com/ie/ie40/gallery`. The page you get to will look something like the one in Figure 29-20.

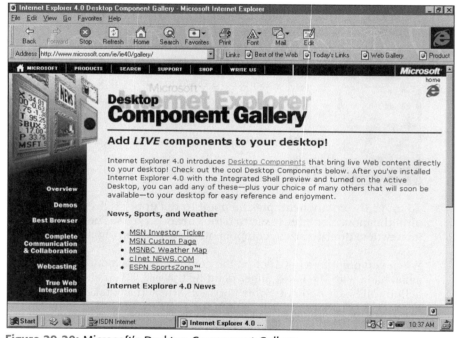

Figure 29-20: Microsoft's Desktop Component Gallery

2. Choose a Desktop Component to add by clicking its name.

3. Read about the component in the page that appears and follow the instructions presented to download the component and set it up on your computer.

For example, in Figure 29-21, I've selected the Stock Quote example. To download it to my desktop, I only have to click the Put it on my Desktop link.

With most components, you'll be given the option to update the component daily (once a day or more often), weekly (less than once a day, but at least once a week), or on some other schedule. For simplicity, you can select Y̲es to update daily (Figure 29-22). I'll show you how to choose other settings and maximize your update efficiency under "Refining Your Update Schedules" later in this chapter.

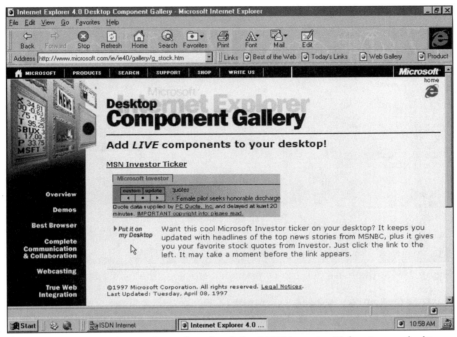

Figure 29-21: Now I'm ready to download the MSN Investor Ticker to my desktop.

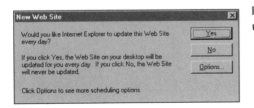

Figure 29-22: If in doubt, choose Y̲es to update your desktop component daily.

In Figure 29-23, you can see where I downloaded several components from Microsoft's Gallery, including c∣net's NEWS.COM, the MSN Investment Ticker, and the MSNBC Weather Map. I sized and positioned them on the desktop using the basic techniques discussed under "Manipulating a Desktop Component" earlier in this section.

Also in Figure 29-23, I eliminated the "Hey! I'm a desktop component" component. I did this through the Desktop tab of the Display Properties dialog box. That is to say, I right-clicked the desktop and chose Properties. Then I clicked the Desktop tab. I selected all my desktop components for display, except that "Hey!...." component, as you can see in Figure 29-24.

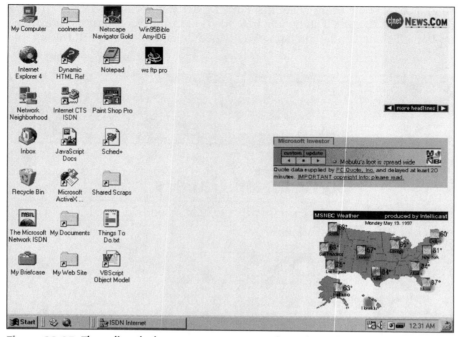

Figure 29-23: Three live desktop components are along the right edge of the screen.

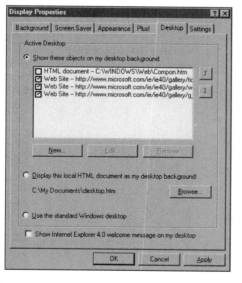

Figure 29-24: Three of my four desktop components will be displayed on the desktop.

If you have a hard time telling which component is which in the Display Properties dialog box, you can see the rest of the URL by clicking it, clicking the Edit button, and then pressing the End key.

In addition to presenting current information from a Web site, most live Desktop Components also act as links to those sites. For example, if I want to get a close look at my weather map, I only have to click the Map. I'm taken straight to the MSNBC Weather site, where I can get a better view of things, as in Figure 29-25. Click the Cancel button after taking a peek.

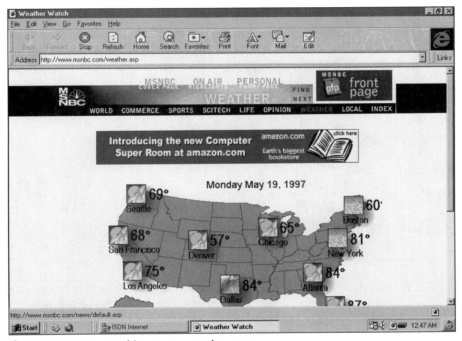

Figure 29-25: Zoomed in on my weather map

Subscribing to Web Sites

Web site subscriptions are another handy new feature of Windows 95/Internet Explorer. When you subscribe to a site, you tell Windows you want to have Web pages that have changed since your last visit downloaded to your PC while you're offline (like, at night while you're asleep!). At some hour you determine, your PC will check every Web site to which you have a subscription. If information in that site has changed, the page will be downloaded to your PC on the spot.

Then when it's convenient for you (say, the next morning), you can look at those changed pages. You needn't wait for them to download to your PC, because they're already on your hard disk in your local Internet cache. In fact, if you download to a portable computer, you can take the machine offline and read the pages wherever it's convenient (on the subway perhaps!).

You can subscribe to any site. And doing so is easy:

1. Connect to the Internet in the usual manner for your PC.

2. Using Internet Explorer 4, browse to any Web site to which you want to subscribe.

3. When you get to the page you want to subscribe to, choose Favorites ➪ Subscriptions ➪ Subscribe from Internet Explorer's menu bar. You're taken to the Subscription dialog box shown in Figure 29-26.

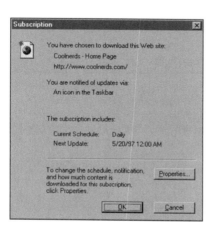

Figure 29-26: The Subscription dialog box

4. If you're content to have the current page checked daily, you can click the OK button. Or, you can click the Properties button to refine the subscription as discussed under the following "Managing subscriptions."

After you choose OK, the Subscription dialog box disappears. Nothing else really happens on the screen. The current Web page will be included in your list of subscriptions, however, as described in the following sections.

Managing subscriptions

You can subscribe to as many, or as few, Web sites as you wish. Do remember, though, when one of the pages in your subscriptions changes, that page is downloaded to the Internet cache on your hard disk. So the more sites you subscribe to, the more disk space will be consumed by downloaded pages.

Activating the subscriptions icon

If you want to be notified, on the desktop, when updated pages are in your Web cache, follow these simple steps:

1. From Internet Explorer's menu bar, choose Favorites ➪ Subscriptions ➪ Options.

2. On the General tab (see Figure 29-27), choose the Show notification icon in the taskbar option.

3. Click the OK button.

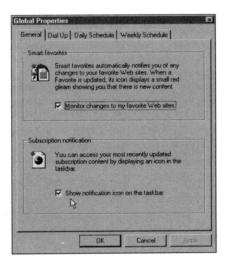

Figure 29-27: The show subscription notification option

The taskbar will now contain a Web page icon, over near the clock. When updated pages are in your collection of subscriptions, that icon will show a red gleam.

Checking your subscriptions

To check your subscriptions, do either of the following:

✦ Click the Subscriptions icon in the taskbar and choose View All Subscriptions (or double-click that icon.)

✦ Or, from Internet Explorer's menu bar choose F̲avorites ➪ S̲ubscriptions ➪ V̲iew All.

Either way, you'll come to the Subscriptions dialog box shown in Figure 29-28. Pages that have changed since you last viewed them are indicated by a red gleam in the upper-left corners of their icons. To view a page, simply click its name. (Or double-click, if you haven't activated single-clicking). Because the page has already been downloaded to your PC, you needn't wait for the page to download now. In fact, you can read these updated pages offline, if you prefer. If you see a message indicating you're offline, click the Stay Offline button, and Internet Explorer 4 will display the downloaded copy of your page.

Desktop Components and Smart Favorites (discussed soon) will be mixed in with your site subscriptions because they, too, are automatically updated periodically.

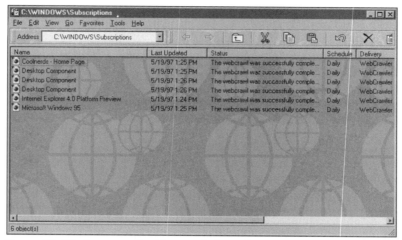

Figure 29-28: Pages marked by a red gleam have changed since you last read them.

Updating subscriptions manually

If, for whatever reason, you want to update all your subscriptions manually, connect to the Internet in the usual manner for your PC. Then click the Subscriptions icon and choose Update Subscriptions Now. Or, open Internet Explorer and choose Favorites ➪ Subscriptions ➪ Update All.

To update a single subscription, open the subscriptions list, right-click the subscription you want to update, and choose Update from the pop-up menu that appears.

Tweaking or deleting a subscription

To change or delete a subscription, first get to the Subscriptions list — either by double-clicking the Subscriptions icon or by choosing Favorites ➪ Subscriptions ➪ View All. To delete a subscription, right-click it and choose Delete.

To change a subscription, right-click it and choose Properties from the pop-up menu. You'll come to a dialog box like the one in Figure 29-29. Use the tabs within the dialog box to view/change options for this one subscription, as summarized in the following:

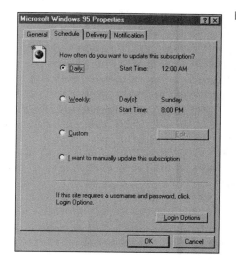

Figure 29-29: Options for a single subscription

✦ **General:** Shows current information about the subscription.

✦ **Schedule:** Choose to update Daily or Weekly, on some other schedule, or not at all (manually).

✦ **Delivery:** Specify how much information you want to download from the subscribed site.

✦ **Notification:** Choose how you want to be notified of changes to the site.

Click the OK button after making your selections.

Managing Favorites Sites

I introduced you to the concept of favorites in Chapter 24, where you first learned to browse the World Wide Web with Microsoft Internet Explorer. As you may recall, when you get to a Web site you want to revisit later, you can choose Favorites ⇨ Add to Favorites to bookmark the site by adding it to your Favorites list.

To return to a favorite site, open the Favorites list and click the site to which you want to return. After you've installed Internet Explorer 4 with Shell Integration, getting to your Favorites folder is simple, because it's available from:

✦ Internet Explorer's menu bar

✦ Most folders' menu bars

✦ The Start menu, as shown in Figure 29-30

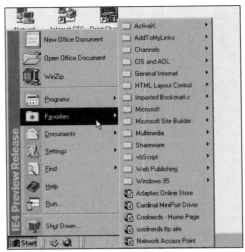

Figure 29-30: Favorites are now available from the Start menu.

As your collection of favorites grows, you may want to start categorizing them into groups to keep the Favorites list from growing too long. This is easy to do:

1. From any folder's menu bar, choose F<u>a</u>vorites ➪ <u>O</u>rganize Favorites.

2. In the Organize Favorites dialog box that appears (Figure 29-31), use the various buttons to create folders, and to move, rename, and delete favorites. You can also drag-and-drop favorites into folders.

3. Click the <u>C</u>lose button when you're done.

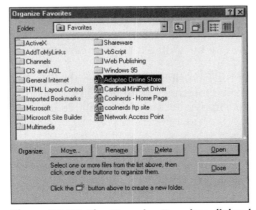

Figure 29-31: The Organize Favorites dialog box

Using smart favorites

Another handy feature of Internet Explorer 4 is the ability to alert you to favorite Web sites that have changed since your last visit. This is similar to subscriptions. With smart favorites, though, the updated pages aren't downloaded to your PC. Instead, the favorite site's icon gets a red gleam.

Hot Stuff You can use a smart favorite as an alternative to a subscription to avoid loading too much Web stuff onto your hard disk.

By default, all the favorites in your Favorites folder are smart favorites. To make a favorite not-so-smart, you actually must right-click it in the Organize Favorites dialog box and deselect the Watch this Site option.

To ensure Windows visits your favorite sites to check for updates, you also must do the following:

1. If the Organize Favorites dialog box is still open, close it.
2. In My Computer or any folder window, choose Favorites ⇨ Subscriptions ⇨ Options.
3. On the General tab, make sure the first option, Monitor changes to my favorite Web sites, is selected as in Figure 29-32.

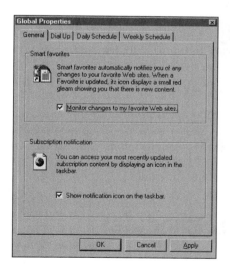

Figure 29-32: Smart favorites will be checked, along with sites to which you've subscribed.

4. Click the OK button.

That's all there is to it. To determine how often Windows checks your favorite sites for changes, follow these steps:

1. Double-click the Subscriptions icon in the taskbar, or choose F<u>a</u>vorites ⇨ <u>S</u>ubscriptions ⇨ <u>V</u>iew All to view all subscriptions.

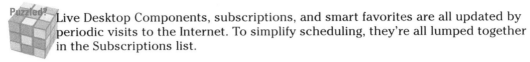

Live Desktop Components, subscriptions, and smart favorites are all updated by periodic visits to the Internet. To simplify scheduling, they're all lumped together in the Subscriptions list.

2. Right-click Smart Favorites and choose P<u>r</u>operties.

3. In the Smart Favorites Properties dialog box that appears (see Figure 29-33), choose how often you want Windows to check for changes to those sites: <u>D</u>aily, <u>W</u>eekly, <u>C</u>ustom, or manually.

4. Click the OK button.

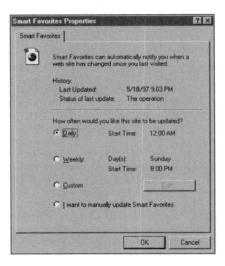

Figure 29-33: Smart Favorites Properties dialog box

That's all there is to it. In the future, whenever you view your list of favorites, pages that have changed since your last visit will be marked with the red gleam. Pages that haven't changed won't display that gleam.

Refining Your Update Schedules

As you've seen, you can opt to have live Desktop Components, subscriptions, and smart favorites updated daily or weekly. Or, you can choose <u>C</u>ustom to update a particular item on some custom schedule other than daily or weekly. Ideally, what you want is to have all these Internet checks and downloads take place while you're away from the computer. Like, maybe when you're sleeping, so you needn't waste time waiting (and waiting, and waiting) for pages to download and sites to be visited. To define, specifically, when daily and weekly Internet visits occur, you change the Global Subscription Properties:

1. Click the Subscriptions icon in the taskbar and choose Global Subscription Properties. Or in Internet Explorer, choose Favorites ➪ Subscriptions ➪ Options from the menu bar.

2. If you don't have a full-time connection to the Internet tab, click the Dial Up tab, choose Yes, and fill in the blanks to define how you'll connect to the Internet. Choose the dial-up networking connectoid that you use to connect to the Internet from the drop-down list next to Connect using. Figure 29-34 shows an example.

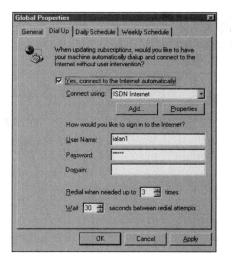

Figure 29-34: Will use my ISDN Internet connectoid to dial into the Internet for updating subscriptions

3. Next, click the Daily Schedule tab.

4. Define when you want daily updates to take place. For example, in Figure 29-35, I've specified I want my daily sites to be checked/updated once a day, at some time between 2:00 A.M. and 5:00 A.M.

5. Click the Weekly Schedule tab.

6. Define when you want weekly updates to take place. For example, in Figure 29-36, I opted to have my weekly updates take place on Monday and Thursday, between 2:00 A.M and 5:00 A.M.

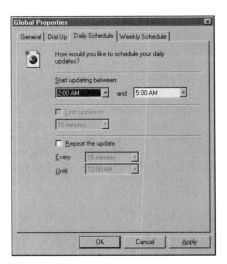

Figure 29-35: Daily updates are to take place one a day, between two and five o'clock in the morning.

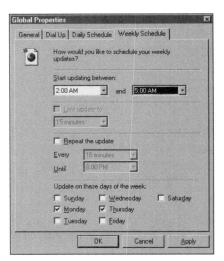

Figure 29-36: Weekly updates will happen on Monday and Thursday between 2:00 A.M. and 5:00 A.M.

7. Click the OK button.

That should do the trick. Just remember to leave your computer and modem turned on at times when updates are to take place. You can turn the monitor off, if you like. But the computer itself must be turned on for the Internet activity to take place.

Danger Zone If your dial-up connectoid requires some kind of human intervention, such as typing in information or clicking an OK button, then it might not work for subscriptions. As a workaround, you can try the Dunce program from `http://www.vecdev.com`.

Tweaking individual subscriptions

If ever you need to check on, or change, when a particular Internet check or update takes place, go to your subscription list. Remember, to do this, you can double-click the Subscriptions icon in the taskbar. Or, choose Favorites ➪ Subscriptions ➪ View All from My Computer or any other menu bar. There, the column labeled Schedule will tell you, at a glance, how often each subscription and Desktop Component, as well as your Smart Favorites, will be checked.

If you want to change any item's schedule, right-click that item and choose Properties. In the Schedule tab, choose which option best describes how often you want to update the item. Remember, if you don't want to use your Daily or Weekly schedule, you can choose Custom, and then click the Edit button and define a schedule unique to that item. If you don't want to update the item automatically at all, you can choose the last option, I want to manually update this subscription. This way, the item will only be updated when you do the manual update described earlier in this chapter under "Updating subscriptions manually."

Summary

Whew! Seems like we covered a whole lot of ground in a short amount of space in this chapter. You probably never imagined that downloading a Web browser could have so much impact on your Windows 95 desktop, and on your own productivity, as well. To summarize the most important points:

✦ Internet Explorer 4.0 with Shell Integration includes features to integrate better the Windows 95 desktop with the Internet.

✦ The Active Desktop can make navigating your own computer similar to browsing the Web, by providing single-click access to desktop icons.

✦ The new Address toolbar also makes it easy to jump to any place on your own computer, or to any Web site, without getting into, or out of, a specific program.

✦ That Active Desktop layer can also house Desktop Components that display up-to-the-minute information from the Internet, as well as links to favorite Web sites.

✦ You can find Desktop Components in Microsoft's gallery at http://www.microsoft.com/ie/ie40/gallery.

✦ Thanks to site subscriptions, you can now have your computer scan favorite sites for changes and download updated pages while you sleep, so you can view those pages offline without waiting.

✦ You can use Smart Favorites to keep track of which sites have changed since your last visit.

✦ For more information on Internet Explorer and the Active Desktop, visit Microsoft's Web site at `http://www.microsoft.com/ie/ie40`.

I think that's enough Internet information to keep you busy for a long time. In the next section, I'll start discussing local area networks — smaller networks that span an office or building rather than the entire planet Earth.

✦   ✦   ✦

Local Area Networks (LANs)

Why Bother with a Local Area Network (LAN)?

If you have two or more PCs in your office or home, the best thing you can do for yourself is hook them together as a *local area network* (LAN). You may think, "Yeah, right. Like I'm really gonna create a LAN just to hook my portable PC to my desktop." You're thinking that because you assume creating a LAN is a big, expensive, complicated undertaking. You think you'll need to shell out big bucks to have someone set it up, and you'll be at that person's mercy every time the LAN goes down. Or worse, you'll have to hire someone full-time just to babysit the LAN.

Put all such thoughts out of your head. LANs were a big complicated mess when DOS was in the picture. But things have gotten much, much easier now that Windows 95 (and Windows NT and Windows for Workgroups) have built-in networking capabilities. You no longer have an operating system (DOS) that's fighting a LAN every step of the way. Instead, you have an operating system that supports and embraces a LAN, which even has all the software you need built right into it.

Advantages of a LAN

Even though setting up a LAN is easier than ever, some investment of time and money still is involved, so you need some justification. Perhaps one of the following advantages of a LAN will solve a problem for you:

✦ If only one PC in the LAN has a printer, CD-ROM drive, or fax/modem, every PC in the LAN can use that hardware.

✦ If several people work on the same document, they can use the documents on one PC without copying and transporting files via floppy disk. Several people often can work on the same document at the same time.

✦ If several people work with the same data — such as a customer list, inventory list, or orders — all this information can reside on one PC. Each user in the LAN will have access to this always current data.

✦ You can set up local e-mail, whereby users can send messages to each other via PC.

✦ Any portable PCs connected to the LAN can regain access to the resources of the LAN even while they're away, thanks to dial-up networking.

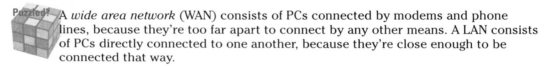 A *wide area network* (WAN) consists of PCs connected by modems and phone lines, because they're too far apart to connect by any other means. A LAN consists of PCs directly connected to one another, because they're close enough to be connected that way.

In short, if you're using floppy disks to transport files from one PC to another — whether to print, fax, modem, whatever — you need a LAN. You'll quickly earn back the time and money you invest in creating the LAN by not having to fumble with floppies anymore.

Why LANs Seem So Complicated

When you read about LANs, you usually are inundated by so many acronyms, technical terms, and product names, you have difficulty understanding what's really involved in setting up a LAN. Maybe I can clear up some confusion about this topic.

Any PC with Windows 95, Windows NT, or Windows for Workgroups on it can hook into the LAN without any third-party software. You don't need Novell NetWare, Banyan-Vines, Microsoft LAN Manager, Lantastic, or other network programs.

If you have relatively few computers (15 or fewer), a simple peer-to-peer LAN probably will work perfectly for you. You won't need to worry about client/server terminology.

The written documentation for LANs can be one of the most confusing elements of networking. Often, when you look up the solution to a problem, the documentation tells you to ask your network administrator — not much help if you *are* the network administrator. Another problem with the written documentation is Step 1 in the instruction manual says something like this: "Make sure the LAN is up, running, and working perfectly, and that you have full administrative rights, before you do anything else. If you have any problems, ask your network administrator."

Isn't this situation a catch-22? You're expecting to set up a LAN, and the instructions tell you to set it all up and grab your local full-time network guru before you do anything else.

In this book, I make no such assumptions. For all intents and purposes, you *are* the network administrator, even if you don't know diddly-squat about LANs at the moment. And I am not assuming the LAN is set up and ready to go. I'm just assuming you have two or more PCs you want to connect in a LAN.

What You Really Need to Know

I don't mean to imply a computer novice should set up a LAN. The job calls for some prerequisite skills and knowledge, summarized in the following list:

✦ You must know how to use My Computer or Windows Explorer to browse around a PC.

✦ You must know how to open a computer case and install a board. If the PC you're connecting to the LAN has an available PCMCIA slot, you must know how to insert and remove PC Cards.

✦ You should get a little practice with Device Manager (refer to Chapter 10) so you can find available resources and tweak some settings if the need arises.

If you don't meet those criteria, you may be better off hiring a pro to do the job. Just make sure this person understands you want to set up a peer-to-peer LAN, using the network capabilities built into Windows 95 (or Windows NT, or Windows for Workgroups). Explain that you're not looking for a dedicated server just yet and you don't need third-party software, such as NetWare. The installer may grumble because this approach seems too easy. But easy is good. Trust me — the simpler, the better.

Planning the LAN

Phase one in setting up a LAN is planning your equipment purchase. You have to choose among several types of cables and network cards. In the interest of keeping things simple, I'll narrow your choices to the items that have emerged as industry standards, which offer the simplest and most flexible solutions to the problem.

Choosing a cable type

The first decision is the kind of cable to use. You have several choices, but you'd do well to stick with TPE cable. This type of cable has many names, including 10BaseT, 10BT, Twisted Pair, Twisted Pair Ethernet, TPE, and RJ-45. But you can recognize the cable because the plugs at the ends look like slightly oversize telephone plugs. The cable resembles the cable that connects your telephone to the wall.

This type of cabling requires an Ethernet hub (also called an Ethernet concentrator) to which each PC in the LAN will connect, as shown in Figure 30-1.

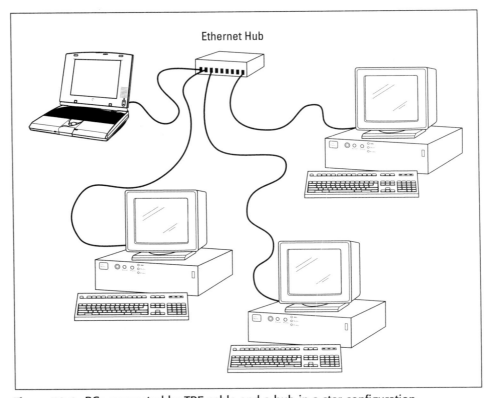

Figure 30-1: PCs connected by TPE cable and a hub in a star configuration

This type of arrangement, in which each PC plugs into a hub, sometimes is called a *star configuration*. I guess this name arose because if you put the hub smack in the middle and spread the PCs around evenly, the configuration would look like a giant asterisk (*), and an asterisk sometimes is called a star. (Now we're *really* getting technical, eh?)

After you decide to use the TPE cable, you must decide where you want to put the hub. Some hubs actually require their own power and, therefore, must be plugged into a wall outlet. You probably should plan to put the hub near a standard power outlet (the same kind you use for a lamp).

Next, you need to measure the distance from each PC to the hub. You must run the cable in such a way that people aren't likely to trip over it. Always round up when you make your calculations. If one PC is just a few feet from the hub, you need a 2-foot or 4-foot cable for this connection. If another PC is about 10 feet from the hub, you need about a 12-foot cable for that connection. You need one cable for each PC you plan to connect to the LAN.

 A cable that's too long still is usable; a cable that's too short is not.

Choosing a network card

In addition to cable, you need one network interface card for each PC in the LAN. This card is a piece of hardware that allows you to connect one PC to a LAN. Like cables, network cards go by several names, including network adapter card, Ethernet card, and NIC. Choosing a network card is fairly easy if you follow these guidelines:

✦ Make sure the card is an Ethernet card.

✦ Make sure the card will fit in the slot you have available — typically, ISA on a desktop PC, an ISA or PCI slot on a Pentium, or a PCMCIA slot on a portable computer.

✦ Choose a card that supports the type of cable you're using (TPE). The hole into which the TPE cable plugs sometimes is called an RJ-45 connector.

✦ The easiest card to install is one that bears the "Designed for Windows 95" plug-and-play logo.

✦ The second easiest card to install is one for which Windows 95 has a built-in driver, which the program can detect and install automatically. The Windows 95 Hardware Compatibility List includes supported Ethernet adapters.

✦ A 32-bit card is faster (and more expensive) than a 16-bit card but not worth fretting over if the LAN is fairly small.

You can mix and match brands and models of network cards however you want, as long as all of them are Ethernet cards. But for simplicity's sake, you may want to buy the same make and model of network card for each PC in the LAN. (You can buy network cards in packs of 5 and 10.) Any laptop PCs you want to hook to the LAN require PC Cards (PCMCIA) rather than traditional internal cards.

Making the Buy

Before you go to the local Comput-O-Rama to buy the stuff for your LAN, you should have your shopping list ready. You need to know the following:

✦ How many ISA (or PCI) Ethernet cards you need, and how many PCMCIA Ethernet cards you need.

✦ What type of plug you need on each Ethernet card (most likely, the RJ-45 plug for TPE cable).

✦ How many Ethernet cables you need and how long each cable should be. Make sure the cables have the proper plugs on each end (the plugs that fit into the RJ-45 socket).

✦ How many slots you need in your Ethernet hub. Allowing for growth never hurts. If you plan to link, say, four computers in your LAN, consider getting a hub with six connection slots.

Figure 30-2 shows an example of a shopping list for connecting four PCs in a LAN. I need four Ethernet cards. But because one of the PCs in my LAN is a laptop, one card must be a PCMCIA-style card. I need four cables (one for each card) and a hub with at least four connection slots.

Things to Pick up at Comput-O-Rama

3   Ethernet cards for desktop PCs [ISA slots]

1   Ethernet card for laptop PC [PCMCIA slot]

2   6-foot TPE cables

2   12-foot TPE cables

1   Ethernet hub with at least 4 slots [6 to allow growth]

Figure 30-2: Shopping list for equipment needed to set up a four-PC LAN

After you buy all this stuff and get it back to where your PCs are, you're ready to move to the next chapter, in which you actually set up that LAN.

Summary

If you have two or more PCs in one location, consider hooking them together in a local area network (LAN):

✦ Computers in a LAN can share resources — printers, drives, CD-ROM drives, folders, and modems.

✦ LANs, which once required highly specialized knowledge, are relatively easy to set up and maintain in Windows 95.

✦ All the networking software you need is built right into Windows 95.

✦ You do need additional *hardware* to set up a LAN. In particular, you need a network card and Ethernet cable for each PC in the LAN, and an Ethernet hub to which to connect all the cables.

✦ When buying a network card, try to find one with the "Designed for Windows 95" logo for quick-and-easy installation.

✦   ✦   ✦

Create Your Own LAN

After you purchase all the hardware you need to turn those independent PCs into a working team, you're ready to start installing. Be forewarned, this process can take a few hours; try to do it when people are not working on the PCs you want to link. Get ready to concentrate. Take the phone off the hook. If other people are around, put a big sign on your back that reads: "Do not talk to me." Your brain will be tied up for a few hours.

Installing the LAN Hardware

At this point, you have hardware (cards and cables) and perhaps software (disks that came with the network cards) in hand. This part is a little tricky. You may have Ethernet cards that were designed for DOS/Windows, or you may have plug-and-play Ethernet cards designed for Windows 95. If you're adding a portable PC to the LAN, you may have a PCMCIA Ethernet card. In the following sections, I'll try to cover all these possibilities. But you also must rely on the card manufacturer's instructions in addition to my instructions.

More Info If the card manufacturer's documentation includes instructions for installing software in DOS or Windows 3.x, you want to *ignore* that section of the documentation. You don't want to use the old real-mode 16-bit drivers if you can avoid them. Instead, you want to use the 32-bit drivers, which are built into Windows 95.

Step 1: Check available resources

Whenever you install new hardware in your PC, you'll probably be asked to choose an Interrupt Request (IRQ) for that device. You also may have to provide an Input/Output (I/O) address. Network cards are no exception.

What is an IRQ?

An Interrupt Request (IRQ) is a channel that's allowed to interrupt whatever the processor is doing at the moment and request immediate attention. The keyboard is a perfect example. Suppose you start some long process and then decide to finish it later. When you press the Esc key, you don't want the processor to ignore you and keep doing what it's doing; you want the processor to stop what it's doing and pay attention to whatever key you are pressing.

Some standards exist for assigning IRQs to devices. IRQ 1, for example, is used for the keyboard on virtually every PC. IRQ 2 is used for the system timer, and IRQs 3 and 4 are for the serial ports (COM 1 and COM 2). The IRQs generally left free are 5, 7, 9, 10, and a few others.

Every time you install some new internal device, such as a sound card or modem, you may need to give that device its own IRQ, so the available IRQs start getting used up. Remembering which IRQs are used and which are available at any given time is tough, so use Device Manager to check for available IRQs before you install any new hardware device.

Before you shut down a PC to install the card, jot down (or print) the resources available on the PC. Follow these steps:

1. Choose Start ➪ Settings ➪ Control Panel.

2. Double-click the System icon.

3. Click the Device Manager tab.

Hot Stuff If this computer is connected to a printer, click the Print button, select System summary, and then choose OK. You get a printed summary of the used IRQ and I/O ports, as well as other information.

4. Double-click Computer at the top of the list and then click the Interrupt request (IRQ) option button.

   The screen shows installed devices, listed by the IRQs the devices are using (see Figure 31-1).

5. Write down any IRQs not already taken — that is, IRQs that do not appear in the list.

   By looking at Figure 31-1, for example, I could write "Available IRQs on this PC: 05, 07, 09, 10."

6. Your network card may want its own area in memory for input/output (I/O), so click the Input/output (I/O) option button to see what's available.

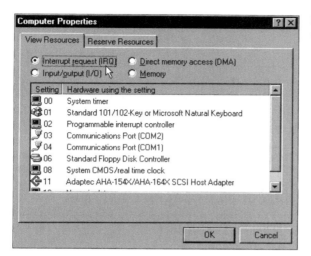

Figure 31-1: Installed devices listed by IRQs

7. Scroll about a third of the way down the list until you see the range 00F0-00FF (see Figure 31-2).

Your network card probably will want an address range below this number, but above 03A. Typically, only a few ranges are already taken, so writing down the ones that are *not* available may be easier. By looking at Figure 31-2, I would write "NOT available I/O ranges: 02F8-02FF, 0330-0333, 0378-037A."

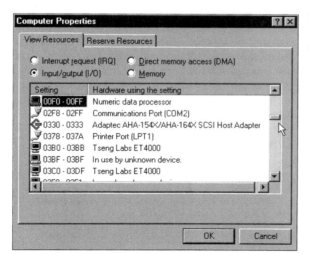

Figure 31-2: I/O addresses above 00FF that already are in use

8. Choose OK twice.

9. Close Control Panel by clicking its Close button.

Remember, the settings you wrote down (or printed) apply only to this PC, so don't let your notes drift too far from this PC. Also make sure you don't confuse these settings with those of any of the other PCs you plan to add to the LAN. While working with each PC, you'll need to refer to the settings several times.

Step 2: Set the board's IRQ

Some ISA cards (not PCMCIA or PCI cards) require you to set dip switches on the board to tell the board which IRQ to use. Now you're getting into a tricky area. You must look at the instructions for the Ethernet card you're installing to determine whether you must set an IRQ yourself — and if so, how you should go about setting this IRQ. The following are possibilities:

✦ If the card's instructions say you don't have to set anything, skip to "Step 3: Shut everything down" later in this chapter.

✦ If the card has dip switches you can adjust manually, and if the directions tell you how to set those switches, follow those instructions to set the dip switches to an available IRQ (in my example, 05, 07, 09, or 10). Then skip to "Step 3: Shut everything down."

✦ If the card requires you to run a program to set the IRQ, do so, following the Ethernet card's instructions. *Make sure you follow only the instructions for setting the dip switches; do not install the DOS or Windows 3.x drivers.* Then read on.

Running the little program that sets dip switches may be somewhat tricky. Most likely, the program will be a DOS program, and you may be unable to run it from a DOS window. Furthermore, you may be required to run the program twice: before you install the board in the PC and after you physically install the board. If you need to run the program before you install the card, follow these steps:

1. Insert into drive A or drive B the floppy disk that came with the Ethernet card, according to the manufacturer's instructions.

2. If you must run the program from a DOS prompt, first try choosing Start ➪ Programs ➪ MS-DOS Prompt.

3. Type the command the instructions tell you to type (for example, **a:\softset2**), and press Enter.

4. If the program complains it cannot be run from a DOS window, type **exit** and press Enter to return to Windows. Then choose Start ➪ Shut Down ➪ Restart the computer in MS-DOS mode ➪ Yes. Again type the command you typed in Step 3, and press Enter.

At this point, you must rely on the Ethernet card manufacturer's instructions to set the IRQ. The screen may tell you how to set the dip switches or jumpers to select a specific IRQ. If the program tells you the best choice is an IRQ that's already taken, don't believe the program — choose an IRQ you know for certain is not taken (in my example, 05, 07, 09, or 10).

If you set the board to a specific IRQ now, write this setting on a piece of paper. You may be asked for the setting later, and you may forget if you don't jot it down. You can write something like "I set the Ethernet card's IRQ to 5" (replacing the 5 with the actual setting you used).

When you complete the manufacturer's instructions on what to do before you install the board, exit the program, if necessary. Type **exit** and press Enter at the C> prompt to return to the Windows 95 desktop.

Step 3: Shut everything down

Before you install the card, you should shut down everything on this PC (and I do mean everything). Follow these steps:

1. Choose Start ➪ Sh_u_t Down.

2. Click _S_hut down the computer?, and click _Y_es.

3. When the screen says it's safe to do so, shut down the PC and all peripherals attached directly to the PC (monitor, printer, external modem, external CD-ROM drive, and so on).

Why it's so confusing

If you read this chapter, you may think this is all terribly complicated and confusing. The reason is networking hardware and software have been evolving from the takes-a-genius technology of the '80s to Windows 95 plug-and-play simplicity.

How complicated things are depends on the age of your hardware. If you buy plug-and-play cards designed for Windows 95 or PCMCIA cards, you needn't mess with IRQs. Also, if you have a Pentium computer with an available PCI slot, you can buy a PCI Ethernet card for that computer, which is

easier to install than the legacy ISA cards. A PCI card is easier to install because it can detect an available IRQ and set itself to use that IRQ.

Older cards require _you_ to do all those things. Your goal is to find an IRQ not being used by any other device. Set the Ethernet card to this IRQ (assuming you can set the IRQ right on the board). The trick is always to specify this IRQ whenever any prompt asks you which IRQ to use for the network card or which IRQ the network is using. (Ugh!)

Step 4: Install the Ethernet card

With everything shut down, you are ready to install the Ethernet hardware. Once again, you should follow the manufacturer's instructions, but the general procedure will be something like the following:

1. If you're installing an internal card (not a PCMCIA card), remove the case from the system unit.

2. Put the card in an available slot.

   If the board contains dip switches, be careful not to change the dip-switch settings accidentally.

3. Replace the cover.

4. Connect one end of an Ethernet cable to the slot on the Ethernet card and the other end to your Ethernet hub.

Step 5: Set the IRQ (if you haven't already)

You probably can ignore this step if you already set the IRQ on the board by setting dip switches. If the board has no dip switches, the hardware manufacturer may require you to run a program to set those switches. Most likely, the instructions will tell you to run the program from DOS, before Windows starts up. Windows 95, of course, has no DOS. But if the card requires you to run a setup program from the DOS prompt to set IRQ switches, you must carefully follow these instructions:

1. Remove any floppies from the floppy disk drives.

2. Turn on the monitor; give it a few seconds to warm up.

3. Turn on the PC, put a finger near the F8 key, and keep your eyes on the screen.

4. As soon as you see the message Starting Windows 95, press the F8 key.

5. Choose Command prompt only by typing **5** and pressing Enter.

6. When you get to the C> prompt, follow the manufacturer's instructions to set the board's IRQ.

   You may need to put a floppy disk in drive A, type **a:\softset2**, and press Enter, for example.

Remember, if the program you're running suggests using an IRQ you know is already in use, *do not* use that suggested setting. Instead, pick an IRQ you know is available (in my example, 05, 07, 09, or 10).

You also may need to provide an I/O address. Make sure you don't pick an address already in use. I determined that I/Os 02F8-02FF, 0330-0333, 0378-037A were not available on my PC, so I would choose any suggested range except one of those.

After you set the IRQ (and optionally, the I/O address), jot down the settings you chose. You may write something like "I set my board to IRQ = 5, I/O address = 0210-021F."

Again, don't let your notes wander from this PC. Keep your notes handy because they have no bearing on any other PC in the LAN. I know I'm harping on this point, but it's not purely a neurotic compulsion. Getting this IRQ and I/O stuff squared away as early in the process as possible is important. Most networks fail simply because the IRQ setting on the board doesn't match the IRQ setting Windows expects, or because the IRQ setting you chose for the network card conflicts with the IRQ setting for some other device installed in the PC. Going back and fixing the mistake can be a lengthy process.

Hot
Stuff
The address range may be expressed without the leading zero and followed by *h*, which stands for *hexadecimal*. So the address range 210-21Fh is the same as 0210-021F. (Dreadfully confusing, I know.)

Follow the instructions to complete and exit the manufacturer's program. When you get to the C> prompt, you can shut down the PC again. Trying to test the card or the LAN makes no sense until at least two of the PCs have their cards installed and are connected to the Ethernet hub.

Step 6: Repeat Steps 1–5 on each PC

The best thing to do now is to repeat the process for each PC in the LAN, starting with "Step 1: Check available resources." The process takes a while. But if you properly install all the network hardware and connect every PC to the Ethernet adapter now, getting everything working right will be much easier later. I've spent many frustrating, hair-pulling hours trying to set up LANs in a hurry. The technique I'm giving you here is slow and cautious, but in the long run, it produces satisfactory results faster.

Telling Windows 95 You're on the LAN

After you install all the Ethernet cards and hook every PC to the Ethernet hub, you need to fire up Windows 95 and tell it, "Hey, look — we're on a LAN now." As long as all the hardware is in place and at least two PCs are connected to the Ethernet hub, Windows 95 will say, "Hey, yeah, cool. Let me install my networking software for you."

This part usually is easy. You need to complete the following procedure on each PC in the LAN (one PC at a time, of course):

1. Gather up your original Windows 95 floppy disks or CD-ROM.

2. Turn on all the peripherals (monitor, printer, external modem, external CD-ROM drive, and so on) for any PC in the LAN.

3. Remove any floppy disks from the floppy drives.

4. Turn on the computer, sit back, and watch the screen.

What you do next depends on what happens onscreen. Windows 95 may detect the new piece of hardware in your PC. If so, follow the instructions onscreen and skip to "Identifying this PC on the LAN" for further information.

If you got all the way to the Windows 95 desktop and Windows didn't detect the new Ethernet card, follow these steps:

1. Choose Start ➪ <u>S</u>ettings ➪ <u>C</u>ontrol Panel.

2. Double-click the Add New Hardware icon.

3. Read the instructions, click Next, choose <u>Y</u>es when you're asked about auto-detection, and then click Next again.

4. Follow the instructions onscreen.

If the Add New Hardware wizard says it didn't find any new devices, you need to install the device. Click the Next button, click Network adapters, click Next again, and select the <u>M</u>anufacturer and Mo<u>d</u>el of your network card. If you can't find your make and model, put the manufacturer's drivers disk in drive A, click <u>H</u>ave Disk, choose OK, and follow the instructions onscreen.

Windows 95 probably will install many files from the floppy disks or CD-ROM, and then ask you to restart the computer. Follow whatever instructions appear onscreen. Then proceed to the following section.

Identify this PC on the LAN

No matter which route you take to install your Ethernet card, you eventually return to the Windows 95 desktop. You may be prompted to enter a user name and password along the way. Type a user name — typically, a person's first name, followed by the first letter of the last name, with no spaces, such as AlanS. Also type a password of up to 15 characters, with no spaces.

 Remember, passwords often are case-sensitive. The password Snorkel, for example, is not the same as snorkel or SNORKEL. Pay attention to the Caps Lock key when you type your password.

Write both the user name and password on a piece of paper, and keep that paper near the PC; you'll need to refer to it in the near future. You can change the user name and password later if you want, but you need to know the password you typed originally.

Any time you're uncertain how to respond to a prompt, you can click the question-mark button in that window, and then click the item about which you're confused. Additional information pops up onscreen.

When you get to the desktop, you should see an icon titled Network Neighborhood; typically, this icon is below the My Computer icon. If you don't see the icon, close all open windows, right-click the desktop, and choose Arrange Icons ⇨ by Name.

If you still don't see the Network Neighborhood icon after arranging the desktop windows, something didn't install correctly. Make sure the hardware (card and cable) are hooked up; then choose Start ⇨ Settings ⇨ Control Panel, and double-click the Network icon. Click Add, click Adapter, click Add again, and follow the instructions onscreen to install your network adapter card.

Your final step is to identify this PC on the LAN and adjust a few settings. Right-click the Network Neighborhood icon, and choose Properties. The Network dialog box appears (see Figure 31-3).

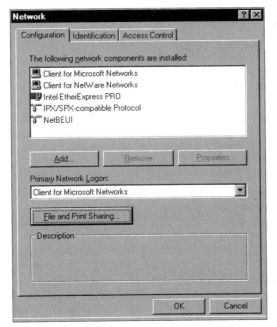

Figure 31-3: The Network dialog box with the Configuration tab selected

Notice the three tabs near the top of the Network dialog box, named Configuration, Identification, and Access Control. Read the following sections carefully for instructions on setting up this PC to run on the LAN.

The Configuration tab

The Configuration tab on your screen should show at least the five options shown in Figure 31-3. If an option is missing, click <u>A</u>dd; select Client, Adapter, or Protocol (depending on which type of component is missing); select the missing component; and then follow the instructions onscreen to install this component.

 The Client for NetWare Networks component is required if you plan to share a CD-ROM drive, even if you probably don't have Novell Netware software on your computer. If this component is missing, use the <u>A</u>dd button to add Client ➪ Microsoft ➪ Client for NetWare Networks.

In the Primary Network <u>L</u>ogon drop-down list, select Client for Microsoft Networks.

Last — and this step is important — click the <u>F</u>ile and Print Sharing button. I suggest you choose both options in the File and Print Sharing dialog box: I want to give others access to my <u>f</u>iles and to allow others to <u>p</u>rint to my printer(s), as shown in Figure 31-4. (All you're doing here is giving yourself the option to share things from this PC later; you're not giving anything away.) Then choose OK to close the dialog box.

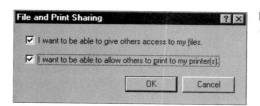

Figure 31-4: Give yourself the option to share stuff later.

The Identification tab

When you finish with the Configuration tab, click the Identification tab. You see a dialog box that looks something like Figure 31-5.

The following list explains how to fill in the blanks:

✦ *Computer name.* Give the computer a unique name of up to 15 characters, with no spaces. You can use any name that identifies the computer or use the name of the person who uses this computer most often. In Figure 31-5, I named the PC CD_Master because I mainly use this PC to create masters of CD-ROM discs.

✦ *Workgroup.* Giving each PC in the LAN the same workgroup name is extremely important, because only PCs that have the same workgroup name can share resources. The name can be up to 15 characters long, with no spaces. In my example, every PC belongs to a workgroup named ALANS_OFFICE. You, of course, can make up your own workgroup name. Just make sure you type the name exactly the same way on each PC.

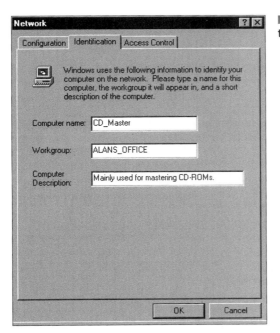

Figure 31-5: The Identification tab of the Network dialog box

✦ *Computer Description.* You can type any description for this computer; no particular rules apply. Just type a brief description you think will further identify this PC to someone on the LAN.

The Access Control tab

The Access Control tab (see Figure 31-6) defines security on this PC.

I strongly suggest you select Share-level access control, which is by far the easiest type of control to manage. If, after using the LAN for a few weeks, you feel you must tighten security, you can change this setting. But unless you're allowing total strangers to dial in to your network, I doubt you'll ever need User-level access control. User-level control is a hassle, because you must list the name of every LAN member who's allowed to use every shared device.

Save the network settings

After you complete all three tabs of the Network dialog box, you're ready to save your choices. Simply click OK at the bottom of the Network dialog box. Depending on your selections, you may need to insert some of the original Windows 95 floppy disks or the CD-ROM. Just follow the instructions onscreen.

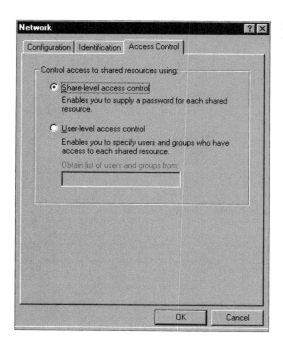

Figure 31-6: The Access Control tab of the Network dialog box

You probably will be prompted to restart the PC as well. Remove any floppy disks from the floppy drives, and follow the instructions to restart the PC.

Know what you get to do next? You get to gather up all those original Windows 95 floppies (or the CD-ROM), and carry them (or it) to the next PC in the LAN. When you get to that PC, start over again, from "Telling Windows 95 You're on the LAN" to this paragraph. Then repeat the process for every PC that's connected to the LAN.

Read my instructions carefully at each PC. If you forget certain little steps, they'll come back and bite ya later, and figuring out what you forgot to do is hard.

When you get to the Identification-tab step, remember to give each PC a different computer name, but the same workgroup name.

After you set up every PC in the LAN, you're ready to test the network.

Testing the LAN

By the time you get to this section, you should have set up the network hardware on every PC in the LAN and identified each PC in the LAN. Every PC is running, showing the Windows 95 desktop, and each desktop shows a Network

Neighborhood icon. (It's late at night, your eyes are tired, your brain is fried, and you wish I'd hurry up and get this over with, right?)

To test your new LAN, follow these steps:

1. Go to any PC in the LAN.

2. Double-click the Network Neighborhood icon.

3. Repeat Steps 1 and 2 for every PC in the LAN.

If everything went well, you see a little icon for every PC in the LAN. In Figure 31-7, for example, you see the four PCs in my little LAN: Cd_master, Comm_center, Pentium_pc, and Travel_pc. Your screen, of course, should list the computer names you assigned to the PCs in your LAN.

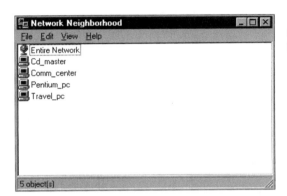

Figure 31-7: Each PC in the workgroup appears in Network Neighborhood.

If you don't see the names of the PCs in your LAN, first try double-clicking the Entire Network option. That action may be enough of a wake-up call to get things going. When you can close the Network Neighborhood folder, reopen the folder, and immediately see all the PCs on your LAN, you're finished. You're ready to move on to Chapter 32 and start sharing resources on the LAN.

If you can't get the network going or if some PCs refuse to appear inside Network Neighborhood, try the troubleshooting techniques in the following section.

Troubleshooting the LAN

As you've seen, setting up a LAN is a complicated ritual, involving many settings and options. Any little wrong setting can cripple the network. The following sections examine possible solutions to various problems that may arise.

You have no Network Neighborhood icon

If one of your PCs doesn't have a Network Neighborhood icon on its desktop, first make sure the icon isn't just hidden. Close all open windows, right-click the desktop, and choose Arrange Icons ➪ by Name. Typically, this action puts the Network Neighborhood icon right below the My Computer icon.

If that procedure doesn't work, something isn't installed — the LAN hardware, the LAN software, or both. Make sure you installed the LAN hardware and the cable from the PC is connected to the Ethernet hub. Then repeat the installation instructions, beginning with "Telling Windows 95 You're on the LAN" earlier in this chapter.

Network Neighborhood is empty

If nothing appears when you open Network Neighborhood, try the following semi-superstitious ritual on each PC:

1. Close all open windows.
2. Choose Start ➪ Shut Down.
3. Select Shut down the computer? and then click Yes.
4. When the screen says it's safe to do so, shut down the PC and all attached peripherals — monitor, printer, external CD-ROM drive, everything.

Next, check the cable that attaches the PC to the Ethernet hub. Make sure the cable is properly plugged into the PC's network card and properly plugged into the hub. If the hub has its own power, make sure the hub is plugged into the wall and is turned on. (See the manual that came with the hub for any additional instructions.)

When you're sure everything is plugged in correctly, follow these steps:

1. Go to any PC in the LAN, and turn on all its external peripherals (monitor, external CD-ROM drive, and so on).
2. Turn on the PC.
3. Watch the screen for any error message that may give you a clue as to what's wrong.
4. When you're prompted, log in, using the appropriate user name and password for that PC.

Life Saver   Logging in to the LAN with a valid user name and password is important. If you just make up a user name and password, Windows will allow you to go to the desktop, but not to the LAN. This situation will make it appear as though the LAN isn't working when, in fact, it may be working perfectly.

5. Repeat Steps 1-4 on each PC in the LAN.

After all the PCs are turned back on, double-click the Network Neighborhood icon on each PC again. You should see an icon for every PC in the LAN. If so, you're finished, and you're ready to start sharing resources on the LAN. Proceed to Chapter 32.

A PC is missing

If Network Neighborhood shows some, but not all, of the PCs in the LAN, you need to troubleshoot the missing PCs. Go to any PC not (but should be) listed, and follow these steps:

1. Shut down Windows.

2. Shut down the entire PC system, including all external peripherals.

3. Make sure the cable is properly plugged into the LAN card on the PC and properly connected to the Ethernet hub.

4. Restart all the external peripherals, restart the PC, and go to the Windows desktop.

5. Open Network Neighborhood on the current PC and on some other PC in the LAN.

If you see the names of both PCs in Network Neighborhood, you're finished. You're ready to move to Chapter 32 and start sharing resources.

If you're still having a problem with one PC, follow these steps on that PC:

1. Right-click Network Neighborhood, and choose Properties.

Life Saver — Make sure the workgroup name on the Identification tab for this PC is spelled exactly like the workgroup name for other PCs in the LAN.

2. Check everything on all three tabs, as discussed in "The Configuration tab," "The Identification tab," and "The Access Control tab" earlier in this chapter, for instructions on setting up this dialog box.

3. After you review all three tabs, choose OK.

4. Follow any instructions that appear onscreen.

If you changed any settings, you probably need to restart this PC and possibly feed it some disks. When you get back to the Windows 95 desktop, open Network Neighborhood again on this PC and on some other PC in the LAN. If you *still* can't see this PC in the LAN, you may have a hardware conflict with your Ethernet card. This problem can be the nastiest of all to solve, which is why I was so obsessed with getting the IRQs right from the beginning. To diagnose and solve this problem, follow these steps:

1. Right-click Network Neighborhood, and choose Properties.

2. Double-click the icon for the network adapter card.

   This icon looks like a tiny board with the letter *P* on it and should show the make and model of your network card. If you see an icon named Dial-Up Adapter, ignore it; it's for Dial-Up Networking only.

3. If your network card has a configurable IRQ and/or I/O address range, you see a tab labeled Resources. Click that tab.

   If you don't see a Resources tab, skip to Step 6.

4. Look at the current Interrupt (IRQ) and/or I/O address range settings.

5. What you do now depends on what you see.

   • If a pound sign (#) appears before the IRQ and I/O settings, as shown in Figure 31-8, those settings are not the problem. Go to Step 6.

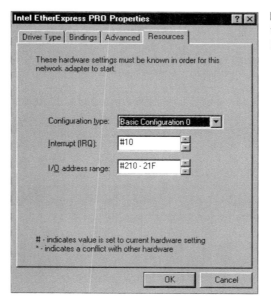

Figure 31-8: The Resources tab of a network card's Properties dialog box

   • If the IRQ setting does not match the setting you wrote down for this computer way back in "Installing the LAN Hardware" earlier in this chapter, use the spin boxes to select the appropriate IRQ. (If the IRQ option is dimmed and unavailable, first set the Configuration type to Basic Configuration 0.) When you choose the right IRQ, you may see a # sign before this setting, but only if the card has dip switches or some kind of program for setting the IRQ.

- If an asterisk (*) appears for either the IRQ or I/O setting, you have a conflict between this piece of hardware and some other piece. Proceed to Step 6, and then read the section "If you have a hardware conflict."

6. Choose OK until you get back to the desktop.

If you have a hardware conflict

If you discover a hardware conflict, you'll have to change the IRQ setting on either the network card or on the device conflicting with the network card. You can use the Troubleshooter to help with this process. Follow these steps:

1. Choose Start ➪ Help.

2. Click the Contents tab.

3. Double-click the Troubleshooting book.

4. Double-click If you have a hardware conflict.

   Or, if you think something else may be the trouble, double-click If you have trouble using the network.

5. Follow the instructions onscreen.

If you still can't seem to get the network working, you may have to start from scratch. Follow these steps:

1. Choose Start ➪ Settings ➪ Control Panel.

2. Double-click the System icon.

3. Click the Device Manager tab.

4. Click the plus sign (+) next to the Network Adapters option (if any).

5. Click the name of the adapter card that's giving you grief.

6. Click the Remove button to remove all drivers for that card.

7. Follow the instructions onscreen.

8. Go back to the Windows 95 desktop, shut down everything, remove the network card from the computer, and start all over with "Installing the LAN Hardware" near the start of this chapter.

This time, pay very close attention to the IRQs you choose; make certain to write down *everything* as you go. If possible, repeat the entire process with a different IRQ this time. If IRQ 5 let you down on the first go-around, for example, use IRQ 7, 9, or 10 (if any one of those settings is available) on the second try.

More Info Chapter 10 discusses general techniques for installing hardware and troubleshooting hardware conflicts.

If all else fails, you may need to call the manufacturer. Optionally, study closely both the instructions that came with the board and the instructions that came with the Ethernet hub. Good luck, and hang in there — I'm sure you'll get everything working.

Summary

This chapter has been all about installing network hardware and getting your LAN up and running. The main points are:

✦ Before you install *any* hardware, use Device Manager to check and, perhaps, print information on used and available IRQs and I/O addresses.

✦ If you're installing a network card that requires you to set an IRQ and other settings right on the board, be sure you do so before installing the card. Refer to the manufacturer's instructions.

✦ You should install the actual card as per the manufacturer's instructions. But ignore any instructions about installing DOS/Windows 3.x drivers for the card.

✦ As you specify IRQ and other settings, be sure to jot down notes. You may be asked for this information several times as you proceed through the installation.

✦ After you've installed all the LAN hardware in all the PCs, you can start setting up the LAN software. Turn on all peripherals and PCs. Then start up each PC. If Windows 95 doesn't detect the new hardware automatically, you can run the Add New Hardware wizard to install the appropriate software.

✦ When identifying PCs on the LAN, be sure to give each computer a unique computer name, but give each computer *the same* workgroup name.

✦ When configuring the LAN software, be sure to click the File and Print Sharing button and enable file and print sharing if you plan to share either anywhere down the road.

✦ After installing all hardware, setting up the software, and restarting each PC in the LAN, you should be able to double-click the Network Neighborhood icon on any PC and see the names of all PCs in the LAN.

✦   ✦   ✦

Sharing Resources on a LAN

By the time you get to this chapter, you should already have set up your LAN, as described in Chapters 30 and 31. Sharing resources on a LAN makes no sense until you can see the PCs listed in Network Neighborhood.

Sharing a Printer

When you share a printer on a LAN, any other PC on the LAN can use that printer. The printer, of course, needs to be physically connected (by a cable) to one PC on the LAN. *Which* PC you use doesn't matter. Throughout this chapter, I refer to whichever PC you use for printing as the *print server*. Mind you, this computer need not be dedicated to printing; it can be anyone's PC on the LAN. If two or more PCs in the LAN have a printer attached, you can share all those printers.

On the print server

Before you can use another PC's printer, you need to go to the PC to which the printer is physically attached, make sure the printer is installed locally at that machine, and then share that PC. Follow these steps:

1. Go to the PC the printer is plugged in to and open My Computer (double-click its icon).

2. Double-click the Printers folder.

3. If the printer you want to share already has an icon in the Printers folder, skip to Step 5.

4. If you haven't already installed the printer on this PC, go ahead and do so, using the Add Printer icon.

When the wizard asks, be sure to tell it you're installing a local printer (a printer that's connected to this PC by a cable). When you finish with the wizard, proceed to Step 5.

5. Right-click the icon for the printer you want to share and choose S̲haring.

Life Saver If you don't see S̲haring as an option when you right-click a printer icon, chances are you just forgot to allow printer sharing on this PC. See "Troubleshooting File and Printer Sharing" later in this chapter.

6. Choose S̲hared As; then type a brief name for the printer and a description, as in the example shown in Figure 32-1.

Optionally, if you want to limit the sharing of this printer to people who know a password, you can type this password.

7. Choose OK.

A little hand appears below the printer's icon, indicating the printer can be shared.

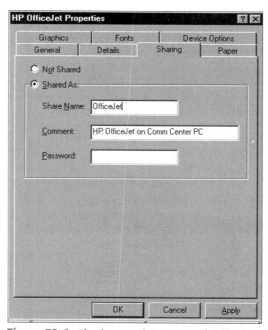

Figure 32-1: Sharing a printer named OfficeJet

On any printer client

Any other PC in the LAN now can act as a *printer client*. By printer client, I mean any PC in the LAN into which the printer is not directly plugged. But before you can print from a particular PC to the shared printer, you need to install a driver for that printer. Follow these steps:

Hot Stuff Gather up your original Windows 95 floppies or CD-ROM for this procedure; you may need them to install a driver for the network printer.

1. Go to any PC that needs access to the shared printer.

   Remember, this printer can be any printer in the LAN *except* the PC into which the printer is physically plugged.

2. Open My Computer (double-click its icon).

3. Double-click the Printers folder.

4. Double-click the Add Printer icon.

5. Click Next.

6. In the second page of the wizard, choose <u>N</u>etwork printer, as shown in Figure 32-2.

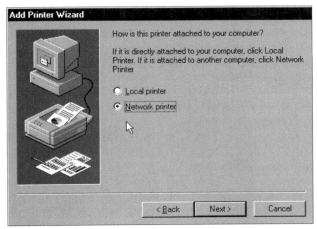

Figure 32-2: Ready to connect to a printer that's connected to some other PC in the LAN

7. Click Next.

8. Click the B<u>r</u>owse button, double-click the name of the PC to which the printer is attached, and then click the name of the shared printer, as shown in Figure 32-3.

Figure 32-3: Connecting to the shared printer named OfficeJet

9. Choose OK.

10. Click Next.

11. Type a name for the printer.

    Optionally, if you want to use this printer as the general default printer when you print from this PC, also choose Yes.

12. Click Next.

13. Complete the remaining options and instructions that the wizard presents.

    When you finish, an icon for the shared printer appears in the Printers folder.

You needn't repeat this process in the future. The newly installed network printer will be available whenever you use this PC (provided the printer and the print server are running at the moment).

Remember, though, you have connected only this PC to the network printer. If you want to connect other PCs to this printer, you must go to this PC and Steps 2-3.

Printing a document

After you install the driver for a network printer, using this printer is no different from using a printer that's physically attached to your computer. You can do the following things:

✦ To print from the program you're currently using, choose File ➪ Print in that program. If necessary, you can select a specific printer in the Print dialog box that appears (exactly how you do this depends on the program you're using).

✦ You can print documents by dragging their icons to the printer's icon.

More Info For more information on printing, refer to Chapter 14.

If the network printer is busy printing someone else's document, your print job waits in the queue until the printer is available. You can go about your business normally, right after you start the print job.

Network printer tips

As mentioned earlier, you can share several printers on a network. To specify which printer you want to use as the default printer for any PC, open the Printers folder (by double-clicking it in My Computer or by choosing Start ⇨ Settings ⇨ Printers). Then click the printer you want to use as the default and choose File ⇨ Set as Default.

When you print from within a program, the program assumes you want to use the default printer. Most programs, though, allow you to choose a different printer on the fly. After you choose File ⇨ Print, select a printer by using the Name drop-down list, the Select Printer button, or whatever tool is available for this purpose.

If you have a problem with a print job, check the print queue on your local printer; open the Printers folder and then double-click the icon for the printer causing the problem. Most likely, the print job still is in your local print queue. You can use commands in the Printer and Document menus to pause or cancel the print job.

Deferred network printing

If, for whatever reason, a network printer becomes unavailable, the icon for that printer is dimmed, but still available. Any print jobs you send to the printer are held in your local print queue until the network printer becomes available. When that printer becomes available, your print jobs start.

Sharing an Entire Hard Disk

You can share an entire hard disk from any PC in the LAN. When you do, every other PC in the LAN has access to everything on that hard disk. This setup is useful when security is not an issue. If you're setting up a LAN between a portable PC and a desktop PC, for example, you may want to share the desktop computer's entire hard disk. This way, you can get to all its contents from the portable even while you're on the road, if you use Dial-Up Networking (refer to Chapter 20).

Sharing a hard disk is like sharing any other device. Two steps are involved: going to the server (the PC which contains the hard disk you want to share) and sharing the disk. Then you can go to any client (any other PC in the LAN) and get to that drive via Network Neighborhood. You also can map a drive letter to the shared drive, as discussed later in this chapter.

On the hard-disk server

The first step in giving multiple computers access to another computer's hard disk is to perform the sharing. Follow these steps:

1. Go to the PC that contains the hard disk you want to share.

2. Open My Computer (double-click its icon).

3. Right-click the icon for the drive you want to share, and choose Sharing.

 If you don't see Sharing as an option when you right-click a drive's icon, chances are you forgot to allow file sharing on this PC. See "Troubleshooting File and Printer Sharing" later in this chapter.

4. Choose Shared As and give the drive a name.

5. Choose Full if you want to add, change, and remove files from this drive (see Figure 32-4).

6. Choose OK.

   A little hand now appears below the icon for the drive, indicating the drive is shared.

From this point on, any other PC in the LAN can connect to this drive.

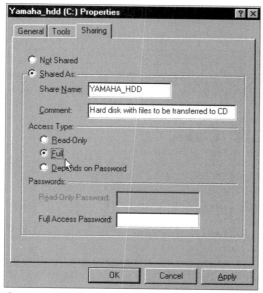

Figure 32-4: Sharing an entire hard disk drive (HDD)

On any hard-disk client

The easiest way to access a shared hard drive from a *client* (a client being any other PC in the LAN) is to start by mapping a drive letter to that shared drive. Follow these steps:

1. Go to any client PC, and double-click Network Neighborhood.

2. Double-click the name of the PC containing the shared drive.

   You see a list of all the shared resources on this PC.

3. Click the name of the shared drive and then choose File ⇨ Map Network Drive.

   Alternatively, right-click the icon for the shared drive and then choose Map Network Drive (see Figure 32-5).

4. In the dialog box that appears, choose any available drive letter to represent this shared drive.

   If you want to reestablish this connection whenever you log on in the future, choose the Reconnect at logon option (see Figure 32-6).

5. Choose OK.

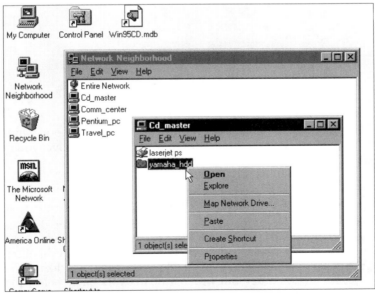

Figure 32-5: Mapping a drive letter to a shared hard disk

Sharing floppy, removable, and zip drives

You can use the techniques described in "Sharing an Entire Hard Disk" to share any type of drive: a floppy drive, a removable Syquest or Bernoulli drive, a zip drive, and even a CD-ROM drive. Then go to any other PC in the LAN and map a drive letter to this shared drive.

When you double-click the icon for the shared drive in My Computer, you see the contents of whatever disk is in this drive. If you gave yourself full permission, you also can create folders on that drive and copy files to those folders — a great way to make

backups of specific folders on many PCs in the LAN.

You also can install programs from the shared drive. Suppose the drive you shared is a floppy drive or CD-ROM drive and you mapped the drive letter G to this drive. To install a program from this shared drive, go to the PC on which you want to install the program, click the Start button, choose Run, and launch the appropriate startup program from drive G (for example, G:\SETUP or G:\INSTALL).

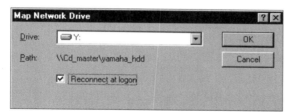

Figure 32-6: Mapping the drive named Y to a shared hard disk on another PC

You can close the Map Network Drive and Network Neighborhood windows now, if you want. You don't need these windows to use the shared drive; you need them only to establish the connection.

Using the shared hard drive

After you map a drive letter to a shared drive, you can treat the drive as though it were connected directly to the current PC. The drive being housed inside some other PC becomes, essentially, irrelevant. When you open My Computer, for example, the drive to which you mapped a letter appears just like the hard disk that's really on your computer, but with a little network cable below the icon (see Figure 32-7). You can move and copy files to this drive as though it were inside this PC.

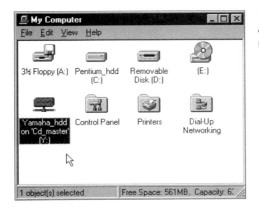

Figure 32-7: The My Computer window after you map a drive letter (Y) to a shared network drive

If I double-click the icon for the Y drive, for example, I see the folders and some files within this drive. Now suppose I size this window and move it to the right, double-click the icon for my local C drive, and then size and move this window to the left. Now I can see the contents of both drives (see Figure 32-8). I can right-drag folders, or files within folders, from one drive's window to the other's to move and copy files at will.

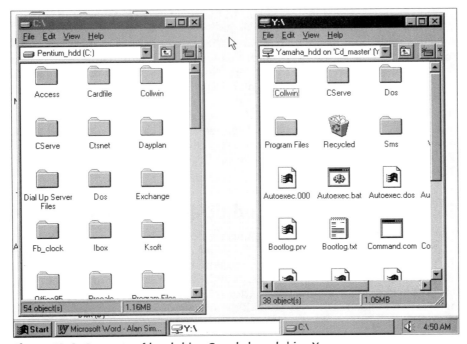

Figure 32-8: Contents of local drive C and shared drive Y

You have all your normal viewing and browsing options in both windows. You can, for example, choose an option from the View menu to change your view of the icons in either window. To see the contents of a folder on either drive, just double-click the folder.

If you start to lose track of which window represents which drive, choose View ➪ Options in My Computer, click the View tab, and then choose Display the full MS-DOS path in the title bar. Each window's title bar now includes the drive letter.

Sharing a CD-ROM Drive

You can share, and connect to, a CD-ROM drive by using exactly the same techniques you use to share and connect to an entire hard disk. A few minor differences exist, however, in the way you use the shared CD-ROM drive:

✦ Because a CD-ROM drive is, by definition, read-only, allowing full access to the drive has no advantage.

✦ What's shared and available at any given moment is the CD-ROM currently in the CD-ROM drive.

✦ Some CD-ROMs have an installation procedure that copies one or more programs to your hard disk. You can install those programs on the local hard disk after you map a drive letter to the shared CD-ROM drive.

Consider this example of using a shared CD-ROM drive. I keep the Microsoft Bookshelf CD-ROM in the CD-ROM drive of my main Pentium computer because Bookshelf is a good resource for writers. Now suppose I want to access Bookshelf from some other PC in the LAN (or all other PCs in the LAN).

The first step is to share the CD-ROM drive. I go to the Pentium computer that houses the CD-ROM drive, open My Computer, right-click the icon for the CD-ROM drive, and choose Sharing. Then I choose Shared As, give the drive a name (PentiumCDROM, for this example), select Read-Only as the access type (see Figure 32-9), and choose OK.

Connecting to the shared CD-ROM drive

Now I can go to any other PC in the LAN and map a drive letter to the shared CD-ROM drive. I go to my portable PC, open Network Neighborhood, and double-click the icon for the Pentium computer. When the shared objects from that computer appear, I right-click the PentiumCDROM icon and choose Map Network Drive. I specify any available drive letter (M, for example) and opt to reconnect at logon. Then I choose OK and close all the remaining open windows.

Shared CD-ROM Drive Troubleshoot

If you have any trouble sharing a CD-ROM drive, check to make certain the Client for NetWare Networks component is installed on all machines. To do so, right-click the Network Neighborhood icon and choose Properties. If you don't see Client for Netware Networks listed as an installed component, use the Add button to install Client ⇨ Microsoft ⇨ Client for NetWare Networks. Follow all instructions that appear on the screen and, after rebooting, try sharing the CD-ROM drive.

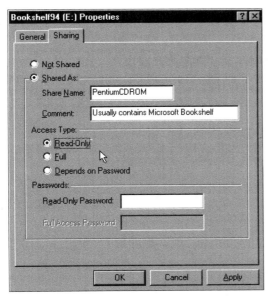

Figure 32-9: Sharing the CD-ROM drive on my Pentium PC

Installing programs from the shared CD-ROM drive

Before I can actually use the Microsoft Bookshelf CD-ROM from the shared CD-ROM drive, I need to install some of its programs to the portable computer's hard disk. This procedure is simple enough. Follow these steps:

1. Choose Start ⇨ Settings ⇨ Control Panel.

2. Double-click the Add/Remove Programs icon.

3. Click the Install button.

4. Click Next, and see whether the wizard finds the appropriate program.

In my example, the program would be on drive M, because this is the drive letter I mapped to the shared CD-ROM drive.

5. If the wizard finds a setup program on some other drive before it gets to the appropriate drive (M, in this case), click the Browse button; select the shared CD-ROM drive in the Look in drop-down list; and then click the setup or install program on that drive, as shown in Figure 32-10.

6. Choose Open.

The Run Installation wizard window states the PC is about to run the selected program (M:\SETUP, in this case), as shown in Figure 32-11.

7. Click the Finish button.

8. Follow any instructions onscreen.

Figure 32-10: Ready to run Setup from the Pentium CD-ROM drive

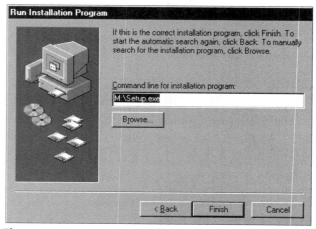

Figure 32-11: Ready to run the setup program on CD-ROM drive M

From now on, I can access Microsoft Bookshelf from either the Pentium PC or the portable PC, so long as the Bookshelf CD-ROM is in the Pentium's CD-ROM drive. All I must do is click the QuickStart buttons that come with Bookshelf. Alternatively, I can choose Start ➪ Programs ➪ Microsoft Multimedia ➪ Bookshelf 95 on whichever PC I am using.

Danger Zone The example of running Microsoft Bookshelf from several PCs is not an endorsement for software piracy. Many programs require special licensing for concurrent use on a LAN, or individual use on multiple PCs. Read your software license agreement for more information. Then comply!

I can repeat the preceding steps on all the PCs in my LAN, if I want, so I can get to the Bookshelf CD-ROM from wherever I am. I can even have all the PCs access Microsoft Bookshelf at the same time.

Sharing a Folder

Sharing drives is great in some situations, but it can be confusing in others. Also, you may want to share some stuff on your hard disk, but keep other people away from other stuff. The simple solution is to share individual folders rather than an entire drive. Other users can map a drive letter to that folder. When they browse the drive letter, the "drive" they see is just that folder, including any subfolders within that folder.

As mentioned earlier, I keep all my ongoing work in a folder named Projects. I keep this folder on one PC and share it. Then, from every other PC in the LAN, I map a drive letter (P) to this folder. When I'm not at my main computer, I always know where to look for a document for some current project: in the P drive.

On the folder server

Technically, a PC that shares folders or files is called a *file server*. But this term can be a little misleading in this context, because it implies just one PC is acting as the server and all the other PCs are clients. In the peer-to-peer type of network discussed in this chapter, any PC can share a folder, and any other PC can connect to that shared folder. So a more accurate term may be *folder server*, which means "whatever PC the folder happens to be on."

The technique for sharing and connecting to a folder is exactly the same as the procedure for sharing and connecting to a drive; you must navigate a little deeper. To share a folder, follow these steps:

1. Go to the PC on which the folder is actually stored.

2. Use My Computer or Windows Explorer to browse to the folder you want to share.

3. When you see the icon for the folder you want to share, right-click that icon and choose S̲haring.

Life Saver If you don't see S̲haring as an option when you right-click a drive's icon, you probably forgot to allow file sharing on this PC. See "Troubleshooting File and Printer Sharing" later in this chapter.

4. Choose S̲hared As, and type a brief, descriptive name for the folder.

You can type a longer description in the Comment box.

5. Select the access type you want to use: R̲ead-Only (other users can see and copy files but not change, move, or delete them), F̲ull (other users can view, change, copy, move, and delete files), or D̲epends on Password (you can define one password to limit some people to read-only access and define another password to give other people full access.

Figure 32-12 shows an example in which I'm allowing full access to my Projects folder.

6. Choose OK.

A little hand appears below the icon for the folder, indicating the folder is shared.

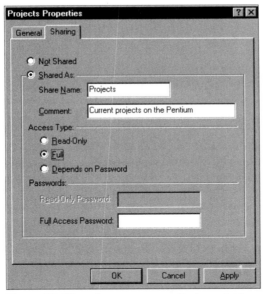

Figure 32-12: Full access to my Projects folder is granted to other LAN members.

On any folder client

Now you can get to the shared folder, via Network Neighborhood, from any PC on the LAN. To simplify future access to this shared folder, you can assign a drive letter to the folder by following these steps:

1. On any PC in the LAN (other than the PC on which the folder is actually stored), double-click Network Neighborhood on the Windows 95 desktop.

2. Double-click the name of the PC containing the shared folder.

3. In the dialog box that appears, right-click the name of the shared folder and then choose Map Network Drive (see Figure 32-13).

4. In the Map Network Drive dialog box, select any available drive letter.

   Optionally, you also can specify whether you want to reconnect to this folder automatically in future logons.

5. Choose OK.

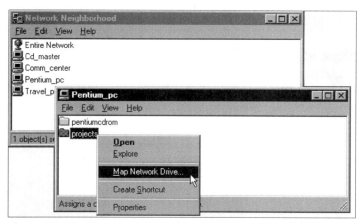

Figure 32-13: About to map a drive letter to a shared folder

You can close all open windows now, if you want.

Using the shared folder

After you connect to a shared folder, you can think of this folder as being its own little drive, from the perspective of the PC you're using. This concept may be confusing at first, but if you think of the drive letter as being a nickname for the folder, understanding it becomes easier.

Whenever I'm on a PC in my LAN, for example, I know drive P is just the nickname for my Projects folder. The folder's real name is \\Pentium_pc\projects; remembering *P* is easier. This is the beauty of assigning a drive letter to a shared folder.

 Any shared resource on the LAN to which you've mapped a drive letter appears with a network-drive icon in My Computer. You have no separate icon for a connected CD-ROM drive or a connected folder.

After you map this drive letter, you can treat the shared folder as you would any drive that's physically connected to your PC. When you open My Computer, you see a network-drive icon for the shared folder (see Figure 32-14). You can double-click this icon to browse the shared folder and to open, copy, move, rename, and delete files normally (assuming you have full access to the shared folder).

Yet another advantage to having all your ongoing projects in a single folder is the simplicity of making backups. Rather than use a slow, noisy tape-backup machine to back up your entire hard disk, you can install a removable hard disk or zip drive. To back up all your current work, drag the Projects folder to the icon for that drive.

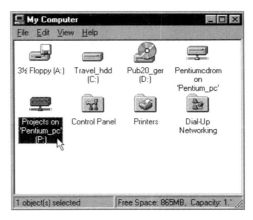

Figure 32-14: The shared folder is drive P, from this computer's perspective.

You also can get to the drive through all the other traditional means of browsing your computer. The connected folder appears as a network-drive icon in Windows Explorer, for example. When you're in a program and choose File ➪ Open or File ➪ Save As, you can use the Drives or Look in icon to navigate to the connected folder.

Figure 32-15 shows the Open dialog box in Microsoft Word. I've opened the Look in: drop-down list and I'm about to open P (my Projects folder) to look for the document I want to open.

You can share as many folders as you want on as many PCs as you want. Just remember, first you must go to the PC on which the folder is stored and share the folder from there. Then you can go to any other PC in the LAN and use Network Neighborhood (or Windows Explorer) to map a drive letter to the shared folder.

You can even share a subfolder within a shared folder. This form of sharing may seem a little strange, because this folder is accessible already. But if you share the subfolder on its own, you can map a drive letter to it and then have easy, one-click access to this folder.

Figure 32-16 shows the Windows Explorer window on my Pentium PC, on which the Projects folder resides. Notice the Projects folder is shared, as always. In addition, I have shared the Windows 95 Book folder within this folder.

After sharing this subfolder, I can go to any other PC in the LAN and, using Network Neighborhood or Windows Explorer, map a different drive letter to the subfolder. Suppose I map the drive letter W to this folder. From then on, whenever I'm in My Computer, Windows Explorer, a program's Open dialog box, or whatever, I can refer to drive W when I specifically want the folder for this book. In other words, I've given the subfolder its own nickname: *W* (see Figure 32-17).

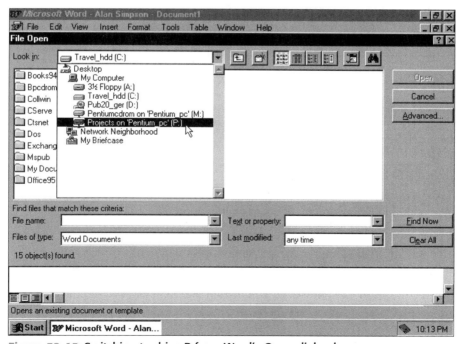

Figure 32-15: Switching to drive P from Word's Open dialog box

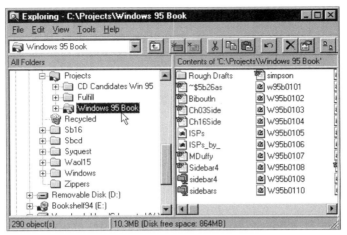

Figure 32-16: The Windows 95 Book subfolder is shared.

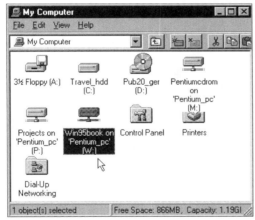

Figure 32-17: Now drive W is a nickname for the Windows 95 Book folder on my Pentium.

This kind of freedom and flexibility takes some acclimation, especially if you've been fighting with floppy disks or dealing with a restrictive dedicated-server type of LAN for a few years. If you remember you can get to any folder from any drive on any PC in the LAN, however, you'll soon find new ways to organize your materials for quick and efficient access.

Disconnecting from a Shared Resource

If you want to disconnect from a shared printer, drive, or folder, follow these steps:

1. Go to the client PC — the one connected to the resource via the network, not physically connected to the source.

2. Open My Computer (double-click its icon).

3. Do one of the following:

   - To disconnect from a shared drive or folder, right-click the appropriate network-drive icon and choose Disconnect.

   - To disconnect from a shared printer, double-click the Printers folder. Then right-click the icon for the printer from which you want to disconnect and choose Disconnect.

4. Close My Computer.

The resource itself remains shared, and any other PCs that were connected to the resource still are connected. If you want to stop sharing the resource, see the following section.

Stopping Resource Sharing

To stop sharing a resource, follow these steps:

1. Go to the resource server — the PC to which the printer is physically attached or the PC that contains the shared drive or folder.

2. Open My Computer (double-click its icon).

3. Do any of the following:

   - To stop sharing a drive, right-click the drive's icon (the sharing hand appears below it) and choose Sharing.

   - To stop sharing a folder, double-click the icon for the drive that contains the shared folder, browse to the shared folder, right-click the folder's icon, and choose Sharing.

   - To stop sharing a printer, double-click the Printers icon, right-click the icon for the shared printer, and choose Sharing.

4. Choose Not Shared from the dialog box that appears.

Danger Zone When you stop sharing a device, you disconnect all users from this device. Disconnecting users from a shared drive or folder can destroy any work they have in progress. Don't do it!

5. If any users are connected to this shared device, you see a warning that you're about to disconnect them; choose No to leave them connected (recommended).

You should disconnect users only if you're sure they're not working on documents stored on the shared drive or folder; otherwise, you run the risk of ruining any work the other users have in progress. Your best bet is to go to each client PC in the network, save any outstanding work, and disconnect that PC from the shared resource first. Then, when you get back to the PC playing the role of server for the shared resource, you can stop sharing the resource without destroying some colleague's hard work.

Shutting Down LAN PCs

After you connect a PC to a LAN, never turn that PC off — unless, of course, you must shut it down to install some new hardware. In this case, you should warn other users to save all their work, so you don't cut them off from a folder they may be using.

But, in general, you don't want other users to lose access to any shared resources that may be on the PC. So if the person who works at this machine is going home for the evening, he or she should turn off the monitor and leave everything else on. The monitor, even if it's just displaying a screen saver, is the biggest power hog in the system. So if you'll be away from the PC for any length of time, shutting down the monitor is a good idea.

Troubleshooting File and Printer Sharing

If you remember these important points, you should be able to troubleshoot any problems you have sharing resources on a LAN:

✦ Before you can share a resource, you must allow sharing from the PC to which the resource is connected. If you can't share a particular resource, right-click Network Neighborhood and choose Properties. Then activate file and printer sharing in the Configuration tab (refer to Chapter 25).

✦ Remember, only PCs with the same workgroup name can share resources in Network Neighborhood. To check (and, optionally, change) a PC's workgroup name, right-click Network Neighborhood on that PC, and then use the Identification tab.

✦ Network Neighborhood displays only shared resources. Before you can connect to a shared resource, you must go to the PC to which the resource is connected and share the resource from there.

✦ To simplify access to a shared drive or folder, you can right-click the resource's icon in Network Neighborhood and map a drive letter to this resource. From then on, the resource appears as a network-drive icon in this PC's My Computer window.

Committing these important points to your brain will help prevent many potential problems and make troubleshooting problems on the fly easier. But other factors also come into play. If you need help with a problem in sharing a resource or connecting to a shared resource, try the Troubleshooter. Follow these steps:

1. Click the Start ⇨ Help.

2. Click the Contents tab.

3. Double-click the Troubleshooting book.

4. Double-click on If you have trouble using the network.

5. Follow the instructions onscreen.

The Troubleshooter is good at helping you define and isolate a problem, as well as taking you right to the settings you must change to eliminate the problem.

Sharing a Fax/Modem

If you have more PCs than fax/modems in your office, you can share any fax/modem so you can send a fax from any PC in the LAN without moving or copying files to another PC.

Sharing a fax/modem is a little trickier than sharing other devices. Before you even attempt to share a fax/modem, you must do three things:

✦ Choose one PC in the LAN to act as the fax server and install the fax/modem on that PC, as discussed in Chapter 15.

✦ Install Microsoft Fax and Microsoft Exchange, as discussed in Chapter 16, on all PCs that will use the fax/modem.

Life Saver   If you have problems installing Microsoft Fax on a PC that doesn't have a modem yet, you can install a standard modem (even though no physical modem may even be attached to the PC). Later, you can delete the fake modem and attach the PC to the shared fax/modem.

✦ You need to have the entire LAN set up and working, as discussed in Chapters 30 and 31.

When the three preliminary tasks are completed, you can proceed with the tasks in the following sections.

On the fax server

I'll refer to the PC to which the fax/modem is physically connected as the *fax server*. Your first step in sharing this fax/modem is to make the modem available for sharing. Follow these steps:

1. Go to the fax server — the PC to which the fax/modem is connected.

2. Double-click the Inbox icon on the desktop or choose Start ➪ Programs ➪ Microsoft Exchange to get into Microsoft Exchange.

3. Choose Tools ➪ Microsoft Fax Tools ➪ Options.

   The Microsoft Fax Properties dialog box appears.

4. Click the Modem tab.

5. Click the name of the modem you plan to share and then click the Set as Active Fax Modem button.

6. Near the bottom of the dialog box, select Let other people on the network use my modem to send faxes.

7. Click the Properties button, choose Shared as, and type a brief name and description for the fax.

   Optionally, you can type a password if you want to limit access to your fax/modem to people who know the password.

8. Choose OK.

   You return to the Microsoft Fax Properties dialog box, in which the fax name appears, dimmed, next to Share name (see Figure 32-18).

9. Optionally, if you want to double-check other settings on this shared modem, click the Properties button near the fax/modem name, check your settings, and then choose OK.

10. Choose OK.

    You return to the Microsoft Exchange window.

11. Click the Close (X) button to close Exchange.

Even though you may not be prompted to do so, I've found restarting the computer at this time is a good idea. Choose Start ➪ Shut Down ➪ Restart the Computer?; then click the Yes button. Wait for the Windows 95 desktop to come back onscreen before you try connecting to the shared modem from another PC in the LAN.

Figure 32-18: Sharing a fax/modem

On any fax client

To give another PC in the LAN access to the shared fax/modem, you first must know the name of the computer on which the fax/modem is installed and the name of the fax/modem. You can see the computer's name in Network Neighborhood. In my case, the computer acting as fax server is named Comm_ctr. The name of the fax/modem is whatever you entered in the Microsoft Fax Properties dialog box (refer to Figure 32-18). The official name you must know is two backslashes, followed by the computer name, followed by one backslash and the fax/modem name. In my example, this name comes out as \\Comm_ctr\SharedFax.

Write the name on a piece of paper and take it with you to any PC you want to give access to this shared modem. Then follow these steps:

1. On any PC you want to give access to the shared modem, open Microsoft Exchange (double-click the Inbox icon or choose Start ➪ Programs ➪ Microsoft Exchange.

2. Choose Tools ➪ Microsoft Fax Tools ➪ Options.

   The Microsoft Fax Properties dialog box appears.

3. Click the Modem tab.

4. Click the Add button.

5. Choose Network Fax/modem from the little list that appears.

6. In the next dialog box, you must type the computer name and fax/modem name, as discussed earlier.

   In my case, I would make the entry shown in Figure 32-19.

7. Choose OK.

   You return to the Microsoft Fax Properties dialog box.

8. Click the name of the shared modem to which you just connected; then click the Set As Active Fax Modem button.

9. Choose OK to return to Microsoft Exchange.

10. Close Exchange.

If you previously had to install a driver for a fake modem, you can get rid of the driver now. Open Control Panel (choose Start ➪ Settings ➪ Control Panel), double-click the Modems icon, click the name of the fake modem driver, and click the Remove button. Then choose Close and close Control Panel.

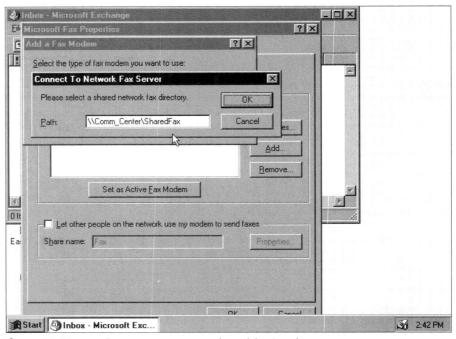

Figure 32-19: Ready to connect to my shared fax/modem

Using the shared fax/modem

The shared fax/modem now is your default modem for sending faxes from this PC. Use the standard technique described in Chapter 16 to create and send a fax at any time — that is, choose Start ➪ Programs ➪ Accessories ➪ Fax ➪ Compose New Fax.

 Chapter 40 discusses Microsoft Exchange in more detail. Chapter 16 discusses faxing in particular.

Your new fax message is added to the Outbox in Microsoft Exchange and sent when the modem becomes available. To check on a fax you sent, open Exchange, and check the Outbox and Sent Items. If the fax still is in the Outbox, you can choose Tools ➪ Deliver Now Using ➪ Microsoft Fax to send it right away (assuming the fax/modem isn't busy at the moment).

Sharing Fonts

Fonts can be a pain on a LAN, because different PCs may have different fonts installed. Suppose Bertha creates a nice document using her cool Avalon Quest font. Then Ellen opens this document on her PC. But Ellen doesn't have the Avalon Quest font on her PC, so Windows replaces that font with something else, such as Times Roman, which doesn't have quite the look and feel Bertha intended.

One way around this problem is to create a single font repository on one PC in the LAN. Figure 32-20 shows one of the PCs, named Comm_ctr, in my LAN. On this computer is a folder named NetFonts. When you open the NetFonts folder, you see it contains two subfolders: one named TrueType and one named Psfonts. The TrueType folder contains TrueType fonts, all of which all have the file extension .TTF. The Psfonts folder contains PostScript Type 1 fonts. (A subfolder named PFM within the Psfonts folder contains PostScript Metric fonts.)

 You need at least version 3.0 of Adobe Type Manager to share PostScript Type 1 fonts on a LAN. Also, this version does not support long folder names. To keep things simple, give your shared fonts folder a DOS-style name, such as NETFONTS (eight characters, no spaces).

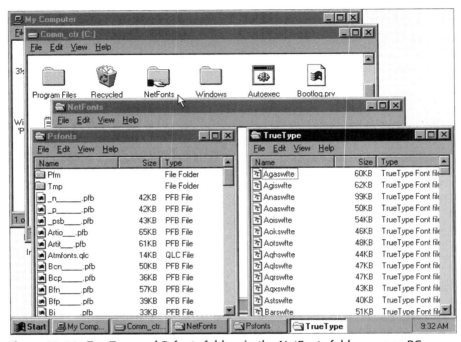

Figure 32-20: TrueType and Psfonts folders in the NetFonts folder on one PC

How you get all your fonts into these two folders is something for which I can't give you step-by-step instructions; different font companies have different installation procedures. But I can give you the following pointers:

✦ Any time you purchase and install a new font, install the font files in the appropriate folder within the NetFonts folder. Later, you can install fonts from that shared folder.

✦ To move existing PostScript fonts into the shared folder, move all the fonts currently in your Psfonts and Psfonts\PFM directory into the Psfonts and Psfonts\PFM subfolders within the NetFonts folder.

✦ If you want to move existing TrueType fonts into the shared folder, move only the .TTF files from the \Windows\Fonts directory, and or \Windows\System directory into that TrueType subfolder in the NetFonts folder. Keep the non-TrueType fonts (fonts that don't have the .TTF file extension) in the Windows\Fonts folder.

✦ Also keep in the Windows\Fonts folder the basic TrueType font files (.TTF), which come with Windows 95. If you're disconnected from the network, you still have those basic fonts with which to work.

Table 32-1 lists the fonts you should store in Windows\Fonts.

Table 32-1 Minimum Fonts in Your Local \Windows\Fonts Folder				
Font Name	*Normal*	*Bold*	*Bold Italic*	*Italic*
Arial	ARIAL.TTF	ARIALBD.TTF	ARIALBI.TTF	ARIALI.TTF
Courier New	COUR.TTF	COURBD.TTF	COURBI.TTF	COURI.TTF
Symbol	SYMBOL.TTF			
Times New Roman	TIMES.TTF	TIMESBD.TTF	TIMESBI.TTF	TIMESI.TTX
Wingdings	WINGDING.TTF			

Whew! (If you don't have a ton of fonts, going to all this trouble may not be worthwhile.) After you set up your NetFonts folder and subfolders and then install (or move) font files into those files, read the following sections for instructions on installing fonts from those shared folders in Windows.

Installing the TrueType fonts

Getting the .TTF font files into a folder on your hard disk is just the first step in installing a font. Again, I can't give you specific step-by-step instructions, because the procedure depends on how the font manufacturer distributes its fonts.

 Once again, I'm not endorsing software piracy here. Before you share a set of fonts, check your license agreement for information on network and concurrent-use details.

The second step is making Windows 95 aware that the .TTF fonts are there — a confusing situation, because this step also is called "installing the fonts." I can give you step-by-step instructions. I'm assuming the .TTF file for the font you want to install already is on the hard disk in the NetFonts\TrueType folder.

Installing TrueType fonts on the font server

On the PC that's playing the role of font server, you need to install TrueType fonts from the local NetFonts\TrueType directory. Follow these steps:

1. Choose Start ➪ Settings ➪ Control Panel.

2. Double-click the Fonts icon.

3. Choose File ➪ Install New Font.

4. Browse to the folder that contains the .TTF files (`c:\NetFonts\TrueType`, in my example), and then deselect the Copy fonts to Fonts folder option, as shown in Figure 32-21.

5. Select the fonts you want to install by Shift+clicking, Ctrl+clicking, or clicking on the Select All button.

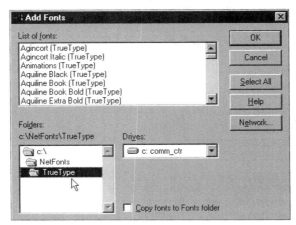

Figure 32-21: Ready to install fonts from C:\NetFonts\TrueType

6. Choose OK.

7. Follow any instructions onscreen.

When you finish, a shortcut symbol appears on fonts you added from the NetFonts\TrueType folder (when you're in Large Icons view). Before you leave this PC, don't forget you must share that folder named NetFonts if you want other PCs on the LAN to have access to these fonts. To share a folder, browse to it in My Computer, right-click the NetFonts icon, and choose Sharing, as discussed earlier in this chapter.

Installing TrueType fonts on any client PC

Now suppose you want to make the same TrueType fonts accessible from some other PC in the LAN. The first thing you must do is map a drive letter to the NetFonts folder. Follow these steps:

1. Go to the PC that will serve as a client to the shared fonts, and double-click Network Neighborhood.

2. Double-click the name of the PC that contains the shared fonts.

3. Right-click the name of the shared folder that contains the shared fonts, and choose Map Drive Letter.

4. Assign a drive letter.

   I chose *F* in Figure 32-22.

5. Choose the Reconnect at logon option.

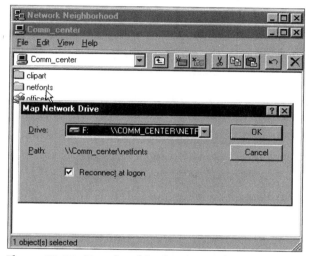

Figure 32-22: Mapping drive letter F to the NetFonts folder

6. Choose OK.

7. Close all open windows.

If you want to make certain you mapped a drive letter correctly, open My Computer on the current PC. You should see a network-drive icon for the NetFonts folder.

The next phase is to tell Windows 95 the TrueType font files (.TTF) are on the shared folder and then install those fonts, so they'll be accessible to all programs on this PC. Follow these steps:

1. Choose Start ➪ Settings ➪ Control Panel.

2. Double-click the Fonts icon.

3. Choose File ➪ Install New Font.

4. Browse to the drive and folder that contains the .TTF files (F:\TrueType, in my example), and deselect the Copy fonts to Fonts folder option; you don't need another copy of those .TTF files on this PC.

   Figure 32-23 shows an example of this procedure on a PC on my LAN.

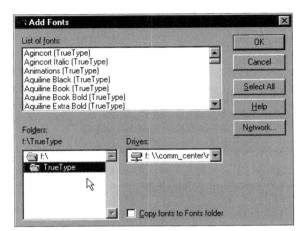

Figure 32-23: Installing fonts from F:\TrueType

5. Select the fonts you want to install by Ctrl+clicking, Shift+clicking, or clicking the Select All button.

6. Choose OK.

7. Follow the instructions onscreen (if any).

You may see a message saying you're pointing to a folder that may not be available later, because you're installing from a network drive. That is OK in this case; you're trying to avoid copying all the .TTF files to every PC in the LAN. Choose OK, and proceed with the installation.

When you finish, you can close all open windows. To test your success, open any program that supports fonts, such as Microsoft Word; then choose a font from that program (in Word, choose Format ➪ Font). Your font list should include all the newly installed fonts.

Remember, if you want every PC in the LAN to have access to the same fonts, you must go to each PC, map a drive letter, and then install the fonts as described in the two preceding sets of steps.

Installing the PostScript fonts

To use PostScript Type 1 fonts, you need a copy of the Adobe Type Manager (ATM) program on every PC that will use the Type 1 fonts. Typically, when you buy a set of Type 1 fonts, you get a copy of the ATM program disk with those fonts.

Danger Zone Only ATM Version 3.0 or later allows you to install fonts without copying them. Also, you must be licensed to use Type 1 fonts on multiple PCs. For more information, contact Adobe at (800) 833-6687.

To find out whether you need to install ATM on a PC, follow these steps:

1. Choose Start ⬦ Programs ⬦ Main.

2. If you don't find the ATM icon, choose Start ⬦ Find, and search for atmcntrl.

3. If you still don't find the ATM logo and atmcntrl file, you must install ATM on this PC.

You must install ATM only one time, so if you found it by using the preceding steps, you do not need to install ATM on this PC. But if you didn't find the program, you'll need to get a copy of the program and install it on your hard disk before you can do anything with Type 1 fonts. The program usually is shipped with any PostScript Type 1 fonts you purchase and often is labeled the ATM Control Panel Program Disk. Typically, you just need to insert that disk into drive A, click the Start button, choose Run, and then run A:\INSTALL.EXE. Remember, you must install a copy of the ATM Control Panel on every PC in the LAN.

Installing PostScript fonts on the server

When you buy a new PostScript Type 1 font, you want to install it on your font server. So go to the PC that acts as your font server and follow these steps:

1. Open the ATM Control Panel window (by double-clicking its icon in the Main program group or by using Find to locate its icon and then double-clicking that icon).

2. In the ATM section, make sure the On option is selected, as shown in Figure 32-24.

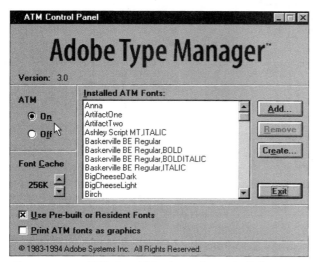

Figure 32-24: ATM should be turned on at all times.

3. Insert into drive A or B the floppy disk containing the fonts you want to install.

4. Click the Add button.

   The Add ATM Fonts dialog box appears.

5. In the Directories list, double-click the drive name for the floppy from which you're installing the fonts.

6. Near the bottom of the dialog box, make sure you specify your shared fonts folder before the psfonts and psfonts\pfm folder names.

   In Figure 32-25, I'm installing the new fonts in `c:\netfonts\psfonts` and `c:\netfonts\psfonts\pfm`.

Danger Zone   When you're installing fonts to the server, you do want to copy files to that PC's hard disk. So make sure the Install without copying files check box is *not* selected. In other words, make sure that check box is empty as in Figure 32-25.

7. Select the fonts you want to install.

8. Click the Add button.

9. After the fonts have been installed, click the Exit button and close Adobe Type Manager.

The fonts now are ready for use on this PC (the one acting as the font server). To make the same fonts accessible to other PCs in the LAN, you need to tell ATM, on each PC, that the new fonts are in the shared-fonts folder.

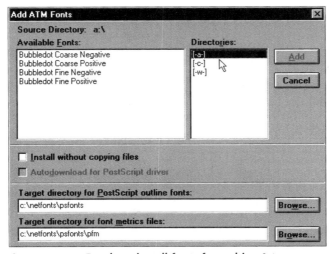

Figure 32-25: Ready to install fonts from drive A to c:\netfonts\psfonts

Installing PostScript fonts on any client PC

Following are two things you must do on the client PC, if you've never done them before:

✦ Map a drive letter to the shared-fonts directory (NetFonts, in my example), as discussed in "Installing TrueType fonts on any client PC" earlier in this chapter.

✦ Install a copy of ATM Control Panel version 3.0 or later on this PC.

Assuming the client PC now has access to drive F (which really is the shared-fonts directory) and you can start ATM on this PC, follow these steps:

1. Start ATM by choosing Start ➪ Programs ➪ Main ➪ ATM Control Panel or by using Find to locate `atmcntrl` and then double-clicking the ATM icon.

2. In the ATM Control Panel, make sure ATM is turned On.

3. Click the Add button.

4. You don't want to copy the font files to the client PC. So do select the check box for the Install without copying files option, as I did in Figure 32-26.

5. In the Directories list, browse to drive F (or whatever drive letter you created for your shared-fonts folder).

6. Browse to the \psfonts\pfm folder on that drive, as shown in Figure 32-26.

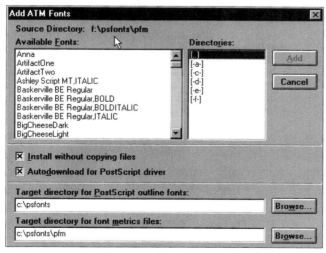

Figure 32-26: Ready to install fonts without copying them to this PC

7. Select the fonts you want to install (you can click the first one and then Shift+click the last one to select them all).

8. Click the Add button.

9. Follow the instructions onscreen, if any.

If the current PC already has a font installed on the shared network drive, for example, you see a message to this effect. Click Cancel if you just want to keep the reference to the local copy of the font intact.

PostScript fonts will not show up in the Fonts folder; only TrueType fonts live there. To verify the installation, you need to open a program that supports Type 1 fonts, such as Microsoft Word. Get to the fonts list (choose Format ➪ Fonts), and you see the PostScript fonts marked with a printer symbol (or some symbol other than *TT* for TrueType; it depends on what program you're using). Figure 32-27 shows an example where the fonts named Anna and ArtifactOne are PostScript fonts. The others are TrueType.

Wow — I'll bet you didn't know you could do so much with a small LAN! The next chapter examines another great advantage of LANs: the capability to send e-mail to other PCs in the LAN.

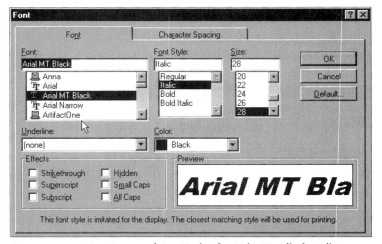

Figure 32-27: TrueType and PostScript fonts in Word's font list

Summary

This chapter has been about using your LAN after you've installed all the appropriate hardware and configured Windows 95 accordingly. In a nutshell:

✦ You can share a printer, drive, folder, or fax/modem on any PC in the LAN.

✦ The computer the shared resource is on or connected to is called the *server*. For example, the PC that has a printer hooked to its parallel port is the *print server*.

✦ Before other LAN members can access a shared resource, you must go to the server of this resource and share the resource. You can do this in My Computer.

✦ Any other PC in a LAN that can use a shared resource is called a *client* to the resource. For example, every PC in the LAN *except* the one to which a printer is connected is a *print client*.

✦ Before a client can use a shared resource, that PC must connect to the shared resource. You can use Network Neighborhood to connect to most shared resources.

✦   ✦   ✦

Setting Up Local E-Mail

Yet another advantage to connecting PCs in a LAN is *local e-mail*, which is an easy-to-set-up type of e-mail that allows members of a workgroup to send messages to one another. Windows 95 comes with the Microsoft Mail Postoffice Workgroup Edition, which is all you need to set up workgroup e-mail. Your incoming local e-mail messages are stored in your Microsoft Exchange Inbox, right along with your MSN (Microsoft Network) messages, incoming faxes, and other types of messages. So managing your local e-mail along with the rest of your messages is easy.

But before you even *think* about setting up local e-mail, make sure you've set up your LAN, as described in Chapters 30 and 31, and that everything is working. You need to do some folder-sharing as well, so you should be familiar with at least that topic from Chapter 32. On top of all this, you must do some planning, as the following section explains.

Phase I: Planning Local E-Mail

You must go through the following preliminary steps before you set up your mail system:

- ✦ Decide who will be the postmaster
- ✦ Decide which PC will be the post office
- ✦ List the names of all the people in the workgroup

These decisions generally aren't too tough to make.

Deciding who will be postmaster

Someone must administer the electronic post office. The responsibilities of this job include the following:

✦ Adding new workgroup members to the post office

✦ Changing information about users

✦ Replacing forgotten passwords

✦ Occasionally checking the status of various post office folders

✦ Occasionally backing up the post office on tape or disk

Deciding where to put the post office

The second choice you must make is where to put the central electronic post office. Every message sent over the local e-mail system will be stored on the post-office PC, so choose a PC with a great deal of available disk space.

Also, if you've decided on a postmaster, you want to make sure he or she can get to the post office PC easily when necessary. Ideally, you would use the post-master's PC as the post office.

Getting a list of workgroup members

The postmaster needs to get an e-mail name and password for each person in the workgroup who will be using the local e-mail system. For starters, I suggest all users use the names and passwords with which they log in. I log in with the name AlanS and the password sesame, for example, so I would use those names as my mailbox name and password.

You also can mark down each person's role in the workgroup, although only one person will be the postmaster and everyone else will be a user. Figure 33-1 shows an example of a four-person workgroup in which Susita Schumack is the post-master (administrator).

Grab your original Windows 95 disk(s)

You may need to install some items from your original Windows 95 disks or CD-ROM, so keep the disks or the CD-ROM handy. If you must install programs from the CD-ROM and you don't have a CD-ROM drive on every PC in the workgroup, share your CD-ROM drive; then map a drive letter from each PC to that CD-ROM drive so you can install programs from that drive. See Chapter 32 if you need help with this procedure.

Name	Mailbox Name	Password	Role
Susita Schumack	SusanS	honcho	Postmaster
Ashley Marie	AshleyM	sesame	User
Alec Fraser	AlecF	sesame	User
Alan Simpson	AlanS	sesame	User

Figure 33-1: A list of e-mail users, mailbox names, and passwords

More Info If your PC is missing any of the components discussed in this chapter, you can install them by using the Microsoft Exchange item in Windows Setup. See "Installing Missing Windows Components" in Chapter 9.

Phase II: Setting Up the Post Office

When you have your plans written down on paper, you're ready to set up your workgroup post office. As usual, setup is the most time-consuming and complicated part of the process, but you must go through it only one time. When you finish, sending and receiving e-mail messages will be a cinch.

To set up the post office, follow these steps:

1. On the PC that will act as the post office, choose Start ➪ Settings ➪ Control Panel.

2. Double-click the Microsoft Mail Postoffice icon.

Danger Zone Make sure you create only one post office, on one PC, for the entire workgroup.

3. In the first wizard screen, choose Create a new Workgroup Postoffice (see Figure 33-2).

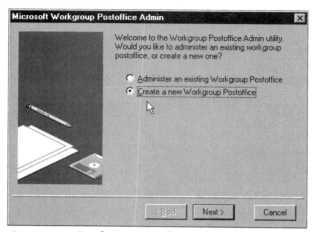

Figure 33-2: Ready to create the workgroup postoffice

4. Click the Next button.

5. In the next wizard screen, type **c:** (your local hard disk) as the post office location, as shown in Figure 33-3, and then click the Next button.

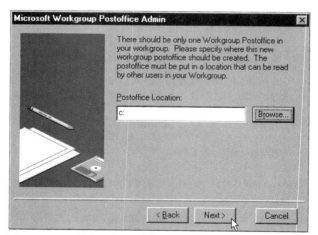

Figure 33-3: Drive C on this computer will be the postoffice location.

6. The next wizard asks whether it should create C:\WGPO0000; click Next to accept.

   The strange name is short for *workgroup* post office number 0000.

7. In the next wizard screen, type the postmaster's name, his or her mailbox name, a password only the postmaster will know, and any of the optional information.

   In Figure 33-4, Susita Schumack is listed as the postmaster.

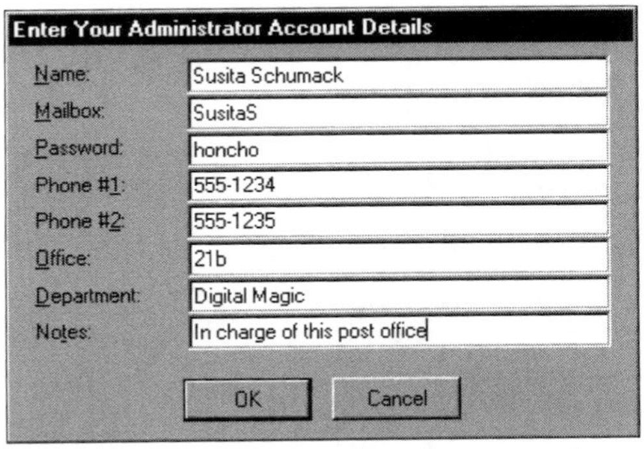

Figure 33-4: Postmaster (workgroup mail administrator) defined

8. Choose OK.

9. You see a reminder about sharing the post office folder; choose OK.

10. Close the Control Panel by clicking on its Close button (X), if you want.

Phase III: Sharing the Post-Office Folder

Now that the wizard has created a post office folder for you (most likely, C:\WGPO0000), you must decide how to share it and give other LAN members unrestricted access to that folder. Follow these steps:

1. On the PC on which you just created the post office, open My Computer (double-click its icon).

2. Double-click the icon for hard disk drive C.

3. Choose View ➪ Arrange Icons ➪ by Name to put the folders in alphabetical order.

4. Right-click the wgpo0000 folder and choose Sharing.

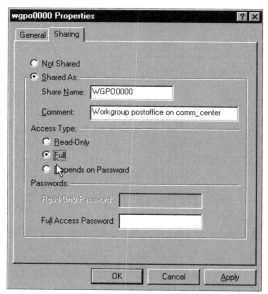 If Sharing isn't an option in your pop-up menu, you probably forgot to allow file sharing on this PC. You need to right-click Network Neighborhood, choose Properties, and turn on File and Print Sharing, as discussed in Chapter 31.

5. Choose Shared As, enter a share name (you can use wgpo0000), type a comment, and choose Full in the Access Type section, as shown in Figure 33-5.

Make sure you leave the boxes in the Passwords section blank.

Figure 33-5: Sharing the new wgpo0000 folder, with full access granted.

6. Choose OK.

A little hand should appear below the wgpo0000 folder icon, indicating the folder is shared.

7. Close all open windows now, if you want, by clicking their Close buttons.

Your post office is almost open for business.

Phase IV: Setting Up User Accounts

Now the postmaster needs to set up an account for each member of the work-group. If you're not the postmaster, you may want to go get this person and help him or her through the process. The postmaster must go through this procedure each time anyone joins the workgroup LAN, deletes an account, or changes a password.

To set up user accounts, follow these steps:

1. On the PC that's acting as the post office, choose Start ⇨ Settings ⇨ Control Panel.

2. Double-click the Microsoft Mail Postoffice icon.

3. Choose Administer an existing Workgroup Postoffice and then click the Next button.

4. Click the Next button to select the suggested wgpo0000 folder.

5. The postmaster needs to enter his or her mailbox name and password.

   In my example, the postmaster enters **SusitaS** and **honcho**. The password appears as asterisks, as shown in Figure 33-6.

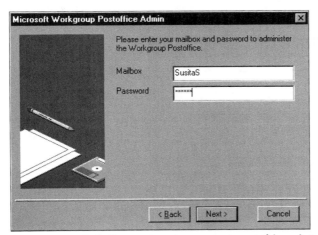

Figure 33-6: Only the postmaster can get past this point.

6. Click the Next button.

   The Postoffice Manager dialog box appears (see Figure 33-7).

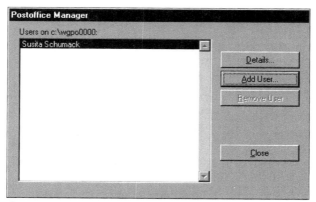

Figure 33-7: The Postoffice Manager dialog box

When you reach the Postoffice Manager dialog box, follow this procedure:

1. Click the Add User button.

2. Fill in the Name, Mailbox, and Password box for one person in the work-group, using the information you jotted down earlier (refer to Figure 33-1).

3. Optionally, fill in other boxes (see Figure 33-8), and choose OK.

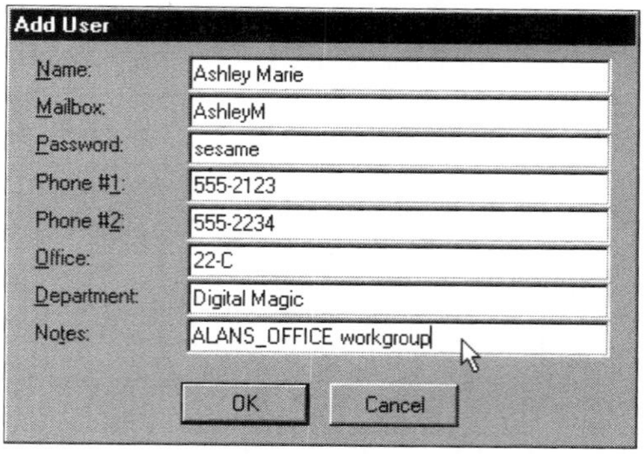

Figure 33-8: One user added to the workgroup post office

4. Repeat Steps 1-3 for each person who will be sending and receiving work-group e-mail.

When you finish, the list in the Postoffice Manager dialog box should include the postmaster's name and the name of each user, as shown in Figure 33-9.

(You don't have to add all users at this time, of course. You can stop at any time and repeat the procedure in this section to add more people later.)

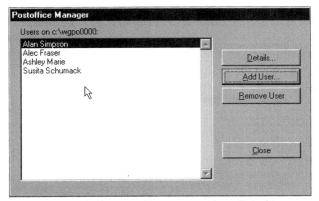

Figure 33-9: My four workgroup members listed in Postoffice Manager

5. To save your new users, click the Close button.

6. Close the Control Panel, if you want.

Phase V: Setting Up E-Mail on Every PC

Microsoft Exchange handles all incoming and outgoing local e-mail messages, along with other types of messages.

Setting up Microsoft Exchange

To set up Exchange to use local e-mail, you need to follow these steps:

1. Choose Start ➪ Settings ➪ Control Panel.

2. Double-click the Mail and Fax icon.

3. If Microsoft Mail is already listed in the information-services list box, skip to Step 13.

4. If Microsoft Mail isn't listed as an information service (see Figure 33-10), click the Add button.

5. In the Add Service to Profile dialog box that appears, click Microsoft Mail.

If Microsoft Mail is not available on this PC, click Cancel; click Cancel again to return to the Control Panel; and go straight to "Installing Microsoft Mail" later in this chapter.

6. Click the OK button.

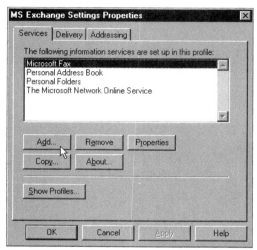

Figure 33-10: Microsoft Mail isn't listed as an information service here.

7. If you are on the post office PC, skip to Step 8.

If you are not on the post office PC, click the Browse button, double-click Network Neighborhood in the list that appears, double-click the name of the post office PC (Comm_center, in my example), and then click the wgpo0000 folder name (see Figure 33-11).

8. Choose OK three times to return to the Control Panel; then close the Control Panel.

9. To identify this particular PC on the LAN, double-click the Inbox icon on the desktop, or choose Start ➪ Programs ➪ Microsoft Exchange.

A dialog box appears, asking for the mailbox name and password for this PC.

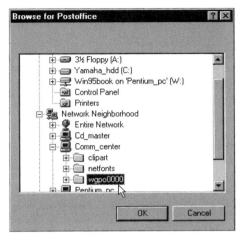

Figure 33-11: Default settings for Microsoft Mail in an Exchange profile

10. Type the appropriate information from the list you made earlier, as shown in Figure 33-12.

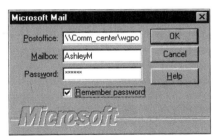

Figure 33-12: Identifying this particular PC's e-mail address

11. Choose OK.

    You go to Microsoft Exchange.

12. Close Exchange.

13. Repeat this procedure on every other PC in the LAN that will send and receive electronic mail.

Puzzled? If you're not prompted to identify this PC's e-mail address, check to make sure the information already entered is correct. Click Start, choose Settings ⇨ Control Panel, then double-click the Mail and Fax icon. Click Microsoft Mail, and then click the Properties button. Check the Connection and Logon tabs, and fill in the appropriate entries. Use the same format I used in Figure 33-12 to enter the path to the Postoffice, mailbox name, and password.

When you complete these steps on every PC in the LAN, your post office is open for business. Skip to "How to Send Local E-Mail" later in this chapter.

Installing Microsoft Mail

Some PCs in the LAN may not have Microsoft Mail installed. To install Microsoft Mail on a PC, first gather up your original Windows 95 disks, or share a CD-ROM drive on the LAN and put your Windows 95 CD-ROM in that drive. (Remember, to install Windows components from a shared CD-ROM drive to another PC, you must map a drive letter to the CD-ROM drive, as discussed in Chapter 31.)

After you collect the original Windows 95 disks or share the CD-ROM drive, follow these steps:

1. Choose Start ➪ Settings ➪ Control Panel.

2. Double-click the Add/Remove Programs icon.

3. Click the Windows Setup tab.

4. Click Microsoft Exchange and then click the Details button.

5. Select both Microsoft Exchange and Microsoft Mail Services, as shown in Figure 33-13.

Figure 33-13: Make sure both Exchange and Mail are selected.

6. Choose OK twice.

7. Follow the instructions onscreen.

When you return to the Control Panel, follow the procedure in "Phase V: Setting Up E-Mail on Every PC" earlier in this chapter.

How to Send Local E-Mail

After the local e-mail system is set up and installed in Microsoft Exchange as an information service on every PC, sending and receiving local e-mail messages is a breeze. Just follow these steps:

1. Double-click the Inbox icon, or choose Start ➪ <u>P</u>rograms ➪ Microsoft Exchange.

2. Choose <u>C</u>ompose ➪ <u>N</u>ew Message.

3. If you know the recipient's mailbox name, type it in the T<u>o</u> box, and skip to Step 4.

   Alternatively, to ensure you have a valid name, click the T<u>o</u> button. If you don't see e-mail recipients' names listed, drop down the <u>S</u>how Names from list and select Postoffice Address List. Then select any number of recipients by clicking each name and then clicking the T<u>o</u> button. When you finish, choose OK.

   In Figure 33-14, for example, someone on the LAN is addressing a message to Alan Simpson.

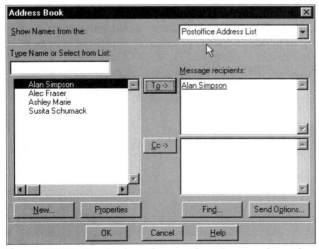

Figure 33-14: Sender has chosen Alan Simpson from the Postoffice Address List.

4. Type a subject and your message, as in the example shown in Figure 33-15.

   Remember, the subject is the brief line the recipient sees in his or her Inbox before opening your message.

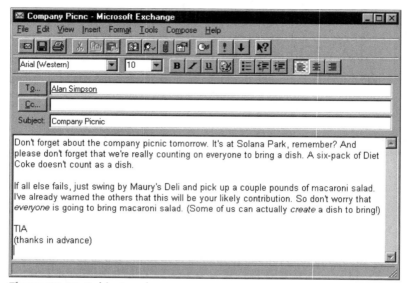

Figure 33-15: Subject and message

5. When you finish typing your message, click the Send button in the toolbar (the first button from the left) or choose File ➪ Send.

Your message is on its way. If you want to make certain the message was sent, stay in Exchange (or reopen it) and make sure you can see the folder list. (Click the Show/Hide Folder List button in the toolbar if you don't see the folder list.) Then click the Sent Items folder. If you don't see your message, perhaps the post office hasn't delivered it yet. To try again, click the Outbox folder, click the message you want to send, and choose Tools ➪ Deliver Now.

Life Saver If you have any problems with your e-mail, try running the Inbox Repair Tool. Click the Start button, point to Programs ➪ Accessories ➪ System Tools and choose Inbox Repair Tool. Click its Help button for information.

Reading Your Local E-Mail

Reading your e-mail messages is the same as reading any other kind of message. Follow these steps:

1. Double-click the Inbox icon on your desktop or choose Start ➪ Programs ➪ Microsoft Exchange.

2. The Inbox opens, displaying all newly received messages.

   When I open the Inbox on my PC, for example, I may see a message sent to me by Ashley Marie (see Figure 33-16).

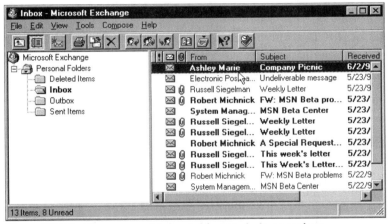

Figure 33-16: Message sent from Ashley Marie in my Inbox

3. To read a message, double-click it.

While you read the message, you can click the buttons in the toolbar to print, delete, reply, forward the message, and so on. Chapter 30 discusses these options, which apply to all messages you receive on your PC.

Changing Your Mail Password

I've been pretty lax about security in telling you how to set up your mail system. As this system is designed, anyone who can log on under your name also can read your mail messages. If you need tighter security, you can change your own password and/or require the user to enter this password before any messages can be opened.

To change your mail password

To change your existing mail password, follow these steps:

1. Open Microsoft Exchange by double-clicking the Inbox icon or choosing Start ➪ Programs ➪ Microsoft Exchange.

2. Choose Tools ➪ Microsoft Mail Tools ➪ Change Mailbox Password.

3. Type your old password.

4. Type your new password twice (once for confirmation).

5. Choose OK.

To require a password

If you want to ensure that only people who know the password (you) can get to your messages, follow these steps to make Microsoft Mail prompt you for a password every time:

1. Choose Start ➪ Settings ➪ Control Panel.

2. Double-click the Mail and Fax icon.

3. Click Microsoft Mail.

4. Click the Properties button.

5. Click the Logon tab.

6. Clear the checkbox titled When logging on, automatically enter password (see Figure 33-17).

Figure 33-17: Clearing the checkbox ensures that Mail always prompts for a password.

7. Choose OK twice to return to the Control Panel.

8. Close the Control Panel.

From now on, whenever you open Microsoft Exchange, you are prompted for a password. You will not be allowed to open your Inbox until you type the password and choose OK.

If you change your mind and don't want to be prompted for a password every time you open your Inbox, click the Remember Password option after you type your mail password and before you click OK.

For most users on the LAN, knowing how to send and read messages is sufficient. You can do many other things with Microsoft Mail, however, especially if you're the postmaster and/or network administrator. The following section discusses basic postmaster responsibilities; Chapter 40 discusses advanced Mail techniques.

Adding, Changing, and Deleting Mail Users

Only the postmaster has the capability to add users, delete users, and change information about users in the workgroup post office. Follow these steps:

1. On the post office PC, choose Start ⇨ Settings ⇨ Control Panel.

2. Double-click the Microsoft Mail Postoffice icon.

3. Choose Administer an existing Workgroup Postoffice and then click the Next button.

4. Click the Next button to accept the suggested post office folder (C:\WPGO0000, for example).

5. Type the postmaster password, and click Next.

6. Select any user name in the list, as shown in Figure 33-18; then click Details to change the user information or click Remove User to delete the user.

   Alternatively, to add a user, click the Add User button and then fill in the form that appears, as discussed earlier in this chapter.

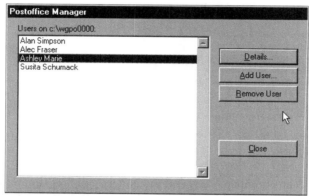

Figure 33-18: The postmaster can add, delete, or change Microsoft Mail users in this dialog box.

7. When you finish making your changes, click the Close button to return to the Control Panel.

8. Close the Control Panel, if you want.

Don't forget, if you added a new PC to the LAN, you also need to set up e-mail on that PC, as discussed in "Phase V: Setting Up E-Mail on Every PC" earlier in this chapter.

Summary

✦ To set up local e-mail for a workgroup, you first must decide which PC will play the role of post office.

✦ Then you need to create a workgroup post office on that PC and share the directory the post office wizard creates.

✦ Next, a person designated as postmaster must create an account for each member of the workgroup.

✦ On each PC, Microsoft Mail must be added to Microsoft Exchange's list of information services.

✦ To send local e-mail, open Microsoft Exchange and choose <u>C</u>ompose ➪ <u>N</u>ew Message.

✦ To read local e-mail, open your Inbox.

✦   ✦   ✦

More Cool LAN Tricks

This chapter explains some features and tricks you can try on your own LAN. Everything discussed in this chapter is optional — you don't have to do any of these things to set up or use a LAN — so feel free to read this chapter at your leisure.

Pop-Up Messages

WinPopup is a handy built-in utility that enables network users to send immediate messages to one another. Unlike e-mail messages, which are stored in the Inbox, pop-up messages appear in the recipient's taskbar immediately.

To set up WinPopup on a PC, you need to install WinPopup from the original floppy disks or CD-ROM (if you haven't already done so). Then drag the WinPopup icon to the Startup folder so the utility starts automatically when you start Windows.

Installing WinPopup

If you're not sure whether WinPopup is on your PC yet, follow these steps to find out and to install it, if necessary:

1. Choose Start ➪ Settings ➪ Control Panel.

2. Double-click the Add/Remove Programs icon.

3. Click the Windows Setup tab.

4. Click Accessories, click the Details button, and then scroll down to see if Win Popup is installed.

5. If WinPopup is already installed, as in Figure 34-1, click the Cancel button and skip to "Adding WinPopup to your Startup folder" later in this chapter.

   If WinPopup isn't already installed, select it so its check-box is checked.

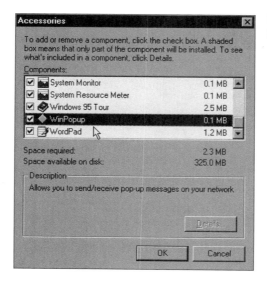

Figure 34-1: WinPopup is already installed in this example.

6. Gather up your original Windows 95 program disks or CD-ROM, and click OK.

7. Follow the instructions onscreen.

After WinPopup is installed on your PC, proceed to the following section.

Adding WinPopup to your Startup folder

The best way to use WinPopup on a LAN is to make sure all LAN members have the utility up and running at all times. The simplest way to do this is to go to each PC and add WinPopup's icon to the Startup folder. Follow these steps:

1. Choose Start ➪ Find ➪ Files or Folders.

2. Type **winpopup.exe** as the file to look for.

3. Click the Find Now button.

When the file is found, it should have a little jack-in-the-box icon.

You can put a WinPopup shortcut right on your desktop. Right-drag the jack-in-the-box icon to the desktop, release the mouse button, and choose Create Shortcut(s) Here.

4. Right-click the Start button, and choose Open.

5. Double-click the Programs icon.

6. Move and size the windows so you can see both the icon for the Startup icon and the icon for WinPopup, as shown in Figure 34-2.

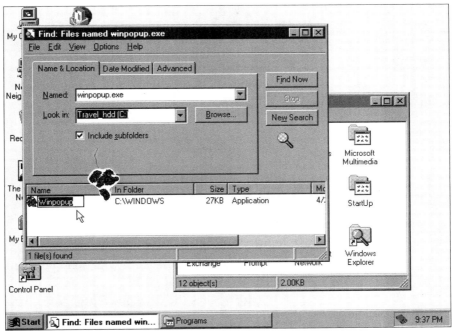

Figure 34-2: Getting ready to right-drag WinPopup to the Startup folder

7. Holding down the right mouse button, drag the WinPopup icon so it covers the Startup folder's icon.

8. Release the mouse button, and choose Create Shortcut(s) Here.

9. Close all open windows.

To ensure that WinPopup starts, restart your PC; choose Start ➪ Shut Down ➪ Restart the computer? ➪ Yes.

Don't forget you must go to each PC in the LAN and repeat this procedure, so all PCs start with WinPopup ready to go.

WinPopup appears onscreen already open, as shown in Figure 34-3. But you can click its Minimize button to reduce it to a taskbar button when you want it out of the way.

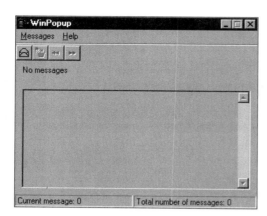

Figure 34-3: WinPopup is fully opened

Sending a pop-up message

To send a pop-up message to someone in your workgroup, follow these steps:

1. Open the WinPopup window, if it isn't open already.

   (By this point, you should be able to click the WinPopup taskbar button to open it.)

2. Choose Messages ➪ Send, or click the envelope button in WinPopup's toolbar.

3. To send the message to a specific person or computer, type that person's log-in name (such as **AshleyM** or **AlanS**) or the name of the computer (for example **comm_center**).

   To send the message to the entire workgroup, click the Workgroup option button; the name of your workgroup appears automatically.

4. Type your message, as in the example shown in Figure 34-4.

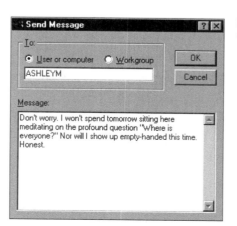

Figure 34-4: A pop-up message to AshleyM in my LAN

5. Choose OK to send the message.

6. Choose OK to respond to the prompt that your message has been sent.

You could minimize the WinPopup window now, but don't close it yet; you want to leave it open so you can receive messages.

Reading pop-up messages

When someone sends you a pop-up message, the WinPopup button in your taskbar informs you that you have a message. Just click this taskbar button to view your message. After reading the message, you can use the various toolbar buttons and the commands in the Messages menu to respond, as follows:

✦ To send a reply, click the Send button.

✦ To delete the message, click the Delete button.

✦ If you have several messages in your bin, click the Previous and Next buttons to scroll through the messages.

When you finish reading your messages, minimize the WinPopup window. But don't close the window if you want to continue getting pop-up messages from other workgroup members.

Personalizing WinPopup

If you want to change the way WinPopup behaves when it receives a message, choose Messages ⇨ Options from within WinPopup. You see the simple dialog box shown in Figure 34-5. Make your changes and then choose OK.

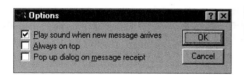

Figure 34-5: Options for personalizing WinPopup

Cutting and Pasting Between PCs

Scraps (refer to "You'll Love These Scraps" in Chapter 4) are great ways to get stuff from one document into another, and using them is fun and easy. But consider the following scenario, using two new LAN members as the example:

Homer is working next to Marge, and he sees something on her screen he wants to paste into his own document. How does Marge cut or copy this object to enable Homer, on the other PC, to paste it into his document? When you find out, please drop me a line, because I'd like to know myself. (Ha, ha — just kidding.)

The answer is, "It depends." For starters, define the goal simply as follows:

Marge (has it) ⇨ Homer (wants it)

If the document Marge is using is in a shared folder (such as the Projects folder I'm always talking about), Marge can choose File ⇨ Save to save her work to disk. Homer can browse to the shared folder, via Network Neighborhood, and double-click the name of Marge's document. A copy of Marge's entire document now appears on Homer's screen. Homer can select whatever he wants and then choose Edit ⇨ Copy to copy the selection into his own Clipboard, even if the document opens as read-only on his PC. When Homer has the stuff in his Clipboard, he can choose Edit ⇨ Paste to paste this object into any document on his PC.

This solution is the simplest, but it works only if the document in question is in a shared folder. If Marge's document isn't in a shared folder, she can copy the document and send it to a shared folder, from which Homer can retrieve the copy. Marge can press Ctrl+A to select her entire document, press Ctrl+C to copy to her Clipboard, press Ctrl+N to create a new blank document, and then press Ctrl+V to paste the selection into that new blank document.

Next, Marge can choose File ⇨ Save As to save the new copy. In the Save As dialog box that appears, she needs to browse to a shared folder Homer can access, enter a file name (such as Homer's Copy), and choose OK. Then Marge can choose File ⇨ Close to get rid of the copy she made for Homer and go back to working on her original document. Now Homer can go to the shared folder, open Homer's Copy, and do with it as he pleases.

If Homer frequently bugs Marge for scraps, a third method may be considered. In this method, Marge creates a shared folder on her own PC, named (for example) Marge's Scraps. Homer maps a drive letter from his PC to the Marge's Scraps folder. Marge can drag any scrap into this shared folder at any time. Homer can go to the Marge's Scraps folder at any time, and cut and paste scraps from this folder into any document of his own. The following sections show you how Homer and Marge would set up and use the shared scraps folder.

Creating a shared scraps folder

Marge wants to cut or copy any portion of any document she's working on to a shared folder named Marge's Scraps. Follow these steps to create this shared folder:

1. On the PC from which you'll be cutting or copying (Marge's PC, in my example), double-click My Computer.

2. Double-click the icon for drive C.

3. Choose File ⇨ New ⇨ Folder.

4. Type a name for the folder (**Marge's Scraps**, for this example).

5. Click just outside this new folder icon to save the new name.

6. Right-click the new folder (Marge's Scraps), and choose S<u>h</u>aring.

Life Saver If S<u>h</u>aring isn't available in the pop-up menu after you right-click, you probably didn't allow for file sharing when you set up this PC. You need to right-click Network Neighborhood, choose P<u>r</u>operties, and use the Configuration tab to allow file sharing. See Chapter 31 (in the neighborhood of Figure 31-3) if you need more information.

7. Choose <u>S</u>hared As.

8. Type a brief Share <u>N</u>ame (**MargeScraps**, for this example).

9. Optionally, type a <u>C</u>omment, choose what type of access you want to offer, and enter a password.

   Figure 34-6 shows my example.

   Read-only access is fine if you want other users to read from this folder, but not rermove anything from it.

10. Choose OK.

11. To create a desktop icon for this folder, right-drag the folder to the Windows 95 desktop, release the mouse button, and choose Create <u>S</u>hortcut(s) Here.

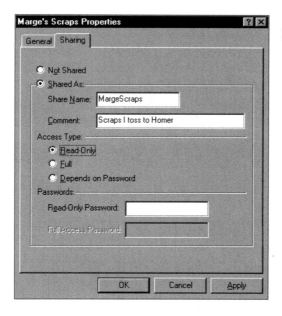

Figure 34-6: Marge will share her new scraps folder.

Within My Computer, you should see your folder with a little sharing hand below it. On the desktop, you should see a shortcut to that folder, as in my example shown in Figure 34-7.

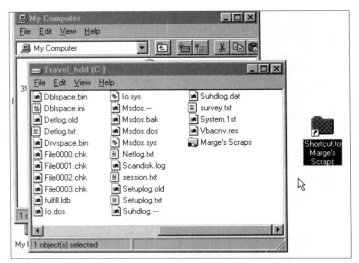

Figure 34-7: New shared Marge's Scraps folder and desktop shortcut

Now Marge can close all her open windows and rearrange desktop icons in alphabetical order (by right-clicking the desktop and choosing Arrange Icons ⇨ by Name). And now she has a place to toss scraps to Homer.

Next, you need to set up the other PC so you can get at the scraps quickly and easily. Follow these steps:

1. On Homer's PC (or any other PC in the LAN that needs Marge's scraps), double-click Network Neighborhood.

2. Double-click the name of the PC on which you created the shared scraps folder.

3. Click the name of the shared scraps folder (Marge's Scraps, in this example).

4. Right-drag the folder to the desktop.

5. Release the mouse button, and choose Create Shortcut(s) Here.

6. Close all open windows.

7. If you want, you can rename the new shortcut by right-clicking its icon and choosing Rename.

In Figure 34-8, I named the shortcut to the shared folder Marge's Scraps. You can, of course, give the shortcut any name you want.

Figure 34-8: Shortcut to Marge's Scraps on Homer's PC

Cutting and copying to the scraps folder

How does Marge get a scrap from whatever document she's working on to the shared folder? She drags it there — that is, she selects the object she wants to share and then drags this object from its current position to the shortcut icon for the shared folder.

In Figure 34-9, Marge selected text from a Word document and dragged this text to the open window for the Marge's Scraps folder.

Pasting from the scraps folder

To get a scrap into your Clipboard so you can paste it wherever you want, follow these steps:

1. On your own PC, open the window for the Marge's Scraps folder.

You may be able to skip Steps 2-4, depending on the program into which you plan to paste the scrap. Some programs allow you to drag a scrap icon into an open document; you may want to try this simpler method first.

2. To open the scrap, double-click it (see Figure 34-10).

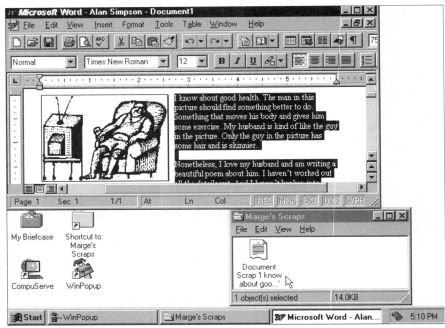

Figure 34-9: Marge dragged the selected text to the shared Marge's Scraps folder.

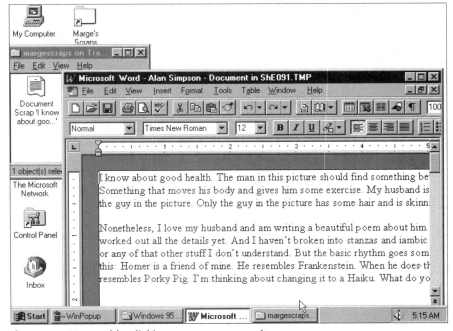

Figure 34-10: Double-clicking a scrap to open it

3. Choose Edit ➪ Select All to select everything within the scrap.

4. Choose Edit ➪ Copy to copy the selection to the Windows Clipboard on your PC.

Now that the scrap is in Homer's Clipboard, Homer can open any document, place the insertion point wherever he wants to put the scrap, and choose Edit ➪ Paste to paste the Clipboard contents at the current insertion-point position.

This scenario is just an example of how two people can cut and paste between their PCs. You simply want to get whatever Person X wants from Person Y's PC to a shared folder. When the object is in a shared folder, Person X can navigate to that shared folder, using Network Neighborhood; then he or she can open, copy, or move the document from that shared folder to his or her own PC or document.

Finding Things on the LAN

Finding things on a single-user PC can be challenging for beginning and casual users, because they need to understand (and keep track of) drives, folders, and filenames. Throw a LAN into the picture, and you add a new dimension — now you also must know on which PC a particular thing is located. You can, however, use several techniques to find things on a LAN, as you'll learn in the following sections.

Long-distance cutting and pasting

If you need to send an object long-distance over phone lines, your best bet is to save the object as a file first. You can use several methods, depending on the application you're using. Some applications allow you to select text or graphics and then choose File ➪ Save As or Edit ➪ Copy To to save the selection to a file. Alternatively, you can select an object and choose Edit ➪ Copy to copy the object to the Clipboard. Then open the Clipboard Viewer (choose Start ➪ Programs ➪ Accessories ➪ Clipboard Viewer) and choose File ➪ Save As from within Clipboard Viewer to save the Clipboard contents to a file.

Regardless of how you get the selection into a file, the next step is to address e-mail to the intended recipient and attach the file to the message you're sending. To see how you do this with the Microsoft Network (MSN), see Chapter 21. You can send mail to the Internet, CompuServe, and America Online from MSN.

Browsing for computers and shared resources

If your LAN is fairly small, you probably will find browsing around with Network Neighborhood is sufficient to find whatever resource you want. Double-click the Network Neighborhood icon; initially, you see a list with Entire Network at the top, followed by a list of PCs in your workgroup. To check out the shared resources on any PC in your own workgroup, double-click the name of the computer you want to browse.

If your workgroup is connected to other workgroups, you can double-click Entire Network to see what other workgroups are available. (Figure 34-11 shows an example in which I have two workgroups going: one named ALANS_OFFICE and the other named MEDIA_LAB.) To explore another workgroup, just click the workgroup's name.

If you find a drive or folder to which you want to connect, you can map a drive letter to it on the spot. Right-click the name of the drive or folder, and choose <u>M</u>ap Network Drive from the shortcut menu that appears.

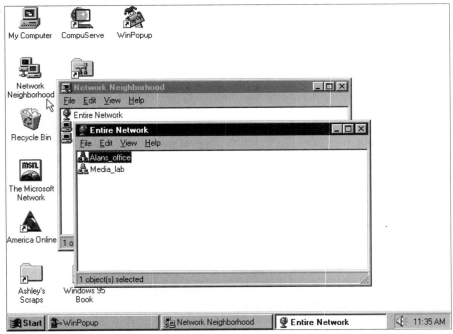

Figure 34-11: Double-clicking Entire Network shows the names of other workgroups.

If you need a reminder on the details of mapping a drive letter, see "Sharing an Entire Hard Disk," "Sharing a CD-ROM Drive," or "Sharing a Folder," as appropriate, in Chapter 32.

Finding a specific computer

If your workgroup has hundreds of computers, browsing for a specific computer can be time-consuming. If you know even part of the name of the computer for which you're looking, you can use Find, rather than Network Neighborhood, to locate a specific computer faster. Follow these steps:

1. On any PC in the workgroup, choose Start ➪ Find.

2. Click Computer.

3. Type the name (or part of the name) of the computer for which you're looking.

4. Click the Find Now button.

   After the little magnifying glass stops spinning, you see a list of computers that match the requested name.

In Figure 34-12, I searched for *comm*. Find located a computer named Comm_center on my LAN.

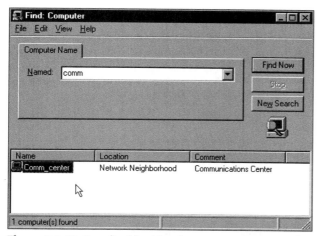

Figure 34-12: Result of looking for a computer named Comm

To explore shared resources on that computer, I would double-click the icon for that PC. Then, to map a drive letter on that PC, I would right-click the appropriate filename and choose Map Network Drive.

Searching for a folder or file

At some point, your LAN may have thousands of folders and files, so searching for something by browsing can take a l-o-o-o-o-o-ng time. But you can speed the process by using the My Computer option with Find. This way, Find will look through your local hard disk and CD-ROM drive (if any), as well as all shared resources to which you mapped a drive letter. Follow these steps:

1. Choose Start ➪ Find.

2. Click Files or Folders.

3. Type all or part of the folder or file for which you're looking.

4. In the Look in list, select My Computer.

5. Click on Find Now.

   The search may take a while, especially if you mapped drive letters to many different resources. But when Find finishes, you see exactly where the folder or file is stored.

Figure 34-13 shows an example in which I searched for a file containing the word *mailing*. Find located a file containing that word in the drive named *P*. To open this file, I double-click its icon, as usual.

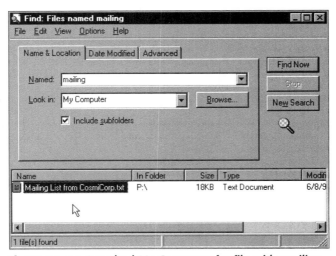

Figure 34-13: Searched My Computer for file with *mailing* in the file name

Managing Other PCs from Your Own PC

Remote Administration enables you to manage other PCs in the LAN from your own PC. Specifically, you can share or unshare folders on some PC other than your own without leaving your chair. On a larger scale, if you set up all the PCs in the LAN for remote administration, you can share and unshare any folder on any PC in the LAN from whichever PC you are using.

In a sense, all the drives and folders on the LAN become yours to do with as you please. You no longer are limited to accessing shared resources on the LAN; you can access any folder, shared or not. You become the grand wazoo of virtually every file and folder on the LAN (the official title is *network administrator* rather than *grand wazoo*).

Before I go into any great detail on Remote Administration, let me give you this warning: Remote Administration can be fairly simple and straightforward, or horrendously complicated. In this chapter, I'll stick with the not-so-complicated stuff that 98 percent of you are likely to find sufficient for your needs. What you learn between here and the end of this chapter, although fairly simple, can make you the grand wazoo of every folder and file on the LAN.

Allowing a PC to be managed remotely

Before you can administer a PC remotely, you must set up that PC so it *can* be administered remotely. This step is a safety net that prevents any person on the LAN from messing with any PC he or she feels like using. So your first step is to complete the following steps:

1. On the PC you want to manage remotely, choose Start ➪ <u>S</u>ettings ➪ <u>C</u>ontrol Panel.

2. Double-click the Passwords icon.

3. Click the Remote Administration tab.

4. Select the <u>E</u>nable Remote Administration of this server option.

5. Type a password (twice) that will allow this PC to be managed from another PC.

   As usual, the password appears in asterisks, as shown in Figure 34-14.

6. Choose OK.

Life Saver If this PC (the one you're sitting at right now) is not set up to allow file sharing, you won't be able to share anything on it from any PC. If you're unsure about the sharing status of files on this PC, right-click Network Neighborhood, choose Properties, click the Configuration tab, and then click the <u>F</u>ile and Print Sharing button. If necessary, refer to Chapter 31, starting with the section titled "The Configuration Tab."

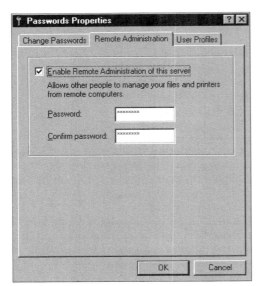

Figure 34-14: This PC can be managed from any other PC in the LAN.

This procedure takes care of the PC you're using right now. If you want to manage the hard disk of another PC on this LAN, you must go to that PC and repeat the procedure. You can assign the same password to each PC, if you want, so you need to remember only one password to get to any PC in the LAN.

Managing a PC remotely

Whenever you're ready to put on your grand-wazoo robe and take control of another PC's drive(s), follow these steps:

1. On your PC (or whatever PC you happen to be using), double-click the Network Neighborhood icon.

2. Right-click the name of the PC you want to manage, and choose Properties from the shortcut menu.

3. Click the Tools tab in the dialog box that appears.

4. Click the Administer button.

5. When you are prompted, type your password for managing that PC and then choose OK.

   You see all the shared resources on that PC, with a new item called C$ included in the list, as shown in Figure 34-15.

That little C$ is your ticket to the remote PC's hard drive. Double-click C$, and you get a view of the entire hard disk on that PC. Figure 34-16 shows an example.

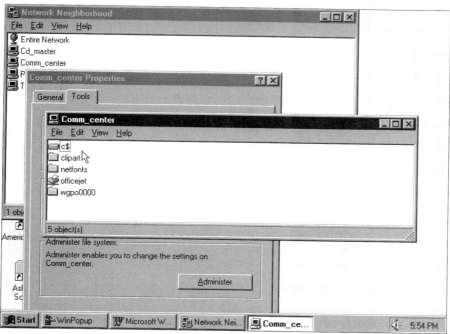

Figure 34-15: C$ and shared resources on comm_center PC

Figure 34-16: Opening C$ shows folders on the
remote PC's hard drive.

Danger Zone Remember, if you disconnect someone from a shared folder he or she is using, you can destroy his or her work. Exercise extreme caution when you unshare a shared folder.

 Life Saver If you accidentally disconnect another user from his work, and he has trouble reopening the file on which he was working when you disconnected him, go to the PC that holds the shared folder, and run ScanDisk on that PC, as discussed in "Find and Repair Disk Errors" in Chapter 11.

To share or unshare a folder on that PC, right-click the folder and choose Sharing. Fill out the dialog box in the usual manner. If you need help with this procedure, see "Sharing a Folder" in Chapter 32. Remember, your action affects everyone in the LAN. After you share a folder, any member of the LAN can connect to that folder and map a drive letter to it. Conversely, when you stop sharing a folder, you disconnect everyone from this folder.

Summary

Following is a review of the main techniques discussed in this chapter:

✦ To send a pop-up message to another LAN member, open WinPopup, click the envelope button, address the message, type the message, and choose OK.

✦ When you receive a pop-up message, open WinPopup to read the message. To reply, click the envelope button. To delete the message, click the trash-can button.

✦ Remember, after you close WinPopup, you won't get messages anymore. A better idea is to minimize WinPopup only when you want it out of the way.

✦ The trick to cutting and pasting between PCs is creating a shared folder both PCs can access. A LAN member can save folders or scraps to the shared folder; then any other LAN member can open and copy objects in that folder.

✦ You can use Network Neighborhood to browse for shared objects on your network.

✦ You can choose Start ➪ Find ➪ Computer to locate a particular PC in your workgroup.

✦ You can tell Find to conduct a search of My Computer when you want to search all local and mapped network drives for a folder or file.

✦ If you want to share folders from a PC without actually going to that PC, you need to activate Remote Administration on that PC. Choose Start ➪ Settings ➪ Control Panel, double-click the Passwords icon, and use the Remote Administration tab to set up a password.

✦ To manage a PC's folders remotely, double-click Network Neighborhood, right-click the name of the PC you want to manage, and choose Properties from the shortcut menu. Click the Tools tab, click the Administer button, and then double-click the C$ drive to gain access to that PC's entire hard disk.

This chapter about wraps it up for networking. I know if you're in a large corporation, your LAN probably is more complicated than the ones discussed in this part of the book. You may have dozens of PCs and workgroups on the LAN, as well as several full-time network administrators. But most of the techniques discussed in this part of the book work on any LAN, large or small.

✦   ✦   ✦

Windows 95 in the Corporate Environment

General Corporate Considerations

I realize some of the people reading this book are MIS managers and similar professionals who are responsible for dozens, perhaps hundreds or even thousands, of PCs. And I'm aware that in a large corporation, upgrading from Windows 3.x to Windows 95 isn't as simple as sticking a disk into a drive and running SETUP.EXE. In this chapter, I discuss some of the challenges Windows 95 presents to corporate MIS managers and the resources and tools available to help you brave those challenges. I do want to make it clear, though, this book is really written for Windows 95 users, not MIS professionals and Network Administrators. I can't cover, in depth, all the countless issues facing MIS professionals in large organizations. But I can make you aware of the many additional resources available to you and point you in the right direction to find those resources.

Why a Corporate Upgrade?

At Microsoft's Tech Ed conference, back around March 1994, I attended a presentation on Windows 95. During the question-and-answer period at the end of the session, an attendee stood and posed the following scenario and question:

"We currently have about 600 users of PCs in our enterprise. Most PCs are running Windows for Workgroups, to which we recently upgraded from Windows 3.1. It took several months and considerable resource expenditure to make the relatively 'simple' switch from Windows 3.1 to Windows for Workgroups.

"But we did it, and now all our PCs are working, people are trained, and everybody seems to be getting the job done without daily crisis intervention from the MIS staff. My question is this: Are you suggesting we now go back, tear all that down, and replace it with Windows 95? And if you *are* suggesting this, could you write a list of specific advantages that would justify the enormous expenditure of resources that yet another upgrade is going to require?"

I was happy *not* to be the speaker who had to respond to this question. The speaker at that session did come up with a fairly good list of justifications, however, which are summarized in the following sections. (I won't try to *sell* you on the idea, though. That's Microsoft's job, not mine!)

Reduced support costs

One potential benefit of switching to Windows 95, even in a large organization, is reduced support costs, as described in the following list:

✦ The intuitive nature of the Windows 95 user interface makes users more independent and, therefore, reduces support costs.

✦ Plug-and-play also reduces support costs by simplifying the hardware-installation process.

✦ The 32-bit operating system offers greater reliability and performance, thereby taking some of the load off support personnel.

✦ Built-in networking allows Windows 95 to work seamlessly with all major networks, including Novell NetWare (see Chapter 37) and Windows NT (see Chapter 36), so network administration is less costly.

More control of desktop PCs

A second justification for large-scale upgrades to Windows 95 centers on the knowledge that MIS managers will have more control of all the PCs in the enterprise, as described in the following list:

✦ User profiles (see Chapter 11) enable multiple users to share a single PC without getting in one another's way.

✦ System policies and group policies can be implemented to reduce a user's ability to change configuration settings (see the "System Policy and Group Policy Editors" sidebar later in this chapter).

✦ Support for remote administration tools and agents is built into Windows 95. System Agent, which comes with Microsoft Plus! (see Chapter 39) can be used to run routine tasks like ScanDisk, defragmentation, and certain kinds of backups automatically at odd hours.

✦ Support for centralized pass-through security, log-on scripts, and validated log on with Windows NT Server (see Chapter 36) and Novell NetWare (see Chapter 37) networks also is built in.

System Policy and Group Policy Editors

System Policies and Group Policies can be used in conjunction with User Policies (see Chapter 11) and network servers to restrict access to Control Panel options, restrict what users can do from the desktop, customize parts of the desktop, and configure some network settings. The Group Policies editor is handy if you already have user groups defined through Windows NT or Novell NetWare, because it enables you to apply policies to those existing groups.

The official documentation for the System Policy Editor and Group Policies is contained within the *Windows 95 Resource Kit*, and is also available online at `http://www.microsoft.com/organizations/corpeval/180.htm`. The System Policies Editor program is available online at `http://www.microsoft.com/windows/common/aa2724.htm`.

The System Policies Editor program is also available on the Microsoft Windows 95 CD-ROM. It's well hidden; you won't find it in Windows Setup or any other "normal" desktop program. To install the System Policies Editor, and Group Policies, click the Start button and choose Settings ⇨ Control Panel and double-click the Add/Remove Programs icon. Click the Windows Setup tab; then click the Have Disk button. In the text box, specify *d:*\Admin\Apptools\Poledit where *d:* is the letter of your CD-ROM drive. Click the component(s) you want to install, and then follow the instructions on the screen.

Improved user productivity

A third reason for a corporation to upgrade to Windows 95 is increased user productivity. Workers will be more productive for the following reasons:

✦ Faster 32-bit processing means more work gets done in less time.

✦ Preemptive multitasking allows multiple hardware devices — such as a printer, a modem, and a floppy disk drive — to work simultaneously.

✦ Dial-Up Networking (see Chapter 20) and Briefcase (see Chapter 18) make it easier for users to work from home or on the road.

✦ Centralized messaging via Microsoft Exchange (see Chapter 40) enables users to take care of incoming and outgoing messages more quickly.

Built-in support for smooth migration

Finally, Microsoft has gone to great lengths to make the transition from Windows 3.x to Windows 95 as smooth, painless, and easy as possible, as described in the following list:

✦ The setup program for Windows 95 automatically detects hardware and installs drivers, so upgrading a single PC is quick and easy.

✦ The setup procedure can be scripted to choose options automatically as the installation proceeds.

✦ *Push installation* enables multiple computers to be upgraded from a server. The administrator needn't even go to the PC being upgraded (see "Update for IS professionals Web site" later in this chapter to get to the right Web page.)

Resources for MIS Professionals

Three major resources are available to MIS professionals who need in-depth knowledge on evaluating, deploying, administering, and maintaining Windows 95 in a corporate environment. In the "books" category Microsoft offers the *Windows 95 Resource Kit*. Subtitled *The Technical Guide for Installing, Configuring, and Supporting Windows 95 in Your Organization*, that behemoth 1,200+ page tome picks up where this book (and other's like it) leave off, and gets deep into technical issues, networking, security, and so forth. You can find the *Windows 95 Resource Kit* at any computer store or book store that sells computer books. Or, you can contact Microsoft Press, the publisher, at (800) MSPRESS. The Resource Kit is also available online as a free downloadable Help file, at `http://www.microsoft.com/windows/software/reskit.htm`.

The corporate evaluation Web site

For those with Internet access, Microsoft offers the Corporate Desktop Evaluation Center (see Figure 35-1). To get there, just point your Web browser to `http://www.microsoft.com/organizations/corpeval`. You will, no doubt, want to check out the Windows 95 product area in this site, which you can find at `http://www.microsoft.com/organizations/corpeval/3_01.htm`.

The news service for system professionals

In addition to the Web site, Microsoft offers a special electronic newsletter for system professionals. When you subscribe, you'll receive e-mail notifications about new and revised content on relevant Web sites, alerts about critical events, issues, the availability of betas and evaluations, and other valuable information. You can subscribe directly from the Corporate Desktop Evaluation Web site at `http://www.microsoft.com/organizations/corpeval` (notice the Subscribe Now link back in Figure 35-1).

More Info A great resource for all kinds of Windows 95 information is at `http://www.microsoft.com/windows95`.

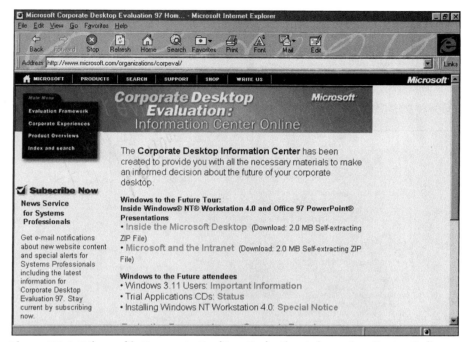

Figure 35-1: Microsoft's Corporate Desktop Evaluation Information Center Online

Update for IS professionals Web site

Another Microsoft Web site bound to interest IS pros is the Update for IS Professionals area at `http://www.microsoft.com/windows/common/aa2718.htm`, shown in Figure 35-2. At this site you can download new and updated service packs, a Windows 95 Support Assistant, Batch Setup scripts and Prompted/ Silent Updates, Windows NT ServerManagement Tools for Windows 95, Microsoft Service for Netware Directory Services, current drivers, Dial-Up Networking Scripting Tool, and much more.

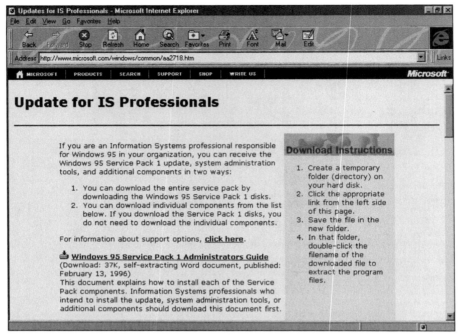

Figure 35-2: The Update for IS Professionals page — another hot spot for system pros

Summary

Large-scale upgrades from Windows 3.x to Windows 95 are bound to be time-consuming and resource-draining undertakings. To encourage such upgrades, Microsoft offers the following justifications:

✦ Support costs are reduced, because users are more independent.

✦ IS managers have more control of desktop PCs and, therefore, can minimize problems caused by inexperienced users fussing with settings.

✦ Workers are more productive, because Windows 95 is faster and offers support for preemptive multitasking.

✦ Microsoft has built-in tools for custom, hands-on, and push installations from a server.

✦ IS professionals and network administrators can find tons of information, software, and product updates at Microsoft's Windows 95 Web site: http://www.microsoft.com/windows95.

✦ Microsoft Press sells *The Windows 95 Resource Kit* to support IS professionals and is making it available as a free download on http://www.microsoft.com/windows/software/reskit.htm.

✦ ✦ ✦

Using Windows 95 on an NT LAN

In Part VIII of this book, I covered all the steps necessary to create a Windows 95 peer-to-peer LAN from scratch. As I discussed, such a LAN is generally sufficient for individuals and small businesses — particularly those who have been "getting by" without any LAN whatsoever. And Windows 95 alone is sufficient for setting up such a LAN — you don't need to purchase or install any additional software.

Larger corporations often need more robust LANs with high-powered network server hardware and tight security. Windows NT Server can take advantage of high-powered hardware and can give the network administrator more flexibility in setting up a security system.

Who This Chapter Is For

In this chapter, I talk about adding a Windows 95 client to an existing Windows NT Server-based LAN. I can't start from scratch and explain how to set up an NT LAN. That's a large topic with many complicated issues involving the selection of compatible hardware and going through an elaborate installation procedure. Whole books are written about setting up and deploying NT LANs — enough room doesn't exist in a book about Windows 95 to cover all that material. Thus, this chapter is written for Windows NT network administrators, and assumes the Windows 95 PC being added to the LAN already has a Network Interface card installed.

> **More Info** If you have access to the World Wide Web, be sure to browse to http://www.microsoft.com/ntserver for more information on using Windows 95 with an NT LAN.

If you have Internet access, and you are thinking about making the move to NT, you can get some good background information on NT Server from Microsoft's Web site. Just point your Web browser to `http://www.microsoft.com/ntserver` where you'll find a home page that looks similar to Figure 36-1. (I say similar to because, like everyone else, Microsoft changes the appearance of their Web site occasionally).

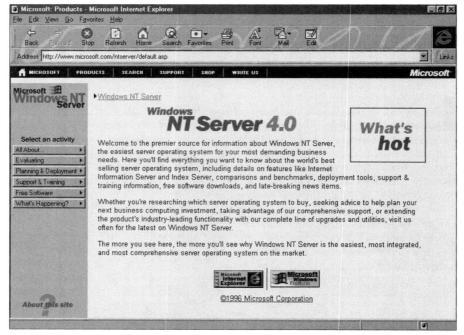

Figure 36-1: Microsoft's Windows NT 4.0 Server Web site

Before I continue, let me mention I use a pure Windows 95 LAN in my own office. So I needed an expert — someone familiar with Windows NT Server 4.0 — to write the rest of this chapter. This expert is Keith Furman of KeithNet Services (`http://www.keith.net`). Thanks, Keith!

Adding a User Account in Windows NT

As a Windows NT Server administrator, your first step in adding a Windows 95 PC to that LAN will be to set up a user account for that PC. To do so, first make sure you are logged on with an account that has administrative access. Then you can use the Administrative Wizard to add the account. You'll find this wizard in the Administrative Tools Folder (see Figure 36-2).

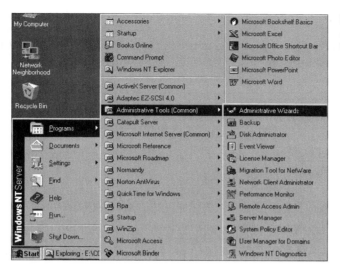

Figure 36-2: Windows NT 4.0 Server Administrative Wizards icon

The Administrative Wizards Application helps you perform various tasks. It can assist with the following administrative functions: Adding User Accounts, Group Management, Managing File and Folder Access, Adding Printers, Adding/Removing Programs, Installing New Modems, Network Client Administrator, and License Compliance. The Add User Accounts Wizard (see Figure 36-3) makes adding a user to NT easy. Here are the steps to follow:

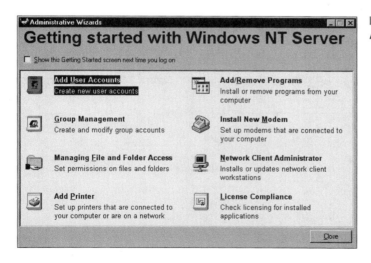

Figure 36-3: Add User Accounts icon

1. Click the Add User Accounts icon in the Administrative Wizard Application. Select the name of the domain to which you would like to add an account. For example, in Figure 36-4 the name of the domain is KEITHNT4S. Select the NT domain name to which your server and the Windows 95 system will be connected.

Figure 36-4: Domain name selected

2. Click the Next button, then add information on the user account you are creating, as shown in the example in Figure 36-5, where:

   • The user's full name is the name of the person for whom you are creating the account.

   • The unique "username" is this person's network name.

   • The optional description is any text to help you remember who this person is in the future.

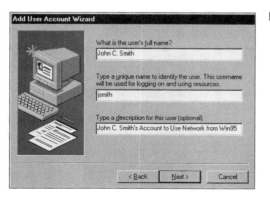

Figure 36-5: User information

3. Click the Next button and enter password information for this user, as in the example shown in Figure 36-6.

No need exists for the password to expire with a Windows 95 account. And no need exists for the user to change the password the first time he or she uses the account. Those options apply mostly for accounts used on Windows NT Server and Workstation.

Figure 36-6: Giving the Wizard password information

4. In the next wizard screen, (see Figure 36-7) you can add this user to one or more Domain Users groups. (Each Domain User group contains specific network access privileges, as defined by the network administrator.) Select which group(s) you want this account to belong to, then click the Next button.

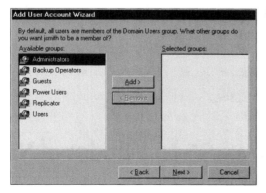

Figure 36-7: Choose Domain Users groups for this new user.

5. In the next wizard screen (see Figure 36-8), choose No Restrictions, or any combination of restrictions presented. If you need more information on restrictions, search for User Management in Windows NT Help.)

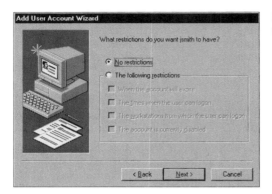

Figure 36-8: Wizard screen for defining user's restrictions

After you complete the last step and click the Next button, you're done. You will see a wizard screen informing you the user has been successfully added (see Figure 36-9). Click the Finish button. You'll be asked if you want to restart the Add User Wizard. In this situation you can choose No, and then move onto the next step of setting up the Windows 95 system to connect to the network.

Figure 36-9: User has been successfully added!

Connecting Windows 95 to Windows NT

After you define the user account in NT, the next steps take place on the Windows 95 PC. You need to know the networking protocol of your LAN, and make sure the Windows 95 PC has its own unique identity. To change the network protocol on the Windows 95 PC, follow these steps:

1. Right-click the Network Neighborhood icon on the Windows 95 desktop, and choose Properties. Or click the Start button and choose Settings ➪ Control Panel, and then double-click the Network icon.

2. Click the Configuration tab and make sure the appropriate protocol is installed. For example, in Figure 36-10, I added the NetBEUI protocol. If the protocol of your NT LAN isn't already listed, use the <u>A</u>dd button to add it now.

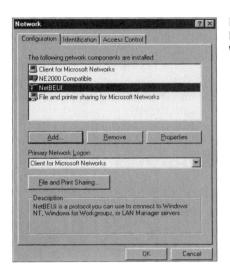

Figure 36-10: Configuration tab of the Network Neighborhood properties on a Windows 95 PC

3. Click the Identification tab and enter a unique name for the Windows 95 PC, the name of your network workgroup, and an optional computer description, as in the example shown in Figure 36-11.

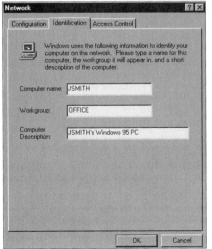

Figure 36-11: Give the Windows 95 PC a unique identity on the network.

4. Click the OK button.

You'll probably be asked to restart the computer. Go ahead and do so. If you're not asked to restart the computer, you can do so manually when you get to the Windows 95 desktop. Just click the Start button and choose Shut Down ➪ Restart the Computer? ➪ Yes. This takes a while, but when the machine finally starts, you'll be prompted for a username and password. Type in the username and password you set up on the Windows NT Server.

When you get to the Windows 95 desktop, the screen will include the Network Neighborhood icon. When you open (double-click) this icon, you'll see the NT Server listed as one of the PCs in the neighborhood.

Sharing Resources in Windows NT

Sharing resources is what networking is all about. Windows NT and Windows 95 enable you to share drives, individual directories (folders), and printers. First, let's look at the steps required to share a drive.

Sharing hard drives in Windows NT

1. To share a hard drive in Windows NT, go to Explorer (My Computer) and right-click the hard drive you want to share. Select Properties and go to the Sharing tab (see Figure 36-12).

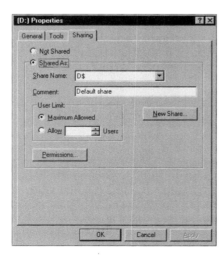

Figure 36-12: The Sharing tab

2. Click the OK button, and give the share a memorable name for future reference. For example, in Figure 36-13, we named the new share server *D*. Note, within this same dialog box, you can also limit the amount of connections for this shared device.

Figure 36-13: New Share named "serverd" defined

3. Click the Permissions button to get to the Access Through Share Permissions dialog box shown in Figure 36-14. By default, the permissions are set for Everyone (all users) to have Full Control of the device (Full Control includes: read and write access).

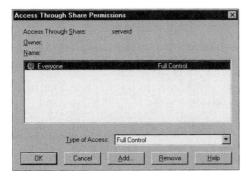

Figure 36-14: Access Through Share Permissions dialog box

4. Remove the Everyone selection — just click it and then click the Remove button.

5. Click the Add button to give the new user access to this shared drive.

6. We will now add access for our sample John Smith user. First, expand the list of Users/Groups displayed on the screen by clicking the Show Users button.

7. Click the user to whom you're assigning permissions (John Smith), then use the drop-down list box near the bottom of the dialog box (see Figure 36-15) to determine which type of access to give this user.

8. Click the OK button.

9. When the New Share dialog box reappears, click its OK button as well.

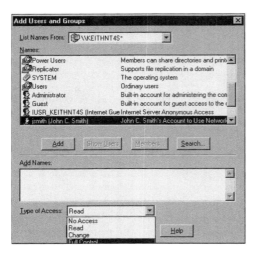

Figure 36-15: Add Users and Groups

The Windows 95 PC now has access to all the shared drive, named *serverd* in this example. Let's look at another way to share information on an NT LAN — sharing only specific directories.

Sharing directories in Windows NT

The procedure for sharing directories in Windows NT 4.0 is similar to sharing an entire hard drive. The steps are as follows:

1. Use My Computer or Windows Explorer to get to the name of the folder (directory) you want to share.

2. Right-click this folder name and choose Properties from the shortcut menu.

3. Select the Sharing tab.

Now you can use the New Share button to share the current directory. The steps from here on are similar to those previously listed under "Sharing hard drives in Windows NT," starting at Step 2.

Sharing printers in Windows NT

Sharing a printer in Windows NT is similar to sharing a drive or directory. To begin, follow these steps:

1. Open the Printers folder in Windows NT.

2. Right-click the printer you want to share, then choose the Sharing option.

3. Choose the Shared option button, and enter a unique name for the printer. For example, in Figure 36-16, I named the shared printer Color.

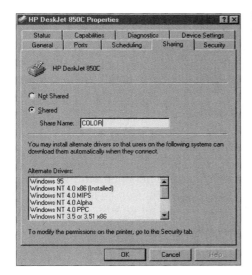

Figure 36-16: Dialog box for sharing a printer

4. To set the permissions of the shared device, click the Security tab, then click the Permissions button and set your permissions following the guidelines presented under "Sharing hard drives in Windows NT" earlier in this chapter.

5. Choose any other options from the tabs as appropriate to your printer and sharing needs, then choose OK.

Remember, the exact options presented to you in the printer Properties dialog box will depend on the make and model of the printer you're sharing. For more information on those options, please refer to the documentation that came with your printer.

Using Shared Resources in Windows 95

Once you've set up a device for sharing on the Windows 95 LAN, the user on a Windows 95 client can get to that resource using the same general techniques described in Chapter 32, "Sharing Resources on a LAN." In a nutshell:

✦ To access a shared drive or directory, double-click the Network Neighborhood icon, and then double-click the server name's icon. All the resources for that server will be listed.

✦ To map a drive letter to a shared drive or directory at this point, right-click the shared resource and select Map Network Drive. Select the drive letter you want allocated to the device.

✦ To access a shared printer, double-click the Network Neighborhood icon, and then double-click the server name's icon. Next, double-click the printer you want to access and follow the wizard to install the appropriate drivers.

Where to Go from Here

Admittedly, this has been a whirlwind tour of setting up and using a Windows 95 PC on an NT LAN. But it will get you started and keep you pointed in the right direction. Remember, the act of *sharing* a device on an NT LAN is something you do in NT. If you need more information, refer to your Windows NT documentation — *not* your Windows 95 documentation.

When a Windows 95 user wants to gain access to a shared device, the techniques described in Chapter 32 will (for the most part) do the trick. What determines whether a given Windows 95 client can get to a shared resource depends on how you, as network administrator, set up the user's account and the permissions for the shared device. So, once again, your NT Server documentation will be your best resource if you have any problems with the techniques described in this chapter.

Summary

To summarize the main steps required to use Windows 95 as a client on an NT LAN:

✦ The first step is to use the Administrative Wizards to set up the new user on the NT LAN. To get to those wizards from the Windows NT Server desktop, click the Start button and choose Administrative Tools (Common) ⇨ Administration Wizards.

✦ Next, choose the first icon — Add New Users — to set up new users coming from the Windows 95 PCs.

✦ On the Windows 95 machine, install a Network Interface card, and then set up the Network Neighborhood properties for the current PC. In particular, you must specify a network protocol on the Configuration tab, and a user name (Computer name) and workgroup name on the Identification tab.

✦ To share a device in NT, open the My Computer or Windows Explorer window, or the Printers folder, and right-click the device you want to share. From the pop-up menu that appears, choose Properties, click the Sharing tab, and click the New Share button to define options for the shared device.

✦ To gain access to a shared drive or directory from a Windows 95 client, double-click the Network Neighborhood icon, then double-click the name of the NT Server machine.

✦ To gain access to a shared printer from a Windows 95 client, double-click the My Computer icon, then double-click the Printers folder.

✦   ✦   ✦

Using Windows 95 on a NetWare LAN

In Part VIII of this book, I showed you how to set up a Windows 95 LAN completely from scratch. I'm well aware, though, that many people, especially those in the corporate environment, already have a Novell NetWare LAN set up; those people need to add Windows 95 PCs as clients to that existing LAN. This is what Chapter 37 is about.

I hired a Novell expert to write this chapter — because I now use a Windows 95 peer-to-peer network in my own office. The expert I hired is Matthew Ronn, of Matthew of MediQual Systems, Inc. (mronn@mediqual.com) and I'd like to thank Matthew now for his contribution. Matthew's contribution here is substantial — he authored nearly 95 percent of this chapter!

Windows 95 and Novell NetWare

As I discussed in Part VIII of this book, you can set up a peer-to-peer LAN using *just* Windows 95 and some LAN hardware — a Network Interface card, cables, and an Ethernet hub. You don't need to purchase any additional software. If you already have a Novell LAN installed from earlier DOS/Windows 3.x days, though, you'll probably want to hold onto all the time and money you've invested in setting up that LAN, and perhaps its security system as well. I wouldn't blame you for wanting to keep that LAN intact!

In this chapter, I assume 1) You are already using a Novell LAN, and 2) You are the network administrator for that LAN. A book on Windows 95 is not the place to discuss the many issues involved in installing, setting up, deploying, maintaining, and so forth, a NetWare LAN. For those of you who are administrators and who have already been through this and are now trying to "stick on" some Windows 95 clients, however, I can offer the following steps and pointers to help you get things moving quickly and smoothly.

More Info Microsoft Press's *Windows 95 Resource Kit,* mentioned in Chapter 35, is one of the most complete resources available for using Windows 95 on a Novell LAN. If you have Internet access, look at `http://www.microsoft.com/windows/common/aa2693.htm` for more information about NetWare and Windows 95.

To connect your Windows 95 PC to a NetWare LAN, your three software options for configuring your PC to communicate on a Novell NetWare network are as follows:

✦ The 32-bit client software that comes with Windows 95, called the Microsoft NetWare client.

✦ The 32-bit client software that comes from Novell is free. On the Web, see `http://support.novell.com/home/client/c3295` for more information.

✦ The old 16-bit NETX or VLM client software that has been used by DOS and Windows 3.1x PCs.

Each approach is reviewed in the following sections. Remember, all I can do is provide a general overview of the techniques in a book geared toward Windows 95. For more complete documentation, refer to your Novell NetWare manuals.

Using the Microsoft NetWare Client

Windows 95 comes with many built-in features and drivers that make it possible to set up your PC with little help from any other source. One of those built-in features is software that allows your PC to connect to a Novell NetWare LAN. Using this approach is convenient because nothing is more frustrating than installing hardware or software on your PC, and then having the system tell you to insert a floppy disk or CD-ROM you don't have available.

The software that comes with Windows 95, which enables you to connect to a NetWare LAN, is called the Microsoft Client for NetWare Networks. All the files you need are right on your Windows 95 installation floppy disks or CD-ROM.

Why would you want to use this client software? This client software works well with Windows 95, NetWare networks, and, in most cases, has worked even better than the client software that comes from Novell. The Microsoft NetWare client enables you to connect to your NetWare LAN by taking advantage of your new 32-bit operating system. It works well with other Microsoft client software that may be installed on your PC. The Microsoft NetWare client also has a nifty feature, which allows your Windows 95 PC to share its files and printers across your NetWare network. That's right! Your PC can look like a NetWare server to other Windows 95 PCs, if you choose.

Let's assume you have successfully installed Windows 95 on your PC; it is up and running and you are ready to connect your PC to your NetWare network. Before you begin, you need to know a few things.

You must know the make and model of your NIC, and whether its settings are hardware or software configurable. Specific NIC settings you need to know are the IRQ, direct memory access (DMA) channel, and memory address. This information can be obtained from the hardware documentation that either came with your NIC card or on a small label affixed to the card itself. If the card is already installed in the Windows 95 PC, you can get the current settings from the device list. Open Control Panel, open the System icon, click the Device Manager tab, click Network Adapters, then click the Properties button.

Logging into a Novell NetWare network requires you to know your Login Name and Password for your NetWare account, as well as the name of the NetWare server or tree you will be logging in to. If you are not the network administrator, you must obtain this information from the administrator.

Installation of the Microsoft Client for NetWare Networks

Now you're ready to install the Microsoft Client for NetWare Networks. You will need to install three network software components: a client, an adapter, and a protocol. Each is an independent component that works with the others to provide your connection to your LAN.

Installing the Microsoft NetWare client

The client component is the software that allows your PC to connect to the appropriate server and LAN resources. It provides an interface to the user for logging in to the network and using its resources, such as disk volumes and printers. Different networks require different client software. Novell NetWare is just one type of network. Follow these steps to install the client software:

Instead of performing the following Steps 1-3, you can right-click the Network Neighborhood icon and choose Properties from the shortcut menu.

1. Click the Start button on the taskbar.

2. Choose Settings ➪ Control Panel.

3. Double-click the Network icon. The Network dialog box appears with the list box labeled The following network components are installed:. This box may either be empty or have other client software installed, depending on your networking needs.

4. Click the Add button. The Select Network Component Type dialog box appears.

5. Select Client from the list of network components and click the Add button. The Select Network Client dialog box appears.

6. Under Manufacturers: select Microsoft.

Puzzled? This may not seem the obvious choice. When you look at the Manufacturers: list box, you may be tempted to select Novell because you want to connect to a Novell network. In this example, however, your choice will be Microsoft, because this is the name of the manufacturer that made the NetWare client software you want to install.

7. Under Network Clients select Client for NetWare Networks (see Figure 37-1).

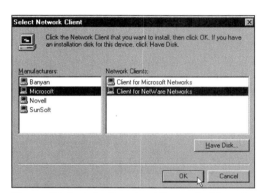

Figure 37-1: Selecting the Microsoft Client for NetWare Networks

8. Click the OK button. This brings you to the next step of installing an adapter.

Installing an adapter for the Microsoft NetWare client

For your PC to communicate with the resources on your network, a software driver must be installed, so your client software knows how to package its information and send it to the NIC. Because you have selected a client in the previous steps, the Select Network Adapters dialog box appears; you can't have a client without an adapter. You have a choice to make here. You can either use drivers for your NIC, which are supplied by Microsoft, or you can use the NIC drivers supplied by the NIC manufacturer. If you're not sure which to use, you may want to check the file dates on the drivers and use whichever one has the most current date.

To find the latest drivers for your NIC or to replace a lost driver disk, you might look for the drivers at the manufacturer's Web site on the Internet or a bulletin board service (BBS) if provided by the manufacturer. If you cannot find adapter drivers from the manufacturer, use the ones listed from Microsoft. Follow these steps to install the adapter software:

1. In the Select Network Adapters dialog box, click the Have Disk button. The Install From Disk dialog box appears and asks for the location of your driver files.

2. Insert the floppy disk containing the drivers for your network adapter card, or click the Browse button and locate the necessary files on your hard disk or CD.

3. Click the OK button.

4. Select your network adapter card from the list that appears.

5. Click the OK button.

This returns you to the Network dialog box.

Installing a protocol for Microsoft NetWare client

The next step is to choose network protocols. Today's networks often use multiple protocols. For instance, a network with NetWare servers and clients may be configured to use the TCP/IP (Transmission Control Protocol/Internet Protocol) protocol as well as the IPX/SPX (Internetwork Packet eXchange/Sequenced Packet eXchange) protocol. IPX/SPX was introduced by Novell, and NetWare networks usually use the IPX/SPX protocol as their primary protocol, although this may change as TCP/IP becomes more popular on NetWare networks.

In the Network dialog box check to see that the IPX/SPX-compatible Protocol appears in the list box labeled The following <u>n</u>etwork components are installed:. If it doesn't, follow these steps to select it:

1. In the Network dialog box, click the <u>A</u>dd button. The dialog box Select Network Component Type appears.

2. Select Protocol from the list of network components. Click the <u>A</u>dd button. The Select Network Protocol dialog box appears.

3. Under <u>M</u>anufacturers: select Microsoft.

4. Under Network Protocols select IPX/SPX-compatible Protocol, as shown in Figure 37-2.

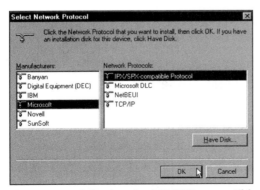

Figure 37-2: Selecting the IPX/SPX-compatible Protocol

Regardless of which protocol you need, you should also add TCP/IP, because this protocol is widely used for both Internet access and on intranets.

5. Click the OK button.

This returns you to the Network dialog box. Don't close this dialog box yet or you'll be prompted to reboot! We're not quite finished here.

Microsoft NetWare client properties

In the Network dialog box, you should now have the three necessary components listed in the list box labeled The following network components are installed: — Client for NetWare Networks, a description of your network adapter card, and the IPX/SPX-compatible Protocol, as shown in Figure 37-3.

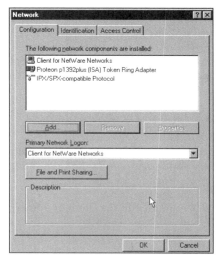

Figure 37-3: Basic Microsoft network components

Configuring Microsoft NetWare client properties

Now it's time to configure the client properties for your Novell client. In the Network dialog box, select Client for NetWare Networks from the list box labeled The following network components are installed:, and click the Properties button. The Client for NetWare Networks Properties dialog box appears. Follow these steps:

1. Click the General tab at the top of the box. In the list box labeled Preferred Server type the name of the Novell NetWare server into which you will log.

2. In the list box labeled First network drive select the letter of your first network drive. The default is the F: drive.

3. There is a check box labeled Enable login script processing. Be sure this box is checked if you want to run your NetWare log in scripts. This check box is checked by default.

4. Click the OK button to return to the Network dialog box.

Configuring Microsoft NetWare adapter properties

Unfortunately, the properties for your adapter are unique to the make and model of your NIC and cannot be specifically described here. You can follow these steps, though, to check for and, if necessary, choose the following settings:

1. In the Network dialog box, select the adapter description in the list box labeled The following network components are installed: and click the Properties button. The dialog box for your adapter's properties appears.

2. Click the Driver Type tab at the top of the dialog box.

3. The radio button labeled Enhanced mode (32-bit and 16-bit) NDIS driver should be selected. This informs you that are using a 32-bit driver—just what you want to speed things along in your 32-bit operating system.

4. Click the Bindings tab at the top of the dialog box.

   Your adapter should be "bound" to the IPX/SPX-compatible Protocol. That is, your adapter card must be told to use the IPX/SPX-compatible Protocol when it communicates over your NetWare LAN. Be sure a check mark appears in the check box. (Your adapter card may be bound to other protocols as well.)

6. Click the Resources tab at the top of the dialog box. These settings are dependent upon the make and model of your NIC. If your NIC needs to be configured by jumpers or switches on the card itself, make certain the settings in these list boxes match those you have set on the card. Note: An asterisk next to a value indicates a conflict with other resources. If you know the resource settings of all the hardware in your PC, this will help you.

If you have any problems with the installed network card, the Windows 95 Device Manager can be a big help in pinpointing conflicts and resource allocations. To get to the Device Manager, open Control Panel, double-click the System icon, and then click the Device Manager tab.

7. Click the Close button. This returns you to the Network dialog box.

Configuring Microsoft NetWare protocol properties

Next, follow these steps to check your protocol properties:

1. In the Network dialog box, select the IPX/SPX-compatible Protocol in the list box labeled The following network components are installed: and click the Properties button. The IPX/SPX Compatible Protocol Properties dialog box appears.

2. Click the Bindings tab at the top of the IPX/SPX-compatible Protocol Properties dialog box. The check box labeled Client for NetWare Networks must be checked. This tells the Microsoft Client for NetWare Networks to use this protocol for its network communication. Click the OK button. This returns you to the Network dialog box.

Completing the Microsoft NetWare client installation

Just a few more things to complete before you're finished:

1. In the Network dialog box, select Client for NetWare Networks in the list box labeled Primary Network Logon:.

2. Click the Identification tab at the top of the Network dialog box to enter information on naming your PC. Enter a name in the list box labeled Computer name:. This must be a unique name on your network, up to 15 characters with no blank spaces.

3. Enter a workgroup name (up to 15 characters, no spaces) in the list box labeled Workgroup:. If you haven't defined workgroups in the past, the simple thing to do is make up a workgroup name, and make certain all the PCs that must share resources have the same workgroup name.

4. You may enter an optional description for this PC in the list box labeled Computer Description. (Do not use any commas in the description!)

5. Click the OK button in the Network dialog box. You may be required to provide Windows 95 system disks.

6. A dialog box labeled System Settings Change appears. Click the Yes button to restart your system. (If you have a floppy in drive A:, remember to remove it before rebooting!)

Installing the service for NDS

If you have a NetWare 4 LAN and you are using Novell Directory Services (NDS), you must add the ability to log in to a directory tree using the Microsoft Client for NetWare Networks. Unfortunately, this service does not come built in with the present version of Windows 95 and must be added as an upgrade or an add-on service.

For more information on the Web see http://www.microsoft.com/windows/common/aa2718.htm. You can also download the necessary file from Microsoft's FTP site by logging in anonymously to ftp.microsoft.com/softlib/mslfiles and downloading the file MSNDS.EXE.

Put this file in its own directory on your PC and execute MSNDS.EXE to extract the files from the archive. Now take the following steps to install the NDS feature:

1. Click the Start button and select Settings ➪ Control Panel and double-click the Network icon. The Network dialog box appears.

2. Click the Add button. The Select Network Component Type dialog box appears.

3. Click Service and click the <u>A</u>dd button. The Select Network Service dialog box appears (see Figure 37-4).

4. Click the <u>H</u>ave Disk button. When the Install From Disk dialog box appears, enter the path for the msnds archive and click the OK button. Click the next OK button and Service for NetWare Directory Services appears in the list box labeled Models:. Click this OK button and the NDS service is installed.

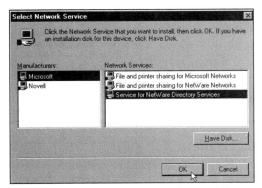

Figure 37-4: Installing support for Novell Directory Services

5. Select Service for NetWare Directory Services from the list box labeled The following <u>n</u>etwork components are installed: and click the <u>P</u>roperties button. Here you may enter the Preferred tree to log in to and the <u>W</u>orkstation default context. Click the OK button to exit.

You will be prompted for Windows 95 disks and then prompted to reboot your PC. Follow the instructions that appear on the screen until you get to the log in window.

Logging in

Once your system has restarted, you see the familiar Windows 95 logo on your monitor. While the logo is displayed, you may press the Esc key; you will see a black DOS screen. Here you can see system messages that tell you what the system is doing while you wait.

Once Windows 95 begins, a dialog box labeled Enter Network Password appears. Enter your NetWare log in name in the field labeled <u>U</u>ser name: and your NetWare password in the field labeled <u>P</u>assword:. Make certain the server you are logging in to is listed correctly in the list box labeled Login <u>s</u>erver:.

More Info   Microsoft uses the term "log on"; Novell uses the term "log in." Both refer to the same action of logging on to a server.

If this is the first time you have used this PC and this log in name to log in to a network, a dialog box labeled Set Windows Password appears. Enter the same password you used when logging into the NetWare network in the list boxes labeled New password and Confirm new password. Click the OK button. Even though you may not be running a Windows 95 network, as far as your PC is concerned, you have a network of one PC and you must log in. Both your system and personal log in scripts will be processed from NetWare. You are now logged in to your NetWare network.

Logging out

You can log out of a server several different ways. Perhaps the most consistent method is to click the Start button and select the Shut Down option. Because you have networking functionality installed on your PC, a choice labeled Close all programs and log on as a different user is available to you. Selecting this simply closes your applications and initiates a new log in session.

You can also right-click any server displayed in Network Neighborhood or Explorer and select Logout from the shortcut menu to log out from that server. Opening a DOS window and typing the command **LOGOUT** will also work.

Providing network resources

With Windows 95's peer-to-peer capability, which works in tandem with the NetWare network, you can share files and attached printers on an individual PC with the rest of the NetWare network. This is a simple way to add a printer to your network. Of course, the catch is your PC must remain on for as long as you want to share your files and/or printer. Also, only other Windows 95 PCs can take advantage of your shared resources.

 Sharing your resources with the network can only be done using Microsoft's Client for NetWare Networks.

Installing the file and printer sharing service

To share a drive or printer on your PC, you must first install the service for sharing printers and files on NetWare networks, so others can access what you are sharing. In Windows 95, a service is a software module that gives the PC the ability to share resources with a network. To install the sharing service for NetWare networks follow these steps:

1. Click the Start button on the taskbar. Select Setttings ⇨ Control Panel.

2. Double-click the Network icon. The Network dialog box appears.

3. Click the Add button. The dialog box Select Network Component Type appears.

4. Select Service from the list of network components and click the Add button. The Select Network Service dialog box appears.

5. Under Manufacturers: select Microsoft. Under Network Services: select File and printer sharing for NetWare networks. Click the OK button.

6. Select File and printer sharing for NetWare networks from the list box labeled The following network components are installed: and click the Properties button. You're taken to the dialog box shown in Figure 37-5, where you must enable Service Advertising Protocol (SAP) if you want users of Novell's NETX and VLM clients to access the shared printer. Note, enabling SAP may put unwanted network traffic on your LAN. Click the OK button.

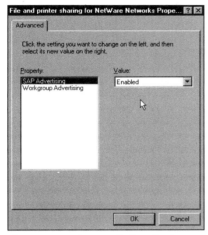

Figure 37-5: Protocols for sharing resources

7. In the Network dialog box, click the File and Print Sharing button. In the File and Print Sharing dialog box, check the box labeled I want to be able to allow others to print to my printer(s). (While you're there, check the box for file sharing if you want to share your files with others.) Click the OK button.

8. In the Network dialog box, click the Access Control tab to allow others to use the files and printers on your PC. User-level access control must be selected and the name of a server must be entered in the list box. Click the OK button here; then click the OK button in the Network dialog box to restart your PC and enable these services.

Next, we'll look at the steps you must follow to share a printer on this LAN.

Sharing a printer

Before you can share your printer with the NetWare network, you must install the file and printer-sharing service on your PC as described in the preceding section. Once your PC has restarted and the file and print-sharing service has been started, you can share a printer attached to your PC. To begin, follow these steps:

1. Click the Start button and select Settings ➪ Printers. The Printers folder appears.

2. Right-click the icon for the printer attached to your PC and select the Sharing option from the shortcut menu. The Printer Properties dialog box appears.

3. Click the Shared As: option and give your local printer a name and a comment, if you wish.

4. Click the Add button to allow users to use your printer. The Add Users dialog box appears (see Figure 37-6). Here you can select users of your NetWare server to allow them to use your printer.

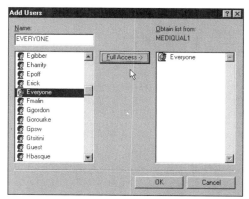

Figure 37-6: Grant printer access to NetWare users

5. When you're satisfied, click the OK button in this dialog box, then click the OK button in the Printer Properties dialog box.

Your printer is now shared. You may repeat the procedure to share any other printer attached to your PC.

Sharing files

If you want to allow file sharing on the NetWare network, you must install the file and printer-sharing service on the PC, as described earlier in this chapter. Once this is done, sharing files on your PC with the NetWare network is similar to sharing printers. When sharing your files, your PC will look like a NetWare server to other Windows 95 clients. To allow NetWare users to access your files, follow these steps:

1. Open Explorer on your PC and right-click a directory you wish to share. This can be the root of your hard drive or a subdirectory.

2. Select the Sharing option from the shortcut menu. The Directory Properties dialog box appears.

3. Click the Shared As: option and give the directory a name and a comment, if you wish.

4. Click the Add button to allow NetWare users to access your directory. The Add Users dialog box appears (see Figure 37-7). Here you can select users of your NetWare server to be allowed full access or read-only access to your directory.

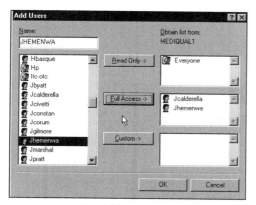

Figure 37-7: Grant file access to NetWare users

5. When you're satisfied, click the OK button in this dialog box, then click the OK button in the Directory Properties dialog box.

Your directory is now shared. You may repeat the procedure to share other directories.

Using the Novell Netware Client 32

Novell provides software for connecting different types of clients to NetWare servers. For example, client PCs may be running DOS, OS/2 or Windows 95, and Novell has developed software that allows each of these to connect to NetWare servers.

To take advantage of the Windows 95 32-bit operating system, Novell provides the NetWare Client 32 client software. This software comes with current available versions of the NetWare NOS, but is also available from Novell if you have older NetWare installations. You can get the NetWare Client 32 software, along with any updates and improvements, free from Novell's Web site at http://www.netware.com, and ftp site at ftp.novell.com.

If you're getting into an intranet, check out `http://www.novell.com/ intranetware/clientwin95.html`.

Why would you want to use this client software? This client software works well with Windows 95 and NetWare networks, and provides a few more NetWare options than the client software from Microsoft. The NetWare Client 32 enables you to connect to your NetWare LAN by taking advantage of your new 32-bit operating system and works well with other installed Microsoft client software on your PC. It also enables you to log in to a NetWare 4.x NDS (Novell Directory Services) tree without having to get add-on products or updates. The NetWare Client 32, however, doesn't support Windows 95 file and print sharing.

Installation of the Novell NetWare Client 32

Once you have your NetWare Client 32 installation disks, you're ready to install the NetWare Client 32 software. You will need to install three network components: Client, Adapter, and Protocol. Each is an independent component that works with the others to provide your connection to your LAN.

Installing the NetWare Client 32

The client component is the software that allows your PC to connect to the appropriate server and LAN resources. It provides an interface to the user for logging in to the network and using its resources such as disk volumes and printers. Different networks require different client software. Follow these steps to install the NetWare Client 32 client software:

1. Click the Start button on the taskbar. Select Setttings ⇨ Control Panel.

2. Double-click the Network icon. The Network dialog box appears with the list box labeled The following network components are installed:. This box may be empty or it may have other client software installed, depending on your networking needs.

3. Click the Add button. The dialog box Select Network Component Type appears.

4. Select Client from the list of network components and click the Add button. The Select Network Client dialog box appears.

5. Click the Have Disk button. The Install From Disk dialog box appears.

6. Insert your floppy disk containing the NetWare Client 32 software or enter the appropriate path name if you have copied these files to your hard drive, and click the OK button. The Select Network Client dialog box appears.

7. Select Novell NetWare Client 32 in the Models: list box and click the OK button.

The client software will be ready after supplying the requested disks.

Installing a NetWare Client 32 adapter

At this point, the Select Network Adapters dialog box is on your screen. Here, you have to choose from among three potential candidates: the drivers supplied by Novell, the ones supplied by Microsoft, or those supplied by the NIC manufacturer. If you have drivers supplied by the adapter manufacturer, we suggest you choose those. Follow these steps to install the adapter software:

1. Click the Have Disk button in the Select Network Adapters dialog box. The Install From Disk dialog box appears asking for the location of your driver files.

2. Insert the floppy disk containing the drivers for your network adapter card, or click the Browse button and locate the necessary files.

3. Click the OK button.

4. Select your network adapter card from the list that appears.

5. Click the OK button.

You'll be returned to the Network dialog box.

Installing a NetWare Client 32 protocol

Because you have selected the Novell NetWare Client 32 software, two default protocols have been selected for you. The IPX/SPX 32-bit Protocol for Novell NetWare Client 32 and the IPX/SPX-compatible Protocol appear in the list box labeled The following network components are installed:.

Novell NetWare Client 32 properties

In the Network dialog box (see Figure 37-8) you should now have the four necessary components listed in the list box labeled The following network components are installed: Novell NetWare Client 32, a description of your network adapter card, the IPX/SPX 32-bit Protocol for Novell NetWare Client 32, and the IPX/SPX-compatible Protocol. Each of these components has its own properties. Many properties can remain at their default values, but a few must be checked and some user input may be required.

Configuring NetWare Client 32 properties

Make certain you are still looking at the Configuration tab in the Network dialog box and follow these steps to insure your client software has the proper settings:

1. In the Network dialog box, select the Novell NetWare Client 32 in the list box labeled The following network components are installed: and click the Properties button. The Novell NetWare Client 32 Properties dialog box appears.

2. Click the Client 32 tab at the top of the box. In the list box labeled Preferred Server type the name of the Novell NetWare server you will be logging in to or type the name of the directory tree and context in the list boxes labeled Preferred tree and Name context, respectively. The Preferred Server option is

used for logging in to a bindery based server; the Preferred tree and Name context options are used for logging in to a NetWare 4.x NDS tree.

3. In the list box labeled First network drive select the letter you want to use for your first network drive. The default is the F: drive.

4. Click the Login tab at the top of the dialog box. Here you may select options regarding how the log in process occurs. Put a check in the box labeled Display script page and check the box marked Run scripts if you want to run your NetWare log in scripts. Choose OK when you're finished to return to the Network dialog box.

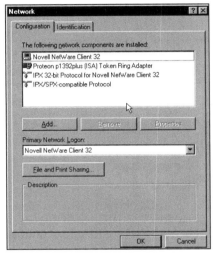

Figure 37-8: Basic Novell network components

Configuring NetWare Client 32 adapter properties

Unfortunately, the properties for your adapter are unique to the make and model of your NIC and cannot be specifically described. A few things can be checked for any adapter, however, as are discussed here.

In the Network dialog box, select the adapter description in the list box labeled The following network components are installed:, and click the Properties button. The dialog box for your adapter's properties appears. Click the Driver Type tab at the top of the dialog box. The radio button labeled Enhanced mode (32-bit and 16-bit) NDIS driver should be selected. This lets you know you are using a 32-bit driver, which is what you want to speed along your 32-bit operating system.

Click the Bindings tab at the top of the dialog box. Your adapter should be "bound" to both the IPX/SPX-compatible Protocol and the IPX/SPX 32-bit Protocol for Novell NetWare Client 32. That is, your adapter card must be told to use both the IPX/SPX-compatible Protocol and IPX/SPX 32-bit Protocol for Novell NetWare Client 32 when it communicates over your NetWare LAN. Be sure a check mark appears in both boxes. (Your adapter card may be bound to other protocols as well.)

Click the Resources tab at the top of the dialog box. Again, these settings are dependent upon the make and model of your NIC. If your NIC must be configured by jumpers or switches on the card itself, make sure the settings in these list boxes match those you have set on the card. Note: An asterisk next to a value indicates a conflict with other hardware.

When you finish checking these various settings, click the Close button to return to the Network dialog box.

Configuring NetWare Client 32 protocol properties

You will want to double-check a few protocol properties before you finish this portion of the setup. First, in the Network dialog box, select the IPX/SPX 32-bit Protocol for Novell NetWare Client 32 in the list box labeled The following network components are installed: and click the Properties button. The IPX/SPX 32-bit Protocol for Novell NetWare Client 32 dialog box appears.

Click the Bindings tab at the top of the dialog box. Be sure the box for Novell NetWare Client 32 is checked. This tells the Novell NetWare Client 32 to use this protocol for its network communication.

Select the IPX/SPX-compatible Protocol in the list box labeled The following network components are installed:, and click the Properties button. The IPX/SPX-compatible Protocol Properties dialog box appears. The settings here may be changed; however, this protocol is for compatibility with Microsoft networking and NetBIOS applications and has no effect on Novell NetWare networking.

When you finish, click the OK button to return to the Network dialog box.

Completing the NetWare Client 32 installation

To complete the installation, stay on the Network dialog box and follow these steps:

1. In the Network dialog box, select Novell NetWare Client 32 in the list box labeled Primary Network Logon:.

2. Click the Identification tab at the top of the Network dialog box to enter information on naming your PC. Enter a name in the list box labeled Computer name:. A unique name must be on your network; this name is limited to 15 characters with no spaces.

3. Enter a workgroup name in the list box labeled Workgroup:, again up to 15 characters in length, with no spaces.

4. You may enter an optional description for this PC in the list box labeled Computer Description:.

5. Click the OK button in the Network dialog box. You may be required to provide Windows 95 system disks.

6. A dialog box labeled System Settings Change appears. Click the Yes button to restart your system.

   Follow the instructions on your screen to reboot your PC until you get to the Windows log on screen. Then move on to the next section.

Logging in — NetWare Client 32

Once your system restarts, you will see the familiar Windows 95 logo on your monitor. Press the Esc key and you will see a black DOS screen. System messages will tell you what the system is doing while you wait.

Once Windows 95 has started on your PC, a list box labeled Novell NetWare Login appears (see Figure 37-9.) Enter your NetWare log in name in the list box labeled Name: and your NetWare password in the field labeled Password:. Be sure the server you are logging in to is listed correctly above your log in name.

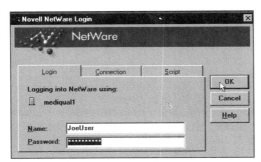

Figure 37-9: Logging into the NetWare network

Click the tab labeled Connection. You have the choice of logging in to a server or an NDS tree. You can select the name of the appropriate resource; if you are logging in as a bindery connection, check the box labeled Bindery connection.

If you checked the box marked Run scripts under the client properties setup, a third tab labeled Script is available. You can choose a specific script to run and to close your script results automatically.

Novell NetWare Client 32 features

With the Novell NetWare Client 32 software installed on your PC, a few more features are available to you. For one, a new program group called Novell has been added to your Programs start menu. Included in this group is the NetWare Login utility, which can be used any time to log in as a new user.

Right-click the Network Neighborhood icon on your desktop. Investigate these utilities. Select Ne<u>t</u>Ware Connections from the shortcut menu and see the available information in the Current NetWare Resources dialog box, including servers, users, connection numbers, connection types, and NDS trees. Note, you can detach from a server from this utility.

Now open Network Neighborhood and double-click the Entire Network icon. Notice two headings now appear — NetWare Directory Services and NetWare Servers. Now you can view each type of NetWare resource according to its type.

Using the Novell Client for NetWare

Another method to connect your Windows 95 PC to a NetWare LAN is to use the real-mode client software provided by Novell, located on the Windows 95 installation disks. Novell provides two client options, called Novell NetWare (Workstation Shell 3.X [NETX]) and Novell NetWare (Workstation Shell 4.0 and above [VLM]). Both are fairly old products; this approach is not recommended. We'll discuss them, though, because some of you may have an old 16-bit application that requires one of these clients. Also, either choice requires only the Windows 95 installation disks and the 16-bit NetWare client disks used for setting up DOS workstations.

The NETX choice applies to Workstation Shell 3.11 and below. It can be used for versions 3.12 and 4.0 if the server is configured to use the 802.3 protocol. Using a real-mode client requires the use of conventional memory and may require the use of memory management such as EMM386.EXE. You cannot use long filenames on NetWare servers using any real-mode client and this client is slower than a protected-mode client.

The VLM choice applies to Workstation Shell 4.0 or greater of NETX.VLM. One attribute of this real-mode client is its ability to run NetWare NDS utilities, such as NWADMIN, NETADMIN, and CX, and to log in to an NDS tree. You still cannot use long filenames on NetWare servers and this client is slower than a protected-mode client.

If you upgraded your DOS PC to Windows 95 and you previously used a NETX client or a VLM client with a bindery-based log in, then the installation program automatically upgrades your software to Microsoft's Client for NetWare Networks. To switch to a real-mode client, you must delete the protected-mode client and do some reinstalling.

Manual installation of the NETX client

If you have upgraded your DOS workstation with a working NetWare Shell 3.X client, then your files are still on your hard drive and can be used to install the Novell NetWare (Workstation Shell 3.X [NETX]) client software manually.

Installing the NETX client

To install the Novell NetWare (Workstation Shell 3.X [NETX]) client software, you must first remove any protected-mode client software that may have been installed by your Windows 95 upgrade procedure.

1. Click the Start button on the taskbar. Select Setttings ➪ Control Panel

2. Double-click the Network icon. The Network dialog box appears. The list box labeled The following network components are installed: should include the Client for NetWare Networks.

3. Select the Client for NetWare Networks and click the Remove button. The Client for NetWare Networks disappears.

4. Click the Add button. The dialog box Select Network Component Type appears.

5. Select Client from the list of network components and click the Add button. The Select Network Client dialog box appears.

6. Under *Manufacturers*: select Novell. Under *Network Clients* select Novell NetWare (Workstation Shell 3.X [NETX]). Click the OK button.

You will be prompted to restart your system. Do so, following the instructions that appear on the screen.

Manual installation of the VLM client

If you have upgraded your DOS workstation with a working NetWare shell 4.0 (or greater) client and you have been logging into a bindery-based network, then Windows 95 will have upgraded your system to use Microsoft's Client for NetWare Networks. You will need your VLM installation disks for DOS-based workstations to install manually the real-mode Novell NetWare (Workstation Shell 4.0 and above [VLM]) client software.

Installing the VLM client

To install Novell NetWare (Workstation Shell 4.0 and above [VLM]) client software, you must first remove any protected-mode client software previously installed by your Windows 95 upgrade procedure.

1. Click the Start button on the Taskbar. Select Setttings ➪ Control Panel.

2. Double-click the Network icon. The Network dialog box appears. See the list box labeled *The following network components are installed:*. This box should have the Client for NetWare Networks listed.

3. Select each network component and click the Remove button. Each component disappears. Click the OK button.

4. When you are asked if you want to restart the computer, click the No button and close Control Panel.

5. Click the Start button on the taskbar. Select Sh<u>u</u>t Down The Shut Down Windows dialog box appears.

6. Select Restart the computer in <u>M</u>S-DOS mode? and click the <u>Y</u>es button.

When the computer restarts in DOS mode, run your VLM workstation installation utility as you would for any DOS PC. During the DOS VLM installation, select support for Windows and answer yes when you are asked whether to replace the NETWARE.DRV file.

Hot Stuff
While you're here, edit your AUTOEXEC.BAT file and add the LOGIN command after your network driver's load. This will prompt you to log in and run your NetWare log in scripts before Windows 95 starts.

When prompted, restart the PC. When you return to the Windows 95 desktop, double-click the Network icon in Control Panel. The Network dialog box appears. Check to see if Windows 95 has automatically detected your Novell NetWare (Workstation Shell 4.0 and above [VLM]) by seeing if it is listed in the list box labeled The following <u>n</u>etwork components are installed:. If Windows 95 has not installed the VLM client, then you must add it manually. Follow these steps:

1. In the Network dialog box click the <u>A</u>dd button. The Select Network Component Type dialog box appears.

2. Select Client from the list of network components and click the <u>A</u>dd button. The Select Network Client dialog box appears.

3. Under <u>M</u>anufacturers: select Novell. Under Network Clients select Novell NetWare (Workstation Shell 4.0 and above [VLM]). Click the OK button. You will be prompted to restart your system.

Installing a NETX adapter
Windows 95 will add an adapter called Existing ODI Driver. This means Windows 95 is using the 16-bit ODI driver, which was loaded in your AUTOEXEC.BAT file. No further configuration is necessary.

Installing a NETX protocol
Windows 95 will add a protocol called Novell IPX ODI Protocol. This means Windows 95 knows to use the IPX/SPX protocol to communicate with NetWare servers. No further configuration is necessary.

Configuring NETX properties
Now you should have the three necessary components listed in the list box labeled The following <u>n</u>etwork components are installed: — Novell NetWare (Workstation Shell 4.0 and above [VLM]), a network adapter card labeled Existing ODI Driver, and the Novell IPX ODI Protocol. The client software does not have properties configurable in Windows 95 because you are using a real-mode client, which is configurable in DOS using DOS commands and the NET.CFG file. The other two

components have their own properties but, because the real-mode client is being used, not too many properties can be changed in Windows 95.

Configuring adapter properties

Select the Existing ODI Driver adapter in the Network dialog box. The Existing ODI Driver Properties dialog box will appear. Click the Driver Type tab. Note, only the real-mode (16-bit) ODI driver option is available. Click the Bindings tab and notice Novell IPX ODI Protocol is currently the only protocol available and must be checked.

Configuring protocol properties

Select the Novell IPX ODI Protocol in the Network dialog box. The Novell IPX ODI Protocol Properties dialog box will appear. By default, the only binding available is to the Novell NetWare (Workstation Shell 4.0 and above [VLM]) and must be checked.

16-bit client features and issues

If you do not run the LOGIN.EXE command from your AUTOEXEC.BAT file and you log in in DOS before Windows 95 starts, no NetWare log in scripts will run. Regardless, you will be prompted by Windows 95 when it starts to log in to a NetWare server, so Windows 95 can reestablish any NetWare settings you have made from Windows 95.

Mapping drives can be done the same way as with other NetWare clients. You can map drives in Network Neighborhood, Explorer, My Computer, or a DOS window. When Windows 95 starts, you are prompted again to log in to your NetWare server. This is done so Windows 95 can take care of mapping drives, and so forth, which you have set up in Windows 95, rather than in DOS.

No shut down option is labeled Close all programs and log on as a different user when using the Start button and Shut Down feature. You may open a DOS window, however, and log in as a new user. Certain log in script commands will function, but drive mappings may not execute correctly when executed from a log in script. The safest way to log in as another NetWare user and execute proper drive mappings is to restart the PC and log in as another user.

The utility NetWare User Tools will function with this configuration. You can attach to servers, map drives, and attach to print queues as you did in Windows 3.1x configurations.

Using Network Resources

The main purpose behind logging in to a network is to use the shared resources available to you on that network. Users primarily need to access network drives and network printers. With Windows 95, both these tasks are completed with greater ease and flexibility than in the past. The following procedures are similar for all the client software previously described.

Mapping network drives

Mapping a network drive means to assign a letter of the alphabet to a shared directory on a network server. This assignment may be made to any directory on any server to which you have access. (You started this mapping process when you selected your First network drive during setup.) By mapping network drives, you can easily refer to a directory on a server by a letter designation, rather than by its full path name. The result is having another drive letter on your PC.

With NetWare, a *map root* assigns a one-letter name to a directory on a network server. When you refer to this directory, it appears as the root directory of the drive. For instance, root mapping is handy when an application requires its files to reside in a first-level directory on a drive. Installing application files at the root of the network drive may not be desired or practical. You will typically install the application in a subdirectory further down the directory tree. Assigning a drive letter as a map root makes it appear to the application and users that the files are at a root of a drive when, in fact, the files may be several levels down in the directory tree.

Windows 95 enables you to perform drive mappings and root mappings. It also gives you many avenues to accomplish these tasks. This is a typical method of mapping a network drive in Windows 95:

1. To map a drive using Explorer, open Explorer by clicking the Start button and selecting Programs ➪ Windows Explorer.

2. In the All Folders box on the left side of your Explorer window, double-click the Desktop icon, then double-click the Network Neighborhood icon, and then double-click the Entire Network icon.

3. Double-click the icon for the desired server and see the volumes for that server appear following the server name.

4. Double-click the volume's yellow folder and keep double-clicking sub-directories until you come to the subdirectory to which you want to map a drive letter.

5. Right-click the desired folder and select the Map the Network Drive option on the shortcut menu. The Map Network Drive dialog box will appear.

6. In the list box labeled Drive: the first available letter of the alphabet will appear. If this is not the letter you wish to use, choose another letter from the drop-down button.

7. Notice, in the list box labeled Path: the fully qualified network name of the desired directory is listed; you may not edit it at this point.

8. Two other options are shown. Check the box labeled Reconnect at logon if you wish to have Windows 95 restore this mapping every time you log on. Otherwise the mapping is temporary. Check the box labeled Connect as Root of the drive if you wish to make this mapping a root mapping.

9. Click the OK button. This drive letter now points to the drive and sub-directory desired. Windows 95 goes ahead and opens that folder for you while you're there (see Figure 37-10).

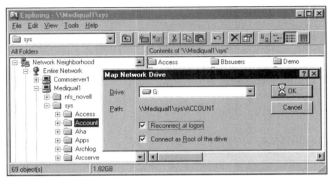

Figure 37-10: Mapping a network drive

Drive mappings can also be initiated from the My Computer utility, Network Neighborhood, and from a DOS window using the MAP command.

Unmapping network drives

You can easily remove a drive mapping from your system with Windows 95 Explorer. Follow these steps:

1. To remove a drive mapping using Explorer, open Explorer by clicking the Start button and selecting Programs ➪ Windows Explorer.

2. Select Tools from the menu and select Disconnect Network Drive from the drop-down menu. The Disconnect Network Drive dialog box will appear.

3. Select the desired drive mapping from the list box labeled Drive: and click the OK button. You may select multiple drive mappings by Ctrl + clicking each drive.

Drive mappings can also be removed from your system using My Computer and Network Neighborhood.

Attaching to network printers

After file sharing, being able to print on network printers is the second most useful procedure you can do on a NetWare network. Windows 95 makes it easy to set up network printing on your PC, and Windows 95 opens that folder for you while you're there. Many ways exist to connect to NetWare printers. Here's one easy way:

1. Click the Start button and select Settings ⇨ Printers. The Printers folder appears.

2. Double-click the Add Printer icon. The Add Printer Wizard starts.

3. Click the Next button, and select Network printer.

4. Click the Next button again. When asked for a Network path or queue name: click the Browse button and a Browse for Printer dialog box appears.

5. Double-click the Entire Network icon, and then the icon for the desired NetWare server. Any available printers will be displayed below that server, as in the example shown in Figure 37-11.

Figure 37-11: Browsing for a network printer

6. Select the desired printer and click the OK button. Click the Next button after indicating whether you ever print from DOS applications.

7. Now you can select the type of printer to which you will be printing. Even though the printer is not connected directly to your PC, you still must install a driver. This is so your PC knows what kind of data to send across the network to the network printer. Select your network printer from the list of Manufacturers: and the model from the list of Printers:. If you have new Windows 95 drivers for your printer, you can click the Have Disk button instead and use your newer drivers on a floppy disk. Click the Next button.

8. You may keep the default Printer name: or type a new one. Click the Next button.

9. You may now print a test page. Click the Finish button and be ready to supply Windows 95 setup disks when requested to complete the installation.

Your printer is now installed. Your Printer's dialog box will have this new printer listed in addition to the Add Printer icon. Right-click your printer icon and a shortcut menu of printing options appears. Many of the options displayed depend on the type of printer you have.

You can look at a printer's properties by right-clicking its icon and by selecting Properties from the shortcut menu. If you look at the properties of your network printer, click the Detail tab, and look at the Print to the following port: list box. Notice your network printer is not assigned to a COM or LPT port. Instead, it has a fully qualified network name as its description. Double-clicking a printer icon in the Printers folder brings up a window, which shows the activity for this printer.

Free Microsoft/Novell Tech Support

Microsoft has tried to make Novell integration as smooth and easy as possible. But one overriding, unpleasant fact exists that can't be ignored: As soon as you start mingling complex products from two different software manufacturers, you're bound to run into little glitches and problems that can drive you up a wall. Fortunately, two great online resources exist, that deal with potential problems — Microsoft's KnowledgeBase at http://www.microsoft.com/kb and Novell's Knowledgebase at http://support.novell.com/search that you can access free. Note, Microsoft's site works best if you browse it with Microsoft's Internet Explorer, version 3.0 or greater.

Summary

If you have an investment of time and money in a Novell Netware LAN, you can use a Windows 95 PC as a client on this LAN. The main points to remember include:

✦ You can use the 32-bit client software that comes with Windows 95 called Microsoft Client for NetWare Networks, or . . .

✦ You can use the 32-bit client software that comes from Novell, or . . .

✦ You can use the old 16-bit NETX or VLM client software that has been used by DOS and Windows 3.1x PCs.

✦ Each of the previous options offers its own unique tools for logging in and for sharing resources.

✦ Use Windows Explorer to map a network drive. To begin, click the Start button and choose Programs ➪ Windows Explorer. In the left pane, double-click the Network Neighborhood icon, click Entire Network, then double-click the desired server.

✦ To attach to a shared printer, double-click the My Computer icon on the desktop, then double-click the Printers folder. Double-click the Add Printer icon and use the wizard to connect to the shared printer.

✦   ✦   ✦

Windows 95 Potpourri

Modern Multimedia

All the earliest programs used one communications medium: text. Text appeared onscreen. You typed text at the keyboard.

Multimedia brings other communications media into the fray — namely pictures, sound, animation, and video. These media allow programmers and multimedia producers to create far more interesting programs for the rest of us to enjoy. But problems have occurred along the way.

Multimedia is something of an irony. Installing and using a multimedia program can be the simplest thing in the world: Just slide the CD-ROM into the CD-ROM drive and sit back. On the other hand, if you've been around the block a few times, you probably know multimedia also can be the most frustrating experience: Slide the disc into the CD-ROM drive and fight for hours trying to get the thing to work.

Many of the problems in multimedia are caused by one simple fact: PC multimedia is too new. PCs were introduced in the late 1970s, so we probably can say PC technology is in the toddler stage of development. The first sound cards and video for Windows programs were introduced in 1991 and 1992. By comparison with PCs, multimedia is in the infant (or, perhaps, zygote) stage of development.

Like real-life zygotes, multimedia has grown rapidly, to say the least. In fact, multimedia hardware and software have been the fastest-growing segments of the PC industry since about 1993. Millions of people just like you are tearing their hair out, trying to get that #$%*$@# game to make some sound.

What Windows 95 Brings to Multimedia

I wish I could say Windows 95 takes care of all the problems posed by multimedia, but no operating system can take care of all the problems. The hardware involved and the ever-changing standards don't allow a single operating system to take care of every conceivable problem.

But although Windows 95 can't solve all the problems, it can increase the likelihood of success. Following are some of the features of Windows 95 that can improve your experience with multimedia:

✦ A built-in CD-ROM File System (CDFS) and cache ensure data from a CD-ROM is read as quickly as possible, allowing for a richer, smoother multimedia presentation.

✦ Better use of memory allows even memory-hungry DOS-based multimedia games to run without requiring you to make elaborate changes in the CONFIG.SYS and AUTOEXEC.BAT files.

✦ Built-in support for a wide variety of *codecs* (compression/decompression methods) increases the likelihood a new multimedia title will run correctly the first time you use it.

✦ Device Manager (see Chapter 10) facilitates diagnosing and correcting the hardware conflicts that cripple multimedia hardware.

What to Look for in a Multimedia PC

Right off the bat, I can say with certainty that older PCs don't have the horsepower needed to run sophisticated multimedia titles. When you're buying a multimedia PC or hardware to upgrade an existing PC, you must look at all the factors on which modern multimedia titles rely. Those factors are:

✦ *Local bus or PCI video.* Historically, one of the biggest constraints on multimedia has been the video subsystem. When you purchase a multimedia PC, be sure to get one that supports local bus video or PCI, so you get the best possible multimedia performance.

✦ *2x or greater CD-ROM speed.* Many new multimedia titles assume you have at least a 2x (double-speed) CD-ROM drive. If possible, consider getting a 4x or faster drive now.

✦ *SVGA with 16-bit color.* The old 64×480 VGA with 16 colors doesn't quite cut it for new titles. Many titles assume you have at least SVGA (Super VGA) capable of displaying at 80×600 resolution and even 16-bit (HighColor) or 24-bit color (TrueColor).

✦ *16-bit audio with MIDI.* Audio cards must be 16-bit and should support MIDI. Few modern multimedia titles run on the old 8-bit sound cards.

If you're the power-hungry type, you may be tempted to get the biggest, fastest CPU and tons of RAM when you buy a multimedia PC, but those features are not major factors in multimedia. Multimedia playback places more demand on other components of the system, especially graphics capability and the CD-ROM drive. If you have to budget, you'd be better off to spend more for local bus or PCI graphics and a fast CD-ROM drive and to skimp a little in the CPU and RAM departments.

Playing with Sound

To do anything with sound, you must install a sound card. You have to consider tons of options when you buy a sound card, but the most important factor is getting a 16-bit (or better) sound card. If you need to upgrade from an 8-bit card or still haven't gotten around to putting a sound card in your system, consider purchasing a "Designed for Windows 95" plug-and-play-compatible board. Such a board greatly simplifies installation and use of that card.

Adjusting the volume

The first thing you need to do with sound is to adjust the volume, so you don't blast your eardrums. On the other hand, you want to make sure there is some volume. Otherwise, when you don't hear any sound from your speakers, you might assume something is wrong and waste a lot of time trying to "fix" your sound card.

You can control volume in six ways. I suggest you try the following methods, in this order, until you get the volume you want:

✦ If your speakers have their own volume control, adjust the volume on the speakers.

✦ Click on the speaker icon in the taskbar, and adjust the slider (see Figure 38-1).

✦ If you're using a multimedia program, search its menus or help system for options that control the volume.

✦ Double-click the speaker icon in the taskbar, and use your installed mixer to adjust the volume.

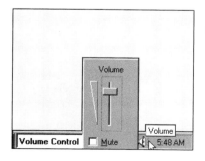

Figure 38-1: Click the taskbar's speaker button to adjust the volume.

✦ Choose Start ➪ Programs ➪ Accessories ➪ Multimedia ➪ Volume Control.

✦ Choose Start ➪ Settings ➪ Control Panel; then double-click the Audio Control (or similar) icon, if it's available.

Life Saver If you have powered speakers and you are having trouble getting the volume and clarity just right, try setting the volume with the speaker power turned off.

Playing a sound clip

If you want to play a sample sound clip, use My Computer, Explorer, or Find to browse to any file with the .WAV (*wave*) or .MID (MIDI) extension; then double-click that file's icon. In Figure 38-2, for example, I've opened a few folders that contain wave files (which have a speaker icon) and MIDI files (which have a musical-note icon). I copied these files from the CD-ROM that came with my sound card.

Double-clicking a wave file launches the Windows 95 Sound Recorder (also visible in Figure 38-2). Double-clicking a MIDI file launches the Windows 95 Media Player program.

Assigning sound effects to events

You can assign sounds, stored in .wav files, to various events that occur in Windows. You can play one sound when Windows starts, another when an error message appears onscreen, and so on.

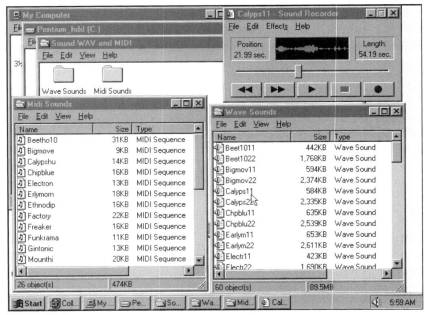

Figure 38-2: A collection of wave and MIDI files on my PC

To assign system sounds, follow these steps:

1. Choose Start ➪ Settings ➪ Control Panel.

    Remember, you also can get to Control Panel by double-clicking the My Computer icon and then double-clicking the Control Panel icon.

2. Double-click the Sounds icon.

    You see the Sounds Properties dialog box, shown in Figure 38-3.

3. Optionally, choose a predefined sound scheme from the Schemes drop-down list near the bottom of the dialog box.

4. Select the name of any event to which you want to assign a sound.

    Events with speaker icons already have sounds assigned to them, but you can change the sounds if you want.

5. Assign a sound to the selected event by choosing a sound from the Name drop-down list or by clicking the Browse button, and then navigating to the wave file of your choice.

6. To preview a sound, click the Play button next to the Preview box.

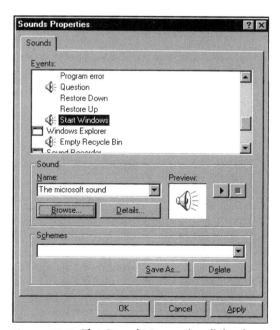

Figure 38-3: The Sounds Properties dialog box

7. For details on a particular sound, click the Details button.

8. Repeat Steps 4-7 to assign sounds to as many events as you want.

9. To save your current mix of sounds, choose <u>S</u>ave and then enter a file name.

10. When you finish, choose OK to return to Control Panel.

11. Close Control Panel, if you want.

The next time one of the events to which you assigned a sound occurs, you'll hear that sound.

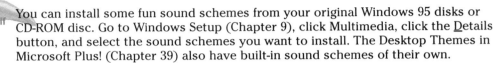

You can install some fun sound schemes from your original Windows 95 disks or CD-ROM disc. Go to Windows Setup (Chapter 9), click Multimedia, click the <u>D</u>etails button, and select the sound schemes you want to install. The Desktop Themes in Microsoft Plus! (Chapter 39) also have built-in sound schemes of their own.

Recording, editing, and playing sounds

Sound Recorder, which comes with your Windows 95 program, enables you to record, edit, and play wave sounds. To start Sound Recorder, you can do either of the following:

✦ Double-click any wave file's icon.

✦ Choose Start ➪ <u>P</u>rograms ➪ Accessories ➪ Multimedia ➪ Sound Recorder.

Figure 38-4 shows how Sound Recorder looks with a sound in its clutches.

Figure 38-4: Sound Recorder

Recording a sound

To record a sound with Sound Recorder, you must hook up a microphone or other input device. I can't give you exact instructions on this procedure, because it depends on your sound card; check the manual that came with the sound card. In general, if you want to record from a microphone, you plug the microphone into the Mic plug on the sound card. If you want to record from a cassette-tape player or audio CD player, you connect that player's Line Out plug to the sound card's Line In plug, using whatever cable is appropriate for your hardware.

Life Saver You can permanently damage sound hardware by plugging in an unacceptable device or by plugging a device into the wrong plug. Refer to your sound-card manual for specific instructions before you plug in any device. Next, you may need to use your mixer or the Windows 95 Volume Control tool to specify the device from which you want to record. The way you perform this step varies from one sound card to the next; refer to your sound-card documentation if you run into any problems. On my systems, I can get to the mixer in two ways: by double-clicking the speaker icon in the taskbar and by choosing Start ➪ Programs ➪ Accessories ➪ Multimedia ➪ Volume Control.

Within the mixer, go to the recording controls (or input controls, as opposed to output or playback controls), and crank up the volume on the input device you plan to use. Then mute, or crank down, all other devices. In Figure 38-5, which shows the mixer for my Sound Blaster card, I selected Line In as the input and cranked up the volume a little. I left all other input devices unselected, so they won't contribute anything to the sounds I want to record.

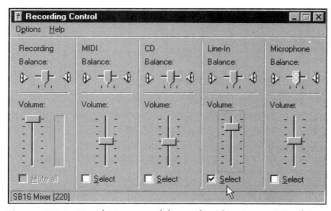

Figure 38-5: Ready to record from the Line In port (only)

Life Saver If you're using a Sound Blaster mixer and don't see the input controls, don't fret; just choose Options ➪ Properties ➪ Recording.

When you have your input device ready to go, display Sound Recorder, and then follow these steps to record a sound:

1. Choose Edit ➪ Audio Properties.

   The Audio Properties dialog box appears, as shown in Figure 38-6.

2. Make sure the recording volume is turned up at least halfway.

3. In the Preferred quality section, choose one of the following options:
   - *CD Quality.* High-quality sound: produces large wave files
   - *Radio Quality.* Medium-quality sound: produces medium-size wave files
   - *Telephone Quality.* Lower-quality sound: produces small wave files.

4. Choose OK to close the dialog box.

5. In Sound Recorder, choose File ➪ New.

6. To start recording, click the Record button (red circle).

   The wave indicator should show the sound as it's being recorded.

7. When you're ready to stop recording, click the Stop button (black square).

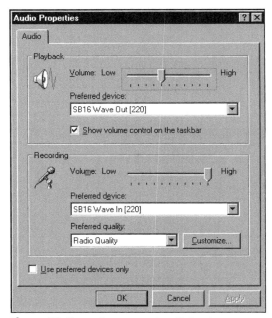

Figure 38-6: Audio Properties dialog box

8. To save the recording, choose File ➪ Save and then enter a filename.

   Sound Recorder automatically adds the .wav extension to whatever filename you type.

The recording stays in Sound Recorder for the time being, so you can play it back and edit it as described in the next two sections.

Playing a sound

After you record a sound (or open a sound file by choosing File ➪ Open), you can easily play it back. Use the control buttons in Sound Recorder as you use the buttons on a tape player. To rewind to the beginning of the sound, for example, click the Seek to Start button; to play the sound, click the Play button. If you're not sure which button is which, point to any button and wait for the tooltip to appear.

Editing a sound

When you have a sound in Sound Recorder, you can have fun playing with the options in the Effects menu (see Figure 38-7).

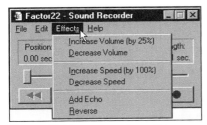

Figure 38-7: Options for editing a sound file

Experiment on your own with these options. Choose any option from the menu; then rewind and click the Play button to hear that effect.

The effects are cumulative. If you choose Effects ➪ Add Echo one time, for example, you hear a little echo. If you choose Effects ➪ Add Echo five times, you get five times as much echo.

Playing audio CDs

Your PC can double as a player for the regular audio CDs you use in your stereo system. To play an audio CD, follow these steps:

1. Put the audio CD in your PC's CD-ROM drive.

2. Choose Start ➪ Programs ➪ Accessories ➪ Multimedia ➪ CD Player.

   The CD Player dialog box appears.

3. If you want to listen to specific tracks (songs), choose Disc ➪ Edit Play List; click the Remove and Add buttons to add and remove playlist tracks (as in the example shown in Figure 38-8); and then click OK.

4. Click on the Play button in CD Player.

5. If you need to adjust the volume, choose View ➪ Volume, or click the speaker icon in the taskbar.

Figure 38-9 shows CD Player playing an audio CD. I have the volume cranked up SO LOUD I CAN HARDLY HEAR MYSELF THINK.

The volume of sound coming from an audio CD may be controlled by your mixer as well as the small Volume indicator slider. For example, if you double-click the little speaker icon and get to the Volume Control dialog box, the slider titled CD will be the one that primarily controls the volume of audio CDs. If this option is muted, you won't hear anything from the audio CD.

When CD Player gets going, you can play with some of the settings in its menu bar. CD Player also has its own help file. If you need help, choose Help from the menu bar or click the question-mark button, and then click the item with which you need help.

You can resume your normal work while CD Player is running. If you want to get the CD Player window out of the way, click its Minimize button. The window shrinks to a taskbar button, and the CD continues to play.

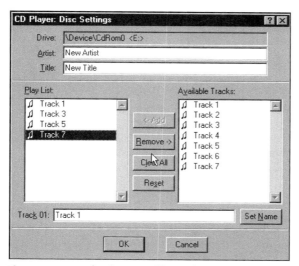

Figure 38-8: Selecting specific tracks on an audio CD

Windows 95 comes with built-in support for CD+, a new standard that will allow audio CDs to be played in a stereo system or a PC. Under CD+, a CD played in a PC also displays song titles and other useful information.

To stop playing a CD, click the Stop button (black square) in CD Player, or close the CD Player window by clicking its Close button (X).

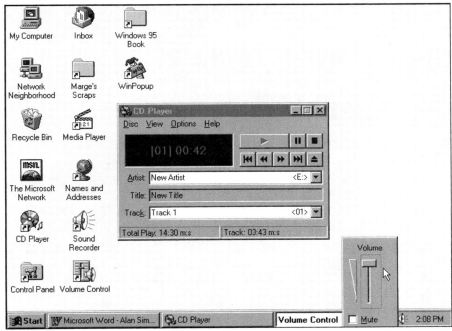

Figure 38-9: The Windows 95 CD Player

Media Player and MIDI

Musical Instrument Digital Interface (MIDI) is electronic sheet music of a sort, which can mimic the sounds of many musical instruments. When you play games or use multimedia titles with great-sounding audio, chances are you're actually listening to MIDI files.

You may have received some sample MIDI sound clips when you purchased your sound card. You can play a MIDI clip simply by double-clicking its icon in My Computer, Windows Explorer, or Find, just as you can play a wave file (as discussed in "Playing a sound clip" earlier in this chapter.) Or you can play a MIDI clip from Media Player by following these steps:

1. Choose Start ➪ Programs ➪ Accessories ➪ Multimedia.
2. Click Media Player to launch that program.
3. Choose Device ➪ 3 MIDI Sequencer.
4. Browse to any folder that contains MIDI clips.
5. Double-click any MIDI (.mid) file.

In Figure 38-10, I've opened a MIDI file named Freaker from my Sound Blaster CD-ROM.

Figure 38-10: Media Player with MIDI file open

6. Click the Play button (tooltips are provided for the buttons).

Hot Stuff You can play wave (.wav), MIDI (.mid), and video (.avi) files from Media Player's Open dialog box.

As you can in Sound Recorder, you can control the volume from your mixer (choose Device ➪ Volume Control from within Media Player) or by clicking the speaker icon in the taskbar. You can use your computer to do other things while the MIDI file is playing.

Features to look for in MIDI boards

If you're just getting into MIDI, or you are considering upgrading your sound/MIDI card, look for the following factors, which enable you to take advantage of Windows 95's MIDI features:

✦ Purchase a card with *general MIDI support*, so your MIDI card plays the right instrument at the right time.

✦ Look for a *standard MIDI port*, into which you can plug any MIDI device (as well as a joystick).

✦ A board that supports *polyphony* provides rich sound. Look for a board that can handle 16-voice to 20-voice polyphony.

✦ *Sampled sounds* provide much better acoustics than wavetable synthesis does. A sampled sound is a recording of the actual instrument, whereas wavetable synthesis produces a mathematical approximation of the instrument's sound.

✦ Support for *MIDI streams* relieves the CPU of some of the burden of playing MIDI; that burden is transferred to the sound card. The result is much better multimedia performance.

Life Saver Any sound card that bears the "Designed for Windows 95" plug-and-play logo is easier to install than an older, nonplug-and-play board.

Recording MIDI

MIDI recording usually is done by professional musicians with MIDI-input hardware and special software. The input device, which usually looks like a piano keyboard, plugs into the MIDI/Game port slot of the sound card.

Windows 95 supports the *general MIDI specification*, to which all MIDI devices adhere; nearly any input device will work. Also worth mentioning is Windows 95 uses a new 32-bit technology called *MIDI streams support,* which allows more music to be played through the PC, with less CPU use. This feature enables music developers to create more advanced music, mixing more instruments. This capability, in turn, enables multimedia developers to include more complex music in their multimedia games and software titles.

In your volume-control box or mixer (refer to Figure 38-5), MIDI input and output volume is controlled by the MIDI, or Synth, channel. You also can control MIDI output volume from the speaker icon in the taskbar.

Advanced MIDI options

If you are a professional musician and you plan to create some MIDI files of your own, be aware of all the settings that influence MIDI in Windows 95. You can get to these settings through Control Panel. Choose Start ⇨ Settings ⇨ Control Panel, and double-click the Multimedia icon. Then click the MIDI tab (see Figure 38-11) to set up custom configurations or add new instruments, or click the Advanced tab to choose and enable MIDI drivers (see Figure 38-12).

To see the properties of a specific MIDI file, browse to the file, right-click its icon, and then choose Properties from the shortcut menu. You can preview the MIDI file from the Properties dialog box that appears (see Figure 38-13).

Digital Video

Windows 95 comes with built-in video-playback capability. In most situations, you'll see digital video played in multimedia titles. Figure 38-14 shows a screen from the movie *Casablanca* in Microsoft's Cinemania 95. Click on the Play button below the picture of Ingrid Bergman to play a short clip from the movie.

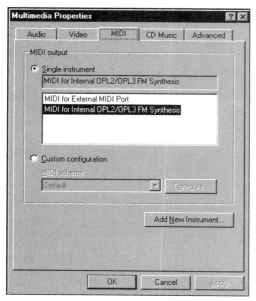

Figure 38-11: MIDI properties are accessible from the MIDI tab.

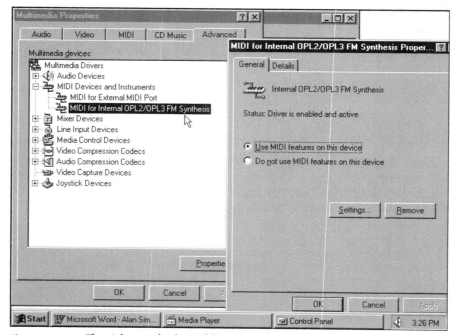

Figure 38-12: The Advanced tab enables you to configure MIDI drivers.

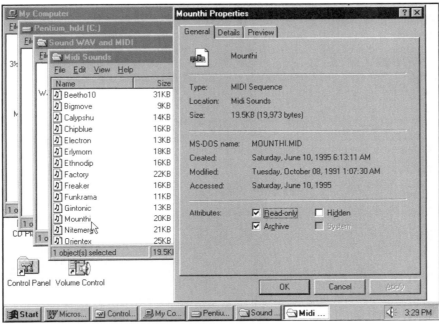

Figure 38-13: Properties of a MIDI file

Figure 38-14: Sample video clip from Microsoft Cinemania 95

You also can buy video clips or download them from many information services. A file that contains a video clip typically has the file extension .avi, Video Clip as its description, and a video-camera icon. In Figure 38-15, I browsed to a collection of video clips on a CD-ROM that contains sample clips from Microsoft and then double-clicked on the filename `cool` to watch the video. The video is paused in the figure, but the mouse pointer is touching the Play button. To restart the video, I just need to click that button.

You also can launch a digital video clip from Media Player. Follow these steps:

1. Choose Start ➪ Programs ➪ Accessories ➪ Multimedia.

2. Click on Media Player.

3. Choose Device ➪ 1 Video for Windows.

4. Browse to a video-clip file.

5. Double-click any video-clip file.

   The first frame of the clip appears in a window.

6. Click on the Play button in Media Player.

   The clip plays in its small window.

7. To open another clip, choose File ➪ Open.

Figure 38-15: Digital video (.avi) clips, one of which is playing.

Adjust the brightness and contrast buttons on your monitor to fine-tune video playback. Your display settings (refer to Chapter 6) also affect the quality of playback.

Controlling video-playback size

Normally, a video clip plays in a small window. You can adjust the size of that window by dragging any corner. Or you can have Windows 95 launch the video at a specific size by following these steps:

1. Choose Start ➪ Settings ➪ Control Panel.

2. Double-click the Multimedia icon.

3. Click the Video tab.

4. Choose an option from the Window drop-down list or click the Full Screen option button, as shown in Figure 38-16.

5. Click the OK button.

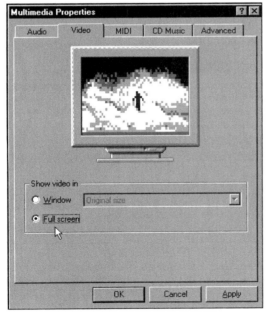

Figure 38-16: Video properties set for full-screen playback

Any video clips you play, whether by double-clicking the filenames or by using Media Player, display in the new size.

Video graininess and jerkiness

When you start playing video at larger sizes, you probably will start to see some degradation in the image. *Graininess,* or *blockiness,* happens because the images must be compressed to fit on a computer disk. If video were stored in an uncompressed format, a single frame of digital video would require an entire megabyte of disk space — an entire CD-ROM would be required to store even a short clip. Furthermore, that CD would need to spin at an awesome speed to feed the data to the PC.

Jerkiness in videos is caused by the speed of the video subsystem, the speed of the CPU, or the speed of the CD-ROM drive. If any of those devices are too slow, the device becomes a bottleneck in getting the huge stream of data into the CPU, decompressed, and out through your screen and sound card.

In terms of software, you can't do much about graininess and jerkiness; the 32-bit multimedia system in Windows 95 decompresses and plays the video as fast as the hardware allows. (When you start buying 32-bit multimedia titles and video clips, however, those elements will run more smoothly.) In terms of hardware, you can throw money at the following options to minimize the problems:

- ✦ Get the fastest CD-ROM player possible; at least 300KB per second is recommended. A fast CD-ROM drive reduces both graininess and jerkiness.
- ✦ A fast 486 or Pentium CPU provides quicker decompression and less jerkiness.
- ✦ A computer with a local-bus or PCI graphics subsytem.
- ✦ A display card with a Display Control Interface (DCI) provider provides the best video performance.

Capturing and editing video

Windows 95 offers no built-in features for capturing (recording), compressing, or editing digital video; you need to buy specialized hardware and software for those purposes. If you're interested in digital video, check with your computer dealer for information on Windows 95-compatible video editing hardware and software.

Writing to CD-ROM

Windows 95 offers no built-in software for mastering (writing to) a CD-ROM disc. CD-ROM is strictly read-only memory, unless you buy special CD-ROM mastering hardware and software. Many such products are readily available at most computer stores.

Be forewarned, though, saving to a CD-ROM is not like saving to a hard disk. On a hard disk, you can store and erase files easily, at will. On a CD-ROM, you have to get everything right the first time: You can't erase what you put on the disc. Having a hard disk with 680M of free space helps. You can store the entire contents of the CD-ROM on the hard disk first, and when you're happy with what's on the hard disk, you can copy the full 680MB (or whatever) to a CD-ROM.

Adding AutoPlay to your CD-ROM production

Windows 95 now offers AutoPlay, a magical feature that enables a user to slide a disc into the CD-ROM drive, sit back, and enjoy the show. No browsing for setup or startup programs is required.

To add AutoPlay to the software you distribute on CD-ROM, just add the text file named AUTORUN.INF to the CD-ROM's directory. Only the following three lines are required:

```
[autorun]
open=pathname\filename.exe paramteers
icon = filename.ico
```

Replace the italicized parameters with actual names from your CD-ROM. For more information, see the *Windows 95 Resource Kit*, published by Microsoft Press.

Windows 95 Codecs

Wave sound (including voice), MIDI, and digital video use some kind of compression/decompression (abbreviated *codec*) scheme to store information on computer disks. Compression is necessary, because audio and video data require huge amounts of storage. Without compression, a single frame of digital video could take up a megabyte of storage. Therefore, a CD-ROM could hold about 680 frames, which represents a short video clip.

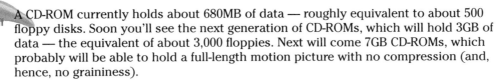 A CD-ROM currently holds about 680MB of data — roughly equivalent to about 500 floppy disks. Soon you'll see the next generation of CD-ROMs, which will hold 3GB of data — the equivalent of about 3,000 floppies. Next will come 7GB CD-ROMs, which probably will be able to hold a full-length motion picture with no compression (and, hence, no graininess).

Windows 95 comes with many popular codecs built right in. To see which codecs are currently installed and to tweak their settings, follow these steps:

1. Choose Start ➪ Settings ➪ Control Panel.

2. Double-click the Multimedia icon.

3. Click the Advanced tab.

4. To view video codecs, click the plus sign (+) next to Video compression codecs.

   To view audio codecs, click the plus sign (+) next to Audio compression codecs.

Figure 38-17 shows an example. If you want to explore or change the settings for a particular codec, click the codec and then click the Properties button. After you explore and/or make changes, click OK to work your way back to Control Panel, and follow the onscreen instructions (if any).

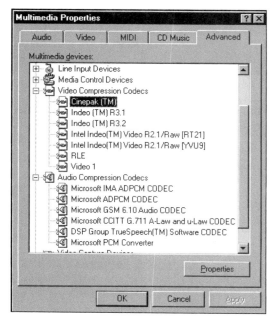

Figure 38-17: Installed codecs

If you buy a hardware device that requires a codec you don't have, you easily can add the appropriate codec to your list. If you buy a video capture board that uses JPEG compression, for example, you can add JPEG to Windows 95. Follow these steps:

1. Choose Start ➪ Settings ➪ Control Panel.

2. Double-click the Add New Hardware icon.

3. Click the Next button.

4. When you are asked about detecting new hardware, click No.

5. Click the Next button to display the list of device categories.

6. Click the Sound, video, and game controllers option, as shown in Figure 38-18.

7. Choose one of the codec options from the Manufacturers list.

   You can choose Microsoft Audio Codecs or Microsoft Video Codecs, for example. Optionally, to install another manufacturer's codec, click Have Disk.

8. In the Models section, click the codec you want to install (see Figure 38-19).

9. Click the Next button.

10. Follow the onscreen instructions.

Figure 38-18: About to install a codec via the Add New Hardware wizard

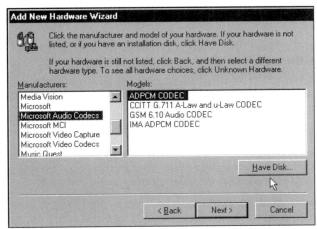

Figure 38-19: Installing a codec via the Add New Hardware wizard

Troubleshooting Multimedia

Multimedia is one of the more difficult things to troubleshoot on a PC. One reason is multimedia involves a great deal of hardware and software, and you can adjust the volume and picture quality in many places. Different multimedia programs also use different techniques to display animation, video, sound, and so on; it's hard to tell whether the problem is in your settings or in the program you're trying to use. If you're having trouble with multimedia, the following checklist can help you diagnose (and perhaps solve) the problem:

✦ If you're having a problem with a specific multimedia program, you may want to set it aside and try a different program. (The troublesome program may be incompatible.)

✦ Make sure all hardware is properly installed and connected properly, per the manufacturers' instructions.

✦ Check the volume of devices outside the PC (such as the volume knobs on your speakers).

✦ Check the status and output volume of all devices in your mixer (choose Start ➪ Programs ➪ Accessories ➪ Multimedia ➪ Volume Control).

✦ Check the volume control in the taskbar (click the speaker icon).

If problems persist, use the Device Manager and the hardware-conflict Troubleshooter (discussed in Chapter 10) to diagnose and solve any conflicts between your multimedia hardware and other devices on your PC.

Summary

Following is a recap of the main points discussed in this chapter:

✦ Like most new technologies, multimedia is plagued with problems affecting both multimedia producers and consumers.

✦ Windows 95 has many built-in features designed to make multimedia richer and easier to use. But even Windows 95 needs speedy modern hardware to do its job.

✦ Most multimedia elements you play probably will be embedded in a game or title stored on a CD-ROM drive.

✦ You can manage small multimedia clips with Windows 95. To play a sound (.WAV), MIDI (.MID), or video (.AVI) clip, you can double-click its filename.

✦ You can control the volume of sound in multimedia in many ways. You can use the volume controls on the speakers, the taskbar's speaker icon, and, perhaps, controls within the program you're using at the moment.

✦ Use the Sounds Properties dialog box to assign custom sounds to Windows events. Choose Start ➪ Settings ➪ Control Panel, and double-click the Sounds icon.

✦ Use Sound Recorder to record, edit, and play wave (.WAV) sounds. Choose Start ➪ Programs ➪ Accessories ➪ Multimedia ➪ Sound Recorder.

✦ Use CD Player to listen to audio CDs. Choose Start ➪ Programs ➪ Accessories ➪ Multimedia ➪ CD Player.

✦ Use Media Player to play MIDI (.MID) sound files and video clips (.AVI files). Choose Start ➪ Programs ➪ Accessories ➪ Multimedia ➪ Media Player.

✦   ✦   ✦

Using Microsoft Plus!

Microsoft Plus! is an optional add-on to Windows 95. If you want it, you need to purchase it separately. If you want to find out more about Plus! before you buy, read this chapter to see what Plus! has to offer, and whether you have the appropriate hardware. If you've already purchased Plus!, you can use this chapter to install and use its features. Here is a brief description of the various goodies Plus! offers:

+ Some fun *desktop themes*, some visual enhancement features, and a 3D pinball game.

+ *System Agent* enables you to schedule programs to run automatically at certain times.

+ *DriveSpace 3* provides disk compression up to 2 gigabytes.

+ *Dial-Up Server* enables you to access your PC from some remote location, using a portable PC and a modem.

+ Internet *Explorer* enables you to explore the Internet using the Windows 95 interface.

System Requirements for Plus!

One of the reasons Plus! is sold as a separate product is it won't work on all hardware. Before you purchase Plus!, you want to make sure your PC meets the minimum requirements:

Processor: 486, or Pentium (no 386s)

Memory (RAM):   8MB

Video display: At least 256 colors. High Color (16-bit) recommended

Installing Microsoft Plus!

Once you have a copy of Microsoft Plus! in hand, you can install it as you would any other program:

1. Click the Start button.

2. Point to Settings, and then click Control Panel.

3. Double-click the Add/Remove Programs icon.

4. Click the Install button on the Install/Uninstall tab.

5. Follow the instructions on the screen, and click the Next button when you're ready to move onto the next screen.

If you opted to install the Internet Explorer, the Internet Setup wizard will start automatically. If you don't have all the information you need to complete the wizard, don't worry. Just choose Cancel and forget about the Internet for now. When you're ready to give the Internet a whirl, see "Set up a Dial-Up Networking Server" later in this chapter.

You'll also be prompted to choose a desktop theme. If you're uncertain which theme you want right now, you can click the Cancel button to keep your current desktop settings. Then you can choose a desktop theme later, following the steps under "Fun with Desktop Themes" a little later in this chapter.

Finally, if your hard disk is already compressed using DoubleSpace or DriveSpace, you'll be given some options to upgrade to DriveSpace 3. You can choose OK to upgrade right on the spot, or choose Notify me again... to leave your current compression scheme intact. To learn more about DriveSpace 3, see "Using Plus! Disk Compression" later in this chapter.

Integrated help for Plus!

Microsoft Plus! has its own online help. But when you install Plus!, its help becomes integrated with the rest of your Windows 95 help. So you can get at the Plus! help from that Start button, as follows:

1. Click the Start button.

2. Click Help.

3. Click the Contents tab.

4. You should now see a book for Microsoft Plus!. Double-click that book to see books within the Microsoft Plus! book, as in Figure 39-1.

You can use the Plus! help normally now. For example, you can double-click any book to see topics within that book. Then you can double-click any topic to explore that topic.

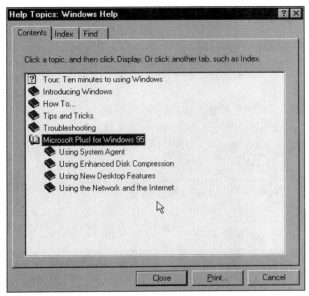

Figure 39-1: Help for Plus! added to Windows 95 help contents

The online help for Plus! is also integrated into the Index and Find tabs of the general Windows help. So let's say, for example, you use the Index or Find tab in Windows 95 to search for the word *Internet*. The results of your search will automatically include relevant topics from both Windows 95 and Microsoft Plus! If you're a little rusty on Windows 95 online help, refer to Chapter 1, starting at the section titled "Your electronic table of contents."

Fun with Desktop Themes

The desktop themes that come with Microsoft Plus! enable you to set up a screen saver, wallpaper, icons, sounds, and other elements, all centered around a theme. To choose a theme:

1. Click the Start button.

2. Point to Settings.

3. Click Control Panel.

4. Double-click the Desktop Themes icon.

You're taken to the Desktop Themes dialog box shown in Figure 39-2. Use the drop-down list button next to Theme to choose a theme. If you have a 256-color display or if you have limited your settings to 256 colors, choose only a 256-color theme. If you're set up for 16-bit or 24-bit color, you can choose any theme.

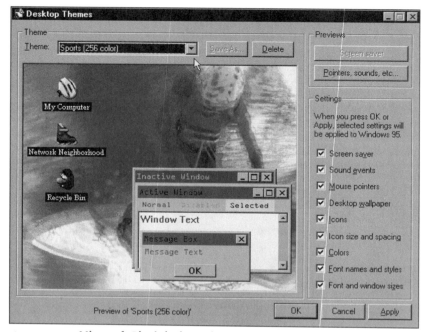

Figure 39-2: Microsoft Plus! desktop themes

If you need to check or change your color settings, right-click the desktop, choose Properties, and click the Settings tab. See Chapter 6 if you need more information.

By default, Plus! will set up all elements of the theme: screen saver, sound events, mouse pointers, and so forth. If you don't want to include an element, just clear its check box. If you want to preview an element before making your selection, click the Screen saver or Pointers, sounds, and so forth, button under Previews.

When you finish making your selection(s), click the OK button to return to the desktop.

If you want to change a particular element of a desktop theme, such as the wallpaper or screen saver, use the standard techniques described in Chapter 6, "Personalizing the Screen." Or follow these steps to get into the appropriate dialog box now:

1. Click the Start button and point to Settings.

2. Choose Control Panel.

3. Double-click the icon for the element you want to change and choose the appropriate tab in the dialog box that appears, as summarized in the following:

If you want to change...	...double-click
Colors	Display ➪ Appearance tab
Fonts	Display ➪ Appearance tab
Icons	Display ➪ Plus! tab
Icon Size and Spacing	Display ➪ Appearance tab (Item)
Mouse pointers	Mouse ➪ Pointers tab
Screen saver	Display ➪ Screen Saver tab
Sound events	Sounds
Wallpaper	Display ➪ Background tab

Using the Plus! Visual Enhancements

Microsoft Plus! also comes with some enhancements to improve the general appearance of your screen. When you install Plus!, options for activating these enhancements are automatically integrated into your Display Properties dialog box. To get to the options:

1. Right-click your desktop and choose Properties. (Or click Start ➪ Settings ➪ Control Panel, and then double-click the Display icon.)

2. Click the Plus! tab in the Display properties dialog box.

The Plus! tab, shown in Figure 39-3, offers the following summarized options:

✦ *Desktop icons:* Click any of the four general desktop icons, and then click the Change Icon button to choose a different picture to represent that icon.

✦ *Show window contents while dragging:* When selected, this option assures you can see the actual contents of any window — not just a ghost image of the window — as you drag the window to a new location on the screen.

✦ *Smooth edges of screen fonts:* When selected, this option eliminates the *jaggies* that often give screen fonts a rough edge.

✦ *Show icons using all possible colors:* Uses whatever color capabilities your system has, rather than just 16 colors, to display icons. Makes for richer-looking icons — but consumes a little memory and slows down screen-refreshing.

✦ *Stretch desktop wallpaper to fit the screen:* Ensures even a small (for example, 640 × 480) screen saver will fill your 800 × 600 or greater screen. To make this work, you must also click the Background tab in the Display Properties dialog box and choose Center under the Wallpaper options.

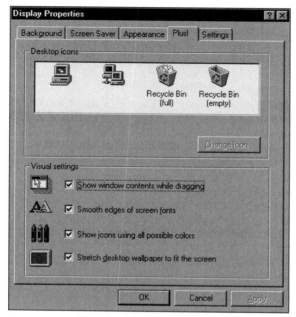

Figure 39-3: Visual Enhancement options on the Plus! tab

When you finish making your selections, choose OK.

Scheduling Programs with System Agent

The System Agent program that comes with Microsoft Plus! enables you to schedule programs to run automatically while you're away from the PC. This is especially good for ensuring your system maintenance tasks, discussed in Chapter 11, are performed on a regular basis.

When you install Microsoft Plus!, System Agent is installed and activated automatically each time you start Windows 95. Initially, System Agent appears as a tiny indicator in the taskbar. To open System Agent, double-click that little indicator. The System Agent opens into a window and displays scheduled tasks, as in the example shown in Figure 39-4.

If you don't see the System Agent indicator in the taskbar, you can follow these steps to open it:

1. Click the Start button.
2. Point to Programs ➪ Accessories ➪ System Tools.
3. Click System Agent.

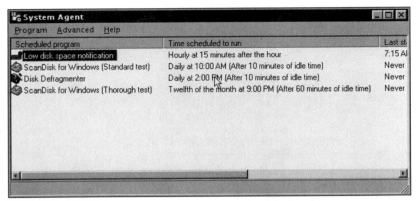

Figure 39-4: The System Agent with some scheduled tasks

Add a scheduled program

If you want to schedule a program to run automatically at some predetermined time, you first need to know the location and filename of that program. If you don't have this information handy, here's how you can find it:

1. Right-click the Start button and choose Open.

2. Double-click the Programs icon. The Programs dialog box that appears contains an icon for each program group and for each program on your Programs menu.

3. Now work your way to the Startup icon for the program you want to schedule. For example, if the program you want to schedule is right on your Programs menu (for example, Microsoft Exchange), you needn't drill down any further. If the program you want to schedule is in the Accessories folder, however, you need to double-click the Accessories icon, so you can find your program's startup icon.

4. When you see the icon for the program you want to schedule, right-click that icon and choose Properties from the shortcut menu that appears.

5. Click the Shortcut tab and look at the Target entry. That's the location and name of the program as needed by System Agent. In Figure 39-5 I've zeroed in on Microsoft Exchange.

6. Now jot down the information in the Target box. For example, in this case I would write C:\PROGRA~1\MICROS~1\EXCHNG32.EXE.

7. Once you've written the information you need, you can back out of your previous selections. Choose Cancel and close open windows until you get back to the desktop.

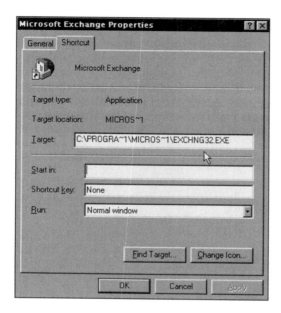

Figure 39-5: The Target option shows the location and name of a program.

Once you know the location and filename of the program you want to schedule, follow these steps to add that program to System Agent:

1. If you haven't already done so, open System Agent.

2. Choose Program ⇨ Schedule a new program from System Agent's menu bar.

3. Click the Browse button.

4. In the Browse dialog box that appears, open folders as appropriate until you find the icon for the program you want to schedule.

In my example, I would first need to click the Up One Level button to get to drive C:, then double-click the Program Files icon (represented by C:\PROGRA~1 in the Target box). Then I'd double-click the Microsoft Exchange icon (represented by \MICROS_1 in the Target description). Finally, I would double-click the EXCHNG32.EXE icon.

5. Type in a Description of your own choosing. Figure 39-6 shows an example using my progress on automating Microsoft Exchange.

6. Now click the When to Run button.

7. Choose options in the "Change Schedule..." dialog box to indicate when you want this program to run. For example, in Figure 39-7, I've set up Exchange to run automatically every day at 1:30 P.M. (That'll remind me to check my e-mail before 4:30 Eastern time).

8. Use the Advanced button and other options on the screen to determine how to handle the various situations each option explains.

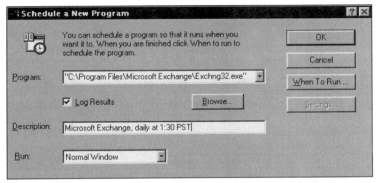

Figure 39-6: Microsoft Exchange is ready to be scheduled.

9. Choose OK as necessary to work your way back to the System Agent window.

The program you just scheduled will be listed with other scheduled programs. You can close System Agent, if you wish, by clicking its Close (X) button. The program will run at the appointed time provided your computer and System Agent are running when the time arrives.

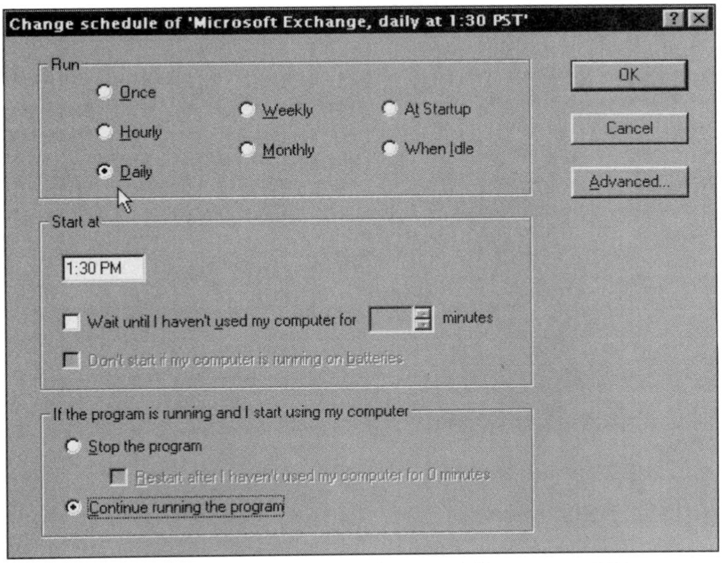

Figure 39-7: Will run Microsoft Exchange daily at 1:30 P.M.

When I say "providing System Agent is running . . .," I mean the System Agent icon must be visible in the taskbar. You needn't open the System Agent icon to make scheduled events occur.

Changing settings for a scheduled program

Some programs, such as DriveSpace and Disk Defragmenter, are specifically designed for use with System Agent. Those programs have special settings you can adjust to decide exactly how you want System Agent to run the program. To change those settings:

1. Open System Agent if it isn't already open.

2. Click the program whose settings you want to change.

3. Choose Program ➪ Properties from System Agent's menu bar.

4. Click the Settings button.

5. In the Scheduled Settings... dialog box that appears, make your selections. Figure 39-8 shows an example using the schedule settings for the ScanDisk program.

6. Choose OK as necessary to work your way back to System Agent.

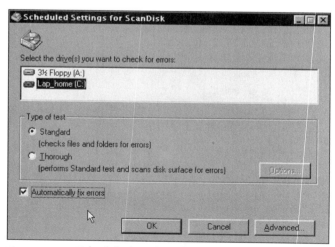

Figure 39-8: Scheduled settings for ScanDisk

Now you can close System Agent by clicking its Close (X) button.

If a scheduled program doesn't have a simple Settings button and Schedules Settings dialog box, you may still be able to control how the program runs by passing *startup commands* to the scheduled programs. Typically, a startup command is a *switch* you add on to the end of the command, outside the quotation marks. For example, adding /a to the Program line for my Exchange program, as follows

"C:\Program Files\Microsoft Exchange\Exchng32.exe" /a

would automatically start Microsoft Exchange and open the Address Book.

To add/change a switch or setting after you've already scheduled a program, open System Agent, right-click the name of the program you want to change, and choose Properties.

To find out what startup switches are available for a program, you must search that program's help or written documentation for appropriate buzzwords, such as *startup* or *switches* or *command line switches*.

To test a scheduled program and any startup options you've defined, open System Agent (if it isn't already open). Right-click the name of the scheduled program you want to test, and choose Run Now from the shortcut menu that appears.

Change a program's schedule

To change the schedule of any program in System Agent:

1. Open System Agent.
2. Right-click the program you want to reschedule.
3. Choose Change Schedule.
4. Make your selections from the Change schedule... dialog box that appears, and then choose OK.

Disable/remove a scheduled program

You can temporarily disable a scheduled program so it does not run at its appointed time, but stays listed in the System Agent dialog box, so you can re-enable it some time in the future. To disable a scheduled program, open System Agent, right-click the name of the scheduled program you want to disable, and choose Disable. The *Time scheduled to run* column in System Agent will show the word *Disabled* for that program. To reinstate the scheduled program, right-click its name again in System Agent, and select the Disable option so it no longer has a check mark.

You can also remove a program from System Agent altogether. Just open System Agent, right-click the name of the program you want to remove, and choose Remove from the shortcut menu. Or click the program you want to remove and choose Program ➪ Remove from System Agent's menu bar.

Disable or enable System Agent

Times may occur when you don't want System Agent to run any of its programs. For example, say you're going to use your PC to give a public presentation and you don't want DriveSpace or "defrag" to pop up in the middle of your presentation. No problem — here's what you do:

1. Open System Agent.

2. Choose Advanced from System Agent's menu bar.

3. Now choose one of the following:

   • Suspend System Agent: Leaves the System Agent indicator in the taskbar as a reminder, but does not allow the agent to run scheduled programs.

   • Stop using System Agent: Choose this option if you want to prevent all scheduled programs from running and to remove System Agent's indicator from the taskbar.

If you opted to suspend the agent, you can click its Close button (X) to close the window. If you opted to stop the agent, you'll be asked for confirmation. Choose Yes, and the System Agent window and taskbar indicator will disappear from your screen.

If you need to re-start System Agent after removing its indicator from the taskbar, click the Start button, point to Programs ➪ Accessories ➪ System Tools, and click System Agent.

Using Plus! Disk Compression

Microsoft Plus! comes with two programs called DriveSpace 3 and Compression Agent. Together, these two programs offer disk compression features unavailable in the DriveSpace program that comes standard with Windows 95 (see "Maximize Your Disk Space" in Chapter 12 for more information on that program). Microsoft Plus! compression offers the following:

✦ Supports compressed drives up to 2 gigabytes (2,048MB) in size, as compared to 512MB in standard DriveSpace.

✦ Compression Agent enables you to compact files more tightly than DriveSpace does.

✦ You can choose settings that enable you to find the best balance between speed and disk space for your PC.

Compressing a drive

To compress a drive using DriveSpace 3, follow these steps:

1. Double-click My Computer.

2. Right-click the icon for the drive you want to compress, and choose Properties from the shortcut menu that appears.

3. Click the Compression tab. You'll see some options like the example shown in Figure 39-9.

Notice you have two choices. You can compress the entire drive, in which case the entire drive will appear larger, though you'll still have only one hard drive (probably drive C). A second choice is to compress just the empty space on the current drive and to treat that new compressed space as a separate drive. For example, if I opted to create a new drive in Figure 39-9, I'd end up with two hard disk drives, one named C: and a new, compressed drive named E: (If you want to keep things simple, choose the first option, Compress Drive).

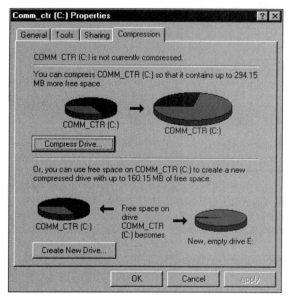

Figure 39-9: Compression options for a sample hard disk

It can take several hours to compress a drive, during which you cannot use the computer at all. You may want to start the job just before leaving work, so you needn't wait around for DriveSpace to finish the job. Once you start compressing, do not shut down Windows or your PC until the compression is finished.

A third possibility is your drive is already compressed using DoubleSpace or the standard DriveSpace. In this case, clicking the Compression tab takes you to a dialog box, which enables you to upgrade your existing compression to DriveSpace 3.

To begin the compression, click whichever button best describes what you want to do. Then follow instructions as they appear onscreen. After compression is complete (which might take several hours), you'll be given a choice of three compression methods:

✦ Standard compression: Compacts data to about half its normal size. This method is the fastest, but conserves the least disk space.

✦ HighPack compression: Compacts a file 10% to 20% more than the standard compression, but takes longer than standard compression.

✦ UltraPack compression: Compresses files more densely than the other two methods, but also takes the longest.

Choose whichever method seems best, given the density/speed trade-off. For example, if keeping things running at top speed is more important than conserving hard disk space, you'll want to select Standard Compression. If disk space is a major problem, you can choose UltraPack. But do note, UltraPack requires you also run the Compression Agent, as described next.

Using the Compression Agent

Once you compress a drive using DriveSpace 3, you can use the Compression Agent to compress files even further. By default, Compression Agent will compress rarely-used files using the UltraPack method. Files you use more frequently will be packed using the faster, HighPack method.

The best way to run Compression Agent is to let System Agent do it for you during odd hours when no one is using the PC heavily. By default, Windows 95 will run Compression Agent at about 10:00 each night. To verify or change that setting, open the System Agent as discussed under "Scheduling Programs with System Agent." Compression Agent will be included in the list, as shown in Figure 39-10.

If you want to run Compression Agent yourself, whether to force a compression now or to explore its Help screens, click the Start button and point to Programs ➪ Accessories ➪ System Tools, and then click Compression Agent.

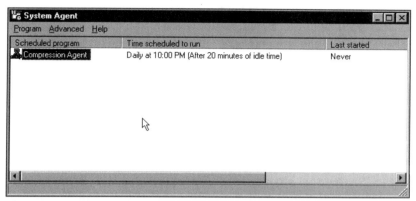

Figure 39-10: Compression Agent added to System Agent

Set Up a Dial-Up Networking Server

The Dial-Up Networking Server component of Microsoft Plus! enables you to configure your Windows 95 PC as a dial-up server. That is, it enables you to set up your PC so it answers the phone when you, or someone else, call in from a Windows 95 PC running the Dial-up Server client (The client comes with standard Windows 95, so you needn't purchase Plus! to dial into an existing server).

When you install Microsoft Plus!, it automatically adds the necessary programs and menu commands you need to set up your dial-up server. Basically, it adds the Dial-Up Server option to the Connections menu in the Dial-Up Networking dialog box (Figure 39-11). For specific instructions on using dial-up networking, see Chapter 20. Pay special attention to the opening sections on Network Neighborhood and sharing resources, and the section titled "Dial-Up Networking."

Figure 39-11: The Dial-Up Server option in Dial-Up Networking

Microsoft Plus! also comes with an early version of Microsoft's Internet Explorer and a (somewhat hidden) version of the Internet kit, which will kick in when you start to set up that version of Internet Explorer. Microsoft Internet Explorer Version 4, however, which is discussed in Part VII of this book, is a significant improvement over that earlier version. So, if you're looking to explore the Internet, I suggest you skip the Internet Explorer on the Plus! disk, and learn about all the latest-and-greatest stuff in Chapters 23-28.

Playing Pinball

After reading this grueling chapter on all the goodies that Plus! offers, you're probably ready to take a break and play a little 3D Pinball:

1. Click the Start button.
2. Point to <u>P</u>rograms ➪ Accessories ➪ Games.
3. Click 3D Pinball to get to the window shown in Figure 39-12.

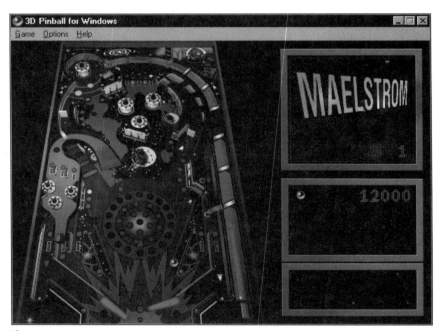

Figure 39-12: 3D Pinball

4. When you're ready to play, choose <u>G</u>ame ➪ <u>L</u>aunch Ball from the menu bar.

Now get your fingers on the Z and / keys, because you'll use those fingers to work the flippers. I trust you can figure out other options on your own, simply by exploring the <u>G</u>ame, <u>O</u>ptions, and <u>H</u>elp commands in the menu bar. I might point out, though, if you switch to full-screen view (<u>O</u>ptions ➪ <u>F</u>ull Screen), you'll need to press the F10 key when you need to get back to the menu bar.

Summary

Microsoft Plus! is an optional add-on package that extends the capabilities of Windows 95. The features in Microsoft Plus! require a 486 or Pentium processor, and preferably a monitor capable of displaying High Color (16-bit). Tools provided by Microsoft Plus! include:

✦ System Agent, which enables you to schedule maintenance tasks to be run at off-hours.

✦ DriveSpace 3, which supports compressed drives up to 2MB in size.

✦ Visual Enhancements, including font smoothing and better color display in icons.

✦ Desktop Themes that enable you to personalize your entire Windows 95 environment.

✦ Dial-Up Networking Server, which enables you to dial into a Windows 95 computer from a remote computer.

✦ Internet Explorer, to connect to the Internet and to explore the World Wide Web.

✦ 3D Pinball, a game that shows off the 3D capabilities of Windows 95.

✦　　✦　　✦

Using Microsoft Exchange

I feel compelled to start this chapter with a confession. When I first began using Microsoft Exchange, I quickly became totally lost and confused. Within minutes of starting Exchange I would have absolutely *no idea* what was happening. I'm telling you because I want you to know if you have this problem, I can relate.

It took me a while to determine the secret to learning Microsoft Exchange. And this secret is: Ignore Microsoft Exchange for a few weeks. That's right, pretend it isn't even there. I know this sounds strange. But after I explain what Exchange *really* is and how to learn about it, my advice might make some sense to you.

What Is Microsoft Exchange?

Microsoft Exchange is a program that manages incoming and outgoing electronic mail and faxes. Exchange is automatically called into play whenever you use one of the following Windows 95 information services:

✦ Faxes sent and received by Microsoft Fax (Chapter 16)

✦ Electronic mail from the Microsoft Network (Chapter 21)

✦ Electronic mail from your local area network (Chapter 33)

And that's not all. Exchange is an open-ended mail receptacle, which manages many other message types as well, including CompuServe mail and Internet mail. The only limitation, in fact, is the availability of software that is capable of talking to the desired service. If you want to check your AOL mail using Exchange and can't, it isn't Exchange's fault — there simply isn't a driver to do this yet.

The reason I recommend you ignore Microsoft Exchange for a few weeks is because you'll find it much easier just to install, and use, any of the messaging services first. As you do so, you'll automatically be introduced to the various components of Exchange relevant to that service. For example, while you're learning to do something *useful*, like send and receive faxes, you'll also be learning a bit about Microsoft Exchange in general. But you'll be learning in a practical, productive manner, which (I think) is the easiest way for most people to learn things.

After you've learned to use services like Microsoft Fax, the Microsoft Network (MSN), Microsoft Mail (local e-mail), Internet Mail or others, *then* you'll find the techniques and concepts described in this chapter make more sense. You'll have some practical experience to which you can anchor the more abstract aspects of Microsoft Exchange.

Starting Microsoft Exchange

You can start Microsoft Exchange in many ways, which, I think, adds to the confusion this program seems to generate. In most situations, Microsoft Exchange starts automatically when some kind of mail or message requires Exchange. You can also fire up Exchange on your own, whenever you want to check your messages, using either of the two following techniques:

✦ Double-click the Inbox icon on the desktop

✦ Choose Start ➪ Programs ➪ Microsoft Exchange.

A dialog box appears telling you Microsoft Exchange is starting. Eventually, this dialog box is replaced by the Inbox for Microsoft Exchange, which looks something like Figure 40-1.

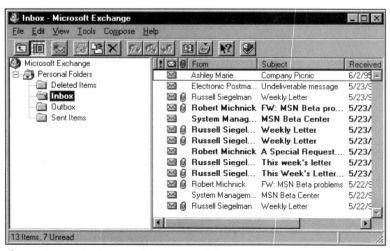

Figure 40-1: The Microsoft Exchange Inbox

What's on the screen

To see all the items shown in Figure 40-1, choose <u>V</u>iew from the menu bar and select any of these items that aren't already selected: Fo<u>l</u>ders, <u>T</u>oolbar, and Status Ba<u>r</u>. Also, I'll be talking about the Show/Hide Folder List, New Message, Address Book, Inbox, and various Reply toolbar buttons, so take a moment to point to (but don't click yet) each button in the toolbar to familiarize yourself with them.

You should be looking at a two-pane view of Exchange now. The left pane lists your personal folders — the folders where your messages are stored. The folder names describe the type of message in each folder:

✦ *Deleted Items:* Contains messages you deleted from one of the other three folders. These "deleted" copies are maintained as a backup, until you're sure you want to delete the messages permanently.

✦ *Inbox:* Stores new messages you've received from other people.

✦ *Outbox:* Stores messages you've written to other people, but have not sent yet.

✦ *Sent Items:* Stores a copy of every message you've sent.

The right pane shows the contents of whatever folder is open. For example, when you click the Inbox folder name, the pane on the right shows messages you've received. Seven columns are across the top pane (although in Figure 40-1, the last column is scrolled out of view.) The columns are:

✦ *exclamation point (!):* This column is marked if the message is marked "Urgent"

✦ *(envelope):* Marked if the message contains both a written message and an attached file

✦ *(paper clip):* Marked if the message contains an attachment (a file)

✦ *From:* Sender's name (if known)

✦ *Subject:* The subject line the sender typed in

✦ *Received:* The date and time the message was received

✦ *Size:* The size of the message in kilobytes (KB)

You can customize, add, and delete columns by choosing <u>V</u>iew ⇨ Columns. You can also instantly sort messages by any column by clicking the appropriate column heading. If you sort the From column heading, for example, messages are alphabetized by sender. In the Inbox, messages you have not read yet are in boldface.

Installing Message Services

While we'd love to jump in and start sending and receiving messages, this isn't possible unless Exchange has first been configured to handle the kind of messages you want. Think of the program as a container that holds many different kinds of messages — Internet mail, CompuServe mail, faxes, and Microsoft Network mail, for instance — and before Exchange can deal with them, you must install software drivers (called services) that let Exchange work with each of them.

This is both Exchange's curse and blessing — its open-ended structure means it is one-stop shopping for your message needs, but you first must get your hands dirty to set it all up.

Your copy of Exchange may have come with some of your message services already configured, but odds are excellent you'll need to finish the job. Whenever you want to add a new service, this is the general procedure:

1. Start Microsoft Exchange using either method described previously.

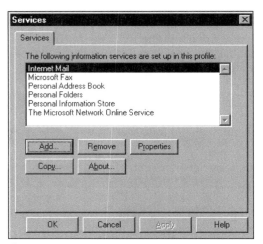

Figure 40-2: The Message Services property sheet

2. Choose Tools ➪ Services. A dialog box like the one in Figure 40-2 will appear with a list of all the services you have installed. Depending on how your system is set up, you may have one, several, or none already in the list of services.

3. Click the Add button. A dialog box appears with a list of all the available services, shown in Figure 40-3. Choose the service you want and click OK.

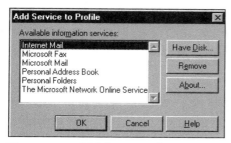

Figure 40-3: Add these services to Exchange to send and receive the appropriate messages types.

4. Follow any directions onscreen to install the desired service. You will probably need to have additional information, such as your logon name, password, or phone number, depending on what kind of service you choose to install.

Setting up Internet Mail

These days, one of the most common messaging systems is Internet e-mail. The Internet offers fast, reliable, and universally accepted electronic mail, which isn't subject to the same kinds of proprietary limitations as systems like MCI Mail, CompuServe, or AOL. Chances are, if you are already connected to the Internet, you already have some kind of program for managing your Internet e-mail. If you don't, I suggest you try either Microsoft Internet Explorer version 3.0 (or higher), available from `http://www.microsoft.com`. Or you might want to try Netscape Navigator 3.0 (or higher), available from `http://home.netscape.com`. Both are top-notch Web browsers with great Internet e-mail messaging built right in. And, to tell you the truth, the best way to do Internet e-mail is probably right from your Web browser.

If you *really* want to use Microsoft Exchange for Internet e-mail, you'll need to install the Internet Mail service in Exchange. Follow the previously listed steps for installing message services, and then complete the property sheet for Internet Mail.

In the General tab, shown in Figure 40-4, you need to enter this information:

✦ *Full name:* Enter the name as you want it to appear in other people's mail systems.

✦ *E-mail address:* This is your address, usually expressed as `yourname@yourprovider.com`.

✦ *Internet Mail server:* You must contact your ISP for the correct name. It is often `yourprovider.com`, the latter half of your e-mail address.

✦ *Account name:* This is the first part of your e-mail address, such as yourname.

✦ *Password:* This is the password your ISP gave you to access your Internet account. Be aware, many ISPs use case-sensitive passwords, so be sure to use the correct upper/lowercase letters here.

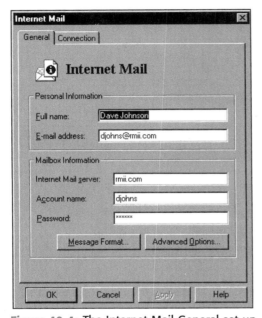

Figure 40-4: The Internet Mail General set-up

In the Connection tab, shown in Figure 40-5, you must finish the set-up:

✦ *Connect using...:* If you use either Dial-up Networking or a local area network (LAN) to connect to the Internet, select Connect using the network.

✦ *Transferring Internet Mail:* If you stay online most of the time through a direct Internet connection (such as a LAN or a free Internet connection) Exchange will work online and check e-mail periodically for you. If you only connect at certain times of the day, check the box that says Work offline and use Remote Mail.

What if you have more than one Internet mail account? Exchange doesn't let you add two identical services. The solution is to create multiple profiles — explained at the end of this chapter — and configure each profile for a different mail account.

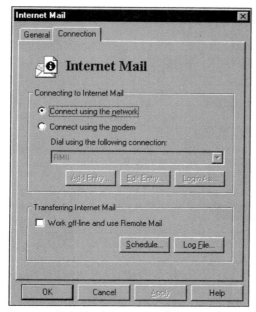

Figure 40-5: The Internet Mail Connection set-up

Setting up CompuServe Mail

You can configure Microsoft Exchange to send mail to and receive mail from your CompuServe account but, to do this, you must download the CompuServe service driver for Exchange. You can get the file from a number of places, but one of the most convenient is Microsoft's Web site at http://www.microsoft.com/windows/software/drivers/other.htm.

Once you install this service, you must fill out its property sheet just like the Internet Mail service. This service has four tabs on the property sheet, but it isn't difficult to fill out; you simply must know some details about your CompuServe account, which you may not have bothered with in years, so get this stuff handy:

✦ On the General tab (see Figure 40-6), fill out your name, CompuServe ID, and password. If you haven't saved the original letter from CompuServe with your password on it, you may need to call CompuServe customer service and get a new one.

Figure 40-6: The CompuServe Mail General set-up

✦ The Connection tab (see Figure 40-7) has modem-specific information. Enter the phone number you use to connect to CompuServe and your modem connection. Or, if you connect to CompuServe through a local area network, consult your company's network administrator for the appropriate information.

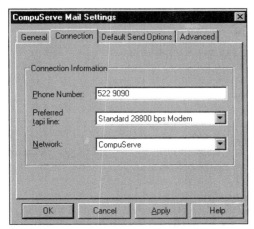

Figure 40-7: The CompuServe Mail Connection set-up

✦ The Default Send Options tab (see Figure 40-8) can be left as it is unless you have unique needs, such as you want sent mail delayed until a certain date.

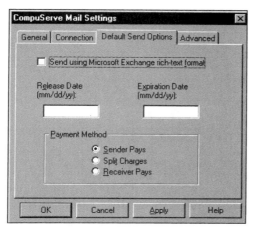

Figure 40-8: The CompuServe Mail Default Send Options set-up

✦ The Advanced tab isn't all that advanced (see Figure 40-9). You'll probably want to deselect Create Event Log; otherwise, your Exchange inbox will fill with messages about the status of Exchange's attempts to send and receive CompuServe e-mail. Also make sure Delete Retrieved Messages is selected, or mail you download from CompuServe will remain on CompuServe's server.

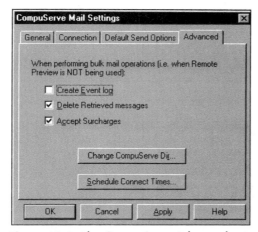

Figure 40-9: The CompuServe Advanced set-up

Installing other services

Internet Mail and CompuServe Mail are the most complicated services to
configure. Others, such as Microsoft Fax and Microsoft Network, do not require as
much work to set up. To learn how to set up Microsoft Fax, see Chapter 16. The
Microsoft Network is discussed in Chapter 21.

Managing Received Messages

The real purpose of Microsoft Exchange is to give you a central place from which
to view, respond to, and send messages. Exchange certainly excels in that
department, because it enables you to whip through your messages quickly. To
read a message, just double-click it. The message appears in a larger window
called the message viewer, as in the example shown in Figure 40-10.

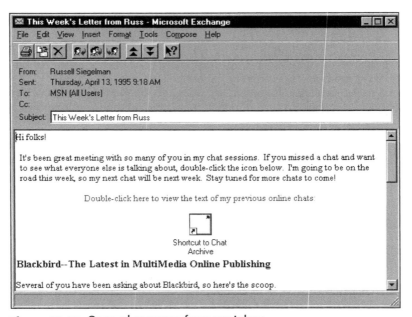

Figure 40-10: Opened message from my Inbox

You can use the toolbar buttons to manage the message as follows:

    ✦ To print a message, just click the Print button in the toolbar.

    ✦ To reply to the sender, just click the Reply to Sender button.

✦ To reply to the sender and all the original recipients, click the Reply to All button.

✦ To forward the message to someone else, click the Forward button.

✦ To delete the message, click the Delete button. The message goes into your Deleted Items folder.

✦ To move the message to some folder other than Deleted Items, click the Move Item button.

✦ To move to the next message, click the Next button.

✦ To move back to the previous message, click the Previous button.

✦ To close the message viewer, click its Close (X) button.

Hot Stuff You can do many of the toolbar functions faster without the toolbar. To delete a message, press the Delete key. To move it to another folder, use the mouse to drag-and-drop it on the desired location.

Now let's take a look at the ways in which you can compose and send messages.

Composing and Sending Messages

You can use Microsoft Exchange as a central area for composing and sending all types of e-mail messages and faxes. Follow these easy steps:

✦ If you're not already in Microsoft Exchange, double-click the Inbox icon or click the Start button and choose Programs ➪ Microsoft Exchange.

Do either of the following:

✦ If you want to reply to a message in your Inbox, click the Reply to Sender or Reply to All button in the toolbar.

✦ If you want to compose a message from scratch, click the New Message button or choose Compose ➪ New Message from Exchange's menu bar.

Either way, you end up at the New Message window shown in Figure 40-11.

This small New Message window offers a ton of features to make quick work of addressing, typing, and sending an e-mail message. I'll talk about those features in the sections that follow. If you're in a hurry, however, plenty of help is available from the New Message window. As in most windows, you can turn the toolbars on and off using commands on the View menu. You can point to any toolbar button to display its tooltip. If you want an explanation of some item in the New Message window, you can click the question-mark button and then click the item with which you want help.

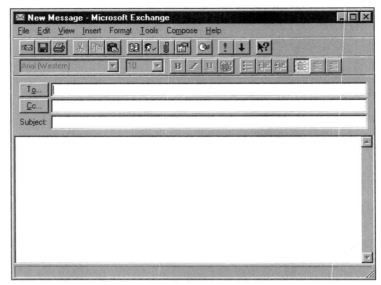

Figure 40-11: Exchange's New Message window

Hot Stuff

If you just want to type and send a quick fax, you can use the Compose New Fax wizard. If you're in Exchange, choose Compose ➪ New Fax from the menu bar. If you're at the desktop, click the Start button and choose Programs ➪ Accessories ➪ Fax ➪ Compose New Fax. See Chapter 16 for more information.

The New Message window also offers a direct route to many of your installed information services. Click the Help command in the menu bar, and choose the topic with which you want help (Figure 40-12.)

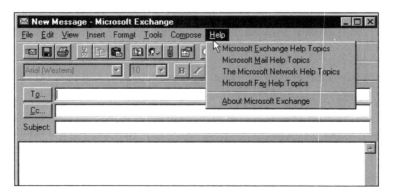

Figure 40-12: The Help menu in the New Message window

Addressing a message

If you're replying to someone else's message, your new message is already addressed to that person. If you're creating a message from scratch, you can click the T<u>o</u> button to address your message. Follow these steps:

Hot Stuff You can also send blind carbon copies of messages. To enable this feature, choose <u>V</u>iew ➪ B<u>c</u>c box from the New Message window's menu bar.

1. Click the T<u>o</u> button.

2. In the drop-down list box to the right of <u>S</u>how names from the option, choose an address book. The options available will depend on which information services you've installed, as follows:

   - *Personal Address Book:* Your personal "little black book" of names and addresses. You need to maintain this book yourself, using the general techniques described under "Setting Up Your Personal Address Book" in Chapter 16.

   - *Microsoft Network:* Names and addresses of MSN members, maintained automatically by MSN. You only have access to this list when you're actually online with MSN.

   - *Postoffice Address Book:* Other members of your local e-mail system or workgroup, maintained automatically by Microsoft Mail.

3. If the list of names is long, type the first few letters of the recipient's name to jump quickly to the appropriate part of the list. When you find the recipient's name, click the T<u>o</u> button.

4. Optionally, to send a copy to another person, select that person's name from the list and click the <u>C</u>c button.

Life Saver If you accidentally copy the wrong name to the recipient column, just click that name and press the Delete (Del) key to remove the name from the column.

5. Repeat Steps 3 and 4 to choose as many recipient and copy-recipient names as you wish. Figure 40-13 shows an example.

6. Choose OK when you've finished selecting recipients' names to return to the New Message window.

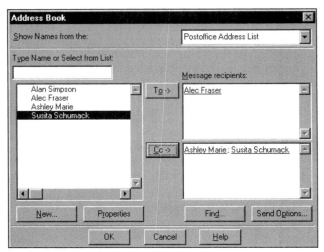

Figure 40-13: Recipient names selected

You can quickly address a message without opening the address book. Simply type part of the recipient's name and click the Check Names icon in the toolbar. Exchange will search the address book and finish the address for you. Be careful, though. If several names exist that match the name for which you're looking (for example, you search for John and several people are named John), Exchange will pick the first one.

You may also type recipients' names without picking them from the address book list. If you enter multiple names, be sure to separate each name with a semicolon (;). The To and cc portions of the New Message window now contain the names of all the recipients.

Filling in the subject

Whatever you type into the Subject line is what appears in the recipient's Inbox. Keep this line brief, so the recipient has some idea what the message is about before he or she opens it. Figure 40-14 shows an example where I selected recipients, typed in a subject, and am ready to type the body of the message.

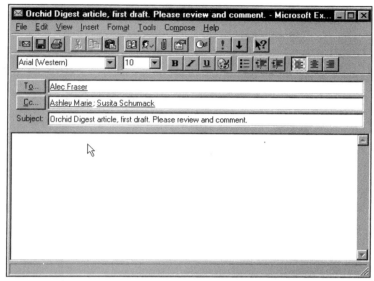

Figure 40-14: Recipients and subject typed in

Typing and editing the message

The large text box is where you'll type your actual message. You can use all the standard Windows text-editing tools and techniques. You can also select text by dragging the mouse pointer through it or by holding down the Shift key while tapping the cursor-positioning keys. Once you've selected text, you can apply any of the formatting features to that text: Font, Size, Bold, Italic, Underline, Color, Bullets, Decrease Indent, Increase Indent, Align Left, Center, or Align Right.

If the formatting features aren't visible, choose <u>V</u>iew ➪ <u>F</u>ormatting Toolbar from the New Message menu bar.

No matter how many formatting flourishes you give your e-mail, it will still arrive as plain text unless the recipient is also using Microsoft Exchange.

Attaching a file to the message

You can attach any file, or combination of files, to a message. The file can be a program, document, another message, whatever. When you attach a file, the attachment appears as an icon in the message. When the recipient receives the message, he or she sees the icon as well. Generally, you should include brief instructions telling the recipient how to use the icon.

Most people center the descriptive text and the icon in a message. If you want to format your message this way, follow these steps:

1. Move the insertion point to the place in your message where you want the descriptive text to appear. (If you need to insert a blank line, press Enter once or twice.)

2. Type the descriptive text, as in the example shown in Figure 40-15.

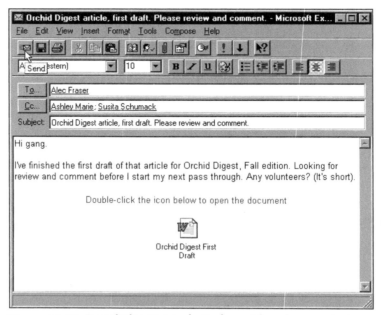

Figure 40-15: Descriptive text and attachment icon in an outgoing message

3. If you want to center the descriptive text, click the Center button in the Formatting toolbar.

4. To make room for the attachment, press the End key to move to the end of the descriptive text line; then press Enter to move down a line.

5. Click the Insert File (paper clip) button in the toolbar.

6. Browse to and select the file you want to insert.

7. Choose OK.

Both the descriptive text and the icon now appear in your message, as shown in Figure 40-15. If you want to add more text, you can press Enter once or twice to insert blank lines. To align the new text to the left margin, click the Align Left button.

More Info You can also insert text from a file, an object, or another message into the body of your message, using options on the Insert menu. For more information, choose Help ⇨ Microsoft Exchange Topics from the New Message menu bar. Then use the Index and Find tabs to search for the topic *insert*.

Assigning properties to the message

You can assign several properties to the message before sending it. Click the Properties button in the toolbar, or choose File ⇨ Properties from the New Message menu bar. Choose your options from the dialog box that appears (see Figure 40-16); and then choose OK.

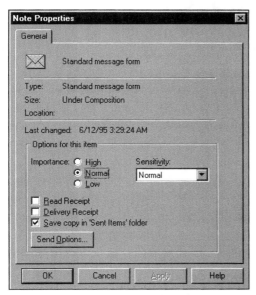

Figure 40-16: Properties assigned to a message

Sending the message

When you're ready to send the message, click the Send button in the toolbar. Exactly when the message gets sent depends on how you set properties for the specific information service you're using to send the message. You can always check the status of a message, and send it immediately if necessary. Follow these steps:

1. If you closed Microsoft Exchange, reopen it by double-clicking the Inbox icon, or choosing Start ⇨ Programs ⇨ Microsoft Exchange.

2. If the Folder List isn't visible, choose View ⇨ Folders or click the Show/Hide Folder List button.

3. Click the Outbox folder.

Any items listed in the Outbox are waiting to be sent.

To send one of the Outbox items immediately, click its name, then choose Tools ➪ Deliver Now. If you have two or more services installed, choose Tools ➪ Deliver Now Using, and then the service you want to use to send the message. Or, you can press Ctrl+M to send and receive mail at any time.

After a message has been sent successfully, it no longer appears in the Outbox. Instead, it appears in your Sent Items folder.

Clearing Out Old Messages

As mentioned earlier, Exchange keeps copies of all the messages you send and receive. Eventually, all these messages will start eating up disk space, so you must clear out old messages occasionally. Follow these steps:

1. Open your Inbox by double-clicking the Inbox icon or choosing Start ➪ Programs ➪ Microsoft Exchange.

2. Make sure you can see the folder list (choose View ➪ Folders or click the Show/Hide Folder List button.)

3. Click the Inbox folder.

4. Select any messages you want to eliminate. You can Ctrl+click and Shift+click to select multiple messages.

5. Click the Delete button in the toolbar.

6. Click the Sent Items folder.

7. Shift+click or Ctrl+click to select any messages you want to eliminate.

8. Click the Delete button to delete the selected messages.

9. Click the Deleted Items folder. The messages in this folder have been deleted from some other folder, but remain on your disk as backups.

10. Shift+click or Ctrl+click to select any messages you want to delete permanently.

11. Click the Delete button.

You see a warning, as shown in Figure 40-17.

Hot Stuff If you believe you should only have to handle a message once, you'll also want a message to erase itself when you delete it. Choose Tools ➪ Options and check the box for Empty the Deleted Items Folder Upon Exiting. If desired, also check Warn Before Permanently Deleting Items. Now you only have to delete a message once and Steps 9, 10, and 11 are unnecessary.

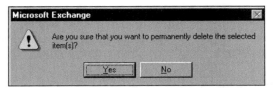

Figure 40-17: Final warning on permanently deleting messages

12. If you're sure you want to delete these messages permanently and reclaim the disk space they're using, choose <u>Y</u>es.

Customizing Exchange

I've directed your attention several times to the property sheet for Exchange's options. You can get there by choosing <u>T</u>ools ➪ <u>O</u>ptions. This dialog box (see Figure 40-18) is worth a second look because you can do so many things to customize the way the program works.

    ✦ *General.* This tab affects the way Exchange tells you about new mail. It also controls what happens to mail when you delete it and which profile is used (see "Understanding Exchange Profiles" later in this chapter for information on profiles). If you use multiple profiles, be sure to select <u>P</u>rompt for a profile to be used.

    ✦ *Read.* This tab controls what happens after you delete or move a mail message. It also affects the style of the message when you reply to someone else's e-mail. Typically, people "quote" the original message — if you want to do this, be sure to select <u>I</u>nclude the original text when replying.

    ✦ *Send.* If you want to know when a recipient has received or read your message, check the appropriate box on this sheet. While it doesn't affect the speed at which mail travels, you can also set it as Private or High Importance if you like — your message will be so marked on the recipient's computer when received.

    ✦ *Spelling.* It is a good idea to turn the spelling checker on from this tab so mail doesn't get sent with misspelled words.

    ✦ *Services.* This tab duplicates the <u>T</u>ools ➪ Ser<u>v</u>ices menu, which you can use to install or modify message services.

    ✦ *Delivery.* This confusing-looking tab performs two functions. First, if you have more than one set of folders installed, the top section determines where new mail is delivered. Most people only have one set of folders and that is, in fact, the default. Second, the bottom determines in what order Exchange will attempt to send a message.

✦ *Addressing.* Similar to the Delivery tab, this sheet prioritizes address lists. The bottom, for instance, determines in which order Exchange will search for addressees. If you have a Microsoft Network and an Internet e-mail address for the same individual, this determines which Exchange tries to use by default.

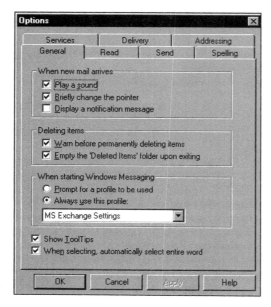

Figure 40-18: The Options dialog box contains property sheets to customize Exchange.

Understanding Exchange Profiles

One aspect of Microsoft Exchange that confuses people is the difference between *information services* and *profiles.* Here are definitions of each of these terms:

✦ *Information service*: A service to which Exchange gives you access, Microsoft Fax, Microsoft Mail, Microsoft Network, and Personal Address Book.

✦ *Profile*: A collection of information settings for a single user of the PC.

If two or more people share a PC, chances are each person will want to set up his or her own Exchange Profile, because buried within the profile is such information as return address, phone number, cover sheet selections, and so forth.

The easiest way to set up a profile is for one user to set up his or her own information services: Fax, personal address book, MSN, and local e-mail, as discussed in the chapters on those topics (Chapters 16, 21, 27). When this profile is set up, another user can copy this profile to a new profile under his or her name, and then tweak the profile to suit personal needs. To copy an existing profile, follow these steps:

1. Choose Start ➪ Settings ➪ Control Panel.

2. Double-click the Mail and Fax icon.

3. In the first dialog box that appears, click the Show Profiles button.

4. To copy the existing profile, click it once and then click the Copy button.

5. Type in a descriptive name for this new profile.

6. Choose OK.

The new profile appears in the list of profile names. For example, in Figure 40-19, I copied the original MS Exchange Settings to Ashley's Exchange Profile. Notice within the same dialog box, you can specify which profile acts as the default profile.

Figure 40-19: Two Exchange profiles are on this computer.

To tweak the settings in Ashley's Exchange Profile, click her profile name in the list and then click the Properties button. A list of information services included in Ashley's profile appears (see Figure 40-20.) In this example, Ashley's profile contains all the same information settings as the MS Exchange Settings profile, because I copied that profile to create Ashley's profile.

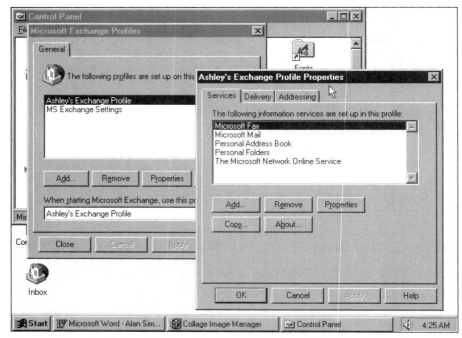

Figure 40-20: Ready to start tweaking Ashley's Exchange Profile

Click any information within Ashley's Exchange Profile (for example, Microsoft Fax, Microsoft Mail, and so on) and then click the Properties button to view and, optionally, to modify the settings to tailor them to Ashley's profile. When you finish, click OK and Close, as appropriate, to work your way back to the Control Panel. (You can also close the Control panel, if you wish.)

Now that you have more than one profile defined on this PC, you'll probably want Windows to prompt you for which profile to use at any given moment. To do so, follow these steps:

1. Open Microsoft Exchange (double-click the Inbox icon or choose Start ➪ Programs ➪ Microsoft Exchange).

2. Choose Tools ➪ Options.

3. Under When Starting Microsoft Exchange choose Prompt for a profile to be used, as shown in Figure 40-21.

4. Choose OK.

From now on, whenever you open Microsoft Exchange, you'll be prompted to choose a profile, as shown in Figure 40-22. Select a profile from the drop-down list and then choose OK.

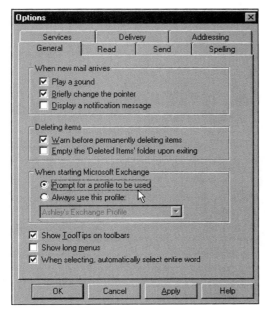

Figure 40-21: Telling Exchange to prompt for a profile

Updating Exchange

Since the release of Windows 95, Microsoft has released a newer version of Exchange. You may want to update to this version of Exchange if you have either a computer with limited memory or use Microsoft Mail in conjunction with Exchange. The new version does the following:

✦ Changes the name from Microsoft Exchange to Windows Messaging

✦ Runs faster on an 8MB computer

✦ Permits access to Microsoft Mail shared folders

✦ Speeds startup time

Aside from these changes, no new features exist in this updated version of the program. If you choose to install the update, you can find it on Microsoft's Web site at `http://www.microsoft.com/windows/software/exupd.htm`. After downloading the file, simply double-click the icon and let the update install. Despite the name change to Windows Messaging, it is identical to the Exchange you to know.

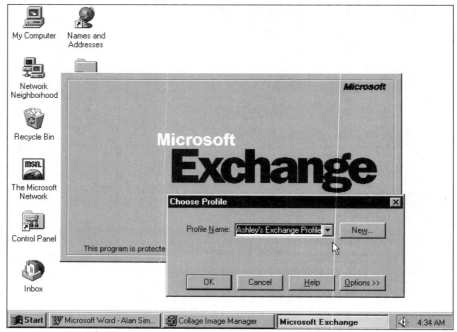

Figure 40-22: Exchange prompting me to pick a profile

Summary

Here are the main points to remember from this chapter:

✦ Microsoft Exchange is a central area for managing incoming and outgoing messages.

✦ The messages are handled by different information services within Exchange: Microsoft Fax, Microsoft Mail, Internet Mail, and Microsoft Network (MSN).

✦ Before any kind of message can be used, the appropriate service must be installed from Tools ➪ Services.

✦ To open Exchange, double-click the Inbox icon on the desktop, or choose Start ➪ Programs ➪ Microsoft Exchange.

✦ The Inbox in Exchange shows messages you've received. Double-click any message to read it.

✦ To reply to a message, click one of the Reply buttons in the toolbar.

✦ To create a message from scratch, click the New Message button in Exchange.

✦ If several people share the same PC, each person can create a separate Microsoft Exchange Profile.

✦   ✦   ✦

Using Microsoft Outlook

O ne of the real gems of the new Microsoft Office suite is a program called Microsoft Outlook. Learning the ins, outs, and back alleys of this program is worthwhile because, if you're like me, you'll leave this one on most of the time. It may well become the cornerstone of your day — a tool that serves as the launching point for most of the other things you do.

What is Microsoft Outlook?

Imagine Microsoft Exchange on steroids. Or, perhaps more appropriately, imagine Exchange after four semesters of night school, where it learned a bunch of new skills to help you though the day. Outlook is a full-featured Personal Information Manager (PIM) combining Exchange's inbox, some features of Office 95's Schedule+ program, and a new and improved Office 97 interface. Outlook performs the following tasks for you:

+ Sends and receives e-mail and faxes

+ Reminds you about appointments and to-dos

+ Keeps a record of what Microsoft Office projects you have worked on and for how long

+ Stores personal reminders on yellow *stickies*

+ Maintains a comprehensive contact database of companies and individuals

This chapter introduces you to many of the techniques you need to get the most from the flexible new program.

Getting around the Outlook window

The first time you start Outlook, you may be overwhelmed by all its tools, panes, icons, and menus. Let's take a short tour of the screen and see what's there. If you don't see essentially the same thing on your screen as what's in Figure 41-1, you can easily remedy this. Select Ｖiew from the menu bar, then ensure the last three options are selected: Ｓtatus Bar, Folde̲r List and Ｏutlook Bar. Aside from the messages in the inbox and list of folders on the left, our displays should be similar.

The pane on the far left of the display is called the Outlook Bar. The *Outlook Bar* is a scrollable list of icons that enable you to get to different parts of the program quickly, much like shortcuts on the Windows desktop.

The next pane contains a list of all the personal folders in Outlook. Unlike Exchange, which lists only e-mail folders here, you'll find much more in Outlook. The choices are:

✦ *Calendar*: This Outlook module contains an appointment calendar and to-do list for managing your time — similar to Schedule+ in functionality, but with a new-and-improved look and feel.

✦ *Contacts*: This module is home to a comprehensive personal address book, far more complete than the one that comes with Exchange.

✦ *Deleted Items*: This is a temporary wastebasket that stores messages you've eliminated from other parts of the program.

✦ *Inbox*: New messages arrive in this folder by default.

✦ *Journal*: This is a logbook that records how you've spent your time — on messages, phone calls, and Microsoft Office applications — while using the computer.

✦ *Notes*: Yellow stickies you can use to create free-form messages to yourself.

✦ *Outbox*: Stores unsent messages.

✦ *Sent Items*: Copies of all the mail you've sent to others.

✦ *Stored*: A filing cabinet, if you will, of messages you want to save.

✦ *Tasks*: A list of all the to-do items. This is another view of the same information stored in the Calendar.

By and large, Outlook looks, and is, similar to Exchange. You can do everything with Outlook you do in Exchange — send, receive, and file mail messages or faxes — and it works the same way. In fact, if you want to learn how to turn your PC into a post office and fax machine with Outlook, check the previous chapter, "Using Microsoft Exchange." Now, let's do some things with Outlook you can't do with Exchange.

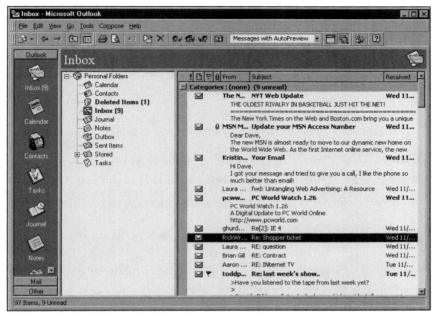

Figure 41-1: Microsoft Outlook in its inbox mode

Outlook's many methods

At least three ways exist to get at most of the dialog boxes in Outlook when you're trying to create a new entry, whether it's a meeting, task, contact, or some other sort of object. While the procedures in the rest of the chapter tend to use only one of these methods, in reality there are others; I've simply chosen the one that seems easiest. Here are more ways to do anything in Outlook:

✦ Choose the appropriate menu item. For instance, to add an appointment to your list of things to do, choose Calendar ➪ New Appointment.

✦ Double-click. Find the time you'd like to place the appointment in your schedule and double-click with the left mouse button.

✦ Right-click. Find the time you want to place your appointment and click with the right mouse button. A context-sensitive menu appears with a list of all the things you can do; New Appointment is one of them.

Remember, many ways exist to accomplish anything in Outlook. Find the way that works best for you — whether it's double-clicking or using the menu — and run with it.

How Mail Is Different

As I said before, Outlook is a pumped-up version of Exchange. So while Outlook sends, receives, and stores messages for you, it does everything a little differently. The most obvious — and useful — difference is the way Outlook displays new mail. By default, new messages are displayed in AutoPreview mode. This shows the first few lines of the message in the inbox, so you can get the gist of a message without opening the file. If you don't like AutoPreview mode, you can select other options from the toolbar. Just click the drop-down menu and you have these options:

✦ *Messages*. This view is the same, plain vanilla view Exchange uses.

✦ *Messages with AutoPreview*. This shows a portion of the new message.

✦ *By Message Flag*. This groups messages according to those that are, and are not, flagged.

✦ *Last Seven Days*. This displays only the last week's messages.

✦ *By Conversation Topic*. This groups together responses and follow-up messages to the same subject line, which makes following a message "thread" and checking for necessary action easier.

✦ *By Sender*. This groups together messages from the same person.

✦ *Unread Messages*. This eliminates the clutter and displays only those messages that have not yet been opened.

✦ *Message Timeline*. This places all your e-mail messages as icons along a timeline to depict the chronology of their arrival graphically (see Figure 41-2).

Managing Your Schedule

Outlook includes a complete Personal Information Manager (PIM). To get to it, simply click the Calendar icon in the Outlook Bar or choose Go ➪ Calendar.

Once you select the Calendar mode, the left side of the screen is unchanged — it still displays folders and the Outlook Bar. As you can see from Figure 41-3, the right side is divided into three zones: a daily schedule down the middle, with a monthly calendar atop a list of to-dos. While the display looks simple, you can do many things in many ways here.

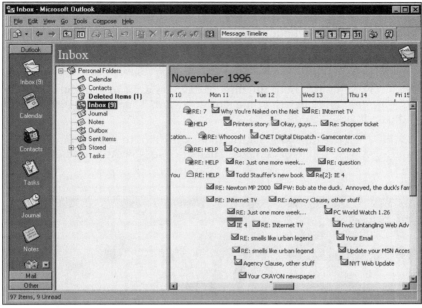

Figure 41-2: The Message Timeline is one of the many new ways to view your mail using Outlook.

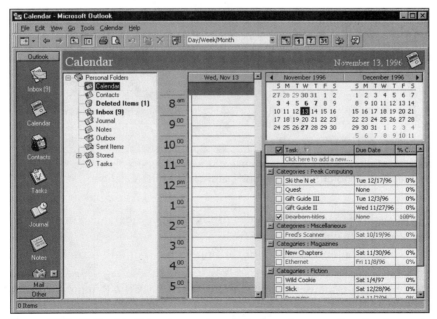

Figure 41-3: Outlook's Calendar mode puts tasks, a two-month calendar, and the day's appointments on the same screen.

Appointments, meetings, and events

You can use Outlook to schedule major events throughout your day and to obtain timely reminders before they occur. To schedule an appointment, for instance, follow these steps:

1. Position the pointer over the time of day you want to schedule an appointment and click the time slot you want. The slot will turn blue to indicate it is selected.

2. Double-click the time slot. Or, right-click the slot to see a context menu offering a wide range of choices. Then choose New Appointment (see Figure 41-4).

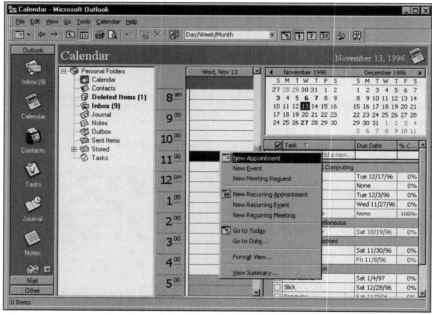

Figure 41-4: Outlook makes extensive use of the right mouse button to simplify tasks like adding appointments, meetings, and tasks to the Calendar.

3. A dialog box appears. Type a descriptive title in the Subject line. This is how the appointment appears onscreen.

4. Or, you can enter a location for the appointment or add extra notes in the large text area at the bottom of the dialog box.

5. If you want a reminder of this appointment, check the Reminder box in the middle of the dialog box. You can click the drop-down box to the right of the Reminder box to set how early the reminder will occur. The default is 15 minutes.

6. If you want to change the start or end time of the appointment, drop-down menus are provided to adjust either the date or time.

7. When you finish setting up the appointment (it should look something like Figure 41-5), click the Save and Close button at the top left of the dialog box.

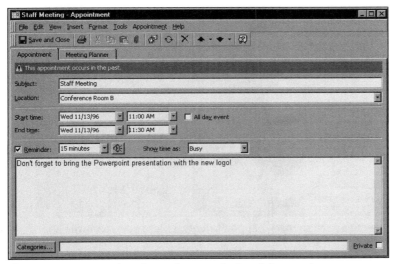

Figure 41-5: A completed appointment before it is saved

The procedure to create meetings and events is essentially the same. Meetings are just like appointments, except you have the ability to invite others. Open a new meeting request as you did for an appointment. Notice an additional line — labeled To: — appears atop the dialog box. Click the To: button and you have the opportunity to add e-mail recipients to the meeting (see Figure 41-6). Recipients will receive an invitation to the meeting you set up.

Events are a bit different than appointments or meetings because they are associated with a day, not a time. Open a new event dialog box just as we did earlier with the right mouse button. Notice the dialog box is similar to the one for appointments, except the dialog box has no start and stop time.

Hot Stuff   If you open a new appointment by accident, you can turn it into an event by clicking the box marked All day event.

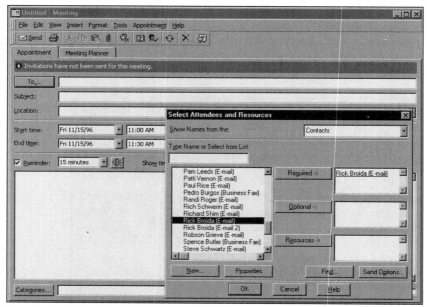

Figure 41-6: Meetings are similar to appointments, except you can invite others via e-mail.

Tasks

Not everything you must do can be scheduled into a specific time of day. While events are useful for marking the entire day — such as COMDEX or Flag Day — the bread and butter of a PIM is the ability to list, sort, and track the myriad of tasks we all must do each day. Go to the post office, get a haircut, and feed the dog are all examples of tasks you may choose to track in Outlook. To create a task, follow these steps:

1. Move the mouse over the task list region of the screen and click with the right mouse button. Choose New Task.

2. A dialog box appears. Name the task in the Subject line and assign a due date, if appropriate. You can add extra details in the large text box, if desired.

3. Click Save and Close to exit.

Displaying Tasks

Outlook gives you great power to track your tasks. You can enter priority and percent complete, for instance, to keep tabs on which tasks are most important and how close to completion they are. You can modify the way the tasks display onscreen as well, to help you track your progress. Choose View ➪ Taskpad Settings ➪ Show Fields. A dialog box like the one in Figure 41-7 enables you to customize the displayed fields. Move the fields you want to see, like % Complete, from the left side of the dialog box to the right and click OK. The Calendar view will update to the requested fields.

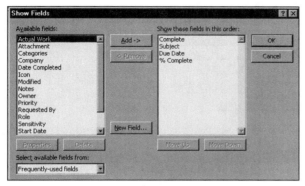

Figure 41-7: The Show Fields dialog box

Using Contacts

Exchange had a rudimentary personal address book, which is still at your disposal in Outlook. But Outlook adds a formidable new tool: Contacts. This full-featured phone book database enables you to track details that go far beyond simple e-mail addresses. Contacts includes fields for addresses, phone numbers, Web pages, company information, and personal data. You don't need to include all this information; just enter what you have or need. You can always add more details later.

To create a Contact entry, follow these steps:

1. Click the Contact icon in the Outlook Bar.

2. Choose Contacts ➪ New Contact from the menu bar. The Contact dialog box opens as shown in Figure 41-8.

3. Enter the individual's name. By default, the name is rearranged into Last, First format in the File as line. The latter is the way the name appears on the Contacts screen.

4. Enter an e-mail address and press Return. Outlook will verify the address is formatted properly and underline it. If the address is formatted incorrectly (perhaps missing a .com, for instance), a dialog box will appear to help you correct the error.

5. Enter a phone number.

6. Click Save and Close to leave the dialog box.

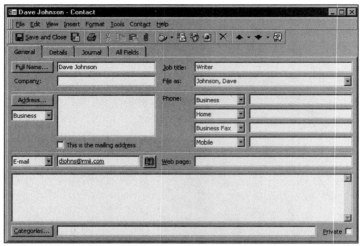

Figure 41-8: The Contact dialog box

When you create a new contact, the first name you enter into the dialog box — the company or an individual's name — is the default name used to file the contact.

You can reopen the contact at any time and enter more data or edit information you've already provided. Simply find the entry on the right side of the screen and double-click the name.

Contacts are good for what?

If you choose to keep all your contact information in Outlook, you can do many neat things with them. Some of these things are accessible from the ever-useful right mouse button. Click the Contacts icon in the Outlook Bar and find a filled-out address. If you're just getting started with Outlook, perhaps you should begin by creating an entry for experimentation. Be sure to enter a phone number, e-mail address, and Web site in the appropriate fields. When you're done, click the entry with the right mouse button. You should see a context-sensitive menu with several options. Some of the most important options include:

AutoDialer

Choose this option and Outlook dials the contact's phone number. To use AutoDialer, follow these steps:

1. Move the mouse over the desired contact and choose AutoDialer from the right mouse button's context menu. The New Call dialog box opens, as in Figure 41-9.

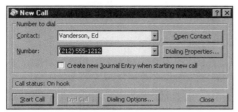

Figure 41-9: Call contacts automatically from the New Call dialog box.

2. If the contact has more than one telephone number, choose the appropriate number from the drop-down menu.

3. If you want to keep a record of the phone call, check the box for Create new Journal Entry when you begin a new call.

4. When you're ready to place the call, click the Start Call button.

5. When the number begins to dial, the Call Status dialog box opens. Click the Talk button, pick up your phone, and wait to begin to talk.

6. If you want to record the call in the Journal, enter any notes you want in the large text box and click Save and Close when you finish with the call.

Outlook even has a speed dial! Add a number to the speed dial list from the New Call dialog box — click the Dialing Options button and enter the name and number. Speed dial is accessed from the toolbar button shaped like a phone.

Explore Web Page

Another way you can use Contacts is to surf to someone's corporate or personal Web page automatically. Simply choose Explore Web Page from the right mouse button menu and Outlook will launch your Web browser and send it directly to the site you entered in the Contact file.

E-mail

You can use Outlook as a personal address book when you send and receive e-mail. If you receive e-mail from a new contact and want to add that person's name to Contacts, the easiest way is to open the e-mail message and right-click the person's name in the From: line as in Figure 41-10. Choose Add to Contacts. A new Contact dialog box opens, with the name and e-mail address filled in already.

When you add a new e-mail address to Contacts, the entire e-mail address often goes in the person's name box. You can correct this Outlook idiosyncrasy before saving the new contact.

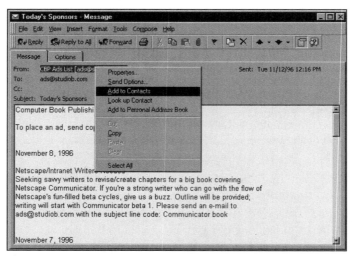

Figure 41-10: Invite people to your meetings from your personal address book.

Keeping a Journal

Have you ever needed to account for your time? Do you want to log all your phone calls — or at least the most important ones — and keep track of who said what? Want to know how long you worked on particular documents for precise invoicing? Outlook's Journal enables you to do all this with little effort.

Configuring the Journal

Before you can begin tracking all these things in Outlook, you must turn it on. To enable the Journal feature in Outlook, follow these steps:

1. Choose <u>T</u>ools ➪ <u>O</u>ptions. The Options dialog box appears as in Figure 41-11.

2. This dialog box has many tabs; click the first one, marked Journal.

3. Check the types of activities you want to appear in the Journal. There are four main areas to configure in this dialog box. They are:

   - *Automatically record these <u>i</u>tems*. This list in the upper-left section determines which kinds of tasks you want recorded in the Journal. Typically, you'll probably want to check e-mail message, although you can also mark items like meeting and task requests. If you check these items, each time you invite someone to a meeting or give someone a task to do, it will show up in the Journal.

- *For these contacts.* The upper-right section lists all the names in your Contacts database. Journal entries will be established for e-mail you send to, or receive from, these people. If you later add names to Contacts, you must revisit this Options dialog box and check mark their names; all names are not selected by default.

- *Also record files from.* This is where you let the Journal track when and how long you use each of the applications from Microsoft Office.

- *Double-clicking a journal entry.* When you double-click a Journal entry, do you want to open the Journal's dialog box — which has additional information about the activity — or just open the document on which you were working?

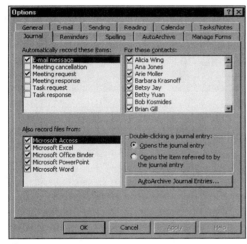

Figure 41-11: The Journal properties in Options

Viewing the Journal

The Journal is now configured. Close the Options box and let's investigate the Journal itself. Click the Journal icon on the Outlook Bar. You'll see a timeline divided into a series of horizontal segments; each segment contains a timeline for a specific activity, such as e-mail, Word documents edited, and meetings requested. You can modify the view to suit your taste. Try these options:

✦ *Expand and collapse timelines.* You should see a plus or minus sign to the left of the Entry Type on each horizontal segment. You can collapse the segment and save space by clicking the minus sign, which will turn into a plus sign, indicating it is collapsed. In Figure 41-12, the Word segment is expanded and Excel is collapsed.

✦ *Change the scale.* By default, the Journal shows a week at a time on the screen. If you spend lots of time in the hot tub, this may be okay, but a large number of events will make this view nearly illegible. The toolbar has day, week, and month views to see more or less on the screen at once. The week-long view, seen in Figure 41-12, is downright claustrophobic; switching to a daily view would give all the documents more elbow room.

✦ *Change the View settings.* You'll find a drop-down menu to the left of the day, week, and month icons in the toolbar. The default is By Type, though you may prefer the more tabular views, like Entry List or Last Seven Days, which show all your combined activities in strictly chronological order. You can switch among any of these views on the fly, so don't worry about experimenting.

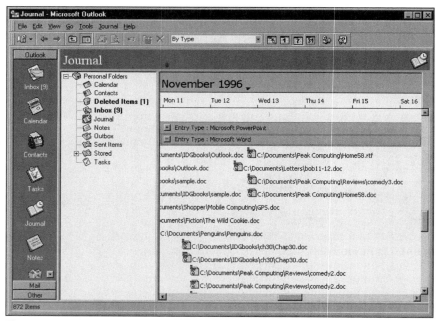

Figure 41-12: The Timeline view shows a chronological depiction of your work.

Using the Journal

We're finally ready to use the Journal. Anything in the Journal can be referenced later to check on notes you've made, how long you worked on the activity, and even load and edit documents. Scroll to a Word document you edited and double-click the icon in the Journal. An e-mail-like dialog box opens, as in Figure 41-13. Notice Outlook displays the person who edited the document — yourself, probably — as well as how long the document was open. If you double-click the document's icon, the document is loaded into Word. Finally, you can add notes in the large text box for future reference.

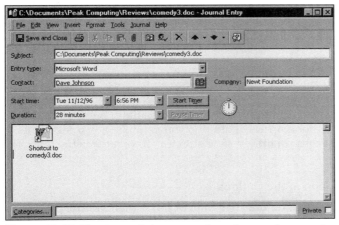

Figure 41-13: The Journal shows you how long a document was edited and who performed the work.

Because each of Outlook's tools are tightly integrated, they can share information. Switch back to Contacts, for instance, and open a name from the database. Click the Journal tab and you'll find a complete history of the messages you've exchanged (see Figure 41-14). This makes keeping an audit trail of the calls, e-mails, and documents you've exchanged a snap.

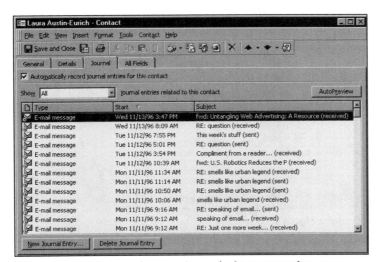

Figure 41-14: Contacts keeps a journal of messages for every person enabled in Options.

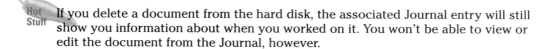

If you delete a document from the hard disk, the associated Journal entry will still **Stuff** **show** you information about when you worked on it. You won't be able to view or edit the document from the Journal, however.

Taking Notes

How many times have you wanted to write yourself a note, but had nowhere to write it? If you keep Outlook open constantly, you can take advantage of its Notes function to write messages on little yellow stickies. To create such a note, follow these steps:

1. Click the Notes icon in the Outlook Bar.

2. Double-click anywhere on the right side of the screen. A note pad appears (see Figure 41-15).

3. Type your message.

4. Click the note's close box in the upper-right corner to close it.

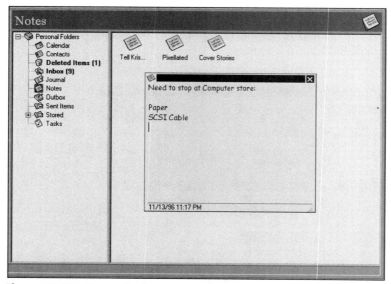

Figure 41-15: The Outlook Notes view

Want to rename a note? Notes take the first line of text as the title: Simply open **Stuff** the note and change the first line to any text you want. You can change the color just as easily; click the control button in the upper-left corner of the note and select Color. Then pick the color you prefer.

Personalizing Outlook

You can change the appearance of Outlook in a number of ways to make it work more to your liking. Some of these — such as turning the Outlook Bar on and off — were discussed at the beginning of this chapter. Now let's see how else we can customize the program.

The Outlook Bar

The Outlook Bar isn't a static, factory-preset icon bar. You can modify it to your heart's content. If you haven't yet noticed, look carefully and you'll see the bar is divided into groups of icons. The default group is called Outlook, but there is also a Mail group and an Other group.

Adding to the Outlook Bar

You can easily add new Groups, such as a Contacts group, by right-clicking the bar and selecting Add New Group. Then name the group, which will appear at the bottom of the screen. You can add icons to new or existing groups easily, as well. You can do this in three ways:

✦ Drag the desired object to the Outlook Bar. You can drag any folder from Outlook into the bar. In this way, you can access a deeply nested mail folder with one click. You can also open My Computer and drag drives or file folders into the toolbar for quick access.

✦ Right-click the Outlook Bar and choose Add to Outlook Bar. A dialog box appears from which you can choose Outlook folders or drives/folders on the hard disk.

✦ Right-click an Outlook folder. One of the menu options is Add to Outlook Bar.

Using categories

Categories provide tremendous control over how you view and store information in Outlook. Using a master list of categories, such as Work, Leisure, and Awaiting Action, for instance, you can file messages and look at only the ones you need at any given time. And using the Inbox Assistant, you can let Outlook automatically file incoming messages in specific folders. You can discard junk mail without reading it or forward messages from mailing lists out of the inbox, so it doesn't get cluttered.

Hot Stuff You may have noticed two ghosted menu items in Outlook's Tools menu: the Inbox Assistant and the Out of Office Assistant. These Microsoft wizards enable you to perform actions automatically on mail based on rules. For more information, choose Help ⇨Contents and Index from Outlook's menu bar, click the Index tab, and search for Inbox Assistant.

Establishing a categories list

The master categories list is found at Edit ➪ Categories. You can add new categories or delete those you don't need by clicking the button marked Master Categories List (see Figure 41-16). To add a new category, type the name of the new category in the New category box at the top and press Return. Delete a category by clicking the desired name and press the Delete button. Reset returns the list to the default entries supplied my Microsoft. This is useful if you accidentally delete important categories and want to return to where you started. When you finish, click OK twice to return to Outlook.

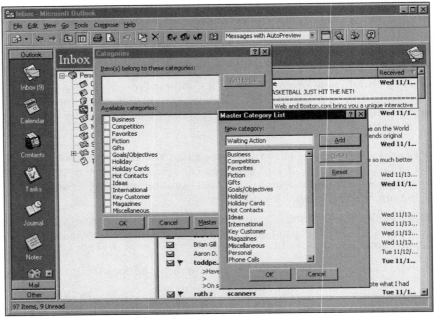

Figure 41-16: Create or modify categories to personalize the way you display Outlook data

Assigning categories

Once you establish categories, you'll want to use them. Right-click a message, contact, journal entry, or any kind of Outlook object, and then select Categories. The category list appears, enabling you to assign the object to one or more categories. Click OK when you finish.

Viewing e-mail by category

You've gone to all the trouble to set-up categories. Now here comes the payoff. To configure your inbox to display messages by category, follow these steps:

1. Choose <u>V</u>iew ➪ <u>G</u>roup By A Group By dialog box appears.

2. At the top is a drop-down menu marked <u>G</u>roup items by. Choose Categories (see Figure 41-17).

3. Click OK.

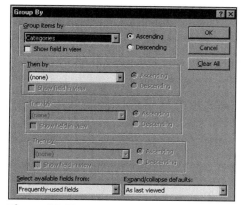

Figure 41-17: Use Categories to sort, filter, and display all the information in Outlook.

Once you set up this category system, you can assign new mail to categories without opening the category list. Simply click the unfiled mail and drag it into the desired category. You can use the plus and minus buttons on each category separator to expand and collapse categories in much the same way as we managed the Journal view.

Categories are arbitrary — you can create new ones or modify the categories Microsoft gave you to your heart's content. The bottom line is you can customize your display, as in Figure 41-18, to help you work the way you want.

Viewing other Outlook objects by category

Who said only e-mail could have all the category fun? Sorting tasks in the Calendar view by categories is also often convenient. The principal is essentially the same. Switch to the Calendar and choose <u>V</u>iew ➪ Taskpad Set<u>t</u>ings. Again choose <u>G</u>roup items by Categories. How about Notes? You bet — just switch to the Notes feature and choose By Category from the drop-down menu in the toolbar. Even Contacts can be grouped by category — how much (or little) you use these categories is up to you.

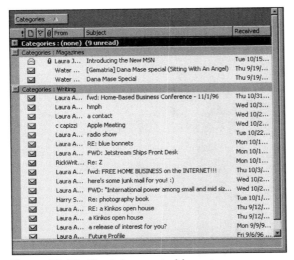

Figure 41-18: The Inbox sorted by category

Summary

This chapter introduced you to the most common and useful features of Outlook. The main points we discussed are:

✦ Microsoft Outlook does everything Exchange does, and more.

✦ You can use the Outlook Bar to switch to Outlook's many applications, like Calendar, Journal, Mail, and Contacts.

✦ Use the right mouse button to place a call or to view the Web site of anyone in the Contact database.

✦ The Journal tracks your time during the day. It can record your phone calls, e-mail, and application editing activities. Remember to first enable the Journal from Options.

✦ You can use the categories to sort and display messages and tasks more easily. You can drag items into category groups or use the right mouse button to select the appropriate category.

In the next chapter, I'll look at the Windows 95 Registry, where all your settings are stored.

✦   ✦   ✦

Dealing with the Windows 95 Registry

Like most users of Windows 95, you probably learned about the Registry when your friends warned you, "Don't mess with that — you might blow up your computer!" So you tried calling customer support for answers to your Registry questions, and you might have heard the response (roughly translating), "Don't mess with the Registry — you might blow up your computer!"

The truth is, computers rarely blow up these days, so you have nothing to worry about. Well, almost nothing. If you mess with the Registry, you run the risk of rendering Windows 95 comatose, with little hope of rescue. With some minimal precautions, however, you can use the Registry safely and at no risk to innocent bystanders. This chapter tells you how.

In this chapter, you will learn about the Registry — what it is and how to use it. You will also learn how to use the Windows 95 Registry Editor. The Registry Editor gives you the power to make changes to the Registry. You can fix problems or, if you're not careful, cause them. You can even remove all the information Windows 95 needs to boot and run. This is why you will also learn how to save backup copies of the Registry and how to recover from Registry disasters. After learning how to manipulate the Registry, you will learn useful tricks for customizing your Windows 95 environment — tricks you can perform only by manually editing the Registry.

What Is the Registry?

The *Registry* is a repository of information for Windows 95 and its applications. What kind of information? Almost anything. For example, when you installed Windows 95, the setup program asked you for your name, and it stored this information in the Registry. Windows 95 also stores information about your hardware configuration in the Registry, such as settings for your modem, printers, video adapters, and so on.

Another example is Explorer, which uses the Registry for several purposes. In Explorer, every file has an icon. Windows 95 uses the Registry to remember which icon goes with which file. When you double-click a file, Explorer looks up information about this file so it can decide which application to launch. Where do you think Windows stores this information? That's right — the Registry.

Most applications store additional information in the Registry, such as user preferences, configuration data, the files you edited most recently, and so on. Each application can store anything it wants.

Out with the old

You may be familiar with .INI files. In Windows 3.1, an application typically stored its configuration data in a text file, such as WINWORD.INI. You could find many of these files cluttering your Windows folder. Windows itself kept information in files, such as WIN.INI and SYSTEM.INI.

Figure 42-1 shows an excerpt from CONTROL.INI, which stores information for the Control Panel. When you upgraded your computer to Windows 95, the setup program read CONTROL.INI and similar files, and copied that information into the Registry. Windows 95 retrieves this same information from the Registry, not from CONTROL.INI.

When you install a new application in Windows 3.1, the setup program often creates new .INI files and modifies existing ones. In some unfortunate situations, it asks you to edit manually one or more .INI files, such as SYSTEM.INI.

Some power users enjoy working with .INI files. The files are plain text files, so you can use any text editor, such as Notepad, to examine or modify a .INI file. Sometimes, the only way to get out of a jam is to edit a .INI file.

In with the new

In Windows 95, the plethora of .INI files is replaced with a single database, the Registry. Because the Registry is a single, centrally located database, it is easy to find the configuration data for a particular application. The Registry does away with the separate .INI files, and allows long names for its Registry entries, so you can find information much more easily than you could with .INI files. Instead of trying to decipher eight-letter filenames, you can search the Registry for a company name, and then look for a full product name. This makes it easier to find information for a particular application.

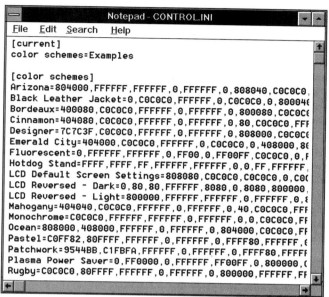

```
─                    Notepad - CONTROL.INI              ▼ ▲
 File   Edit   Search   Help
[current]                                                    ↑
color schemes=Examples

[color schemes]
Arizona=804000,FFFFFF,FFFFFF,0,FFFFFF,0,808040,C0C0C0,
Black Leather Jacket=0,C0C0C0,FFFFFF,0,C0C0C0,0,800040
Bordeaux=400080,C0C0C0,FFFFFF,0,FFFFFF,0,800080,C0C0C0
Cinnamon=404080,C0C0C0,FFFFFF,0,FFFFFF,0,80,C0C0C0,FFF
Designer=7C7C3F,C0C0C0,FFFFFF,0,FFFFFF,0,808000,C0C0C0
Emerald City=404000,C0C0C0,FFFFFF,0,C0C0C0,0,408000,80
Fluorescent=0,FFFFFF,FFFFFF,0,FF00,0,FF00FF,C0C0C0,0,F
Hotdog Stand=FFFF,FFFF,FF,FFFFFF,FFFFFF,0,0,FF,FFFFFF,
LCD Default Screen Settings=808080,C0C0C0,C0C0C0,0,C0C
LCD Reversed - Dark=0,80,80,FFFFFF,8080,0,8080,800000,
LCD Reversed - Light=800000,FFFFFF,FFFFFF,0,FFFFFF,0,8
Mahogany=404040,C0C0C0,FFFFFF,0,FFFFFF,0,40,C0C0C0,FFF
Monochrome=C0C0C0,FFFFFF,FFFFFF,0,FFFFFF,0,0,C0C0C0,FF
Ocean=808000,408000,FFFFFF,0,FFFFFF,0,804000,C0C0C0,FF
Pastel=C0FF82,80FFFF,FFFFFF,0,FFFFFF,0,FFFF80,FFFFFF,0
Patchwork=9544BB,C1FBFA,FFFFFF,0,FFFFFF,0,FFFF80,FFFFF
Plasma Power Saver=0,FF0000,0,FFFFFF,FF00FF,0,800000,0
Rugby=C0C0C0,80FFFF,FFFFFF,0,FFFFFF,0,800000,FFFFFF,FF ↓
←                                                          →
```

Figure 42-1: Windows 3.1 uses CONTROL.INI to store Control Panel data.

What is in the Registry?

Because the Registry stores information for every application, it needs a way to organize this information. To keep one application's data from interfering with the data from another application, the Registry uses a tree-like arrangement, similar to the way files and folders reside on a disk drive.

Where a disk drive uses folders, the Registry has *keys*. Just as a folder can contain other folders, a key can have its own subkeys. Instead of files, the Registry has *values*. For example, the Control Panel stores its information under the key, Control Panel. This key has subkeys for Appearance, Colors, and so on. The Appearance subkey has its own subkey — Schemes — to record all the named color schemes you can define in the Appearance tab of the Control Panel's Display applet. Each named color scheme is a separate value, as you can see in Figure 42-2.

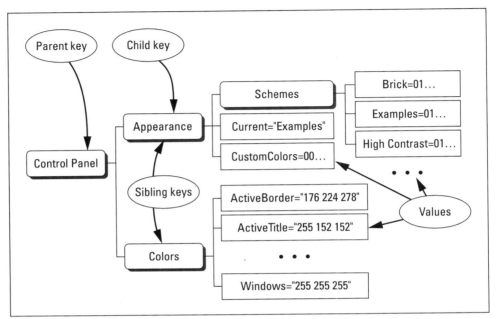

Figure 42-2: The Control Panel stores its Registry data in a tree under the Control Panel key.

More Info In the Registry, a key has no relation to the keys on your keyboard, your car keys or house keys, or any other key you are likely to encounter in real life. A key is just one more bit of techno-jargon you need to learn. In computerese, a program uses a key to look up information. For example, when you look up a word in a dictionary, you are using the word as a key to search through the dictionary. A key in the Registry is similar — programs look up configuration data using keys and subkeys. The Registry stores the actual data (like the definitions in the dictionary) in a key's values.

Keys in the Registry are like relatives in a family tree. One key can be the *parent* of several *child* keys. All the child keys that share a parent are *siblings*.

The information for a key is its *values*. Every value has a name, a type, and data. For example, the Appearance key has a value — Current — the name of the current color scheme. The data for the Current key is the word *Examples* in Figure 42-3. A value's type says whether the data are ordinary text, a number, or something else. Just to be complicated, the Registry uses special names for these types. Table 42-1 lists the types you will see in the Registry.

More Info DWORD is short for *double word*, which is another way of saying *number*. A *word* is a unit of computer storage. A double word is two adjacent words. But don't let this confuse you. Just remember, when the Registry says DWORD, it means number.

Table 42-1	
Registry Value Types	
Type	**Registry Jargon**
Ordinary text	String
Numbers	DWORD
Everything else	Binary

To refer to a specific Registry key, use a *path*, which is analogous to a file path. A Registry path is a series of key names, separated by backslashes. Every Registry path starts with a *root key*, one of six special keys that Windows 95 defines. The root key is similar to a drive letter in file paths. For example, HKEY_CURRENT_USER\Control Panel\Appearance\Schemes is a Registry path that starts with the root key HKEY_CURRENT_USER, and follows the keys Control Panel, Appearance, and Schemes.

That's enough theory. Now it's time to start getting your hands dirty. You can begin by learning how to use the Registry Editor to view and modify Registry entries.

Using the Registry Editor

You can look at what's in the Registry by running the Registry Editor. From the Start menu, choose Run..., type **regedit** and press Enter (or click the OK button). You will see a window that looks similar to Figure 42-4 .

Hot Stuff While you read this chapter, you might find dragging the regedit icon onto your desktop more convenient. You can find regedit in the Windows folder.

The left pane shows several keys (HKEY_CLASSES_ROOT, and so on). You can expand each key, to reveal subkeys, in much the same manner as Explorer. Click the little plus sign to expand a key and view its subkeys. You can also press the plus sign on the numeric keypad to expand a key. Click the minus sign to collapse the subkeys or press – on the keypad.

When you select a Registry key, the Registry Editor displays the full path to that key in the status bar, at the bottom of the window. If you cannot see the status bar, select <u>V</u>iew ⇨ Status Bar from the menu bar.

The Registry always contains six standard, top-level keys. Every Registry path must start with one of these root keys, just as a complete filename starts with a drive letter. Table 42-2 lists the root keys in Windows 95.

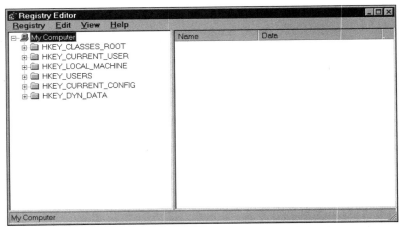

Figure 42-3: To run the Registry Editor, choose Run... from the Start menu, type **regedit** and press Enter.

Table 42-2
Standard Root Keys

Key name	Description
HKEY_CLASSES_ROOT	File associations (short for HKEY_LOCAL_MACHINE\ Software\Classes). Explorer uses this information to choose icons, respond to double-clicks, and display context menus.
HKEY_CURRENT_USER	Information for the current user (short for HKEY_USERS*current user name*). Applications store their preferences here.
HKEY_LOCAL_MACHINE	Information that applies system-wide. Windows 95 stores information about hardware configurations here. Applications can also store information that pertains to the computer, not to users.
HKEY_USERS	Information for all users. If you configured Windows 95 for multiple users, each user has a subkey under this key. When the user logs in, that user's subkey becomes HKEY_CURRENT_USER.
HKEY_CURRENT_CONFIG	Current configuration of the local machine (short for HKEY_ LOCAL_MACHINE\Config*current configuration*). When you boot Windows 95, it determines your hardware configuration and sets this key to the appropriate subkey of HKEY_LOCAL_ MACHINE\Config. This is important only if you use multiple configurations, such as a laptop computer that may or may not use a docking station.
HKEY_DYN_DATA	System data that vary at run time, such as information about plug-and-play devices.

You can use the Registry Editor to view, create, or modify Registry entries (keys and values). The following sections tell you how to use the Registry Editor.

 Before you make any changes to the Registry, carefully read the section, "Backing Up Your Registry," later in this chapter. The Registry Editor has no Undo function. Always back up the Registry before modifying it.

Creating a new key

To create a new key, select the parent key, and choose New ➪ Key from the context menu, or choose <u>E</u>dit ➪ New ➪ Key from the menu bar. The Registry Editor creates the key and gives it a name like New Key #1. Change the name to the desired name and press Enter.

Notice the key automatically has a value, named (Default Value), but this value has no data. This is why the Registry Editor displays the data as (value not set).

Deleting a key

Select the key you want to delete and press the Delete key, choose Delete from the context menu, or choose <u>E</u>dit ➪ Delete from the menu bar. The Registry Editor confirms whether you want to delete the key.

When you delete a key, you also delete all its subkeys and values. The Registry Editor does not have an Undo feature. When you delete a key, that key is gone for good. Always make a backup copy of the Registry before you delete any keys.

Renaming a key

To change a key name, select that key, press F2, and type the new key name, followed by Enter. You can also choose <u>E</u>dit ➪ Rename from the menu bar or choose Rename from the context menu. All the subkeys that share a common parent key must have different names. The Registry Editor will not let you assign a key name that is the same as a sibling key's name.

Values

When you select a key, the Registry Editor displays a list of values in the right pane. Notice the columns, labeled Name and Data. A key can have any number of values, although most keys have none. The Registry Editor always displays one key, named (Default). For its data, you usually see (value not set), which is the Registry Editor's way of saying this key does not really have a default value.

 If you are a programmer, you should know the real name of the default value is an empty string. The Registry Editor displays the name as (Default) because this is easier to read. Think of it as the equivalent of, "This value name intentionally left blank." You should never create a value with the name (Default) because this would be confusing.

To see an example of a key with several values, expand HKEY_CURRENT_USER, then expand Control Panel, and select the Colors key. In the right pane of the Registry Editor, you can see a list of names and strings, where the strings contain mysterious-looking numbers. This is where Windows 95 stores the color choices you make in the Display Control Panel applet.

Try this experiment: In the Control Panel, double-click the Display icon, then select the Appearance panel. Look at the value for Window in the Registry Editor. You might see something like "255 255 255" for the data, as you can see in Figure 42-4. This means your current window background color is white. In the Display applet, change the color to bright green. Click the Apply button to see all your windows change color. In the Registry Editor, press F5 to refresh the window. Notice how the Window value changes to "0 255 0", which is the color value for green. Restore the original value in the Display applet before you go blind.

Note   Any changes you make in Windows 95 proper update the Registry immediately. Even if the Registry is "open" with regedit. As you'll see in a moment, though, the opposite isn't always true. That is, changing the contents of the Registry with regedit doesn't necessarily update all of Windows 95 immediately.

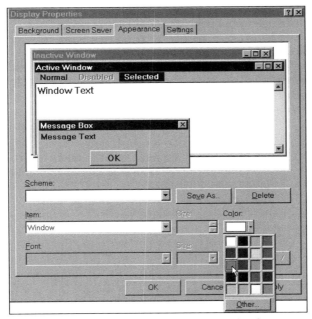

Figure 42-4: Change the Window color to bright green, and watch how the value changes in the Registry.

Modifying a value

You can change any value in the Registry. Just double-click the name or select the value name and press Enter. The Registry Editor pops up a dialog box where you can type a new value.

The Registry stores information for Windows 95, but changing the information does not always cause an immediate change to Windows. For example, while you are still viewing the Control Panel\Colors key, try changing a value by hand. For example, double-click the Window name, and enter **192 192 192** as the string data. Figure 42-5 shows you what this dialog box looks like. Press Enter or click OK. Notice the Registry Editor has the new values, but your desktop looks the same. None of the windows adopt this new color.

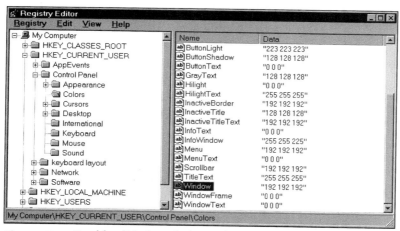

Figure 42-5: Double-click the Window value and type **192 192 192**. You need to restart Windows 95 to see the effect of this change.

Exit and restart Windows 95. Now you can see the new window background color (which is gray). This is because when Windows 95 starts, it reads the Registry to learn what color to make its windows. After that, it doesn't check the Registry again until an application tells it the color information has changed.

The moral of this story is you can change values in the Registry Editor, but Windows 95 may not act on the new values until you exit and restart Windows. Restarting Windows every time you make a minor change to the Registry would be tedious, so an application, such as a Control Panel applet, can inform Windows of a change to the Registry. In this case, Windows reads the new value from the Registry and redraws every window. This is how you can change color schemes without restarting Windows.

For an example of editing a DWORD value, select the HKEY_CURRENT_USER\
Control Panel\Desktop key, and double-click the ScreenSaveUsePassword value.
You can enter the new DWORD value as an ordinary number (decimal) or as a
hexadecimal (base 16) value. Click the Cancel button or press the Esc key to exit
the dialog box without making any changes. Figure 42-6 shows you the Edit
DWORD Value dialog box.

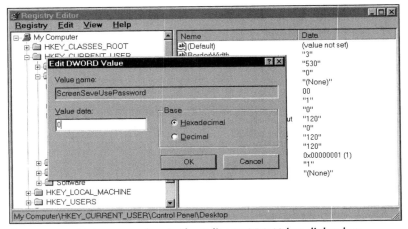

Figure 42-6: Enter a number in the Edit DWORD Value dialog box.

To see an example of the Edit Binary dialog box, select the Control
Panel\Appearance key, and double-click the CustomColors value. Notice the data
for CustomColors is a series of pairs of letters and numbers. Each pair represents
one byte of data. When you edit the binary data, just type to insert new bytes. Use
the arrow keys to move around in the dialog box. The Delete key deletes the next
byte, and the Backspace key removes the previous byte. You can also select many
bytes at once and delete them or type to replace them with new data. Figure 42-7
shows you the Edit Binary Value dialog box.

Instead of double-clicking a value to modify it, you can also select the value name
and press Enter. Or you can choose Edit ➪ Modify from the menu bar, or choose
Modify from the context menu.

When you modify a value, make sure the new value is what you want. The Registry
Editor does not have an Undo feature.

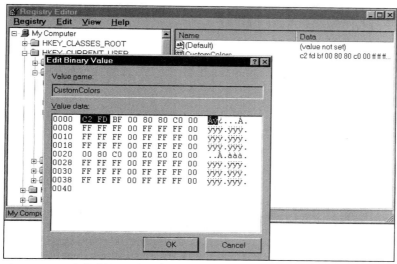

Figure 42-7: Edit binary data by inserting and deleting bytes in the Edit Binary Value dialog box.

Adding a new value

Most of the changes you will make to the Registry will be modifications of existing values. Sometimes, though, you will need to add a new value to a key. Choose Edit ➪ New or choose New from the context menu. The cascading menu gives you the choice of creating a new String value, Binary value, or DWORD value. Choose the type of value you want to create, and the Registry Editor creates the value with default data and a name like New Value #1. Type a new name for the value and press Enter.

The Registry Editor creates a String value with an empty string as the data. A DWORD value gets zero as the data, and a new Binary value gets a zero-length value for its data. You can modify the default data, as described in the previous section, "Modifying a value."

Deleting a value

To delete a value, select the value you want to delete (or select multiple values). Then press the Delete key. You can also choose Delete from the context menu or from the Edit menu in the menu bar. The Registry Editor confirms whether you really want to delete the values.

The Registry Editor does not have an Undo feature. When you delete a value, that value is gone. If you make a mistake, you might damage your Registry in a way that prevents Windows 95 from starting. Always make a backup copy of the Registry before you try editing it by hand.

Backing Up Your Registry

Before you make any changes to the Registry, you should make a backup copy. Some of the entries in the Registry are vital for Windows 95 and, if you accidentally delete the wrong key, you might be unable to start your computer.

Windows 95 makes one backup copy for you. Look in your Windows folder (usually C:\WINDOWS), and find the files, USER.DAT and SYSTEM.DAT. These system files are usually hidden in Explorer, so you may first have to choose <u>V</u>iew ➪ Options and select Show all files.

The USER.DAT and SYSTEM.DAT files together comprise the Registry. Windows 95 always keeps a backup copy of these files, named USER.DA0 and SYSTEM.DA0. (That's a zero at the end of the name, not the letter *O*.) Every time Windows 95 starts successfully, it creates new USER.DA0 and SYSTEM.DA0 files from USER.DAT and SYSTEM.DAT. After that, it does not touch these files until the next time you boot Windows 95. In other words, you know the Registry entries in USER.DA0 and SYSTEM.DA0 are valid for starting Windows 95. If you have a subsequent problem and cannot start Windows 95, you can try using the USER.DA0 and SYSTEM.DA0 files to restore the Registry, as described in the next section, "Restoring a Damaged Registry."

Windows 95 does not change USER.DA0 or SYSTEM.DA0 to reflect any changes to the Registry that occur while Windows 95 is running. This helps ensure USER.DA0 and SYSTEM.DA0 contain a valid backup of the Registry in case an application, for example, stores invalid information in the Registry and prevents Windows 95 from running. You have a guarantee the Registry was valid when Windows 95 created the USER.DA0 and SYSTEM.DA0 files, so they are probably safe to use.

Sometimes, though, you want to make additional backups of the Registry. For example, say you are about to make some manual changes to the Registry, perhaps you want to implement one of the ideas from the section, "Useful Registry Tricks," later in this chapter. You want to save the Registry in its current state, not the state it was in when you started Windows 95 this morning (or yesterday, or last week, or whenever you booted your PC).

To make a manual backup of the Registry, simply copy the USER.DAT and SYSTEM.DAT files to a safe place. Remember to select Show all files in Explorer, so you can see the USER.DAT and SYSTEM.DAT files in the Windows directory. If you are using a DOS window, or a BAT file, you can make these files visible by changing their file attributes, as shown in the following:

```
C:\Windows>md backup
C:\Windows>attrib -h -r -s system.dat
C:\Windows>copy system.dat backup
        1 file(s) copied
C:\Windows>attrib -h -r -s user.dat
```

```
C:\Windows>copy user.dat backup
        1 file(s) copied
C:\Windows>attrib +h +r +s system.dat
C:\Windows>attrib +h +r +s user.dat
```

Do not delete the USER.DA0 and SYSTEM.DA0 files. You never know when you might need them.

User profiles

If you configure Windows 95 for multiple user profiles, then each user has a separate Registry tree under the HKEY_USERS root key. If you click Cancel in the logon directory, Windows 95 uses the default user profile, which corresponds to the ".Default" Registry key.

Each user has a separate USER.DAT file in the user's logon folder, which is typically under Profiles, that is, `C:\Windows\Profiles\Jane\USER.DAT`. Windows 95 divides the Registry into two files to separate the system-wide settings (SYSTEM.DAT) from the entries that vary for each user (USER.DAT). Windows 95 copies the appropriate USER.DA0 file when you log on.

Because SYSTEM.DAT contains the global, system-wide Registry entries, a single SYSTEM.DAT file exists. Thus, to make a backup copy of the Registry when you have multiple user profiles, you need to copy SYSTEM.DAT in the Windows folder, and you must copy the current user's USER.DAT file in that user's logon folder.

Exporting and importing Registry entries

Instead of copying the entire Registry, you will often find saving a copy of only one key and its subkeys and values easier. For example, if you want to experiment with the settings under Control Panel\Appearance, you can save just those keys and values without copying the entire Registry. This can make undoing your changes easier. You can import the saved key to restore the original settings without copying the entire Registry.

To export a key, and its subkeys and all their values, select the parent key and choose Registry ➪ Export Registry File. The dialog box shows the Export range as the key you selected. Enter a filename and click OK. The exported file is not a Registry file, but a text file you can view or edit in any text editor.

More Info If you are familiar with .INI files, you will recognize the format of a Registry export file (.REG). The most striking difference is the section names in a .REG file are complete key paths, for example, [HKEY_CURRENT_USER\Software\Microsoft]. Also, .REG files can contain binary and DWORD values, such as "dword:0000016d".

To import the entries from an export file, choose Registry ➪ Import Registry File. Importing a Registry file merges the exported file with the entries already in the Registry. Figure 42-8 illustrates how values in the export file take precedence over values in the Registry, but any values or keys not present in the export file are unaffected by importing that file. (You can also double-click a .REG file on the desktop, or anywhere else, and its contents will merge with the Registry.)

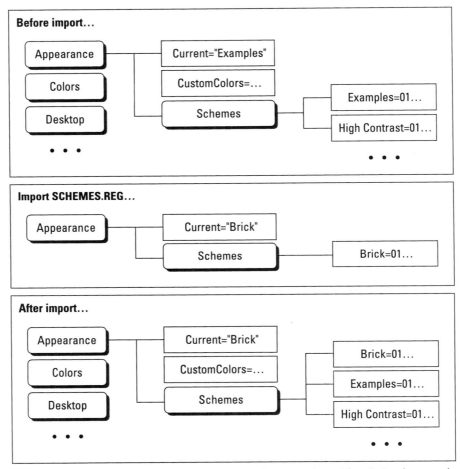

Figure 42-8: Import Registry entries to merge those entries with existing keys and values in the Registry

You can also save a copy of the entire Registry by exporting all its keys. Click the All button for the Export range to export the entire Registry. If you must save the entire Registry, though, it's easiest to copy the file without bothering with exporting and importing keys. Exporting is most useful when you need to save only a few keys.

Restoring a Damaged Registry

Disaster strikes — you try to start your computer, but all you get is an error message:

```
Registry File was not found. Registry services may be
inoperative for this session.
```

Or worse, while Windows 95 is booting, it stops dead in its tracks, with no error messages, no explanations, but with one bewildered user. The first thing to try is to boot in Safe Mode. When you see "Starting Windows 95..." press the F8 key. Use the arrow keys to change the menu selection to Safe Mode and press Enter. Windows automatically restores the Registry from the last backup and the most you've lost is one session's worth of changes.

If you're the hands-on type, you can restore the Registry yourself. Boot to Command Mode and change directories to the Windows directory. Then type the following commands:

```
C:\Windows>attrib -h -r -s system.dat
C:\Windows>attrib -h -r -s system.da0
C:\Windows>copy system.da0 system.dat
        1 file(s) copied
C:\Windows>attrib -h -r -s user.dat
C:\Windows>attrib -h -r -s user.da0
C:\Windows>copy user.da0 user.dat
        1 file(s) copied
```

If you made a manual copy of the Registry (always a good idea before you attempt any experiment), you can restore the manual copy in a similar manner. If you have multiple-user profiles, remember to restore USER.DAT to the appropriate users' folders under Windows\Profiles.

If one of the Registry files becomes damaged while you are running Windows 95, you may see an error message from Windows (as in Figure 42-9). In most cases, you can let Windows automatically restore the backup copy of the Registry, which is USER.DA0 or SYSTEM.DA0. If all else fails, you can restore the Registry files from the last system backup you performed.

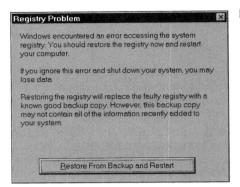

Figure 42-9: If Windows detects a damaged Registry file, it prompts you to restore the Registry from its backup copy (USER.DA0 or SYSTEM.DA0).

How Do Applications Use the Registry?

Applications typically use the Registry in one of two ways. The most common way is to store application-specific information, such as user preferences. The details depend on the application. Sometimes, you can learn about an application's Registry settings by reading the application's help files or other documentation. Usually, though, this information is not documented, and you should not try manually editing the application's Registry entries.

If you are curious, you can use the Registry Editor to browse the Registry entries for an application. Look under the key, HKEY_CURRENT_USER\Software. You will see a list of software companies, including Microsoft. The exact list depends on which software products you have installed on your computer. The subkeys under a company's key represent the company's products. For example, HKEY_CURRENT_USER\Software\Netscape may have a subkey for Netscape Navigator. Some products have subkeys for different versions of the product. For example, the key for Microsoft Money 95 is HKEY_CURRENT_USER\Software\Microsoft\Money\4.0.

Try running the Registry Editor now. Look at the entries under Software, to see which products have Registry entries. See if you can find a match between the Registry entries and your preferences and options in an application.

Another kind of application presents a user interface to the Registry entries that other programs create and use. Several of the Control Panel applets work like this. These applications relieve you of the burden of editing the Registry manually by providing a nice, easy-to-use interface. In addition to modifying Registry entries, these applications might also tell Windows 95 about the new Registry entries, so you needn't restart Windows for the new settings to take effect.

The standard Control Panel applets do not cover all the useful Registry entries, though. The next section describes another applet you can download from the Internet. This applet helps by giving you a useful interface to several Registry entries. The remaining sections in this chapter describe Registry entries for which no Control Panel applet exists. For these situations, you must edit the Registry manually, which you learned about earlier in this chapter.

Power toys

The *Tweak UI power toy* is a Control Panel applet that enables you to control several aspects of your Windows 95 environment. It is one of several power toys, which are simple tools Microsoft offers free, but without support. You can download the power toys from Microsoft's Web site. You can currently find these power toys at `http://www.microsoft.com/windows/software/powertoy.htm`. As with any URL, this address can be ephemeral so, if it doesn't work, look around the main Microsoft Web site for any information on software downloads, the Windows 95 software library, or power toys.

The Tweak UI power toy is a useful tool for working with several Registry entries and other preferences for your Windows 95 environment. Without the Tweak UI power toy, you would need to edit the Registry manually. Now that you've read this far, you know how to do this, but why should you? The Tweak UI power toy is easier to use, and you needn't remember the Registry names and values.

For example, if you have turned off the Tip of the Day feature and you want to re-enable it, you can do so in the Registry. Find HKEY_CURRENT_USER\Software\ Microsoft\Windows\CurrentVersion\Explorer\Tips, and edit the Show value to change it to anything other than zero. For example, set the first byte to 01, so the value of Show is "01 00 00 00." The next time you start Windows 95, Explorer will show you the Tip of the Day. Remembering the Registry key isn't easy, though, so the Tweak UI power toy makes it easier. Select the Explorer page and check the Tip of the day box. Figure 42-10 shows this example of using the Tweak UI power toy.

The Tweak UI power toy also has settings for the mouse, changing the arrow icon for shortcuts, choosing icons and drives to appear on the desktop, and more. Download the Tweak UI power toy and try it yourself.

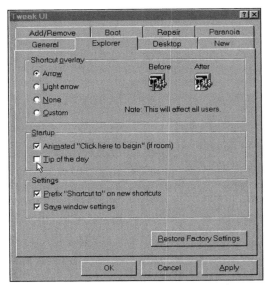

Figure 42-10: The Tweak UI power toy enables you to modify your Windows 95 environment easily.

Useful Registry Tricks

This section describes several ways you can use the Registry to customize your Windows 95 environment. The situations when you need to edit the Registry manually are few, but sometimes you have no other choice. In the following situations, the Registry Editor is often your only choice.

Moving an application

Sometimes you need to move an application from one folder to another, often from one drive to another. One way to do this is to uninstall the application and reinstall it to a new location. This means you lose all the preferences you have laboriously customized. Instead, you can move all the files by hand, and then update the application's Registry entries by hand.

Let's say you plan on moving an application from C:\AppDir to D:\AppDir after buying a new disk drive. The first step is to move all the files. The next step is to update the application's Registry entries.

In the Registry Editor, choose Edit ⇨ Find.... Type **C:\AppDir** and press Enter. The Registry Editor searches for a Registry entry that contains "C:\AppDir" and selects the first one it finds. Press Enter to edit the value's data, and type the new folder name, **D:\AppDir** and press Enter. Now press F3 to repeat the search. You can make this go faster by copying the new folder name to the Clipboard, so you can quickly paste it (by pressing Ctrl+V) when you change values.

Keep repeating this — F3, Enter, Ctrl+V, Enter — until the Registry Editor can no longer find any occurrences of the old application path. Congratulations! You have now moved the application without sacrificing your preferences. Some applications keep additional information in .INI and other files. Consult your application's documentation for details. You may need to edit those files to change C:\AppDir to D:\AppDir the same way you changed the Registry.

If you find the repetition tedious, you can export the Registry to a temporary .REG file, and use a text editor to replace the file paths. Then import the edited .REG file. Many text editors have powerful search and replace functions, which can make this task easier.

Before making any changes to the Registry, remember to make a backup copy. Exporting and importing the entire Registry opens the possibility of a major catastrophe, and you must be prepared.

File associations

You can easily create new file associations from Explorer by choosing View ⇨ Options and clicking the File Types tab. When you create a file association, Windows 95 creates two or more entries in the Registry — one entry for the file type, and one for each extension.

The (Default) value for the extension is the name of the key for the file type. This is how you can have several different extensions for the same file type. Figure 42-11 illustrates how file associations work.

When you double-click a file, Explorer looks up the file extension under the HKEY_CLASSES_ROOT. It uses the (Default) key to learn the file type, which it also looks up under HKEY_CLASSES_ROOT. From there, Explorer learns which command it must run to open this file. The file type can also specify an icon, a context menu, property sheet information, and so on.

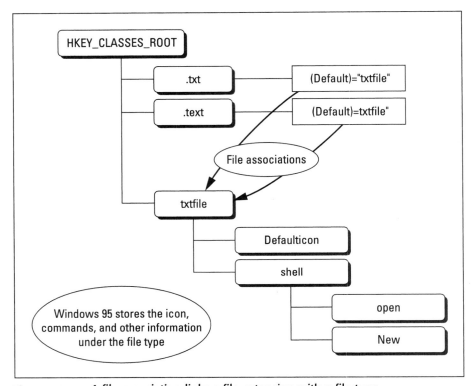

Figure 42-11: A file association links a file extension with a file type.

When you use <u>V</u>iew ➪ Options..., Explorer automatically creates both kinds of Registry keys for you. But what happens if you change your mind and want to use different extensions for a file type? Explorer does not have a simple way to change the filename extensions it associates with a file type. For this, you must edit the Registry manually.

Let's say you want to add a new extension (say, .TEXT) to the existing extensions for plain text files. First, you need to learn which Registry key Windows 95 uses for text files. Open the Registry Editor and expand HKEY_CLASSES_ROOT. Look for an extension Windows 95 currently uses for text files, such as .TXT. The data for the (Default) value is the name of the file type key. As you can see in Figure 42-12, this key name is "txtfile".

Now you can create a new key for .TEXT files. Select HKEY_CLASSES_ROOT, and choose <u>E</u>dit ➪ New ➪ Key. Enter **.TEXT** and click OK to create the new key. In the value pane, double-click the (Default) name. The Registry Editor prompts you for a new value. Enter **txtfile** and click OK. You have now created a new Registry key and value.

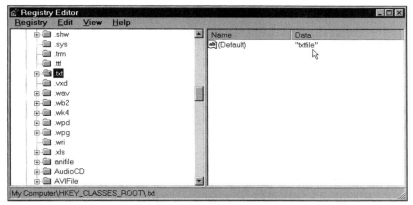

Figure 42-12: Add a new extension for a file type by creating a Registry entry under HKEY_CLASSES_ROOT.

Go to the Explorer window and choose View ➪ Options.... Look for Text Document, and notice TEXT is now one of the extensions it lists. When you double-click a .TEXT file, Explorer treats this file as a plain text file and opens it using Notepad or another text editor you may have installed.

Icon for BMP files

You already know you can specify a different icon for different kinds of files using My Computer or Windows Explorer. (Choose View ➪ Options, click the File Types tab, choose a registered file type, click the Edit button, and then click the Change Icon button.) For bitmap (.BMP) files, you can take things a step further, and display a miniature of the bitmap as the file's icon. Find the key, HKEY_CLASSES_ROOT\Paint.Picture\DefaultIcon. Set the (Default) value to %1. After this, Windows 95 displays the actual bitmap as the file's icon, as you can see in Figure 42-13. Change the view to large icons to get a better view of the miniature bitmaps.

You should do this only if you have a fast CPU and a fast disk. Reading and reducing the bitmaps can take a long time, especially for a folder containing many bitmap files, such as the Windows folder. With a Pentium-class machine, though, you probably won't notice much slowdown.

If you want to change the icon back, use the Explorer's View ➪ Options menu item to select a new icon for all bitmap files.

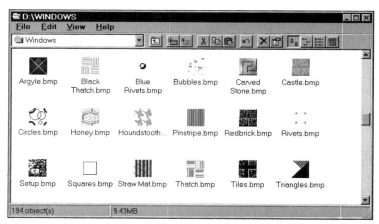

Figure 42-13: Display a miniature bitmap as a BMP file's icon

Cleaning up your desktop

Not every user likes the Windows 95 desktop and its icons. You can remove all the icons from your desktop in one swift move. Find the Registry key, HKEY_CURRENT_USER\Software\Microsoft\Windows\CurrentVersion\Policies\Explorer and create a DWORD value, with the name NoDesktop. Change the data to 1. When you restart Windows, your desktop will be completely clean of icons. And you won't be able to drag files to the desktop.

If you ever want to revert to the original Windows 95 desktop, change the NoDesktop value to zero (0), and restart Windows.

If you want to change many of the policy settings, the simplest way to do this is to use the System Policy Editor, which comes on the Windows 95 CD-ROM. The normal setup program does not install the Policy Editor, so you must do this manually. Look in the `Admin\AppTools` folder. The Policy Editor can give you a lot of control over the Windows 95 environment and desktop, but if you only want to eliminate the icons on your desktop, you will probably find the simplest way is to give the Policy Editor a miss and edit the Registry directly.

Tips of the day

Did you know Windows 95 stores its tips of the day in the Registry? Look at HKEY_LOCAL_MACHINE\SOFTWARE\Microsoft\Windows\CurrentVersion\Explorer\Tips, and you will see a list of string values. Each name is a number, such as "31". You can change the existing tips or add new tips. If you add new tips, make sure the numbers immediately follow those of the existing tips. You may need to hunt for the highest numbered tip because the tips are listed in alphabetical, not numerical, order.

Remember, the tips are under HKEY_LOCAL_MACHINE, so these changes affect everyone who uses the same machine.

Special folders

You can also look up useful information in the Registry for use elsewhere in Windows 95. For example, expand the key HKEY_CLASSES_ROOT\CLSID. You will notice a long list of subkeys with strange names, such as {21EC2020-3AEA-1069-A2DD-08002B30309D}. Windows 95 uses these strange key names to keep track of information when you link data in applications, for special files and folders, and so on. The specific values are cryptic because they are used by applications, not users. You needn't remember any of these special values, but you can use three of them in a special way.

When you choose the <u>S</u>ettings ➪ <u>C</u>ontrol Panel item from the Start menu, Windows 95 opens the Control Panel, which looks and acts like a folder, albeit a special folder. You can take advantage of this similarity between the Control Panel and folders by creating a Control Panel shortcut in your Start menu. By adding the Control Panel to the Start menu, the Control Panel applets become individual menu items. This means you can start one particular applet without opening the Control Panel folder.

This trick requires knowledge of the magic name for the Control Panel folder. You can learn this name by searching the Registry. Select the HKEY_CLASSES_ROOT\CLSID key and choose <u>E</u>dit ➪ Find. Type **Control Panel,** make sure the Data box is checked, and click OK. Windows 95 searches for Control Panel as the value data and finds the key with this value. The key name is the magic identifier for the Control Panel. You can create a folder in your Start menu and give the folder any name you like, but make the name's extension the same as the magic key name, for example, "Ctrl Panel.{21EC2020-3AEA-1069-A2DD-08002B30309D}".

To copy the key name without making a mistake, select the key name in the Registry Editor and start to rename it (press F2 or choose the Rename menu item). Select the entire text and press Ctrl+C to copy the name to the Clipboard. Then press Esc so you don't accidentally change the name of the key. You can then set the name of the new folder by typing **Ctrl Panel.** followed by Ctrl+V to paste the magic name.

Windows 95 recognizes the magic name (by looking it up in the Registry) and what started life as an ordinary folder becomes a magic Control Panel folder. You can now use the Ctrl Panel menu item in your Start menu to invoke any particular Control Panel applet, as shown in Figure 42-14.

You can do the same for your dial-up networking and printers folders. Look for the value data "Dial-up Networking" and "Printers" to find the magic key names.

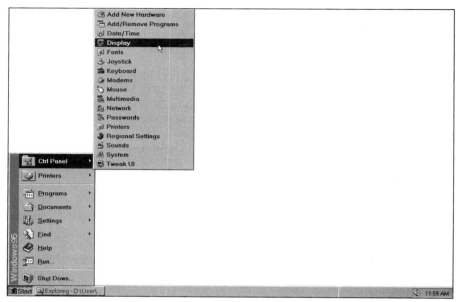

Figure 42-14: Start a Control Panel applet from your Start menu without opening the Control Panel folder.

Summary

This information has become a bit technical. But, remember, most of you will probably never have to edit the Registry directly. But should the occasion arise, here are some important points to remember:

◆ The Registry is a collection of information about your Windows 95 preferences and all the application programs on your PC.

◆ The Registry is automatically updated when you change preferences or install new programs, so a need to change the Registry yourself rarely occurs.

◆ The Registry replaces the initialization (.INI) files used in earlier versions of Windows.

◆ Information within the Registry is organized in a tree-like hierarchy, much like the way folders and files on a disk are organized.

◆ Always back up your Registry before making any changes to it manually.

◆ To edit the Registry, use the regedit program that comes with Windows 95. To start regedit, click the Start button, choose <u>R</u>un, type **regedit**, and then click OK.

◆   ◆   ◆

Appendixes

✦ ✦ ✦ ✦

In This Part

✦ ✦ ✦ ✦

Installing Windows 95

If you just purchased your PC, and it came with Windows 95 preinstalled, you needn't do anything in this appendix — you can go straight to Chapter 1 and start enjoying the new Windows.

I suspect most of you, however, currently have DOS and perhaps Windows 3.x on your PC, and you now need to install Windows 95. This appendix is written for you.

System Requirements for Windows 95

To use Windows 95, your PC must meet *at least* the following specifications:

Processor	386, 486, or Pentium
Memory (RAM)	4MB (8MB preferred)
Available hard disk space	30MB (40MB preferred)
Video display	VGA minimum; SVGA recommended

Hot Stuff If you already have Internet access, you can download a System Check program that will automatically determine if your PC is ready for Windows 95. Point your Web browser to `http://www.microsoft.com/windows/common/aa2677.htm` to download the program.

Preinstallation Housekeeping

If you've been using your PC for a while with DOS or DOS/Windows 3.x, now may be a good time to do a little spring cleaning and get rid of any old junk taking up space on your hard disk. Don't delete DOS or your existing version of Windows, however, and don't delete any programs you want to use after you install Windows 95. Delete only old projects you don't need anymore and any programs you no longer use. The process is sort of like moving to a new house; take this opportunity to eliminate some unnecessary clutter and extra baggage.

When you've whittled down your hard disk to DOS, Windows 3.x, programs you use frequently, and works in progress, consider doing the following: (If you don't know how to do these things, you can look them up in your DOS manual or just skip them.)

✦ If you know how to modify CONFIG.SYS and AUTOEXEC.BAT, comment out any commands that load TSR programs, such as antivirus utilities, pop-up tools, undelete utilities, screen savers, and any other extra goodies that use memory, but aren't required to make your system run.

 To comment out a command, type **rem**, followed by a space, at the beginning of the line.

✦ After you modify CONFIG.SYS and AUTOEXEC.BAT, shut down your PC, and then restart it to activate those changes and get a fresh start.

✦ If your computer has any time-out features, such as the suspend features used on portable PCs, disable those features now.

✦ If you have an antivirus program handy, run it now to check for, and delete, dormant viruses that may still be lurking on your hard disk.

✦ Make sure any external devices (modems, external CD-ROM drives, and so on) are connected and turned on, so Windows 95 can detect them during installation.

✦ Run SCANDISK or CHKDSK to tie up any loose ends caused by dangling file fragments.

✦ Run DEFRAG with full optimization to maximize the efficiency of your hard disk.

✦ If possible, back up the entire hard disk at this point.

✦ Run MSD, and make sure your system has what it takes to install and use Windows 95.

✦ If your PC is connected to a local area network (LAN), check to make sure you're connected to the LAN properly, so Windows 95 can see your LAN during installation.

If you discover your system doesn't meet the minimum system requirements, don't try to install Windows 95 until you upgrade your computer to meet the requirements. If you need help upgrading, contact your local computer dealer or repair service.

Starting the Installation

Now you're ready to begin the installation procedure. Gather your Windows 95 installation disks or CD-ROM, and (if you haven't already done so) start your computer in the usual manner. Then follow these steps:

1. If you have any programs running, close them; if you know of any TSR programs that are running and know how to terminate them, do so now.

2. If you are installing from floppy disks, put Windows 95 Disk 1 in drive A or B of your PC.

   If you're installing from a CD-ROM, put the Windows 95 compact disc in the CD-ROM drive.

3. If you are installing from a DOS-only PC (a PC that has no version of Windows on it), ignore the following steps; skip to "Installing on a DOS-only PC" later in this chapter.

4. If you haven't already done so, start Windows in the usual manner (type **win** at the DOS command prompt).

5. When you get into Windows, close all open windows *except* Program Manager.

6. Choose <u>F</u>ile ➪ <u>R</u>un.

7. Type *x*:**\setup**, in which *x* is the location of your Windows 95 disk.

   If you're installing from a floppy disk in drive A, for example, type **a:\setup**. If you're installing from a CD-ROM in CD-ROM drive D, type **d:\setup**.

8. Press Enter or click OK.

Start reading the onscreen instructions, and skip to "The routine-check phase" later in this chapter.

Installing on a DOS-only PC

If you're installing Windows 95 on a PC that doesn't have Windows 3.x on it, follow these steps to begin:

1. Make sure the DOS command prompt (C>) is on your screen and Windows 95 Disk 1 is in drive A or drive B, or the Windows 95 CD-ROM is in the CD-ROM drive.

2. Switch to the drive that contains the Windows 95 disk.

   If the Windows 95 Disk 1 is in drive A, for example, type **a:** and press Enter; you should see an A> prompt. If the Windows 95 CD-ROM is in drive D, type **d:** and press Enter; you should see a D> prompt.

3. Type **setup** and press Enter.

Start reading the onscreen instructions, and proceed with the following section.

The routine-check phase

In the first phase of the installation, the Setup program makes a routine check of your system. If you already ran SCANDISK and DEFRAG, this phase goes by quickly. If Setup finds any problems during this phase, you need to respond to any prompts that appear.

If you're installing from floppy disks, you probably will be prompted to remove and insert floppies after the routine check is complete. Follow the onscreen instructions.

About the Setup wizard

After copying some files to your hard disk, Setup starts the Setup wizard. The wizard handles most of the installation procedure. Various wizard screens ask questions and keep you informed as the installation proceeds, as in the example shown in Figure A-1.

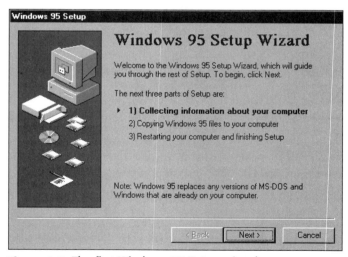

Figure A-1: The first Windows 95 Setup wizard screen

Most of the wizard screens contain buttons labeled Back and Next. In general, you want to read each screen, follow any instructions, make any selections presented on each screen, and then click the Next button. Click the Back button only if you need to return to a previous screen and change some earlier selections.

The installation procedure has several phases. The following sections describe each of these phases. For actual instructions on what to do next, always do what the screen tells you to do.

The Information-Collection Phase

The first step the wizard performs involves gathering information about you and your PC. The wizard screens are self-explanatory, but the following sections discuss your options in various screens.

Choosing a directory

When you are asked to choose a directory (see Figure A-2), you should choose C:\WINDOWS to replace your current version of Windows (if any).

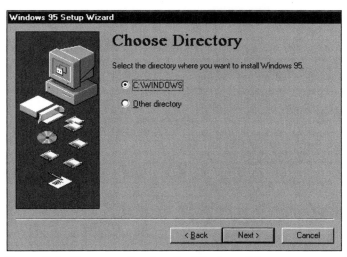

Figure A-2: Choose a directory for Windows 95.

I know you'll be tempted to keep the "old Windows" until you're sure about the new version and, indeed, you can choose Other directory and put Windows 95 in its own directory (such as Win95). But my experience has been that trying to keep two operating systems — or two versions of an operating system — on one hard disk is more trouble and more confusion than it's worth. I suggest you accept the suggested directory (C:\WINDOWS), and then click Next.

Setup takes a moment to prepare the directory and to check for installed components and available space.

Providing setup options and user information

You'll be given a choice of options for setting up Windows 95, as in the example shown in Figure A-3.

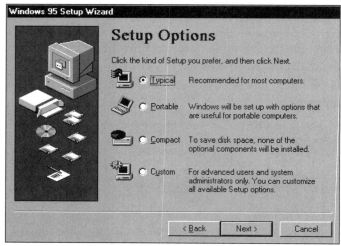

Figure A-3: Choose a Typical (desktop) or Portable (laptop) installation.

The options are self-explanatory. You probably will want to choose Typical if you're installing on a desktop PC. If you're installing on a laptop PC, choose Portable. You needn't worry about which components are installed right now; you can go back and add components at any time, as discussed in "Installing Missing Windows Components" in Chapter 9.

After you click Next, you are prompted to type your name and (optionally) your company name. Fill in the text boxes as they appear, and click Next to proceed through the wizard screens.

Analyzing your computer

Eventually, you reach the wizard screen that begins the hardware-analysis phase (see Figure A-4). You may see a list of hardware components. If you have any of the listed components, click the appropriate check boxes. Then click Next to start the hardware analysis.

Figure A-4: Ready to begin hardware analysis

The hardware analysis may take several minutes. Read the instructions onscreen during that phase to learn what you must do in case problems arise.

Getting connected

When the hardware analysis is complete, the Get Connected wizard screen appears (see Figure A-5).

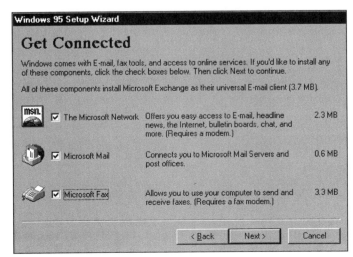

Figure A-5: The Get Connected wizard screen

You should choose options for which you have the appropriate hardware, as summarized in the following list:

✦ If you have a modem, choose The Microsoft Network.

✦ If you are on a LAN, choose Microsoft Mail.

✦ If you have a fax modem, choose Microsoft Fax.

Click the Next button to proceed.

Specifying Windows components

The next wizard screen (see Figure A-6) enables you to decide which components to install. Chances are you'll be better off making those decisions after you learn about all the various optional components. Installing components at any time in the future is easy, so you can safely choose Install the most common components (recommended), and then click Next to move along.

Figure A-6: Choose optional components or just move along.

Identifying the PC

You may be prompted to identify your computer on the network. If so, the following list explains how to fill in the blanks:

✦ *Computer name.* Type any name you feel like giving this PC — a brand name, pet name, your name, whatever.

✦ *Workgroup.* If you're a member of a LAN and also a member of a workgroup (a local departmental LAN), you must type the correct workgroup name. If you're unsure of your workgroup name, ask your network administrator. If you're not a member of a workgroup, you can leave this box blank or type **Workgroup**.

✦ *Computer Description.* Type any description you want to use.

Click the Next button after you fill in the blanks.

Creating a startup disk

If you have a blank floppy disk handy, creating an emergency startup disk is a good idea. This way, if your hard disk ever crashes, you can start your PC from the floppy.

To create the startup disk, choose the Yes option, and follow the instructions onscreen. When the startup disk is complete, I suggest you label it Windows 95 Startup and store it in a safe place.

If you don't have a floppy handy right now, you can create a startup disk later. For now, you can choose the No option, and then click Next to move along. Try to remember to create the startup disk soon, though, because if you ever need it, you'll *really* need it. And by then, you won't be able to create a new startup disk. The section titled "Making an Emergency Startup Disk" in Chapter 9 tells you how to create a startup disk at any time after the installation is complete.

The File-Copying Phase

After the information-gathering and startup-disk phases are complete, you move to Phase 2, which involves copying files (see Figure A-7).

Click the Next button, and follow the onscreen instructions. This phase takes several minutes. If you're installing Windows 95 from floppy disks, you'll be instructed to remove and insert disks as you go along.

Finishing Setup

After all the files have been copied, you're ready to start Phase 3 of the installation. Remove the floppy disk, if any, from the disk drive, and click Finish in the last wizard screen (see Figure A-8).

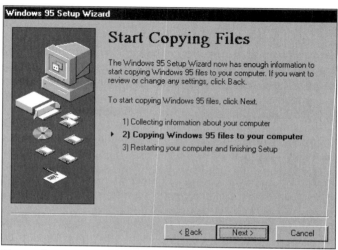

Figure A-7: Beginning Phase 2 (copying the files)

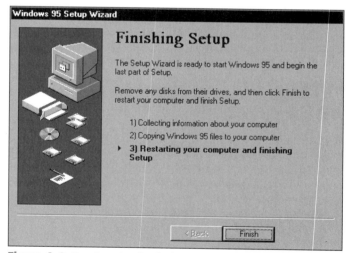

Figure A-8: Starting the final phase of installation

Windows 95 may take several minutes to start and to set up all your programs, the help system, and so on. Be patient.

You'll be given the opportunity to specify your time zone; do so, as the screen instructs you.

Toward the end of the installation, Windows 95 attempts to detect and install your hardware and it may ask questions about specific items. If you can answer those questions, do so. If you are unsure about any hardware item, don't panic, and don't guess — just choose the Not Installed option. You can always install a hardware device later, after you gather information about that device. For information on installing hardware, see Chapter 10 — *after* you finish installing Windows 95 and have read the basics in Chapters 1–5 or so.

When you get to the Welcome to Windows 95 window (see Figure A-9), the installation process is complete. Congratulations — you're in for some fun.

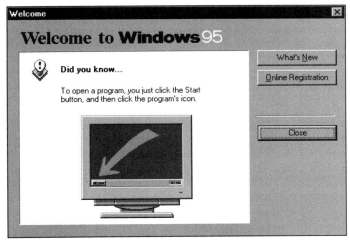

Figure A-9: Windows 95 is installed!

If you're a former Windows 3.x user who wants a summary of what's new and different in Windows 95, read Appendix B. If you're ready to get right into the program, start with Chapter 1.

Upgrading from Windows 3.x

To upgrade your DOS or Windows 3.x PC to Windows 95, follow the installation instructions presented in Appendix A. This appendix isn't a how-to thing. Rather, it's a discussion of *why* you might want to upgrade your system to Windows 95 and answers to some common questions.

Why Bother?

I guess the first question everyone asks is "Why should I bother upgrading to Windows 95 when my DOS/Windows 3.x PC is working fine?" Well, there are several answers to that question. The most important question, though, centers around the differences between 16-bit software and 32-bit software.

You've probably noticed a lot of cool new software is available for Windows 95 and Windows NT. Getting the Windows 3.x version of that program may not be easy and, in some instances, may not even be possible. Contrary to popular belief, this is not a marketing ploy to force you to buy new hardware and software. Rather, it's because of a more fundamental change to the way computing is done nowadays. The old DOS/Windows 3.x combo represented a 16-bit operating system. Windows 95 (and NT) are 32-bit operating systems.

A 32-bit operating system gives programmers — the guys who create the programs you buy and use — more creative leeway. Creating a 16-bit version of a new 32-bit program is a lot of work and may take months to complete. For this reason, the Windows 3.x version of some cool new program is often unavailable for many months after the 32-bit version has already been released.

Furthermore, things programmers can do in the 32-bit world are virtually impossible to do in the 16-bit world. "Backpedaling" a 32-bit program down to a 16-bit operating system often requires removing some cool features of the program. So many people who wait months for the Windows 3.x of a program are disappointed because the 16-bit version isn't as good as the 32-bit version.

The bottom line is the PC is an evolving technology, with the constant goal being to create more powerful, and yet more user-friendly, machines the general public can use. The switch from the 16-bit world to the 32-bit world was a big step in this evolution. To make this step yourself, you must abandon your old 16-bit DOS/Windows 3.x operating system and replace it with a 32-bit operating system. This may not be what you want to hear, but it's the truth.

So, let's look at some specifics and, hopefully, answer some questions that may pop up before, and after, you upgrade.

Before the Upgrade

If you haven't already upgraded to Windows 95, you may be wondering whether it's worth doing so. What new advantages — and new headaches — are likely to result from this upgrade? The questions and answers in this section deal with those questions.

What is Windows 95?

Windows 95 is more of a replacement for the DOS and Windows products you probably use now than an upgrade of those products. Windows 95 is a completely new and separate product, and also a major improvement (in my opinion). Earlier versions of DOS/Windows were tied to the early 16-bit PC and AT (286) computers. Windows 95 is a clean break from all that, taking advantage of the 32-bit technology offered in the 386, 486, and Pentium microprocessors.

What benefits will I get from upgrading?

Upgrading offers many benefits and, I suspect, within a few weeks of doing so, you'll wonder how you ever got along without Windows 95.

One immediate improvement is an easier, more intuitive interface (when you get the hang of it). Multitasking also is better; you can print, format a disk, and download files with your modem at the same time. Better multimedia is almost guaranteed. Plug-and-play technology means you can buy new gadgets and gizmos, plug them in, and use them — all without the conventional headaches involved in installing new devices.

Will my existing hardware and software work?

If you currently use DOS and Windows 3.x, the answer to this question almost certainly is yes. You can check the hardware requirements at the beginning of Appendix A, if you're not sure. But most likely, if your PC runs Windows 3.x now, it'll run Windows 95 just fine.

Many 16-bit programs will run fine on a Windows 95 PC. The only truly "troublesome" programs tend to be DOS games and some custom software. If you have a 16-bit program with which you absolutely cannot part, you may want to check with the creator or manufacturer of that program to make sure it will run in Windows 95. Or, to see if they've made a Windows 95 version of that program.

Most older hardware components will also continue to function after you upgrade to Windows 95. However, the components will probably work better if you replace the current 16-bit driver for that program with a new 32-bit driver. In many cases, Windows 95 will make this replacement for you, automatically and behind the scenes. So the conversion will be painless. But, once again, it never hurts to ask the hardware manufacturer for information on making the change to Windows 95.

What about my local area network?

Windows 95 is compatible with most existing LAN software, including Windows networks and Novell networks. If your PC is connected to a LAN, you should leave it connected to the LAN when you install Windows 95. This way, Windows 95 can detect your LAN hardware and software and adjust to it automatically. You'll still be on the LAN after you complete the upgrade.

If you don't have a LAN, but you're considering setting up one, Windows 95 is a *must-have* product. You probably can set up the LAN yourself, using the built-in LAN capabilities (no extra programs are required!).

Is Windows 95 OK for laptop PCs?

Windows 95 is the operating system of choice for portable PCs. A special installation option is designed for portables, and many new features make portable computing easier and more productive. (Part V of this book is about portable computing.)

A few options for portable computers require special hardware. Onscreen power management, for example, requires Advanced Power Management 1.1 (APM 1.1). If you don't have APM 1.1, however, your existing power-management tools will still work. Hot docking — the capability to dock and undock a portable PC without powering down — requires a special plug-and-play BIOS. If your PC doesn't have the fancy BIOS, don't fret. You'll find docking and undocking your PC are much easier under Windows 95; you'll just need to power down to do so.

What is plug-and-play?

The phrase *plug-and-play* has been around for a while, even though it has never been meaningful. (I remember buying a plug-and-play network card that promised I could plug it in and forget it. After fighting with this card for hours, I realized the promise really was "Plug it in and forget you ever bought it, 'cause it ain't gonna work — ever.")

Microsoft is trying to formalize a plug-and-play specification that really *is* plug-and-play. That is, when you buy a new piece of hardware — such as a modem, network card, scanner, CD-ROM drive, or sound card — you can literally plug it into your PC and start using it. You won't have to hassle with complex installations, CONFIG.SYS and AUTOEXEC.BAT files, and IRQs.

Because the term *plug-and-play* has been used loosely for several years, Microsoft had to come up with a special logo to identify products that really are Windows 95 plug-and-play-compatible. These devices bear a logo that specifically says "Designed for Windows 95."

Will plug-and-play devices work on my existing PC?

You needn't buy an entirely new PC to use "Designed for Windows 95" plug-and-play devices. When you install a plug-and-play device in your existing PC, you still get the benefits of easy, automatic installation.

How does Windows 95 compare with Windows for Workgroups?

Windows for Workgroups (version 3.11) was a successor to Windows version 3.1. The major difference between 3.11 and 3.1 is the 3.11 version offers built-in networking; versions 3.1 and 3.11 require DOS and are the older 16-bit operating systems. Windows 95 is a 32-bit operating system and does not require DOS.

Windows 95 offers the same built-in Windows networking that Windows for Workgroups offers. If you have PCs connected in a Windows for Workgroups network now, you can add a Windows 95 PC to your existing LAN or upgrade any PC on the LAN.

How does Windows 95 compare with Windows NT?

Windows NT is geared toward high-end workstations with a great deal of RAM (at least 16MB) and disk space (200MB just for the operating system). The product works with high-end processors, such as those in the Dec Alpha and MIPS machines. NT also offers symmetric multiprocessing, which means if your PC has several processors, NT uses them all at the same time.

Windows 95 is the operating system of choice for modern desktop and portable PCs. The product runs only on PCs that sport 386, 486, and Pentium microprocessors. The hardware requirements of Windows 95 are much more modest; about 4MB of RAM (although 8MB is recommended) and about 40MB of extra hard disk space (for the operating system) will do the trick.

How did we get to version 95?

For years, I've been asking software manufacturers, "Why don't we stop with the random version-numbering system and start using the year, the way we do with cars?" Under that system, the version number would be a point of reference. We all know how old a '76 Volkswagen is, for example, but how old is QuasiCalc 6.01?

Nobody ever listened to me, of course. But someone at Microsoft apparently came up with the same idea, so we now have year numbers instead of version numbers. (No, this change does not mean an upgrade will come out every year — I asked. Microsoft may skip some years.)

After the Upgrade

After you upgrade to Windows 95, a new crop of questions may arise as you explore the new terrain. This section deals with those issues.

What happened to Program Manager?

Program Manager, in Windows 95, is set up more like a menu than a window. If you click the Start button and then point to (or click) Programs, you should see your original program groups. To open one of those groups, point to it or click it. To start a program, click its icon in the menu.

You may miss your old buddy Program Manager for a few days, but I recommend you get used to the new Start-button method of launching programs. Two clicks launch virtually any program. And as Part I of this book explains, you can set up shortcuts to programs you use frequently.

You'll also learn to appreciate the Documents menu and the entire document centric approach, both of which enable you to forget about programs. If you want to open and edit an existing document, choose that document from the Documents menu or double-click the document's icon. I never use the old method of opening a program, and then choosing File ⇨ Open to open a document. Now, every document is just one or two clicks away.

What happened to File Manager?

File Manager has been replaced by Windows Explorer. To launch Explorer, click the Start button, point to Programs, and click Windows Explorer. You'll see the similarity with File Manager immediately.

Windows 95 also has two great alternatives to Explorer: My Computer and Find. Find is especially good, because you don't even need to know where a particular file is located to open it; you can type part of the name of the file you want, and Find finds it for you. Double-click the document's icon and, bingo! — the file is open and ready for editing.

What happened to DOS?

Windows 95 has no DOS to start up from and no DOS to exit to. When you want to shut down your PC, click the Start button, choose Shut Down, click Shut down the computer?, and then click Yes. Wait a few seconds. When all your work is saved, a big message onscreen tells you it's safe to turn off the PC.

If you need to get to a DOS command prompt, click the Start button, point to Programs, and choose MS-DOS prompt. From the C> prompt that appears, you can use whatever DOS commands you're familiar with. When you want to return to Windows, type **exit** and press Enter.

If you come across a DOS program that absolutely refuses to run from a window, you must take a different route to the C> prompt. Click the Start button, click Shut Down, click the option titled Restart the computer in MS-DOS mode?, and then click Yes. You should be able to run that feisty DOS program from the C> prompt that appears. (Use this method as a second resort. You'll get better performance if you can run the DOS program by using the first method.)

Should I really learn to use this new interface?

Yes, you really should learn the new user interface. You, no doubt, will have many temptations to bring the old Program Manager back to your desktop, but I think you'll be better off learning to use the new Start-button technique of launching documents and programs. From there, you can learn about creating shortcuts to things you access often.

What happened to directories?

Directories still exist, but they're called *folders* now. In Explorer and other browsing tools, folders are identified by a little manila-file-folder icon. (I think a file-drawer icon would be a better analogy, though, because a folder may contain several files.)

How do I use those long filenames?

In case you haven't heard, Windows 95 no longer limits you to those dinky eight-character filenames. Now you can use up to 255 characters, including spaces, to identify a folder or file. Instead of naming a file QTR01TXS.XLS, for example, you can name it First Quarter Taxes.xls.

Only 32-bit programs (programs designed for Windows 95 and Windows NT) enable you to type these long filenames, however. When you use the 16-bit version of a program, you still are limited to typing eight-character filenames, with no spaces.

What's on the CD-ROM?

The CD-ROM in this book is brought to you by Software USA, distributors of outstanding shareware for Windows users. I think you'll enjoy these high-quality, try-before-you-buy programs, and you'll like how easy it is to find, install, and run the sample programs from Software USA's special browser. The CD-ROM contains a sampling of programs from all five of Software USA's special interest groups, as summarized in the following:

- ✦ Home and Office
- ✦ Children's programs
- ✦ Education
- ✦ Games
- ✦ Lifestyles

Using the CD-ROM

Using the CD-ROM couldn't be easier. Just remove the CD-ROM from its protective holder in the back of the book. Then follow these simple steps:

1. Insert the CD-ROM into your CD-ROM drive.
2. Wait a few seconds as the browsing program loads.

If, for whatever reason, your PC isn't set up to autostart CDs, follow these steps instead:

1. Insert the CD-ROM into your CD-ROM drive.
2. Open My Computer (double-click the My Computer icon on your Windows 95 desktop).
3. Right-click the icon for your CD-ROM drive and choose Explore from the shortcut menu that appears.

4. Scroll down to, and double-click, the icon for the program named smartcd.exe.

The browser window will open up looking like Figure C-1.

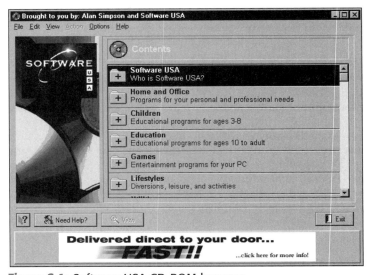

Figure C-1: Software USA CD-ROM browser

If you don't want to listen to the browser's background music, choose <u>O</u>ptions ➪ Background Music from its menu bar.

You'll see a list of Special Interest Groups (categories), each preceded by a file folder icon with a plus sign in it. To look at more detail in a category, click that category's icon. For example, in Figure C-2, I've clicked the Home and Office Special Interest Group, and you can see a list of programs within that category (Web Wizard, Font Lister, and so forth).

To learn more about a particular program, double-click the program's name, or highlight the program name and click the View button. A brief description of the program appears, as in Figure C-3. Note, too, beneath the description are some tabs, which provide more information.

✦ **Details**: Description of the program.

✦ **Screenshot**: A sample screen display.

✦ **Requirements**: Hardware needed to run this program.

✦ **Publisher**: Person or company that publishes the program.

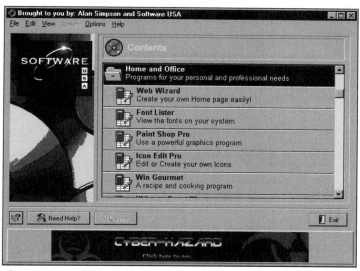

Figure C-2: Exploring offerings in the Home and Office special interest group

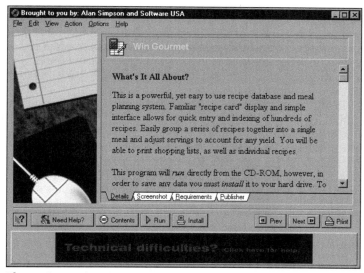

Figure C-3: A description of Win Gourmet, one of the programs in the Home and Office special interest group

While you're viewing information about a single program, you can use the buttons listed here to try the program, or to explore some more:

✦ **Contents**: Takes you back up to the level of program Special Interest Groups.

✦ **Run**: Enables you to run the program immediately, without even installing it on your hard disk.

✦ **Install**: Takes you step-by-step through the procedure necessary to install the program on your hard disk.

Life Saver   Not all programs can be run directly from the CD-ROM. If the program you're currently viewing fits this category, the Run button will be dimmed and unavailable. To try the program, you must first install it using the Install button.

Plenty of online help is available as you browse through the CD-ROM's offerings. Just go to the Contents screen and open the Software USA folder for information about shareware and Software USA, and for answers to Frequently Asked Questions (FAQs). To close the browser, click its Close button (X), or choose File ⇨ Exit from its menu bar.

About Software USA

Software USA is a private club of shareware enthusiasts. Benefits of membership to this club include monthly mailings of top-notch shareware, technical support by phone, and an extensive library of top-notch shareware programs. All programs have been hand-selected by a sophisticated selection committee, which allows only the best products to reach your hands. No demos, teasers, time-wasters, or nasty viruses allowed — only fully functioning programs with complete try-before-you-buy capability! If you want to purchase a program, you must register with the publisher and pay their fee. If you don't like a program, simply don't buy it!

As a Software USA member, you'll pay a small volume charge that's automatically billed to your credit card, covering shipping, handling, and duplication. Cost of membership is $19.95 per month if you join a special interest group, such as Home and Office, Children's, Games, Education, Lifestyles, or Hot Picks and Features. Or, you can receive *all* the programs in all the special interest groups for a low $24.95 per month. You'll receive as many as 50 programs per month, which comes out to as little as 50 cents per program!

To join, or to get more information, contact:

Software USA, 9909 Huenekens Street, San Diego, CA 92121
Phone: (619) 455-6200; Fax: (619) 455-0039

If you have access to the Internet, you can also contact Software USA through any of these addresses:

Web Site: http://www.softusa.com
General Information and Sales: sysop@softusa.com
Customer Support: custserv@softusa.com
Webmaster: sysop@softusa.com

Programs on the CD-ROM

The CD-ROM in this book contains some samples of the types and quality of programs mailed each month to members of Software USA. Several programs from each special interest group, as well as some additional useful utility programs, are included and are listed in the following pages.

Home and Office Special Interest Group

Are you looking for programs to help you with your business or personal finances? This special interest group offers programs that help you manage money, resources, employees, events, recipes, addresses, and more. Desktop publishing programs in this group help you create and print professional-quality flyers, pamphlets, booklets, and newsletters. You'll also find some fonts and clip art in this special interest group. The CD-ROM you already own offers these samples from the Home and Office special interest group:

Web Wizard

Try your hand at creating your own home page for the World Wide Web. Web Wizard will ask you a few simple questions, and then create a file containing HTML (Hypertext Markup Language). You may then view the file using Netscape Navigator, Microsoft Internet Explorer, or any other Web browser. (Publishing the page requires an Internet account with home page).

Font Lister

Are so many fonts installed on your computer that you don't know what they all look like? With FontLister you can view a list of all the fonts (installed or not) on your system. You can delete unwanted fonts or install new ones. You can even print out a fontbook (a list of your fonts) for quick and easy reference!

Paint Shop Pro

This is the complete Windows graphics program for image creation, viewing, and manipulation. Features include painting with eight brushes, photo retouching, image enhancement and editing, color enhancement, image browser, batch conversion, and scanner support. Included are 20 standard filters and 12 deformations. Supports plug-in filters. Over 34 file formats.

Web site: http://www.jasc.com

Icon Edit Pro

Tired of looking at the same old desktop? Now there is Icon Edit Pro, a powerful, yet easy to use, icon editor and browser for Windows 95. With Icon Edit Pro, you can create icons up to 256 colors and choose from several different sizes. You can mark, move, mirror, or rotate any rectangular area to create your own personalized icons.

Web site: http://pcwww.uibk.ac.at/subz/c40551

Win Gourmet (Cuisine)

A powerful, but simple to use, recipe database and meal-planning system. Familiar recipe card display and simple interface enables quick entry and indexing of recipes. Easily group a series of recipes together into a single meal and adjust servings to determine any yield. Prints shopping lists, too!

Web site: http://www.smisoftware.com

Ultimate Event Planner

Helps you plan any event where you have timelines to keep, budgets to maintain, contacts to track, guests to invite, and other details to handle. Provides a single place to store and organize all the important events in your business and personal life.

Children's Special Interest Group

Kids love to learn and have fun with the computer. Software USA's programs make learning and playing easy and fun. This group of programs will best be enjoyed by children in the age range of toddlers to sixth grade. Members of this special interest group will receive about ten programs per month. Programs cover counting and reading, shape recognition, problem solving, adventure and general knowledge. Perfect for families with young children. The CD-ROM you already have includes these programs:

Child's Play 2

This children's paint program will keep your little ones busy for hours. Includes incredible paint tool effects, rubber stamps, sound effects, and various screen erasers. Also loads, saves, and prints their masterpieces.

Roxie's Math Fish

A multimedia game designed to teach your child addition, subtraction, multiplication, and division. With attractive animation and excellent sound effects, Roxie the cat will play "Go Fish" with your child, gently helping him or her to choose the correct card. The mouse cursor changes in different areas of the screen providing for intuitive play. This game is used in schools.

Primary Learning

Primary Learning presents ten educational exercises for children, ages 6 through 14. These educational programs teach spelling, math, and geography.

Hansel and Gretel

Your kids can sit back and enjoy the story of *Hansel and Gretel* as the narrator reads aloud. They can color pictures, too!

Web site: http://www.tellitagan.com

Web site: http://members.aol.com/latticewrk/lattice.htm

Education Special Interest Group

Educators and teachers select programs in this Special Interest Group, focusing on students from seventh grade to college level. Learn music, facts, languages, and more. The CD-ROM you now own includes the following programs:

Guitar Teacher

A system for studying, saving, and printing guitar chord diagrams. Print chord charts. Supports Sound Blaster, MIDI audio boards, 7 chord formulas (with 6 alternatives per chord), 504 chords, formula and voicing displayed, right- or left-handed fingering. The program also includes a guitar tuner, as well as instruction on tuning and chord structure. Please note that you must have a sound card installed on your computer in order to play chords.

Math Flight

Practice basic arithmetic with activities, including addition, subtraction, multiplication, division, mixed addition/subtraction, and mixed multiplication/division. You can also print arithmetic operation tables.

Web site: http://www.datacom.ca/~ron

Presidents of the United States

Provides an overview of every United States President. Look up biographical information, dates in office, and other interesting presidential facts. A great source of information for students.

SouthAmeriGeo

Learn all the countries and capitals of South America and parts of Central America. Has both teaching and quizzing modes.

Web site: http://www.hway.net/jcvrosen/advantage.html

Selingua

Selingua is a vocabulary training program with extensive built-in dictionaries. More than 2,000 words in English, German, Spanish, French, and Swedish. Can be used by native speakers of any of those languages.

Games Special Interest Group

This special interest group offers fun and exciting entertainment programs, including Action, Arcade, Adventure, Simulation, and Strategy games, as well as Sports and Puzzles. Included on the CD-ROM in the back of this book.

DX-Ball

Break all the bricks on the screen to gain points and continue to the next board. Catch blue bonuses for good options, red ones for bad options, and gray ones for mixed blessings. See the title screen of the game for a complete table of bonuses and their functions.

Age of Sail

The navies of the era provided in this game varied greatly in leadership and crew training. Great details of each ship in the fleet help provide you with strategies to battle with the other ships. Gives you strong seaman skills.

Web site: `http://www.empire-us.com/aos/index.htm`

Quiver

Aliens have stolen orbs, allowing them to return to your world's distant past. You must stop them from altering your planet's past — and present!

Web site: `http://www.esdgames.com`

Lifestyles Special Interest Group

Sports, leisure activities, and general human interest programs are what the Lifestyles' special interest group is all about. Software covering everything from hobbies like cross-stitching to sports to entertaining programs that help you customize your answering machine message. Representative programs from this group, which are on the CD-ROM you now own, include:

Golf League Recorder

Would you like to improve your Golf Game? Try Golf League Recorder! Golf League Recorder tracks your and your golf buddies' scores and tracks performance. You enter in the scores for the local golf course and it helps you identify your problem holes. In addition, this program is fully customizable and even allows 9-hole rounds.

Jigsaws Galore

The ultimate Windows jigsaw puzzle game! Ten puzzles are included and the user has the ability to design custom puzzles. Puzzles can be set to varying difficulty from 4 to 4,000 pieces. Cheating is allowed if you need help, although the game is so much fun you probably wouldn't ever want to cheat!

Web site: http://www.dgray.com

Professional Bartender

A complete bartending program to assist both the professional and amateur bartender.

Web site: http://www.delve.com/aardvark.htm

Screen Loupe

Need to get a quick close-up of your screen? Just move your mouse over any portion of the screen to get a closer view. Screen Loupe enables you to view any section of the screen at 2X, 4X, or 8X magnification. Great for visual impaired, elderly, educational uses, and just for fun.

Lagoon Screen Saver

Hilarious screensaver of a cartoon undersea world.

Web site: http://www.slagoon.com

Noteworthy Player

Play MIDI files created with Noteworthy Composer.

Web site: http://www.ntworthy.com

Utilities

Many shareware programs don't fall into any particular special interest group. Instead, these general programs, often called *utilities*, help you get more from your computer and Windows 95. As examples of the kinds of programs you'll get from Software USA, the CD-ROM in this book includes the following utility programs:

Runtime Libraries

A collection of files required to run a variety of shareware programs. Easily installed. If you already have one of these files installed, the program will tell you and you can skip the reinstallation.

WinZip 6.2

WinZip 6.2 for Windows 95 and NT. Features built-in ZIP & UNZIP. Handles MIME, UUencode, XXencode, BinHex, TAR, gzip, and so forth. Now with the WinZip Self-Extractor Personal Edition. Includes tight integration with the Windows 95 shell: drag-and-drop TO or FROM the Explorer or ZIP and UNZIP without leaving the Windows Explorer.

Web site: http://www.winzip.com

System Analyst for Windows (SAW)

SAW is a Windows diagnostic utility that shows pages of useful system information. Help files explain most of the terms used. Display/save/print report. Monitors system resources/events/errors in the background. Automatic install/uninstall. Full information given before installation.

ACDSee

ACDSee is two tools in one. As an image viewer, ACDSee stands unsurpassed in its ability to decode and display many different image formats quickly. High-quality output is another advantage of ACDSee, with single- and double-pass dithering algorithms, which enable you to make optimal use of your display's capabilities. An important feature is incremental display, whereby images are displayed on the fly as they are decoded.

You can scroll, zoom, or use any other function while ACDSee is decoding, which means you spend less time waiting and more time doing. ACDSee also gives you the capability to view a sequence of images automatically, as in a slide show. If you use ACDSee as an image-viewing helper application, you can reduce window clutter by configuring ACDSee to show all images in the same window, instead of starting a new program instance for each image.

Web site: http://www.acdsys.com/acd

Keyboard Shortcuts: Quick Reference

If you frequently use the keyboard in your work, you may find you often have to take your hands off the keyboard to perform some simple mouse operation — for example, opening a drop-down list in a dialog box. You could, in fact, press Alt+down arrow to open the drop-down list.

If you take a minute to review the common keyboard shortcuts summarized in this appendix, you may find a technique that enables you to keep your typing fingers on those home keys.

Feature/Action	*Keyboard Shortcut*
Accessibility: Filter Keys	Hold down right Shift key for 8 seconds
Accessibility: High Contrast	Left Alt+left Shift+Print Screen
Accessibility: Mouse Keys	Left Alt+left Shift+Num Lock
Accessibility: Sticky Keys	Tap Shift 5 times
Accessibility: Toggle keys	Hold down Num Lock for 5 seconds
Beginning of line	Home
Bottom of document	Ctrl+End
Bypass auto-play on CD-ROM	Hold down Shift while inserting CD-ROM

Feature/Action	Keyboard Shortcut
Bypass startup programs	Hold down Shift during startup
Cancel	Esc
Check box: toggle on or off	spacebar
Close document window	Ctrl+F4
Close failed (hung) program	Ctrl+Alt+Delete
Close folder and all parent folders	Hold down Shift and click Close (X)
Close program window	Alt+F4
Command-prompt startup	Press F8 at Starting Windows prompt message
Context menu	Shift+F10
Copy to Clipboard	Ctrl+C
Cut to Clipboard	Ctrl+X
Cycle through program windows	Alt+Tab
Delete	Delete
Delete; no Recycle Bin	Shift+Delete
Drag-and-drop, copy item	Ctrl+drag
Drag-and-drop, create shortcut	Ctrl+Shift+drag
Drag-and-drop, move item	Alt+drag
End of line	End
Explore object	Shift+double-click
Explorer: Collapse selection	- (gray minus key)
Explorer: Expand all below	* (gray asterisk key)
Explorer: Expand selection	+ (gray plus key)
Explorer: Go To	Ctrl+G
Explorer: Go To Parent	Backspace
Explorer: Next pane	F6
Explorer: Open combo box	F4
Explorer: Refresh	F5
Explorer: Scroll without moving selection	Ctrl+arrow key
Find	F3

Feature/Action	Keyboard Shortcut
Help	F1
Insert/Overwrite: toggle on or off	Insert
Menu	F10
Microsoft Natural keyboard: Cycle through	Win+Tab taskbar buttons
Microsoft Natural keyboard: Explorer	Win+E
Microsoft Natural keyboard: Find Computer	Ctrl+Win+F
Microsoft Natural keyboard: Find File/Folder	Win+F
Microsoft Natural keyboard: Minimize All	Win+M
Microsoft Natural keyboard: Run	Win+R
Microsoft Natural keyboard: System Properties	Win+Break
Microsoft Natural keyboard: Undo Minimize All	Shift+Win+M
Microsoft Natural keyboard: Windows Help	Win+F1
Minimize all open windows (from taskbar or desktop)	Alt+M
New document	Ctrl+N
Next open program window	Alt+Tab
Next option in dialog box or form	Tab
Next tab of dialog box	Ctrl+Tab
OK	Enter
Open document	Ctrl+O
Open drop-down list	Alt+down arrow
Open Look In list	F4
Open property sheet	Alt+Enter or Alt+double-click
Open With: display verb list	Ctrl+right-click
Option buttons	space bar
Paste	Ctrl+V
Preceding option in dialog box or form	Shift+Tab
Preceding tab of dialog box	Ctrl+Shift+Tab
Print	Ctrl+P
Refresh	F5

Feature/Action	Keyboard Shortcut
Rename	F2
Save document	Ctrl+S
Select All	Ctrl+A
Select text	Shift+any direction key
Select to beginning of document	Shift+Ctrl+Home
Select to end of document	Shift+Ctrl+End
Select to end of line	Shift+End
Select to start of line	Shift+Home
Start menu (open)	Ctrl+Esc
Top of document	Ctrl+Home
Undo	Ctrl+Z

Glossary

:-): Your basic smiley symbol (when viewed from the side — lean your head left), often used in e-mail messages to mean "just kidding."

<g>: In an e-mail message, means "grin" or "just kidding."

10BASE-T: A type of cable used to connect computers together in a local area network. Typically plugs into an RJ-45 slot on a network adapter card and Ethernet hub.

16-bit: The addressing scheme used in the original IBM PC and AT (286) computers. The main reason for the old 640K limit.

256-color: The minimum number of colors many modern programs will accept. To change your color settings, right-click the desktop, choose Properties, and then click the Settings tab.

32-bit: The addressing scheme used in 386, 486, and Pentium processors. Enables a wider range of addresses and processes data more quickly.

A

Active Desktop: An added bonus to Microsoft's Internet Explorer 4, which replaces the Windows 95 wallpaper with an interactive layer that can provide easy access to the Internet information services, sites, and local documents.

active window: The window currently capable of accepting input. The active window is said to *have the focus*. The active window can cover other windows on the desktop.

AOL (America Online): A popular information service offering e-mail, special-interest groups, Internet access, and other services.

anonymous FTP: A service that enables Internet users to upload and download files freely across the Internet, without identifying themselves or typing passwords.

API (Application Programming Interface): A set of routines programmers can call from higher-level languages. These routines access capabilities of the operating system.

ASCII (American Standard Code for Information Interchange): A standard for describing characters that allows different makes and models of computers to communicate with one another. An *ASCII file* or *ASCII text file* is one containing only ASCII characters, no pictures or formatting codes.

associate: To tie a filename extension to a program. For example, the .doc filename extension is usually associated with Microsoft Word. When you double-click a document with the .doc extension, Windows automatically opens Microsoft Word and opens the file on which you double-clicked.

At Work: Microsoft Corporation's initiative to get all office equipment — including PCs, telephones, fax machines, and copy machines — to interact with one another.

B

backward compatibility: The ability to use documents, settings, and so forth, from earlier products. For example, Windows 95 is backwardly compatible with DOS and Windows 3.x.

baud: The speed of a modem. The higher the baud rate, the faster the modem.

BBS (Bulletin Board Service): A service you can contact via telephone lines using your modem and a communications program, such as HyperTerminal. Most offer special interest groups, shareware, freeware, and other services.

binding: A process that establishes a communication channel between a network adapter card's driver and the driver for a network protocol. In Windows 95, bindings are available via the Network icon in the Control Panel.

BIOS enumerator: In a plug-and-play system, the BIOS enumerator identifies all hardware on the motherboard.

bps (bits per second): A measure of a modem's speed, also expressed as *baud*.

bookmark: To mark a page on the World Wide Web for easy return in the future. In Microsoft Internet Explorer, the term *favorite* is more common than the term *bookmark*.

BRB: Abbreviation for Be Right Back, often used in Internet chats.

browse: To look around at drives, folders, and files using My Computer, Windows Explorer, or a dialog box's Browse button. To look around the Internet using a program like Microsoft Internet Explorer.

bus: A device that controls other devices. For example, when you plug a new board into a PC, you're actually plugging it into a bus.

byte: The amount of space required to store one character. For example, the word *cat* requires three bytes of storage; the word *Hello* requires five bytes.

C

cache: Pronounced *cash*. Refers to an area in RAM where frequently accessed data is stored to speed access.

CD-ROM (Compact Disc Read-Only Memory): CD-style disks used in CD-ROM readers on a PC. Unless you have special equipment, you can only read information *from* a CD-ROM. You cannot add, change, or delete files.

CDFS (Compact Disc File System): The system Windows 95 uses to manage files stored on a CD-ROM.

character: A single letter, digit, or punctuation mark. For example, nine characters are in the following boldface text: **Hello123!**.

chat: A means of communicating over a network (including the Internet) by typing messages back and forth. Requires a special program like Microsoft Chat.

CIS (CompuServe Information Service): A popular information service offering e-mail, special-interest forums, Internet access, and other services.

click: To press and release the main mouse button after positioning the mouse pointer onto whatever you want to click. The main mouse button is usually the one that rests comfortably under your index finger.

client: A computer on a LAN that uses some resource shared by another computer on the LAN. The computer to which the shared resource is physically connected is called the *server*.

Clipboard: An area in memory where objects can be stored temporarily, for cut and paste procedures. Typically, you select an object (by clicking it) or select text (by dragging the mouse pointer to it). Then to copy to the Clipboard, choose Edit ⇨ Copy, or press Ctrl+C. Move to wherever you want to put the object/text, and choose Edit ⇨ Paste or press Ctrl+V to copy the Clipboard's contents to the insertion point position. To open the Clipboard, click Start and choose Programs ⇨ Accessories ⇨ Clipboard Viewer.

close: To remove an object from the screen so it's no longer visible. Typically, closing an object removes it from memory (RAM) and saves it to the hard disk.

CMOS: Memory maintained by a small battery within the PC. Often used to manage settings that come into play before the operating system is loaded. When you see a message, such as "Press <Del> to run Setup," pressing the Delete (Del) key at this point takes you to the CMOS settings of that PC.

codec: A system to compress/decompress digital video and sound to minimize the amount of disk space required for storage.

computer name: The name assigned to a computer, up to 15 characters in length. To assign a name to a computer, open Control Panel, double-click the Network icon, and click the Identification tab.

connectoid: An icon inside the Dial-Up Networking folder that contains the information necessary to connect, by modem, to a particular online service or Internet Service Provider (ISP). The Dial-Up Networking folder exists inside the My Computer folder.

context menu: The menu that appears when you right-click an object. Also called a *shortcut menu* or a *pop-up menu*.

context-sensitive help: Onscreen help relevant to what you're currently trying to do. In Windows 95, you typically use the Help key (F1) or question-mark (?) button to receive context-sensitive help.

control: Any button, list, or text box within a dialog box that enables you to control how the computer will behave.

Control Panel: The place in Windows 95 where you choose your own settings and preferences, add new hardware and software, and alter profiles. Click Start and choose Settings ⇨ Control Panel. Or open My Computer and double-click the Control Panel icon.

CTI (Computer/Telephone Integration): Using a PC in combination with the telephone system. For example, voice mail (see *telephony*).

Ctrl+Click: To hold down the Ctrl (control) key while you click objects with your mouse.

Ctrl+Drag: To hold down the Ctrl (control) key while you drag an object with your mouse.

cyberspace: A nickname for the Internet or all the networks of the world. The place where e-mail messages travel to get from sender to recipient.

D

DDE (Dynamic Data Exchange): A means by which two separate programs can exchange data and commands. Available in early Windows, DDE has been superseded by OLE in more recent versions of Windows.

default: A selection that will be used unless you specify otherwise. For example, when you print, the job is sent to the *default printer* unless you specifically request a different printer.

default printer: The printer used when no other printer is specified. To define the default printer, open My Computer, and then double-click the Printers folder. Right-click a printer's icon and choose Set As Default from the shortcut menu. Only one printer can act as the default printer.

desktop: Basically, your entire screen when Windows 95 is running.

desktop component: A program that can be placed on Internet Explorer 4's Active Desktop. Several desktop components are available from `http://www. microsoft.com/ie/ie40/gallery`.

desktop icon: An icon that appears right on the desktop, such as My Computer and Recycle Bin. You can also add your own *shortcut* icons to the desktop.

desktop theme: A combination of sounds, wallpaper, screen saver, and icons to give your entire desktop an appearance. The Microsoft Plus! package comes with several desktop themes.

device: A general term for any gizmo or gadget you put into a computer or attach to a computer with a cable.

device driver: (see *driver*)

dialog box: A box with options, which appears on the screen, so you can make additional selections. For example, choosing File ⇨ Open from a program's menu bar typically displays that program's Open dialog box.

DHCP (Dynamic Host Configuration Protocol): A protocol for TCP/IP configuration, often used for Internet connections.

digital video: Video stored in binary format on a disk, rather than in the analog format of a VHS tape.

dimmed: An option or command that's grayed because it's unavailable in the current context. For example, Copy and Cut commands are dimmed when an object or text is selected. On the Edit menu, Paste is dimmed when the Clipboard is empty.

directory: (see *folder*)

directory server: A place on the Internet where people who want to communicate gather. Used in conjunction with a communications program like Microsoft NetMeeting.

DLL (Dynamic Link Library): A file containing API routines programmers can access using procedure calls from a higher-level language.

DMA channel (Direct Memory Access channel): A direct channel for transferring data between a disk drive and memory, without involving the microprocessor.

dock: To put a portable PC into a docking station or port replicator.

docking station: A unit that connects a portable computer to larger desktop accessories, such as full-sized keyboard, monitor, and disk drives.

document: Typically a file you create while using some program. For example, when you use a word processing program to type a letter, that letter is a *document*.

document-centric: An operating system design that focuses on the documents people create and use, as opposed to the programs needed to create/edit those documents.

DOS (also MS-DOS): The original Disk Operating System for the IBM PC. Purely textual interface where you type commands, rather than clicking icons with a mouse. Still used to create many games because DOS enables quick screen updating useful in simulations and animations.

driver (also called a *device driver*): A small program that makes a hardware device work. For example, to print, you typically need a printer (hardware) and a driver (software) for that printer.

Dial-Up Networking: A service that lets a PC dial into another PC or local area network and access its shared resources. The PC that dials the phone is called the *dial-up client*. The PC that answers the phone is called the *dial-up server*.

domain: In Windows NT, a group of computers sharing a common domain database and security policy controlled by a Windows NT Server domain controller.

domain name: On the Internet, the last part of an e-mail address. For example, in alan@coolnerds.com the coolnerds.com part is the Internet domain name.

domain controller: In a local area network, the Windows NT computer that authenticates logons, controls security, and then maintains the master domain database.

DNS (Domain Name System): A database used by Internet TCP/IP hosts to resolve host names and IP addresses. Enables users of remote computers to access one another by host names rather than IP address.

double-click: To point to an object with the mouse pointer, and then press and release the main mouse button twice in rapid succession (click-click!). The main mouse button is usually the one that rests comfortably under your index finger.

drag: To hold down the mouse button while moving the mouse, usually to move an icon or selection to some new location on the screen. Right-drag means to drag using the secondary mouse button (usually the mouse button on the right side).

drag-and-drop: A mouse technique of dragging an object from one location and dropping it in another.

drop-down list: A text box with a down-arrow box attached, so you can choose an option from a list rather than typing in an option. To open the drop-down list, click the drop-down list arrow, or press Alt+down arrow.

DSP (Digital Signal Processing): A feature of modern telephony boards that allows hardware to be updated to new standards using software only. Prevents the hardware from becoming obsolete each time a new modem or compression standard comes on the market.

download: To copy something from another computer onto your own computer.

E

e-mail: Electronic mail sent over a local area network (LAN) or a wide area network (WAN).

e-mail address: The address that uniquely identifies you on a network, much as your street address uniquely identifies the location of your home (see *Internet address*).

edit: To change something, such as a letter you've written.

editor: A program that enables you to change something, like a letter you've written.

EPS (Encapsulated PostScript): High-resolution graphics file that can only be printed on PostScript printers.

Ethernet: The most widely used network protocol for PCs.

Ethernet cable: The cable used to attach a PC's network adapter card to an Ethernet concentrator.

Ethernet concentrator: A device to which all PCs in a local area network connect via Ethernet cables.

Ethernet hub: Another name for an Ethernet concentrator.

event: Any activity from the mouse, keyboard, or a program the computer can detect. Mouse clicks and key presses are events.

Explorer: A browsing tool in Windows 95 you can get to by clicking the Start button, pointing to Programs, and choosing Windows Explorer.

F

factoid: A small fact, or a fact that could change with time.

FAQ (Frequently Asked Questions): A document you can browse on the Internet or download from a fax-back service to answer common questions about a topic.

FAT (File Allocation Table): The filing system used by DOS and 16-bit versions of Windows. Windows 95 uses a 32-bit implementation of FAT called VFAT (Virtual File Allocation Table).

file: The basic unit of storage on a disk. For example, when you create and save a letter, that letter is stored in a *file*. Each file within a folder has its own unique filename.

file sharing: Allowing multiple PCs on a local area network access to the same set of files on one PC. To allow file sharing on a PC, you must make sure file sharing is enabled in the network properties (right-click Network Neighborhood and choose Properties). Then to share a drive or folder, right-click the item's icon in My Computer, and choose Sharing.

file system: The overall structure in which files are named and organized. Windows 95 uses VFAT for the hard disk, CDFS for CD-ROM drives.

flame: To rant and rave on the Internet or another information service.

FTP (File Transfer Protocol): A service that allows file transfers over a TCP/IP connection. Commonly used to upload/download files across the Internet.

FTP site: A place on the Internet with files you can download — using an FTP program — to your own computer.

folder: An area on the disk containing its own set of files. Called a *directory* in DOS and earlier versions of Windows.

font: A lettering style. To add, view, and remove fonts in Windows 95, click Start, choose Settings ⇨ Control Panel, and then double-click the Fonts folder. To assign a font to text in a program, select the text. Then choose Format ⇨ Font from the program's menu bar.

free space: The amount of unused space on a disk. To see how much free space is available, open My Computer, click a drive icon, and look at the status bar, or run ScanDisk on the drive. To gain free space, delete unwanted files and empty the Recycle Bin.

G

gateway: (see *IP Router*)

graphics: Pictures (as opposed to text).

graphics accelerator: A hardware device that speeds complex graphics rendering onscreen.

H

hack: To get past a password or other security device. A hacker is a person who gets into places in Cyberspace. Also a general term for *programmer* or computer enthusiast.

Help key: The key labeled F1 near the top of the keyboard. Pressing F1 usually brings up context-sensitive help.

High Color: A scheme that shows near photographic-quality color on your PC. Also called *16-bit color*. To change your color settings, right-click the desktop, choose Properties, and then click the Settings tab. Not all hardware supports High Color, however.

home page: The first page you come to on a World Wide Web site on the Internet. Clicking the Home button in a Web browser returns you to the home page.

host: Any device attached to the Internet using TCP/IP. For example, the computer that answers the phone in dial-up networking. In direct-cable connection, the PC with the shared resources you want to access.

hot docking: The capability to connect a portable computer to its docking station without powering down the portable PC. Requires a special plug-and-play BIOS.

hot swapping: A characteristic of some PC cards that allows insertion/removal of the card without powering down the PC.

HPFS (High Performance File System): The file system used by the OS/2 operating systems. Supports long filenames, but no security.

HTML (Hypertext Markup Language): A set of tags used to add boldface, italics, lists, images, and hyperlinks to Web pages, e-mail messages, and newsgroup postings.

HTTP (Hypertext Transport Protocol): The protocol used in the World Wide Web to allow documents to call one another.

hub: Short name for an Ethernet concentrator or Ethernet hub. A device into which all PCs on the local area network connect via cable.

hyperlink: A hot spot on a Web page or in some other document that, when clicked, takes you to some new page or location on the Internet.

I

Icon: Any little picture on the screen. Typically you can right-click an icon to see its options and properties. Double-clicking an icon usually opens it into a window.

in-place editing: A technique that enables you to edit an embedded document without leaving the program you're in currently. The tools of the object being edited come to the current program's menu bar and toolbar.

INI file: A text file that holds information necessary to initialize a program. In Windows 95, these settings are stored in the Registry, but the original INI files are maintained to support backward compatibility.

Internet: A worldwide network of computers into which anyone can tap. Home of such popular services as the World Wide Web, FTP, Usenet Newsgroups, and Internet e-mail (among others).

Internet address: A person's mailing address on the Internet. If you have an MSN account, your Internet address is your MSN name followed by @msn.com.

Internet Explorer: A program included in the Microsoft Plus! kit that enables you to explore the Internet from your Windows 95 PC. Requires a modem, Microsoft Network (MSN) account, or an account with an ISP.

Internet mail: e-mail sent through the Internet via a direct ISP connection or a connection through some other service such as MSN, CompuServe, or America Online.

Internet Service Provider: (see *ISP*)

Interrupt: A condition that disrupts ongoing processing to call attention to a process that needs processor resources.

I/O device: Any hardware device that provides input to, or output from, the central processing unit. Printers, mice, keyboards, monitors, and disk drives are all I/O devices.

IP address: An address used to identify a computer uniquely on the Internet. A series of numbers, such as 123.45.67.890, assigned by an Internet Service Provider (ISP).

IP Router: A computer connected to several TCP/IP networks that can route or deliver packets between networks. Also called a *gateway*.

IPX/SPX: A network transport protocol used by Novell Netware networks. In Windows 95, the NWLINK.VXD module implements the IPX/SPX protocol.

IRQ (Interrupt Request Line): The line a hardware device uses to call attention to the processor. Typically, each hardware device must have its own IRQ. To view IRQ usage in Windows 95, click Start and choose Settings ⇨ Control Panel. Double-click the System icon, click the Device Manager tab, and then double-click Computer at the top of the list.

ISDN (Integrated Services Digital Network): Provides Internet access at up to 128K, more than twice the speed of 56K modems. Requires special arrangements with your Internet Service Provider and local telephone company.

ISP (Internet Service Provider): A service that connects your PC to the Internet via your modem and telephone line (see *Appendix C*).

J

JPEG (Joint Photographic Experts Group): Compression/decompression scheme used for digital video (see *MPEG*).

K

K or **KB** or **Kilobyte**: 1,024 bytes (characters).

kernel: The part of an operating system that manages the processor.

L

LAN (local area network): Computers connected to one another with cables and network adapter cards, rather than by modems and telephone lines.

legacy: Older hardware devices that don't conform to the Designed for Windows 95 plug-and-play specification.

local area network: (see *LAN*)

local printer: A printer that's physically connected, via a cable, to the current PC.

localization: Adapting software to the language and formats of a specific country or culture.

LOL: Abbreviation for *Laugh Out Loud,* often used in Internet chats.

lurk: To hang around and read messages in an Internet newsgroup without really contributing to the group. This is a good thing to do for a while when you're new to a newsgroup.

M

map a drive letter (also called *map network drive*): To assign a shortcut drive-letter name, such as *M:* or *P:,* to a shared device in a local area network. To map a drive letter, double-click Network Neighborhood, double-click a computer's icon, and right-click a shared device, and then choose Map Network Drive from the shortcut menu.

MAPI (Messaging Application Programming Interface): Allows programs to access the messaging capabilities of the operating system. For example, many programs offer a File ⇨ Send option, which interacts with the MAPI and enables you to send messages directly from that application.

memory: Generally refers to RAM in PC lingo, as opposed to some other type of memory (such as disk storage).

Memphis: Code name for the next major release of Windows 95, sometimes referred to as Windows 97, Windows 98, and Windows 90x.

menu: A list of options. Clicking the Start button displays the Start menu.

message: The general term for any kind of correspondence, such as a note or letter, that takes place over computers.

message box: Any box that appears on the screen to display a message.

Microsoft Network: (see *MSN*)

MIDI (Musical Interface Digital Interface): A standard for playing music on a PC's sound board.

MIME (Multipurpose Internet Mail Extensions): A protocol that allows e-mail messages to contain more than plain text.

miniport driver: A 32-bit virtual driver that allows the easy addition and removal of hardware, without rebooting the entire system. Windows 95 and Windows NT both support miniport drivers.

MMX: A new feature of Pentium processors that helps multimedia applications run faster and better.

modem: A device that connects your PC to a telephone line.

MPEG (Motion Picture Experts Group): A modern compression/decompression scheme for digital video that may, someday, allow video to run as smoothly on a PC as it does on a TV/VCR.

MS-DOS: (see *DOS*)

MSN (Microsoft Network): An information service provided by Microsoft Corporation.

Mwave: IBM's implementation of the DSP standard that allows modem and telephony hardware to be updated via software, so the actual hardware doesn't become obsolete when standards improve.

My Computer: A browsing tool to find resources on your own PC. Usually the first icon on the desktop. Also displays icons for shared resources on other PCs to which you've mapped a drive letter.

N

NDIS (Network Driver Interface Specification): The interface for network drivers. All transport drivers call the NDIS interface to access network adapters.

net (the net): A slang expression for *the Internet.*

NetBEUI transport (pronounced *net buoy*): Stands for NetBIOS Extended User Interface, a local area network transport protocol provided in Windows 95.

NetBIOS (Network Basic Input/Output System): A program that allows input/output requests to be sent to, and received from, another computer on a local area network.

netiquette: Network etiquette, polite and proper conduct on the Internet.

netizen: A citizen of a network or the Internet.

network: Two or more computers connected to one another with cables or modems and telephone lines. A local area network (LAN) is generally PCs close to one another and connected without modems and telephone lines. A wide area network (WAN) is composed of computers connected with telephones and modems. A LAN can connect to a WAN.

network adapter card: A hardware device that enables you to connect a PC to other PCs in a local area network.

network adapter driver: A small program that controls a network adapter card.

network administrator: The person in charge of managing a local area network, including accounts, passwords, e-mail, and so on.

Network Neighborhood: A desktop icon, which, when double-clicked, displays shared resources on other PCs in the same workgroup on your local area network. Network Neighborhood enables you to browse shared resources on the LAN in much the same way My Computer enables you to browse resources on your own computer. If you use Network Neighborhood to map a drive letter to a shared resource, that resource will then be available in your My Computer window.

network printer: A shared printer physically connected to some other PC in the LAN. Opposite of a *local printer*.

newbie: Someone who is just beginning to learn how to use the Internet.

newsgroup: An electronic bulletin board on the Internet where people post messages to one another.

NDIS (Network Driver Interface Specification): The interface for network driver adapters in all Windows networks.

NIC (Network Interface Card): Another name for a *network adapter* or *network adapter card*.

NT: The shortcut name for *Windows NT*, Microsoft's 32-bit operating system for high-end workstations and non-Intel processors, such as the Dec Alpha and Power PC.

NTFS: The file system used by Windows NT.

O

Object: An individual chunk of data you can manipulate on the screen, which can be a chart, picture, sound, video, or chunk of text.

object-oriented: An operating system that allows chunks of data to be manipulated as individual objects and easily moves/copies from one program to another.

object package: (see *package*)

OLE (pronounced *olay*): The acronym without words, OLE originally stood for *object linking and embedding,* a feature of Windows that enables you to take an object from one program (such as a chart in a spreadsheet program), and to link or embed that object into another program's document (such as a word processing report). OLE's capabilities extend beyond simple object embedding. Now if you ask a Microsoft person what OLE stands for, he or she will likely say "nothing . . . it's just olay."

OOP: Object-oriented programming language used to control an object-oriented operating system.

Option button: A small, round button in a dialog box that generally enables you to select only one option of many. Also called *radio buttons* (because only one button can be "pushed in" at a time).

OSR 2: A special version of Windows 95 that ships only on new computers manufactured after 1996. For more information, see
`http://www.microsoft.com/windows/pr/win95osr.htm`.

P

package (also called an *object package*): An icon that represents a linked or embedded object. Double-clicking the icon opens and displays the contents of the package.

packet: A chunk of information sent over a network. This typically includes a *header* describing the source and destination address, an ID number, and information used for error control.

page: 1) Internet: an electronic document in the World Wide Web or Gopher; 2) RAM: a fixed-sized chunk of memory; 3) BBS: "page the sysop" means to sound a beep on the system operator's PC.

password: A string of characters that enables you to access protected data.

path: The location of a folder described in terms of its drive folder and subfolder. For example, in c:\winword\mydocuments\Letter to Mom.doc, the c:\winword\mydocuments\ part is the path to the file named Letter to Mom.doc. Also a DOS command used to identify directories to search, now handled by the Registry in Windows 95.

PC Card: A credit card-sized adapter card that fits into the PCMCIA slot of a portable or desktop PC.

PCI (Peripheral Component Interconnect): A local bus system that allows quick and easy installation of devices and supports high-speed graphics processing. Used in many Pentium and Apple Power PC computers. The successor to the older ISA, EISA, and VL bus systems.

PCMCIA (Personal Computer Memory Card International Association): A standard that defines how PC Cards must be designed to work in the PCMCIA slot of a portable or desktop PC.

peer-to-peer network: A way to connect several PCs into a local area network where any PC can act as either client or server.

plug-and-play: A general term for devices that are (supposedly) easy to plug into your PC and use. In Windows 95, a device that really *can* be plugged in and used immediately. The latter devices bear the Designed for Windows 95 logo.

plug-and-play BIOS: A Basic Input/Output System capable of configuring plug-and-play devices during power up and also during run time.

point: *To point to* an object means to move the mouse until the mouse pointer is touching that object.

pointing device: A mouse or trackball used to move the mouse pointer around on the screen.

PPP (Point-to-Point Protocol): An industry standard method of connecting PCs through telephone lines. PPP is often used to connect a PC to the Internet and to connect one PC to another during dial-up networking.

pop-up menu: The menu that appears when you right-click an object. Also called a *context menu* or a *shortcut menu.*

port: A slot on the back of your PC into which you plug a cable that connects to some external device. Mice, keyboards, monitors, external modems, external CD-ROM drives, printers, and all other external devices plug into a port on a PC.

port replicator: A compact-sized docking station for a portable computer that allows easy connection to a full-sized keyboard, mouse, monitor, and other devices.

Postoffice: The place where an e-mail message is stored until the recipient reads the message. In a workgroup, only one PC can play the role of Postoffice.

preemptive multitasking: A scheduling technique that allows the operating system to take control of the processor at any time. Allows multiple hardware devices, such as modem, printer, screen, and floppy disk to operate simultaneously.

primary mouse button: On a right-handed mouse, this is typically the button on the left. If you reverse the mouse buttons for left-handed use, the primary mouse button becomes the mouse button on the right. The idea is to use whichever mouse button rests comfortably under your index finger as the primary mouse button.

printer driver: A small program that allows a PC to drive a printer (to make the printer work).

printer fonts: Fonts built into the printer, rather than stored on disk. Also called *resident fonts.*

printer sharing: Allowing your printer to be used by other members of a local area network. On the local PC (the one to which the printer is connected) print sharing must be enabled through Network Neighborhood properties. Then the printer must be installed as a local printer, and then shared via the Printers folder in My Computer. Other LAN members must then use the Add New Printer icon in their own Printers folder, and the Network Printer option, to connect to that shared printer.

private key: A password you create to manage your own *public keys*.

program: Software that makes the computer perform a specific task or helps you perform some job using the PC.

properties: The characteristics of an object. You can usually get to an object's properties by right-clicking the object's icon and choosing Properties from the shortcut menu that appears.

property sheet: A specialized dialog box or tab within a dialog box, that enables you to view and change an object's characteristics. For example, right-clicking the Windows 95 desktop and choosing Properties, opens the Display Properties sheet.

protocol: An agreed-upon set of rules by which two computers can exchange information over a network. Windows 95 supports three protocols: NetBEUI, TCP/IP, and IPX/SPX.

public key: Passwords shared by people who need to secure privacy in their fax and e-mail transmissions. To read someone else's private transmissions, you must get a public key from that person. To create your own secured messages, you need to create a public key and to send it to your intended recipients.

R

RAM (Random Access Memory): Super-fast memory that stores whatever programs and document you're working with currently. The term *memory* is often used as a synonym for RAM.

real mode: The general term for a 16-bit device driver loaded into memory from the CONFIG.SYS or AUTOEXEC.BAT file. Windows 95 attempts to replace all real-mode drivers with its own 32-bit virtual drivers, which provide better performance.

refresh: To update something on the screen so it shows current data. Can typically be accomplished by pressing the F5 key or choosing View ➪ Refresh from a menu bar.

RegEdit (Registry Editor): A program you can use to manipulate the Registry directly, without using Control Panel or any property sheets. To open, you must click the Start button, choose Run, then type **regedit,** and then press Enter.

registered file type: A type of document file associated with a specific program, based on its filename extension. For example, all .DOC files are registered to (associated with) the Microsoft Word for Windows program. Extensions on registered file types are hidden unless you use View ⇨ Options in My Computer to turn off the option titled Hide MS-DOS file extensions for file types that are registered.

Registry: The place where Windows 95 stores all settings and preferences you choose through Control Panel, and all associations between filename extensions and programs.

remote administration: The ability for a person to control sharing and other settings on someone else's PC from his or her own PC in the LAN. The PC being administered must grant this permission via the Passwords icon in Control Panel.

rich text: Text that contains special formatting like **boldface** and *italics*.

resource: An item that can be shared in a LAN. For example, disk drives, folders, CD-ROM drives, printers, and modems are all useful resources that can be shared.

right-click: To point to an object, and then click the secondary mouse button (typically the mouse button on the right side of the mouse).

right-drag: To hold down the secondary mouse button while dragging an object across the screen.

root directory: The topmost folder on a disk, typically named \. For example, C:\ represents the root directory of drive C:.

S

SCSI (Small Computer Standard Interface, pronounced *scuzzy*): An interface specification that allows multiple disk drives, CD-ROM drives, and other devices to be connected to one another, and then connected to a single port on the PC.

search engine: A special service on the World Wide Web that helps you find information on a particular topic. Alta Vista at `http://www.altavista.com` is a search engine.

secondary mouse button: On a right-handed mouse, this is typically the button on the right. If you reverse the mouse buttons for left-handed use, the secondary mouse button becomes the mouse button on the left. The button that rests comfortably under your middle or ring finger.

select: To specify on which object(s) you plan to perform some operation. Usually you select one object by clicking it. To select multiple objects, you can use Ctrl+Click or Shift+Click. Or you can drag a frame around the objects. To select text, drag the mouse pointer through the text.

selection: An object (or objects) already selected and, hence, framed or highlighted in some manner.

server: In a LAN, the PC with some resource connected directly to it. For example, if your PC has a printer attached to it, and you let other LAN users print to your printer, your PC is acting as the *print server*. The other PCs are *clients* to that server.

share: To allow multiple users on a local area network to use a single device, such as a printer or modem, that's attached to only one PC in the LAN. You can also share disk drives, CD-ROM drives, and folders.

shareware: Programs you're allowed to try — and use — for a while, without charge. If you like the program, the authors hope you'll *register* and send in some money. In return, you get a noncrippled version of the program or mailings when bigger and better versions are available.

shortcut: 1) An icon on the desktop that enables you to open a folder, document, or program without going through the Start menu; 2) An alternative to using the mouse, often called a *keyboard shortcut*.

SLIP (Serial Line Internet Protocol): A method used to connect a PC to an Internet Service Provider. PPP is preferred over SLIP when connecting to the Internet with Windows 95.

smart favorites: Icons that point to favorite places on the Internet, which also show a gleam when information on this site has changed. A feature of Internet Explorer 4 and the Active Desktop (see *Chapter 29*).

smiley: A series of characters that, when turned on its side, looks like a facial expression. For example, this is the basic :-) smiling face smiley. Also called *emoticon*.

snail mail: The new term for what we used to call *mail*. Any mail that involves paper, as opposed to e-mail.

spamming: Using the Internet as a means of advertising. A *spam* is an e-mail or newsgroup posting that's true intention is to advertise some product or service.

Start button: The button that appears in the taskbar, which you can click to start a program, open a recently saved document, get help, and so forth.

Start menu: The first menu to appear after you click the Start button in the taskbar.

status bar: The bar along the bottom of a program's window that provides information about the status of various options within that program. Can typically be turned on or off using a command on the program's View menu.

string: Textual rather than numeric data. For example, 123.45 is a number, whereas *My dog has fleas* is a string (of characters).

subfolder: A folder contained within another folder. The containing folder is called the *parent folder.*

subnet: Any smaller network connected to the Internet.

subnet mask: A value that enables the recipient of Internet packets to distinguish the network ID portion of the IP address from the ID of the host.

SVGA (Super Virtual Graphics Array): The type of display card and monitor that gives you high resolution, rich color, and graphics. An improvement over standard VGA.

system menu: A menu you can open by clicking the icon in the upper-left corner of a window or by pressing Alt+Spacebar. Enables you to move and size a window using the keyboard rather than the mouse.

sysop: The term used for the person who operates a bulletin board.

T

TAPI (Telephony Application Program Interface): A standardized set of procedures programmers can use to enable their programs to interact with the modem and dialing properties on your PC.

TCP/IP (Transmission Control Protocol/Internet Protocol): The primary communications protocol used on the Internet. Allows a Windows 95 PC to participate in UNIX-based bulletin boards and other information services. Can also be used to allow a non-Windows PC (such as an OS/2 computer) to connect to a Windows local area network.

telephony: The interaction between PCs and telephones. A *telephony board* is a device you can add to your PC to support voice mail, fax-on-demand, and similar services.

text file: A file that contains only ASCII text codes like letters, numbers, spaces, and punctuation — no hidden codes. Text files should be created and edited with text-only editors, such as NotePad.

thread: 1) A series of messages about a topic posted to an information service; 2) An executable chunk of program code that can run simultaneously with other threads in a microprocessor.

TIA (Thanks In Advance): Often used to close an e-mail message.

title bar: The colored area across the top of the window that shows the window's name and offers the Minimize, Maximize, and Close buttons, and system menu. To move a window, drag its title bar. You can also maximize/restore a window by double-clicking its title bar.

toolbar: A set of buttons and other controls that provide one-click access to frequently used menu commands. A program's toolbar usually appears below its menu bar. In many windows, you can choose <u>V</u>iew ➪ Toolbar to show/hide the toolbar.

tooltip: A little label that appears below a button after you rest the mouse pointer on that button for a few seconds.

tray: The name originally given to the Windows 95 taskbar.

True Color: A scheme that shows photographic-quality color on your PC. Also called 24-bit color. To change your color settings, right-click the desktop, choose <u>P</u>roperties, and then click the Settings tab. Not all hardware supports True Color, though.

U

UART: Pronounced *wart,* a chip used on a modem or serial device that determines the top speed of serial communications. The latest UART — 16550A — offers the highest speeds.

UNC (Uniform Naming Convention): A method of identifying a resource by its computer name, followed by a resource name. The computer name is preceded by two backslashes, for example, *\\Comm_Center\MyStuff.*

Unimodem: A universal driver for modems.

upload: To copy something from your own computer to some other computer on a network.

URL (Uniform Resource Locator): The address of a single page on the World Wide Web or other resource on the Internet.

Usenet: A service on the Internet that enables people to communicate via newsgroups. Each newsgroup is like an electronic bulletin board where members post messages to one another.

V

VDM (Virtual DOS Machine): An environment used to run 16-bit DOS and Windows 3.x programs in Windows 95.

VESA (Video Electronic Standards Association): A group that defines standards for video displays (see *VL*).

VGA (Virtual Graphics Array): The type of display card and monitor that gives you rich color and graphics.

virtual driver: A 32-bit Windows 95 device driver that can be loaded into upper memory via the Registry (as opposed to a real-mode driver, which must be loaded into conventional or upper memory via CONFIG.SYS or AUTOEXEC.BAT).

virtual memory: Disk space used as RAM when RAM runs out.

virus: A computer program specifically designed to do damage on whatever PC it lands. High-tech vandalism.

VL (VESA Local bus): A standard that allows high-speed connections to monitors and other devices. Often used in modern 486 computers. PCI — another standard — is used in Pentium computers.

V*x*D: A 32-bit Windows 95 virtual device driver, often used as a filename extension on the device driver's filename. The *x* indicates the type of device being driven. For example, .VPD is a printer driver; .VDD is a display driver.

W

WAOL: A Windows program for accessing the America Online information service.

WAN (Wide Area Network): A large network that extends beyond the boundaries of an office or building. The Internet is a WAN.

wart: (see *UART*)

Web: Short for *World Wide Web*.

Web browser: A program, such as NCSA Mosaic or Netscape Navigator, that enables you to access the Internet's World Wide Web.

whiteboard: A simple drawing program that can be used by several people at the same time. Microsoft Chat comes with a whiteboard.

WinCIM (Window CompuServe Information Manager): A program used to access the CompuServe information service from a PC that uses Windows.

window: The space on a screen that holds one program or dialog box. Double-clicking an icon typically opens that icon into a window.

Windows NT: Microsoft's 32-bit operating system for high-end workstations and non-Intel processors. For example, computers that use the Dec Alpha, MIPS, or PowerPC chips can run the Windows NT operating system. Only Intel PCs with 386, 486, or Pentium chips can run Windows 95.

WINS (Windows Internet Name Service): A naming service that resolves Windows network computer names to Internet IP addresses.

workgroup: A collection of computers in a LAN that all share the same workgroup name. When you first open Network Neighborhood, it displays other computers in your same workgroup. You determine to which workgroup a PC belongs by using the Identification tab in network properties (right-click Network Neighborhood and choose Properties).

workstation: A PC with unusually high processing capabilities, often used for computer-aided design and similar calculation-intensive and graphics-intensive jobs. May use a non-Intel microprocessor, such as the Dec Alpha, or multiple 486 or Pentium processors.

World Wide Web: A popular place on the Internet, where you can browse through documents that contain text, graphics, and even multimedia.

Z

zipped file: A file that has been compressed to speed transmission across telephone lines. The file must be *unzipped* on your computer after you receive it, using a program such as WinZip or PKZip (see *Appendix D* or `http://www.winzip.com`).

INDEX

Numbers and Symbols

A

IDG BOOKS WORLDWIDE, INC.
END-USER LICENSE AGREEMENT

READ THIS. You should carefully read these terms and conditions before opening the software packet(s) included with this book ("Book"). This is a license agreement ("Agreement") between you and IDG Books Worldwide, Inc. ("IDGB"). By opening the accompanying software packet(s), you acknowledge that you have read and accept the following terms and conditions. If you do not agree and do not want to be bound by such terms and conditions, promptly return the Book and the unopened software packet(s) to the place you obtained them for a full refund.

1. **License Grant.** IDGB grants to you (either an individual or entity) a nonexclusive license to use one copy of the enclosed software program(s) (collectively, the "Software") solely for your own personal or business purposes on a single computer (whether a standard computer or a workstation component of a multiuser network). The Software is in use on a computer when it is loaded into temporary memory (RAM) or installed into permanent memory (hard disk, CD-ROM, or other storage device). IDGB reserves all rights not expressly granted herein.

2. **Ownership.** IDGB is the owner of all right, title, and interest, including copyright, in and to the compilation of the Software recorded on the disk(s) or CD-ROM ("Software Media"). Copyright to the individual programs recorded on the Software Media is owned by the author or other authorized copyright owner of each program. Ownership of the Software and all proprietary rights relating thereto remain with IDGB and its licensers.

3. **Restrictions on Use and Transfer.**

   (a) You may only (i) make one copy of the Software for backup or archival purposes, or (ii) transfer the Software to a single hard disk, provided that you keep the original for backup or archival purposes. You may not (i) rent or lease the Software, (ii) copy or reproduce the Software through a LAN or other network system or through any computer subscriber system or bulletin-board system, or (iii) modify, adapt, or create derivative works based on the Software.

   (b) You may not reverse engineer, decompile, or disassemble the Software. You may transfer the Software and user documentation on a permanent basis, provided that the transferee agrees to accept the terms and conditions of this Agreement and you retain no copies. If the Software is an update or has been updated, any transfer must include the most recent update and all prior versions.

4. **Restrictions on Use of Individual Programs.** You must follow the individual requirements and restrictions detailed for each individual program in Appendix C of this Book. These limitations are also contained in the individual license agreements recorded on the Software Media. These limitations may include a requirement that after using the program for a specified period of time, the user must pay a registration fee or discontinue use. By opening the Software packet(s), you will be agreeing to abide by the licenses and restrictions for these individual programs that are detailed in Appendix C and on the Software Media. None of the material on this Software Media or listed in this Book may ever be redistributed, in original or modified form, for commercial purposes.

5. Limited Warranty.

(a) IDGB warrants that the Software and Software Media are free from defects in materials and workmanship under normal use for a period of sixty (60) days from the date of purchase of this Book. If IDGB receives notification within the warranty period of defects in materials or workmanship, IDGB will replace the defective Software Media.

(b) **IDGB AND THE AUTHOR OF THE BOOK DISCLAIM ALL OTHER WARRANTIES, EXPRESS OR IMPLIED, INCLUDING WITHOUT LIMITATION IMPLIED WARRANTIES OF MERCHANTABILITY AND FITNESS FOR A PARTICULAR PURPOSE, WITH RESPECT TO THE SOFTWARE, THE PROGRAMS, THE SOURCE CODE CONTAINED THEREIN, AND/OR THE TECHNIQUES DESCRIBED IN THIS BOOK. IDGB DOES NOT WARRANT THAT THE FUNCTIONS CONTAINED IN THE SOFTWARE WILL MEET YOUR REQUIREMENTS OR THAT THE OPERATION OF THE SOFTWARE WILL BE ERROR FREE.**

(c) This limited warranty gives you specific legal rights, and you may have other rights that vary from jurisdiction to jurisdiction.

6. Remedies.

(a) IDGB's entire liability and your exclusive remedy for defects in materials and workmanship shall be limited to replacement of the Software Media, which may be returned to IDGB with a copy of your receipt at the following address: Software Media Fulfillment Department, Attn. *Windows 95 Bible,* IDG Books Worldwide, Inc., 7260 Shadeland Station, Ste. 100, Indianapolis, IN 46256, or call 1-800-762-2974. Please allow three to four weeks for delivery. This Limited Warranty is void if failure of the Software Media has resulted from accident, abuse, or misapplication. Any replacement Software Media will be warranted for the remainder of the original warranty period or thirty (30) days, whichever is longer.

(b) In no event shall IDGB or the author be liable for any damages whatsoever (including without limitation damages for loss of business profits, business interruption, loss of business information, or any other pecuniary loss) arising from the use of or inability to use the Book or the Software, even if IDGB has been advised of the possibility of such damages.

(c) Because some jurisdictions do not allow the exclusion or limitation of liability for consequential or incidental damages, the above limitation or exclusion may not apply to you.

7. U.S. Government Restricted Rights.
Use, duplication, or disclosure of the Software by the U.S. Government is subject to restrictions stated in paragraph (c)(1)(ii) of the Rights in Technical Data and Computer Software clause of DFARS 252.227-7013, and in subparagraphs (a) through (d) of the Commercial Computer—Restricted Rights clause at FAR 52.227-19, and in similar clauses in the NASA FAR supplement, when applicable.

8. General.
This Agreement constitutes the entire understanding of the parties and revokes and supersedes all prior agreements, oral or written, between them and may not be modified or amended except in a writing signed by both parties hereto that specifically refers to this Agreement. This Agreement shall take precedence over any other documents that may be in conflict herewith. If any one or more provisions contained in this Agreement are held by any court or tribunal to be invalid, illegal, or otherwise unenforceable, each and every other provision shall remain in full force and effect.

Installing the CD-ROM

To use the CD-ROM, remove the disc from its protective holder. Then follow these simple steps:

1. Insert the CD-ROM into your CD-ROM drive.
2. Wait a few seconds as the browsing program loads and displays the contents of the CD-ROM.

If, for whatever reason, your PC isn't set up to autostart CDs, follow these steps instead:

1. Insert the CD-ROM into your CD-ROM drive.
2. Open My Computer (double-click the My Computer icon on your Windows 95 desktop).
3. Right-click the icon for your CD-ROM drive and choose Explore from the shortcut menu that appears.
4. Scroll down to, and double-click, the icon for the program named smartcd.exe.

The browser window opens, displaying the contents on the CD-ROM.

Please see Appendix C for complete instructions and information about using the software on the CD-ROM.

IDG BOOKS WORLDWIDE REGISTRATION CARD

Visit our
Web site at
http://www.idgbooks.com

ISBN Number: 0-7645-3069-0

Title of this book: Windows 95 Bible, 2nd Edition

My overall rating of this book: ❏ Very good [1] ❏ Good [2] ❏ Satisfactory [3] ❏ Fair [4] ❏ Poor [5]

How I first heard about this book:

❏ Found in bookstore; name: [6] _____   ❏ Book review: [7] _____

❏ Advertisement: [8] _____   ❏ Catalog: [9] _____

❏ Word of mouth; heard about book from friend, co-worker, etc.: [10]   ❏ Other: [11] _____

What I liked most about this book:

_____

_____

What I would change, add, delete, etc., in future editions of this book:

_____

_____

Other comments:

_____

Number of computer books I purchase in a year: ❏ 1 [12]   ❏ 2-5 [13]   ❏ 6-10 [14]   ❏ More than 10 [15]

I would characterize my computer skills as: ❏ Beginner [16] ❏ Intermediate [17] ❏ Advanced [18] ❏ Professional [19]

I use ❏ DOS [20] ❏ Windows [21] ❏ OS/2 [22] ❏ Unix [23] ❏ Macintosh [24] ❏ Other: [25]_____

(please specify)

I would be interested in new books on the following subjects:

(please check all that apply, and use the spaces provided to identify specific software)

❏ Word processing: [26] _____   ❏ Spreadsheets: [27] _____

❏ Data bases: [28] _____   ❏ Desktop publishing: [29] _____

❏ File Utilities: [30] _____   ❏ Money management: [31] _____

❏ Networking: [32] _____   ❏ Programming languages: [33] _____

❏ Other: [34] _____

I use a PC at (please check all that apply): ❏ home [35] ❏ work [36] ❏ school [37] ❏ other: [38] _____

The disks I prefer to use are ❏ 5.25 [39] ❏ 3.5 [40] ❏ other: [41]_____

I have a CD ROM: ❏ yes [42]   ❏ no [43]

I plan to buy or upgrade computer hardware this year: ❏ yes [44]   ❏ no [45]

I plan to buy or upgrade computer software this year: ❏ yes [46]   ❏ no [47]

Name: _____   Business title: [48] _____   Type of Business: [49] _____

Address (❏ home [50] ❏ work [51]/Company name: _____)

Street/Suite# _____

City [52]/State [53]/Zip code [54]: _____   Country [55] _____

❏ **I liked this book!** You may quote me by name in future
IDG Books Worldwide promotional materials.

My daytime phone number is _____

**IDG
BOOKS**
WORLDWIDE

THE WORLD OF
COMPUTER
KNOWLEDGE®

❏ YES!

Please keep me informed about IDG Books Worldwide's World of Computer Knowledge. Send me your latest catalog.

BESTSELLING
BOOK SERIES
FROM IDG

Free Gift!

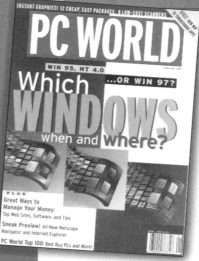

Order your

Sample Issue

of PC WORLD, the world's leading monthly computer magazine.

Just complete and send the postage-paid card below. You'll receive a FREE sample issue of PC WORLD and a FREE IDG Books/PC WORLD CD Wallet – perfect for transporting your CDs.

▲ Detach here and mail ▲

Free Gift/Sample Issue Reservation

☑ **YES!** Please rush my FREE CD Wallet and my FREE sample issue of PC WORLD! If I like PC WORLD, I'll honor your $19.97* invoice to get 11 more issues (12 in all). That's 72% off the regular newsstand rate. If I decide PC WORLD is not for me, I'll write "cancel" on the invoice and owe nothing. The sample issue and CD Wallet are mine to keep.

ORDER TODAY!

Please allow 6 to 8 weeks for delivery of your first issue.

International (non-U.S.) Orders: Please place this card in an envelope with the appropriate postage and mail to: PC World, PO Box 55029, Boulder, CO 80322-5059.

*Subscriptions: If you choose to subscribe, Canadian and Mexican orders will be billed an additional $20 U.S. per subscription for postage. Canadian orders will also be billed 7% GST (#R124669680). All other international orders will be billed an additional $46 U.S. for postage.

Printed in the USA. Savings based on annual newsstand rate of $71.40.

Name

Company

Address

City   State   Zip

7BWAI

Get the most from your PC.

Every issue of PC WORLD is packed with the latest news and information to help you make the most of your PC.

- Hot PC News
- Top 100 PC & Product Ratings
- Applications Tips & Tricks
- Buyer's Guides
- Consumer Watch
- Hardware and Software Previews
- Internet & Multimedia Special Reports
- Problem-solving Case Studies
- Monthly @Home Section

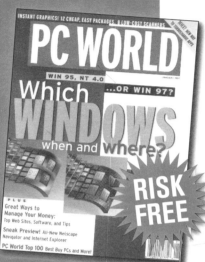

YOUR FREE GIFT!

As a special bonus with your order, you will receive the IDG Books/PC WORLD CD wallet, perfect for transporting and protecting your CD collection.

Send Today for your sample issue and FREE CD wallet.

Plug into PC WORLD Online now!
http://www.pcworld.com

IIııIıIIııııIIııIıIıIIıIIıııIIIıIıııIIııIIıIıIıI